The Mexico Handbook

The Mexico Handbook

Economic and Demographic Maps and Statistics

James B. Pick and
Edgar W. Butler

Routledge
Taylor & Francis Group
LONDON AND NEW YORK

First published 1994 by Westview Press, Inc.

Published 2019 by Routledge
52 Vanderbilt Avenue, New York, NY 10017
2 Park Square, Milton Park, Abingdon, Oxon OX14 4RN

Routledge is an imprint of the Taylor & Francis Group, an informa business

Library of Congress Cataloging-in-Publication Data
Pick, James B.
The Mexico handbook : economic and demographic maps and statistics / James B. Pick and Edgar W. Butler.
p. cm.
Rev. ed. of: Atlas of Mexico / James B. Pick, Edgar W. Butler, Elizabeth L. Lanzer.
Includes references and index.
Contents: Overview—Population—Urbanization—Marriage, fertility, and family planning—Migration—Mortality, health, and housing—Social characteristics—The economy—Labor force —Development—Politics.
1. Mexico—Maps. 2. Mexico—Economic conditions—1982- —Maps. 3. Mexico—Social conditions—1970- —Maps. 4. Mexico—Population—Maps. 5. Mexico—Statistics. I. Butler, Edgar W. II. Pick, James B. Atlas of Mexico. III. Title.
G1545.P5 1994 <G&M>
912.72—dc20

94-12195
CIP
MAP

ISBN 13: 978-0-367-29385-7 (hbk)
ISBN 13: 978-0-367-30931-2 (pbk)

To my wife, Patricia M. Butler

E.B.

To my wife, Rosalyn Laudati

J.P.

Contents

Figures

Maps

Tables

Acknowledgments

This project could only have been accomplished through the support, cooperation, and collaboration of many individuals and institutions.

We would first like to acknowledge the superb geographic information system (GIS) assistance, computer analysis, and technical work of our graduate research assistant, Sandra Tint. She demonstrated truly remarkable abilities and talents in data entry, data management, and data analysis. Her contributions to GIS development, programming, and utilization were outstanding. This book would not have been possible without her superb effort and dedication.

We would like to acknowledge the support and backing of the University of Redlands in this endeavor. The Jones Computer Center provided excellent facilities and support personnel. At Jones, we would particularly like to thank Dr. Dave Bragg and Ken Caron. We appreciate greatly the entire staff and administration of Whitehead Center for their constant interest, help, and support. We especially thank Karen Philabaum, Joy Terry, and Pam Stanley for staff support. Our thanks also go to Dr. Hub Segur, former Dean James Waddell, and Interim Dean Anne-Marie Feenberg for providing research grants to James Pick for the project and for their support and encouragement. We appreciate Provost Frank Wong's campus-wide interest and support for GIS.

At the University of California, Riverside, we would like to thank the Intramural Research Program and the UCR Mexico Collaborative Research and Training Group for research funds to Edgar Butler that assisted in carrying out this project. Thanks also to Dr. Arturo Gomez-Pompa, former director of the University of California Mexico–United States Research Program, for encouragement. The office staff in the Department of Sociology at UCR—Cathy Carlson, Robin Whittington, Anna Marie Wirc, Terry deAnda, and Renee DeGuirre—assisted in many ways the completion of this project.

In Mexico, we owe a special debt of gratitude to Dr. Carlos Jarque Uribe, who has been a constant source of inspiration to us. He has constantly made available to us data and information and has been extremely supportive of our efforts over the years. Prior to being in charge of INEGI (Instituto Nacional de Estadistica, Geografia, e Informatica) and since being president of INEGI, he has demonstrated his generosity, intelligence, and enthusiasm. At INEGI, Fernando Zepeda Bermudez was personally involved in our project far beyond what one could expect. We also thank Act. Jose Arturo Blancas Espejo, Act. Roy A. Campos Esquerra, Biol. Armando Cortes Ortiz, Lic. Alejandro del Conde Ugarte, Act. Antonio Escobedo Aguirre, Lic. Daniel Garcia Agoitia, Juan M. Ling Chong, Act. Miguel Angel Mejia Tapia, Act. Susana Perez Cadena, Lic. Alfonso Sandoval Arriaga, Lic. Tomas Ramirez Reynoso, Lic. J. Walter Rangel Gonzalez, Act. Elsa Reseno Perez, Eduardo Sojo Garza, and Ing. Alfonso Zarco Munoz. We would like to express our gratitude to them and to all the other professional and talented persons at INEGI in Aguascalientes who so willingly gave up some of their valuable time to allow us to spend a week touring, learning, and being supported in our endeavors. The great cooperation of the president and persons at INEGI greatly enriched our work and our understanding of Mexico. For those of you at INEGI—you have our eternal gratitude for your time and willingness to share with us your work!

The maps in this volume were produced with software by Strategic Mapping, Inc.; we have learned to appreciate the utility of their package as well as their support and advice. We gratefully acknowledge the GIS technical advice of John Chow and Grace Law.

We thank Dr. Tonatiuh Guillen Lopez, Dr. Beatriz Figueroa, and Dr. Brigida Garcia for research advice and assistance.

Also, we appreciate the assistance of Westview Press, in particular Dean Birkenkamp, friend as well as Vice President and Group Director, Editorial Acquisitions; Lynn Arts; and Michelle Starika Asakawa. We, the authors—James B. Pick and Edgar W. Butler—truly are aware that this book would not have been completed without those persons noted above. Also, we acknowledge that any deficiencies that may be noted are solely our responsibility.

James B. Pick
Edgar W. Butler

The Mexico Handbook

1

Overview

- Introduction
- Mexico Database Project
- Methods
- GIS Methodology
- The Base Maps
- Handbook Variables

Introduction

This *Handbook* was developed as part of the continuation of a larger project devoted to developing a database on Mexico. The database project brings together a large array of data on economics, population, housing, and a variety of other information gleaned from a variety of governmental and private sources. This *Handbook* utilizes some information from the previously published *Atlas on Mexico* (Pick, Butler, and Lanzer 1989). However, most data, statistics, and maps presented in this volume are updated using the 1989, 1990, and 1991 Mexican economic, population and housing, and agricultural censuses. Furthermore, since there has been a limited amount of systematic mapping and analysis of other kinds of data such as that on political events, tourism, etc., from the 1990s, the volume systematically includes such statistics and maps from a variety of additional sources. All information presented here is from our much larger Mexico Database Project.

The *Handbook* is primarily a descriptive volume that we hope will further enhance an understanding of Mexico, broaden U.S. perspectives on Mexico, and interest others in using the statistics and maps that we have brought together in one information system (Butler et al. 1989a; Pick, Butler, and Tint 1993). While the *Handbook* focuses on descriptive information, some analyses are presented in the form of simple correlations and, in some instances, statistics and maps present more sophisticated multivariable analyses.

Virtually all information included in this work is available to the U.S. and Mexican public in the form of census publications, annual statistical volumes (anuarios), electronic media, and numerous other publications. However, while not difficult, the logistics of gathering the data from scattered sources, documents, files, and reports is very time consuming. Some data included in this volume are available only in electronic mode. In every instance we note the source and how to obtain information for those who may be interested in more detail than presented here. Finally, to our knowledge, no one else has systematized into one database such comprehensive recent information on Mexico.*

In addition to this Overview chapter, the *Handbook* contains ten additional chapters, each offering statistics, maps, and figures along with text. Each map is accompanied by statistics used to generate the map and the specific source of data. Also, on occasion, notation will be made of the potential source of error in the data if they are considered to be suspect. Further, the exact definition of each original variable is provided, along with an explanation of how multidimensional variables were constructed. The text accompanying each map has as its goal explicating important trends, noting regional differences if they exist, and pointing out major relationships with other important dimensions.

The *Handbook* is derived from the larger database on Mexico that has been utilized by us in a variety of research projects. Results of these research endeavors

---

* The data utilized in this volume are available on diskette from the Mexico Database Project, c/o James B. Pick, Department of Management and Business, University of Redlands, 1200 East Colton Avenue, P. O. Box 3080, Redlands, California 92373-0999, USA.

are cited throughout the volume; in addition, the References list all the publications from the project.

Most statistics and maps presented here are for the 32 Mexican federal entities, i.e., 31 states plus the Federal District. For this volume, the Federal District is also referred to as a state. In addition, there are several sections that present statistics and maps for geographical units smaller than states. For example, information on the Mexico City "conurbated district" includes data on the *delegaciones* of the Federal District and a number of *municipios* from the state of Mexico that surround much of the Federal District. *Municipios* are geographical units somewhat similar to counties in the U.S. They are defined by the Mexican census as the base unit of territorial division and political/administrative organization of the nation (INEGI 1984–1986; Pirez 1981). They were established by the 1917 Constitution with the intent of giving more emphasis to regions and localities. Partly because *municipio* boundaries have not been substantially altered since 1917, there is an unequal number of them among the states. For example, there are 571 *municipios* in the state of Oaxaca and 222 in Puebla, versus only four in Baja California and 38 in Coahuila. This variation in number presents problems for certain research study designs. For example in the Mexico City conurbated area *delegaciones* and *municipios* contain large populations.

Our view is that the *Handbook* will be of use to planners, researchers, businessmen, decision makers, as well as laypersons who are interested in Mexico. We have found that even the most knowledgeable person about Mexico can be surprised at some of the data and spatial distributions uncovered in our presentation.

The *Handbook* is divided into eleven major sections. This Overview chapter describes the overall volume, presents a brief overview of the Mexico Database Project, database methodology, mapping techniques, and the base maps referred to throughout the volume. The second chapter focuses on the Mexican population. It features maps of the total population in 1900 and 1990 and presents historical data showing population in 1900 and 1990 and presents historical data showing population change by state beginning in 1900 through 1990. There also is an emphasis on population growth by various units between 1970 and 1990. The chapter also includes an examination of the population of Mexico City by *delegaciones* and *municipios*. Several maps in the chapter explore the age structure in 1990, population density for the states, and the sex ratio.

Chapter 3 presents statistics, maps, and text on urbanization. Urbanization in 1990 is examined and data illustrate rural-urban change between 1900 and 1990. Additional analyses are concerned with urbanization change between 1950 and 1990. Some maps locate the large cities and capital cities of Mexico in 1990 and data illustrate population change in these cities between 1980 and 1990. Focus also is on Mexican cities along the U.S. border. Finally, population density in Mexico City and projections for urban growth in the conurbated region are made for the period between 1990 and 2010. The text also examines some emerging literature on Mexican urbanization.

Marriage, Fertility, and Family Planning are emphasized in Chapter 4. Marriage variables examined consist of women who are currently married, those in common law marriages (*union libre*), and women who are currently divorced or separated. These data were derived from the *Encuesta Nacional de Fecundidad*

(ENFES 1989). Fertility dimensions included in the *Handbook* include the crude fertility rate, a standardized fertility rate, and cumulative fertility rates by age categories. Also in this chapter are several family planning factors including sterilization and IUD usage. Chapter 5 explores a whole host of migration dimensions including an analysis of migration streams to and from Mexico City. Legal migration from Mexico to the U.S. also is presented.

Mortality, health, and housing dimensions are examined in Chapter 6. Hospitals and clinics and children receiving No Weekly Meat or Eggs are shown for the states and Mexico City. The infant mortality rate by state and a series of crude and standardized mortality rates are illustrated for the states. Literacy, education, indigenous language, religion, consumption of goods and services, and crime are presented in Chapter 7.

The Economy and Labor Force are extensively examined in Chapters 8 and 9. Economic dimensions explored in Chapter 8 include an illustration of peso devaluation from 1960–1990, several measures of natural resource, agricultural, and manufacturing production, and economic development. Also, electrical energy capacity, information on communications and transportation, and corporations, taxes and duties collected, and Mexican-U.S. trade. Chapter 9 focuses more on Mexican labor force dimensions such as the economically active population, under and unemployment, occupational distributions, labor force by industry, income levels, and the future projected size of the labor force.

Chapter 10 describes the Salinas economic plan and presents information on tourism and the development of maquiladoras along the U.S. border. Chapter 11 focuses on political events in Mexico with an emphasis on the 1988 Mexican presidential election, the 1991 elections for congressional delegates, opposition vote, and presents several projections for the 1994 presidential election.

Mexico Database Project

The Mexico Database Project is based upon the assumption that systematized information is necessary for Mexico to take full advantage of its population and natural resources. The Mexico Database Project is a computerized Geographic Information System (GIS) on the states, *municipios*, and *delegaciones* of Mexico. The goal of the Database Project is to make available systematized information of these units of Mexico for administrative, planning, policy decisions, and research purposes.

So far the project has produced several dozen articles and three books. The project's first book was the *Atlas of Mexico* published by the Westview Press in 1989. This *Handbook* is a new volume that enlarges and updates the information and findings of the earlier published volume. Also published by Westview Press in 1991 was a book entitled *Sucesion Presidencial: The 1988 Mexican Presidential Election* (Butler and Bustamante 1991d). Articles published utilizing the database have focuses on fertility, migration, socioeconomic dimensions, election results and projections, the labor force and projections, Mexico City, Oaxaca, and an analysis of continuity and change. Works in progress include an *Atlas of Mexico City*, a book on urbanization in Mexico, an analysis of the Mexican borderlands and maquiladoras, and more extensive political analyses. This volume thus represents only a very small portion of the work already accomplished using the Mexico Database.

Methods

This *Handbook* utilizes data from a variety of sources, including the Mexican censuses from 1895–1990. In addition, the *Encuesta Nacional de Fecundidad (ENFES)* of 1987 was used to develop the fertility section of this volume. Also the *Resumen General* census publications were especially valuable (SPP and INEGI, various years). Further, *Anuarios Estadisticos* (SPP and INEGI various years) were systematically consulted. A variety of other publications were utilized and are referred to at the appropriate place in the text and are listed in the References. Once data from various sources were gathered, they were processed for statistical and mapping purposes.

The text emphasizes simple interpretation and comparisons. Simple descriptive statistics are often referred to. For longitudinal data series, trends and changes over time are pointed out. At times, the text refers to other maps showing similarities and/or contrasts. To assist in comparisons, a correlation matrix was computed for the entire set of variables included in the *Handbook;* at times these correlations are referred to clarify relationships. Generally, the correlation coefficient examines the relationship between two variables with a range from -1.0 to +1.0 (Afifi and Azen 1972; Blalock 1979). Also reported for many dimensions is the arithmetic average for the states—the mean. Finally, to present some idea of relative homogeneity among variables, the coefficient of variation (CV) is reported. The CV is a measure of related variables that takes into account deviation relative to the mean (Afifi and Azen 1972; Blalock 1979). The coefficient is defined as 100 times the ratio of the standard deviation to the mean. Thus the CV allows a relative comparison of variation among all variables. In the text, a CV of less than 20 is treated as small or narrow; a CV between 21 and 99 is considered middle range, while a CV of 100 and greater is considered as large.

GIS Methodology

Background

In the late 1980s, the Mexican Database Project designed and built a population-demographic GIS that contained over 300 attributes, based mostly on the 1980 Mexican population census, as well as on data from the economic censuses, the anuario estadistico series, on federal government sources on tourism, energy, economics, and on political data from Mexican periodicals and political parties (Butler et al. 1987; Pick et al. 1989a). That project was based on the ArcInfo GIS software running on a large VAX minicomputer. This hardware platform offered multi-user and remote dial-up capabilities. The GIS included about eight national coverages, including a coverage of the 32 federal entities, a coverage of Mexico's 2,323 municipios, a coverage of major cities, coverages for the historical growth in the Mexican railways, a specialized coverage of the Mexican/U.S. border, etc. The national GIS data and outputs were made available in hardcopy form (Pick et al. 1989a) and provided in diskette form to numerous requesters (Mexico Database Project 1990).

Based on drawbacks to the earlier approach, the authors decided in early 1992 to develop an entirely new GIS for Mexico, focusing mainly on population/economic data from the late 1980s and 1990s. Since the overlap of attributes between the new Mexico GIS and the earlier Mexico GIS was perhaps 10 percent, the research team decided that the GIS should be designed afresh, starting with a full analysis of contemporary GIS alternatives. Fortunately, the data requirements could be clearly researched before constructing the GIS, since the INEGI schedule of censuses included the economic census in 1989, the population census in 1990, the agricultural census in 1991. In addition, the data from the fairly recent 1987 Encuesta de Fecundidad y Salud (ENFES) were available (ENFES 1989); the Anuario Estadistico series produced fairly regular variables in a wide variety of areas; and hardcopy and computerized sources were well documented in other specialized areas, such as maquiladora and energy statistics. The advance knowledge of the data sources and their specific attributes enabled precise formulation of system specifications.

The authors sought to build a more user-friendly GIS system, that did not require as much technical expertise or complex system management knowledge as for the earlier Mexican Database Project. The new approach broadens the potential user base and enables better system maintenance over time. Another advantage was improved capability to export the GIS system (not only the hardcopy output but the entire hardware/software system) to requesters at other research centers and corporations. Another requirement built into the new design was ease in transport and conversion of the GIS attribute data for input into standard statistical processing software.

System Configuration

The present GIS system has the following components:

1. Hardware base consisting of the Macintosh, with Summagraphic digitizer and Postscript laser printer for map output (Apple Laserwriter with 4 MB of memory). Adoption of high performance Macintosh laptops for most project members, with other having desktop Macintoshes. All Macintoshes, including laptops, had at least 10 MB of main memory and 80 MB of hard disk.
2. A menu-based commercial software package with a contemporary micro-based user interface and digitizing capabilities (AtlasPro from Strategic Mapping Inc.). Preference given to acquiring commercial digitized coverages, if available, rather than performing in-house digitizing.
3. Use of a micro spreadsheet (Excel) as the primary storage for the GIS database. Reliance on the spreadsheet for data transformation and pre-processing. Smaller tables can then be produced by selecting and "peeling away" columns from the master spreadsheet.
4. Portability from the master spreadsheet directly into a major commercial statistical packages, in this case SPSS/Macintosh.

A conceptual overview of the GIS system may be helpful in understanding this design. The overview shows the major components of attributes, coverages, and outputs (see Figure 1.1). The attributes, i.e., study variables, are socioeconomic characteristics such as mortality rate, number of corporations, bean production, etc. These are arranged in master spreadsheets that encompass hundreds of attributes, in fact as large as the memory capacity of the micros allows. The attributes are geographically keyed to one or more *coverages*. A coverage, also called a base map, is a set of geographical features that can be linked to attributes. For instance, one coverage in the Mexican GIS is the boundaries of the 32 federal entities, i.e., states. The attribute spreadsheet file stores data on the 32 federal entities. The GIS software, in this case AtlasPro, reads in the attribute data and links it with a particular coverage to produce output. The output may be in the form of printed output, as in this case from a Postscript printer, or screen displays. It is important to note that the GIS contains many attributes as well as many coverages. The coverage being used must be matched with an appropriate attribute file. In some cases, several coverages can be used simultaneously and superimposed on the same map, referred to as a *map overlay*.

The system configuration avoided standard third generation languages. In their place, spreadsheet commands and macro language were used in database construction, data entry and data manipulation, and the menu-based commands in AltasPro were utilized for GIS construction and manipulation. The approach allowed very rapid development and implementation of a database.

Systems Design of Records and Files

The GIS was organized carefully into layers of files, all keyed to a master ordering of major attributes (see Figure 1.2). The master ordering was by subject matter categories as determined by the authors. The ordering was largely carried over from prior major publications of the research team (Pick, Butler, and Lanzer 1989a) and from releases of the GIS data (Mexico Database Project 1990). Although standard subject matter orderings, such as the Library of Congress, could have been adopted, instead project-based customized ordering was selected to suit the particular needs of users. In this case, the customized ordering proved beneficial, and is highly recommended. It should be noted that the ordering applies only to *major attributes*, i.e., those that are intended for mapping. Another category of attributes we called *subsidiary attributes*, i.e., those attributes used for computing major attributes but not intended for mapping. Subsidiary attributes associated with a major attribute were located in spreadsheet columns to the right of the major attribute, unless the subsidiary had already been entered. Another file structure feature was to maintain the master database in three huge master spreadsheet files (see Figure 1.2). The master spreadsheet for Mexico City contains the master data to support mapping for any of three sub-coverages.

Figure 1.1 Conceptual Diagram of Mexican GIS

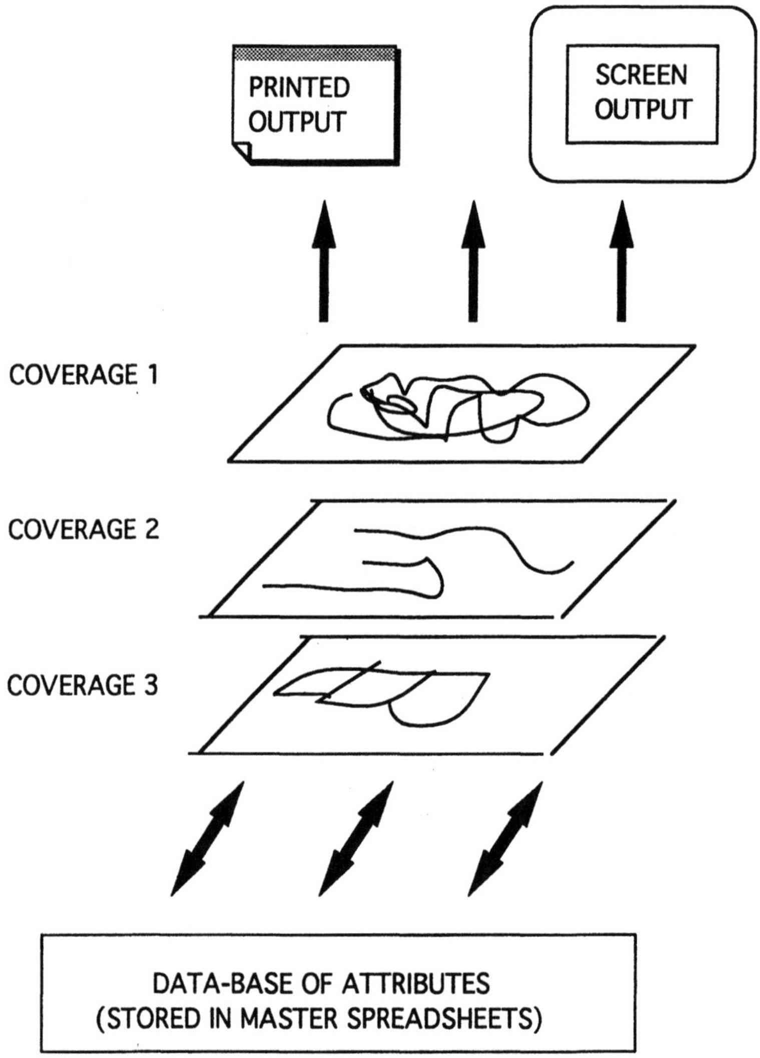

Figure 1.2 System Diagram of Mexican GIS

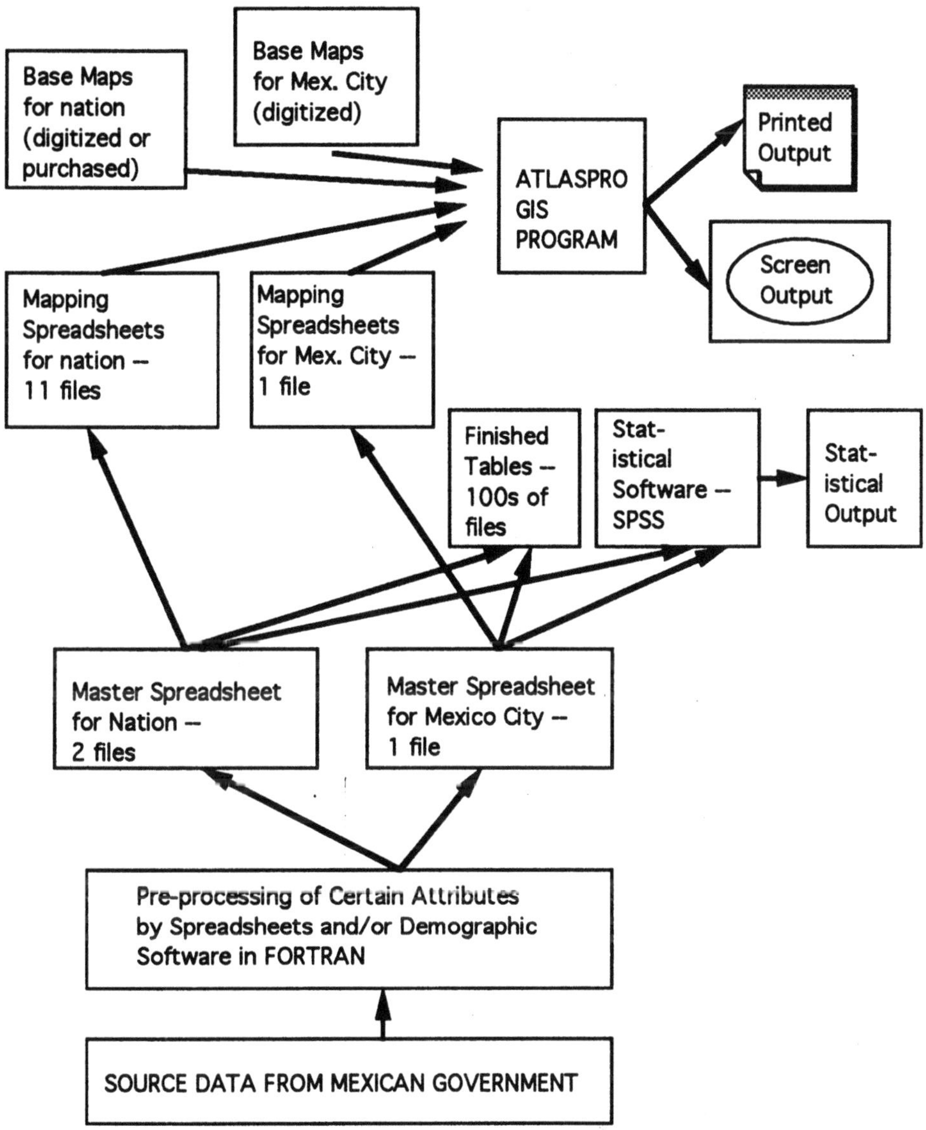

Acquisition of Census and Other Data

The *Handbook* is based on the following Mexican census and survey data:

1. The Mexican Population Census of 1990 appeared highly consistent in its content and organization with the Population Census of 1980, with the exception that the 1990 census included small areas for all of Mexico for the first time. These areas known as AGEBs had been planned but not reported for the 1980 Population Census. The overall consistency in design with the 1980 and earlier population censuses convinced the authors to include many attributes that spanned several censuses, in order to facilitate longitudinal comparisons. For example, the complete set of major occupational and industry categories were included for both the 1980 and 1990 censuses was fully incorporated into the Mexico GIS, with exactly equivalent aggregation of categories, to achieve consistency of longitudinal comparison.
2. An attempt was made to incorporate data mostly gathered in the 1987–1991 time frame. The reason was to encourage consistency for cross-sectional studies.
3. Some attributes were chosen that are not available in U.S. government censuses and surveys, for example housing units using the kitchen as a bedroom, children receiving no weekly meat or eggs, religion, population speaking native language, and decision-making on contraceptive sterilization. These were included in order to stimulate planning and research perspectives different from those available on U.S. data.
4. Fertility and mortality data were entered in both crude and age standardized forms. Indirect standardization was performed as part of the pre-processing of the data, based on FORTRAN programs. It is important to note that adjustments for the differences in age structure do not correct for the fundamental reporting problems inherent in the Mexican vital statistics registration system.
5. Generally, unspecified attribute categories were excluded from the GIS. The reason is that the data storage in the GIS would have to be increased greatly to accommodate the unspecified attribute categories, while the proportions unspecified in the 1989–1991 censuses had dropped greatly from the level in the 1980 census of population. For most research or reference purposes, the small benefits of adjusting for the unspecified categories were minimal. For particular research studies that require adjustments for unspecified population, users could always supplement the master spreadsheet(s) with particular unspecified attribute categories and utilize spreadsheet calculations to make appropriate adjustments.

The entire data set from the *Handbook* is available in diskette form with a standard directory and file organization (see Figure 1.2). A detailed codebook accompanies the data.

Applications of the Handbook Data

The *Handbook* data are intended for a multidisciplinary and multi-use environment. Among the major applications are the following:

1. Source of computerized information and maps for businesses and policy makers.
2. Information base for GIS descriptive studies by a variety of academic disciplines.
3. Data and exploratory maps for demographic and other research studies.
4. In some cases, the data will be incorporated into a GIS system for use in teaching of social science, management, Latin American studies, and introductory geography and geographic information systems.

Each type of user has different objectives and requirements in using these data. For instance, business users tend to emphasize *currency* of the information and capability to upgrade the information with new data releases, geographic detail for regions of interest to their business, speed and portability of access. These users are less interested in the source of the information than having the right information and maps for the right decision makers. Demographic, economic, and other social science researchers tend to emphasize the sources of demographic data, data accuracy including unspecified categories, the accuracy of data transformations such as standardizations, and ease in transporting the attribute data into demographic and statistical routines. In such an environment of multi-application and multi-use, the authors inevitably faced compromises on choice of attributes. It is hoped that the attributes selected for inclusion will be useful to the broadest group of readers.

The Base Maps

This particular section presents the base maps that are essential in understanding subsequent text, statistics, and maps included in this volume. The base maps delineate state and regional boundaries that are referred to throughout the *Handbook*. Base Map 1.1 outlines the state boundaries of Mexico and the legend lists the states in alphabetical order with a designated number. This base map was used for producing all other state maps found in this volume. These state boundaries were delineated from a source map produced by Strategic Mapping (1991).

A second base map (Map 1.2) identifies one version of regions in Mexico; this regional map is used for subsequent text notations. The regions are (1) northwest, (2) north, (3) northeast, (4) west, (5) central, (6) gulf, (7) pacific south, and (8) southeast. These regions are very similar to those proposed by Bassols (1961) and by us (Fukurai et al. 1989). The states included in each region are listed in Table 1.1.

While these regions are adopted consistently in text discussion, individual states within these regions differ radically from each other on some dimensions; when this occurs, individual state differences within regions are noted. Thus, the regional map should be viewed only as a very rough guide for three reasons. First, there are others who have delineated Mexico into different regions based upon economic variation (Scott 1982; J. Wilkie 1970; R. Wilkie 1984), as well as others at earlier points in time (Rodriquez 1960). Second some researchers on Mexico argue that regions in Mexico vary by dimensions, characteristics or variables included in the analysis. Third, many other people familiar with Mexico believe that states vary so much from each other that it does not make sense to delineate regions because regionalization in Mexico does not exist. On the other hand, there are often used expressions by Mexicans to describe people from various areas, e.g., *Nortenos* for people from the northern border states and *Chilangos* for people from the Mexico City area. After examining the material in this volume, the reader may come to his/her own conclusion regarding the utility of base regions for particular purposes.

In addition to the eight base regions shown on Map 1.2, two somewhat other unique regions are referred to on occasion in the text. The border region includes the states of Baja California, Sonora, Chihuahua, Coahuila, Nuevo Leon, and Tamaulipas from the three northern base regions. These states are considered as a unique region in order to identify and interpret communalities and trends relevant to states bordering the U.S. in phenomena such as income levels, fertility, etc. (Stoddard 1983; Whetten and Burnight 1956; Pick et al. 1987).

Coverages for Mexico City

The problem of alternative coverages for Mexico City was solved by creating three overlapping sub-coverages with increasing geographical extents: (1) the Federal District, i.e., the highly urbanized core of Mexico City (see Map 1.3); (2) the present metropolitan boundaries of Mexico City (referred to as the Central Metropolitan Zone, or CMZ) (see Map 1.4); and (3) the broadest coverage consisting of the Federal District and most municipios in the state of Mexico (referred to as the Conurbated Area) (see Map 1.5). The CMZ coverage is shown in Map 1.4. Coverages (2) and (3) (see Map 1.5) were based on the areal classifications in a major mid-80s study of Mexico City (Garza 1987). Table 1.2 indicates the names and number codes for the small areas in Maps 1.3, 1.4, and 1.5.

The conurbated Mexico City is a second unique region. This region consists of the Federal District and a number of *municipios* from the state of Mexico. The Federal District and its *delegaciones* are shown in Map 1.3. The Federal District with the addition of *municipios* from the state of Mexico is illustrated by Map 1.4. This definition of greater Mexico City is that of INEGI (1992). Map 1.5 shows the total region utilized for population projections by Garza (1987). In 1990, Mexico City as delineated by INEGI contained 15,047,685 people, which consisted of 18.5 percent of the total Mexican population. Obviously, this region had to be distinguished because of this extensive population base and because of its economic, industrial, finance, communications, and transportation importance (Pick et al. 1989a).

MAP 1.1
STATES OF MEXICO

1	AGUASCALIENTES	21	PUEBLA
2	BAJA CALIFORNIA	22	QUERETARO
3	BAJA CALIFORNIA SUR	23	QUINTANA ROO
4	CAMPECHE	24	SAN LUIS POTOSI
5	COAHUILA	25	SINALOA
6	COLIMA	26	SONORA
7	CHIAPAS	27	TABASCO
8	CHIHUAHUA	28	TAMAULIPAS
9	DISTRITO FEDERAL	29	TLAXCALA
10	DURANGO	30	VERACRUZ
11	GUANAJUATO	31	YUCATAN
12	GUERRERO	32	ZACATECAS
13	HIDALGO		
14	JALISCO		
15	MEXICO		
16	MICHOACAN		
17	MORELOS		
18	NAYARIT		
19	NUEVO LEON		
20	OAXACA		

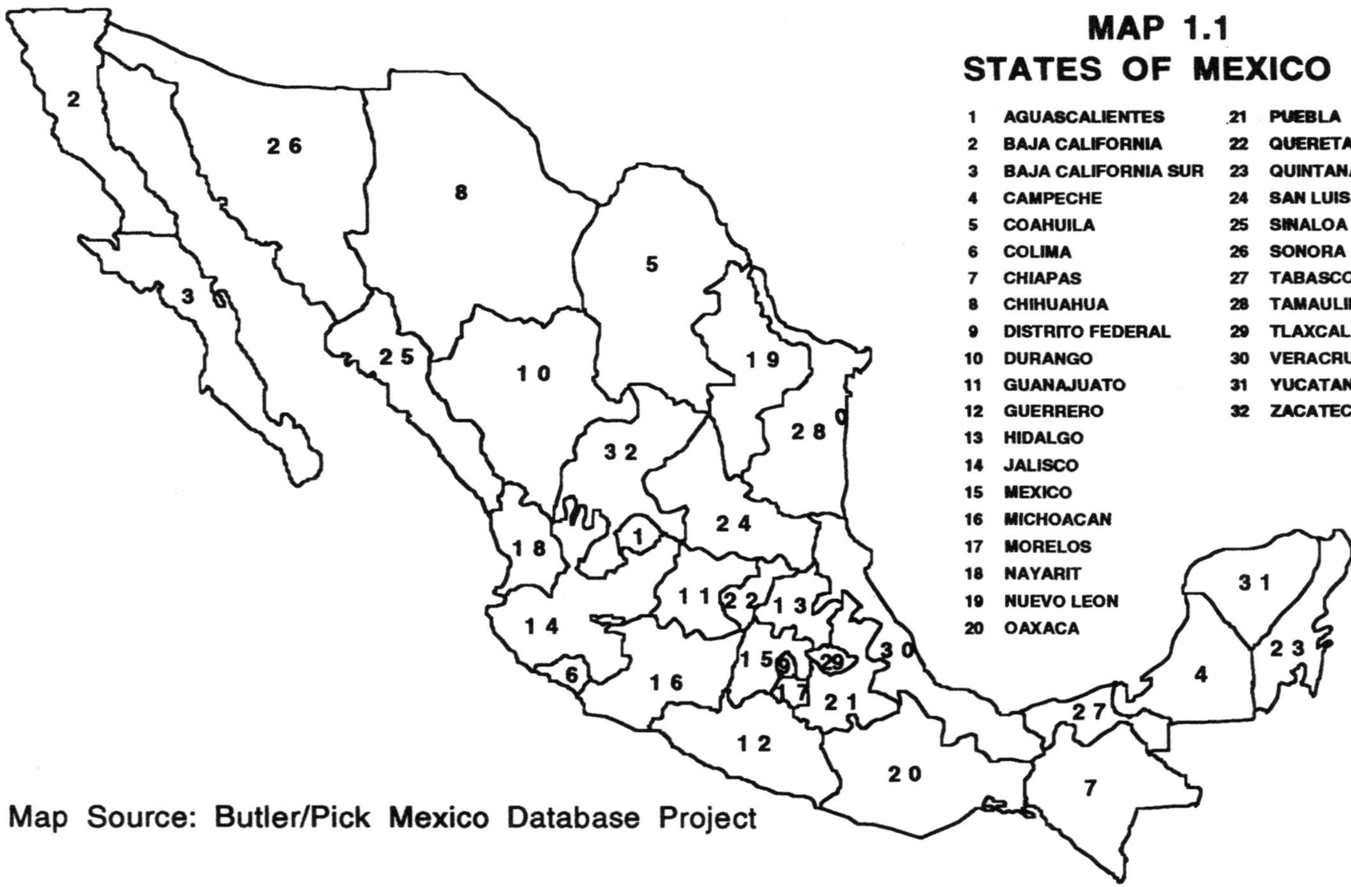

Map Source: Butler/Pick Mexico Database Project

Table 1.1 Mexican Regions

Region Number	Name	States
1.	NORTHWEST	Baja California Baja California Sur Sinaloa Sonora Narayit
2.	NORTH	Coahuila Chihuahua Durango San Luis Potosi Zacatecas
3.	NORTHEAST	Nuevo Leon Tamaulipas
4.	WEST	Aguascalientes Colima Guanajuato Jalisco Michoacan
5.	CENTRAL	Distrito Federal Hidalgo Mexico Morelos Puebla Queretaro Tlaxcala
6.	GULF	Tabasco Veracruz
7.	PACIFIC SOUTH	Chiapas Guerrero Oaxaca
8.	SOUTHEAST	Campeche Quintana Roo Yucatan

SOURCE: 1976–77 World Fertility Survey.

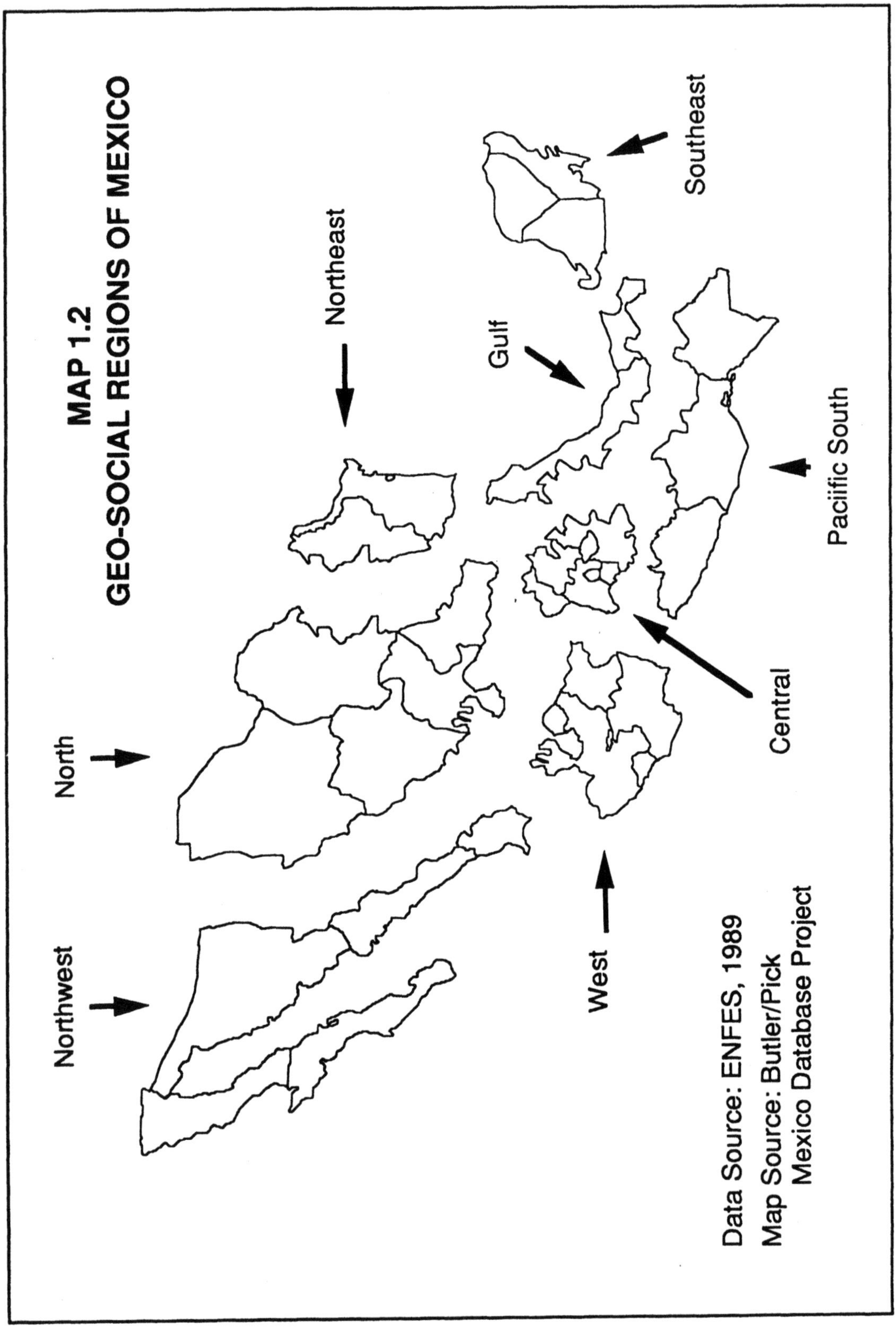

MAP 1.2
GEO-SOCIAL REGIONS OF MEXICO

Table 1.2 Delegacions and Municipios in Mexico City Coverages

No.	State			
1	ALVARO OBREGON			
2	AZCAPOTZALCO			
3	BENITO JUAREZ			
4	COYOACAN			
5	CUAJIMALPA			
6	CUAUHTEMOC			
7	GUSTAVO A. MADERO			
8	IZTACALCO	*		
9	IZTAPALAPA			
10	MAGDALENA CONTRERAS			
11	MIGUEL HIDALGO			
12	MILPA ALTA			
13	TLAHUAC			
14	TLALPAN			
15	VENUSTIANO CARRANZA			
16	XOCHIMILCO			
17	ACOLMAN			
18	ATENCO			
19	ATIZAPAN DE ZARAGOZA			
20	CHALCO			
21	CHICOLOAPAN		**	
22	CHIMALHUACAN			
23	COACALCO			
24	CUAUTITLAN DE R. RUBIO			
25	CUAUTITLAN IZCALLI			
26	ECATEPEC			
27	HUIXQUILUCAN			
28	IXTAPALUCA			
29	JALTENCO			
30	LA PAZ			
31	MELCHOR OCAMPO			
32	NAUCALPAN			
33	NEXTLALPAN			
34	NEZAHUALCOYOTL			
35	NICOLAS ROMERO			***
36	TECAMAC			
37	TEOLOYUCAN			
38	TEPOTZOTLAN			
39	TEXCOCO			
40	TLALNEPANTLA			
41	TULTEPEC			
42	TULTITLAN			
43	ZUMPANGO			
44	AMECAMECA			
45	ATLAUTLA			
46	AXAPUSCO			
47	AYAPANGO			
48	CHIAUTLA			
49	CHICONCUAC			
50	COCOTITLAN			
51	COYOTEPEC			
52	ECATZINGO			
53	HUEHUETOCA			
54	ISIDRO FABELA			
55	JILOTZINGO			
58	JUCHITEPEC			

Table 1.2 List of Regional States (Continued)

No.	State	
59	NOPALTEPEC	
60	OTUMBA	
61	OZUMBA	
62	PAPALOTLA	
63	SAN MARTIN DE LAS PIRAMIDES	
64	TEMAMATLA	
65	TEMASCALAPA	
66	TENANGO DEL AIRE	***
67	TEOTIHUACAN	
68	TEPETLAOXTOC	
69	TEPETLIXPA	
70	TEZOYUCA	
71	TLALMANALCO	

NOTE: * Federal District
** CMZ
*** Conurbated Area.

MAP 1.3
FEDERAL DISTRICT

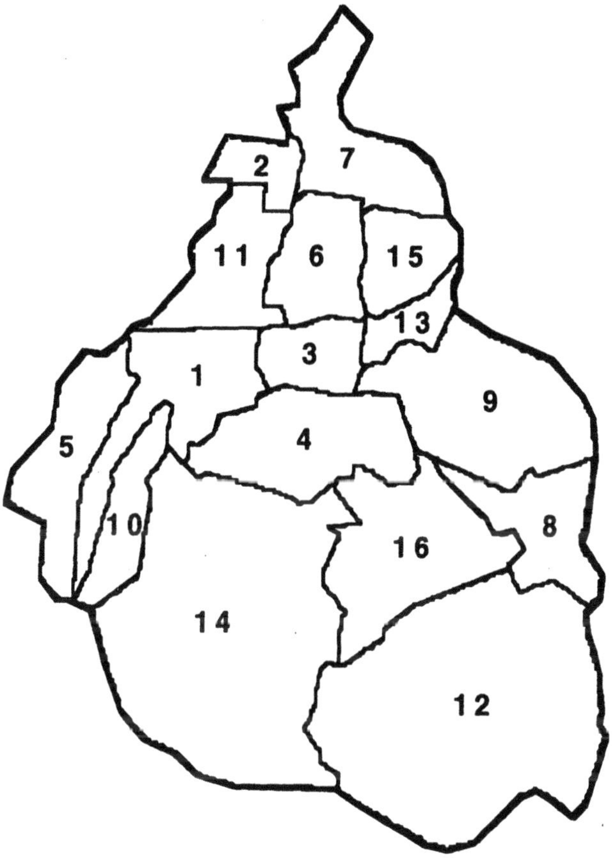

Map Source: Butler/Pick Mexico Database Project

MAP 1.4
CENTRAL METROPOLITAN ZONE (CMZ)

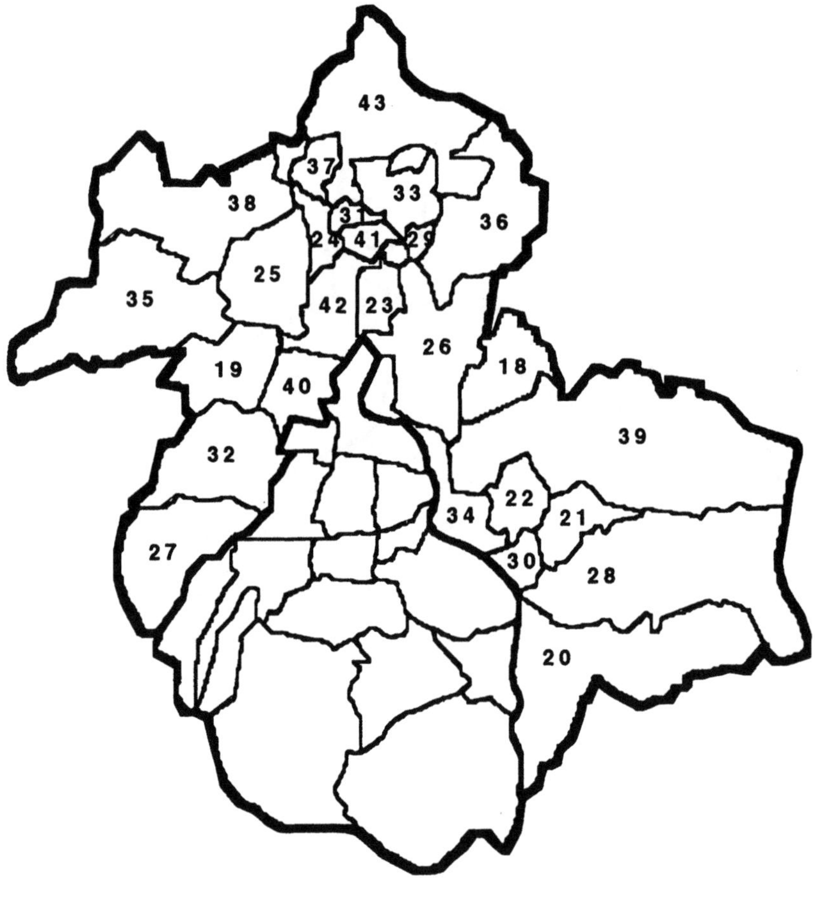

Map Source: Butler/Pick Mexico Database Project

MAP 1.5
CONURBATED AREA

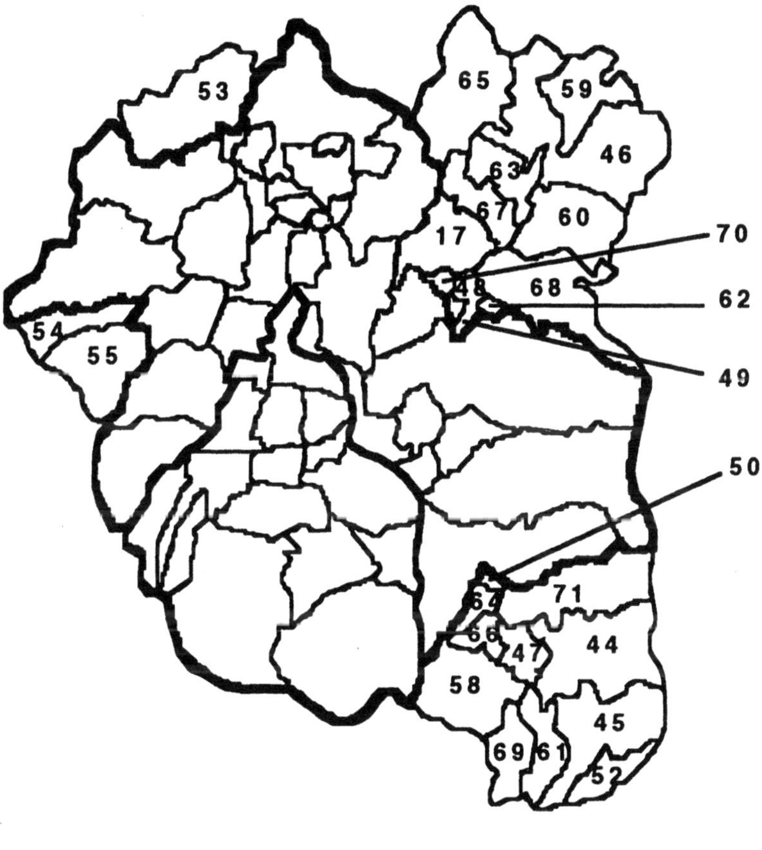

Map Source: Butler/Pick Mexico Database Project

Handbook Variables

The dimensions presented in this volume are only a few of the multitude available from numerous Mexican government publications and reports from private agencies. This work primarily utilizes the 1989, 1990, and 1991 agricultural, population and housing, economic censuses and information gleaned from various *Anuarios Estadisticos* up through 1991, and the ENFES survey of 1987. However, available in these and a variety of other sources is information covering lengthy time periods of Mexican history, especially beginning in 1895 with the first Mexican census. In addition to the variables and time periods presented here, the Mexico Database Project contains a substantially larger computerized database on Mexico. This volume, then, is only illustrative of the range of variables and time period actually contained in the Mexico database. Plans are for a similar book on Mexico City and the borderlands region.

The range of dimensions and time periods contained in the *Handbook* were constrained by cost considerations rather than by database information. For those who are interested in obtaining the computerized database, or who would like to obtain data tables, maps, graphics, data analysis from the larger database, information may be obtained by communicating with the authors.

2

Population

Introduction

Chapter 2 examines the growth and characteristics of the Mexican population, currently the third largest nation in the western hemisphere. Population distribution is analyzed during this century by region and state. Longitudinal comparisons are made of regional and state demographic growth. The population of Mexico City is mapped and examined by small areas. The 1990 national age structure is presented including three major age categories and dependency ratio, i.e., a measure of the proportion of children and elderly to working age population. The chapter concludes by investigating the nation's 1990 sex ratio and population density.

Total Population

The Mexican population increased from 13.6 million in 1900 to 81.2 million in 1990. The annual rate of natural increase over ninety years was 2.0 percent. However, as seen below, the decennial growth has fluctuated considerably, with slower growth before 1940 and after 1980.

Year	Population (in 1000s)	Decennial Growth Rate
1900	13,607	
1910	15,160	11.4
1921	14,335	-5.0
1930	16,553	14.9
1940	19,654	18.7
1950	25,791	31.2
1960	34,923	35.4
1970	48,225	38.1
1980	66,847	38.6
1990	81,250	21.5
		Average: 22.8

SOURCE: SPP and INEGI, *Mexican Censuses of Population, 1900–1990.*

The slow growth early in the century was due to higher fertility and higher mortality rates than at present. Population grew most rapidly in the 1960–1980 period, due mostly to a high level of fertility combined with reduced mortality. The recent slowing of growth reflects a substantial lowering of age-adjusted fertility rates starting in the latter part of the 1970s. Nevertheless, the absolute population increase of 14.4 million in the 1980s was very large, approximating the absolute growth increments for the 60s and 70s (see Table 2.1). Figure 2.1 and Table

2.1 show the population trends by region.

Maps 2.1, 2.2, and 2.3 show the population distribution by state for 1900, 1950, and 1990. Apparently, the distribution pattern has been remarkably stable over the ninety years, even though the total population grew six times (Butler, Pick, and Fukurai, in press). This stability may be the result of relatively less international and internal migration during the century than in some other countries including the United States (see Bogue 1985).

There are four regional patterns of population change that are evident over the ninety year period: (1) population concentration in the Federal District and State of Mexico, (2) increasing importance of northern border states, (3) population deconcentration of certain central states, and (4) population change in Oaxaca and Michoacan.

Population Concentration in the Federal District and State of Mexico. During 1900–1990, there was successively a population build-up in the Federal District, until about 1970, followed by population deconcentration from the Federal District into in the state of Mexico beginning around 1970 to present. This trend is apparent in the high pre-1970 growth curve for the Federal District and in the very rapid growth for the state of Mexico starting in 1970 (see Figure 2.1 and Table 2.2). That state's rapid growth accounted for a large part of the large absolute increase in the population of the central consolidated region in the 70s and 80s (see table for Figure 2.1 and Table 2.1). Another way to view this is that the Federal District grew at a 3.6 percent annual rate from 1900 to 1950, before reducing to an annual rate of .9 percent for the past two decades. Comparable rates for the state of Mexico are 2.0 percent and 4.7 percent respectively. The effect relates to deconcentration of the urban center and growth of peripheral areas typical of a large metropolis in a developing nation (Berry 1981, Chapter 3).

The state of Mexico became the most populous state in the census for the first time in 1990, with 9.8 million residents. After decreasing from 6.9 percent of the national population in 1900 to 5.4 percent in 1950, the state of Mexico rose to 12.1 percent in 1990. On the other hand, the Federal District was not formed in 1900, so its population must be estimated. The smaller city, versus metropolitan, population of Mexico City was 491,304 in 1900, 3.1 percent of the nation. By 1950, its population accounted for 11.8 percent of Mexico, in 1970 equalled 14.3 percent, and in 1990 equaled 10.1 percent.

Increasing Importance of Northern Border States. The six northern border states increased in importance in the first nine decades of the twentieth century, growing by 6.5 fold, versus 6 fold for the nation. However, within the border area, the four states overlapping the northeast and northwest regions grew 8.7 fold. In the northwest, the 34 fold growth of Baja California has been especially dramatic, and has underpinned the growth of that region. Baja California's position adjacent to populous California has been a major factor attracting inmigrants. On the other hand, the two states of Chihuahua and Coahuila that overlap the north region grew over the ninety years only 3.4 fold—considerably lower than for the nation. These states have rougher terrain, fewer transportation linkages, and weaker economic connections with the U.S. than the other border states.

Population Deconcentration from Certain Central States. It is clear from the maps that the states of Durango, Zacatecas, and San Luis Potosi in the southern north region and five other adjoining states to the south of Guanajuato, Queretaro, and Hidalgo increased at slow growth rates during the twentieth century. These states grew about half as fast as the nation. While the six states comprised 24 percent of the Mexican population in 1900, they only accounted for 14 percent in 1990. The proportional decrease is largely due to outmigration to Mexico City and relatively weak economies. In the past two decades, these states have all continued to show sluggish population increase, except for Queretaro, which was fourth nationally in growth rate. The reason for Queretaro's growth is proximity to Mexico City's northwestern sprawl. Thus it is receiving increasing spillover from the metropolis. Two other central states, Tlaxcala and Puebla, showed similar patterns of slow growth from 1900 to 1990.

Population Change in Oaxaca and Michoacan. Oaxaca's national population proportion declined from 7.0 percent in 1900 to 3.7 percent in 1990, while Michoacan decreased from 6.9 percent to 4.4 percent. These states' relative decline is due to very high lifetime outmigration, especially to the Federal District (Fukurai et al. 1989) as well as to a high standardized mortality rate for Oaxaca.

Figure 2.1
Population by Consolidated Region, Mexico: 1900–1990
(in thousands)

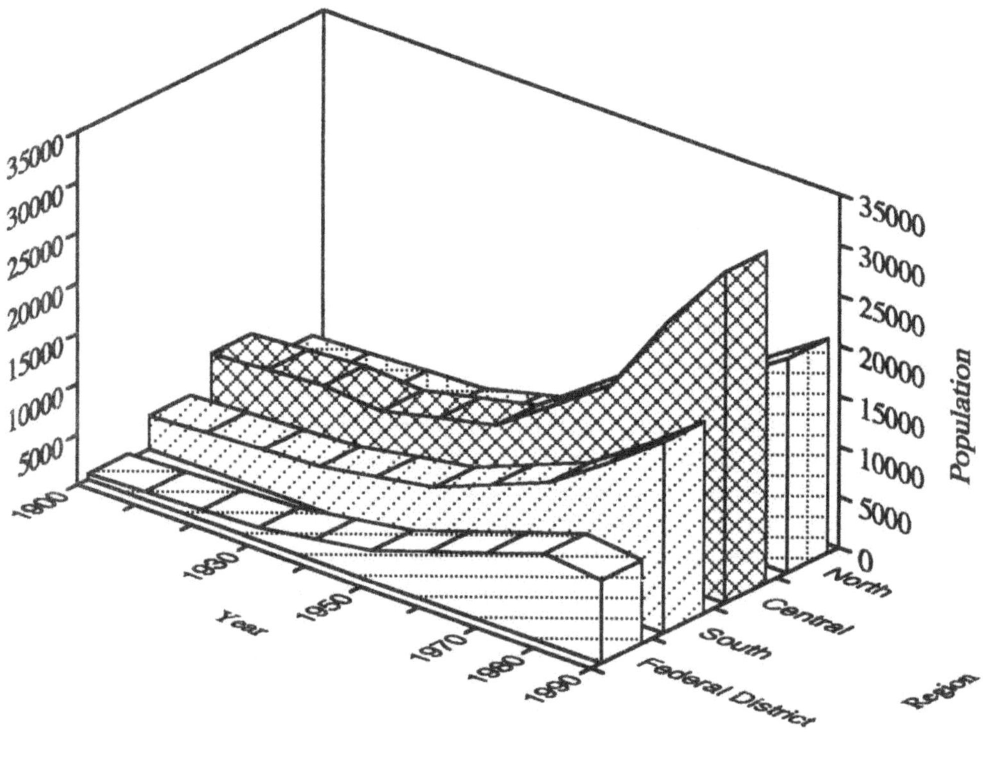

Table 2.1 Population by Region 1900–1990 (in thousands)

A. Region	1900	1930	1950	1970	1980	1990
NORTHWEST	716	975	1,724	3,908	5,483	6,831
NORTHEAST	543	762	1,458	3,151	4,438	5,348
NORTH	2,033	2,371	3,718	5,900	7,556	9,043
WEST	3,319	3,486	4,799	8,470	11,113	13,982
FEDERAL DISTRICT	542	1,230	3,050	6,874	8,831	8,236
CENTRAL	3,125	3,390	4,712	9,058	14,703	18,838
GULF	1,141	1,601	2,403	4,584	6,451	7,730
SOUTHEAST	396	481	666	1,098	1,710	2,391
SOUTH PACIFIC	1,789	2,256	3,248	5,182	6,563	8,851
TOTAL	13,608	16,552	25,778	48,226	66,848	81,250
B. Region						
NORTH (Consolidated)	3,296	4,108	6,900	12,959	17,477	21,222
CENTRAL (Consolidated)	6,444	6,876	9,511	17,528	25,816	32,820
FEDERAL DISTRICT	542	1,230	3,050	6,874	8,831	8,236
SOUTH (Consolidated)	3,326	4,338	6,317	10,864	14,724	18,972
TOTAL	13,608	16,552	25,778	48,225	66,848	81,250

NOTE: Population for Quintana Roo in 1900 was included in Yucatan. Population for Baja California Sur in 1900 was included in Baja California. In panel B, north consolidated includes the northwest, northeast, and north regions from panel A. The central region in panel B includes the west and central regions from panel A. The south region in panel B includes the gulf, southeast, and south pacific regions from panel A.

SOURCE: SPP AND INEGI, Mexico Censuses of Population, 1900–1990.

Table 2.2 Total Population, 1900-1990

No.	State	1900	1930	1950	1970	1980	1990	Relative Pop. Growth 1900-90
1	AGUASCALIENTES	102,416	132,900	188,075	338,142	519,439	719,659	603
2	BAJA CALIFORNIA	47,624	48,327	226,965	870,421	1,177,886	1,660,855	3387
3	BAJA CALIFORNIA SUR		47,089	60,864	128,019	215,139	317,764	NA
4	CAMPECHE	86,542	84,630	122,098	251,556	420,553	535,185	518
5	COAHUILA	296,938	436,425	720,619	1,114,956	1,557,265	1,972,340	564
6	COLIMA	65,115	61,923	112,321	241,153	346,293	428,510	558
7	CHIAPAS	360,799	529,983	907,026	1,569,053	2,084,717	3,210,496	790
8	CHIHUAHUA	327,784	491,792	846,414	1,612,525	2,005,477	2,441,873	645
9	DISTRITO FEDERAL	541,516	1,229,576	3,050,442	6,874,165	8,831,079	8,235,744	1421
10	DURANGO	370,294	404,364	629,874	939,208	1,182,320	1,349,378	264
11	GUANAJUATO	1,061,724	987,801	1,328,712	2,270,370	3,006,110	3,982,593	275
12	GUERRERO	479,205	641,690	919,386	1,597,360	2,109,513	2,620,637	447
13	HIDALGO	605,051	677,772	850,394	1,193,845	1,547,493	1,888,366	212
14	JALISCO	1,153,891	1,255,346	1,746,777	3,296,586	4,371,998	5,302,689	360
15	MEXICO	934,463	990,112	1,392,623	3,833,185	7,564,335	9,815,795	950
16	MICHOACAN	935,808	1,048,381	1,422,717	2,324,226	2,868,824	3,548,199	279
17	MORELOS	160,115	132,068	272,842	616,119	947,089	1,195,059	646
18	NAYARIT	150,098	167,724	290,124	544,031	726,120	824,643	449
19	NUEVO LEON	327,937	417,491	740,191	1,694,689	2,513,044	3,098,736	845
20	OAXACA	948,633	1,084,549	1,421,313	2,015,424	2,369,076	3,019,560	218
21	PUEBLA	1,021,133	1,150,425	1,625,830	2,508,226	3,347,685	4,126,101	304
22	QUERETARO	232,389	234,058	286,238	485,523	739,605	1,051,235	352
23	QUINTANA ROO		10,620	26,967	88,150	225,985	493,277	NA
24	SAN LUIS POTOSI	575,432	579,831	856,066	1,281,996	1,673,893	2,003,187	248
25	SINALOA	296,701	395,618	635,681	1,266,528	1,849,879	2,204,054	643
26	SONORA	221,682	316,271	510,607	1,098,720	1,513,731	1,823,606	723
27	TABASCO	159,834	224,023	362,716	768,327	1,062,961	1,501,744	840
28	TAMAULIPAS	218,948	344,039	718,167	1,456,858	1,924,484	2,249,581	927
29	TLAXCALA	172,315	205,458	284,551	420,638	556,597	761,277	342
30	VERACRUZ	981,030	1,377,293	2,040,231	3,815,422	5,387,680	6,228,239	535
31	YUCATAN	309,652	386,096	516,899	758,355	1,063,733	1,362,940	340
32	ZACATECAS	462,190	459,047	665,524	951,462	1,136,830	1,276,323	176
	National Total	13,607,259	16,552,722	25,779,254	48,225,238	66,846,833	81,249,645	497
	Mean	453,575	517,273	805,602	1,507,039	2,088,964	2,539,051	629
	Median	327,861	410,928	691,846	1,154,401	1,552,379	1,930,353	527
	S.D.	342,800	409,424	669,871	1,395,786	1,993,948	2,216,375	591
	C.V.	75.58	79.15	83.15	92.62	95.45	87.29	94
	Minimum	47,624	10,620	26,967	88,150	215,139	317,764	176
	Maximum	1,153,891	1,377,293	3,050,442	6,874,165	8,831,079	9,815,795	3387

DEFINITION: Relative Population Growth 1900-1990 is the ratio of total population 1990 minus the total population 1900 to the total population 1900 times 100.

NOTE: NA = does not apply.
Baja California Sur was a territory and included with Baja California in 1900.
Quintana Roo was a territory and included with Yucatan in 1900.

SOURCE: 1900 Mexican Census of Population; 1930, 1950 and 1970 Mexican Censuses of Population, Resumen General; 1980 Mexican Census of Population, Volume 1, Table 2; 1990 Mexican Census of Population, Table 2.

MAP 2.1
TOTAL POPULATION, 1900

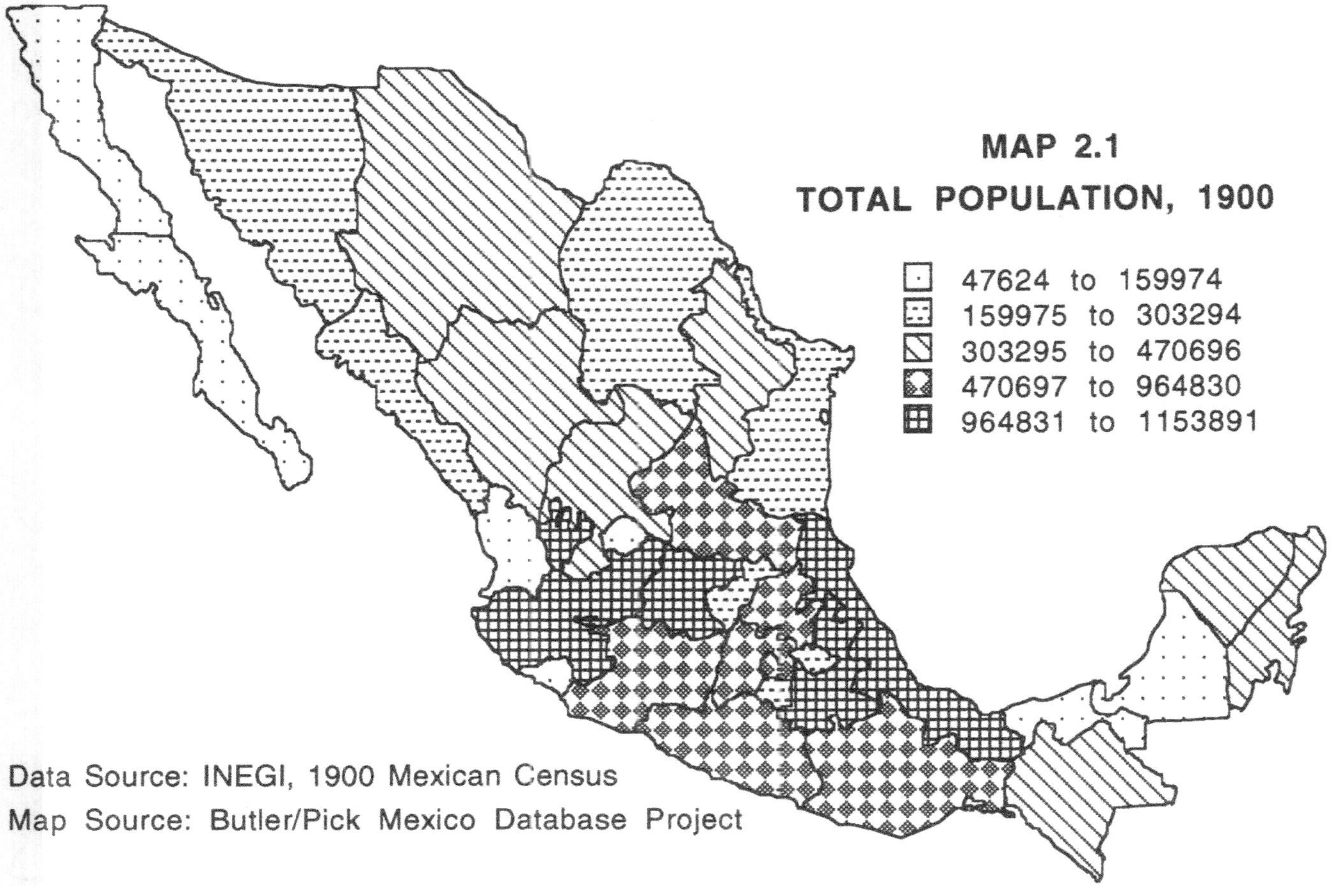

Data Source: INEGI, 1900 Mexican Census
Map Source: Butler/Pick Mexico Database Project

MAP 2.2
TOTAL POPULATION, 1950

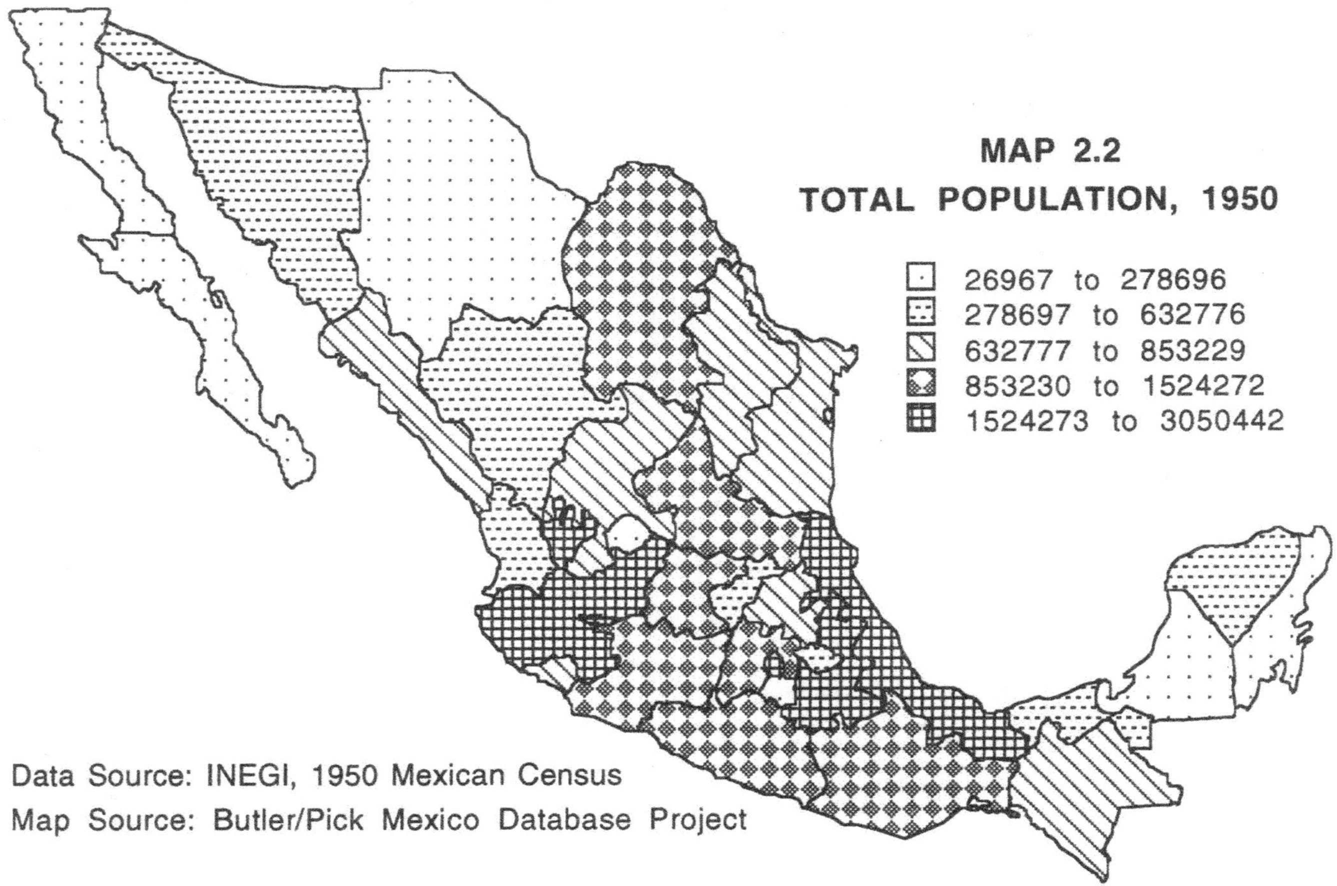

Data Source: INEGI, 1950 Mexican Census
Map Source: Butler/Pick Mexico Database Project

MAP 2.3
TOTAL POPULATION, 1990

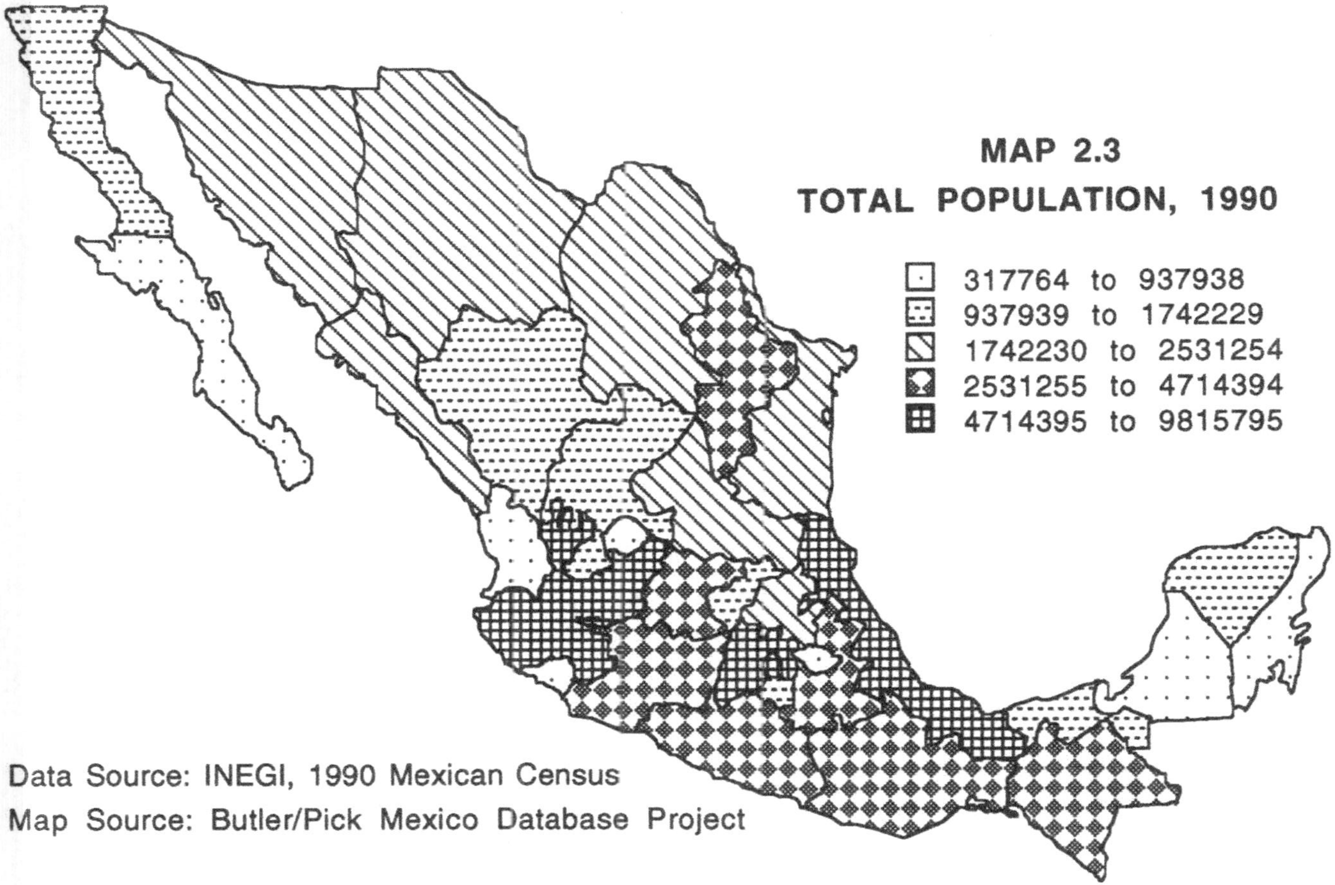

Data Source: INEGI, 1990 Mexican Census
Map Source: Butler/Pick Mexico Database Project

Total Population of Mexico City, 1990

Mexico City is the world's largest city. In 1990, the Central Metropolitan Zone (CMZ) had a population of 15,047,685 (INEGI 1993b). This consists of the total population of the delegacions in the Federal District and the municipios in the state of Mexico, as shown in Table 2.3 and Map 2.4. Also as seen in Table 2.3, the population of the Mexico City Conurbated Area was 15,440,746. Map 2.2 presents population for the CMZ. This is 71 percent more populous than the 1970 count of 8,799,937 (INEGI 1985). Although the 1990 Census accuracy for Mexico City has been questioned regarding undercount (Corona 1991), it is the only recent total count for the population of the metropolis. The criticism has focused on scheduling and follow-up to the enumeration (Corona 1991). Nevertheless, this book analyzes some Mexico City data from the 1990 census, due to the uniqueness and national importance of the census data.

The distribution of population reveals several important patterns:

Northward Population Center. The population is most heavily concentrated in the northern half of the Federal District and the municipios of Atizapan de Zaragoza, Naucalpan, Ecatepec, and Nezahualcoyotl, adjoining the northern half of the Federal District. The northward location of this population center is due to historical and topographical reasons. In the southern Federal District, there is the rough terrain of major mountains and volcanoes, and a less stable geologic base for human settlement and building. Historically, industrial development took place towards the north (Garza 1987). This spread of the most populous areas across two federal entities (Federal District and state of Mexico) may account for some of the conflict in governance of Mexico City.

Northwestern Expansion. There is a substantial thrust of population growth away from the population center towards the northwest. The population concentrations in this northwestern growth corridor approach those of the Federal District. This finger extends about half way into the state of Mexico.

Population Expansion to the East. Another large corridor of population growth extends to the southeast of the Federal District, all the way to the Mexico/Puebla state border. This corridor includes in its southern extension the large and very poor municipio of Chalco, most of which is an urban slum. Chalco is delimited to the south by a large volcanic zone.

Growth Barrier to the South and Southwest. The large volcanoes to the south and southwest form a natural barrier to metropolitan expansion in those directions. It is ironic that this natural barrier is also one of the causes of thermal inversion in the atmosphere, leading to the severe air pollution of the metropolis, especially during the dry season (Schteingart 1988).

Table 2.3 Total Population of Mexico City, by delegacion and municipio, 1990

No.	State	1990	No.	State	1990
1	ALVARO OBREGON	642,753	58	TEOLOYUCAN	41,964
2	AZCAPOTZALCO	474,688	59	TEOTIHUACAN	30,486
3	BENITO JUAREZ	407,811	60	TEPETLAOXTOC	16,120
4	COYOACAN	640,066	61	TEPETLIXPA	12,687
5	CUAJIMALPA	119,669	62	TEPOTZOTLAN	39,647
6	CUAUHTEMOC	595,960	63	TEXCOCO	140,368
7	GUSTAVO A. MADERO	1,268,068	64	TEZOYUCA	12,416
8	IZTACALCO	448,322	65	TLALMANALCO	32,984
9	IZTAPALAPA	1,490,499	66	TLALNEPANTLA	702,807
10	MAGDALENA CONTRERAS	195,041	67	TULTEPEC	47,323
11	MIGUEL HIDALGO	406,868	68	TULTITLAN	246,464
12	MILPA ALTA	63,654	69	ZUMPANGO	71,413
13	TLAHUAC	206,700	70	TIZAYUCA	NA
14	TLALPAN	484,866		Conurbation Total	15,440,746
15	VENUSTIANO CARRANZA	519,628			
16	XOCHIMILCO	271,151		Mean	223,779
17	ACOLMAN	43,276		Median	48,858
18	AMECAMECA	36,321		S.D.	337,432
19	ATENCO	21,219		C.V.	150.79
20	ATIZAPAN DE ZARAGOZA	315,192		Minimum	2,387
21	ATLAUTLA	18,993		Maximum	1,490,499
22	AXAPUSCO	15,803			
23	AYAPANGO	4,239		Central Metropolitan Zone Total	11 ,458,685
24	COACALCO	152,082			
25	COCOTITLAN	8,068		Mean	266,481
26	COYOTEPEC	24,451		Median	131,926
27	CUAUTITLAN IZCALLI	326,750		S.D.	350,791
28	CUAUTITLAN DE R. RUBIO	48,858		C.V.	131.64
29	CHALCO	282,940		Minimum	4,239
30	CHIAUTLA	14,764		Maximum	1,490,499
31	CHICOLOAPAN	57,306			
32	CHICONCUAC	14,179		Federal District Total	8,235,744
33	CHIMALHUANCAN	242,317			
34	ECATEPEC	1,218,135		Mean	514,734
35	ECATZINGO	5,808		Median	461,505
36	HUEHUETOCA	25,529		S.D.	383,344
37	HUIXQUILUCAN	131,926		C.V.	74.47
38	ISIDRO FABELA	5,190		Minimum	63,654
39	IXTAPALUCA	137,357		Maximum	1,490,499
40	JALTENCO	22,803			
41	JILOTZINGO	9,011			
42	JUCHITEPEC	14,270			
43	MELCHOR OCAMPO	26,154			
44	NAUCALPAN	786,551			
45	NEXTLALPAN	10,840			
46	NEZAHUALCOYOTL	1,256,115			
47	NICOLAS ROMERO	184,134			
48	NOPALTEPEC	5,234			
49	OTUMBA	21,834			
50	OZUMBA	18,052			
51	PAPALOTLA	2,387			
52	LA PAZ	134,782			
53	SAN MARTIN DE LAS PIRAMID	13,563			
54	TECAMAC	123,218			
55	TEMAMATLA	5,366			
56	TEMASCALAPA	19,099			
57	TENAGO DEL AIRE	6,207			

SOURCE: INEGI, 1990 Mexican Census of Population, Volumes for Federal District and the State of Mexico.

MAP 2.4
TOTAL POPULATION
MEXICO CITY (CMZ), 1990

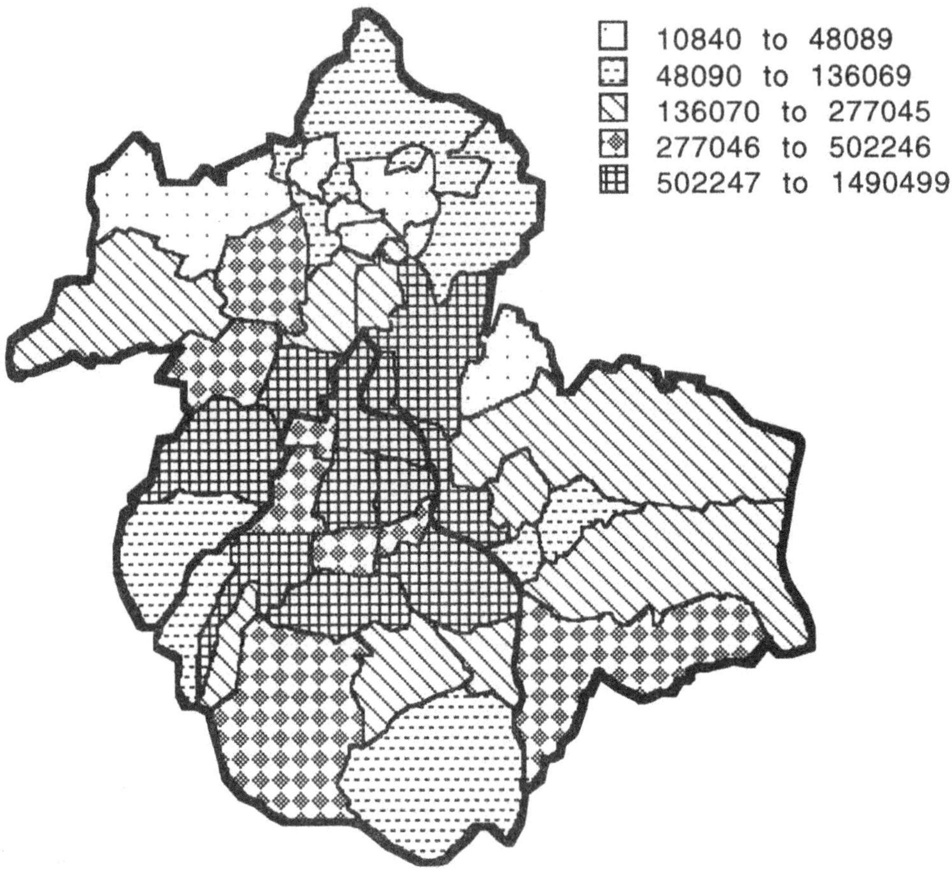

Data Source: INEGI, 1990 Mexican Census

Map Source: Butler/Pick Mexico Database Project

Population Growth, 1970–1990

Mexico's population grew by 33 million in the 1970s and 1980s. The statewide pattern of absolute growth of the population correlates closely to the patterns of population size in 1950 and 1990 (compare Map 2.5 with Maps 2.2 and 2.3). On the other hand, relative population growth appears keyed to economic strength and social attractiveness, which is contrary to population size.

Absolute Population Growth

The absolute population growth corresponds closely to population size, since the states only had moderate variation in relative growth rates, as determined by a coefficient of variation in relative growth of 84 (see Table 2.4). The moderate variation is due to low rates of internal migration, compared say to the U.S. (see section 3 of Chapter 5 and compare to Bogue 1985 and U.S. Bureau of the Census 1992b). Hence, most population growth is due to fertility, which has low variation among states (see Chapter 4).

There is a sharp difference in population growth between the Federal District and the surrounding state of Mexico. The Federal District grew over the twenty years by 1.4 million persons, far less than the 6.0 million in population added to the state of Mexico. However, as seen in Table 2.1 and Map 2.5, the mid 80s populations of these two federal entities were comparable. This reflects the massive outward expansion of Mexico City beyond Federal District boundaries during this period.

In addition to the state of Mexico, other states with rapid relative growth during this period, Quintana Roo and Baja California Sur, experienced large absolute population increases compared to their base populations. For instance, Quintana Roo had a 1970 population of 88,150 and grew by 405,127 persons during the twenty years. Likewise, Baja California Sur started in 1970 with a 128,019 population and grew by 189,745 persons. Clearly, these absolute demographic increases have a great impact on the economic and social structure of these states, as well as on the natural environment.

The six border states grew by 5.4 million persons. That increase was largely concentrated in urban areas, including major impacts on border cities (see Chapter 3 sections 3 and 7).

Relative Population Increase

The relative population increase reflects growth in states surrounding the Federal District, in the two Bajas, and in many southeastern states (see Table 2.4 and Map 2.6). The state of Mexico had the largest relative growth—2-1/2 times over the two decades. Several other states surrounding Mexico City, Queretaro, Tlaxcala, and Morelos, approximately doubled in size. Aguascalientes, a small state with good living standards, also grew rapidly.

Baja California Sur, the third most rapidly growing Mexican state, increased in size by 2–1/2 times. Its growth must be ascribed to several factors including a favorable climate, small starting population size, proximity to the United States, and relatively good living standards. Baja California approximately doubled in size over the twenty years, a rate of growth fairly close to the national average. Its annual growth rate of 3.2 percent over the past two decades was much less than its very rapid rate of 14.4 percent during the period from 1930 to 1970.

In the southeast, from 1970 to 1990, the state of Quintana Roo led the nation in growing by nearly six fold, at an annual rate of 8.6 percent. This reflects high fertility and inmigration due to its prominence in tourism (see Chapter 10, sections 3 and 4), favorable environmental conditions, and above-average income (see Chapter 9). Campeche in the southeast and Chiapas in the south also over doubled in size, largely due to high fertility (see section 3 of Chapter 4).

The north region and adjoining Nayarit grew slowly in population from 1970 to 1990. This region has topographical barriers and is economically poor. Several other states, in particular Michoacan and Oaxaca, continued their twentieth century patterns of slow growth (see Table 2.1).

The pattern of population growth 1970–1990 closely resembles the patterns for lifetime and 1985–1990 inmigration, hotels/motels, and urban change 1950–1990. On the other hand, it is opposite from the patterns of aged population, mortality, and unemployment. These associations appear plausible, since Mexico has grown in recent decades by migratory movement of younger population to areas of greater employment opportunities.

Table 2.4 Population Growth, 1970-1990

No.	State	Population 1970	Population 1990	Population Growth Absolute	Population Growth Relative
1	AGUASCALIENTES	338,142	719,659	381,517	1.1283
2	BAJA CALIFORNIA	870,421	1,660,855	790,434	0.9081
3	BAJA CALIFORNIA SUR	128,019	317,764	189,745	1.4822
4	CAMPECHE	251,556	535,185	283,629	1.1275
5	COAHUILA	1,114,956	1,972,340	857,384	0.7690
8	COLIMA	241,153	428,510	187,357	0.7769
6	CHIAPAS	1,569,053	3,210,496	1,641,443	1.0461
7	CHIHUAHUA	1,612,525	2,441,873	829,348	0.5143
9	DISTRITO FEDERAL	6,874,165	8,235,744	1,361,579	0.1981
10	DURANGO	939,208	1,349,378	410,170	0.4367
11	GUANAJUATO	2,270,370	3,982,593	1,712,223	0.7542
12	GUERRERO	1,597,360	2,620,637	1,023,277	0.6406
13	HIDALGO	1,193,845	1,888,366	694,521	0.5818
14	JALISCO	3,296,586	5,302,689	2,006,103	0.6085
15	MEXICO	3,833,185	9,815,795	5,982,610	1.5607
16	MICHOACAN	2,324,226	3,548,199	1,223,973	0.5266
17	MORELOS	616,119	1,195,059	578,940	0.9397
18	NAYARIT	544,031	824,643	280,612	0.5158
19	NUEVO LEON	1,694,689	3,098,736	1,404,047	0.8285
20	OAXACA	2,015,424	3,019,560	1,004,136	0.4982
21	PUEBLA	2,508,226	4,126,101	1,617,875	0.6450
22	QUERETARO	485,523	1,051,235	565,712	1.1652
23	QUINTANA ROO	88,150	493,277	405,127	4.5959
24	SAN LUIS POTOSI	1,281,996	2,003,187	721,191	0.5626
25	SINALOA	1,266,528	2,204,054	937,526	0.7402
26	SONORA	1,098,720	1,823,606	724,886	0.6598
27	TABASCO	768,327	1,501,744	733,417	0.9546
28	TAMAULIPAS	1,456,858	2,249,581	792,723	0.5441
29	TLAXCALA	420,638	761,277	340,639	0.8098
30	VERACRUZ	3,815,422	6,228,239	2,412,817	0.6324
31	YUCATAN	758,355	1,362,940	604,585	0.7972
32	ZACATECAS	951,462	1,276,323	324,861	0.3414
National Total		48,225,238	81,249,645	33,024,407	0.6848
Mean		1,507,039	2,539,051	1,032,013	0.8841
Median		1,154,401	1,930,353	761,926	0.7472
S.D.		1,395,786	2,216,375	1,058,756	0.7413
C.V.		92.62	87.29	102.59	83.85
Minimum		88,150	317,764	187,357	0.1981
Maximum		6,874,165	9,815,795	5,982,610	4.5959

DEFINITION: Population Growth 1970-90 is the ratio of total population 1990 minus the total population 1970 to the population 1970.

SOURCE: SPP and INEGI, 1970 and 1990 Mexican Censuses of Population, Resumen General.

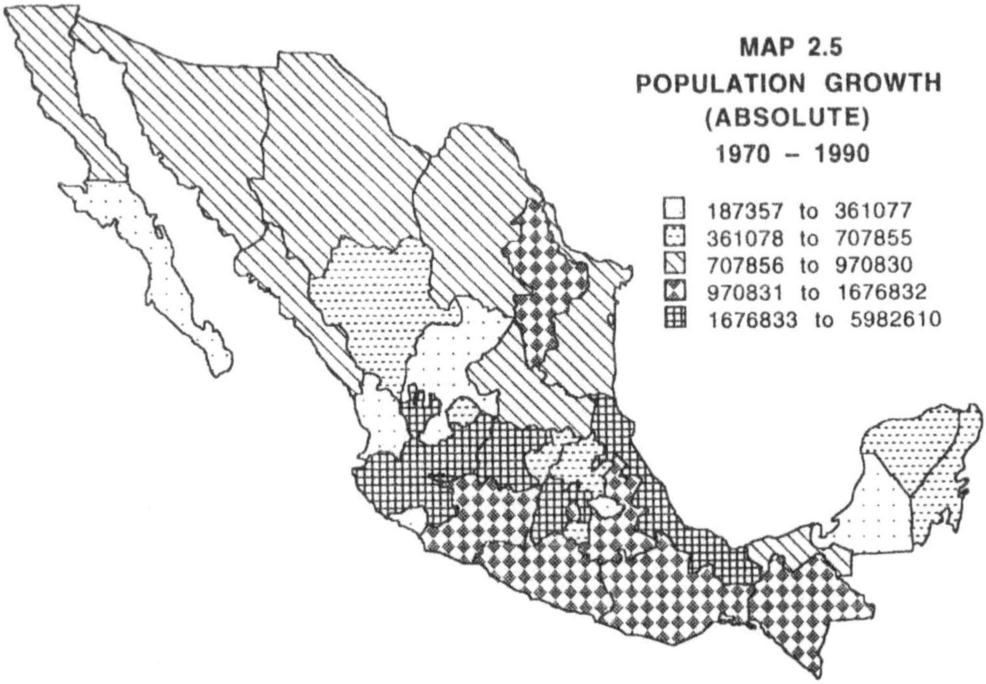

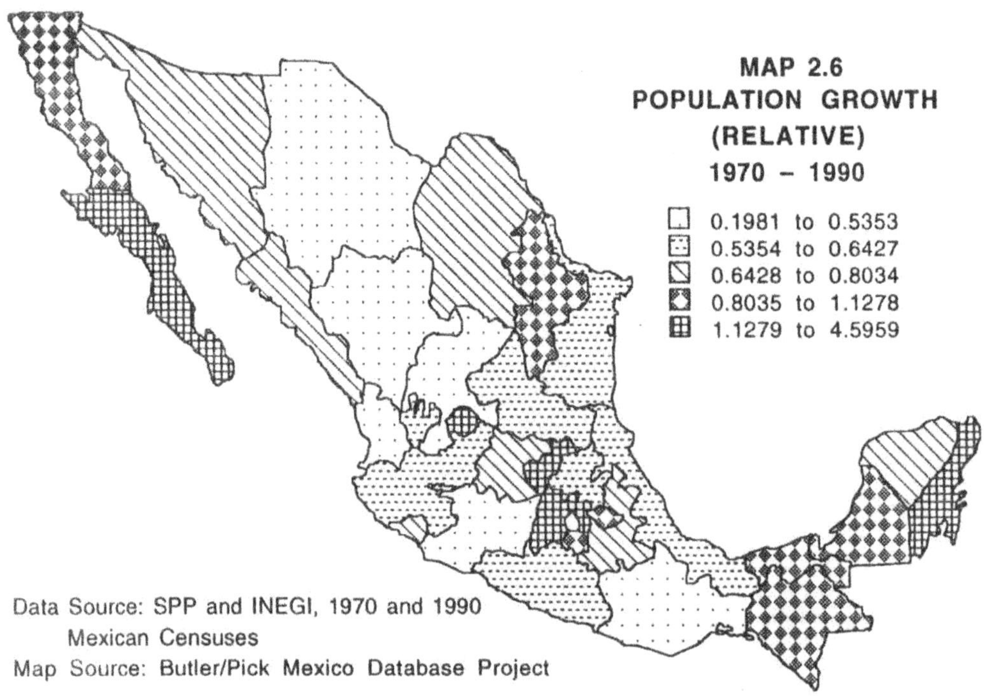

Data Source: SPP and INEGI, 1970 and 1990 Mexican Censuses
Map Source: Butler/Pick Mexico Database Project

Age Structure, 1990

Population 0–17 Years

As shown in Table 2.5, the percentage of younger population in Mexico is highest in the pacific south region. Other states with young age structure include Tabasco, Guanajuato, and Zacatecas. These areas are characterized by high fertility, low extent of female economic activity, low education, lower levels of economic development, and greater emphasis on agriculture. These associations are supported by several theories proposing that fertility is influenced by the intermediate characteristics of education, female economic activity, and educational level (Kasarda et al. 1986). In the central region, there is a very low proportion young in the Federal District, only 38 percent, and somewhat higher proportions in the surrounding states of Mexico and Morelos, while the rest of the central region is above average. This "ring" pattern illustrates the theoretical mechanism discussed above, in particular the underlying influence of the metropolis' lower fertility (see Map 2.7). Because of its high urbanization and economic prosperity, it was anticipated that fertility, and hence proportion of young population, would be low in the border region. The border states have uniformly low proportion young, which reflects its high urbanization and economically prosperity.

In comparing the patterns of young population in 1990 and 1980 (Pick et al. 1989a), several differences are apparent. In 1990, there is a more uniformly high proportion of young population in the south region. Another difference is that the above "ring effect" noted for the central region for 1990 is barely evident in 1980. In addition there is uniformly moderate proportion of young in the southeast region in 1990 versus an erratic pattern for 1980. These "changes" may be a result of population amount or a more accurate 1990 census.

Population 18–64 Years

Geographic trends shown on Map 2.8 for the proportion of working age population (age 18 to 64) are strongly opposite to those for young population. In the border states, Federal District, state of Mexico, and the large populous state of Veracruz, there are the highest proportions of working age population. On the other hand, the Bajio states of Zacatecas, Hidalgo, and Guanajuato, plus Michoacan and the south region, have smaller working age populations. These states are economically among the poorest and tend to have high net outmigration rates (see Chapter 5, section 8).

Generally, higher proportions of working age population are associated with high educational levels and with attributes of economic prosperity such as the proportion of professionals or tertiary sector. It is inversely related to a variety of fertility and marginality indicators.

Comparing the 1990 patterns for working age population with those for 1980, there is a reduced proportion of working age in the south region in 1990. For the central region, the opposite of the "ring pattern" noted above for young population appears for 1990, but is not evident in 1980.

Population Age 65 or Older

Map 2.9 illustrates that Mexico's older population is concentrated in the west and southern north regions, as well as in Baja California and Yucatan. These concentrations are partly due to historical age-specific migration patterns, but this is difficult to establish since census migration statistics do not take account of age (INEGI various volumes). The highest proportion of elderly, about 5 percent, are in Yucatan, Zacatecas, and Nayarit, while the lowest proportion, only 2.1 percent, is in Quintana Roo.

The 1990 geographic distribution appears very similar to 1980. At the same time, there was an overall ten percent increase in the proportion of elderly from 3.8 percent in 1980 to 4.2 percent in 1990. By contrast, the elderly component was 12.6 percent of the U.S. population in 1990 (U.S. Bureau of the Census 1992a).

Dependency Ratio

The dependency ratio measures the ratio of dependents, i.e., children, adolescents, and elderly, to working age population. It is important to note that for Mexico the age structure is such that dependents consist mostly of the young rather than the elderly (compare the columns in Table 2.5). The nation's dependency ratio for 1990 of 1.01 is much lower than the similar mean of 1.18 for 1980. This reduction is the result of a lowering of fertility in the late 70s and 80s, leading to a relative age-structural shift from the 0–17 to the 18–64 category. The 1990 Mexican dependency ratio is 63 percent higher than the dependency ratio of .62 for the U.S. in 1990 (U.S. Bureau of the Census 1992a). Although there is low overall variation in dependency ratio (coefficient of variation equals 11), the percentage range between the lowest value for the Federal District and the highest value for Guerrero is 56 percent. The Federal District's ratio of .62 is the result of an age structure weighted towards working age population. From a social welfare viewpoint, the District's low dependency is beneficial in countering some already unmanageable problems (Schteingart 1988).

Not surprisingly, the pattern of distribution for dependency ratio shown in Map 2.10 very closely resembles that for young population (see Map 2.7). The associations of dependency ratio with other attributes very closely resemble those for young population, and the reader is referred to them. Dependency is a crucial indicator of the social burden faced by Mexican people. The national pattern of dependency ratio portrays areas where there is greater governmental challenge to plan and provide educational and social services keyed to dependents.

Table 2.5 Age Structure, 1990

No.	State	Age 0 - 17 Population	Age 0 - 17 Ratio	Age 18 - 64 Population	Age 18 - 64 Ratio	Age 65+ Population	Age 65+ Ratio	Dependency Ratio	Total Population
1	AGUASCALIENTES	345,937	0.4807	342,365	0.4757	29,112	0.0405	1.0955	719,659
2	BAJA CALIFORNIA	688,797	0.4147	883,202	0.5318	56,633	0.0341	0.8440	1,660,855
3	BAJA CALIFORNIA SUR	138,779	0.4367	164,683	0.5183	10,798	0.0340	0.9083	317,764
4	CAMPECHE	249,356	0.4659	257,894	0.4819	20,332	0.0380	1.0457	535,185
5	COAHUILA	867,895	0.4400	1,012,832	0.5135	80,152	0.0406	0.9360	1,972,340
6	COLIMA	195,544	0.4563	209,064	0.4879	19,537	0.0456	1.0288	428,510
7	CHIAPAS	1,644,086	0.5121	1,456,590	0.4537	98,955	0.0308	1.1967	3,210,496
8	CHIHUAHUA	1,040,747	0.4262	1,270,274	0.5202	98,694	0.0404	0.8970	2,441,873
9	DISTRITO FEDERAL	3,093,651	0.3756	4,718,249	0.5729	394,930	0.0480	0.7394	8,235,744
10	DURANGO	655,663	0.4859	633,148	0.4692	57,770	0.0428	1.1268	1,349,378
11	GUANAJUATO	1,944,920	0.4884	1,822,473	0.4576	171,688	0.0431	1.1614	3,982,593
12	GUERRERO	1,310,331	0.5000	1,172,453	0.4474	106,772	0.0407	1.2087	2,620,637
13	HIDALGO	909,266	0.4815	832,361	0.4673	82,930	0.0439	1.1245	1,888,366
14	JALISCO	2,451,533	0.4623	2,548,190	0.4805	256,654	0.0484	1.0628	5,302,689
15	MEXICO	4,501,215	0.4586	4,997,403	0.5091	294,916	0.0300	0.9597	9,815,795
16	MICHOACAN	1,730,771	0.4878	1,607,477	0.4530	167,572	0.0472	1.1809	3,548,199
17	MORELOS	539,236	0.4512	599,168	0.5014	52,754	0.0441	0.9880	1,195,059
18	NAYARIT	389,588	0.4724	384,587	0.4664	40,743	0.0494	1.1189	824,643
19	NUEVO LEON	1,285,843	0.4150	1,671,178	0.5393	125,122	0.0404	0.8443	3,098,736
20	OAXACA	1,491,198	0.4938	1,378,887	0.4567	143,135	0.0474	1.1853	3,019,560
21	PUEBLA	2,000,107	0.4847	1,928,755	0.4675	186,527	0.0452	1.1337	4,126,101
22	QUERETARO	514,040	0.4890	491,547	0.4676	38,791	0.0369	1.1247	1,051,235
23	QUINTANA ROO	228,936	0.4641	244,863	0.4964	10,166	0.0206	0.9765	493,277
24	SAN LUIS POTOSI	967,365	0.4829	934,132	0.4663	92,817	0.0463	1.1349	2,003,187
25	SINALOA	1,022,990	0.4641	1,080,305	0.4901	88,467	0.0401	1.0288	2,204,054
26	SONORA	786,520	0.4313	949,950	0.5209	73,057	0.0401	0.9049	1,823,606
27	TABASCO	740,215	0.4929	709,349	0.4724	46,773	0.0311	1.1095	1,501,744
28	TAMAULIPAS	953,360	0.4238	1,181,007	0.5250	97,198	0.0432	0.8895	2,249,581
29	TLAXCALA	366,333	0.4812	358,750	0.4712	35,347	0.0464	1.1197	761,277
30	VERACRUZ	2,838,249	0.4557	3,104,480	0.4985	258,863	0.0416	0.9976	6,228,239
31	YUCATAN	612,442	0.4494	670,312	0.4918	76,106	0.0558	1.0272	1,362,940
32	ZACATECAS	635,519	0.4979	574,179	0.4499	63,530	0.0498	1.2175	1,276,323
National Total		37,140,432	0.4571	40,240,107	0.4953	3,376,841	0.0416	1.0069	81,249,645
Mean		1,160,639	0.4632	1,257,503	0.4882	105,526	0.0415	1.0412	2,539,051
Median		888,581	0.4650	942,041	0.4812	81,541	0.0422	1.0543	1,930,353
S.D.		973,908	0.0306	1,163,844	0.0303	89,992	0.0070	0.1235	2,216,375
C.V.		83.91	6.61	92.55	6.20	85.28	16.97	11.86	87.29
Minimum		138,779	0.3756	164,683	0.4474	10,166	0.0206	0.7394	317,764
Maximum		4,501,215	0.5121	4,997,403	0.5729	394,930	0.0558	1.2175	9,815,795

DEFINITION: Dependency ratio is the population age 0-17 and age 55+ to age 18-64.

SOURCE: INEGI, 1990 Mexican Census of Population, Resumen General, Table 2.

MAP 2.7

POPULATION AGE 0 - 17, 1990

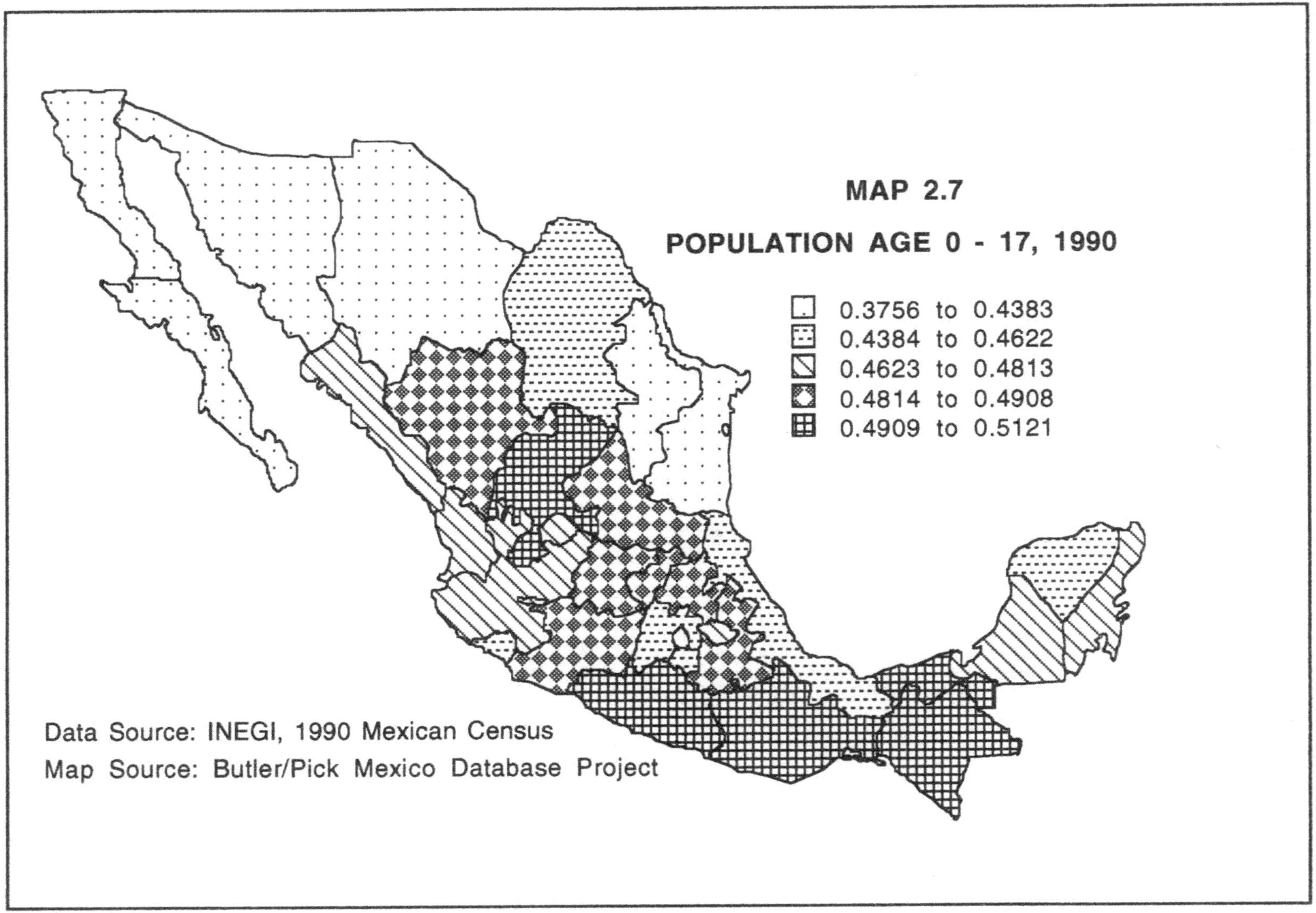

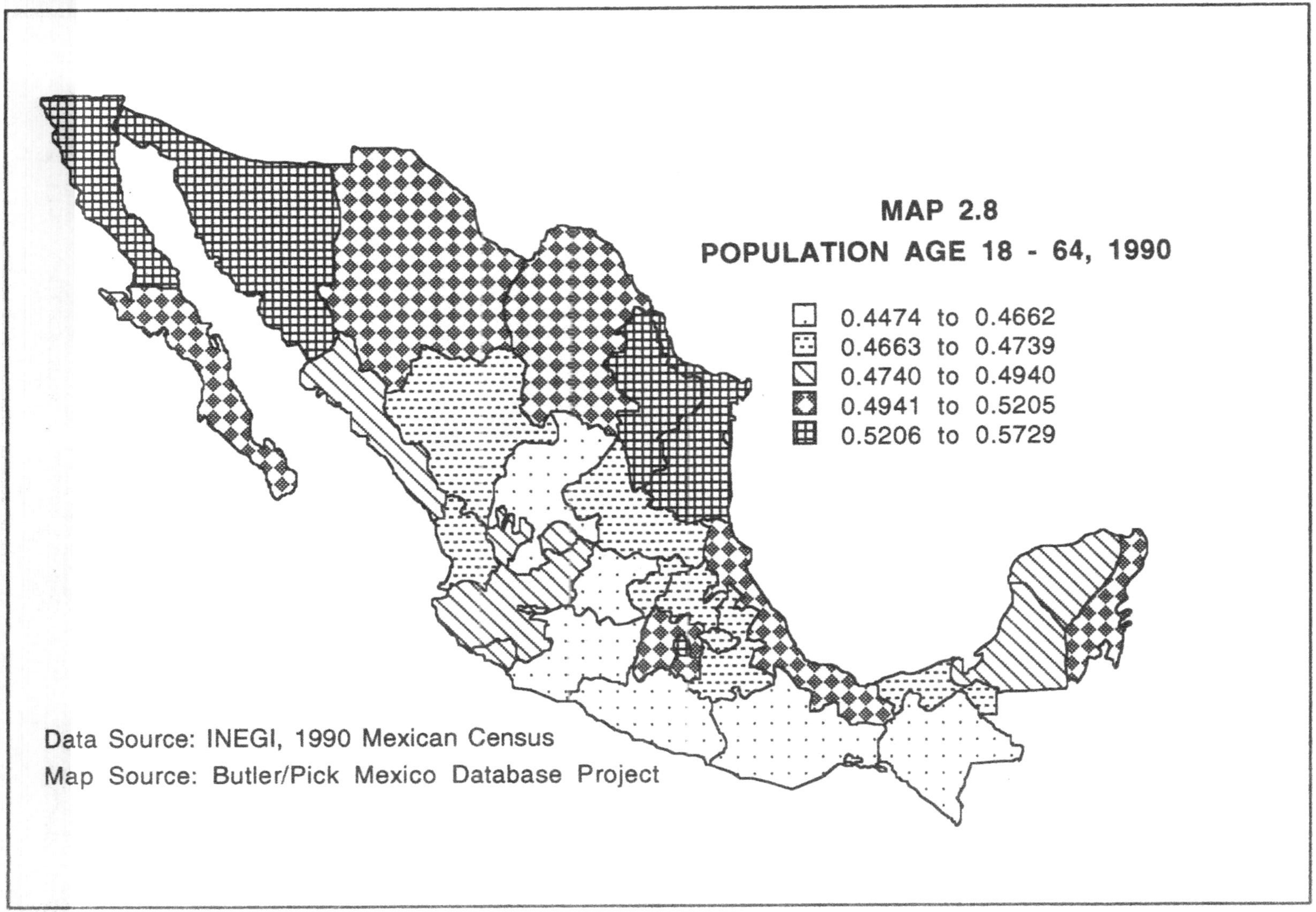
MAP 2.8
POPULATION AGE 18 - 64, 1990
0.4474 to 0.4662
0.4663 to 0.4739
0.4740 to 0.4940
0.4941 to 0.5205
0.5206 to 0.5729
Data Source: INEGI, 1990 Mexican Census
Map Source: Butler/Pick Mexico Database Project

MAP 2.9
POPULATION AGE 65 OR OLDER
1990

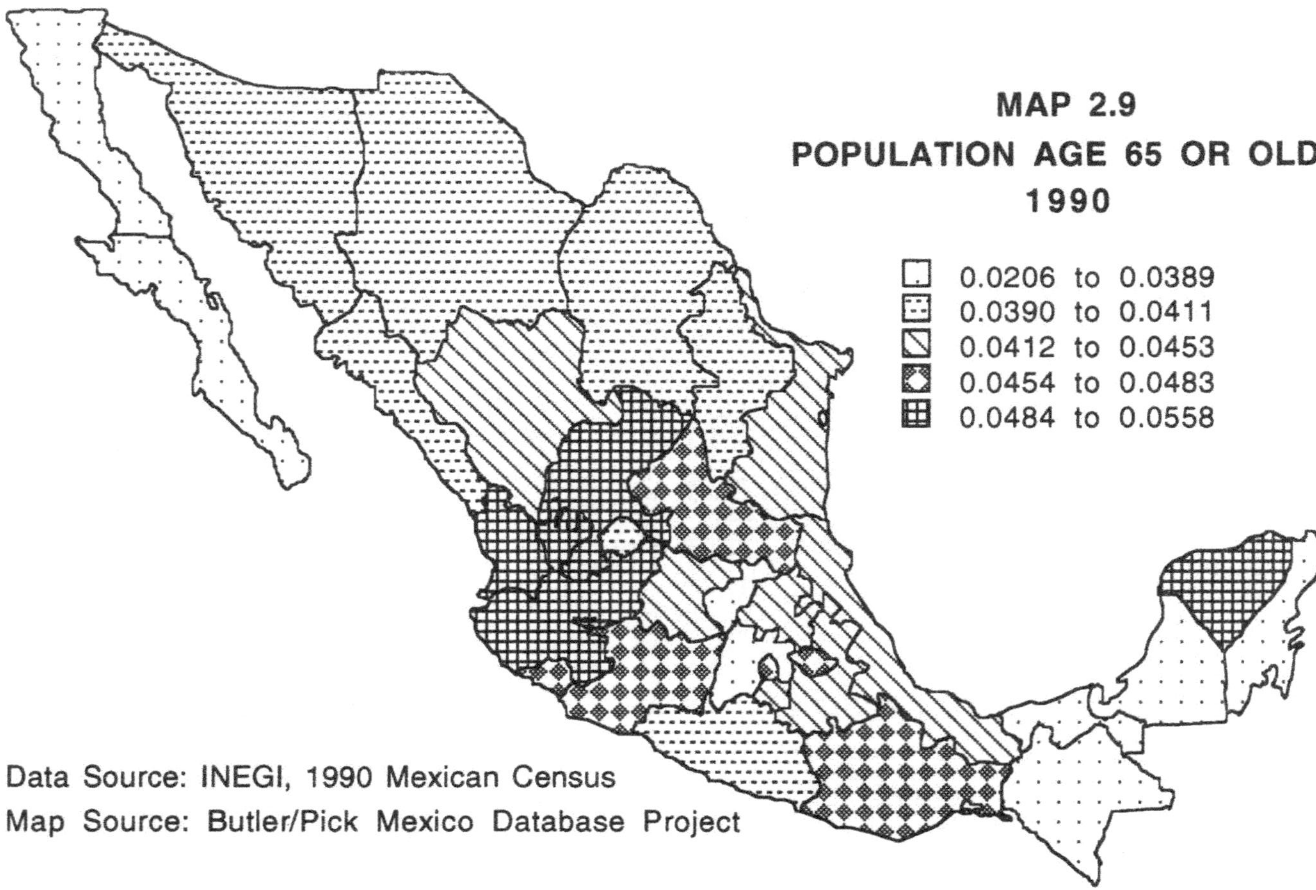

Data Source: INEGI, 1990 Mexican Census
Map Source: Butler/Pick Mexico Database Project

MAP 2.10
DEPENDENCY RATIO, 1990

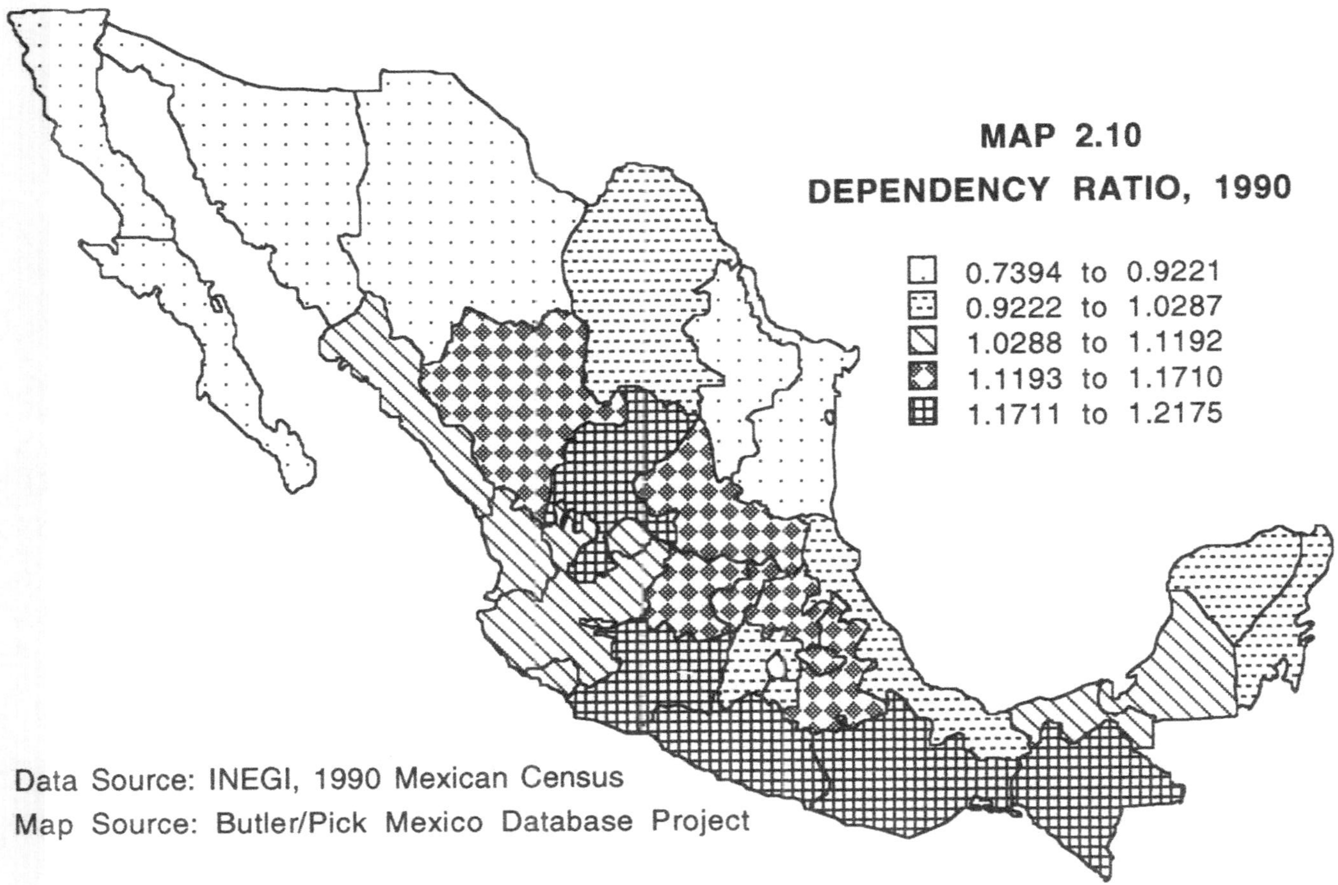

Data Source: INEGI, 1990 Mexican Census
Map Source: Butler/Pick Mexico Database Project

Sex Ratio, 1990

The sex ratio is the proportion of males to females. A sex ratio over 1.00 implies a preponderance of males, while one under 1.00 indicates more females. Mexico's sex ratio in 1990 was .9646, which is slightly lower than the 1980 level of .9772 and much lower than the 1950 sex ratio of 1.0499. Mexico's 1990 level is slightly higher than the comparable value of .9511 for the U.S. in 1990 (U.S. Bureau of the Census 1992a). The significant drop over 40 years is due to greater proportion of older age population, which tends to have a lower sex ratio, e.g., more females. The sex ratio is positively correlated with population growth, inmigration, and economic activity and inversely correlated with the proportion elderly, mortality, and unemployment.

As reported in Table 2.6 and seen in Map 2.11, 1990 sex ratios were highest in the states of Quintana Roo and Baja California Sur. These are population growth states. They received high numbers of inmigrants in the 1980s who tended to be youthful with high sex ratios. Likewise, Campeche experienced high growth and inmigration in the 1980s. Sonora and Sinaloa had high 1990 sex ratios, which may be related to gender differentials in migration or mortality. Chiapas' high sex ratio is not due to migration, which had low rates in the 1980s. Rather, the elevated ratio may relate to the extremely high proportion of labor force in agriculture, that may tend to draw or retain male workers in the state.

The lowest sex ratio of .9171 is for the Federal District. This is due to the Federal District's age structure of very small proportion of young and high proportion of elderly. An older age distribution favors a low sex ratio, since, as a general rule, females tend to have lower mortality than males at older ages (Keyfitz and Flieger 1990).

The west region's very low sex ratio of .9414 is due in part to an older age composition. The west has the highest regional concentration of elderly population (see Map 2.9). Sex ratios are also low in Guerrero, Oaxaca, and Veracruz. Those states may have experienced relatively greater male net outmigration.

The 1990 sex ratio pattern closely compares to that for 1980. An exception is the sharp rise in Baja California's sex ratio from .9725 to 1.0040. This may be partly due to enumeration differentials between the 1980 and 1990 censuses. In particular, Baja California's enumeration was criticized in 1980.

Table 2.6 Sex Ratio, 1990

No.	State	Male Population	Female Population	Sex Ratio
1	AGUASCALIENTES	350,218	369,441	0.9480
2	BAJA CALIFORNIA	832,090	828,765	1.0040
3	BAJA CALIFORNIA SUR	161,833	155,931	1.0379
4	CAMPECHE	268,772	266,413	1.0089
5	COAHUILA	979,097	993,243	0.9858
6	COLIMA	212,543	215,967	0.9841
7	CHIAPAS	1,604,773	1,605,723	0.9994
8	CHIHUAHUA	1,213,302	1,228,571	0.9876
9	DISTRITO FEDERAL	3,939,911	4,295,833	0.9171
10	DURANGO	664,766	684,612	0.9710
11	GUANAJUATO	1,926,735	2,055,858	0.9372
12	GUERRERO	1,282,220	1,338,417	0.9580
13	HIDALGO	929,138	959,228	0.9686
14	JALISCO	2,564,892	2,737,797	0.9368
15	MEXICO	4,834,549	4,981,246	0.9706
16	MICHOACAN	1,718,763	1,829,436	0.9395
17	MORELOS	583,785	611,274	0.9550
18	NAYARIT	411,057	413,586	0.9939
19	NUEVO LEON	1,542,664	1,556,072	0.9914
20	OAXACA	1,477,438	1,542,122	0.9581
21	PUEBLA	2,008,531	2,117,570	0.9485
22	QUERETARO	516,168	535,067	0.9647
23	QUINTANA ROO	254,908	238,369	1.0694
24	SAN LUIS POTOSI	987,315	1,015,872	0.9719
25	SINALOA	1,101,621	1,102,433	0.9993
26	SONORA	915,088	908,518	1.0072
27	TABASCO	749,982	751,762	0.9976
28	TAMAULIPAS	1,111,698	1,137,883	0.9770
29	TLAXCALA	375,130	386,147	0.9715
30	VERACRUZ	3,077,427	3,150,812	0.9767
31	YUCATAN	673,892	689,048	0.9780
32	ZACATECAS	623,663	652,660	0.9556
National Total		39,893,969	41,355,676	0.9647
Mean		1,246,687	1,292,365	0.9772
Median		954,118	976,236	0.9743
S.D.		1,078,171	1,138,627	0.0305
C.V.		86.48	88.10	3.1250
Minimum		161,833	155,931	0.9171
Maximum		4,834,549	4,981,246	1.0694

DEFINITION: Sex Ratio is the male population to the female population.

SOURCE: INEGI, 1990 Mexican Census of Population, Resumen General, Table 2.

MAP 2.11
SEX RATIO, 1990

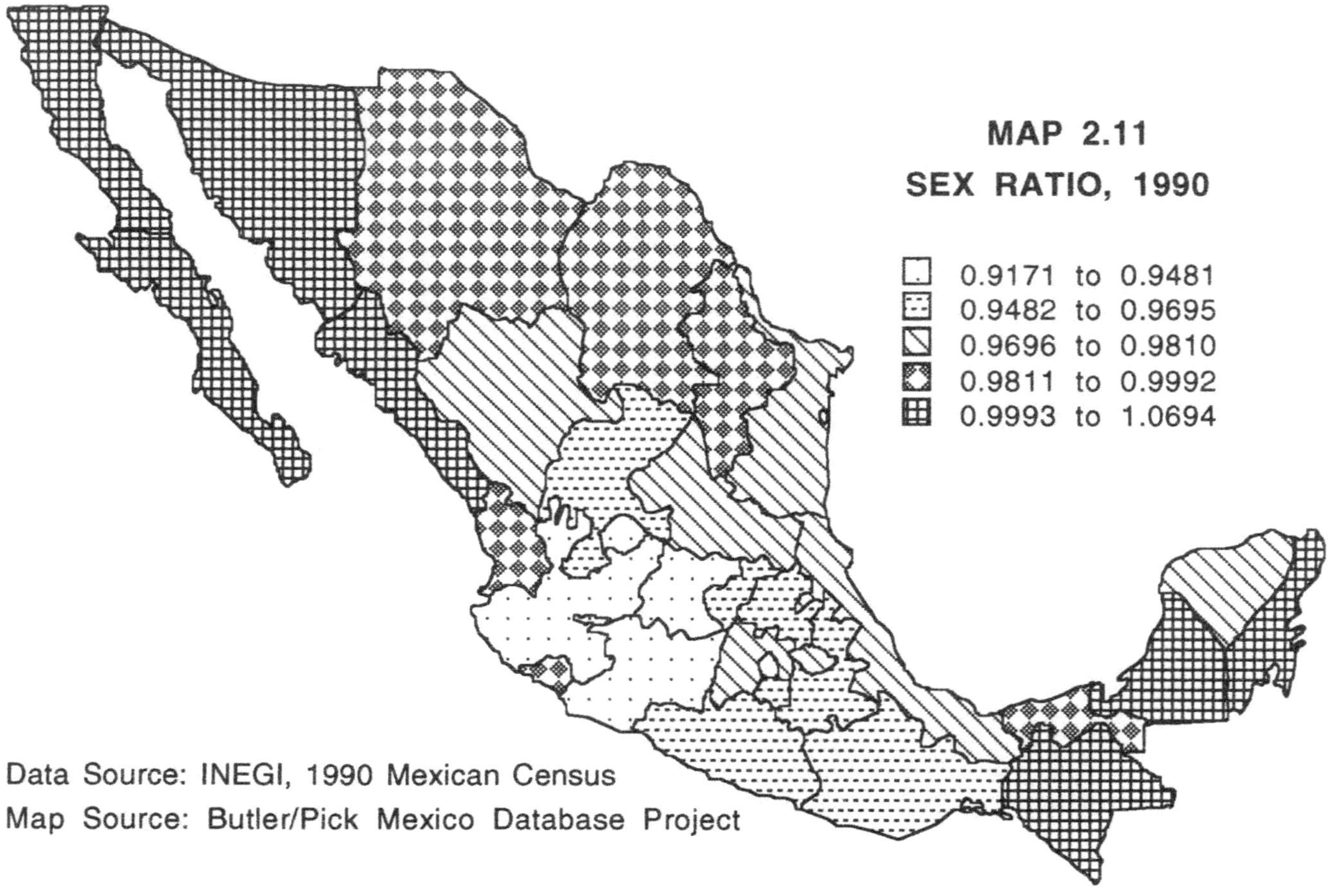

Data Source: INEGI, 1990 Mexican Census
Map Source: Butler/Pick Mexico Database Project

Population Density, 1990

Mexico's 1990 population density was 41.3 persons per square kilometer (km). The density grew by 22 percent from 1980 to 1990. Excluding the Federal District, the population density was 37.1. High population density is associated with indicators of economic prosperity including economic activity, tertiary sector employment, and presence of business consultants. It has opposite patterns from fertility, youthful age structure, and dependency.

The Mexican states show large variation in population density (see Table 2.7). The Federal District's density is by far the highest at 5,494 persons/km^2. Its density reflects the population concentration of one of the world largest cities. Mexico, Morelos, and Tlaxcala, "overspill" states from metropolitan Mexico City, are next in density level at 457, 242, and 194 persons/km^2 respectively.

As shown in Map 2.12, at the low extreme are Baja California Sur and Quintana Roo, with densities of only 4.3 and 9.8 persons/km^2 , respectively. These states had the lowest 1990 populations and lack major cities. However, they grew rapidly in the 1980s, so their population density nearly doubled from 1980 to 1990. Such high growth may partly reflect the environmental attractiveness of low density land areas, as well as the impact of increased employment in the tourism sector.

If the nation is viewed as a whole it may be divided into four zones of decreasing density: (1) the Federal District, Mexico, Morelos, and Tlaxcala; (2) the rest of the central flank of the country running from Veracruz on the east side to Michoacan and Colima on the west; (3) portions of Mexico above and below the central flank, consisting of Sinaloa, Nayarit, the eastern part of the north, the northeast, and south regions; and (4) the southeast region and a modified "northwest" region, consisting of Baja California, Baja California Sur, Sonora, Chihuahua, and Durango.

Explanation of these differences stems from combinations of historical settlement patterns, location of cities, climate, agriculture, and topographical features such as mountains and deserts. These four density zones are briefly discussed below.

Federal District/Mexico/Morelos/Tlaxcala. This includes the urbanized core of the nation, that developed in pre-colonial Mexico. It also includes "overspill" states that have received migrants from the urban core (see Maps 2.4 and Chapter 5).

The Rest of the Central Flank. This region generally has adequate rainfall and reasonable temperatures. It has many major, and mostly older cities, which developed for a variety of historical reasons.

Portions of Mexico Above and Below the Central Flank. In the north, the climate is generally of mediocre attractiveness and agriculture is often limited by dryness. In addition, density is reduced by the presence of the Sierra Madre Oriental mountains along its eastern side. The northeast region is somewhat below the median in density. Its topographic and climatic features have average attractiveness, allowing moderate agricultural production, largely irrigated. The south is heavily agricultural with a substantial indigenous population. In this zone, there are fewer larger cities for equivalent land area than in the central flank.

Northwest and Southeast. The "northwest" is quite arid with limited natural or irrigated agriculture. It also has substantial mountainous areas. Its states are physically much larger than the states of the central flank. The southeast is an area with a hot, tropical climate. In recent Mexican history, it has lacked substantial city development except for Merida because of its remoteness; in addition it has not had adequate transportation to the remainder of Mexico, a low extent of industrialization, and presence of native and agricultural-based cultures.

Table 2.7 Population Density, 1990

No.	State	Area (Square Kilometers)	Total Population	Density
1	AGUASCALIENTES	5,589	719,659	128.8
2	BAJA CALIFORNIA	70,113	1,660,855	23.7
3	BAJA CALIFORNIA SUR	73,677	317,764	4.3
4	CAMPECHE	51,833	535,185	10.3
5	COAHUILA	151,571	1,972,340	13.0
6	COLIMA	5,455	428,510	78.6
7	CHIAPAS	73,887	3,210,496	43.5
8	CHIHUAHUA	247,087	2,441,873	9.9
9	DISTRITO FEDERAL	1,499	8,235,744	5,494.2
10	DURANGO	119,648	1,349,378	11.3
11	GUANAJUATO	30,589	3,982,593	130.2
12	GUERRERO	63,794	2,620,637	41.1
13	HIDALGO	20,987	1,888,366	90.0
14	JALISCO	80,137	5,302,689	66.2
15	MEXICO	21,461	9,815,795	457.4
16	MICHOACAN	59,864	3,548,199	59.3
17	MORELOS	4,941	1,195,059	241.9
18	NAYARIT	27,621	824,643	29.9
19	NUEVO LEON	64,555	3,098,736	48.0
20	OAXACA	95,364	3,019,560	31.7
21	PUEBLA	33,919	4,126,101	121.6
22	QUERETARO	11,769	1,051,235	89.3
23	QUINTANA ROO	50,350	493,277	9.8
24	SAN LUIS POTOSI	62,848	2,003,187	31.9
25	SINALOA	58,092	2,204,054	37.9
26	SONORA	184,934	1,823,606	9.9
27	TABASCO	24,661	1,501,744	60.9
28	TAMAULIPAS	79,829	2,249,581	28.2
29	TLAXCALA	3,914	761,277	194.5
30	VERACRUZ	72,815	6,228,239	85.5
31	YUCATAN	39,340	1,362,940	34.6
32	ZACATECAS	75,040	1,276,323	17.0
National Total		1,967,183	81,249,645	41.3
Mean		61,474	2,539,051	241.7
Median		58,978	1,930,353	42.3
S.D.		54,106	2,216,375	962.6
C.V.		88.01	87.29	398.3
Minimum		1,499	317,764	4.3
Maximum		247,087	9,815,795	5,494.2

DEFINITION: Population density is the ratio of total population to total area in square kilometers.

SOURCE: INEGI, 1990 Mexican Census of Population, Resumen General, Table 2.

MAP 2.12
POPULATION DENSITY, 1990

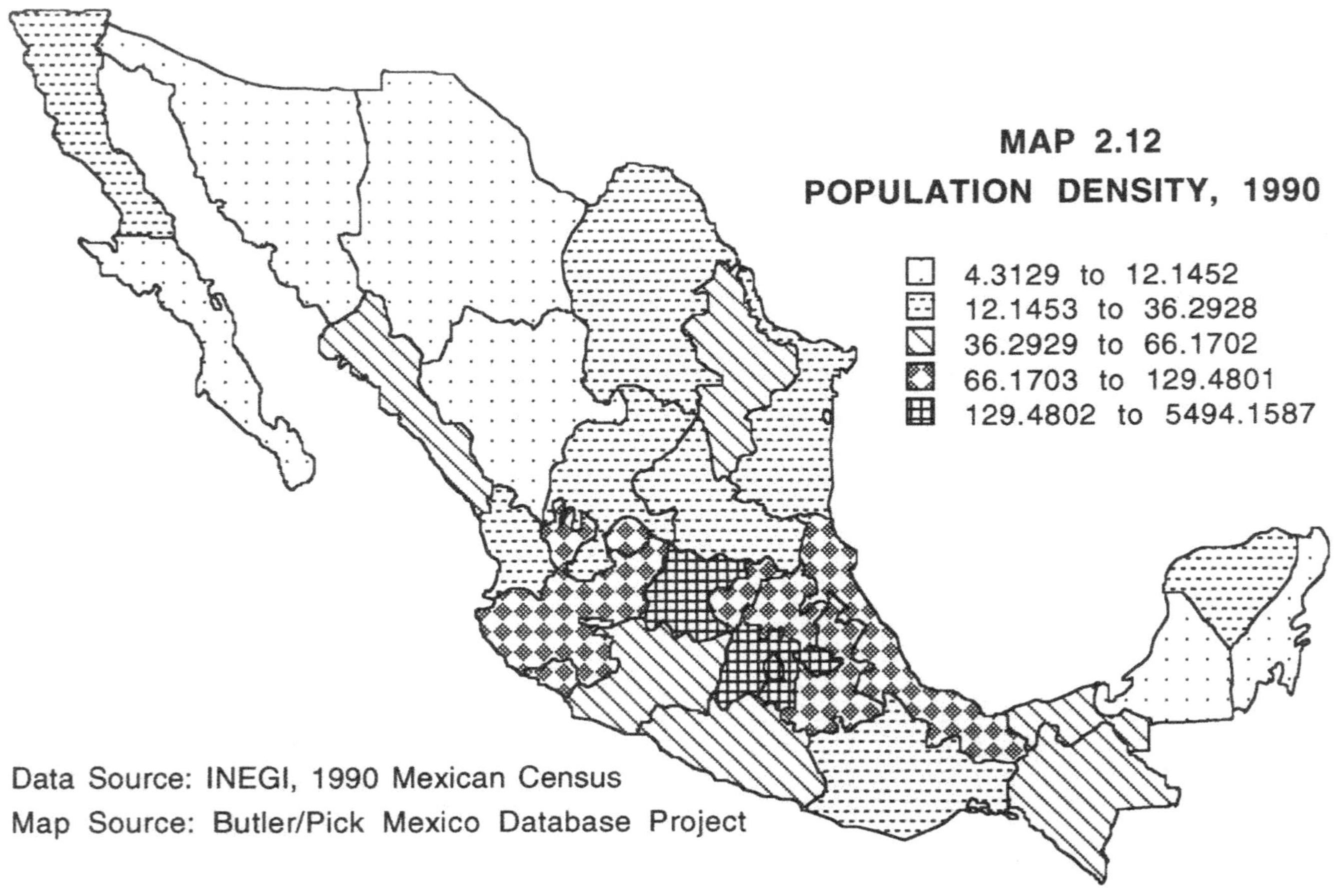

Data Source: INEGI, 1990 Mexican Census
Map Source: Butler/Pick Mexico Database Project

3

Urbanization

Introduction

This chapter examines urbanization, large cities, density, projected population, and border city growth and change. Urbanization includes the levels of urbanization throughout the twentieth century and the change in urbanization in the latter half of the century. There is a special section on the 59 largest Mexican cities, i.e., metropolitan areas above 100,000 population. This section also examines change in city populations during the decade of the 80s. Population density of Mexico City also is examined. A population projection of Mexico City to year 2010, encompassing the larger conurbation, is presented and discussed. Finally, the population of the Mexican border cities is examined, including twin cities facing each other across the U.S.-Mexican border. This reveals substantial growth in the population of border cities during the 1980s.

Urbanization, 1930, 1950, and 1990

Mexican urbanization increased greatly during the twentieth century. Urbanization is measured by the urban ratio, in particular the ratio of population living in places of 2,500 or more to total population. National urbanization increased from 28 percent in 1900 to 71 percent in 1990 (see Figure 3.1). The rural ratio is equal to one minus the urban ratio so its decrease is the converse of urbanization. This fundamental change reflects massive rural to urban migration throughout the century. The change has been associated with alterations in economic and work patterns, life style, as well as environmental impacts. Paralleling Mexico's urban increase is growth in its major cities.

The growth in urbanization shown in Figure 3.1 may be divided into two segments: the 1900–1940 period of moderate urban increase and the 1940–1990 period of rapid urban growth. In the first four decades, the national urban population increased from 19 percent in 1900 to 34 percent in 1940, averaging .4 percent in annual growth. However, during 1940 to 1990 the urban ratio doubled, growing by 1.5 percent annually. However, in the 1980s, the annual growth rate was only .7 percent. The 1980s' slowdown may have resulted from environmental and social limits reached in the carrying capacities of the larger metropolitan areas, as well as the inherent slowing as certain cities and states approached 100 percent urbanization.

The geography of urbanization has changed only slightly during the twentieth century. This is reflected in minor differences in the urban patterns for 1930, 1950, and 1990 (see Maps 3.1, 3.2, and 3.3). Urban ratios for the three time points are very significantly intercorrelated. The steadiness in urban patterns over many decades is not unique for Mexico—some other Mexican socioeconomic characteristics have also been stable in the twentieth century (Butler and Pick 1991; Butler, Pick, and Fukurai in press). The stability in urban patterns may be due to Mexico's relatively non-mobile population during the century. Also, the patterns of origin and destination states for rural-urban migration streams have been rather stable.

Urban patterns by state (see Table 3.1) reflect the urban growth for the nation and for states. The coefficient of variation in the absolute size of urban population is consistently much higher than the CV for the urban ratio. For instance, in 1990, the CV for raw urban population is 107, versus a CV of 23 for urban ratio. Both coefficients of variation are reduced, compared to values for 1930 and 1950. Because the urban patterns for 1930, 1950, and 1990 are highly intercorrelated, only the 1990 pattern is discussed here. However, the conclusions below on geographical patterns in 1990 urbanization apply as well for the two earlier dates.

The 1990 urban geographical pattern is analyzed by state, by region, and by metropolitan area. By state, the highest urban ratios are for the Federal District (.997), Nuevo Leon (.920), and Baja California (.909). These values reflect the major urban centers of Mexico City, Monterrey, and Tijuana, as well as Ensenada. In terms of absolute size of urban population, the largest states by far are Mexico and the Federal District, followed by Jalisco, Veracruz, and Nuevo Leon. Unlike the others, Veracruz does not contain any of Mexico's largest metropolises, but as seen in Map 3.5 it contains several large cities.

The least urban states are Oaxaca (urban ratio of 0.394), Chiapas (.404), Hidalgo (.448), and Zacatecas (.459). These states contain only two of Mexico's top 59 cities (see Map 3.5 and Table 3.2) and are agricultural, poor states.

Urbanization only partially corresponds to the outlines of standard regions. It is highest in the border region, being 71.7 percent urban. The central region is high only in its population core, consisting of the Federal District and Mexico plus Morelos, an area that has an urban ratio of 91.0 percent. Half of the national urban population is located in the border region and the population core of the central region.

The pacific south and gulf regions have the lowest urbanization. The south's urban ratio of 44.6 percent reflects its agricultural and less developed nature. This 1990 level is equivalent to the national urban ratio for 1950. The gulf region has an urban ratio of 55.0 percent. On the other hand, the west and southeast regions are moderate overall in urbanization.

Alternatively, Mexico's statewide urban pattern may be regarded vis-a-vis the location of the largest cities (compare with Map 3.5). Given that Mexico City corresponds to the Federal District and substantially to the state of Mexico; Guadalajara to the state of Jalisco; and Monterrey to the state of Nuevo Leon; then these five states accounted for 27 percent of the nation's urban population in 1990.

Urbanization in 1990 is associated with economic prosperity and urban indicators, and inversely related to marginality and rural indicators. In particular, the urban ratio has significant relationships with the urban indicators of education, literacy, vehicle ownership, and telephones. It is also significantly associated with the economic features of high monthly income, tertiary employment, professional/technical, administrative/managerial and service occupations, female economic activity, and number of corporations. It varies inversely to dependency ratio, annual fertility rate, literacy change 1950–1990, as well as to the marginality indicators of low income, households without toilet, households without electricity, crowding, and no meat and eggs. It is interesting that urbanization varies oppositely to home ownership, since the reverse pattern is expected in the United States.

Figure 3.1
Urban and Rural Population
Mexico: 1900-1990

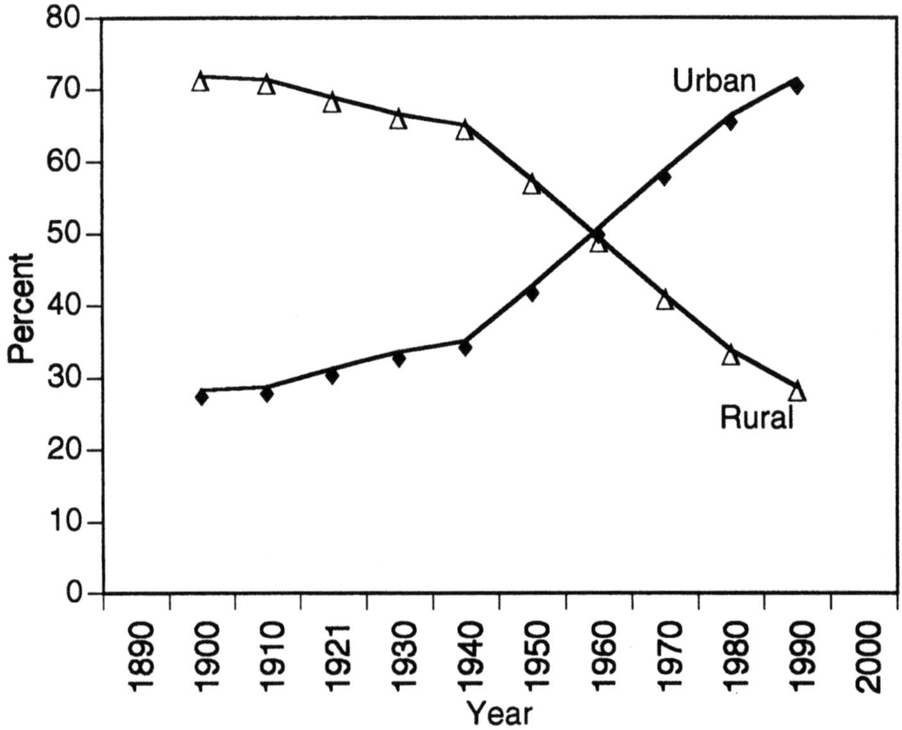

Supporting Data

Year	Urban	Rural
1890		
1900	28.3	71.7
1910	28.7	71.3
1921	31.2	68.8
1930	33.5	66.5
1940	35.0	65.0
1950	42.6	57.4
1960	50.7	49.3
1970	58.7	41.3
1980	66.3	33.7
1990	71.3	28.7

SOURCE: Estadisticas Historicas de Mexico, 1985; INEGI, 1992a.

Table 3.1 Urbanization, 1930-1990

No.	State	1930		1950		1980		1990		% Change Urbaniz. 1950-90
		Pop. Places 2500+	Urban Ratio	Pop. Places 2500+	Urban Ratio	Pop. Places 2500+	Urban Ratio	Pop. Places 2500+	Urban Ratio	
1	AGUASCALIENTES	72,735	0.5473	103,262	0.5490	365,545	0.7037	550,697	0.7652	0.2162
2	BAJA CALIFORNIA	26,268	0.5435	146,391	0.6450	1,004,194	0.8525	1,509,794	0.9090	0.2640
3	BAJA CALIFORNIA SUR	16,979	0.3606	20,022	0.3290	149,973	0.6971	248,665	0.7825	0.4535
4	CAMPECHE	38,155	0.4508	70,069	0.5739	292,006	0.6943	374,780	0.7003	0.1264
5	COAHUILA	227,276	0.5208	413,978	0.5745	1,204,971	0.7738	1,697,321	0.8606	0.2861
6	COLIMA	27,402	0.4425	67,559	0.6015	258,586	0.7467	357,034	0.8332	0.2317
7	CHIAPAS	92,627	0.1748	209,133	0.2306	702,969	0.3372	1,296,742	0.4039	0.1733
8	CHIHUAHUA	162,099	0.3296	373,357	0.4411	1,410,799	0.7035	1,889,766	0.7739	0.3328
9	DISTRITO FEDERAL	1,135,123	0.9232	2,884,133	0.9455	8,831,079	1.0000	8,213,843	0.9973	0.0518
10	DURANGO	94,248	0.2331	180,486	0.2865	595,544	0.5037	774,417	0.5739	0.2874
11	GUANAJUATO	336,663	0.3408	552,516	0.4158	1,771,604	0.5893	2,525,533	0.6341	0.2183
12	GUERRERO	97,336	0.1517	199,251	0.2167	883,394	0.4188	1,369,536	0.5226	0.3059
13	HIDALGO	114,933	0.1696	179,892	0.2115	506,275	0.3272	845,718	0.4479	0.2364
14	JALISCO	494,452	0.3939	836,124	0.4787	3,304,635	0.7559	4,340,432	0.8185	0.3398
15	MEXICO	202,956	0.2050	367,679	0.2640	6,007,404	0.7942	8,285,207	0.8441	0.5801
16	MICHOACAN	275,330	0.2626	455,789	0.3204	1,530,083	0.5333	2,186,354	0.6162	0.2958
17	MORELOS	33,219	0.2515	118,354	0.4338	699,331	0.7384	1,023,228	0.8562	0.4224
18	NAYARIT	58,703	0.3500	99,008	0.3413	414,528	0.5709	511,731	0.6205	0.2792
19	NUEVO LEON	172,175	0.4124	413,911	0.5592	2,197,288	0.8744	2,850,657	0.9199	0.3607
20	OAXACA	195,901	0.1806	293,953	0.2068	757,871	0.3199	1,191,303	0.3945	0.1877
21	PUEBLA	319,524	0.2777	539,233	0.3317	1,899,938	0.5675	2,652,779	0.6429	0.3112
22	QUERETARO	46,276	0.1977	69,196	0.2417	350,623	0.4741	627,839	0.5972	0.3555
23	QUINTANA ROO	2,790	0.2627	7,247	0.2687	133,511	0.5908	364,374	0.7387	0.4700
24	SAN LUIS POTOSI	158,712	0.2737	260,452	0.3042	786,023	0.4696	1,105,023	0.5516	0.2474
25	SINALOA	90,651	0.2291	177,522	0.2793	1,049,545	0.5674	1,412,447	0.6408	0.3615
26	SONORA	116,225	0.3675	231,424	0.4532	1,067,861	0.7054	1,443,067	0.7913	0.3381
27	TABASCO	38,790	0.1732	79,558	0.2193	405,950	0.3819	745,718	0.4966	0.2773
28	TAMAULIPAS	147,367	0.4283	380,281	0.5295	1,445,960	0.7513	1,823,704	0.8107	0.2812
29	TLAXCALA	56,632	0.2756	110,315	0.3877	320,480	0.5758	582,351	0.7650	0.3773
30	VERACRUZ	392,926	0.2853	679,380	0.3330	2,743,286	0.5092	3,501,726	0.5622	0.2292
31	YUCATAN	185,867	0.4814	285,567	0.5525	782,041	0.7352	1,071,618	0.7863	0.2338
32	ZACATECAS	110,291	0.2403	166,678	0.2504	426,432	0.3751	586,317	0.4594	0.2090
National Urban Population		5,540,631		10,971,720		44,299,729		57,959,721		
National Total Population		16,552,722		25,779,254		66,846,833		81,249,645		
National Urban Ratio		0.3347		0.4260		0.6627		0.7134		0.2874
Mean		173,145	0.3355	342,866	0.3993	1,384,367	0.6137	1,811,241	0.6912	0.2919
Median		112,612	0.2815	204,192	0.3372	784,032	0.5901	1,244,023	0.7195	0.2836
S.D.		211,127	0.1575	503,820	0.1676	1,788,364	0.1732	1,943,224	0.1605	0.1033
C.V.		121.94	46.94	146.94	41.97	129.18	28.22	107.29	23.22	35.39
Minimum		2,790	0.1517	7,247	0.2068	133,511	0.3199	248,665	0.3945	0.0518
Maximum		1,135,123	0.9232	2,884,133	0.9455	8,831,079	1.0000	8,285,207	0.9973	0.5801

DEFINITION: Urbanization is the ratio of population living in localities of the stated population total to the total population of the state.

SOURCE: 1930 and 1950 Mexican Census of Population, Resumen General; 1980 Mexican Census of Population, Volume 2, Table 2, 1990 Mexican Census of Population, Resumen General, Table 3.

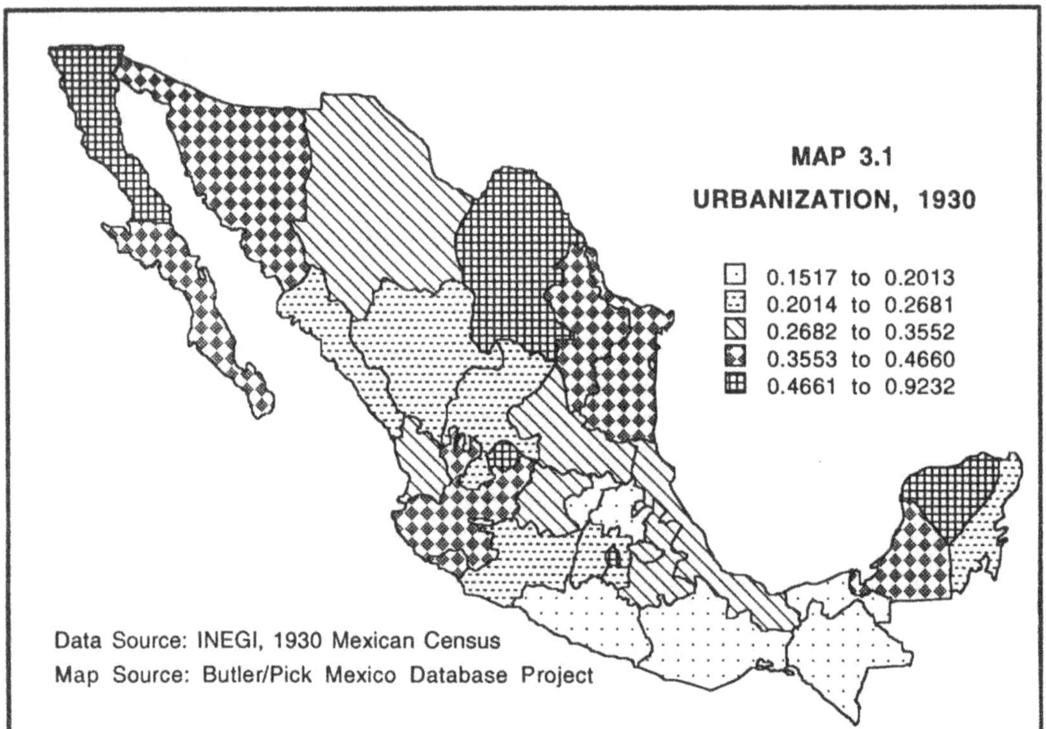
MAP 3.1
URBANIZATION, 1930
0.1517 to 0.2013
0.2014 to 0.2681
0.2682 to 0.3552
0.3553 to 0.4660
0.4661 to 0.9232
Data Source: INEGI, 1930 Mexican Census
Map Source: Butler/Pick Mexico Database Project

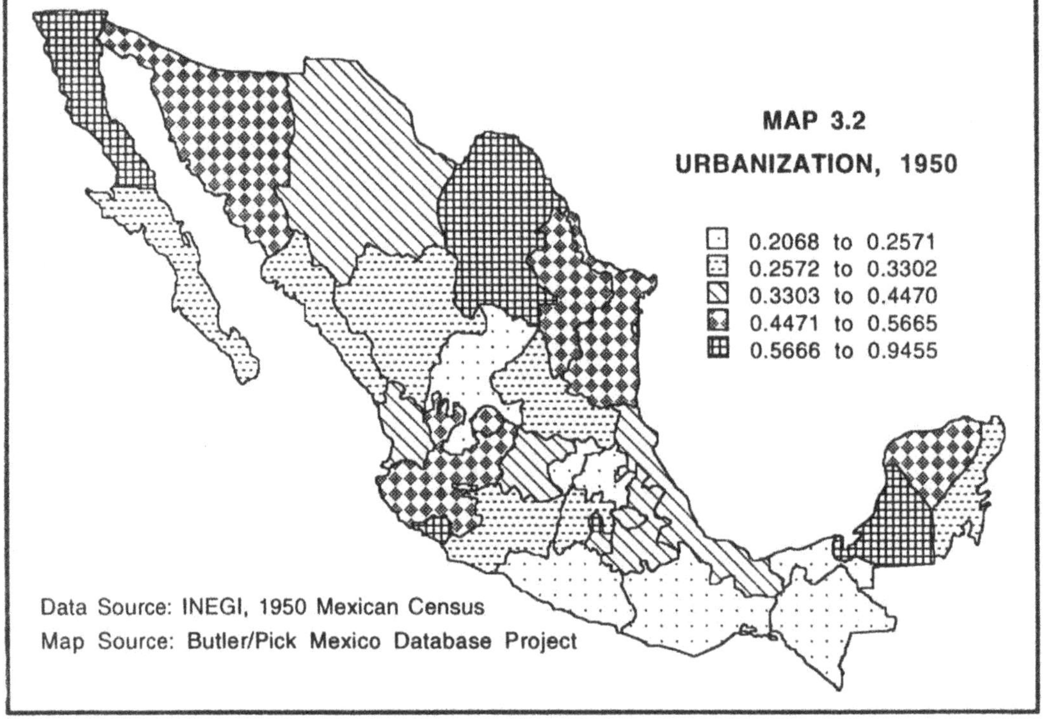
MAP 3.2
URBANIZATION, 1950
0.2068 to 0.2571
0.2572 to 0.3302
0.3303 to 0.4470
0.4471 to 0.5665
0.5666 to 0.9455
Data Source: INEGI, 1950 Mexican Census
Map Source: Butler/Pick Mexico Database Project

MAP 3.3

URBANIZATION, 1990

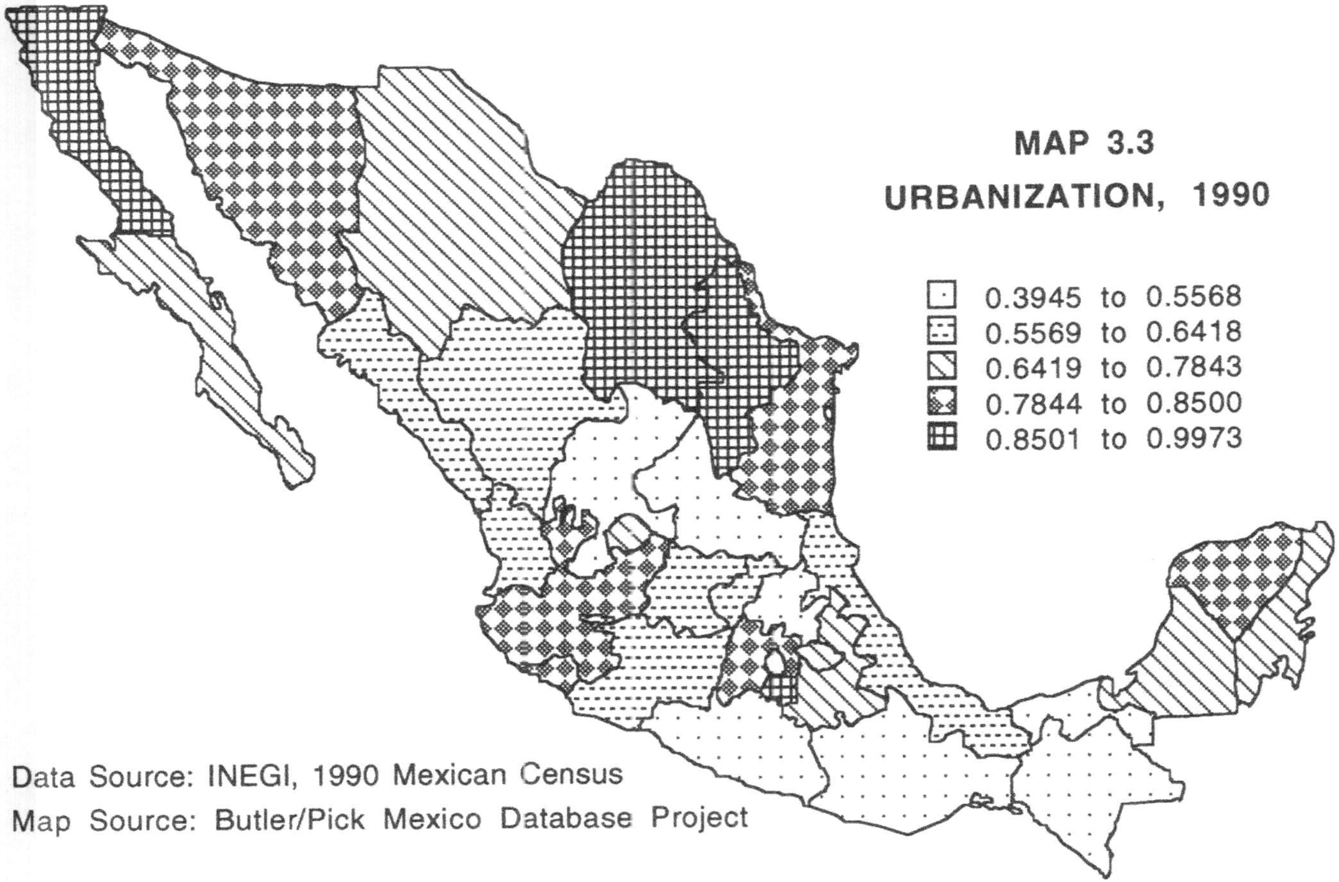

Data Source: INEGI, 1990 Mexican Census

Map Source: Butler/Pick Mexico Database Project

Urbanization Change, 1950–1990

Urbanization change is the difference in the urban ratio in 1990 minus the urban ratio in 1950 (see Table 3.1 and Map 3.4). The national urbanization change 1950–1990 was .287, which implies a two-thirds increase from the .426 proportion urban in 1950. Urbanization increased for all Mexican states, with a moderate coefficient of variation of 35. This reflects partly the fact that the major cities are located throughout the nation (see Map 3.5) and the rates of city growth have been fairly consistent over the past four decades.

At the upper extreme of urban change, the state of Mexico, had growth of 58 percent over the four decades. It is revealing to cast this increase in absolute terms—the state of Mexico gained 7.9 million urban residents from a starting 1940 urban population base of only 368,000! There were large urban increases in other states surrounding the CMZ, namely Queretaro, Morelos, and Tlaxcala. That growth may be explained by urban "overspill" from the metropolis. Urbanization also grew sharply from 1950 to 1990 in the states of Baja Sur and Quintana Roo. They were among the most rapidly growing states in population from 1950 to 1990, with the preponderance of the population growth located in urban areas.

The lowest urbanization change 1950–1990 was in the Federal District, which grew by 5.2 percent over the forty years. However, since the Federal District was already 94.6 percent urbanized in 1950, only a small further change was possible. Other states with low urban growth in the range of 13 to 22 percent were Campeche, Aguascalientes, Chiapas, Oaxaca, and Zacatecas. Except for Aguascalientes, these states lack cities in Mexico's top 20. Urban migrants may not be attracted to these less populous cities. Also, the agricultural nature and poverty in the latter three states may have deterred inmigration to their urban areas.

The patterns of urbanization change 1950–1990 do not correspond to standard regions. This contrasts with urbanization, which had some distinctive regional patterns.

Urbanization change 1950–1990 has relatively few significant relationships to other characteristics discussed in this book. It is positively related to population growth 1970–1990, secondary education, construction workforce, and automobile production, as well as to both lifetime and 1985–1990 inmigration and net migration. The associations with inmigration are plausible, since net inmigration has been a component of change in much of the urban population growth. This attribute is inversely associated with lifetime and 1985–1990 outmigration, elderly population (age 65 plus), population density, and low income. The inverse effect with population density may be interpreted as the influence of natural carrying capacity limits on urban growth, while low income may be interpreted as an economic disincentive for rural to urban migrants. The reverse association with elderly population may reflect locational preferences of the elderly for less urbanized areas or a population residue, i.e., long-time rural residents.

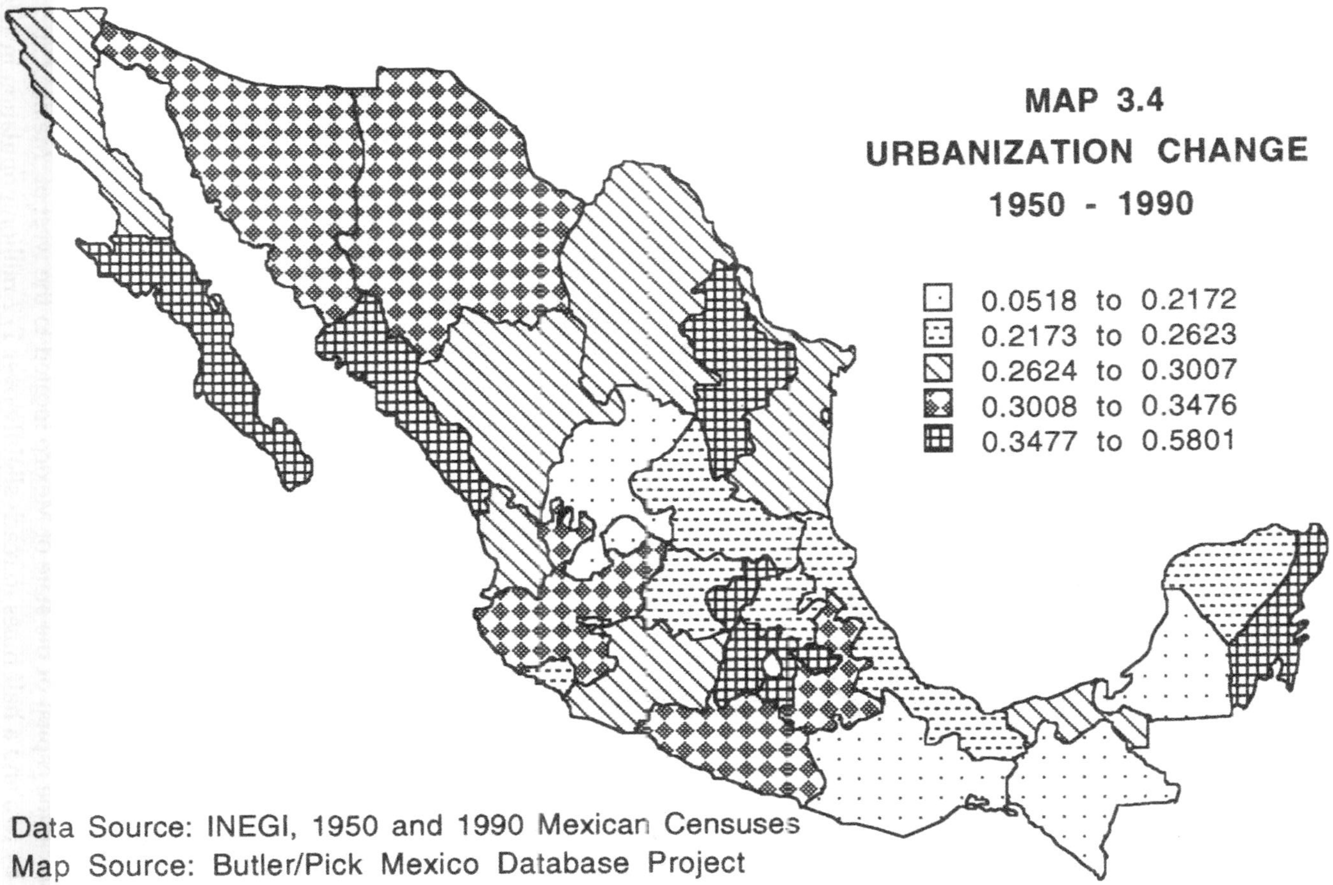

Data Source: INEGI, 1950 and 1990 Mexican Censuses
Map Source: Butler/Pick Mexico Database Project

Large Cities, 1990

Mexican population in 1990 was almost half concentrated in large cities. A large city is defined here as having a population greater than 100,000. There were 59 large cities in 1990, an increase of thirteen cities from 1980. It is important to note that our city definition changed somewhat from 1980 to 1990. For 1980, the city concept corresponds to the city definition in the Mexican Census, except for the largest cities that are defined according to the *Estadisticas Historicas de Mexico.* In 1990, city is defined in accord with a special INEGI compilation (INEGI 1993b). The city units were A.M., i.e., Area Metropolitana, for the largest three cities, M.U. ("Mancha Urbana"), or urban grouping, for certain other cities, in particular where several smaller cities constitute a common urban unit; and the 1990 census city definition for the others. Although these city definitions vary somewhat between years, they appear close enough to enable the present study to examine changes over time. Another confounding factor in this comparison is that some cities annexed land areas or even surrounding smaller cities over time. Nevertheless, the city sizes for the last three censuses are analyzed and some longitudinal comparisons are made.

In 1990, the 59 large cities contained 48 percent of the national population, thirteen percent more than in 1980. This implies that the growth in large cities was faster in the eighties than the national urban growth. Urbanization only increased by five percent during the decade.

The twelve largest cities in 1990 contained 26,749,195 persons, or 33 percent of the population. A decade earlier, the twelve largest cities contained a nearly identical one third of the population. This implies that 1980s' growth in major cities has been concentrated in cities smaller than the top twelve, as well as in the thirteen new large cities added over the decade. The nation's largest city is the Mexican City metropolis, totaling 15 million population containing 18.5 percent of the nation's population. This high proportion of population in one city places Mexico City in the category of a primate city (Jefferson 1939; Berry 1981). It is both the economic, financial, governmental, and cultural heart of the nation, as well as the locus of awesome environmental problems and vast amounts of poverty, crime, and social disorganization (Schteingart 1988; Garza 1987). Because of its size and importance, many of Mexico City's features are mapped and discussed in detail in this volume.

Mexico City's population grew more slowly than the nation as a whole in the 80s. It grew by 12.7 percent, much less than the 21.5 percent national growth. Although some critics contend that the 1990 census may have undercounted the population of the largest cities (Corona 1991), it is highly unlikely that adjustments to undercount would alter the fundamental conclusion of its relatively slower growth.

The next eleven largest cities grew during the 80s by 40.2 percent increment. These cities offered inmigrating people and businesses much more attractive environmental conditions, amenities, and in some cases a better business and job outlook than Mexico City. By far the most rapid growth in the top twelve occurred in Toluca, the capital of the state of Mexico located to the west of Mexico City. It grew by two and a half times to reach slightly over 1/2 million population in 1990. Another rapidly growing city in the top twelve was Tijuana, which grew by 63 percent to a size of 699,000 in 1990. If it continues its 80s' growth rates in the 1990s, it will pass one million population by the mid-90s and stand alongside San Diego as a major bi-national metropolis (see Table 3.4). The more slowly growing of the top twelve cities, besides Mexico City, are the metropolises of Monterrey and Guadalajara, the interior cities of Leon, San Luis Potosi, and Chihuahua, as well as Merida. These cities grew by about a third in the 80s.

The geographical distribution of the large cities (see Map 3.5), corresponds to the pattern of urban population in Map 3.3. Map 3.5 shows the 37 largest cities, i.e. with populations larger than 200,000. Table 3.2 presents population and other attributes for the 59 largest cities, i.e. more than 100,000 in population. The numbering on Map 3.5 is by rank order of population size and corresponds to lefthand rank order column in Table 3.2. The largest concentration of major cities is across the central flank of the nation. In Map 3.3, Mexico City is surrounded by three other large cities in three surrounding states, including the fourth largest city in Mexico—Puebla. Large cities are relatively sparse in the south and southeast regions, with the largest ones being Acapulco and Merida. The border states contain sixteen of the 59 large cities, half of which are on or very near the U.S. border. Nevertheless, the interior border state cities contain substantial population. Many of them have benefited from proximity to the U.S. and the growth in maquiladora industry. It is important to mention that the nation's most rapidly growing states of Baja Sur and Quintana Roo added newly classified 100,000 + cities in the 1980s—La Paz in Baja Sur and Cancun in Quintana Roo. Both these cities' economies are principally focused on tourists. Also, the expanding state of Mexico added the new large city of Buenavista.

Table 3.2 also identifies the most rapidly growing cities in the 80s. Although these changes have some definitional and annexation inconsistencies, they are nevertheless worthwhile to consider. The cities with the highest *relative* growth in the 80s were Toluca, Mexico; Cuernavaca, Morelos; Tuxtla, Chiapas; Monclova, Coahuila; and Queretaro, Queretaro. All of them over doubled in size. Toluca, Cuernavaca, and Queretaro received their growth from the outward spread of Mexico City. Tuxtla, Chiapas's largest city, experienced rapid growth from a combination of expanded tourism, international immigration from Central America, and other types of population influx. Monclova's growth is largely the result of expanding maquiladora industry in a border state.

The sex ratios in the major cities varied largely in accord with statewide patterns. The highest sex ratio was for Cancun, with a ratio of 108. High ratios are characteristic of much of the southeast of the country. There are also high sex ratios in most of the northwestern border cities, including Nogales (102), Tijuana (100), Monclova (100), and Juarez (98). These higher ratios may stem from the labor composition of the cities, the historical frontier nature of this part of the county, as well as from the presence of prospective or returning international migrants, who are predominantly male.

Table 3.2 Large Cities, 1990

No.	City	State	1990 Pop.	1990 No. Households	1990 Sex Ratio	1980 Pop.	% Change 1980-1990
1	Mexico City AM	D.F./Mexico *	15,047,685	3,133,834	94.17	13,354,271	12.68
2	Guadalajara AM	Jalisco *	2,870,417	557,378	93.80	2,192,557	30.92
3	Monterrey AM	Nuevo Leon *	2,558,494	529,242	98.41	1,913,075	33.74
4	Puebla MU	Puebla *	1,157,386	238,388	92.31	772,908	49.74
5	Juarez	Chihuahua	789,522	176,902	98.02	544,496	45.00
6	Leon	Guanajuato *	758,279	128,951	94.93	593,002	27.87
7	Tijuana	Baja California	698,752	155,710	100.40	429,500	62.69
8	Torreon/G. P. MU	Coahuila/Durange	689,212	141,370	94.37	445,053	54.86
9	San Luis Potosi MU	San Lius Potosi *	613,181	122,928	92.31	471,047	30.17
10	Merida MU	Yucatan *	532,964	118,328	91.94	400,142	33.19
11	Toluca MU	Mexico *	517,150	103,102	93.05	199,778	158.86
12	Chihuahua	Chihuahua *	516,153	116,669	94.17	385,603	33.86
13	Acapulco de Juarez	Guerrero	515,374	109,144	93.05	301,902	70.71
14	Tampico/C. M. MU	Tamaulipas	490,003	112,556	92.68	400,401	22.38
15	Aguascalientes MU	Aguascalientes *	455,234	86,000	93.05	293,152	55.29
16	Veracruz MU	Veracruz	447,202	105,594	89.39	367,339	21.74
17	Cuernavaca MU	Morelos *	446,739	97,223	93.42	192,770	131.75
18	Saltillo MU	Coahuila *	441,739	89,842	97.63	284,937	55.03
19	Mexicali	Baja California *	438,377	99,140	98.02	341,559	28.35
20	Queretaro MU	Queretaro *	431,905	82,356	93.42	215,976	99.98
21	Morelia	Michoacan *	428,486	86,912	91.94	297,544	44.01
22	Culiacan	Sinaloa *	415,046	82,333	94.93	304,826	36.16
23	Hermosillo	Sonora *	406,417	86,769	98.41	297,175	36.76
24	Durango	Durango *	348,036	70,988	92.68	321,148	8.37
25	Oaxaca MU	Oaxaca *	295,658	49,761	89.04	154,223	91.71
26	Jalapa MU	Veracruz *	291,038	66,050	87.27	204,594	42.25
27	Tuxtla	Chiapas *	289,626	60,982	93.05	131,096	120.93
28	Matamoros	Tamaulipas	266,055	59,089	94.17	188,745	40.96
29	Reynosa	Tamaulipas	265,663	59,085	97.24	194,693	36.45
30	Irapuato	Guanajuato	265,042	49,549	92.68	170,138	55.78
31	Mazatlan	Sinaloa	262,705	56,331	95.31	199,830	31.46
32	Villahermosa/Centro	Tabasco *	261,231	57,531	93.42	158,216	65.11
33	Monclova MU	Coahuila	254,376	54,479	100.00	115,786	119.69
34	Cajeme/C. O.	Sonora	219,980	46,664	95.69	165,572	32.86
35	Nuevo Laredo	Tamaulipas	218,413	47,546	95.31	201,731	8.27
36	Celeya	Guanajuato	214,856	41,048	92.68	141,675	51.65
37	Tepic	Nayarit *	206,967	43,705	91.94	145,741	42.01
38	Coatzacoalcos	Veracruz	198,817	45,174	96.46	233,935	
39	Ciudad Victoria	Tamaulipas *	194,996	42,014	95.69	140,161	39.12
40	Uruapan	Michoacan	187,623	36,858	92.68	122,828	52.75
41	Orizaba MU	Veracruz	174,179	38,489	91.20	114,848	51.66
42	Pachuca	Hidalgo *	174,013	37,608	90.84	110,351	57.69
43	Ensenada	Baja California	169,426	40,694	97.24	120,483	40.62
44	Cancun	Q. Roo	167,730	39,832	108.33		
45	Los Mochis/Ahome	Sinaloa	162,659	32,975	94.17	122,531	32.75
46	Poza Rica de Hidalgo	Veracruz	151,739	33,425	89.39	166,799	-9.03
47	Campeche	Campeche *	150,518	33,748	93.80	128,434	17.19
48	Cordoba MU	Veracruz	148,481	31,889	89.04		
49	Zacatecas MU	Zacatecas *	146,484	29,309	93.80		
50	Zamora MU	Michoacan	145,597	27,794	91.94		

Table 3.2 Large Cities, 1990 (Continued)

No.	City	State	1990 Pop.	1990 No. Households	1990 Sex Ratio	1980 Pop.	% Change 1980-1990
51	Colima MU	Colima *	142,844	31,050	94.52		
52	Minatitlan	Veracruz	142,060	31,032	94.17		
53	Tehuacan	Puebla	139,450	27,236	92.68		
54	Tapachula	Chiapas	138,858	29,541	91.20		
55	La Paz	Baja Calif. Sur *	137,641	30,008	100.40		
56	Salamanca	Guanajuato	123,190	23,649	94.55		
57	Buenavista	Mexico	114,653	22,180	99.20		
58	Cuautla	Morelos	110,242	23,555	91.20		
59	Nogales	Sonora	105,873	22,797	101.61		
Total City Population			38,652,436			28,752,571	
Population of Mexico			81,249,645			81,249,645	
Proportion of Population in Cities			0.475724368			0.3538793	
Mean City Population			655126.03	136175.19	94.38	625055.89	49.02
S.D.			1949754.56	405166.79	3.52	1937721	33.03
C.V.			297.62	297.53	3.73	310.00763	67.38
Minimum City Population			105,873	22,180	87.27	110,351	-9.03
Maximum City Population			15,047,685	3,133,834	108.33	13,354,271	158.86

NOTE: Three state capitals are not populous enough to appear; Chilpancingo, Guerrero; Chetumal, Quintana Roo; and Tlaxcala, Tlaxcala.
G.P. = Gomez Palacio.
C.M. = Cuidad Madero.
C.O.= Cuidad Obregon.
* City is capital of state.

SOURCE: INEGI, 1993b; Estadisticas Historicas de Mexico, 1985.

MAP 3.5

LARGE CITIES, 1990

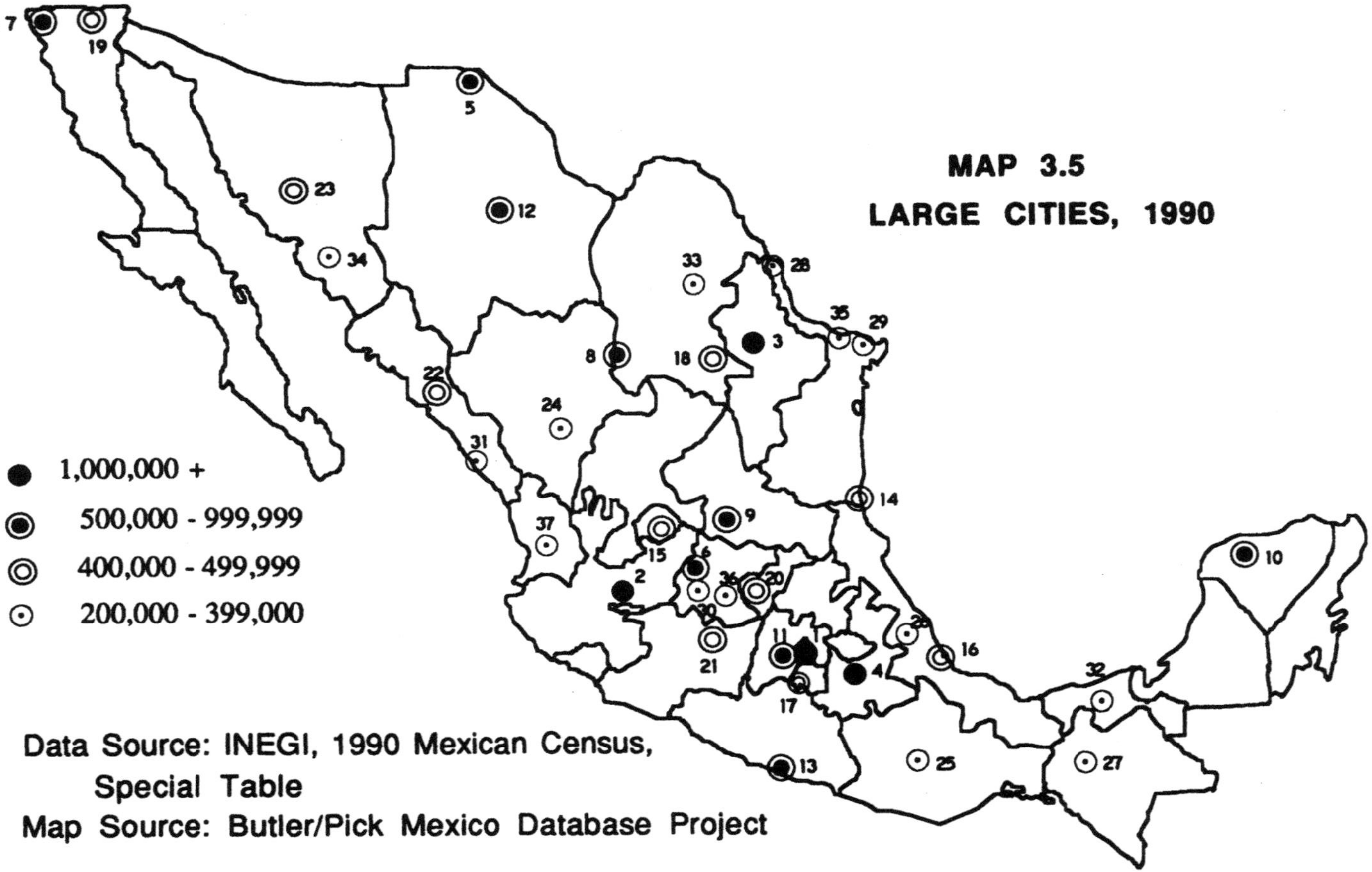

Data Source: INEGI, 1990 Mexican Census, Special Table

Map Source: Butler/Pick Mexico Database Project

Population Density, Mexico City, 1990

Population density for Mexico City is calculated as the population per hectare. This density measure may be converted into the density units for national and state population densities, i.e., population per square kilometer, by multiplying the present measure by 100. Mexico City's high density level is reflected in the Federal District's 1990 density of 5,494 persons per square kilometer and high densities for the state of Mexico as well as adjacent Morelos and Tlaxcala (see Chapter 2).

Caution must be exercised in analyzing urban population densities, since a portion of land areas may be uninhabitable for natural or other reasons. Overall, in 1980, the land area in 32 sub-areas of Mexico City is one third urban, with about equal proportions for the Federal District and state of Mexico. As seen in Table 3.3, the area that is classified as urban varies considerably among the geographical sub-areas. Although the land in several sub-areas is 100 percent urban, there is considerable variation. For instance, in the Federal District, the five delagaciones of Cuajimalpa, Magdalena Contreras, Milpa Alta, Tlahuac, and Tlalpan contain major portions mountainous, i.e., volcanic terrain, which is largely uninhabitable. Their land area is only 15.8 percent urban. Although the urban land classifications for the sub-areas changed between 1980 and 1990, the 1980 classifications are the most recent available to the authors (Garza 1987). Hence, they will be referred to in interpreting the population density of Mexico City.

Generally, the population density pattern shows a concentric pattern, with the highest densities centered in the north section of the Federal District and with reduction to low densities at the periphery of the metropolis (see Map 3.6). Compared to the pattern of total population in Map 2.4, the population density pattern is more concentrated and falls off more evenly in a concentric gradient. An exception is in the south and southwest, where the density falls off sharply from high to low values. There are several explanations for this pattern. First, the sub-areas located at the center of this pattern tend to have high proportions of urban land. For instance, the delegacions that were 100 percent urban land in 1980 are located in the north part of the Federal District. The proportion of urban land generally decreases radially the further away from the center. Second, the distribution of population is also centered in the north of the Federal District and falls off radially away from the center, although in a more irregular manner (see Map 2.4). Third, the sharp density drop in the south and southwest is due to uninhabitable mountainous/volcanic terrain, which rises swiftly and dramatically.

The region of very high density in the northern Federal District has distinctive patterns. The highest densities are in the delegacions of Azapotzalco, Gustavo Madero, Milpa Alpa, and Iztapalapa. These surround the moderately dense Venustiano Carranza, which contains substantial park areas. This high density zone also extends outside the Federal District into the municipio of Nezahualcoyotl in the state of Mexico (see Table 3.3). The north center of the District, consisting of the Miguel Hidalgo, Benito Juarez, and Coyoacan delegacions, also has high density.

The lowest densities are in the southern parts of the Federal District and adjoining municipios to the southwest. These delegacions all abut against the southern volcanic barrier. It should be mentioned that the densities within the *urban land areas* of these southern delegacions and municipios may be high, rivaling densities to the north. It is also important to distinguish the mostly economically prosperous southeast delegacions of Magdalena Contreras and Tlalpan from the poor sub-areas of Milpa Alpa, Tlahua in the District, and Chalco in the state of Mexico. The urban adaptations of architecture and housing developments based on volcanic materials in the former is changed to a struggle for urban poor to achieve shelter and urban services for the latter.

The northwest population corridor already noted (see Chapter 2) is less evident for population density. The reason is that much of the land in the corridor section remains rural. For instance the populous municipio of Naucalpan consisted of only 39 percent urban land area in 1980. With expected population growth in this corridor in the future (see next section), Naucalpan and other adjacent municipios may be expected to have a rising proportion of population and become much more dense.

Projected Population Growth in Mexico City, 2010

This section is based on population projections for Mexico City from 1980 to 2010 presented in *Atlas de la Ciudad de Mexico* (Garza 1987). Although projections were based on somewhat higher fertility assumptions than would be present today, the projection is useful in anticipating the pattern and spread of population for the Mexico City conurbation in the future. As seen in Map 3.7 and comparing to Map 2.4 for 1990, the projected 2010 population has shifted the most populous areas to the north and northwest of the Federal District. The northwest corridor, apparent for 1990 population, has opened up with large populations in the outlying northwest municipios of Atizapan de Zaragoza, Cuautitlan Izcali, and Nicolas Romero. Projected population of these three municipios in 2010 is 2.39 million, which compares to a 1980 population of .51 million. Other municipios in the northwest are also projected to have high relative population growth.

Rapid growth is also projected in municipios north of the tip of the Federal District. These include Cuautitlan de Romero Rubio, Coacalco, and Tecamac. These three municipios are projected to grow from .77 million in 1980 to 1.49 million in 2010. Unlike municipios outside the Federal District to the northwest and north, municipios in the east of Mexico City are not projected to have very large populations. However, several eastern municipios are projected to grow rapidly, in particular Chicoloapan and Chimalhuacan, which are estimated to grow from .09 million to .55 million.

In summary, Garza (1987) forecasts a much larger metropolis overall, with several key patterns. First, a shift in the population centroid of the metropolis towards the northwest, with major population centers developing, outside of the Federal District, along a northwestern population corridor. Second, a shift toward the amassing of more population to the north of the tip of the Federal District. Third, the eastern part of the metropolis remains relatively unpopulous, but several fringe areas undergo high *relative* population increase. The results of this projection are subject to considerable error. However, the projection may serve as a helpful guide to considering future growth and change in the metropolis.

Table 3.3 Population Density, Mexico City, 1990

No.	State	Land Area In Hectares (1)	%	Urb. Land Area In Hectares (2)	%	% (3)	Population Density
	DISTRITO FEDERAL	150300.0	46.53	62500.98	56.06	41.58	1452.74
1	ALVARO OBREGON	8586.9	2.65	4580.06	4.11	53.50	74.8527
2	AZCAPOTZALCO	3434.0	1.06	3434.00	3.08	100.00	138.2318
3	BENITO JUAREZ	2711.9	0.84	2711.90	2.43	100.00	150.3783
4	COYOACAN	5711.7	1.79	5771.79	5.18	100.00	110.8973
5	CUAJIMALPA	7776.7	2.41	2208.58	1.98	28.40	15.3881
6	CUAUHTEMOC	3309.3	1.02	3309.30	2.97	100.00	180.0864
7	GUSTAVO A. MADERO	8921.7	2.76	7503.15	6.73	84.10	142.133
8	IZTACALCO	2366.1	0.73	2162.61	1.94	91.40	189.4772
9	IZTAPALAPA	11940.9	3.70	8155.63	7.31	68.30	124.823
10	MAGDALENA CONTRERAS	7042.5	2.18	2380.36	2.14	33.80	27.6949
11	MIGUEL HIDALGO	4746.6	1.48	3954.62	3.55	83.00	85.7178
12	MILPA ALTA	27828.0	8.62	807.01	0.72	2.90	2.2874
13	TLAHUAC	9123.5	2.82	2536.33	2.27	27.80	22.6558
14	TLALPAN	30547.0	9.46	5070.80	4.55	16.60	15.8728
15	VENUSTIANO CARRANZA	3442.1	1.07	3442.10	3.09	100.00	150.9625
16	XOCHIMILCO	12743.1	3.94	4472.83	4.01	35.10	21.2783
	STATE OF MEXICO	172793.0	53.47	48996.15	43.94	28.37	746.12
17	ATIZAPAN DE ZARAGOZA	7495.0	2.32	3685.15	3.31	49.17	42.0536
18	COACALCO	4497.0	1.39	1034.85	0.93	23.01	33.8185
19	CUAUTITLAN IZCALLI	10200.0	3.16	3625.06	0.62	35.54	32.0343
20	CUAUTITLAN DE R. RUBIO	4069.0	1.26	695.01	3.25	17.08	12.0074
21	ECATEPEC	12617.0	3.91	8912.08	7.99	70.63	96.5471
22	CHALCO	27359.0	8.47	1962.60	1.76	7.17	10.3418
23	CHICOLOAPAN	4728.0	1.46	585.21	0.52	12.38	12.1206
24	CHIMALHUANCAN	3368.0	1.04	1925.45	1.73	57.16	71.9469
25	HUIXQUILUCAN	10993.0	3.40	1063.35	0.95	9.67	12.0009
26	IXTAPALUCA	20613.0	6.38	1568.40	1.41	7.46	6.6636
27	NAUCALPAN	15490.0	4.80	6083.67	5.46	39.27	50.778
28	NEZAHUALCOYOTL	6200.0	1.92	4918.37	4.41	79.32	202.5992
29	LA PAZ	3692.0	1.14	1501.53	1.35	40.67	36.5065
30	TULTITLAN	7170.0	2.22	2295.03	2.06	32.01	34.3743
31	TLALNEPANTLA	8245.0	2.55	6024.86	5.40	73.07	85.2404
32	NICOLAS ROMERO	25967.0	8.04	3115.53	2.79	11.99	7.0911
Total		323003.0	100.00	111497.13	100.00	34.52	2198.86

DEFINITION: Population density is the ratio of population to land area in hectares.

NOTE: Percentage (3) is the urban land ratio, ie., (2)/(1).

SOURCE: Garza, 1987.

MAP 3.6
POPULATION DENSITY
MEXICO CITY, 1990

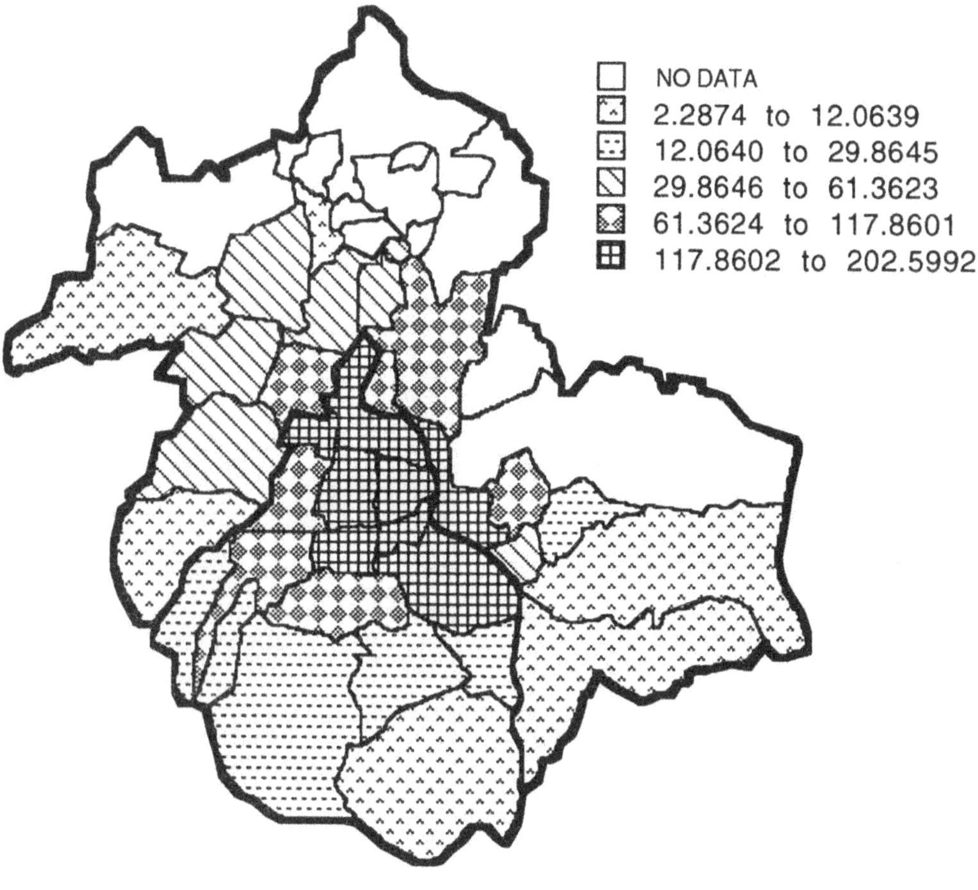

Data Source: INEGI, 1990 Mexican Census;
land areas from Garza, 1987
Map Source: Butler/Pick Mexico Database Project

MAP 3.7
PROJECTED POPULATION
CONURBATED AREA
2010

NO DATA
6421 to 25863
25864 to 66594
66595 to 322690
322691 to 648368
648369 to 26637788

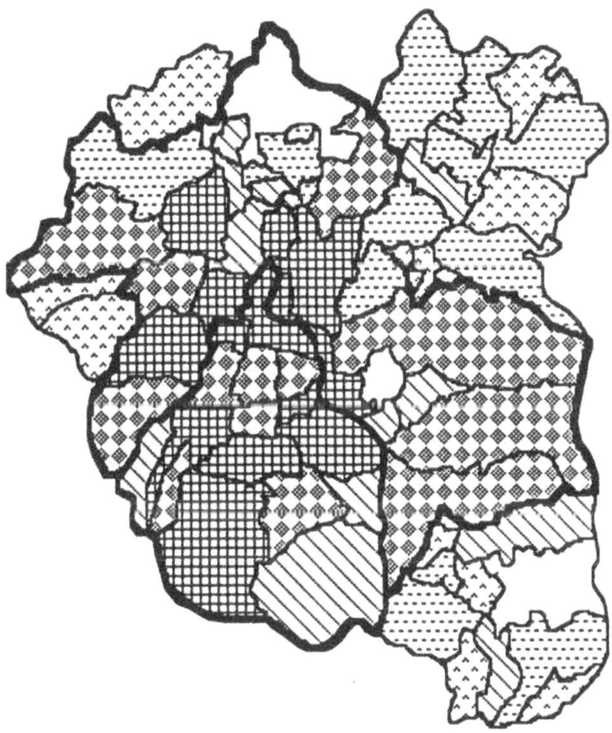

Data Source: Garza, 1987

Map Source: Butler/Pick Mexico Database Project

United States-Mexican Border Cities and States

Mexican states and cities on the U.S. border have been overshadowed in importance in the history and development of Mexico. Today, these areas have emerged as vitally important economic, social, and political entities. A major factor in the greater importance of the border is the growing Mexican-U.S. economic exchange and co-production centered in this area. Growth in the past decade in the maquiladora sector of the Mexican economy is one important indicator of this relationship (see Chapter 10).

Although border populations grew rapidly early in the century, since 1970, the portion of national population in the border region has remained constant. The proportion of national population in the border region was almost exact one sixth of national population from 1970 to 1990. Mexico's population in the border region between 1970 and 1990 is presented below.

State	1970 Pop.	1980 Pop.	1990 Pop.	% Growth 1970–1990	% Growth 1980–1990
Tamaulipas	1,457	1,924	2,250	54	17
Nuevo Leon	1,695	2,513	3,099	83	23
Coahuila	1,115	1,557	1,972	77	27
Chihuahua	1,613	2,005	2,442	51	22
Sonora	1,267	1,850	2,204	66	19
Baja Calif.	870	1,178	1,661	91	41
Total Border Region	8,017	11,027	13,628	70	24
Nation	48,225	66,847	81,250	68	22
% in Border	0.166	0.165	0.168		

NOTE: The population figures are in thousands.
SOURCE: INEGI, *1990 Mexican Census of Population.*

While the border region grew in the 70s and 80s at about the national rate within the region, Baja substantially exceeded the nation's growth, while Tamaulipas lagged the nation. Partly, this is explained by differences in regional economic partnerships with the U.S. While Tamaulipas is located along the south Texas border, an economically depressed region, Baja adjoins California, which during the 70s and 80s had a large and prosperous regional economy. Baja has also served as the major channel for the large Mexican migration flows between Mexico and the U.S. (Lorey 1990). This flow has implied an increase in temporary and longer term residence in Baja for migrants at various stages of their moves (see Pick et al. 1990a).

The border may also be conceived as a narrow band adjacent to the 2,000 mile U.S.-Mexican border. In such a view, the eight major metropolitan areas of twin

U.S.-Mexican cities rise in importance (see Map 3.8 and Table 3.4). In 1990, the twin cities had a bi-national population of 6.4 million persons, of which 2.9 million resided in Mexico and 3.5 million in the U.S.. These cities are developing into new urban and metropolitan forms that extend into economics, politics, and familial/social structure (Tamayo and Fernandez 1983; Gonzalez-Arechiga and Ramirez 1990; Arreola and Curtis 1993). They are becoming important economic entities, since they are the loci for most of Mexico's maquiladora plants (see Chapter 10) and offer unique international trade and commercial services.

The population figures referred to for the twin cities for the U.S. cities based on the U.S. Census concept of urbanized area (U.S. Bureau of the Census 1992). An urbanized area includes the central city and any contiguous cities. It differs from a metropolitan area by not corresponding to county boundaries.

In the 1980s, both the Mexican and U.S. border city components grew more rapidly than their respective nations. The Mexican component's growth rate of 42 percent was much higher than Mexico's 22 percent growth, while the U.S.'s border city component's growth of 25 percent exceeded U.S. decennial growth of 10 percent. However, Mexican population in border cities constituted 21 percent of the Mexican border region population, while the equivalent U.S. portion was only seven percent. This implies that Mexican border population is much more "bunched up" next to the border line, while in the U.S. the border region population is more spread out.

Twin cities show considerable variation. The largest twin city is the San Diego/Tijuana, with an 1990 population of 3.0 million. This twin city is a major North American metropolis. For example, its *combined* 1990 population total would rank it as the 12th largest metropolitan area in the United States, between Miami-Fort Lauderdale at 3.2 million and Atlanta at 2.8 million (U.S. Bureau of the Census 1991) and second in size in Mexico. It holds nearly half of the border twin cities' population, and it is increasing its economic importance, both in North America and globally (Arreola and Curtis 1993). Although Tijuana grew rapidly in the 80s, the population of this twin city is still nearly 80 percent U.S. citizens. Second in population size is Ciudad Juarez/El Paso, which had a combined population of 1.4 million in 1990, equivalent to about one quarter of the border twin cities' population. In contrast to San Diego/Tijuana, Ciudad Juarez/El Paso is about 60 percent Mexican citizens. The Mexican city of Ciudad Juarez is roughly the size of Tijuana, but has the largest maquiladora sector in Mexico (see Chapter 10).

The twin city of Mexicali/Calexico had a population one sixth the size of San Diego/Tijuana. It is 96 percent Mexican citizens. This is due largely to the agricultural nature of Imperial County on the U.S. size, which so far has limited population growth. Mexicali/Calexico grew in the 80s at about 3/4 the rate of San Diego/Tijuana. The slower growth may be due to a hotter, inland location and less accessible transportation.

There are three twin cities in the east between the states of Texas, U.S., and Tamaulipas, Mexico. The two eastern ones, Matamoros/Brownsville and Reynosa/McAllen, are similar in many respects. They are fairly balanced between the two sides, with populations in the roughly half million range. They grew during the 1980s at about 30 percent, a rate about at the average for border cities. These twin cities are not as prosperous as Tijuana/San Diego and Ciudad Juarez/El

Paso, because south Texas is a poor section of the U.S. and Tamaulipas is only moderate in prosperity in Mexico. The third twin city of Nuevo Laredo/Laredo resembles the others although it is somewhat smaller at 1/3 million persons and grew more slowly in the 80s—by only 16 percent.

The smallest twin cities are Piedras Negras/Eagle Pass and Nogales/Nogales. Both are predominantly Mexican citizens in population. Nogales/Nogales grew rapidly in the 80s, in fact the most rapidly at 53 percent of the eight twin cities. This growth was due in large part to the influx of maquiladora industry into the city (see Chapter 10). By contrast, Piedra Negras Negras/Eagle Pass grew at an average rate for the twin cities.

The Mexican portions of the twin cities grew more rapidly in the 80s than the U.S. part. In particular, Mexican segments grew by 42 percent, while the U.S. growth was 25 percent. This differential reflects varying nationwide population growth rates in the two nations, as well as the build-up of maquiladora industry on the Mexican side of the border. The Mexican cities of Nogales, Sonora, grew by 60 percent, and Tijuana grew by 63 percent, exceeding by far the average growth rate for the major Mexican cities (see Table 3.2), or increased at about 2–1/2 times the rate of the border region as a whole.

Table 3.4 U.S. - Mexico Twin Cities, 1990

No.	Twin City, State	Population	Twin Cities Population *	Percent	Twin Cities Pop. Growth 1980-90**
1	Matamoros, Tamaulipas	266,055	383,731	6.03	33.34
2	Brownsville, Texas, UA	117,676			
	Brownsville, Texas, City	98,962			
3	Reynosa, Tamaulipas	265,663	528,855	8.31	29.53
4	McAllen, Texas, UA	263,192			
	McAllen, Texas, City	84,021			
5	Nuevo Laredo, Tamaulipas	218,413	342,064	5.38	16.42
6	Laredo, Texas, UA	123,651			
	Laredo, Texas, City	122,899			
7	Piedras Negras, Coahuila	96,198	116,849	1.84	31.49
8	Eagle Pass, Texas, City	20,651			
9	Ciudad Juarez, Chihuahua	789,522	1,360,539	21.39	34.54
10	El Paso, Texas, UA	571,017			
	El Paso, Texas, City	515,187			
11	Nogales, Sonora	105,873	125,362	1.97	53.47
12	Nogales, Arizona, City	19,489			
13	Mexicali, Baja California	438,377	457,010	7.18	28.38
14	Calexico, California, City	18,633			
15	Tijuana, Baja California	698,752	3,047,169	47.90	38.59
16	San Diego, California, UA	2,348,417			
	San Diego, California, City	1,109,962			
	Total		6,361,579		34.15
	Mexico Total		2,878,853	45.25	41.52
	U.S. Total		3,482,726	54.75	24.75

SOURCE: U.S. Census of Population, General Population Characteristics, CP-1, 1992; INEGI, 1993b.
UA=urbanized area.

* For U.S. component of twin cities, urbanized areapopulation included where applicable, otherwise city population included.

** In 1980-90 growth calculations, for U.S. component, city populations used exclusively for consistency.

MAP 3.8
UNITED STATES-MEXICAN BORDER CITIES AND STATES, 1990

Data Sources: INEGI, 1990 Mexican Census;
U.S. Census Bureau, 1990 United States Census
Map Source: Butler/Pick Mexico Database Project

4

Marriage, Fertility, and Family Planning

Introduction

Chapter 4 concentrates on the dimensions of marriage, fertility, and family planning. Data are largely from the *Encuesta Nacional Sobre Fecundidad y Salud* (ENFES) and from the 1990 Mexican Population and Housing Census.

Marriage attributes include women currently married, women with common law marriage, and women divorced and separated. Fertility dimensions are crude and standardized fertility rates, cumulative fertility measures, and gross reproduction rate. Family planning variables include women using contraceptives and women sterilized.

Many other attributes on these dimensions are available in specialized fertility, contraception, and family surveys, including the ENFES, governmental surveys from INEGI, and health surveys. The 1990 Census of Population and Housing and *Cuaderno de Poblacion* series contain a wealth of additional information.

Marriage

Women Currently Married, 1987

Marriage showed a very steady trend in the 1980s and was also very even in its geographical distribution (see Table and Map 4.1). The number of marriages increased from 493,151 in 1980 to 642,201 in 1990, for an annual rate of increase of 2.6 percent, which approximates the decennial rate of increase in population of 2.0 percent. Likewise, the marriage rate, in marriages per thousand, barely fluctuated from 7.38 in 1980 to 7.90 in 1990. Similarly, as seen in the table below, type of union, i.e., marriage versus common law marriage (i.e., union libre), has not varied substantially since the mid 70s. The table shows the marital status distribution for women of fertile age for four demographic surveys from 1976 to 1987.

Marital Status	WFS Survey 1976	National Prevalence Survey 1979	National Demographic Survey 1982	ENFES Survey 1987
Married	51.6	55.4	51.5	51.4
Common Law Marriage	8.4	8.8	9.0	9.4
Divorced/ Separated	4.5	4.3	4.2	4.8
Widowed	4.5	4.3	4.2	4.8
Single	33.1	29.5	32.5	32.6
TOTAL	100.0	100.0	100.0	100.0

NOTE: Figures represent percent of respondents. The data is for women of fertile age, i.e., 15–49 years.
SOURCE: ENFES, 1989.

The age distribution of marital status for the fertile age groups, seen in Figure 4.1, shows a dramatic decline in the single status from 80 percent for 15–19 age group to 5 percent for the 45–49 age group, with a parallel increase in the married proportions from 12 percent to 70 percent (ENFES 1989). On the other hand, the proportion of women in common law marriage is relatively steady over the fertile age range, increasing from 6 to 10 percent. The steadiness in this category may reflect the conversion of common law marriages, across the spectrum of ages, into legal marriages. The separated, widowed, and divorced components are small, but slowly increase with age.

The marriage rate is remarkably stable geographically (see Table 4.3 and Map 4.4). This is reflected in its coefficient of variation of only fourteen. The marriage rate is highest in the northeast, west, and southeast regions. It is relatively very low in the Federal District and the gulf and pacific south regions. The low value for Mexico/Mexico City corresponds to late 70s survey results of the low proportion of married population in the Federal District (see Pick et al. 1989a). Traditional marriages may be low in the gulf and pacific south regions because of the high concentration of common law marriages (see Map 4.2). In fact, the national pattern of marriage rate is remarkably opposite from that of common law marriage, even though the measure of common law marriage is different. This contrast implies that the pattern for rate of marital union (legal and consensual) may be more smooth in geographic pattern than either subcomponent. As seen in Table 4.1, the proportions of fertile-age women currently married in the ENFES Survey of 1987 were also remarkably stable.

Common Law Marriage, 1976–1977

The data presented here are from the World Fertility Survey (WFS) of 1976–1977 (SPP 1979a,b,c). The older data are included, since these data on common law marriages far surpass the more recent survey data. According to the WFS data, the statewide mean for common law marriages at first union in 1976–77 was 17.5 percent (Table 4.2). As reported in Figure 4.2, there is substantial variation in common law marriages by region and by state. There is great variation in common law marriages, ranging from none reported in Aguascalientes to a high of 49 percent in Guanajuato.

States with the highest levels were Guanajuato, Hidalgo, Veracruz, and Nayarit, all in the range of 39–49 percent. Map 4.2 shows that these states are irregularly located across Mexico's central flank, and do not correspond to standard regions. There is moderate to high common law marriage in the pacific south region, averaging 23 percent. In the Federal District, eleven percent of women have a common law first union. States with less than five percent common law marriage at first union were located in the west, except for Guanajuato. In the border region, values were distributed along a gradient from high in the west to low in the east.

Table 4.1 Women Currently Married, 1987

	Residential Zone	Percent
1	ZONE I	51.00
2	ZONE II	51.90
3	ZONE III	50.90
4	ZONE IV	52.30
5	ZONE V	51.00
Mean		51.42
Median		51.00
S.D.		0.6380
C.V.		1.24
Minimum		50.90
Maximum		52.30

NOTE:

Zone I
- Baja California Sur
- Baja California
- Sonora
- Sinaloa
- Nayarit
- Chihuahua
- Durango
- Zacatecas
- Aguascalientes
- San Luis Potosi

Zone II
- Coahuilla
- Nuevo Leon
- Tamalipas

Zone III
- Veracruz
- Chipas
- Tabasco
- Campeche
- Quintana Roo
- Yucatan
- Tlaxcala
- Puebla
- Oaxaca

Zone IV
- Coalima
- Jalisco
- Michoacan
- Guanajuato
- Queretaro
- Hidalgo

Zone V
- Distrito Federal
- Mexico
- Guerrero
- Morelos

DEFINITION: Proportion of surveyed women age 15–49 who are currently married.
SOURCE: Encuesta Nacional Sobre Fecundidad y Salud, 1989, Table 4.2.

MAP 4.1
WOMEN CURRENTLY MARRIED, 1987

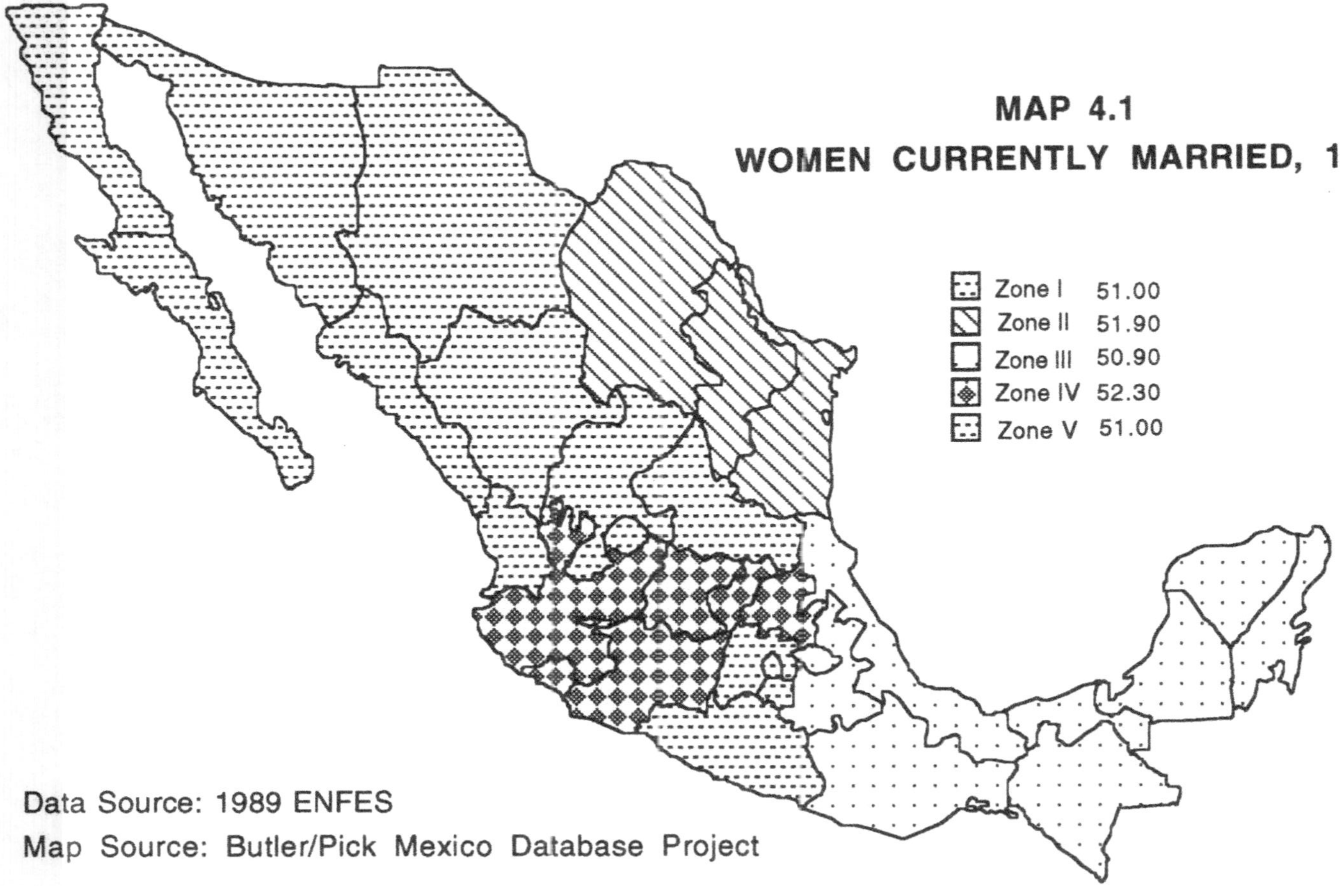

Data Source: 1989 ENFES
Map Source: Butler/Pick Mexico Database Project

Figure 4.1
Percentage Distribution of Fertile Age Women by Marital Status, 1987

Supporting Data

	Single	Common Law Married	Married	Widowed	Divorced	Separated
15–19	80.1	6.1	12.3	0.0	0.0	1.5
20–24	41.2	11.4	44.6	0.2	0.2	2.6
25–29	18.2	11.3	64.6	0.6	0.9	4.3
30–34	9.2	9.8	72.9	1.9	2.2	4.0
35–39	8.5	11.0	70.0	2.1	1.8	6.9
40–44	4.2	7.9	74.1	6.6	0.7	6.5
45–49	4.8	10.0	69.5	7.6	1.9	6.2

SOURCE: Encuesta Nacional sobre Fecundidad y Salud, 1987.

Figure 4.2
Women with Common Law Marriage, 1987

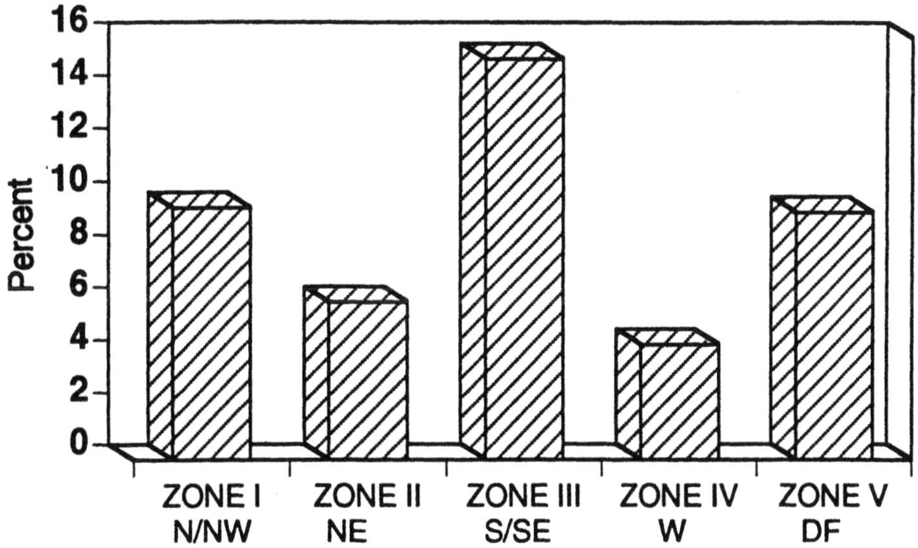

Supporting Data

	Residential Zone	Percent
1	ZONE I (N and NW)	9.60
2	ZONE II (NE)	6.00
3	ZONE III (S and SE)	15.20
4	ZONE IV (W)	4.40
5	ZONE V (DF)	9.40
Mean		7.80
Median		7.80
S.D.		2.55
C.V.		32.64
Minimum		4.40
Maximum		15.20

DEFINITION: Zone I: northern and northwestern states;
Zone II: northeastern states;
Zone III: south and southeastern states;
Zone IV: western states;
Zone V: Federal District.

NOTE: Zones correspond to state groupings shown in Table 4.1.

SOURCE: Encuesta Nacional Sobre Fecundidad y Salud, 1989, Table 4.2.

Table 4.2 Common Law Marriage (Union Libre), 1976-77

No.	State	Percent Common Law Marriages
1	AGUASCALIENTES	0.0000
2	BAJA CALIFORNIA	0.2500
3	BAJA CALIFORNIA SUR	ND
4	CAMPECHE	ND
5	COAHUILA	0.1300
6	COLIMA	ND
7	CHIAPAS	0.3480
8	CHIHUAHUA	0.1370
9	DISTRITO FEDERAL	0.1100
10	DURANGO	0.1370
11	GUANAJUATO	0.4900
12	GUERRERO	0.0810
13	HIDALGO	0.4450
14	JALISCO	0.0510
15	MEXICO	0.1070
16	MICHOACAN	0.0380
17	MORELOS	0.1840
18	NAYARIT	0.3920
19	NUEVO LEON	0.0750
20	OAXACA	0.2570
21	PUEBLA	0.1570
22	QUERETARO	0.0540
23	QUINTANA ROO	0.0860
24	SAN LUIS POTOSI	0.1540
25	SINALOA	0.3020
26	SONORA	0.1560
27	TABASCO	0.1560
28	TAMAULIPAS	0.1050
29	TLAXCALA	ND
30	VERACRUZ	0.3960
31	YUCATAN	0.0250
32	ZACATECAS	0.0790
Mean		0.1751
Median		0.1370
S.D.		0.1340
C.V.		76.52
Minimum		0.0000
Maximum		0.4900

DEFINITION: Ratio is the percent of survey respondents with common law marriages for first union.

NOTE: ND = no data.

SOURCE: 1976-77 World Fertility Survey.

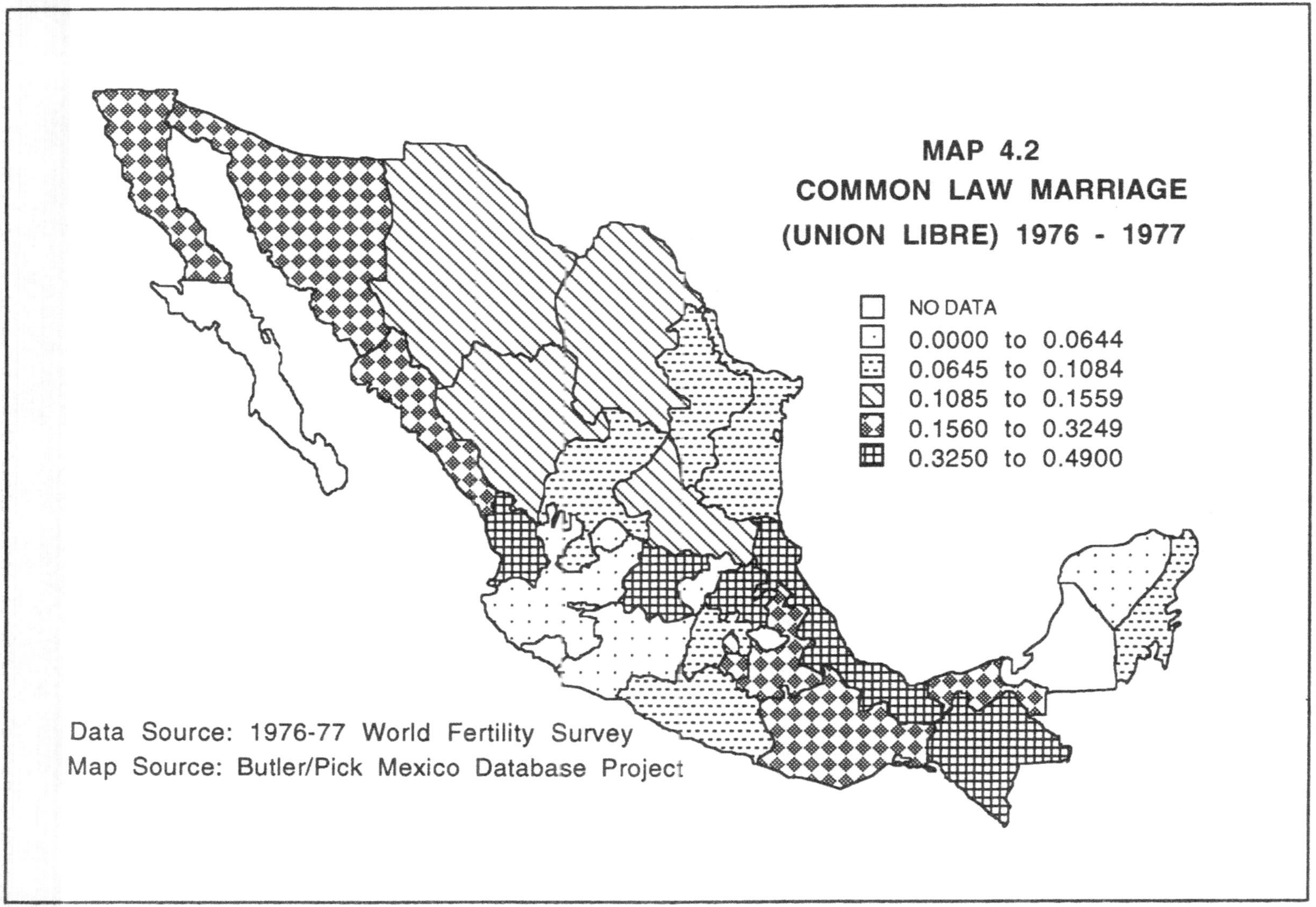
MAP 4.2
COMMON LAW MARRIAGE
(UNION LIBRE) 1976 - 1977
NO DATA
0.0000 to 0.0644
0.0645 to 0.1084
0.1085 to 0.1559
0.1560 to 0.3249
0.3250 to 0.4900
Data Source: 1976-77 World Fertility Survey
Map Source: Butler/Pick Mexico Database Project

Divorce Rate, 1990

There is very small proportion of divorced population in Mexico, although it has increased rapidly over the past decade. The number of divorces grew from 21,674 in 1980 to 46,254 in 1990, at a compounded annual rate of 7.6 percent. The divorce rate in 1990 was only .57 per 1000 population or one divorce for every fourteen marriages. However, the divorce rate was much lower in 1980, only .32. By contrast, in the United States in 1990, the marriage rate was 9.8 per 1000, while the divorce rate was 4.7 per 1000, a much higher level than for Mexico (National Center for Health Statistics 1992b). Thus, in the U.S. there was one divorce for every two marriages. The reasons for Mexico's low divorce rate include its dominant Catholic religion (see Chapter 7), as well as cultural norms favoring traditional marriage and not sanctioning divorce.

Divorce took place for a wide range of marital durations. As seen in Figure 4.3, divorces appear somewhat weighted towards marital durations of 1–5 years, although the proportion of divorce over the next four years of marital duration is only somewhat lower. As shown in Figure 4.4, divorce occurred mostly through the courts, although one seventh of divorces was administrative. The most important judicial ground applying to about half of divorces was mutual consent.

In the ENFES Survey of 1987, the geographic pattern of divorce was similar to that for the divorce rate in 1990 (also see Table 4.3 and Maps 4.3 and 4.4). The table below shows the proportion of fertile aged women separated and divorced in 1987.

	Separated	Divorced
Zone I (northern and northwestern states)	5.0	1.1
Zone II (northeastern states)	4.5	1.0
Zone III (south and southeastern states)	4.7	0.3
Zone IV (western states)	2.5	0.3
Zone V (Federal District)	3.3	1.6

NOTE: Zones correspond to state groupings shown in Map 4.1. Figures are per 100 women age 15–49.
SOURCE: ENFES, 1989.

The geographical distribution of separated women (see Map 4.5) reveals that separation is highest in the north/northwest and south/southeast, and is much lower in the western states and 4 state "Federal District" area. This may reflect the traditional Catholic structure in the western states, while also reflecting greater acceptance of marital separation in the more modern north/northwest and also in the less advanced south/southeast. The 1987 ENFES data reveal opposite geographical patterns for proportions of women separated and married (compare Map 4.5 to Map 4.1).

Figure 4.3
Duration of Marriage at Time of Divorce, 1989

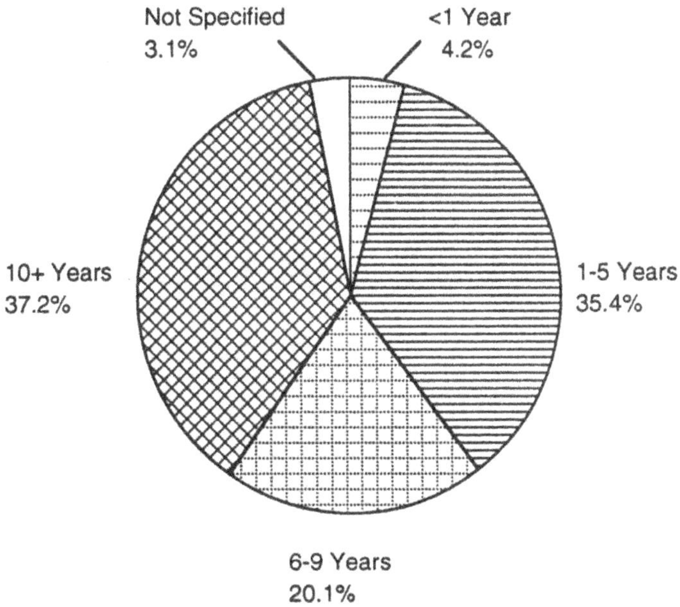

Figure 4.4
Grounds for Divorce, 1989

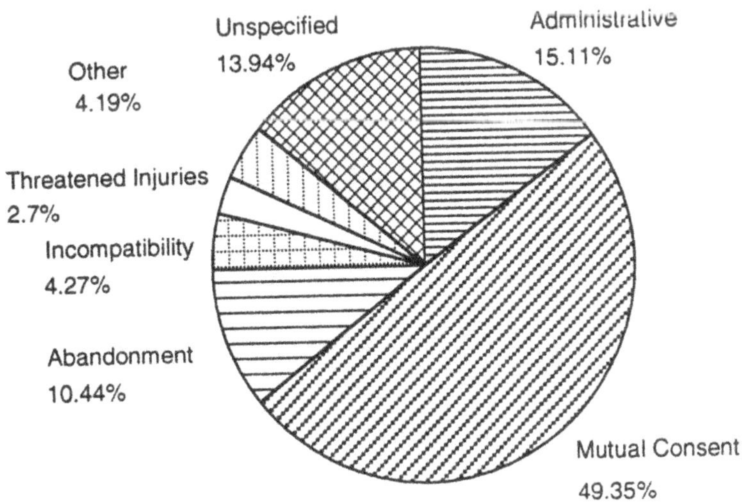

SOURCE: INEGI, Cuaderno de Poblacion, 1992.

Table 4.3 Marriage and Divorce Rates, 1990

No.	State	Marriage Rates	Divorce Rates
1	AGUASCALIENTES	8.3331	0.4586
2	BAJA CALIFORNIA	9.4229	0.9694
3	BAJA CALIFORNIA SUR	7.6252	0.8465
4	CAMPECHE	9.1968	0.4484
5	COAHUILA	9.8026	1.0186
6	COLIMA	7.8971	1.1762
7	CHIAPAS	5.5396	0.5133
8	CHIHUAHUA	8.6507	1.6635
9	DISTRITO FEDERAL	7.2346	0.6812
10	DURANGO	8.4669	0.4506
11	GUANAJUATO	8.7925	0.4017
12	GUERRERO	8.3823	0.1320
13	HIDALGO	7.0564	0.3220
14	JALISCO	9.2317	0.5441
15	MEXICO	7.1941	0.3793
16	MICHOACAN	9.5964	0.4470
17	MORELOS	8.0264	0.7648
18	NAYARIT	7.5026	0.5566
19	NUEVO LEON	9.6965	0.8139
20	OAXACA	7.1189	0.1682
21	PUEBLA	6.1465	0.3410
22	QUERETARO	8.5290	0.4186
23	QUINTANA ROO	9.3984	0.8819
24	SAN LUIS POTOSI	7.9344	0.4673
25	SINALOA	7.9186	0.8158
26	SONORA	7.7648	0.6240
27	TABASCO	7.9900	0.8330
28	TAMAULIPAS	9.0630	0.5681
29	TLAXCALA	10.0042	0.4243
30	VERACRUZ	6.0974	0.4897
31	YUCATAN	9.1515	1.0529
32	ZACATECAS	9.7178	0.5657
	National Total	7.9040	0.5693
	Mean	8.2651	0.6324
	Median	8.3577	0.5504
	S.D.	1.1509	0.3163
	C.V.	13.93	50.02
	Minimum	5.5396	0.1320
	Maximum	10.0042	1.6635

DEFINITION: These rates equal marriages or divorces per 1,000 population.

SOURCE: 1991 Anuario Estadistico, Tables 3.1.17 and 3.1.18.

MAP 4.3
MARRIAGE RATE, 1990

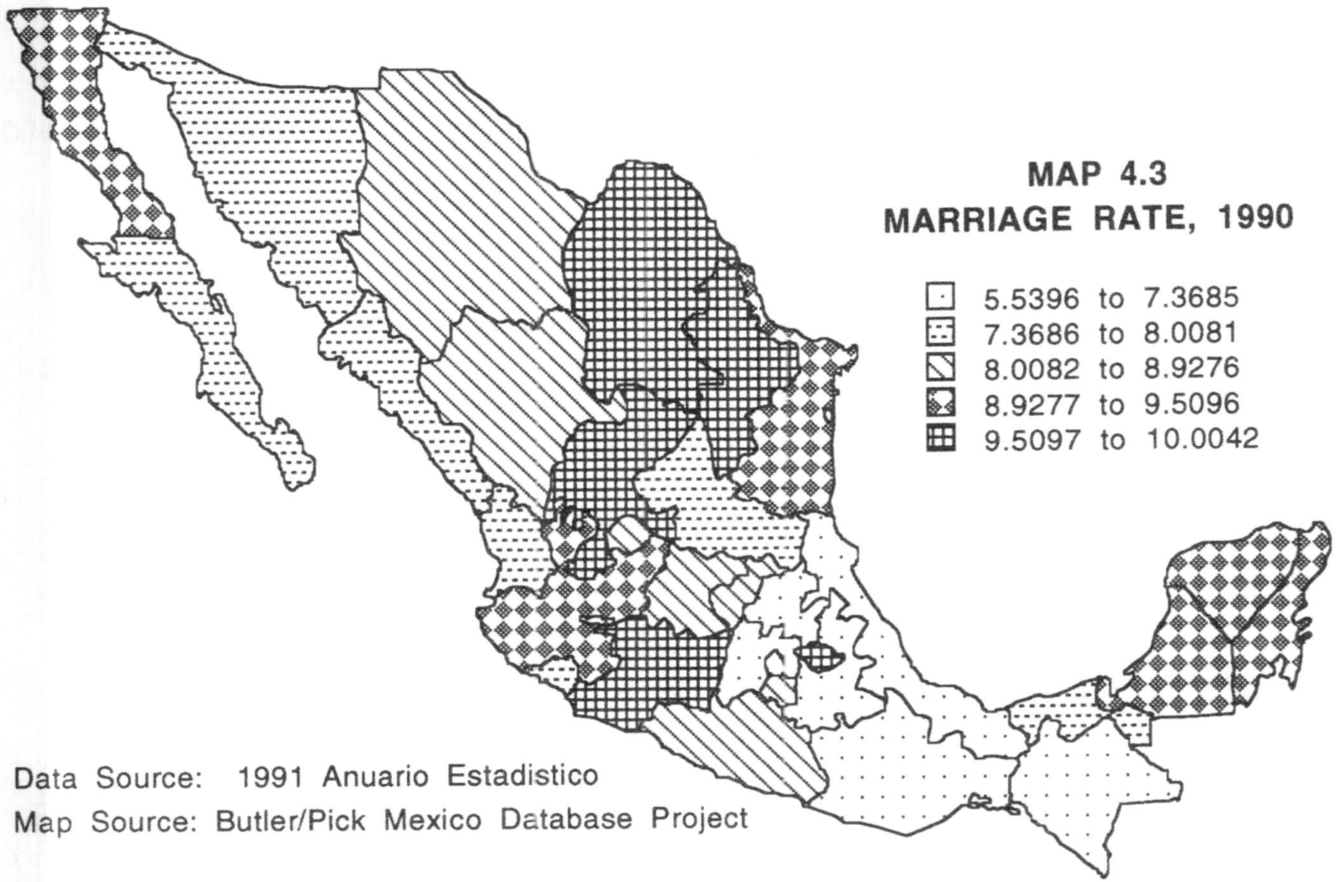

Data Source: 1991 Anuario Estadistico
Map Source: Butler/Pick Mexico Database Project

MAP 4.4
DIVORCE RATE, 1990

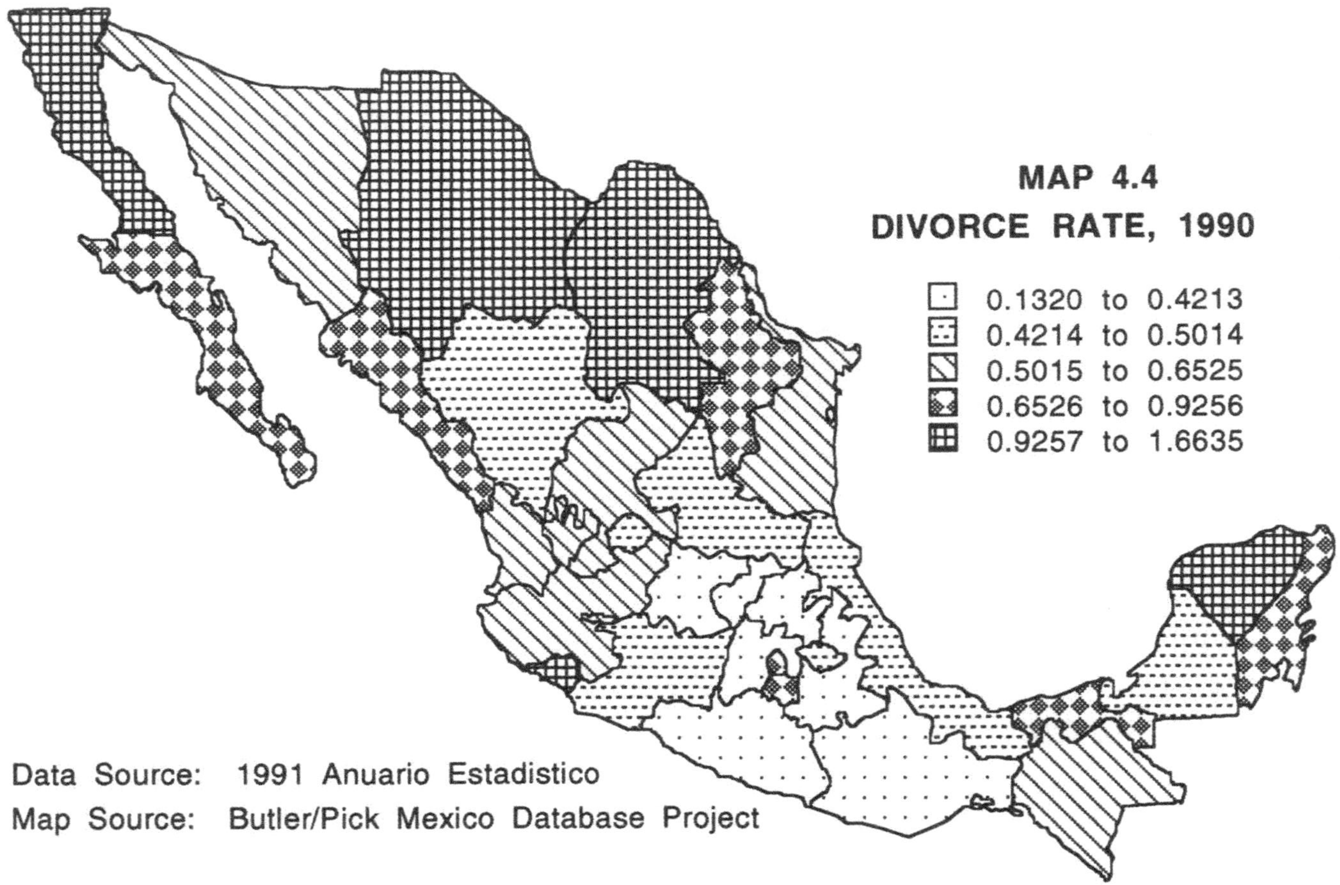

Data Source: 1991 Anuario Estadistico
Map Source: Butler/Pick Mexico Database Project

MAP 4.5
WOMEN SEPARATED, 1987

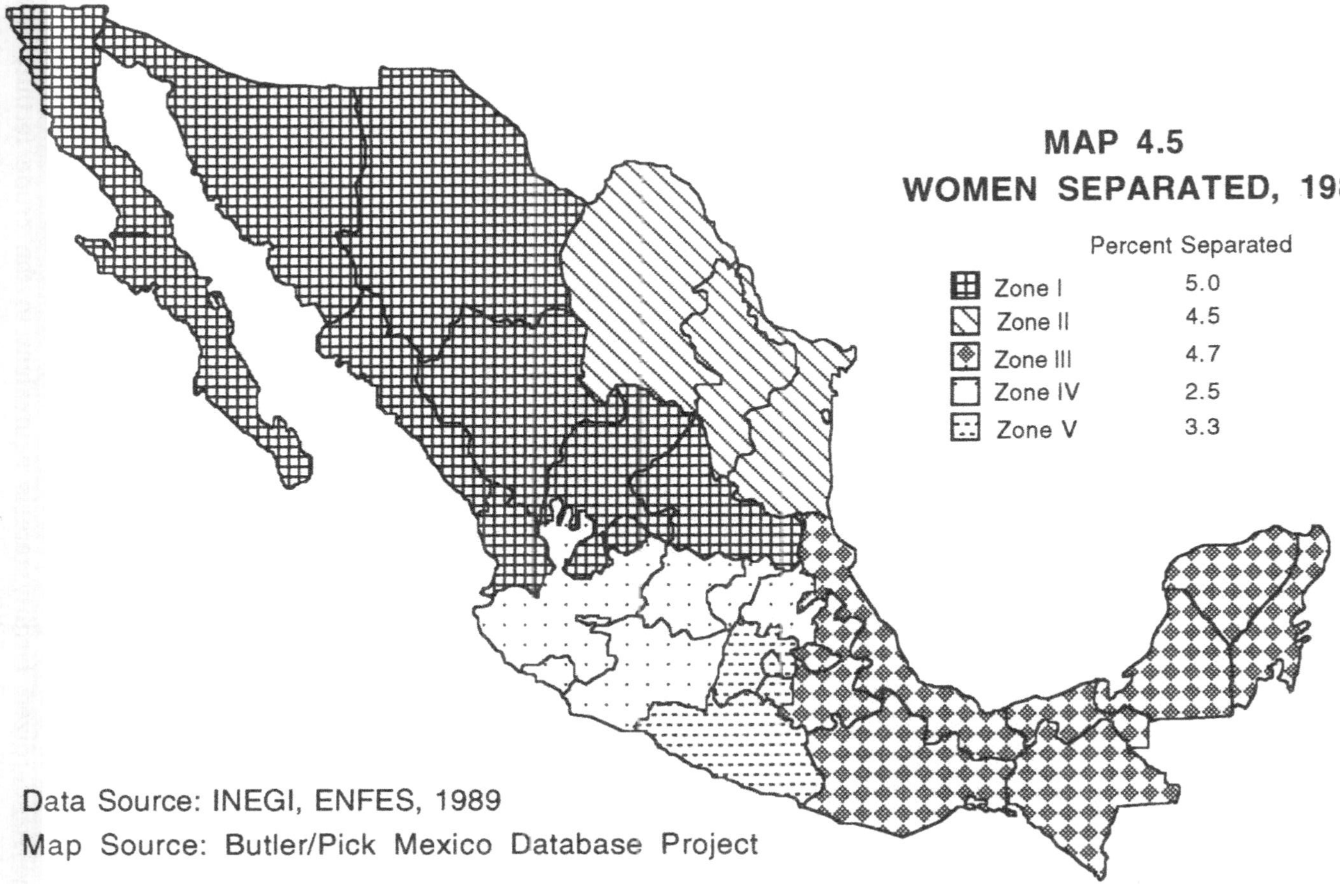

Data Source: INEGI, ENFES, 1989

Map Source: Butler/Pick Mexico Database Project

Fertility

Crude Fertility Rate, 1990

Crude fertility is the ratio of births to total population. It indicates the volume of current reproduction. Mexico's crude fertility rate was fairly steady in the 1950s and 1960s, followed by sharp declines in the 1970s and 1980s. The crude birth rate and decennial change by year are shown below.

Year	Crude Birth Rate (Per 1000)	Decennial Change
1950	45.6	
1960	46.1	1.1
1970	44.2	4.3
1980	35.0	-20.8
1990	28.7	-18.0
1993	29.0	

SOURCE: 1950–1980 data, *Estadisticas Historicas de Mexico* ; 1990 data, 1990 *Mexican Census;* 1993 data, *Population Reference Bureau.*

The 1993 crude fertility rate of 29 is somewhat higher than the average of 26 for Latin American nations, but much lower than the rates of 16 for the United States and 15 for Canada (Population Reference Bureau 1993).

The statewide mean for 1990 crude fertility is 33.1 (see Table 4.4). This mean exceeds the national average because several very populous states have the lowest rates, in particular Nuevo Leon at 26.3 and the Federal District at 28.4. The rates are low in those states, because of the presence of the large metropolises of Monterrey and Mexico City, that historically have had very low fertility rates. On the other hand, Jalisco's crude fertility at 32.6 is average, pointing to lack of comparable low fertility in the metropolis of Guadalajara. Crude fertility is highest in the states of Quintana Roo, Chiapas, Michoacan, and Puebla. Since the geographic pattern closely resembles that for standardized fertility (compare Maps 4.6 and 4.7), more detailed discussion of the geographic pattern is done in the section on standardized fertility.

Crude fertility rate in 1990 is very highly correlated with 1990 standardized fertility rate. As a result, the relationships with other variables are very similar to those for standardized fertility rate. These relationships are discussed below under standardized fertility, and all those discussed carry over to crude fertility rate.

Standardized Fertility Rate, 1990

The standardized fertility rate is equivalent to the crude fertility rate adjusted for state to state differences in the population age distribution. More specifically, the standardized fertility rate for each state is adjusted by a factor d/Summation(F_a P_a), where d represents the total births in the state, F_a is the age-specific fertility rate for the nation and P_a is the population of a five-year age group in the state. It is essential to standardize the crude fertility rate, because otherwise the age structure of individual states have an undue influence on the state's fertility, e.g., in a state with a young population, the state's fertility rate may appear unduly high from a greater proportion of women in the highly fertile twenties age range. It is important to mention that, since the age distribution of the population has slight variation between states (note the low CVs in Table 2.5), indirect standardization in this instance has only a modest effect on values.

The mean standardized fertility in 1990 is 33.9, with a coefficient of variation of 15. It should be noted that the indirect standardization increased the coefficient of variation in fertility rates by 43 percent.

The geographical pattern for standardized fertility rate reveals distinctive directional and regional patterns. There is generally a gradient from low rates in the north to high rates in the south, with a major exception in the very low rate for the Federal District and high rate for Durango. The Federal District and its surrounding states of Mexico and Morelos are seen on the map as an "island" of low fertility in the lower central part of the nation. This strong north-south continuum is similar to that for several prominent modernization indicators, including urbanization (see Map 3.3) and income (see Chapter 9). The border region has quite low rates (27.7 on average), while the pacific south has very high rates, averaging 41.5. The south is 50 percent higher in fertility than the border! The south's high fertility is an important demographic force countering the south's net outmigration (see Maps 5.5 and 5.8). Michoacan also resembles the south region, since it has very high fertility as well as net outmigration. The southeast region varies considerably from higher rates in Quintana Roo to moderate rates in Campeche and lower rates in Yucatan. This may be partly accounted for by the greater modernization of Yucatan as reflected in such indicators as urbanization and high income.

The geographical distribution of standardized fertility has changed little in the 1980s, even though rates dropped throughout the nation. This is seen by comparing the present map with the 1979 standardized fertility seen in Map 3.2C in *Atlas of Mexico* (Pick et al. 1989a). Some minor differences noted are the *relative* rise in fertility during the decade for the states of Chiapas, Quintana Roo, and Veracruz. Durango persists over the decade in having much higher fertility than its neighbors. One explanation may be Durango's relatively low prevalence of sterilization (see Map 3.3E in *Atlas of Mexico*), a contraceptive method that moved into predominance in Mexico in the 1980s.

Standardized fertility varies oppositely from indicators of modernization and economic prosperity. This is seen by its inverse relationships to literacy, urbanization (r = - .79 with 1990 urban ratio), literacy, education (- .78 with 1990 higher education), female economic activity (.78), vehicle and telephone ownership, professional/technical, administrative, and service occupations, and high monthly income. It also varies oppositely from cardiovascular and cancer mortality, which are often associated with more advanced economies. Another important reverse association is with lifetime net migration. In other words, the higher 1990 fertility, the more likely the state has been a net provider of lifetime outmigrants. However, there is no such correlation with 1985–1990 net migration. There is also a positive association with population native to state.

Standardized fertility has direct relationships to assorted other variables. It is strongly associated with crowding (r = .83). This may be indicative of larger family size as a result of high fertility. It is also associated with several attributes of low modernization, including housing lacking toilets, low income, and home ownership (sic), that are pointed out elsewhere to be associated with poorer conditions, and with agricultural occupation (.72).

Cumulative Fertility to Women Age 20–29, 1990

Cumulative fertility is the total number of living births to a woman of a designated age. Cumulative fertility for women age 20 to 29 had a statewide average of 1.47 in 1990. This compares to a statewide mean of 1.77 in 1980. The national cumulative fertility rates for women age 20–29 dropped from 1.67 in 1980 to 1.40 in 1990, a sixteen percent decrease in the eighties, which is comparable to the decrease in crude fertility rate. The variation between states is quite low (CV = 15) and comparable to that for standardized fertility rate (see Table 4.5).

The ordering of states in cumulative fertility, age 20–29, is similar to that for standardized fertility, with the lowest values in the Federal District and border states of Baja California, Nuevo Leon, and Tamaulipas and highest levels in the southern and southeastern states of Chiapas, Oaxaca, Guerrero, and Tabasco.

As shown on Map 4.8, the geographical distribution is highly similar to that for standardized fertility. This is reflected in a highly significant correlation between the two measures of .80. The similarity in patterns reflects geographical persistence of fertility patterns over time and, in this case, regardless of period versus cohort fertility measure. Because the patterns are so similar, explanations of pattern given for standardized fertility rate apply here as well.

Cumulative Fertility to Women Age 45–49, 1990

Cumulative fertility to women age 45–49 in 1990 represents nearly all fertility from the cohort of women born in the World War II era of 1940–1945. The national value is 5.46, or five and a half births on average per woman (see Table 4.5). Cumulative fertility for women 45–49 varies almost six times as much as for women 20–29. The reason for the much greater variation may be that women in their twenties have more similar scheduling for early fertility, whereas women's later fertility preferences and outcomes, i.e., in their thirties and forties, differ much more across the nation.

The state range for completed fertility varies by over 3 children per women, from a low of 4.0 children in the Federal District to a high of 7.3 children per woman in Zacatecas.

Comparing the patterns of cumulative fertility for women 45–49 to those of 20–29 reveals similarities as well as differences. The similarities include low fertility in the border region, Federal District and surrounding states of Mexico and Morelos, and high fertility in Zacatecas and Nayarit. However there is a major difference in the area of highest levels (see Map 4.9). For women age 45–49, the highest fertility is in selected states in the west and southern north regions, including Michoacan, Guanajuato, Aguascalientes, Durango, and Zacatecas. These states, except for Aguascalientes, have experienced slow population growth (see Table 2.2) and high net outmigration (see Map 5.8). The states have generally moderate cumulative fertility for women 20–29, which may reflect generational differences in childbearing preferences. For the women age 45–49, cumulative fertility is moderate in the south, southeast, and gulf regions, in contrast to high cumulative fertility for younger women. This regional-generational shift may again reflect changes in childbearing preferences, fertility control, and cultural traditions.

As with cumulative fertility for younger women, there is a strong comparison with the geographical pattern in 1980 (see Map 3.2F in *Atlas of Mexico* by Pick et al. 1989a). Overall in the nation, cumulative fertility for women 45–49 was 6.26 in 1980, dropping to 5.46 in 1990. The west and southern north area of high fertility is similar to that for 1980, as well as the low fertility in the south, southeast, and gulf. By contrast, the border region has relatively much higher cumulative fertility in 1980, averaging 6.61 in 1980, versus only 5.17 in 1990, for a drop of 22 percent versus 13 percent nationally. This sharp drop reflects partly the rapid economic advance in the 80s in the border area.

The relationships of cumulative fertility for women 45–49 are similar to those for standardized fertility and for 20–29 year old cumulative fertility. Several relationships only present for cumulative fertility in the older age group are inverse associations with contraceptive use (r = - .53), lifetime net migration (- .48), and gross state product (- .46). The latter relationship reflects an inverse effect with modernization. It is somewhat surprising that the reverse association with contraception use is not present for cumulative fertility for younger women.

Total Fertility Rate, 1984–1986

Total fertility rate (TFR) is a measure of the total childbearing per woman across the fertile age groups. It differs from cumulative fertility by being the sum of the age-specific fertility rates (Keyfitz and Flieger 1971). An age specific fertility rate is the number of births to women for an age group, divided by the population of women in the age group. For instance, the age specific fertility rate for women 20–24 equals the ratio of the number of births to 20–24 year old women to the population of 20–24 year old women. Total fertility rate may be calculated, based on the age-specific fertility rates for women at a particular point in time—this is referred to as a *period* TFR. However, if the fertility rates are calculated, over many decades, for a group of women born at the same time that ages together, the TFR is referred to as a *cohort* TFR. The variable shown in Map 4.10 and Table 4.6 is an average of the period TFRs for the three years, 1984–1986.

The change in the TFR is shown below for Mexico for the last quarter century.

Year	TFR-National Total	TFR-Rural	TFR-Urban
1966–1970*	6.95	7.96	6.08
1970–1974**	6.48	7.90	5.93
1975–1979	5.24	6.67	4.45
1984–1986***	3.80	5.85	3.47 (est.)
1990–1993****	3.70		
1993****	3.40		

* Cohort Rate, World Fertility Survey, 1976–77
** Cohort Rate, National Prevalence Survey, 1979
*** Period Rate, Encuesta Nacional de Fecundidad, 1987
**** Period Rate, Population Reference Bureau, 1990–1993

The substantial drop in TFR over the past quarter century parallels the drop in crude fertility rate and reflects the progress of the nation through the demographic transition, including widespread adoption of contraception. The difference in TFR between urban and rural areas is very large. It points to an issue in Mexican population control, which is the continuing high levels of fertility in rural areas, that tend to produce more children than are supportable in rural areas.

The TFR by Zones from the ENFES survey of 1987 shows regional differences, with the survey's western and south/southeastern regions having substantially higher TFRs than the other three regions (see Table 4.6). The low levels in the northeast reflect the region's high urbanization and prosperity. It is important to again point out the sharp north-south differences in fertility.

By contrast, the TFR in the United States was 2.58 in 1990, having dropped from 3.07 in 1970 (National Center for Health Statistics 1993a). Hence, the standardized fertility differential between Mexico and the U.S. as measured by the TFR narrowed to about forty-three percent in 1990.

Table 4.4 Crude and Standardized Fertility Rates, 1990

No.	State	Number of Births 1990	Total Population 1990	Crude Ann. Fertility Rate 1990	Standardized Ann. Fertility Rate 1990
1	AGUASCALIENTES	24,160	719,659	33.5715	34.0460
2	BAJA CALIFORNIA	49,229	1,660,855	29.6408	26.8435
3	BAJA CALIFORNIA SUR	9,316	317,764	29.3174	27.4346
4	CAMPECHE	17,602	535,185	32.8896	33.8954
5	COAHUILA	59,735	1,972,340	30.2864	29.3859
6	COLIMA	12,927	428,510	30.1673	30.4936
7	CHIAPAS	123,625	3,210,496	38.5065	41.1915
8	CHIHUAHUA	69,642	2,441,873	28.5199	27.2934
9	DISTRITO FEDERAL	233,828	8,235,744	28.3918	25.0740
10	DURANGO	47,823	1,349,378	35.4408	38.1413
11	GUANAJUATO	135,978	3,982,593	34.1431	36.4937
12	GUERRERO	97,905	2,620,637	37.3592	42.2665
13	HIDALGO	68,558	1,888,366	36.3055	39.5883
14	JALISCO	173,030	5,302,689	32.6306	33.9672
15	MEXICO	317,814	9,815,795	32.3778	30.6112
16	MICHOACAN	135,996	3,548,199	38.3282	42.3536
17	MORELOS	38,797	1,195,059	32.4645	32.7604
18	NAYARIT	27,186	824,643	32.9670	36.2529
19	NUEVO LEON	81,573	3,098,736	26.3246	24.1875
20	OAXACA	106,766	3,019,560	35.3581	40.7176
21	PUEBLA	156,577	4,126,101	37.9479	41.0452
22	QUERETARO	39,761	1,051,235	37.8231	38.7470
23	QUINTANA ROO	19,783	493,277	40.1053	36.7845
24	SAN LUIS POTOSI	66,628	2,003,187	33.2610	36.3196
25	SINALOA	67,287	2,204,054	30.5287	31.0172
26	SONORA	52,603	1,823,606	28.8456	27.8152
27	TABASCO	54,306	1,501,744	36.1620	36.5197
28	TAMAULIPAS	67,327	2,249,581	29.9287	28.7000
29	TLAXCALA	27,031	761,277	35.5074	36.9812
30	VERACRUZ	194,105	6,228,239	31.1653	31.7822
31	YUCATAN	40,874	1,362,940	29.9896	31.6846
32	ZACATECAS	40,896	1,276,323	32.0420	35.5861
	National Total	2,658,668	81,249,645	32.7275	
	Mean	83,083		33.0718	33.9369
	Median	63,182		32.7601	34.0066
	S.D.	70,325		3.5436	5.2208
	C.V.	84.64		10.72	15.38
	Minimum	9,316		26.3246	24.1875
	Maximum	317,814		40.1053	42.3536

DEFINITION: Crude fertility rate is the ratio of births for the year 1990 to the population in 1990, multiplied by 1,000. Standardized fertility rate is calculated from the annual fertility rate 1990 by indirect standardization, based on a state's population age structure in 1990 and a standard population (see text for explanation).

NOTE: The number of births for Chiapas is for 1989 due to inaccuracy in 1990.

SOURCE: INEGI, 1991 Annuario Estadistico, Table 3.1.10.

MAP 4.6

CRUDE FERTILITY RATE, 1990

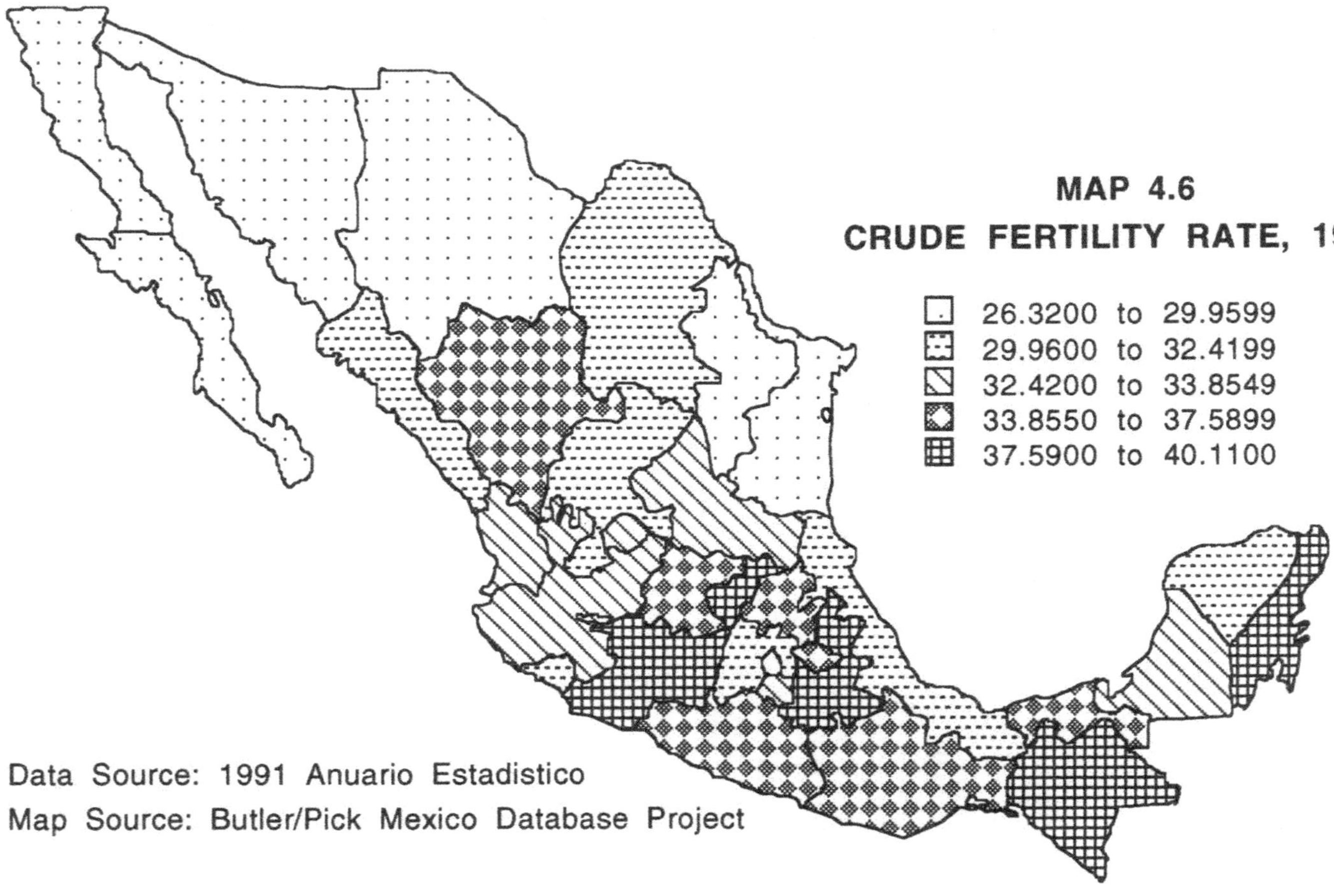

Data Source: 1991 Anuario Estadistico

Map Source: Butler/Pick Mexico Database Project

MAP 4.7
STANDARDIZED FERTILITY RATE
1990

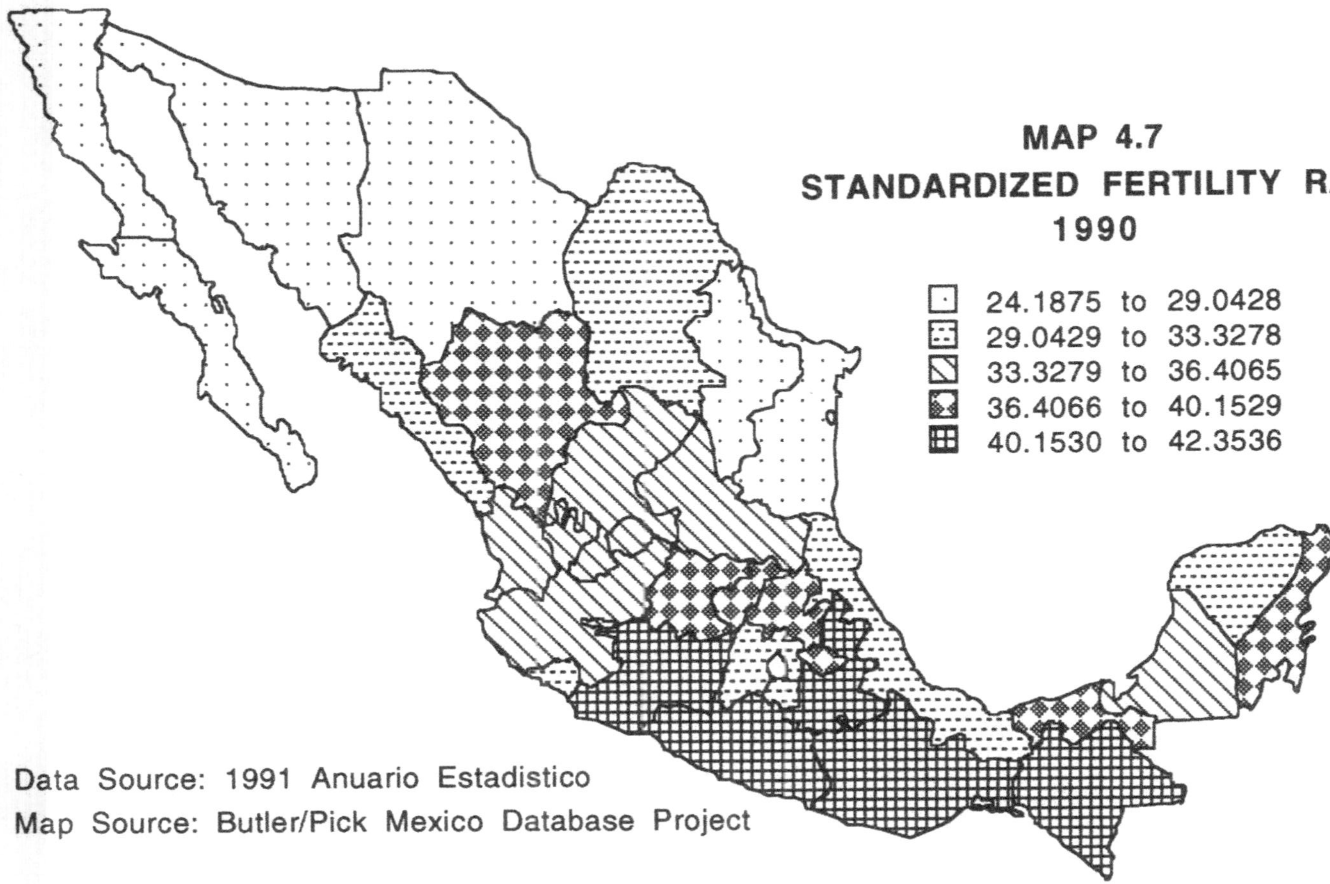

Data Source: 1991 Anuario Estadistico
Map Source: Butler/Pick Mexico Database Project

Table 4.5 Cumulative Fertility, 1990

No.	State	Cumulative Fertility to Women Ages 20-29	Cumulative Fertility to Women Ages 45-49
1	AGUASCALIENTES	1.3204	6.3509
2	BAJA CALIFORNIA	1.2602	5.0553
3	BAJA CALIFORNIA SUR	1.3780	5.3458
4	CAMPECHE	1.6810	5.3830
5	COAHUILA	1.3549	5.4084
6	COLIMA	1.3764	5.9804
7	CHIAPAS	2.0153	5.7099
8	CHIHUAHUA	1.3192	5.2447
9	DISTRITO FEDERAL	0.9633	3.9738
10	DURANGO	1.5666	6.4267
11	GUANAJUATO	1.4135	6.6222
12	GUERRERO	1.8133	5.8938
13	HIDALGO	1.6862	5.7512
14	JALISCO	1.2533	5.8915
15	MEXICO	1.3707	5.2876
16	MICHOACAN	1.4704	6.3489
17	MORELOS	1.4004	5.2473
18	NAYARIT	1.5468	6.2249
19	NUEVO LEON	1.0910	4.9922
20	OAXACA	1.7561	5.5420
21	PUEBLA	1.5882	5.7506
22	QUERETARO	1.4923	6.2370
23	QUINTANA ROO	1.6241	5.6072
24	SAN LUIS POTOSI	1.5253	6.1016
25	SINALOA	1.4064	6.0563
26	SONORA	1.2809	5.2345
27	TABASCO	1.7728	5.8886
28	TAMAULIPAS	1.2377	5.0772
29	TLAXCALA	1.5276	6.0416
30	VERACRUZ	1.5259	5.2778
31	YUCATAN	1.4521	5.0236
32	ZACATECAS	1.4664	7.3249
	Mean	1.4668	5.6969
	Median	1.4593	5.7303
	S.D.	0.2141	0.6245
	C.V.	14.60	10.96
	Minimum	0.9633	3.9738
	Maximum	2.0153	7.3249

DEFINITION: Cumulative fertility is defined as the number of children ever born to women in a designated age group to the total number of women in that age group.

SOURCE: INEGI, 1990 Census of Population, Resumen General, Table 24.

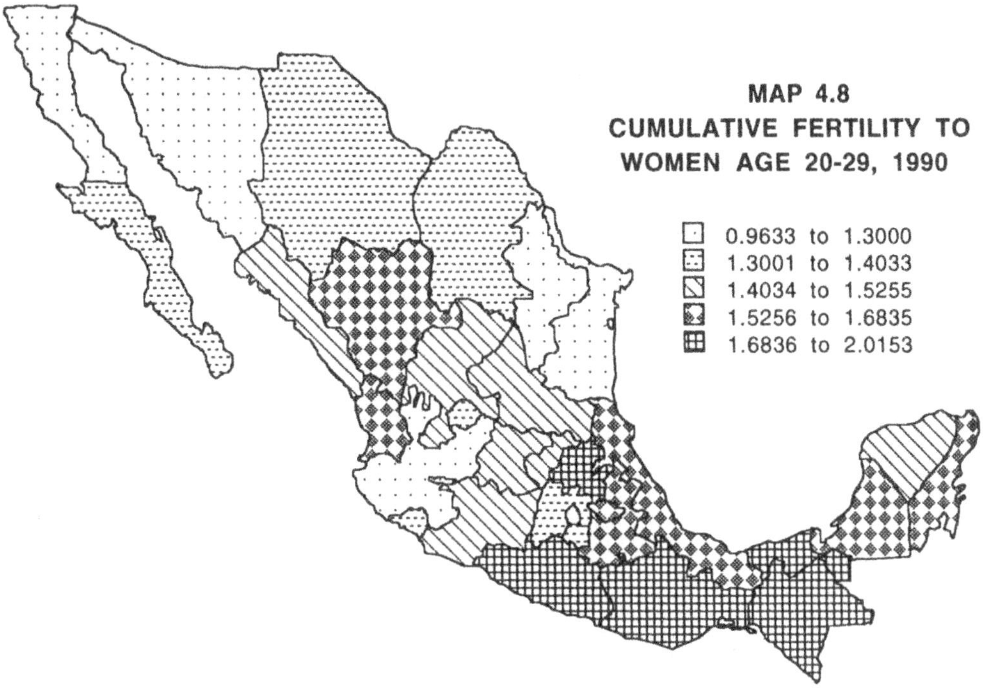
MAP 4.8
CUMULATIVE FERTILITY TO
WOMEN AGE 20-29, 1990
0.9633 to 1.3000
1.3001 to 1.4033
1.4034 to 1.5255
1.5256 to 1.6835
1.6836 to 2.0153

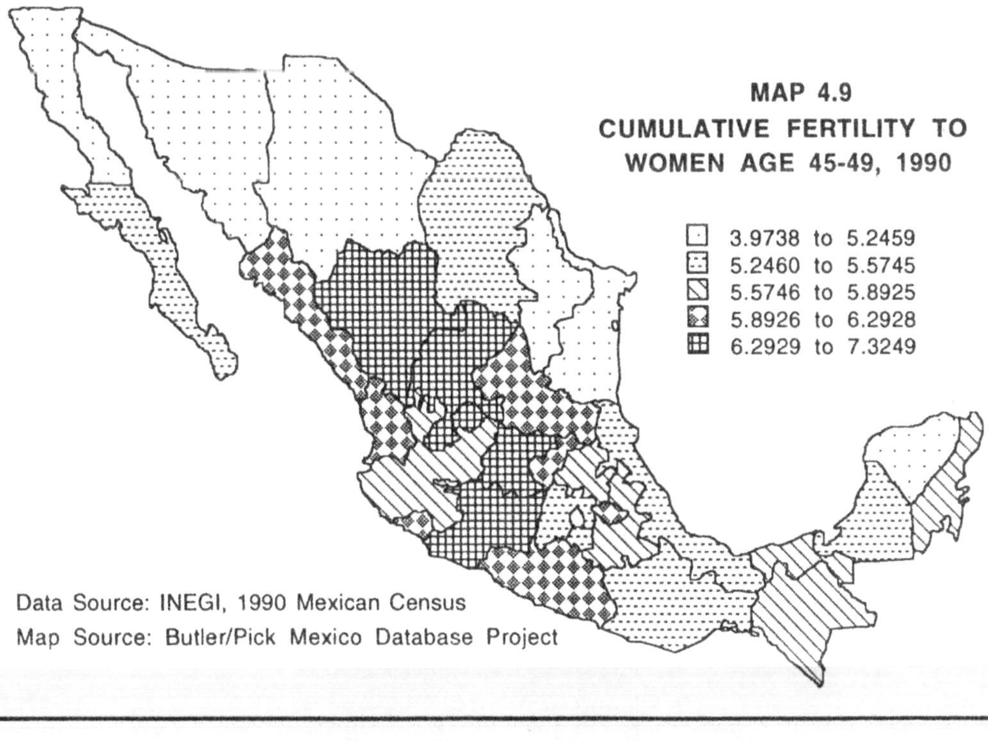
MAP 4.9
CUMULATIVE FERTILITY TO
WOMEN AGE 45-49, 1990
3.9738 to 5.2459
5.2460 to 5.5745
5.5746 to 5.8925
5.8926 to 6.2928
6.2929 to 7.3249
Data Source: INEGI, 1990 Mexican Census
Map Source: Butler/Pick Mexico Database Project

Table 4.6 Total Fertility Rate, 1984 - 1986

	Residential Zone	Percent
1	ZONE I (N and NW)	3.83
2	ZONE II (NE)	3.22
3	ZONE III (S and SE)	4.59
4	ZONE IV (W)	4.90
5	ZONE V (DF)	3.38
Mean		3.98
Median		3.83
S.D.		0.7380
C.V.		18.52
Minimum		3.22
Maximum		4.90

DEFINITION: The total fertility rate (TFR) is a measure of the number of births a woman would have if she experienced the set of current schedule of age-specific birth rates throughout her lifetime. The table indicates the average TFR over the three years, 1984–1986.

NOTE: Zones correspond to state groupings shown in Table 4.1.

SOURCE: Encuesta Nacional Sobre Fecundidad y Salud, 1989, Table 5.4.

MAP 4.10
TOTAL FERTILITY RATE
1984 - 1986

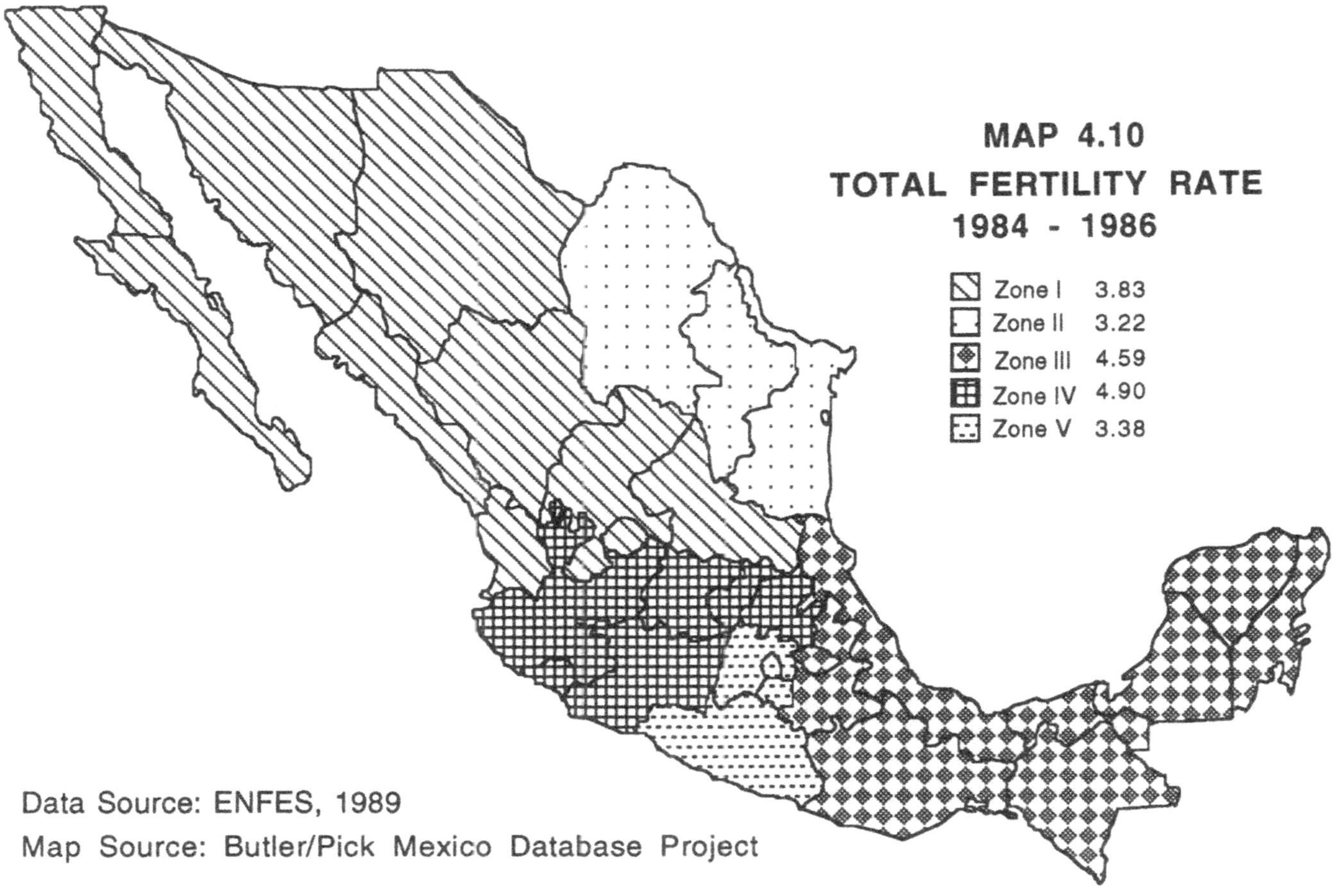

Data Source: ENFES, 1989
Map Source: Butler/Pick Mexico Database Project

Family Planning

Introduction

Family planning has been a strong influence in reducing fertility in Mexico. As shown in Figure 4.5, the use of contraception among Mexican women of childbearing age increased substantially in the late 70s and 80s. e.g., the proportion of women in a union who used any contraceptive method increased from 30 to 53 percent between 1976 and 1987. The prevalence level of 53 percent compares with 1993 levels of 59 percent for Latin America and 74 percent for the United States (Population Reference Bureau 1993). Likewise, the proportion of women using modern methods about doubled from 1976 to 1987, and the 1987 level of 45 percent compares to 1993 levels of 49 percent for Latin America and 69 percent for the U.S. This increase in contraceptive utilization has been one of the key intermediate factors in Mexico's sharp fertility reduction in the 70s and 80s.

The type of contraception adopted by Mexican women has shifted away from the birth control pill and towards female sterilization. As seen in Figure 4.6, pill use declined by half from 1976–1987, while female sterilization approximately quadrupled. Although traditional methods dropped considerably from 1976 to 1982, this category increased somewhat in the mid 80s. Its small resurgence may be related to increased use of condoms, due to the growing AIDs epidemic.

Female sterilization has moved into first place as the dominant form of contraception. By contrast male sterilization accounted for only 1.5 percent of contraceptive methods in use in 1987. There are major differences in contraception by age of women. As seen in Figure 4.7, for women under 30 in 1987, the most important methods were IUD and pills, followed by traditional methods and female sterilization. On the other hand for women over 30, half of contraceptive methods was female sterilization, accompanied by reduced prevalences of traditional methods, IUD, and pills.

There is a high level of knowledge of birth control, as seen in Figure 4.8, although this knowledge is only partly converted into actual use. On the average for modern methods, 81.3 percent of women in 1987 knew modern methods, but a much lower proportion had used the methods. Knowledge of efficient birth control varies slightly geographically, based on the 1976/77 WFS Survey (see Map 3.3C in *Atlas of Mexico*).

Women Using Female Sterilization, 1987

Female sterilization is the leading contemporary birth control method in Mexico. On the average, 18.6 percent of women in a union used female sterilization in 1987. This use varies considerably by place of residence. In particular, the percentages were 23.5 percent for metropolitan areas, 21.9 percent for non-metropolitan cities of 20,000 or more, 18.1 percent for places of 2,500 to 19,999 population, but only 11.9 percent for places of 2,500 or less population.

The proportion of women using female sterilization also varies considerably geographically. As reported in Table 4.7 and seen in Map 4.11, sterilization use is highest in the northeast and Mexico City regions (also including Guerrero). The high rates in these regions reflect the influence of the large metropolises of Monterrey and Mexico City. On the other hand, sterilization use is low in the western and south/southeast regions. The low level of use in the west is unexplained, but might be due to more traditional contraceptive and childbearing practices in the region, due to the high proportion of Catholic population (see Map 7.8). In comparison to the geographical pattern of sterilization use in 1976/77 (see Map 3.3E in Pick et al. 1989a), there is high use of sterilization in the Mexico City metropolitan region and in the northeast. However, the west region in 1980 has relatively higher level of use of female sterilization.

Female Contraceptive Sterilization Decision by Person Other Than the Woman, 1987

Who decides on female contraceptive sterilization is an important behavioral dimension of the leading contraceptive method in Mexico (ENFES 1989). Overall, in forty percent of instances, the woman decides alone, in forty-eight percent of cases the woman decides in consultation with someone else, and in 13 percent of instances another person decides. Included in the latter case are 3.7 percent of instances where the woman is not in agreement with the decision (ENFES 1989).

This decision-making varies greatly by place of residence, with 90 percent of women in metropolitan areas deciding (alone or in consultation), versus 82 percent deciding in rural places of less than 2,500 persons (ENFES 1989). The decision making is even more dramatically influenced by educational level, with female decisions for 93 percent of cases with the woman having secondary or more education, but in only 66 percent of instances for women without formal education.

The geographical differences in this decision-making process are seen in Figure 4.9, which shows the proportion of female contraceptive sterilization decisions made by another person other than the woman. The rates are highest in the south and southeast, which may reflect the low educational levels and rural nature of the south and southeast. The levels are also high in the northeast, which is surprising since it is an economically more advanced region. The lowest levels for about ten percent of this variable are in the west region and Mexico City region. The explanation for Mexico City is that the high economic and educational levels lead to reduced decision-making by other than the woman herself.

Figure 4.5
Percentage of Women Who Use Contraceptive Methods, 1976-1987

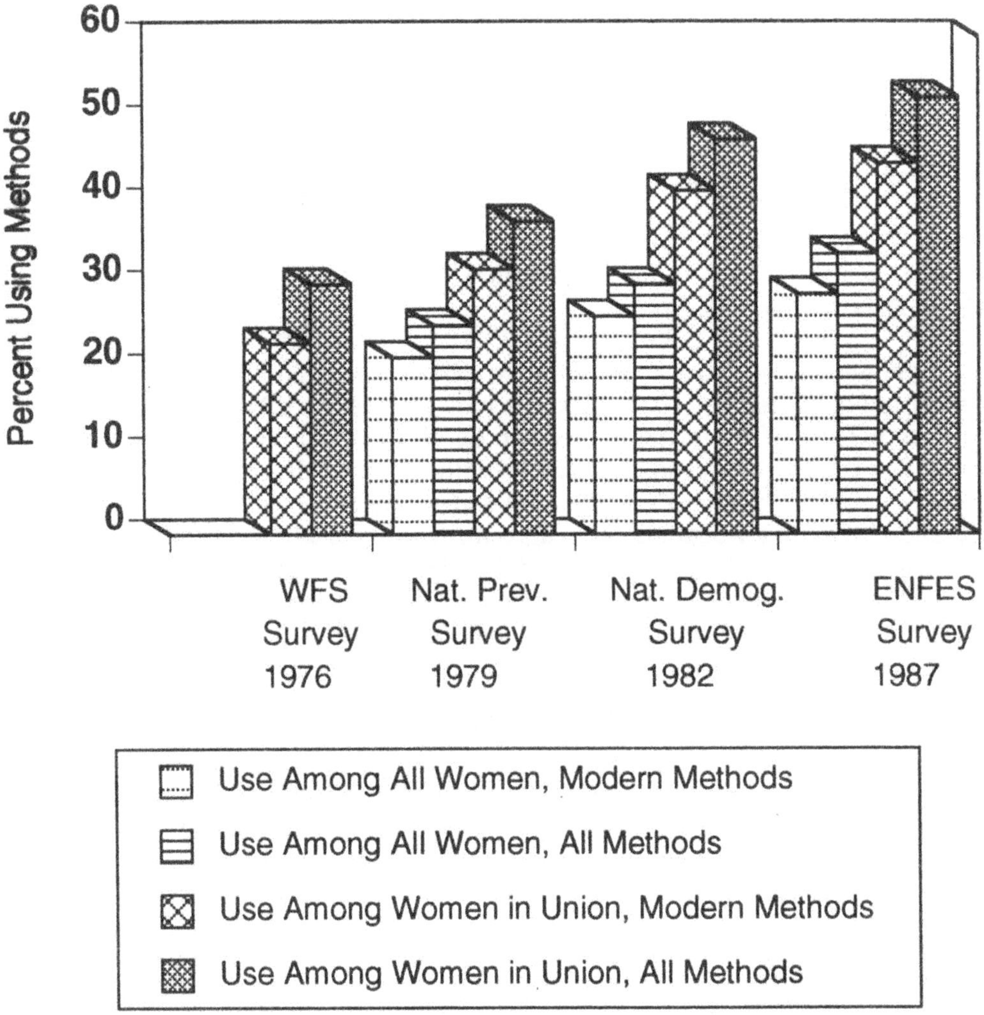

SOURCES: World Fertility Survey, 1976-77; National Prevalence Survey, 1979; National Demographic Survey, 1982; Encuesta Nacional de Fecundidad (ENFES), 1989.

Figure 4.6
Percentage of Women Using Contraceptive Methods by Method of Active Use, 1976 - 1987

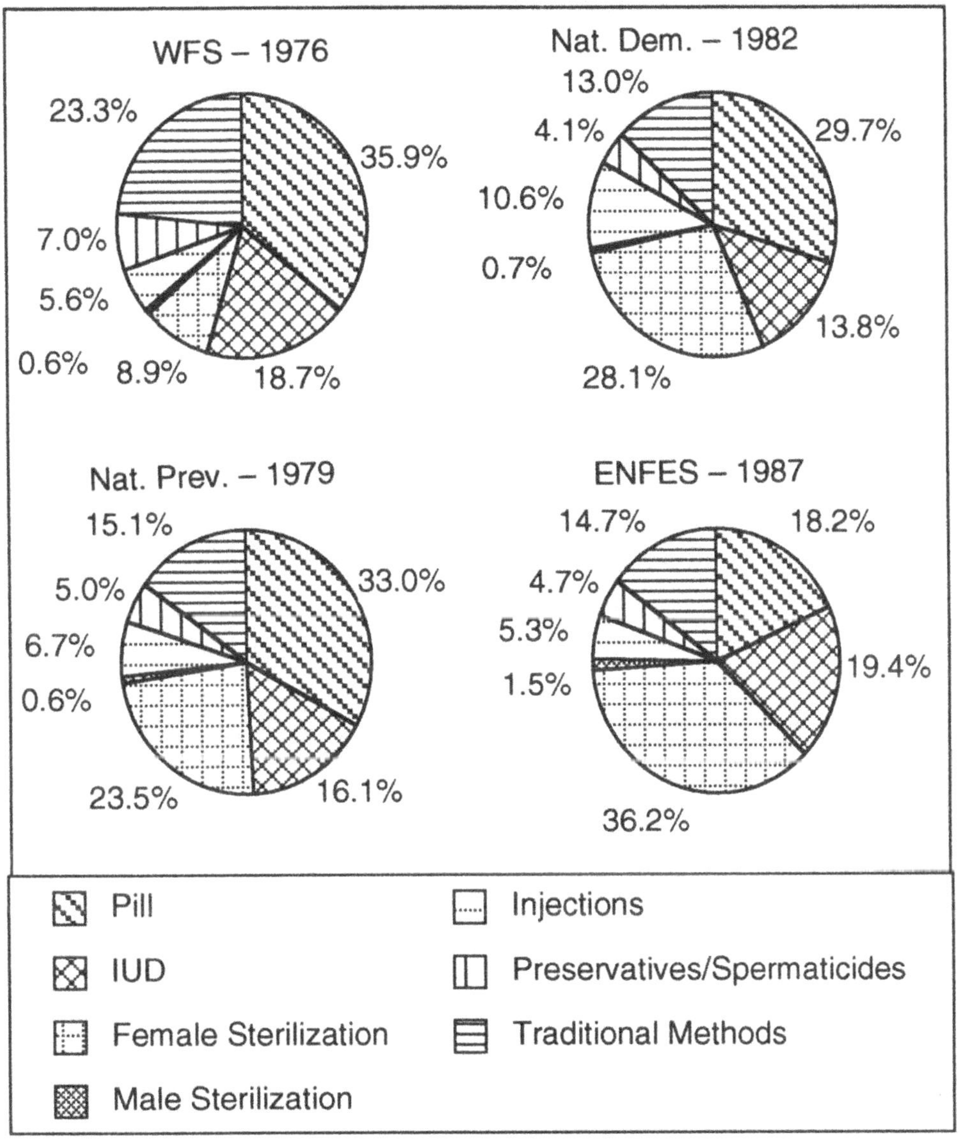

DEFINITION: Women are of fertile age and currently utilizing contraception. Traditional Methods include condoms, rhythm, withdrawal, etc.

NOTE: WFS = WFS Survey, 1976; Nat. Dem. = National Demographic Survey, 1982; Nat. Prev. = National Prevalence Survey, 1979; ENFES = Encuesta Nacional Sobre Fecundidad y Salud, 1989.

Figure 4.7
Contraceptive Use for Women in Union by Present Method According to Age, 1987

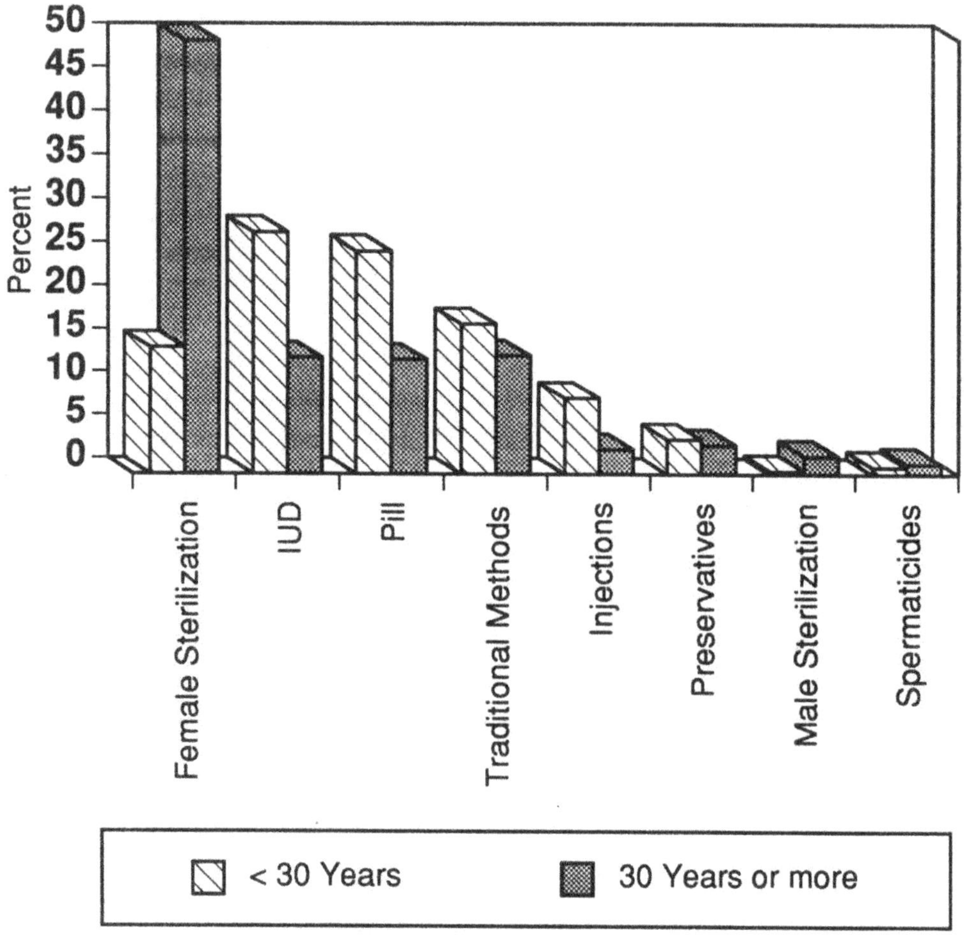

DEFINITION: Applies to all women respondents. Women are in the age range 15-49 years.

SOURCE: Encuesta Nacional Sobre Fecundidad y Salud, 1989.

Figure 4.8
Women Who Know About and Use Contraceptives by Method, 1987

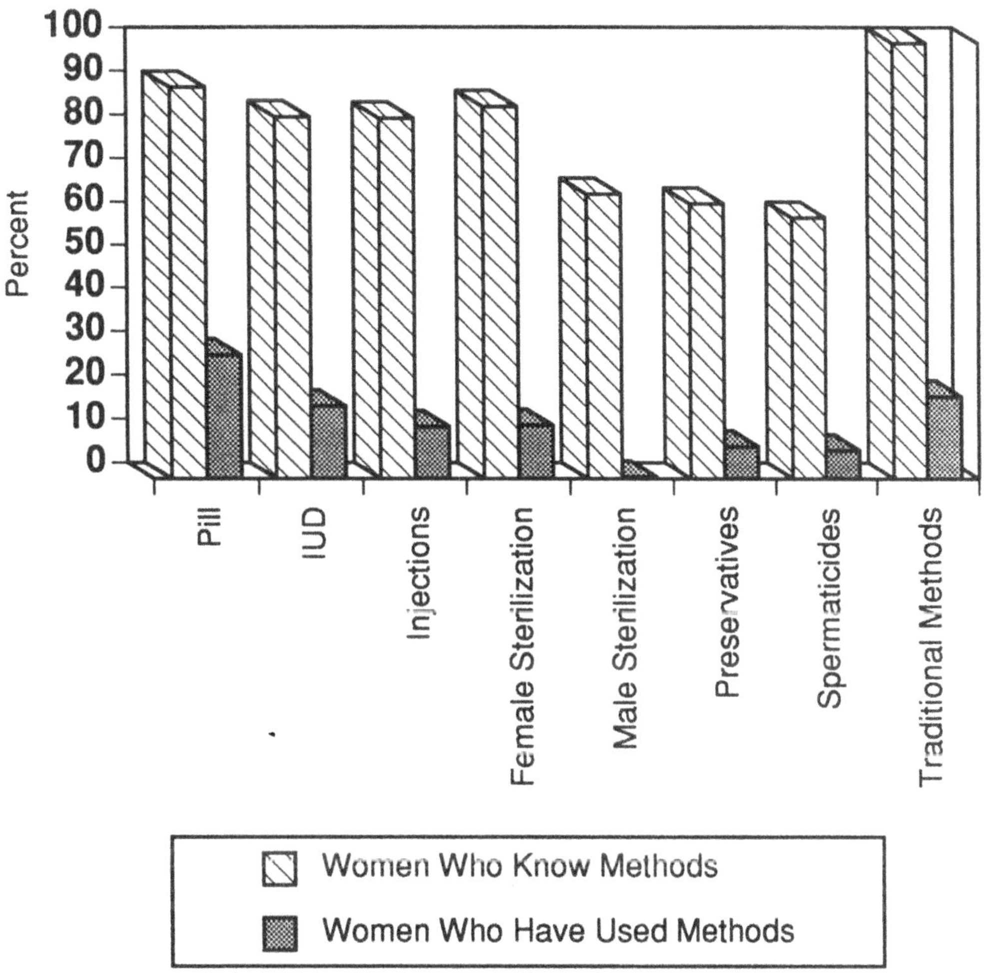

DEFINITION: Applies to all women respondents. Women are in the age range 15-49 years.
SOURCE: Encuesta Nacional Sobre Fecundidad y Salud, 1989.

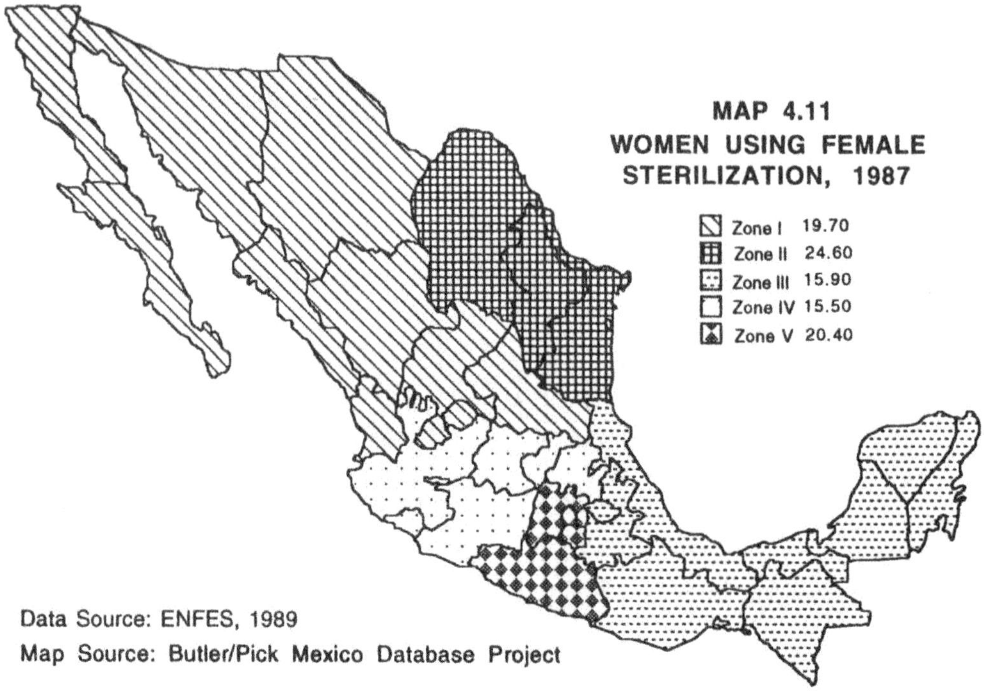

Table 4.7 Women Using Female Sterilization, 1987

Residential Zone	Percent
1 ZONE I (N and NW)	19.70
2 ZONE II (NE)	24.60
3 ZONE III (S and SE)	15.90
4 ZONE IV (W)	15.50
5 ZONE V (DF)	20.40
Mean	19.22
Median	19.70
S.D.	3.7225
C.V.	19.37
Minimum	15.50
Maximum	24.60

DEFINITION: Proportion of women in union who are currently utilizing female sterilization for contraception.

NOTE: Zone I: northern and northwestern states;
Zone II: northeastern states;
Zone III: south and southeastern states;
Zone IV: western states;
Zone V: Federal District and nearby states.
Zones correspond to state groupings shown in Map 4.1.

SOURCE: Encuesta Nacional Sobre Fecundidad y Salud, 1989, Table 8.2.

Figure 4.9
Female Contraceptive Sterilization Decision By Person Other Than the Woman, 1987

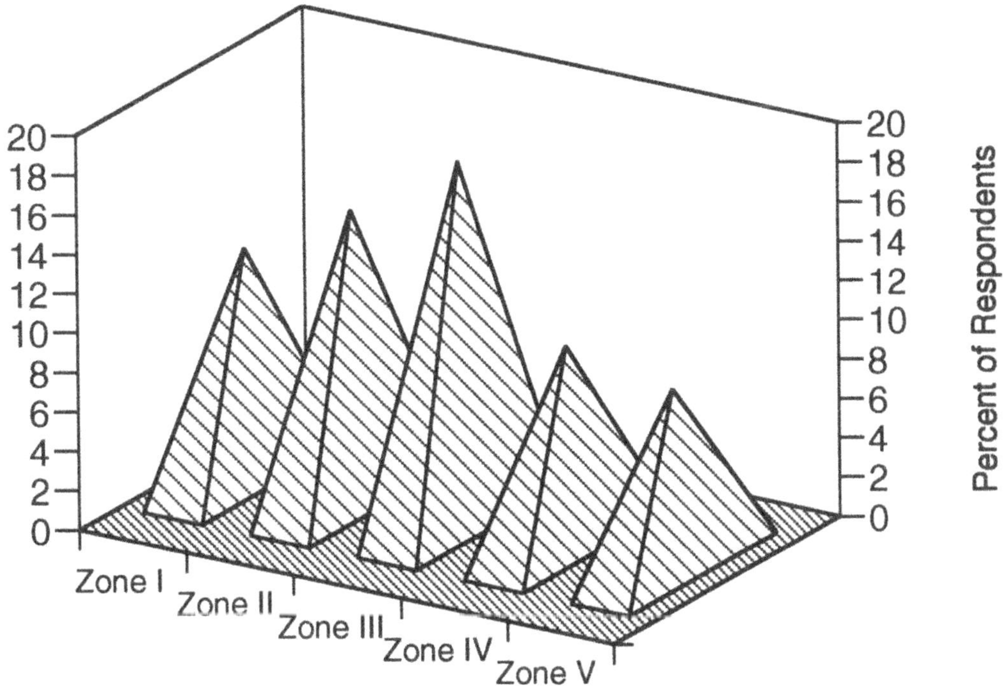

Supporting Data

	Residential Zone	Percent
1	ZONE I (N and NW)	11.60
2	ZONE II (NE)	14.70
3	ZONE III (S and SE)	18.30
4	ZONE IV (W)	10.10
5	ZONE V (DF)	9.10
Mean		12.76
Median		11.60
S.D.		3.7507
C.V.		29.39
Minimum		9.10
Maximum		18.30

DEFINITION: Zone I: northern and northwestern states;
Zone II: northeastern states;
Zone III: south and southeastern states;
Zone IV: western states;
Zone V: Federal District.

NOTE: Zones correspond to state groupings shown in Map 4.1.

SOURCE: Encuesta Nacional Sobre Fecundidad y Salud, 1989, Table 8.2.

5

Migration

Introduction

This chapter concentrates on migration patterns as determined by analysis of the 1990 Mexican census of population. Population native to state reflects the extent to which the population is historically rooted in a particular state. By contrast, migration streams in the past five years, i.e., from 1985 to 1990, show the leading population movements among states. Other information is presented on lifetime inmigrants and outmigrants over the past five years. In addition, other analyses examine lifetime and past five years net migrants, that is the difference between inmigration and outmigration. Finally, data are presented on the percentage of inmigration to Mexico City between 1985 and 1990. This reveals where in Mexico City migrants moved to, and provides finer detail on destination of migrants to Mexico's two most populous states—the state of Mexico and the Federal District.

Population Native to State, 1990

Population native to state in 1990 measures the stability/mobility of the population. For an individual, it measures state residential stability from time of birth. Table 5.1 shows the national level for population native to state in 1990 to be 81.5 percent (also see Map 5.1). This implies a surprising amount of geographic stability, given Mexico's rapid population growth in the twentieth century (see Butler et al. 1993). This is virtually unchanged from the comparable figure of 82.2 percent in 1980. There is small variation in 1990, as reflected in a coefficient of variation of 16.

States with the highest proportions of natives are Chiapas, Yucatan, Oaxaca, and Guerrero, all in the range of 94–95 percent. Chiapas, Oaxaca, and Guerrero are the most rural states in Mexico (see Table 3.1), and would be expected to have low rates of inmigration. Yucatan, however, was highly urbanized in 1990 (79 percent), yet had a fairly low rate of inmigration 1985–1990 (3.2 percent). The high nativity in Oaxaca may be ascribed largely to its high proportion of indigenous population, the highest in the nation in 1990. States with the smallest native population are Quintana Roo (41 percent), Baja California (51 percent), Mexico (60 percent), and Baja Sur (67 percent). The former high proportion of native population in Quintana Roo has been reduced by the very high inmigration into the state in the 70s and 80s (see Tables 5.3 and 5.4). That proportion was reduced in the 80s by four percent from 45 percent in 1980. The state's inmigration is due to the large expansion in tourism in Quintana Roo. Nevertheless, the state still retains a high proportion of native born population (see Chapter 7). Mexico, surrounding the Federal District, grew vastly in the 80s as the result of overspill from the District and migration from other populous states (see Map 5.2). Baja California and Baja Sur, also high inmigration states in the 70s and 80s, have low native to state.

By region, proportions of native population are highest in the pacific south. In the west, central and gulf regions comprising the central region, there is a broad ring of states with high rates of native population that surrounds the central metropolitan zone, plus Morelos and Queretaro that have low proportion native to state. The lower nativity in the ring's center may be interpreted as the influence of migration into Mexico City and surrounding states that received some metropolitan overspill in the 80s. In particular, Queretaro in the 80s experienced a drop of five percent in population native to state, which reflect the sixth highest net inmigration in that decade among the states. In the west region, rapidly growing Aguascalientes and Colima have low native to state. The northwest and northeast regions are low in proportion native to state. This may reflect their roles as receiving states for streams of internal migration for various times in the twentieth century (see Butler and Pick 1991). The north region has increasing levels of nativity, moving from north to south.

An explanation of the differences in proportions native to state is that massive rural-to-urban migration in the twentieth century left rural states with high proportions native, while inmigration to urban and growing states served to reduce proportions native. This conclusion is supported by the strong negative correlation of - .61 between 1990 population native to state and urbanization. An implication is that urban states have served as "melting pots" of inmigrants, while rural areas are more stable. In sum, this variable reflects Mexico's historical patterns of interstate and rural/urban migration. Nativity is lower in the U.S. than in Mexico. The comparable U.S. figure for native to state in 1990 was 67.1 percent (U.S. Bureau of the Census 1992b). This indicates Americans' greater geographic mobility than Mexicans.

Table 5.1 Population Native to State, 1990

No.	State	Population Native To State	Total Population	Ratio
1	AGUASCALIENTES	575,429	719,659	0.7996
2	BAJA CALIFORNIA	842,893	1,660,855	0.5075
3	BAJA CALIFORNIA SUR	214,427	317,764	0.6748
4	CAMPECHE	402,837	535,185	0.7527
5	COAHUILA	1,664,638	1,972,340	0.8440
6	COLIMA	306,278	428,510	0.7148
7	CHIAPAS	3,052,859	3,210,496	0.9509
8	CHIHUAHUA	2,032,497	2,441,873	0.8324
9	DISTRITO FEDERAL	6,143,892	8,235,744	0.7460
10	DURANGO	1,191,518	1,349,378	0.8830
11	GUANAJUATO	3,616,666	3,982,593	0.9081
12	GUERRERO	2,452,357	2,620,637	0.9358
13	HIDALGO	1,684,231	1,888,366	0.8919
14	JALISCO	4,505,395	5,302,689	0.8496
15	MEXICO	5,855,061	9,815,795	0.5965
16	MICHOACAN	3,214,309	3,548,199	0.9059
17	MORELOS	846,161	1,195,059	0.7080
18	NAYARIT	688,075	824,643	0.8344
19	NUEVO LEON	2,354,322	3,098,736	0.7598
20	OAXACA	2,834,795	3,019,560	0.9388
21	PUEBLA	3,748,152	4,126,101	0.9084
22	QUERETARO	860,061	1,051,235	0.8181
23	QUINTANA ROO	201,342	493,277	0.4082
24	SAN LUIS POTOSI	1,798,974	2,003,187	0.8981
25	SINALOA	1,915,813	2,204,054	0.8692
26	SONORA	1,497,010	1,823,606	0.8209
27	TABASCO	1,348,501	1,501,744	0.8980
28	TAMAULIPAS	1,680,533	2,249,581	0.7470
29	TLAXCALA	664,490	761,277	0.8729
30	VERACRUZ	5,597,605	6,228,239	0.8987
31	YUCATAN	1,279,661	1,362,940	0.9389
32	ZACATECAS	1,163,676	1,276,323	0.9117
	National Total	66,234,458	81,249,645	0.8152
	Mean	2,069,827	2,539,051	0.8133
	Median	1,672,586	1,930,353	0.8468
	S.D.	1,652,329	2,216,375	0.1276
	C.V.	79.83	87.29	15.69
	Minimum	201,342	317,764	0.4082
	Maximum	6,143,892	9,815,795	0.9509

DEFINITION: Ratio is the population native to state to the total population.

SOURCE: INEGI, 1990 Mexican Census of Population, Resumen General, Table 4.

MAP 5.1
POPULATION NATIVE TO STATE
1990

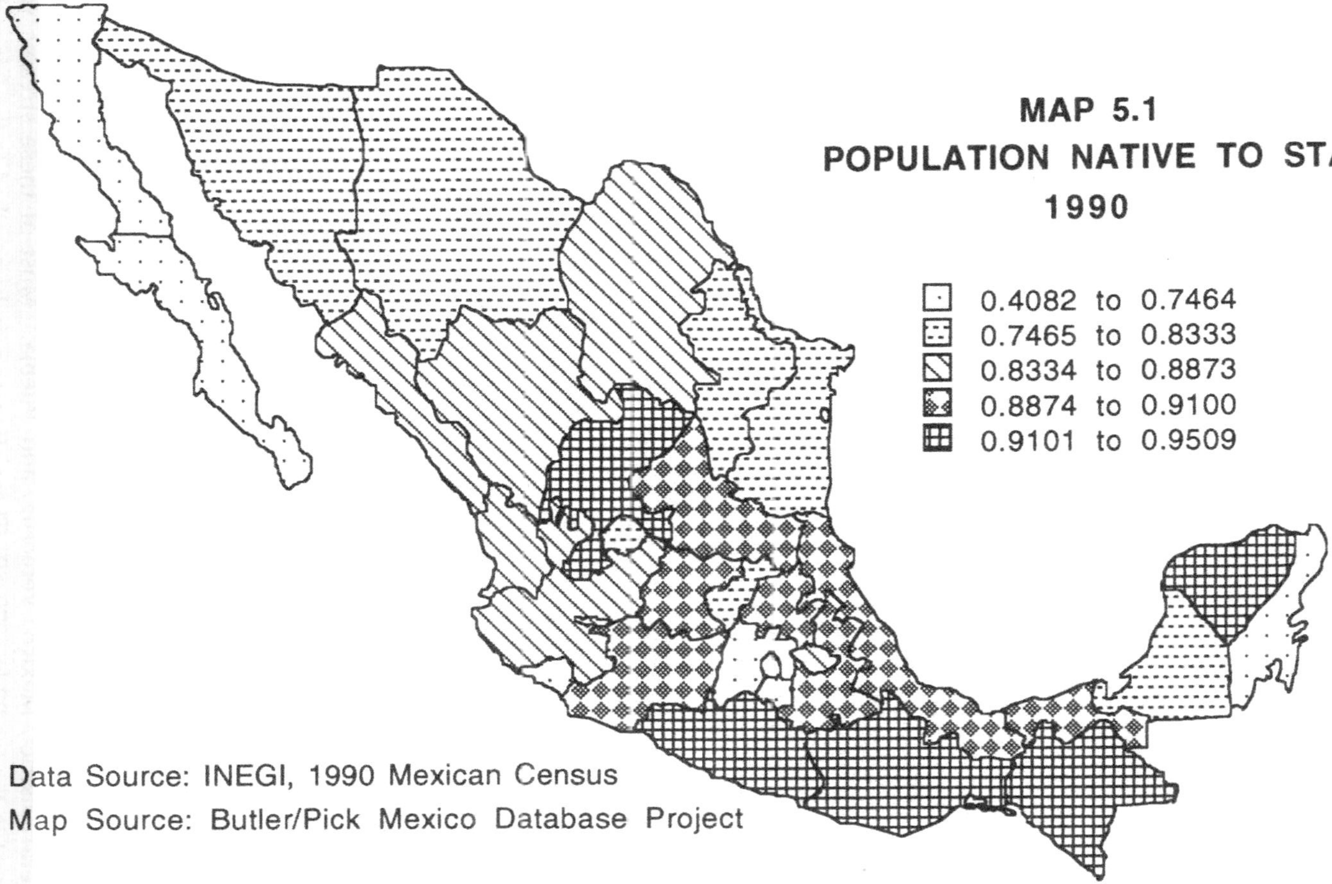

Data Source: INEGI, 1990 Mexican Census

Map Source: Butler/Pick Mexico Database Project

Migration Streams in Previous Five Years, 1990

The largest 23 interstate migration streams are shown for the period 1985–1990 in Maps 5.2 (enlargement of central region) and 5.3 (rest of nation). By number, these streams comprise only 2.3 percent of the nation's 992 interstate streams, while they comprise 37.5 percent of migrants. This is larger than the 21.4 percent of migrants in 1979–80. This implies that the largest streams grew in relative importance in the 1980s. The data exclude foreign in- and outmigrants, as well as 1985–1990 migrants who did not specify states of migration origin and destination. Since unspecified respondents are excluded, the data are identical to those utilized for net lifetime migration.

The largest stream of 548,975 persons is from the Federal District to the state of Mexico (see Table 5.2). This stream constitutes 15.8 percent of all 1985–1990 migrants. The size of this stream grew by about 50 percent from 1979–80, when it accounted for 9.9 percent of migrants. This stream has been present for several decades and represents a continuation of metropolitan overspill from the Federal District into the state of Mexico (Van Arsdol et al. 1976; Schteingart 1988). At the same time, the second largest stream of 80,905 is the reverse one from the state of Mexico to the Federal District. It constitutes 2.3 percent of migrants, a relative level similar to 1979–80. Some of this flow may be from remaining rural areas in the state of Mexico.

There are a number of major flow patterns for the top 23 streams. There is a major migration from the Federal District to states other than Mexico in the central flank, specifically Puebla, Jalisco, Guanajuato, Michoacan, Veracruz, Morelos, Hidalgo, and Queretaro. This flow of 270,415 migrants, or 7.8 percent of total migration, represents a more distant "overspill" from the Federal District. It grew sharply over the decade from 3.0 percent in 1979–80.

It is important to note that, among the top 23 streams, total migration flow *into* the Federal District was reduced from 7.5 percent of migrants in 1979–80 to only 4.0 percent in 1985–1990. On the other hand, the total migration flow *out of the Federal District* nearly doubled relatively from 12.9 percent in 1979–80 to 23.6 percent in 1985–1990. It may be said that flow away from the Federal District to the rest of the central region is the dominant feature in the nation's internal migration flows in the late 80s. The reasons for such huge outflow are the pressing urban and environmental problems of the metropolitan center (Schteingart 1988).

In the major 23 patterns, there are several specific streams into outlying states of the 1980s. In particular, these streams were from Sinaloa and Jalisco into Baja, from Yucatan into Quintana Roo, from Durango into Chihuahua, and from Veracruz into Tamaulipas. The Baja flows were noted for the 1950s (Whetten and Burnight 1956) and were shown to be consistent throughout the twentieth century (Butler and Pick 1991). The other patterns feeding outlying states are not well documented, nor did they occur for 1979–80.

Excluding streams between the Federal District and Mexico, there are a number of other migration streams evident between the populous central states of the Federal District, Mexico, Veracruz, and Puebla. Most of these streams were present in the top 23 in 1979–80. These streams may be ascribed to the fairly close proximity of these very populous states.

The remaining top streams are two from the southern region. Specifically, the streams are from Oaxaca to Mexico and Veracruz. The prominent Oaxaca-to-Federal-District stream in 1979–80 is not evident for 1990. The migration out of the south region diminished in the 1980s from 3.2 percent of migrants in 1979–80 to only 1.5 percent of migrants in 1985–1990. It would seem that the rootedness of the southern population, apparent with the pattern for native to state, has increased in the past decade.

Major internal migration streams were studied by Whetten and Burnight (1956), based on the 1950 Census, and were examined for the 1980 Census in *Atlas of Mexico* (Pick et al. 1989a). Comparison of the 1950 results with the present streams is somewhat hampered by the 1950 streams being *lifetime* streams, for *non-contiguous* states. Nevertheless, comparison shows that over a 40 year period, migration *into* the Federal District diminished from huge to moderate levels, while migration *out of* the Federal District increased greatly. Flows to the border were more apparent at the beginning and end of the forty year period.

Table 5.2 Migration Streams in Previous Five Years, 1985–1990

No.	From	To	Volume
1	DISTRITO FEDERAL	MEXICO	548,975
2	MEXICO	DISTRITO FEDERAL	80,905
3	SINALOA	BAJA	39,867
4	DISTRITO FEDERAL	PUEBLA	38,213
5	DISTRITO FEDERAL	JALISCO	37,330
6	DISTRITO FEDERAL	GUANAJUATO	35,766
7	DISTRITO FEDERAL	MICHOACAN	35,528
8	YUCATAN	QUINTANA ROO	35,108
9	DISTRITO FEDERAL	VERACRUZ	34,876
10	PUEBLA	MEXICO	34,199
11	VERACRUZ	MEXICO	32,795
12	DISTRITO FEDERAL	MORELOS	32,463
13	DURANGO	CHIHUAHUA	32,270
14	VERACRUZ	TAMAULIPAS	31,464
15	PUEBLA	DISTRITO FEDERAL	31,200
16	HIDALGO	MEXICO	29,191
17	DISTRITO FEDERAL	HIDALGO	28,686
18	VERACRUZ	DISTRITO FEDERAL	28,355
19	DISTRITO FEDERAL	QUERETARO	27,553
20	VERACRUZ	PUEBLA	26,776
21	OAXACA	MEXICO	26,573
22	OAXACA	VERACRUZ	25,962
23	JALISCO	BAJA CALIFORNIA	25,749
Total (Top 23)			1,299,804
Total			0.3743

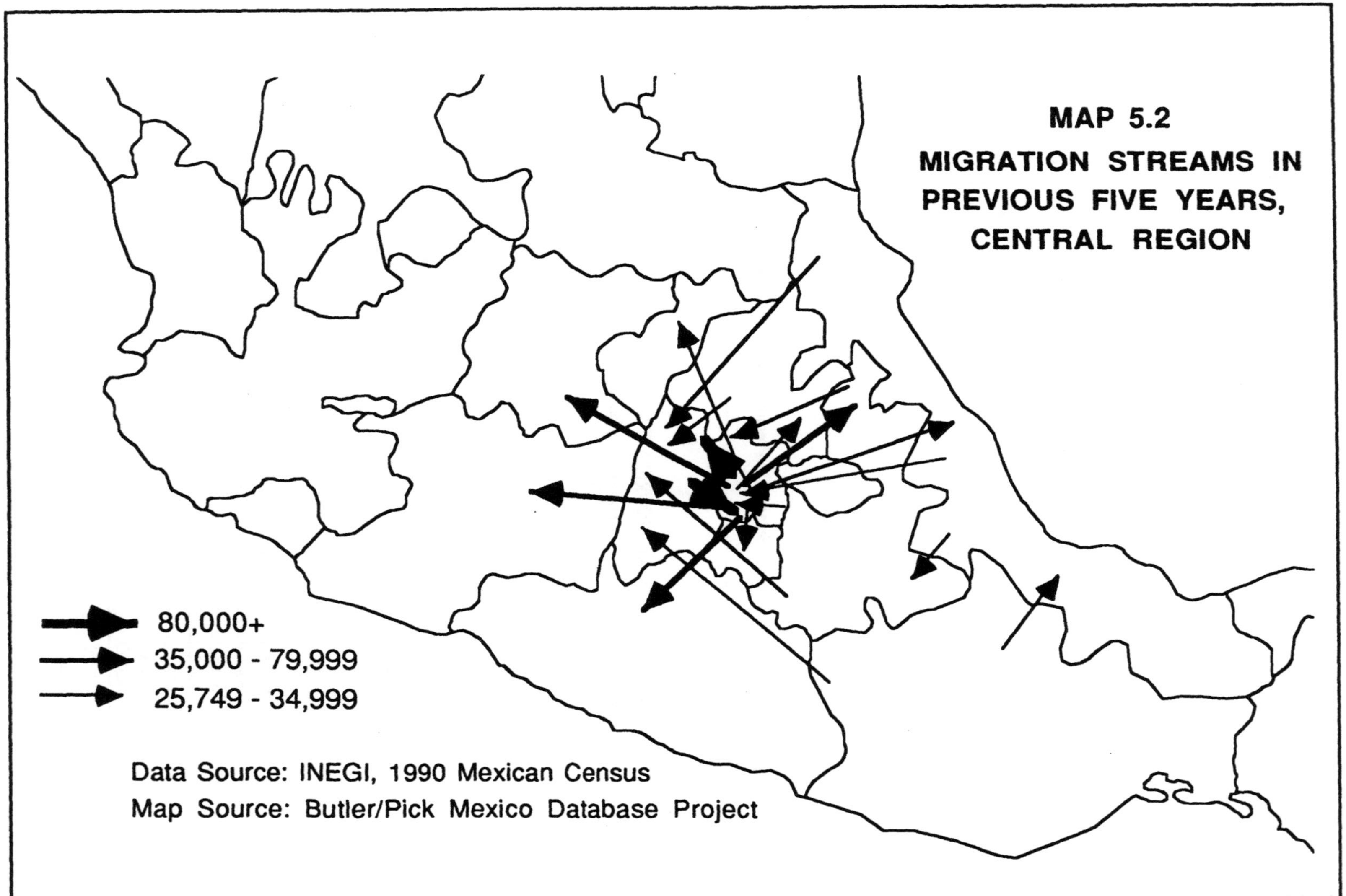
MAP 5.2
MIGRATION STREAMS IN PREVIOUS FIVE YEARS, CENTRAL REGION
80,000+
35,000 - 79,999
25,749 - 34,999
Data Source: INEGI, 1990 Mexican Census
Map Source: Butler/Pick Mexico Database Project

MAP 5.3
MIGRATION STREAMS IN LAST FIVE YEARS, PERIPHERAL AREAS

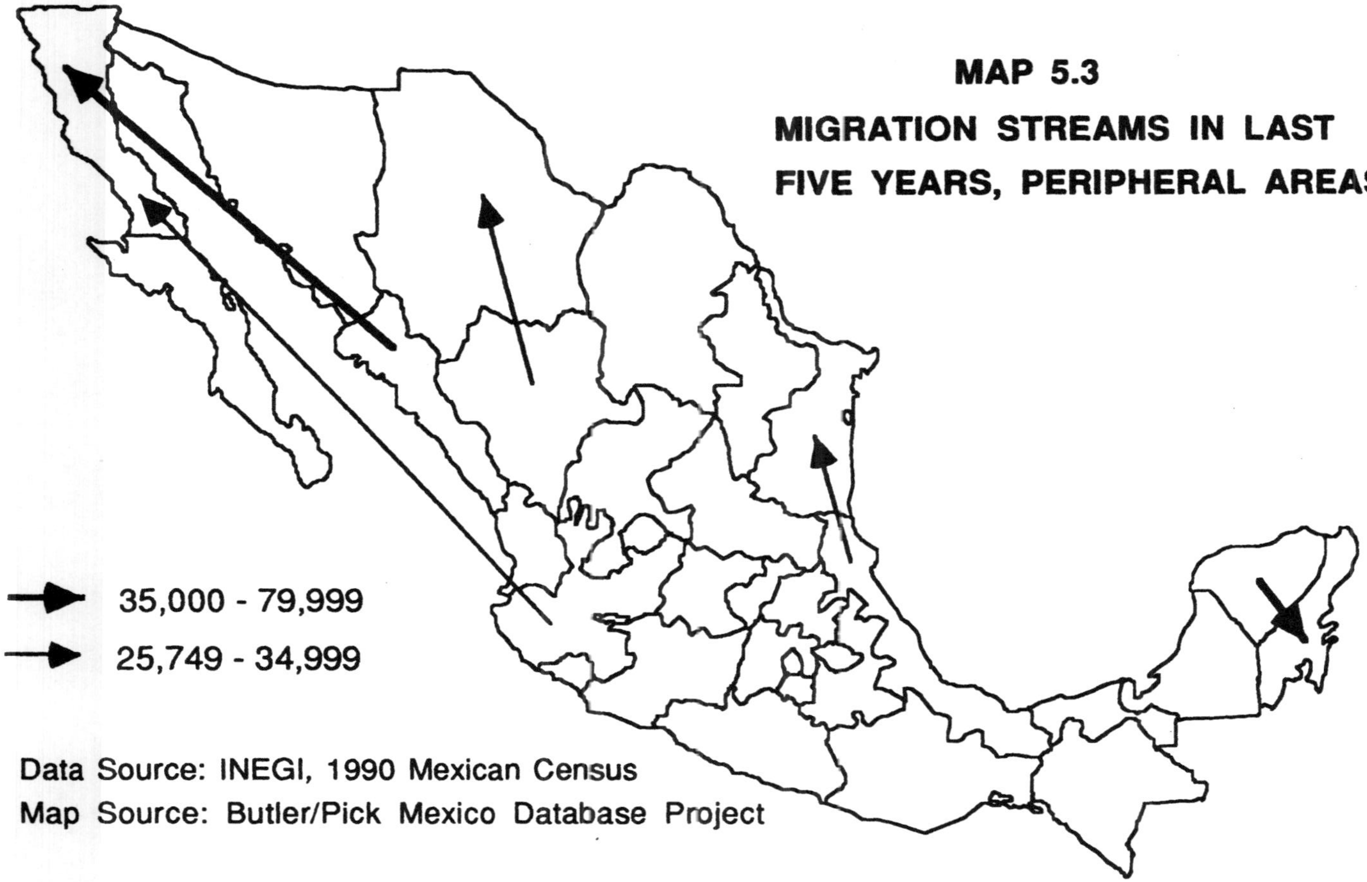

Data Source: INEGI, 1990 Mexican Census
Map Source: Butler/Pick Mexico Database Project

Inmigrants Per Capita, Lifetime, 1990

Lifetime migration is the ratio of inmigrants to a state to the population of the state. The mean state lifetime inmigration for 1990 was .1670 (see Table 5.3). This may be compared to the national proportion of all lifetime inmigrants to national population. The national proportion in 1990 was .1720, which implies that about one sixth of Mexican in 1990 had inmigrated to their present state of residence from another state. The proportion of lifetime inmigration increased by 36 percent in the 80s from a comparable figure of .1265 in 1980. This comparison must be viewed cautiously, since in the 1980 but not in the 1990 census there was a large proportion of unspecified respondents on migration. The Mexican rate of lifetime inmigration is lower by comparison with mobility rates for Americans (Bogue 1985).

Lifetime inmigration has a significant opposite correlation of - .48 with lifetime outmigration. This is plausible, since the relative economic attractiveness of states has remained rather steady and migration steams flows have been fairly consistent in the twentieth century. As seen in Map 5.4, lifetime inmigration is correlated with attributes reflecting economic prosperity including economic activity, tertiary employment, high income, service industry, hotels, tourism, and vehicle ownership. On the other hand, it varies in the opposite direction from attributes of economic poverty including low monthly income, dependency ratio, no meat and eggs in the household, lack of a toilet in the housing unit, and agricultural occupation. The variation in lifetime inmigration of 74 is moderate, although substantially less than for lifetime outmigration. Lifetime inmigration is highest in Baja California, Baja Sur, Mexico, and Quintana Roo—relatively prosperous states that grew very rapidly in the 80s, Rates in these states average about 50 percent, which implies that one half of the population migrated from another state at some point in life. Other states with high lifetime inmigration include Morelos, the Federal District, Colima, Tamaulipas, and Nuevo Leon. It is interesting that the Federal District's rate of .2417 is twenty percent higher than in 1980. This partly reflects the fact that the Federal District in the 80s continued to attract inmigrants, even though its rate of outmigration in the 80s surged to an unprecedented high level. By comparison, earlier in the century, the Federal District consistently attracted inmigrants.

Inmigration is lowest in the pacific south and is also low throughout the gulf region and parts of the central and north regions. Lifetime inmigration is only .0455 for the pacific south region, implying that only one in every twenty two residents inmigrated from other states. Reasons include poverty of the region and the strength of indigenous cultures in the area. The gulf region has a low lifetime inmigration rate of .0940. It also has a high proportion of indigenous population, although economically it is more prosperous than the pacific south. Several states in the Bajio area of Mexico also have low inmigration.

Outmigrants Per Capita, Lifetime, 1990

Lifetime outmigration was equivalent in volume to lifetime inmigration, with a national outmigration proportion of .1719. The statewide mean for net outmigration is .1636. The coefficient of variation of 55 indicates a moderate level, lower than for lifetime inmigration (see Table 5.3). States with the highest lifetime outmigration are the Federal District (in second place with a rate of .3823) and the states in the Bajio area of Zacatecas, Durango, Hidalgo, and San Luis Potosi (see Map 5.5). Given the very large population of the Federal District, the outmigration rate implies that there were about two lifetime outmigrants for every five 1990 residents. Many outmigrants moved to the surrounding state of Mexico, contributing to its massive population growth especially over the past two decades. Lifetime outmigration losses in the Bajio approximate one third of present population. This region has become a poor one during the twentieth century, a push factor for departure. States with the least outmigration are the growth states of Quintana Roo, Baja California, and Mexico, as well as Nuevo Leon, which has grown rapidly, especially before 1970.

Lifetime outmigration is associated with unemployment, elderly population, and marginality indicators of no meat and eggs and housing lacking a toilet. These characteristics are typical of the impoverished Bajio states. It varies oppositely from economic activity, high income, sex ratio, and urban and population growth over the past several decades. The inverse association with sex ratio may reflect lower sex ratios in more prosperous states. Lifetime outmigration does not have significant associations with occupation or industry variables.

By region, lifetime outmigration is lowest in the southeast and gulf, and in the border region, except for Chihuahua. It is highest in the four Bajio states, and also very high in the south. Other regions are inconsistent in lifetime inmigration. The central region has among the highest lifetime outmigration for the Federal District and among the lowest for Mexico, factors reflecting in part the large-scale movement of population from the Federal District to the state of Mexico, where population remained resident.

Net Migration Per Capita, Lifetime, 1990

Lifetime net migration is the difference of net inmigration minus net outmigration. It was highest in 1990 in the growth states of Quintana Roo, Baja California and Mexico and lowest in the adjoining states of Zacatecas, Durango, Hidalgo, and San Luis Potosi, plus the southern state of Oaxaca.

As shown in Table 5.3 and Map 5.6, it is also important to consider the *volume* of lifetime net migration. Volume is largest by far for the state of Mexico, followed by Baja California and Nuevo Leon. These states are ones that, during the twentieth century, received very large influxes of rural to urban migration (all three states), migration to the border (Nuevo Leon, Baja), and migration from metropolitan overspill (Mexico). In all three states, there were rapidly growing cities during the century, resulting the first, third, and seventh largest Mexican metropolises in 1990 (see Table 3.2). The state of Mexico has by far the largest volume of net migration, with a net of 3.3 million persons migrating over a lifetime. In other words, the net migration accounted for one-third of the state's 9.8 million residents in 1990. States with the largest negative volume of net migration, i.e., representing net outmigrants, were the Federal District, Michoacan, Oaxaca, Zacatecas, and Guanajuato. The Federal District's outflow has already been addressed, in the 1980s, in the migration streams shown in Map 5.2. The four others are poor states including the latter two Bajio states. Many migrants from these four states moved to the CMZ.

Lifetime net migration is positively associated with economic prosperity and growth. In particular, it has significant associations with high income, economic activity, service industry, and population growth in the 70s and 80s. It is also related to secondary education, service industry, and hotels. It is inversely related to economic poverty variables of low monthly income and agricultural occupation, as well as to marginality indicators such as housing without a toilet and no meat and eggs.

Lifetime net migration is highly correlated at .88 with net migration 1985–1990. This is plausible both because of historical stability in migration trends (see Butler and Pick 1991), as well as due to the statistical weighting of lifetime migration volume towards more recent years.

Table 5.3 Lifetime Migration, 1990

No.	State	Lifetime Inmig.	No. of Per Capita Lifetime Inmig.	Lifetime Outmig.	Lifetime Outmig.	No. of Lifetime Net Inmig.	Per Capita Lifetime Net Inmig.
1	AGUASCALIENTES	138,380	0.1923	109,121	0.1516	29,180	0.0405
2	BAJA CALIFORNIA	747,730	0.4502	97,184	0.0585	650,122	0.3914
3	BAJA CALIF. SUR	96,857	0.3048	25,099	0.0790	71,679	0.2256
4	CAMPECHE	115,483	0.2158	66,603	0.1244	48,818	0.0912
5	COAHUILA	284,522	0.1443	369,688	0.1874	-85,468	-0.0433
6	COLIMA	115,085	0.2686	62,177	0.1451	52,888	0.1234
7	CHIAPAS	107,030	0.0333	229,372	0.0714	-124,375	-0.0387
8	CHIHUAHUA	348,686	0.1428	189,204	0.0775	158,981	0.0651
9	DISTRITO FEDERAL	1,990,652	0.2417	3,148,776	0.3823	-1,159,935	-0.1408
10	DURANGO	146,822	0.1088	398,027	0.2950	-251,606	-0.1865
11	GUANAJUATO	302,141	0.0759	702,486	0.1764	-401,178	-0.1007
12	GUERRERO	128,359	0.0490	520,755	0.1987	-392,755	-0.1499
13	HIDALGO	184,613	0.0978	520,671	0.2757	-336,285	-0.1781
14	JALISCO	709,202	0.1337	679,772	0.1282	28,852	0.0054
15	MEXICO	3,884,249	0.3957	574,694	0.0585	3,308,693	0.3371
16	MICHOACAN	269,392	0.0759	866,331	0.2442	-597,704	-0.1685
17	MORELOS	339,297	0.2839	123,695	0.1035	215,457	0.1803
18	NAYARIT	122,312	0.1483	164,097	0.1990	-41,872	-0.0508
19	NUEVO LEON	707,462	0.2283	212,403	0.0685	494,673	0.1596
20	OAXACA	168,049	0.0557	696,724	0.2307	-528,859	-0.1751
21	PUEBLA	350,504	0.0849	734,739	0.1781	-384,812	-0.0933
22	QUERETARO	179,214	0.1705	163,411	0.1554	15,620	0.0149
23	QUINTANA ROO	273,611	0.5547	17,690	0.0359	255,856	0.5187
24	SAN LUIS POTOSI	186,262	0.0930	539,674	0.2694	-353,675	-0.1766
25	SINALOA	267,124	0.1212	327,042	0.1484	-60,192	-0.0273
26	SONORA	296,657	0.1627	169,103	0.0927	127,235	0.0698
27	TABASCO	143,088	0.0953	163,209	0.1087	-20,321	-0.0135
28	TAMAULIPAS	521,399	0.2318	321,740	0.1430	199,382	0.0886
29	TLAXCALA	93,595	0.1229	162,477	0.2134	-68,972	-0.0906
30	VERACRUZ	583,665	0.0937	873,351	0.1402	-290,155	-0.0466
31	YUCATAN	74,617	0.0547	207,325	0.1521	-132,753	-0.0974
32	ZACATECAS	100,117	0.0784	526,380	0.4124	-426,519	-0.3342
	National Total	13,976,176		13,963,020		0	
	Mean	436,756	0.1722	436,344	0.1658	0	0.0062
	Median	226,693	0.1383	275,556	0.1500	-51,032	-0.0330
	S.D.	724,082	0.1219	557,076	0.0906	692,922	0.1834
	C.V.	165.79	70.76	127.67	54.64		
	Minimum	74,617	0.0333	17,690	0.0359	-1,159,935	-0.3342
	Maximum	3,884,249	0.5547	3,148,776	0.4124	3,308,693	0.5187

DEFINITION: Lifetime inmigrants is the number of migrants into a state for the lifetimes of current residents. Lifetime outmigrants is the number of migrants out of a state for the lifetimes of current residents. Foreign migration is excluded from all migration variables, but unspecified population is included. Lifetime net migrants is the difference of lifetime inmigrants minus lifetime outmigrants. In calculating lifetime net migrants, the unspecified population is excluded, in order that lifetime net migrants sum to zero for the nation.

SOURCE: INEGI, 1990 Mexican Census of Population, Resumen General, Table 5.

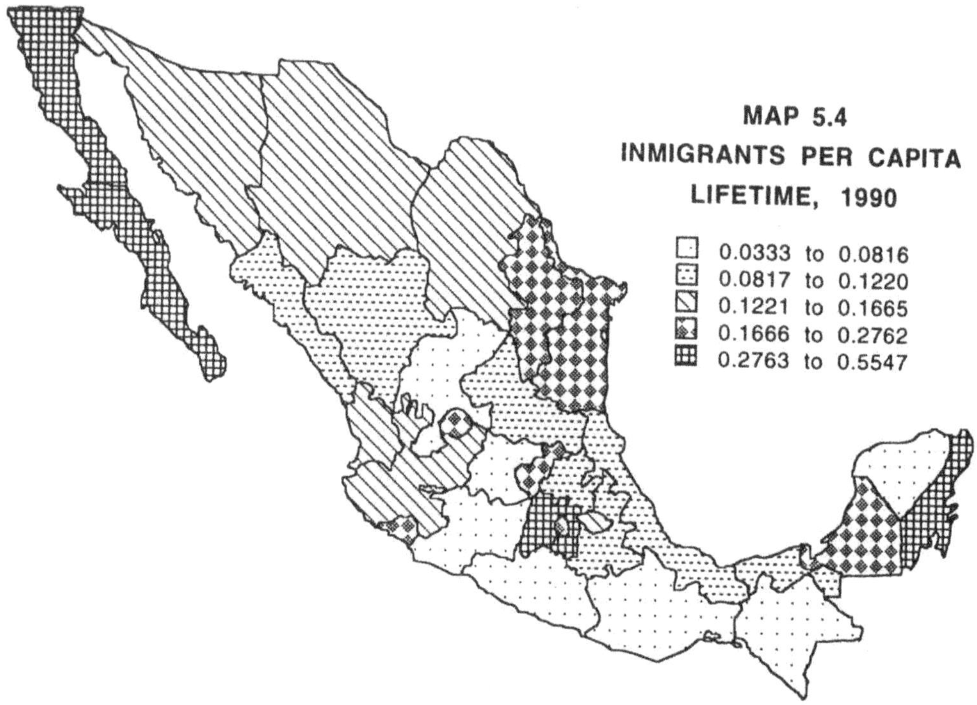
MAP 5.4
INMIGRANTS PER CAPITA
LIFETIME, 1990
0.0333 to 0.0816
0.0817 to 0.1220
0.1221 to 0.1665
0.1666 to 0.2762
0.2763 to 0.5547

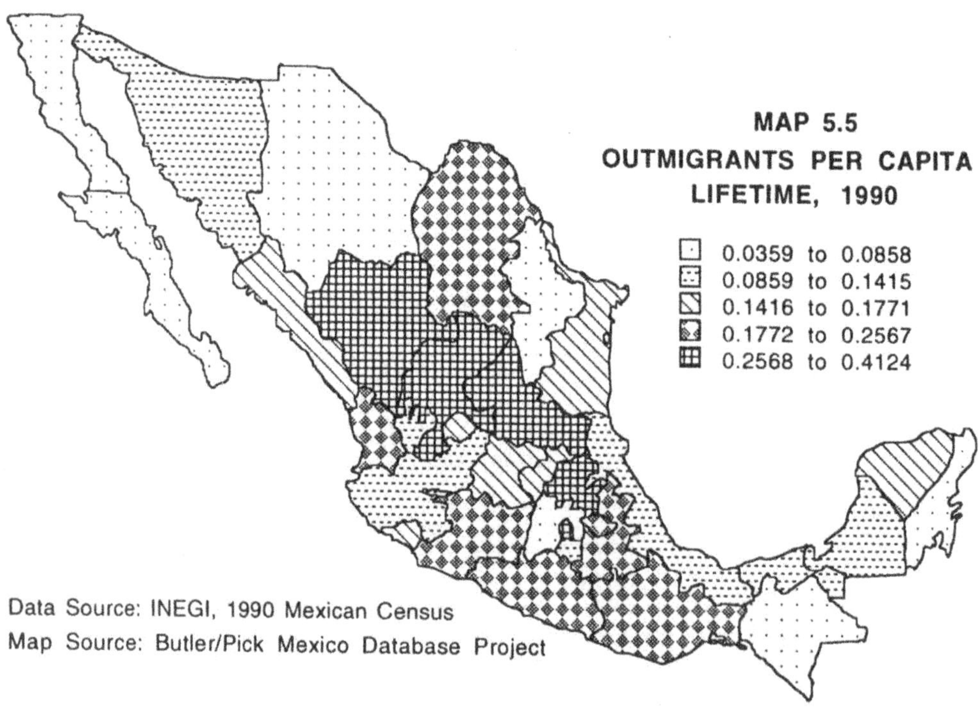
MAP 5.5
OUTMIGRANTS PER CAPITA
LIFETIME, 1990
0.0359 to 0.0858
0.0859 to 0.1415
0.1416 to 0.1771
0.1772 to 0.2567
0.2568 to 0.4124
Data Source: INEGI, 1990 Mexican Census
Map Source: Butler/Pick Mexico Database Project

MAP 5.6
NET INMIGRANTS PER CAPITA
LIFETIME, 1990

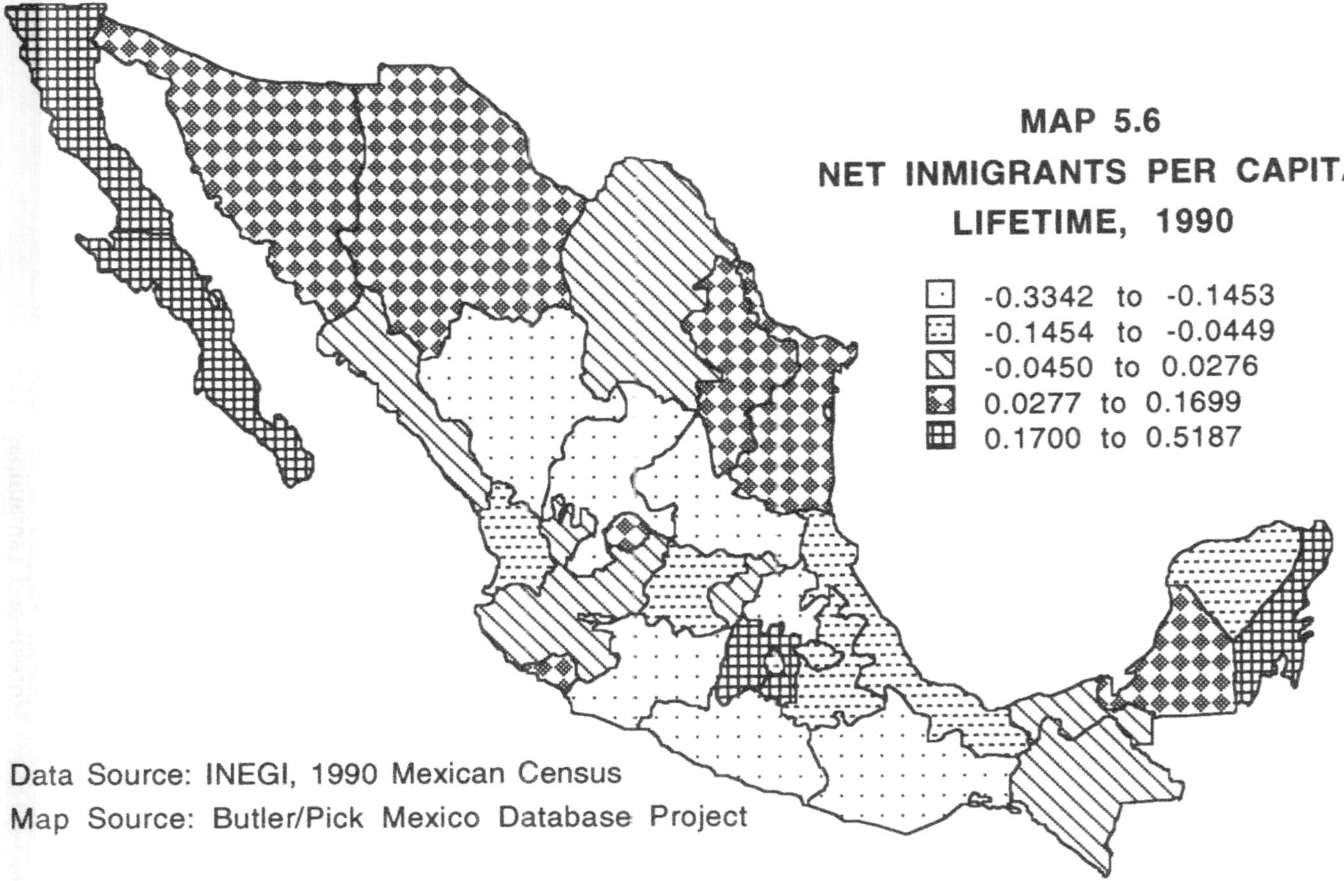

Data Source: INEGI, 1990 Mexican Census
Map Source: Butler/Pick Mexico Database Project

Inmigration in the Past Five Years, 1990

This variable measures the ratio of inmigrants from 1985–1990 to population age five years on older in 1990. It had a mean value of .0579 as seen in Table 5.4. The coefficient of variation of 72 is moderate. States with the highest inmigration 1985–1990 were Quintana Roo at .2250 and Baja California at .1549 (see Map 5.7). Although the state of Mexico was in third place at .0919, it grew by far the most in inmigration volume, by 787,000 persons in 1985–1990. The states lowest in inmigration 1985–1990 were the southern states of Chiapas, Guerrero, and Oaxaca, which experienced only about two percent inmigration. Other low states included Zacatecas and Hidalgo from the Bajio area. These inmigration patterns correspond closely to lifetime inmigration patterns already discussed.

Inmigration 1985–1990 is very significantly correlated at .92 with lifetime inmigration. Relationships with other variables are very similar to those already discussed for lifetime inmigration.

In comparing five year inmigration rates for 1985–1990 with one-year inmigration rates for 1979–80, it is interesting that rates were about forty percent higher for the 1979–80 period (see Pick et al. 1989a, Table 4.3). It may be that the economic depression of the mid 1980s slowed rates of inmigration.

Outmigration in the Past Five Years, 1990

The ratio of outmigrants in the period 1985 to 1990 to the population age five years and older in 1990 (see Table 5.4 and Map 5.8) had a mean value of .0413. The coefficient of variation is substantially lower than for inmigration 1985–1990. The state with by far the highest outmigration rate 1985–1990 was the Federal District at .1405, i.e., about one out of seven residents outmigrated over the five years. Other high outmigration states included Durango, Zacatecas, and states in the south. States with the lowest outmigration were the northern border states of Baja, Chihuahua, and Nuevo Leon, as well as Aguascalientes and Chiapas. Chiapas' low outmigration in 1985–1990 is consistent with its low lifetime outmigration (see Map 5.5).

In *volume* of outmigrants 1985–1990, the Federal District dominated with about one million outmigrants. Other major outmigrant states in volume were Mexico and Veracruz.

Outmigration 1985–1990 is highly correlated with lifetime outmigration at .69. It is also associated with population density, commercial workforce, gross state product, and telephones. It varies inversely with urbanization change 1950–1990 and construction workforce.

Rates of outmigration are also comparatively lower in 1985–1990 than in 1979–80, with the economic depression of the 80s as one probable cause (see Pick et al. 1989a, Table 4.3). The geographic pattern looks quite similar to that for 1979–80, with major differences being the reductions in outmigration rates for Baja and Baja Sur, as well as for Morelos and Tamaulipas.

Net Migration in the Past Five Years, 1990

Net outmigration is the difference between the rates of net inmigration 1985–1990 and net outmigration 1985–1990. It is highest for Quintana Roo, Baja California, and Mexico (see Table 5.4 and Map 5.9). The inmigration rate of .18 for Quintana Roo implies a compounded annual net inmigration rate in the late 80s of 3.4 percent. By far the lowest net migration rate 1985–1990 was for the Federal District, which decreased by ten percent net over the five years. This reflects a population *deconcentration* from the central part of the CMZ, with most of the outflux going to the state of Mexico.

Net migration, 1985–1990 is correlated at .88 with lifetime net migration. The associations with other variables are similar to those for lifetime net migration. Net migration 1985–1990 is associated with population growth in the past two decades, population density, urbanization change 1950–1990, hotel/motel services, and gross state product. It has reverse associations with population density, mid century total population, unemployment and low monthly income.

Table 5.4 Migration in Previous Five Years, 1990

No.	State	No. of Inmig.*	Per Cap. Inmig.*	No. of Outmig.*	Per Cap. Outmig.*	No. of Net Inmig.*	Per Cap. Net Inmig.*
1	AGUASCALIENTES	44,012	0.0711	17,452	0.0282	26,527	0.0428
2	BAJA CALIFORNIA	220,848	0.1549	40,309	0.0283	180255	0.1264
3	BAJA CALIF. SUR	29,539	0.1070	11,735	0.0425	17725	0.0642
4	CAMPECHE	34,500	0.0756	24,697	0.0541	9762	0.0214
5	COAHUILA	69,278	0.0400	80,748	0.0467	-11554	-0.0067
6	COLIMA	31,123	0.0837	18,356	0.0492	12747	0.0343
7	CHIAPAS	43,947	0.0162	69,824	0.0258	-27502	-0.0101
8	CHIHUAHUA	118,343	0.0559	40,146	0.0189	77933	0.0368
9	DISTRITO FEDERAL	299,285	0.0406	1,035,758	0.1405	-737523	-0.1000
10	DURANGO	41,301	0.0353	82,359	0.0704	-41211	-0.0352
11	GUANAJUATO	98,926	0.0291	94,976	0.0280	3443	0.0010
12	GUERRERO	46,959	0.0211	120,236	0.0540	-73619	-0.0330
13	HIDALGO	67,114	0.0412	85,909	0.0528	-18945	-0.0116
14	JALISCO	178,259	0.0389	138,366	0.0302	39645	0.0086
15	MEXICO	787,020	0.0919	271,421	0.0317	514946	0.0601
16	MICHOACAN	106,146	0.0349	121,134	0.0399	-15532	-0.0051
17	MORELOS	91,322	0.0871	39,613	0.0378	51614	0.0492
18	NAYARIT	35,934	0.0505	38,769	0.0545	-2904	-0.0041
19	NUEVO LEON	114,049	0.0415	66,247	0.0241	47597	0.0173
20	OAXACA	74,083	0.0285	138,780	0.0533	-64888	-0.0249
21	PUEBLA	126,056	0.0354	139,132	0.0390	-13446	-0.0038
22	QUERETARO	67,976	0.0757	29,264	0.0326	38593	0.0430
23	QUINTANA ROO	92,895	0.2250	18,969	0.0459	73841	0.1788
24	SAN LUIS POTOSI	64,531	0.0375	77,650	0.0451	-13251	-0.0077
25	SINALOA	83,139	0.0432	105,330	0.0548	-22519	0.0115
26	SONORA	72,307	0.0453	53,840	0.0337	18281	-0.0051
27	TABASCO	47,965	0.0372	54,412	0.0422	-6597	-0.0051
28	TAMAULIPAS	115,424	0.0584	75,599	0.0383	39697	0.0201
29	TLAXCALA	35,906	0.0542	25,028	0.0378	10830	0.0163
30	VERACRUZ	163,924	0.0302	236,281	0.0436	-72695	-0.0134
31	YUCATAN	38,395	0.0323	47,384	0.0399	-9020	-0.0076
32	ZACATECAS	36,731	0.0334	68,784	0.0625	-32230	-0.0293
	National Total	3,477,237		3,468,508		0	
	Mean	108,664	0.0579	108,391	0.0446	0	0.0134
	Median	70,793	0.0414	69,304	0.0411	270	-0.0014
	S.D.	137,609	0.0419	179,373	0.0211	168922	0.0491
	C.V.	126.64	72.35	165.49	47.39		
	Minimum	29,539	0.0162	11,735	0.0189	-737523	-0.1000
	Maximum	787,020	0.2250	1,035,758	0.1405	514946	0.1788

DEFINITION: Inmigrants in previous five years are the number of migrants into a state in the previous five years. Outmigrants in previous five years are the number of migrants out of a state in the previous five years. Foreign migration is excluded from all migration variables. For in- and outmigrants, unspecified population is included. Net migrants is the difference of inmigrants minus outmigrants. In calculating net migrants in previous five years, the unspecified population is excluded, in order that net migrants sum to zero for the nation.

NOTE: * in previous five years.

SOURCE: INEGI, 1990 Mexican Census of Population, Resumen General, Table 5.

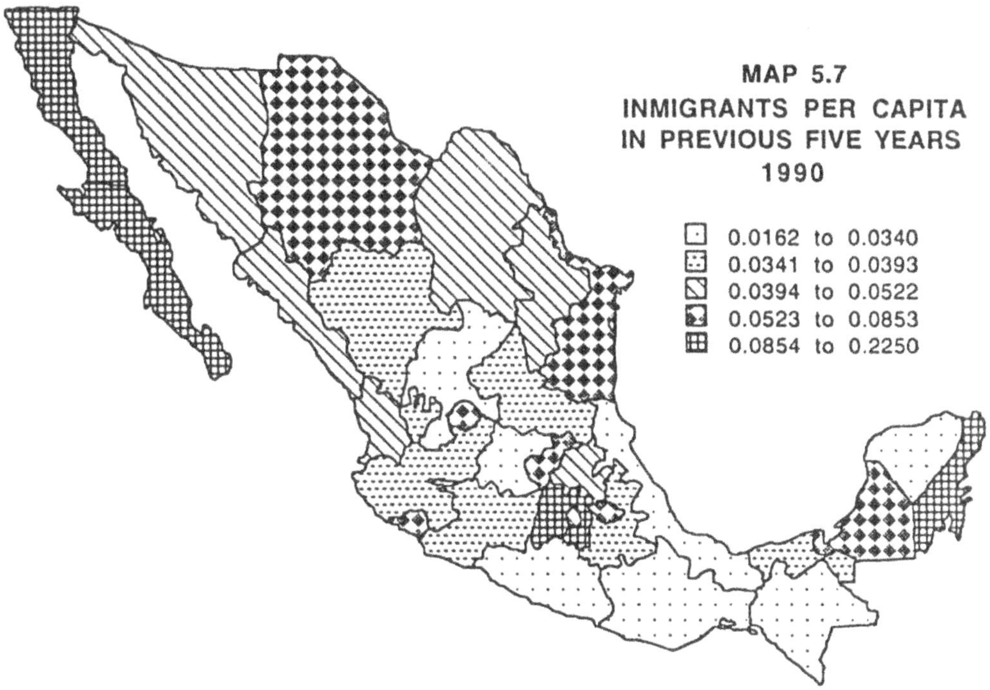
MAP 5.7
INMIGRANTS PER CAPITA
IN PREVIOUS FIVE YEARS
1990
0.0162 to 0.0340
0.0341 to 0.0393
0.0394 to 0.0522
0.0523 to 0.0853
0.0854 to 0.2250

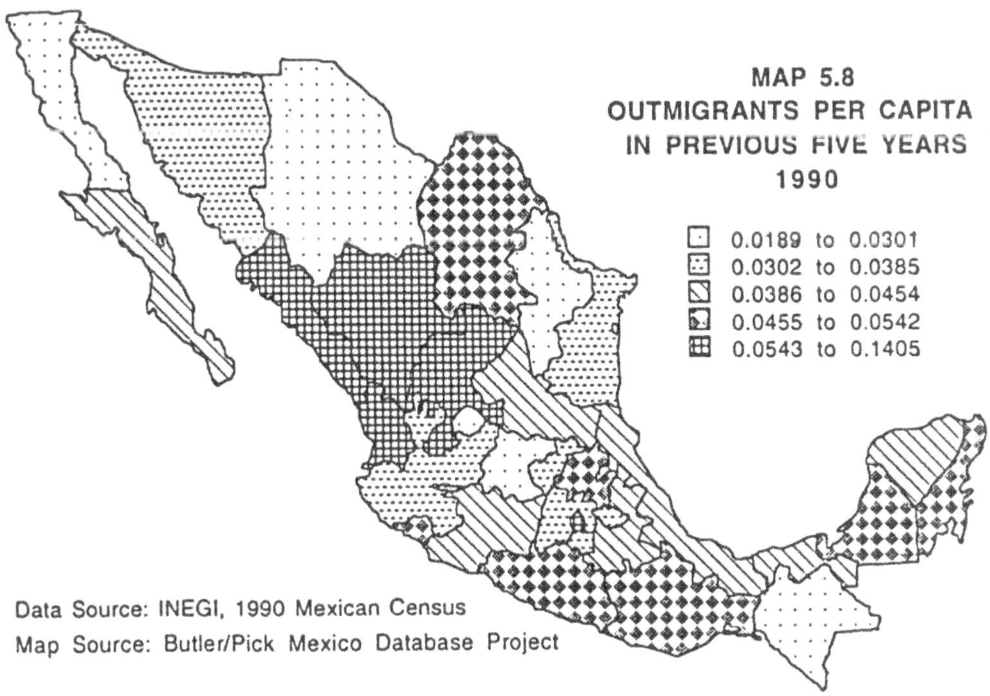
MAP 5.8
OUTMIGRANTS PER CAPITA
IN PREVIOUS FIVE YEARS
1990
0.0189 to 0.0301
0.0302 to 0.0385
0.0386 to 0.0454
0.0455 to 0.0542
0.0543 to 0.1405
Data Source: INEGI, 1990 Mexican Census
Map Source: Butler/Pick Mexico Database Project

MAP 5.9
NET INMIGRANTS PER CAPITA
IN PREVIOUS FIVE YEARS, 1990

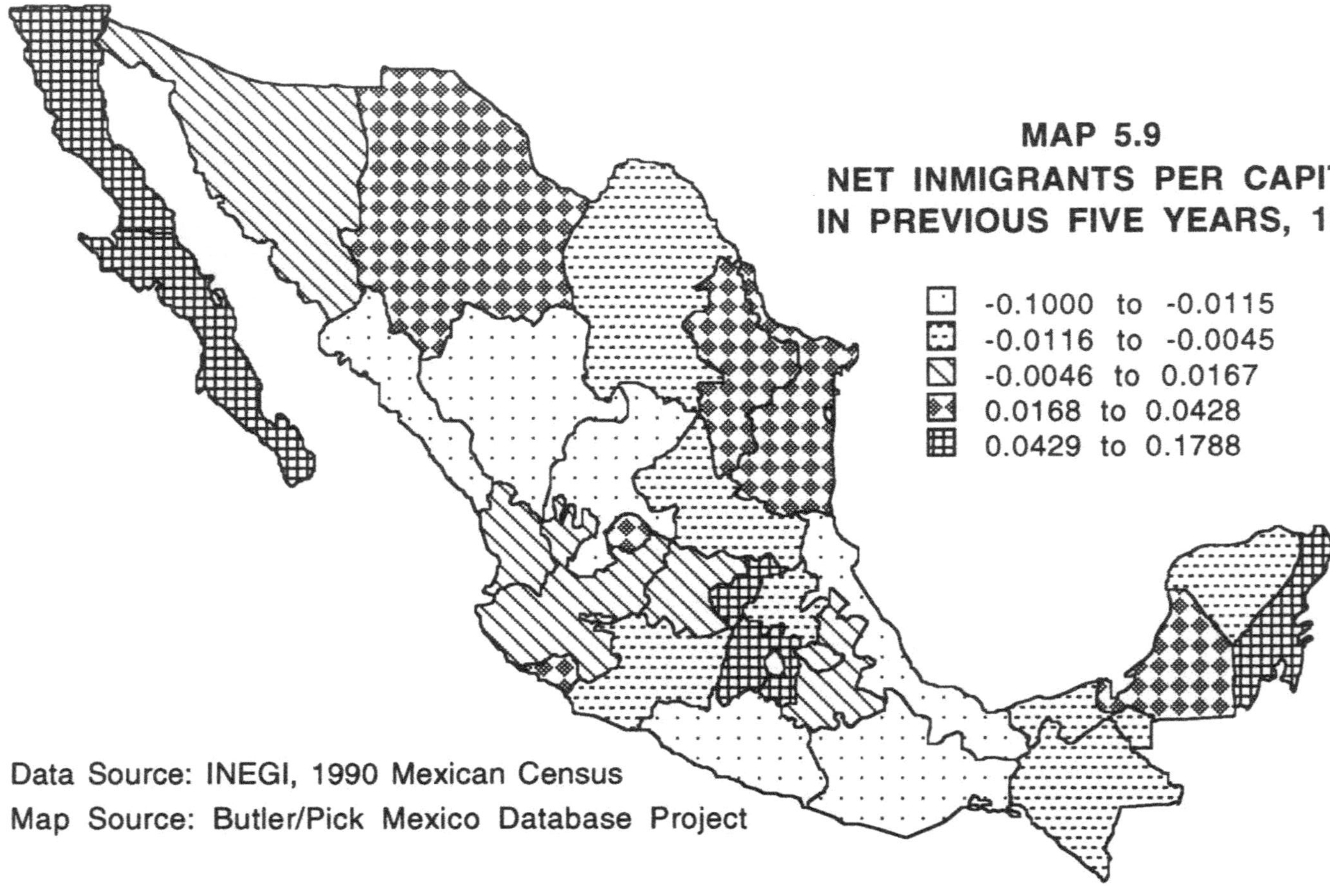

Data Source: INEGI, 1990 Mexican Census
Map Source: Butler/Pick Mexico Database Project

Percent Inmigrants to Mexico City in the Past Five Years, 1990

This attribute shows the percentage of inmigrants to Mexico City in the past five years. The high extent of migration is reflected in the mean percentage of 29.7 percent. The migration patterns are quite different for the Federal District versus the state of Mexico areas (see Map 5.10). This difference reflects a similar major differential in the statewide patterns between the Federal District and state of Mexico. The state of Mexico in the 1985–1990 period had 9 percent inmigration, while the Federal District experienced 4 percent inmigration.

Areas with the highest percentage of inmigrants are located in the state of Mexico, at or near the north and northeast boundaries of the Federal District. The highest net inmigration is for the municipio of Atenco, located to the northeast of the District. This municipio in 1990 was under-populated compared to neighboring municipios (see Map 2.4). The high inmigration may reflect its low population and available land space. Other municipios with over 50 percent inmigration 1985–1990 are Amecameca, Nezahualcoyotl, Cuautitlan Izcalli, Tultitlan, and Tlalnepantla, all located to the District's north and northeast. The high inmigration in this zone reflects lack of natural barriers to population growth and an economically more attractive area immediately outside the Federal District.

Looking at the broad pattern of Mexico City inmigration, the Federal District has low rates of inmigration, in the range of 2 to 11 percent. This district is encircled by part of the state of Mexico with high inmigration municipios in the range of 34 to 89 percent inmigration. At the outer edge of Mexico City to the north and west are municipios with moderate inmigration rates in the range of 11 to 34 percent. These state of Mexico municipios included in the CMZ have far higher inmigration rates than the municipios in the rest of the state. This broad pattern reflects the huge volume of movement from the Federal District to Mexico City (see Table 5.2, which reveals an over 1/2 million migrant stream from the District to the state of Mexico). The pattern of inmigration reflects the preferred destination of many of these stream migrants to the half ring closely surrounding the District. Comparing the pattern of Mexico City's 1985–1990 inmigration with the total population distribution in 1990 (Map 2.4), the pattern points to probable future population growth in the half ring around the District, especially in the north and northeast.

MAP 5.10
INMIGRANTS PER CAPITA
IN PREVIOUS FIVE YEARS
MEXICO CITY (CMZ), 1990

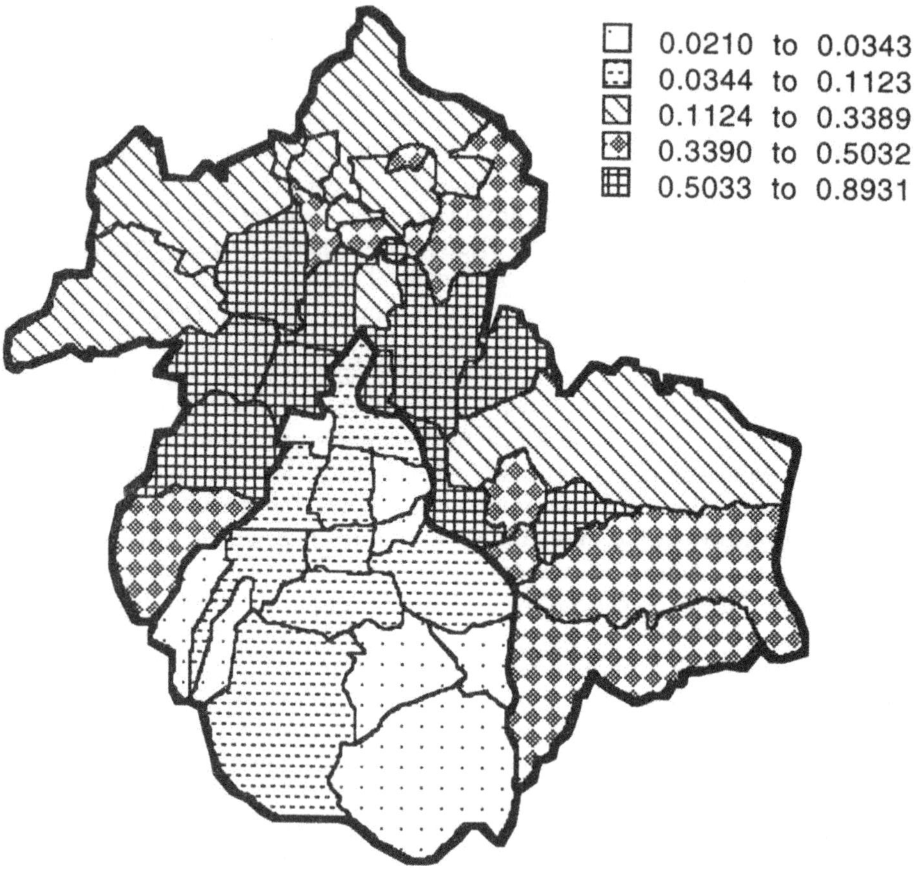

Data Source: INEGI, 1990 Mexican Census

Map Source: Butler/Pick Mexico Database Project

Immigration of Mexicans to the United States, 1930–1988

Legal immigration of Mexicans to the United States fluctuated greatly during the twentieth century (Lorey 1990). Levels of legal immigration from 1930 to 1985 are shown in Table 5.5 and Figure 5.1. Although immigration was quite low in the Depression years of the 1930s, it increased only slightly during World War II and the early postwar years. A sharp rise in legal immigration commenced in 1953 and 1954 with the start of the Bracero Program. This program was sponsored and approved by the U.S. government. It was designed to bring Mexican legal immigrants into the U.S. to work in low skilled jobs especially in agriculture. As seen in the figure, in the 1970s and first half of the 1980s, the level of legal immigration of Mexicans to the U.S. rose even more. This increase was related to the expanding job opportunities for lower skilled workers in the American economy, especially in the southwestern states. The data shown in Figure 5.1 do not include undocumented immigration from Mexico to the United States.

Figure 5.1
Immigration of Mexicans to the United States
1930 - 1985

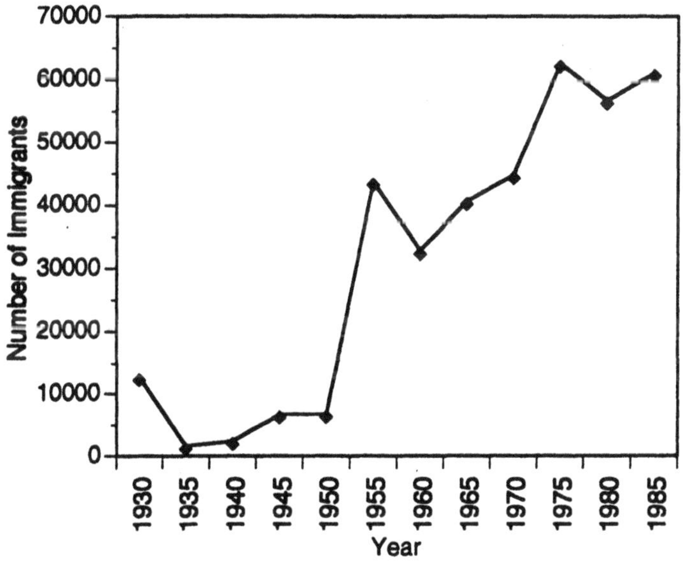

NOTE: Mexican immigrants are defined as nonresident aliens with Mexico as nation of last permanent residence and admitted to the U.S. for permanent residence.

SOURCE: Lorey, 1990.

Table 5.5 Immigration of Mexicans to the United States, 1930–1985

Year	Mexican Immigrants	% of Total Immigration to the U.S.	Year	Mexican Immigrants	% of Total Immigration to the U.S.
1930	12,703	5.3	1958	26,791	10.6
1931	3,333	3.4	1959	22,909	8.8
1932	2,171	6.1	1960	32,708	12.3
1933	1,936	8.4	1961	41,476	15.3
1934	1,801	6.1	1962	55,805	19.7
1935	1,560	4.5	1963	55,986	18.3
1936	1,716	4.7	1964	34,448	11.8
1937	2,347	4.7	1965	40,686	13.7
1938	2,502	3.7	1966	47,217	14.6
1939	2,640	3.2	1967	43,034	11.9
1940	2,313	3.3	1968	44,716	9.8
1941	2,824	5.5	1969	45,748	12.8
1942	2,378	8.3	1970	44,821	12.0
1943	4,172	17.6	1971	50,324	13.6
1944	6,598	23.1	1972	64,209	16.7
1945	6,702	17.6	1973	70,411	17.6
1946	7,146	6.6	1974	71,863	18.2
1947	7,558	5.1	1975	62,552	16.2
1948	8,384	4.9	1976	74,449	14.8
1949	8,083	4.3	1977	44,646	9.7
1950	6,744	2.7	1978	92,681	15.4
1951	6,153	3.0	1979	52,479	11.4
1952	9,079	3.4	1980	56,680	10.7
1953	17,183	10.1	1981	101,268	16.9
1954	30,645	14.7	1982	56,106	11.2
1955	43,702	18.4	1983	59,079	10.7
1956	61,320	19.1	1984	57,557	10.6
1957	49,321	15.1	1985	61,077	10.7

NOTE: Mexican immigrants are defined as nonresident aliens with Mexico as nation of last permanent residence and admitted to the U.S. for permanent residence.

SOURCE: Lorey, 1990.

6

Mortality, Health, and Housing

Introduction

This chapter examines mortality, health, and housing. Mortality includes infant mortality, which indicates the force of mortality relative to fertility in the first year of life. Crude and standardized mortality are measures of the overall impact of mortality on the population as a whole. Standardization adjusts mortality for age structural differences from state to state. Mortality is analyzed for the five major causes of death categories in Mexico, namely cardiovascular, respiratory, nutritional/metabolic/endocrine/immunity, trauma, and cancer. For these death causes, geographic and longitudinal changes are noted, as well as comparison among causes.

The section on health examines the national levels of hospitals and health personnel in the late 80s. It includes a variable from the 1980 census that was not included in 1990—no meat and eggs, i.e., the proportion of the population lacking these dietary items. Housing indicators analyzed include housing density and crowding, several characteristics of housing units, and home ownership. These variables reflect the lifestyle of Mexicans and are linked to urban and economic conditions.

Mortality

Infant Mortality Rate, 1990

The infant mortality rate measures the mortality of infants in the first year of life. It is defined as the ratio, for a one year period, of deaths to persons under one year of age to 1,000 live births. In 1993, Mexico's infant mortality rate is estimated at 38 (Population Reference Bureau 1993). This represents a one quarter decrease from the rate of 50 in 1988 (Population Reference Bureau 1988). The infant mortality rate tends to be related to health and medical care conditions, and more generally to economic development levels, for a nation or other geographic unit (Rabell et al. 1986). The sharp drop from 1988 to 1993 reflects medical and public health advances, as well as economic improvements in Mexico during the Salinas Administration. By comparison, in 1993 the infant mortality rate of Latin America is estimated at 49, and the rates for the United States and Japan are put at 8.6 and 4.4 respectively.

In Mexico, there are severe inadequacies in information on infant mortality. Data from the vital statistics system, which registers births and deaths, are incomplete, so that the system tends to underestimate infant mortality (Bruch et al. 1980; Rabell et al. 1986). The official national infant mortality rate, reported by this system for 1990 was 25, which is about 34 percent lower than the 1993 estimated rate of 38 (Population Reference Bureau 1993).

The historical Mexican national infant mortality rate has dropped substantially since 1950 as shown below.

Year	Infant Mortality Rate and Range
1950 (1)	170–230
1960 (1)	130–170
1970 (1)	65–95
1980 (2)	74
1980 official (3)	39
1990 official (3)	25
1993 (4)	38

SOURCE: (1) Aguirre and Camposortega, 1982; (2) Rabell et al., 1986; (3) INEGI 1982 and 1993; (4) Pop. Ref. Bureau , 1993.

Clearly over a 43 year period, the infant mortality rate dropped substantially, by as much as five-fold. This is in line with long term health and economic improvements.

As seen in Table 6.1, the official infant mortality rate was 25 in 1990. The statewide mean was 23, with moderate coefficient of variation of 36. The lowest infant mortality in the range of 6 to 9 is in the states of Durango, Guerrero, and Sinaloa. These states were also among the lowest in official infant mortality in 1979 (see Pick et al. 1989a, Table 5.1). The low rates in these states do not correspond to the patterns of infant mortality as estimated by Rabell (1986), especially for Durango and Guerrero, which Rabell estimated as higher than average. The highest infant mortality rates are in the central states and Guanajuato, which are in the range of 34–40. The Federal District has a moderate infant mortality rate of 24. There is moderate resemblance in the geographic pattern with the official rates in 1980, but little correspondence to the 1979 infant mortality as estimated by Rabell (Pick et al. 1989a, Table 5.1; Map 6.1, this volume). This variable is obviously subject to large errors related to inadequacies in the registration systems for infant deaths as well as for births (Bruch et al. 1980; Rabell et al. 1986). Results should be regarded very cautiously, as a means to present official trends. For more accurate estimates at a much earlier time point, the reader is referred to the 1979 estimated rates by Rabell and others (1986). Because of the likely errors in 1990 official infant mortality, the relationships with other variables will not be discussed, except to mention that the official rates are very highly correlated with crude and standardized mortality rate and with standardized respiratory mortality rate. The high correlation with respiratory mortality rate may be an artifact, resulting from the coincidence of high respiratory mortality concentrated in the central states of Mexico.

Crude and Standardized Mortality Rates, 1990

The crude mortality rate is the ratio of deaths to 1,000 population. The standardized mortality rate is the crude rate adjusted for age structural differences through indirect standardization, a technique explained in Chapter 4. The technique adjusts the crude mortality rate for a given population, in this case Mexican states, by reference to a standard population (Keyfitz and Flieger 1971). For the indirect standardization performed in this chapter, the standard population selected is Mexico, 1990. The method adjusts the crude death rate of the given population by a factor that is the ratio of the number of deaths in the given population divided by the number of deaths based on the mortality rates of the standard population and the age structure of the given population. Later in the chapter the same method is applied to cause-specific death rates, such as mortality from trauma.

Among Mexican states, there are not large differences in age structure. This is reflected in low coefficients of variation in the age structure variables shown in Table 2.5. Consequently, indirect standardization has only slight effects on mortality patterns, and the maps for crude mortality rate and standardized mortality rate are highly similar (compare Maps 6.2 and 6.3). Hence, the remainder of this discussion only concerns standardized mortality rate, but applies as well to the crude mortality rate, unless discrepancies are noted.

The national crude mortality rate in 1993 was estimated at 6 (Population Reference Bureau 1993). As seen in the following table, the crude death rate for Mexico decreased greatly in the second half of the twentieth century, and life expectancy at birth improved. In comparison, the 1990 U.S. crude death rate was 8.6 (National Center for Health Statistics 1993b).

Year	Crude Mortality Rate	Life Expectancy At Birth		
		Overall	Male	Female
1950	16.1	49	48	51
1960	11.5	59	58	60
1970	10.1	62	60	64
1980	6.3	66	63	69
1993	6.0	70	66	73

SOURCE: 1950–1980, Rabell et al. 1986; 1993, Population Reference Bureau , 1993.

From 1950 to 1993, life expectancy was extended overall by 21 years, a remarkable increase. Also, the gender difference in life expectancy, i.e., female minus male life expectancy, lengthened from three years in 1950 to seven years in 1993. By comparison, U.S. life expectancy at birth was 72 years for males and 79 years for females in 1990 (National Center for Health Statistics 1993b).

The average standardized mortality rate in 1990 was 5.0. There was relatively little variation in the rate by state (see Table 6.2). The highest rates, above 6, are in the states of Puebla, Oaxaca, and Chihuahua. These states have differing locations and levels of urban and economic development. The cause of high mortality in these states must be found in specific causes of death, as well as in possible errors in the vital statistics reporting systems in the states. The lowest rates are in the states of Guerrero, Sinaloa, Quintana Roo, and Nayarit. These states are less urban and industrialized, and tend to have reduced mortality from cardiovascular and cancer mortality.

The geographical distribution of 1990 standardized mortality closely resembles that for 1980 (compare Map 6.3 with Map 5.1C in Pick et al. 1989a). Several major differences between the two years are the rise in mortality in the states of Sonora, Guanajuato, and Chiapas. In Sonora, this rise may be due to increasing mortality for cardiovascular and cancer mortality stemming from greater industrialization, urbanization, and modernization. Shifts in these states may be due in part to better reporting of mortality in the registration system.

Standardized and crude mortality are closely intercorrelated (.78). In addition, standardized mortality is closely related to infant mortality (.63), standardized respiratory mortality (.69), and standardized cardiovascular mortality (.41). Standardized mortality does not reveal significant associations with many other variables, except it is inversely related to underemployment.

Standardized Mortality Rate from Cardiovascular Diseases, 1990

The analyses described in this section are for the standardized mortality rates by leading causes of death—cardiovascular, trauma, cancer, nutritional/metabolic/endocrine/immunity diseases, and respiratory. The geographic patterns for the first two are similar, but differ for the others. As seen in the table below, the distribution of causes of death in Mexico changed in the 1980s.

	1979		1990		Change
Cause of Death	No. Deaths	%	No. Deaths	%	in Percent 1979–90
Cardiovascular Diseases	69,327	16.2	88,982	21.0	4.8
Trauma	63,641	14.9	58,904	13.9	-1.0
Nutritional, Metabolic, Endocrine, Immunity Diseases	24,033	5.6	45,575	10.8	5.2
Respiratory Diseases	59,475	13.9	44,277	10.5	-3.4
Cancer	27,865	6.5	42,017	9.9	3.4
Infectious and Parasitic Diseases	61,138	14.3	40,996	9.7	-4.6
Digestive Diseases	29,938	7.0	33,238	7.9	-0.9
Diseases of Infancy	26,941	6.3	23,063	5.5	-0.8
Undefined Diseases	29,658	6.9	9,716	2.3	-4.6
Others	36,201	8.4	35,449	8.4	0.0
TOTAL	428,217	100.0	422,803	100.0	

SOURCE: INEGI, *1983 and 1991 Anuarios Estadisticos.*

The leading causes of death in 1990 were cardiovascular, followed by trauma, nutritional/metabolic/endocrine/immunity, respiratory, and cancer. These five causes accounted for two thirds of Mexican deaths in 1990. There have been some major shifts in cause of death 1979–1990, with increases in cardiovascular, nutritional, and cancer, and decreases in respiratory and infectious/parasitic diseases. This shift reflects social changes that took place in the 1980s. In particular, declines in respiratory and infectious parasitic categories reflect improved environmental conditions regarding sanitation, pollution, and public health. On the other hand, the increase in cardiovascular mortality may stem from dietary and lifestyle changes, while the relative increase in cancer deaths may stem from environmental and dietary alterations. The decrease in undefined diseases reflects improved statistical accuracy in designation of cause of death.

Overall, trends in cause of death reflect the benefits from greater emphasis on sanitation and public health, but deterioration stemming from dietary, stress, and pollution factors. Despite an increase in population size, the total number of deaths decreased slightly between 1979 and 1990, which reflects a substantial lowering in the crude mortality rate. This also reflects age structural shifts in the 1980s.

For the leading cause of death, cardiovascular, there are sharp regional contrasts (see Table 6.3 and Map 6.4). Standardized cardiovascular mortality is by far the highest in the border states, with the highest rate of 1.47 in Baja California, a rate almost one and a half that of the statewide mean. The high rates in the border region reflect dietary, pollution, stress and other factors favorable to cardiovascular diseases. The proximity to the United States may be influential in the higher cardiovascular disease, and may reflect the influence of American lifestyle and diet south of the border and especially in border cities.

The region with the lowest cardiovascular mortality is the pacific south. Its average rate is twenty-six percent lower than the statewide mean. The south's lack of pollution, lower level of occupational stress, and traditional diet that is more vegetable-based may account for some of the reduction. The central region, except for the Federal District, is below average in cardiovascular mortality. On the other hand, the Federal District is somewhat above average. The much lower cardiovascular rates in Mexico City compared to the border may be due to factors other than urban stress and pollution, including diet and greater availability of medical care.

It is interesting that cardiovascular mortality remains low in Quintana Roo, Mexico's fastest growing state, which is increasingly modernizing. On the other hand, the high mortality for this disease entity in Tabasco appears unexplained.

Patterns of cardiovascular mortality in 1979 and 1990 are highly correlated (see Pick et al. 1989a, Map 5.1D). Several changes, however, should be noted. The most notable shifts are Baja California's and Tabasco's much higher rates in 1990 and Durango's sharp decrease during the decade. The Federal District is moderate in level both years and has risen somewhat.

The future shifts in cardiovascular mortality in Mexico may partly reflect the extent of penetration of American diet and lifestyle into Mexico, a factor that may partly depend on the spread of U.S. business and commerce under NAFTA.

Standardized cardiovascular mortality rate shows very distinctive and strong relationships with many other characteristics. Generally, it is associated with factors of urbanization and modernization but inversely related to indicators of poverty, rural areas and agriculture, and illiteracy. In particular, it shows very strong association with urbanization, literacy, secondary education, consumer goods including motor vehicles and telephones, mortgages, professional and managerial occupation, and high income. It varies oppositely to crowding, no meat and eggs (this is plausible medically), no toilet, and cumulative fertility. It has a very high correlation of .86 with standardized cancer mortality rate. This may be due to geographical similarities in related causative factors, including diet and environmental factors.

Standardized Mortality Rate from Trauma, 1990

The second largest cause of death in 1990 was trauma, which includes accidents, homicide, suicide, and other related causes. The mean standardized death rate for trauma was .73. The coefficient of variation at 20 is low and approximates that for the other causes of death. The states with the highest trauma mortality are Colima, Chihuahua, and Nayarit, with rates about one third above the mean. The lowest trauma mortality is in Nuevo Leon, Yucatan, and Baja Sur. The highest and lowest states are the same as for 1979 (see Pick et al. 1989a).

As shown in Map 6.5 the geographical differences in trauma mortality do not correspond to standard regions. Instead there are distinctive "areas" of contiguous states. The largest "area" for high trauma mortality comprises six states in the southern west, central, and pacific south. Likewise, another "area" of high trauma mortality consists of three states in the western north and southern northwest regions. These two "areas" overlap with rougher terrain, i.e., the major north-south mountain ranges, which may partially account for higher accident rates. Also, road systems in these states are below the national norm. Other states with high trauma mortality are the neighbor states of Tabasco and Campeche, and Baja California. Besides accidents, higher homicide and suicide rates may contribute to the elevated levels. The states with the lowest trauma death rates are the neighboring border states of Coahuila/Nuevo Leon, as well as Veracruz, Chiapas, Yucatan and Baja Sur.

Comparing trauma death levels for 1990 with those for 1979 (see Map 5.1G in *Atlas of Mexico*), there is a similarity in the large southern "area." However, the three-state high-trauma "area" in the north in 1990 was not present in 1979. The rise in trauma death rate in this northern area may involve changes in crime rates or possibly represents longitudinal shifts in accuracy of the vital statistics reporting systems. States with the lowest trauma show general correspondence between the two time points.

There are relatively few correlations with other characteristics. This may reflect the lack of correspondence with other attributes or underlying factors of trauma mortality including safety regulations, hostile terrain, homicide, suicide, etc.

There are positive associations with underemployment (.56) and congressional vote in 1992 for other parties, i.e. , leftist parties (.43). The latter association may be an artifact due to the coincidence of leftist voting occurring in states with mountains and rough terrain, poor roads, and higher crime. Trauma mortality is inversely associated with business consulting (- .42) and value of corporations (- .35). These effects may indicate some tendency for corporations (and corporate consultants) to locate in states with better terrain and roads and lower crime. However, there are many extraneous reasons as well for corporations to choose locations.

Standardized Mortality Rate from Nutritional, Metabolic, Endocrine, and Immunity Diseases, 1990

This cause of death category increased in prominence from 1979 to 1990. In this section "nutritional, metabolic, endocrine, and immunity" is abbreviated as "NMEI." It moved from ninth place in 1979 to third place in 1990, with the number of deaths nearly doubling. The general causative factors are complex across a class of diseases and the causation is not addressed in the literature on Mexican mortality. However, the increase in AIDS mortality may have influenced the rising mortality.

The state mean rate is .53, with a coefficient of variation of 20. The states with the highest NMEI mortality are Baja California, Chihuahua, and Coahuila in the north and the Federal District and Puebla, all with rates of .66 to .69. The lowest rates in the range of .32 to .35 are for Guerrero, Quintana Roo, and Zacatecas (see Table 6.3 and Map 6.6).

The areal pattern reveals high rates in the border region, except Nuevo Leon, and the central region. There are low to moderate rates for the other states and regions, except for a high rate in Colima. This pattern may reflect the influence in the border region of proximity to the U.S. In particular, U.S.-influence diet and lifestyle might lead to an increase in diet- and metabolic-related diseases, while the AIDS cases in Mexico may be more concentrated in the border states.

NMEI mortality rate has few correlations with other characteristics. It is not correlated with other causes of death. There are several direct associations with pork production, bean production, radio stations, business consulting, and value of new mortgages. These associations do not appear to be directly explainable. Rather, they may be artifacts, related to the coincidence of regional patterns.

Standard Mortality Rate from Respiratory Diseases

Respiratory diseases constitute a major cause of death, that dropped considerably from 1979 to 1990. As a percentage of deaths, this cause dropped by about one quarter in the 1980s. The reason for the drop may relate to improved medical care for respiratory diseases. The influence of national changes in air pollution on the drop is difficult to estimate, although there have been some notable attempts especially in Mexico City to reduce air pollution.

The state mean standardized death rate for respiratory is .46. The respiratory rate has the highest coefficient of variation at 30 among causes of death. This reflects sharper differences in environmental and public health conditions. The states subject to the highest respiratory mortality in the range of .80 to .83 are Mexico and Puebla. These rates are eighty percent higher than the statewide mean. These states encompass highly polluted urban areas of Mexico City and Puebla and have climatic conditions favoring air pollution conditions. It is interesting that the Federal District's rate of .59 is only twenty percent above the mean. Since the Federal District is badly impacted by air pollution, its reduced respiratory mortality may reflect improved medical and public health services compared to other surrounding states. It is noteworthy that the level of the Federal District *relative* to the mean for each year, increased by one third from

1979 (see Table 5.3 in Pick et al. 1989a). This increase doubtless reflects longitudinal increase in impacts from air pollution contaminants in the District.

By region, respiratory mortality is highest in the central, west, and part of the Border region (see Map 6.7). It is by far the highest in the central region. That region has an average rate of .68—forty percent above the mean. Although other factors play a role, the polluting effects of the two major metropolises of Mexico City and Puebla influence an entire region. Rates are elevated in the states of Jalisco and Guanajuato. It is important to note that Jalisco contains the major metropolis of Guadalajara, another source of pollution and that Guanajuato may be part of an extended zone from Jalisco to the central region. In the border region, respiratory mortality varies considerably, with the highest mortality located in Sonora, Chihuahua, and Nuevo Leon. On the other hand, the gulf, southeast, and pacific south regions have moderate to low respiratory mortality. In those regions, the environmental and pollution factors are quite favorable. There is remarkable similarity to the geographic pattern in 1979 (see Map 5.1E in Pick et al. 1989a).

Standardized respiratory mortality is positively associated with absolute population growth 1970–1990, economically active population, cement production, and manufacturing work force. These are indicators typical of large cities, which may have more deteriorated air and worse environmental conditions. It varies oppositely from hotels/motels and five star hotels, attributes that reflect Mexico's coastal tourist areas, which tend to have less polluted air and environments.

Standardized Mortality Rate from Cancer, 1990

Standardized cancer mortality accounted for the fifth largest number of deaths in 1990, a large increase from 1979 when it was in seventh place. In 1990, cancer accounted for ten percent of deaths, an increase of fifty-two percent from 1979. This rapid rise may be due both to decrease in the respiratory and infectious disease categories, as well as a shift in Mexico to a more modernized lifestyle that tends to encourage higher incidences of cancer.

The mean standardized mortality rate was .52, with a low coefficient of variation of 21. The rates were highest in the six border states and lowest in Guerrero, Guanajuato, Oaxaca, and Tlaxcala, all rural and less prosperous states. Cancer mortality rate in the Federal District is .59, one sixth above the mean.

As illustrated in Map 6.8 the regional pattern of cancer deaths closely resembles that for cardiovascular mortality. This is reflected in a highly significant correlation between the two causes of death of .86. Since the two patterns are so similar, discussion under cardiovascular deaths fits, except for the following difference. For cancer, there are much higher rates in Baja Sur and Tabasco than for cardiovascular.

Likewise, the associations with other characteristics are very similar to those for cardiovascular mortality. Generally, as with cardiovascular, high cancer rates are directly related to attributes of urbanization, modernization, economic prosperity and vary inversely from attributes of agricultural/rural, underdevelopment, poverty, and marginality.

For cancer as well as cardiovascular causes, mortality is linked to "improved" lifestyle and modernization. As the nation in the future becomes even more modernized as a result of economic improvements, trade agreements, and adoption of advanced nations' goods and lifestyles, it is likely that these two causes of death will rise in prominence.

Table 6.1 Infant Mortality Rate, 1990

No.	State	Infant Mortality Rate
1	AGUASCALIENTES	28.4400
2	BAJA CALIFORNIA	27.5400
3	BAJA CALIFORNIA SUR	20.4000
4	CAMPECHE	22.3300
5	COAHUILA	16.2400
6	COLIMA	25.8400
7	CHIAPAS	16.5700
8	CHIHUAHUA	25.8300
9	DISTRITO FEDERAL	24.1900
10	DURANGO	6.8800
11	GUANAJUATO	36.3400
12	GUERRERO	7.8600
13	HIDALGO	22.3800
14	JALISCO	24.0400
15	MEXICO	35.9200
16	MICHOACAN	17.4300
17	MORELOS	22.2200
18	NAYARIT	12.3600
19	NUEVO LEON	17.3300
20	OAXACA	23.4500
21	PUEBLA	36.9300
22	QUERETARO	34.2500
23	QUINTANA ROO	21.6300
24	SAN LUIS POTOSI	22.9300
25	SINALOA	8.0400
26	SONORA	21.6100
27	TABASCO	25.6300
28	TAMAULIPAS	16.1900
29	TLAXCALA	39.7300
30	VERACRUZ	20.4400
31	YUCATAN	24.0700
32	ZACATECAS	21.2000
	National Total	24.6096
	Mean	22.6950
	Median	22.3550
	S.D.	8.1596
	C.V.	35.95
	Minimum	6.8800
	Maximum	39.7300

DEFINITION: Infant mortality rate equals 1,000 times the number of infant deaths divided by the number of births in 1990.

SOURCE: 1991 Anuario Estadistico, Tables 3.1.10 and 3.1.13.

MAP 6.1
INFANT MORTALITY RATE, 1990

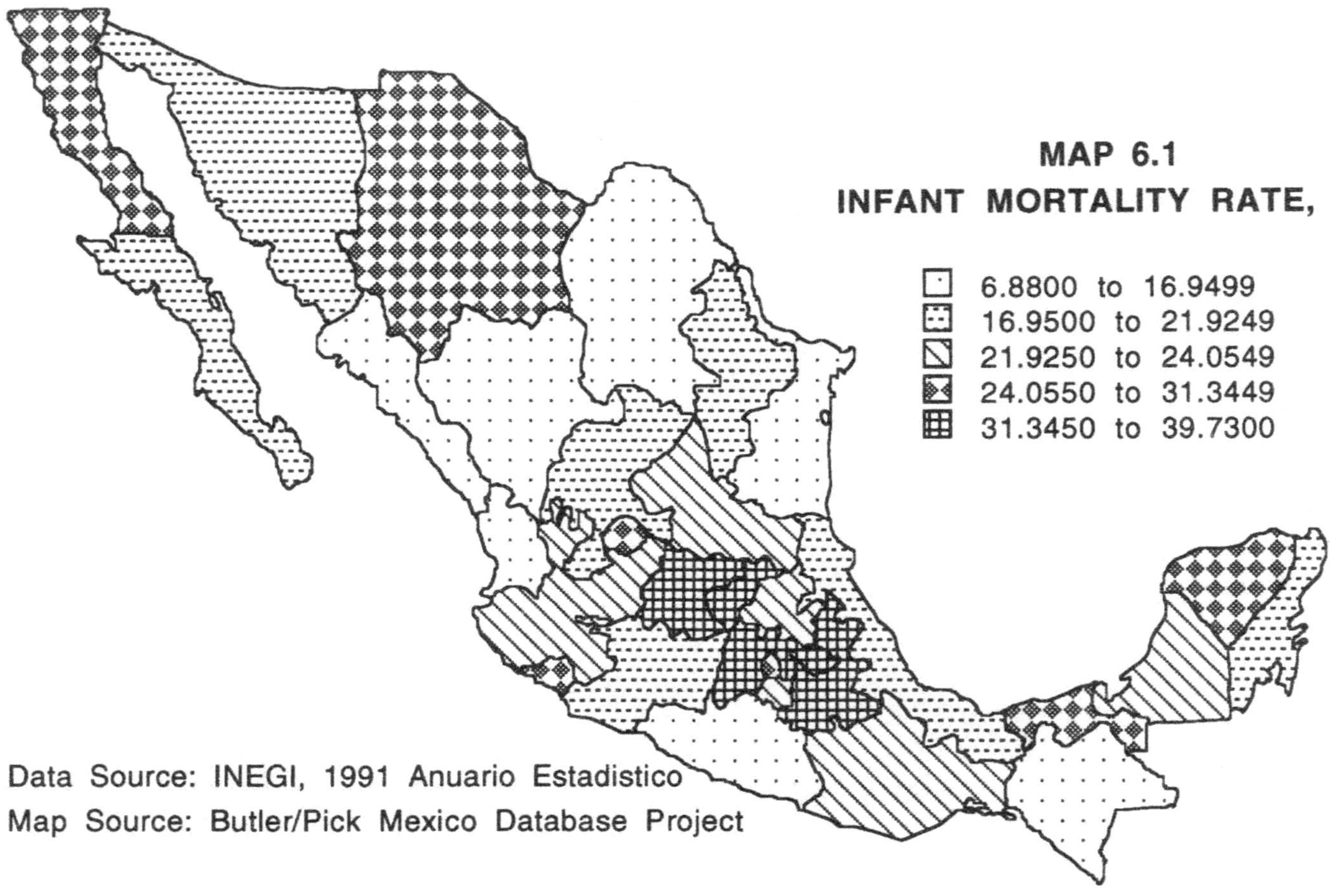

Data Source: INEGI, 1991 Anuario Estadistico

Map Source: Butler/Pick Mexico Database Project

Table 6.2 Crude and Standardized Mortality Rates, 1990

No.	State	Number of Deaths 1990	Total Population 1990	Annual Mortality Rate 1990	Standardized Annual Mortality Rate 1990
1	AGUASCALIENTES	3,409	719,659	4.7370	4.8311
2	BAJA CALIFORNIA	8,602	1,660,855	5.1793	5.8126
3	BAJA CALIFORNIA SUR	1,324	317,764	4.1666	4.6262
4	CAMPECHE	2,404	535,185	4.4919	4.6885
5	COAHUILA	9,485	1,972,340	4.8090	4.9540
6	COLIMA	2,417	428,510	5.6405	5.5327
7	CHIAPAS	16,677	3,210,496	5.1945	5.7061
8	CHIHUAHUA	14,239	2,441,873	5.8312	6.0024
9	DISTRITO FEDERAL	44,741	8,235,744	5.4325	5.2248
10	DURANGO	5,815	1,349,378	4.3094	4.2357
11	GUANAJUATO	22,288	3,982,593	5.5964	4.2614
12	GUERRERO	8,928	2,620,637	3.4068	3.4090
13	HIDALGO	10,029	1,888,366	5.3109	5.2050
14	JALISCO	30,004	5,302,689	5.6583	5.3603
15	MEXICO	50,090	9,815,795	5.1030	5.9199
16	MICHOACAN	17,296	3,548,199	4.8746	4.5916
17	MORELOS	6,178	1,195,059	5.1696	5.0117
18	NAYARIT	3,872	824,643	4.6954	4.3579
19	NUEVO LEON	13,711	3,098,736	4.4247	4.6025
20	OAXACA	19,535	3,019,560	6.4695	6.0041
21	PUEBLA	27,524	4,126,101	6.6707	6.3269
22	QUERETARO	5,710	1,051,235	5.4317	5.7068
23	QUINTANA ROO	1,604	493,277	3.2517	4.2486
24	SAN LUIS POTOSI	10,251	2,003,187	5.1173	4.7422
25	SINALOA	8,653	2,204,054	3.9259	4.0756
26	SONORA	9,176	1,823,606	5.0318	5.2638
27	TABASCO	6,818	1,501,744	4.5401	4.8982
28	TAMAULIPAS	11,010	2,249,581	4.8942	4.8347
29	TLAXCALA	4,361	761,277	5.7285	5.4479
30	VERACRUZ	31,211	6,228,239	5.0112	4.9713
31	YUCATAN	7,752	1,362,940	5.6877	5.1072
32	ZACATECAS	6,068	1,276,323	4.7543	4.2991
	National Total	421,182	81,249,645	5.1838	
	Mean	13,162		5.0171	5.0081
	Median	9,052		5.0674	4.9627
	S.D.	12,028		0.7500	0.6659
	C.V.	91.38		14.95	13.30
	Minimum	1,324		3.2517	3.4090
	Maximum	50,090		6.6707	6.3269

DEFINITION: Crude mortality rate is the ratio of deaths for the year 1990 to the population in 1990, multiplied by 1,000. Standardized mortality rate is calculated from the annual mortality rate 1990 by indirect standardization, based on a state's population age structure in 1990 and a standard population (see text for explanation).

NOTE: The national total excludes 1,621 deaths of unspecified state location.

SOURCE: 1991 Anuario Estadistico, Table 3.1.10.

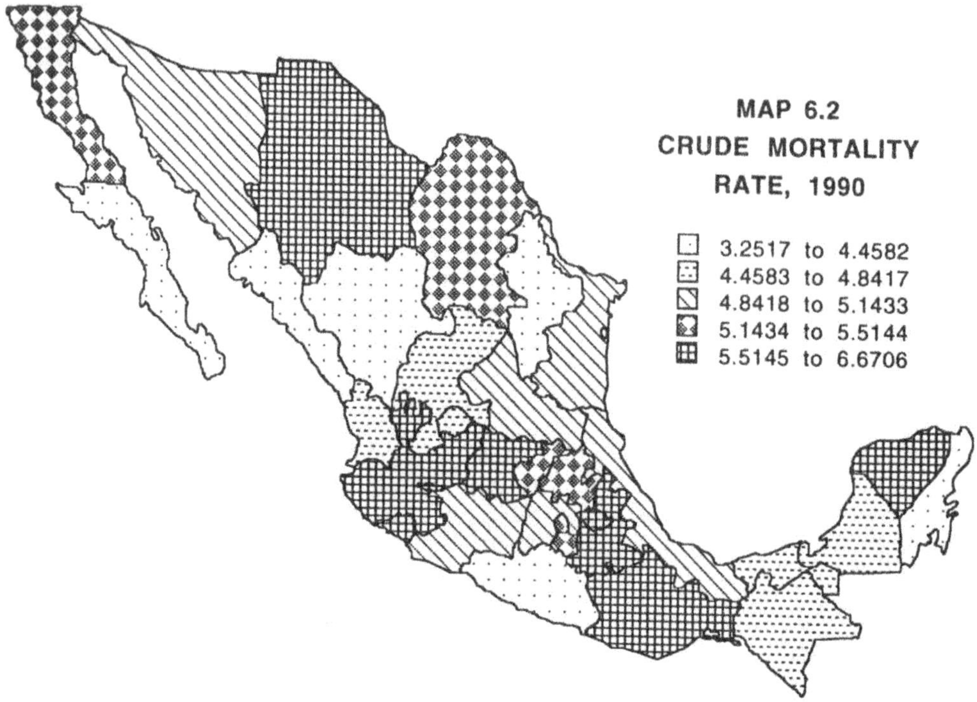

MAP 6.2
CRUDE MORTALITY RATE, 1990

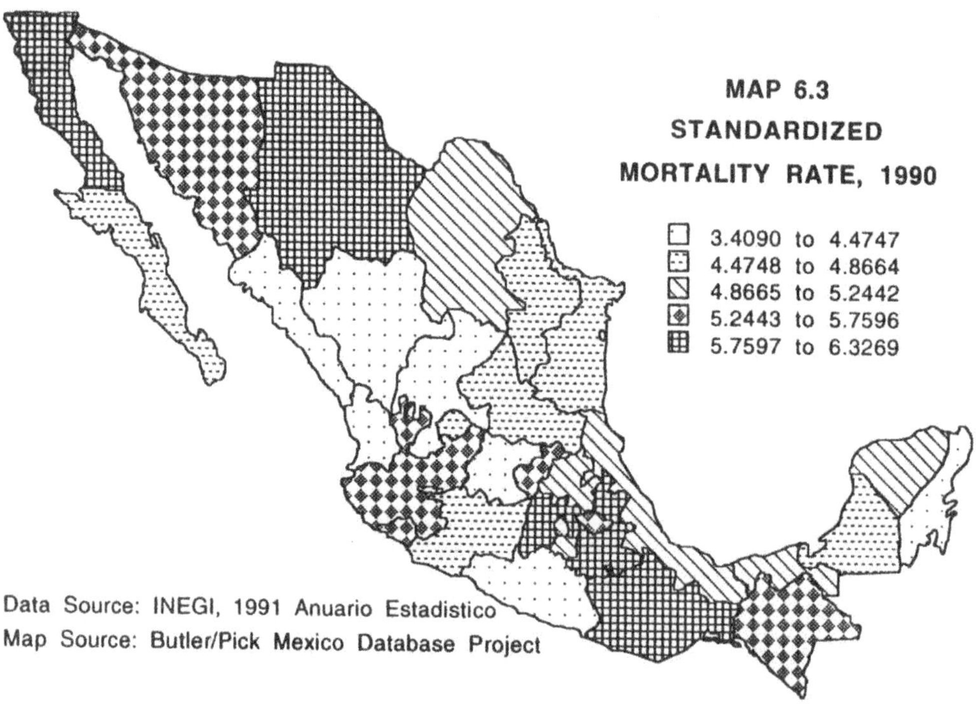

MAP 6.3
STANDARDIZED MORTALITY RATE, 1990

Data Source: INEGI, 1991 Anuario Estadistico
Map Source: Butler/Pick Mexico Database Project

Table 6.3 Standardized Mortality Rates for Leading Causes of Death, 1990

No.	State	Standardized Mortality Rate Cardiovascular Diseases	Trauma	NMEI* Diseases	Respiratory Diseases	Cancer
1	AGUASCALIENTES	1.0938	0.6390	0.5382	0.4352	0.5750
2	BAJA CALIFORNIA	1.4725	0.8312	0.6638	0.4918	0.6903
3	BAJA CALIFORNIA SUR	1.0474	0.5485	0.6017	0.4053	0.6549
4	CAMPECHE	1.0333	0.7887	0.4065	0.3439	0.4421
5	COAHUILA	1.2837	0.6015	0.6724	0.4550	0.6565
6	COLIMA	1.1535	0.9990	0.6439	0.3981	0.5727
7	CHIAPAS	0.8896	0.5957	0.4938	0.4734	0.4275
8	CHIHUAHUA	1.4578	0.9861	0.6734	0.4947	0.6674
9	DISTRITO FEDERAL	1.1794	0.5307	0.6832	0.5860	0.5908
10	DURANGO	1.0265	0.8102	0.4333	0.3990	0.5232
11	GUANAJUATO	0.7046	0.6644	0.4497	0.5264	0.3310
12	GUERRERO	0.5854	0.8764	0.3237	0.2386	0.2892
13	HIDALGO	1.0267	0.6882	0.5633	0.5745	0.4377
14	JALISCO	1.1862	0.7817	0.5904	0.5968	0.6078
15	MEXICO	1.0140	0.8625	0.6151	0.8629	0.4693
16	MICHOACAN	0.9440	0.9436	0.4731	0.4360	0.4964
17	MORELOS	1.0359	0.8188	0.5480	0.4228	0.5127
18	NAYARIT	0.9940	0.9427	0.4113	0.3128	0.5331
19	NUEVO LEON	1.3641	0.4617	0.4852	0.5098	0.6334
20	OAXACA	0.9217	0.8902	0.5570	0.4601	0.3714
21	PUEBLA	1.0399	0.6228	0.6857	0.8325	0.4227
22	QUERETARO	1.0106	0.6816	0.6278	0.6737	0.4502
23	QUINTANA ROO	0.7407	0.7727	0.3330	0.2956	0.4058
24	SAN LUIS POTOSI	1.0346	0.6364	0.4781	0.4760	0.4720
25	SINALOA	1.0966	0.7326	0.3897	0.3313	0.6510
26	SONORA	1.4366	0.6884	0.5459	0.5548	0.7037
27	TABASCO	1.2852	0.7974	0.4309	0.4300	0.5043
28	TAMAULIPAS	1.2550	0.6583	0.6077	0.4472	0.6465
29	TLAXCALA	0.9440	0.6347	0.5971	0.7995	0.3759
30	VERACRUZ	1.1508	0.6151	0.5541	0.3735	0.5142
31	YUCATAN	1.2448	0.4902	0.5019	0.4804	0.5718
32	ZACATECAS	1.0055	0.7611	0.3506	0.4591	0.5191
	Mean	1.0831	0.7298	0.5290	0.4868	0.5225
	Median	1.0379	0.7105	0.5470	0.4596	0.5167
	S.D.	0.2058	0.1430	0.1073	0.1454	0.1100
	C.V.	19.00	19.60	20.28	29.87	21.05
	Minimum	0.5854	0.4617	0.3237	0.2386	0.2892
	Maximum	1.4725	0.9990	0.6857	0.8629	0.7037

DEFINITION: Annual cause—specific mortality rate is the ratio of deaths in 1990 due to a specific cause to the population in 1990, multiplied by 1,000. The standardized cause—specific mortality rate is calculated from the annual cause—specific mortality rate 1990 by indirect standardization, based on the state's population age structure in 1990 and a standard population (see text for explanation).

NOTE: NMEI=Nutritional, Metabolic, Endocrine, and Immunized.

SOURCE: INEGI, 1991 Anuario Estadistico.

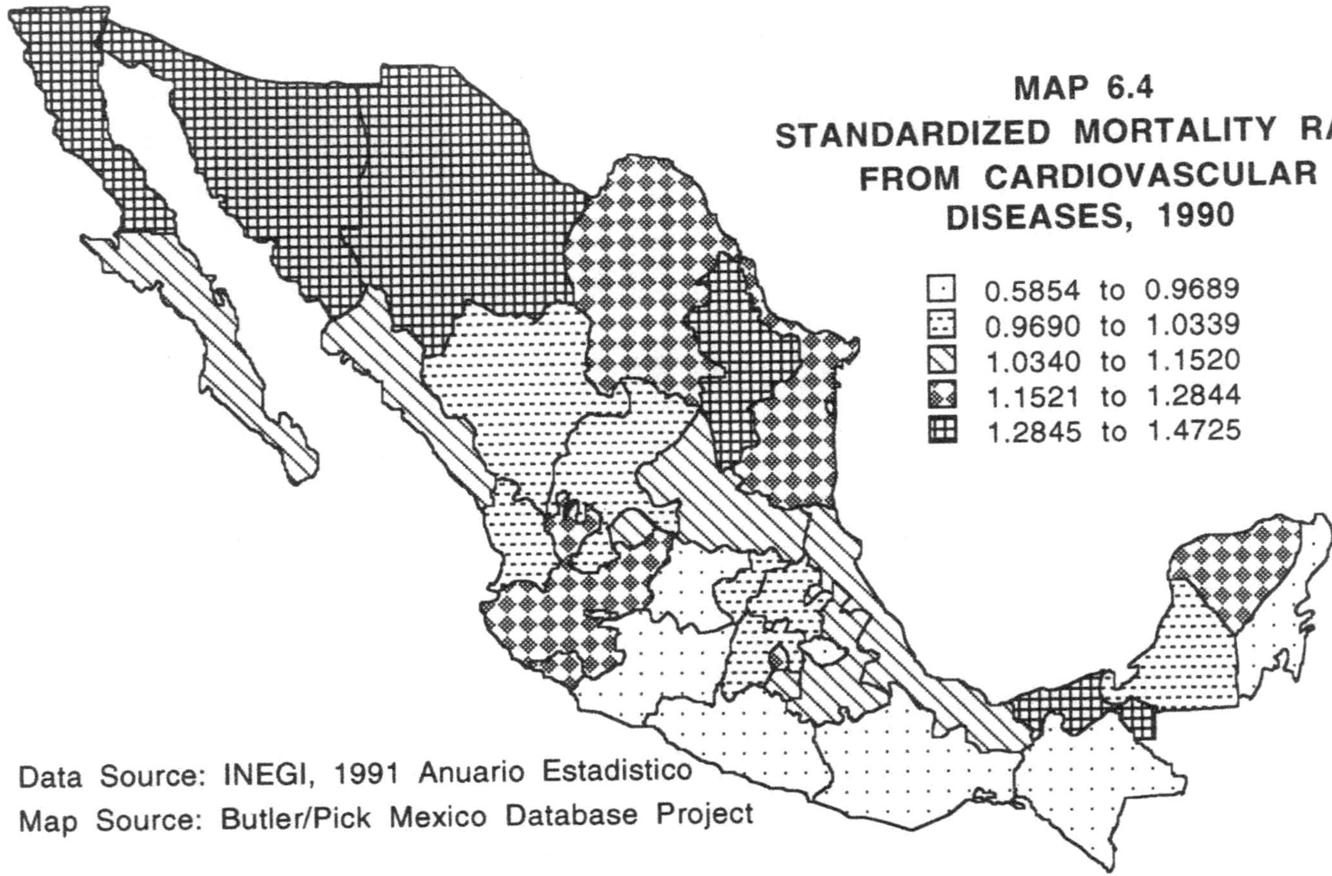

MAP 6.4
STANDARDIZED MORTALITY RATE FROM CARDIOVASCULAR DISEASES, 1990

Data Source: INEGI, 1991 Anuario Estadistico
Map Source: Butler/Pick Mexico Database Project

MAP 6.5
STANDARDIZED MORTALITY RATE FROM TRAUMA, 1990

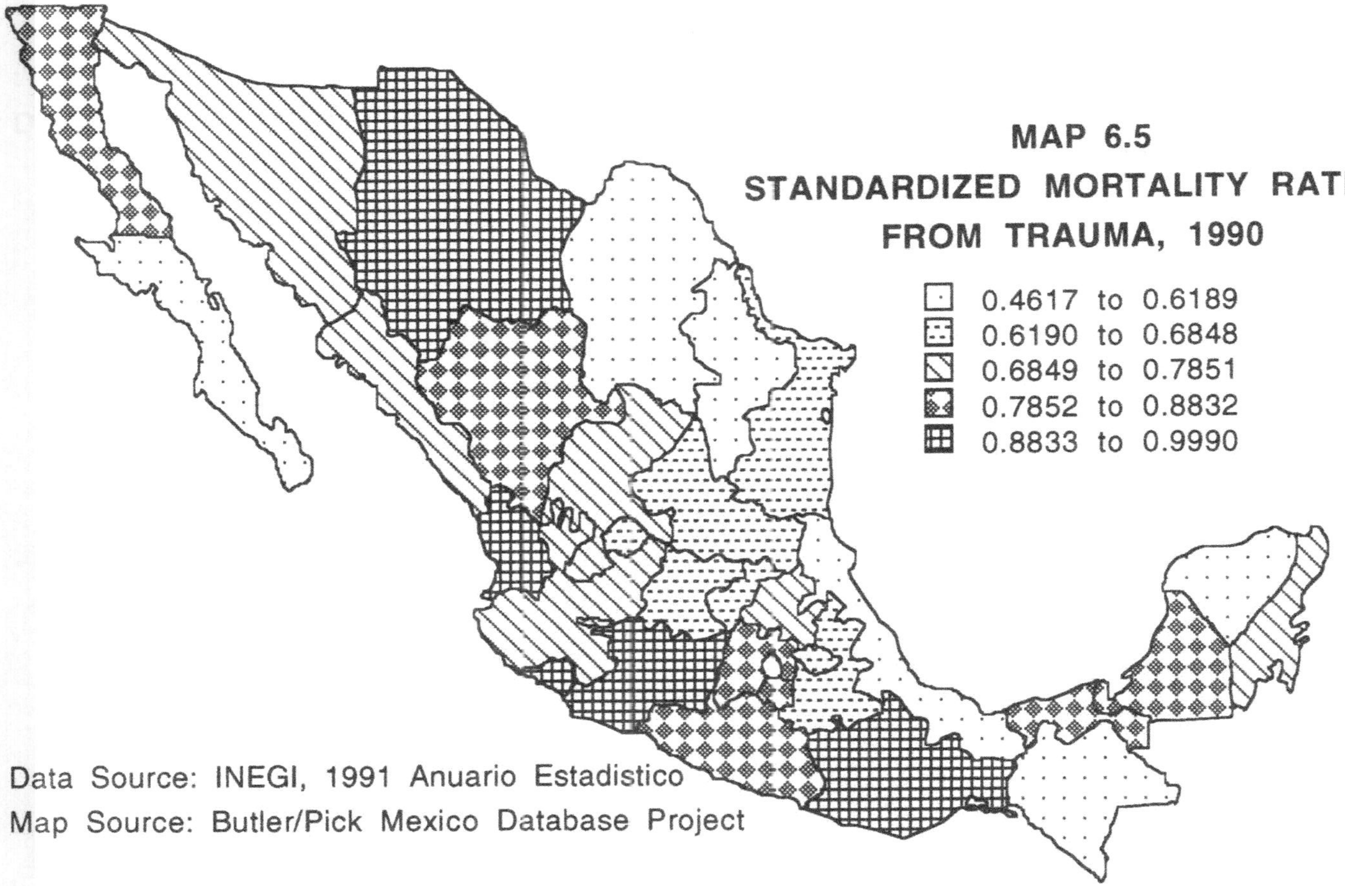

Data Source: INEGI, 1991 Anuario Estadistico
Map Source: Butler/Pick Mexico Database Project

MAP 6.6
STANDARDIZED MORTALITY RATE FROM NUTRITIONAL, METABOLIC, ENDOCRINE AND IMMUNITY DISEASES, 1990

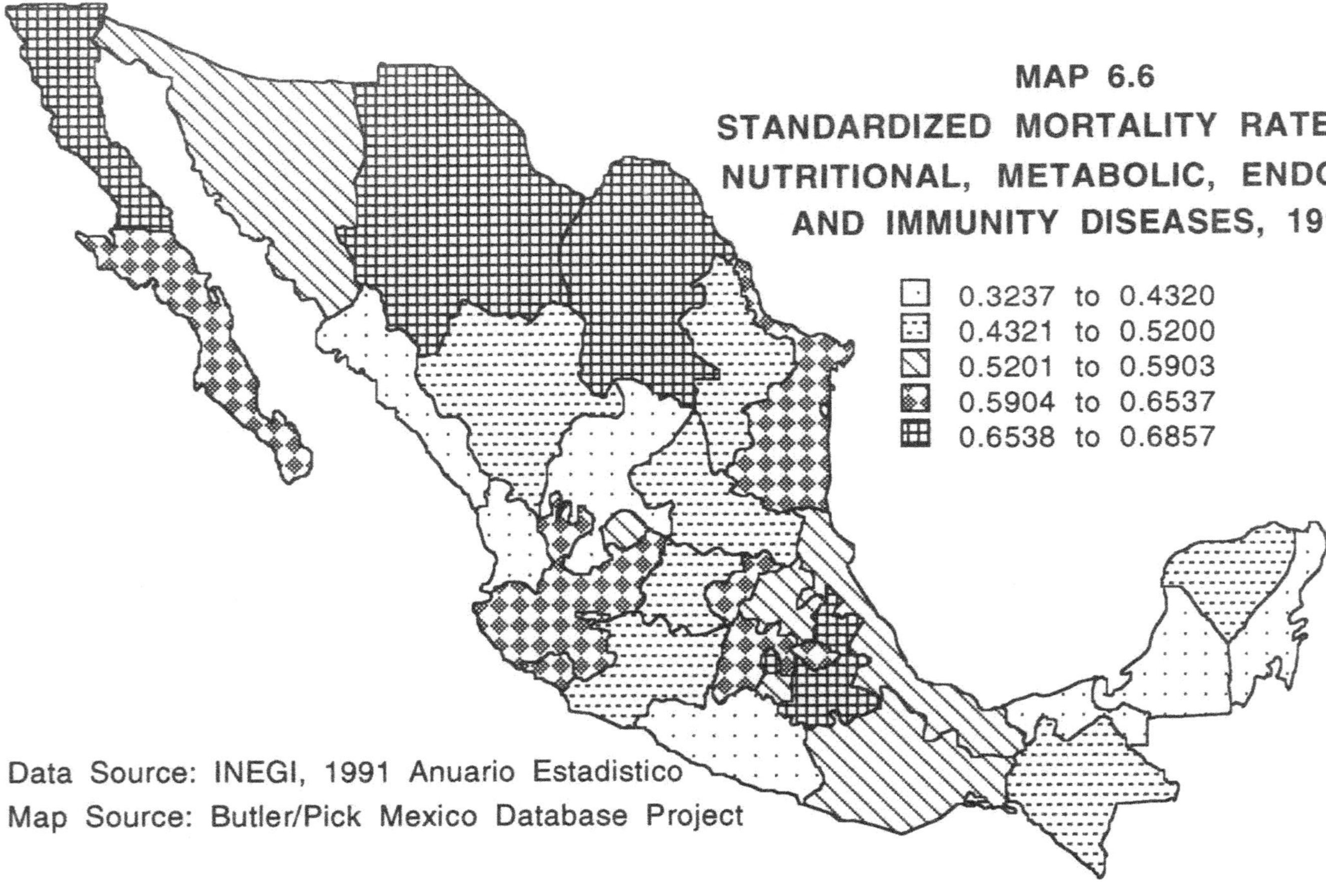

Data Source: INEGI, 1991 Anuario Estadistico
Map Source: Butler/Pick Mexico Database Project

MAP 6.7
STANDARDIZED MORTALITY RATE
FROM RESPIRATORY
DISEASES, 1990

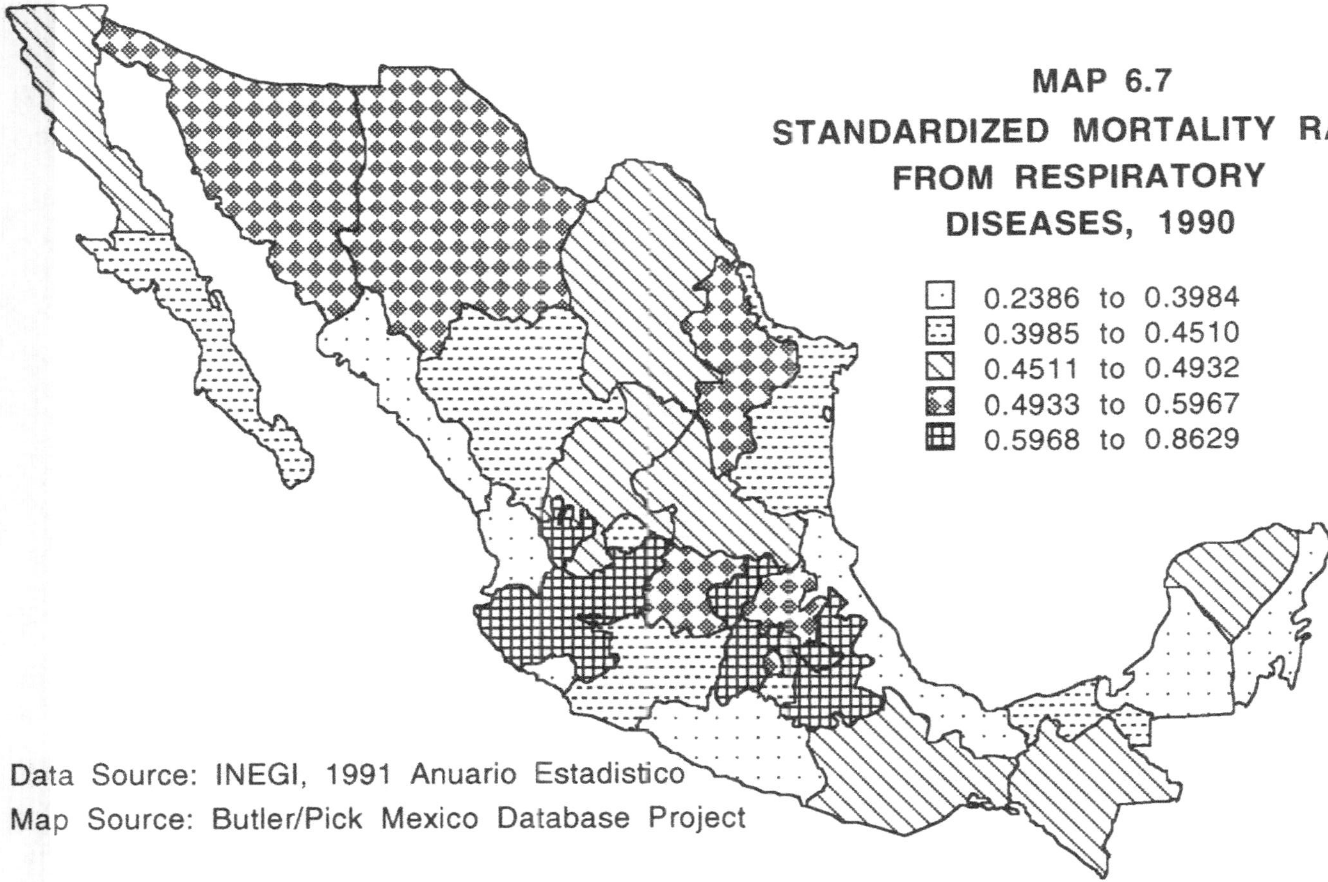

Data Source: INEGI, 1991 Anuario Estadistico
Map Source: Butler/Pick Mexico Database Project

MAP 6.8

STANDARDIZED MORTALITY RATE FROM CANCER, 1990

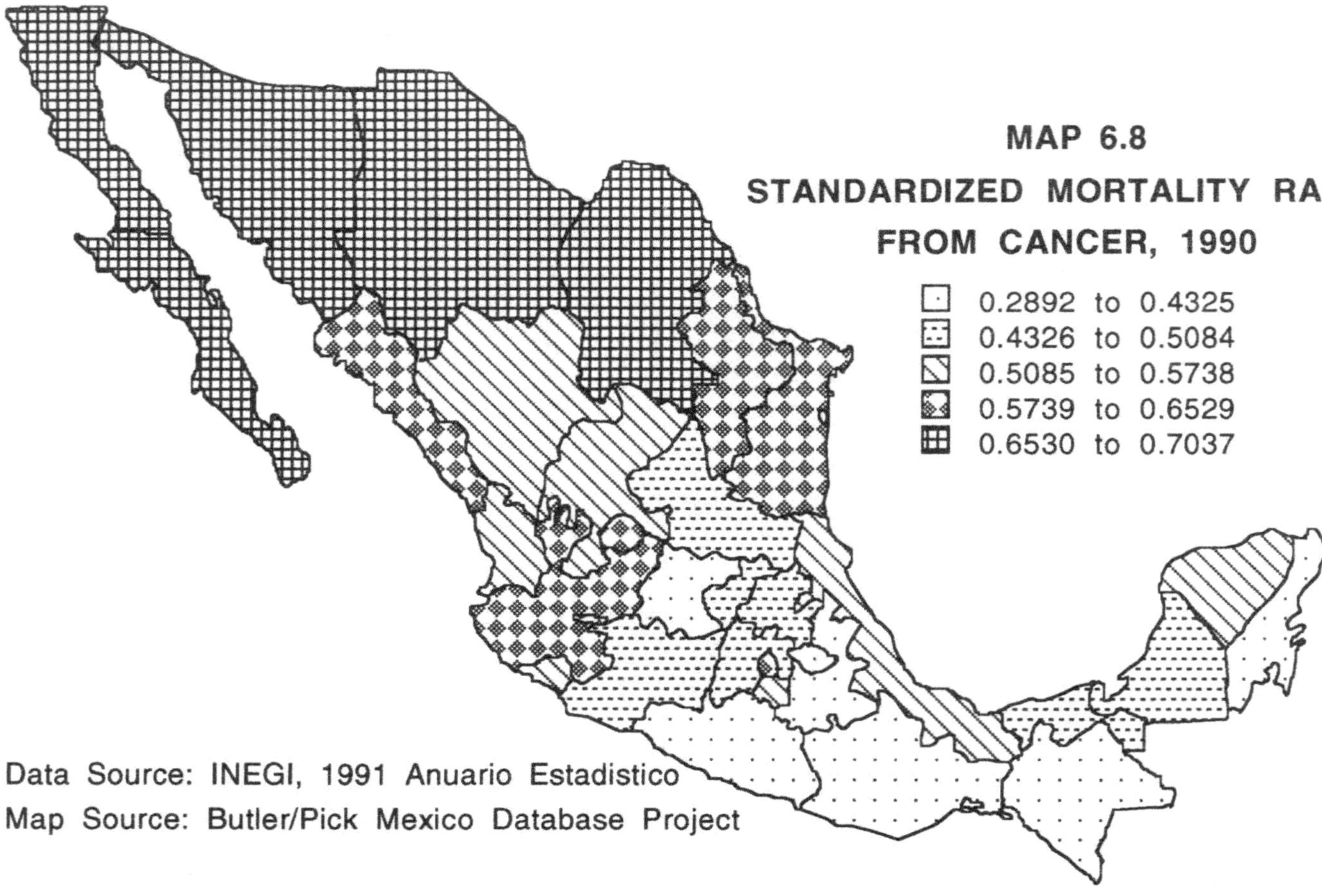

Data Source: INEGI, 1991 Anuario Estadistico
Map Source: Butler/Pick Mexico Database Project

Health

Hospitals, Clinics, and Medical Personnel, 1985–1989

Mexico's medical establishments and personnel shifted in the late 80s, with modest overall per capita increases. The figures discussed refer to the public sector, that is, to hospitals, clinics, and medical personnel sponsored by the federal government. Over 90 percent of these are located in three federal agencies, Secretariat of Health (Secretaria de Salud), Mexican Institute of Social Security (Instituto Mexicano del Seguro Social), and the Institute of Security and Social Services of State Workers (Instituto de Seguridad y Servicios Sociales de los Trabajadores del Estado). Thus, the federal government accounts for the preponderance of medical care in Mexico.

Overall in the late 80s, federal medical facilities and health personnel increased by roughly ten percent on a per capita basis (see Table 6.4 and Figure 6.1). There were 804 hospitals in 1989, or about one hospital per 100,000 persons. Although the number of hospitals remained steady from 1985–1989, there was a slight shift from general to specialty hospitals (see Table 6.4 and Figure 6.2). However, the number of hospital beds per capita declined, a reflection partly on the shift to more specialized hospitals. The nation's 12,000 outpatient clinics increased per capita about nine percent from 1985–1989.

Mexico had 59,000 federal-based doctors in 1989, a one fifth increase since 1985. The greatest growth took place in general practice, versus specialty physicians. On the other hand, the nation's 4,200 federal-based dentists had no per capita growth in the late 80s. In the remaining categories of personnel, "pasantes," i.e., medical assistants, decreased by about a fourth 1985–1989, while the undesignated category rose sharply.

Although the geographic pattern for health facilities and personnel are not presented in this volume, the geographic distribution for hospitals and clinics in 1980 was given in *Atlas of Mexico* (Map 5.2A). That distribution indicated the highest per capita levels of hospitals and clinics to be in the pacific south and in the states of Baja Sur, Aguascalientes, Queretaro, and Quintana Roo. Those broad geographic patterns are assumed to continue in the 1990s as well.

Children Receiving No Meat or Eggs, 1980

This characteristic measures the proportion of population of children under six who received no weekly meat or eggs in 1980. The attribute serves as an indicator of childhood undernourishment. This characteristic was not included in the 1990 census of population. It is included here because it is a variable that reflects on health conditions for children, as well as indicating marginality.

The national proportion of 10 percent indicates that a significant proportion of children in Mexico had a deficient diet in 1980. There is moderate variation in the variable. At the high extreme are Zacatecas, Guanajuato and Queretaro, in which about a fifth of children received no weekly meat or eggs. At the other extreme, less than five percent of the children in Baja California and Baja California Sur were undernourished (see Table 6.5).

Map 6.9 show that the entire northwest region has consistently low values. This is a region of high income combined with good availability of meat and diary products. The Federal District and states of Mexico and Nuevo Leon have low values at 3.4, 6.5, and 5.6. These values reflect the presence of urban centers with high income levels. There is a nine-state region with high values, that includes the rest of the central region, except Morelos, the southern north region, plus Guanajuato and Aguascalientes. The pacific south is also high, while the gulf and southeast regions are low to moderate.

The pattern of children receiving no meat or eggs is strongly associated, in expected directions, with urbanization, as well as education and literacy. Comparing the geographic distributions for the present variable and urbanization in 1990 (Map 3.3), they appear opposite, with several minor differences.

Table 6.4 Hospitals, Clinics, and Medical Personnel of the Federal Government of Mexico, 1985-1989

	POP.	HOSPITALS AND CLINICS					MEDICAL AND DENTAL						
							Physicians						
		General Hosp.	Specialty Hosp.	Outpat. Clinics	Tot.	Hospital Beds	General Practice	Specialists	Tot.	Dentists	"Pasantes"	Other	Total Med./Dent. Personnel
1985	74,048*	740	80	10,135	10,955	60,617	24,622	21,275	45,897	3,932	12,615	6,930	69,374
1986		720	85	10,121	10,926	61,383	25,075	22,241	47,316	4,925	12,375	9,745	74,361
1987		685	97	10,529	11,311	59,560	25,757	21,644	47,401	4,838	14,985	5,758	72,982
1988		692	105	11,122	11,919	59,302	36,332	24,291	60,623	5,054	7,425	16,297	89,399
1989 **	79,810*	692	112	11,880	12,684	61,251	34,733	24,671	59,404	4,196	9,562	11,351	84,513
%Change 85-89	7.8	-6.5	40.0	17.2	15.8	1.0	41.1	16.0	29.4	6.7	-24.2	63.8	21.8
%Change 85-89 /capita***	0.0	-13.2	29.9	8.8	7.4	-6.2	30.9	7.6	20.1	-1.0	-29.7	52.0	13.0

* Estimated
** Provisional
*** Per capita figures based on estimated population levels in table.
NOTE: "Pasantes" are medical assistants.
SOURCE: Anuarios Estadisticos, 1988-1991.

Figure 6.1
Medical/Dental Personnel Vs. Hospital Beds in Mexico, 1985 - 1989

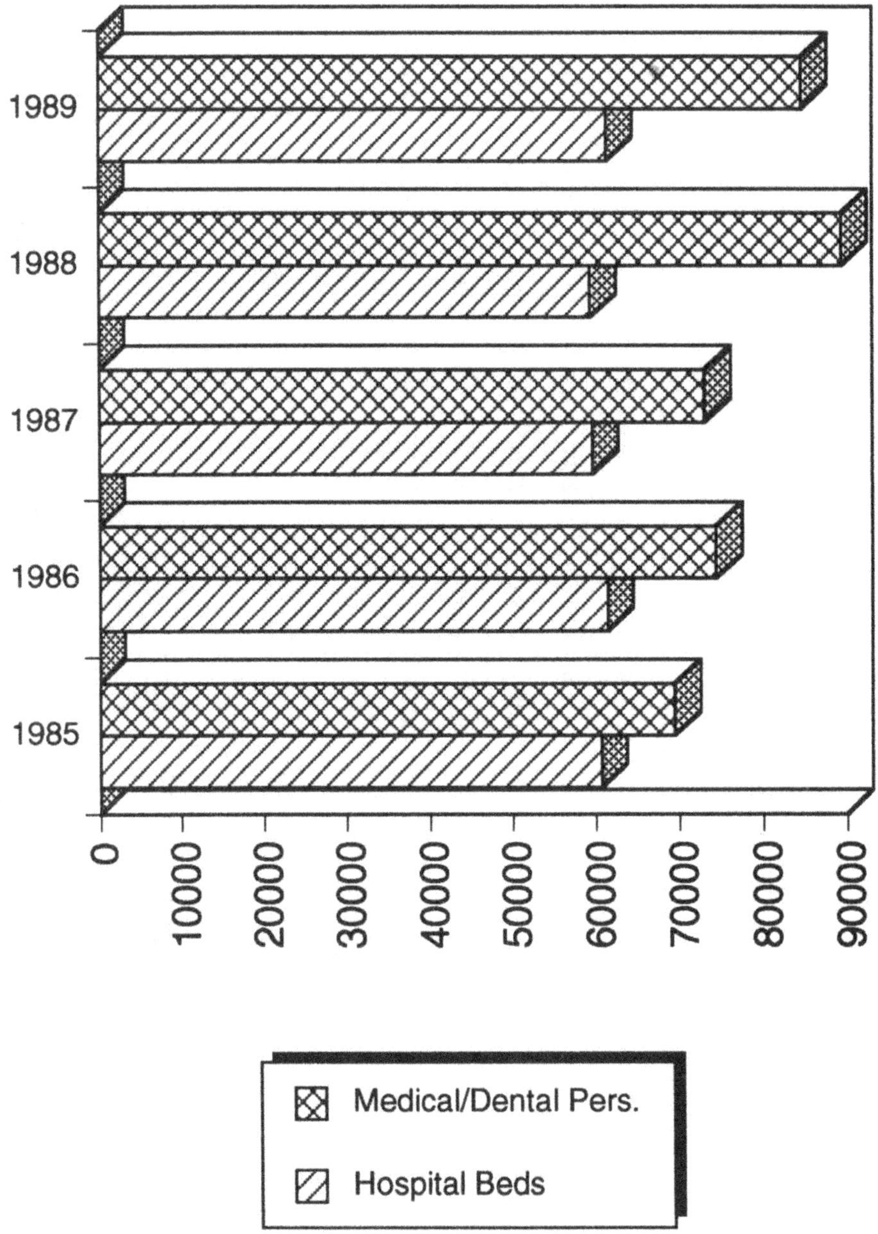

Source: Anuarios Estadisticos, 1988 - 1991.

Figure 6.2
General and Specialty Hospitals of the Federal Government in Mexico, 1985 - 1989

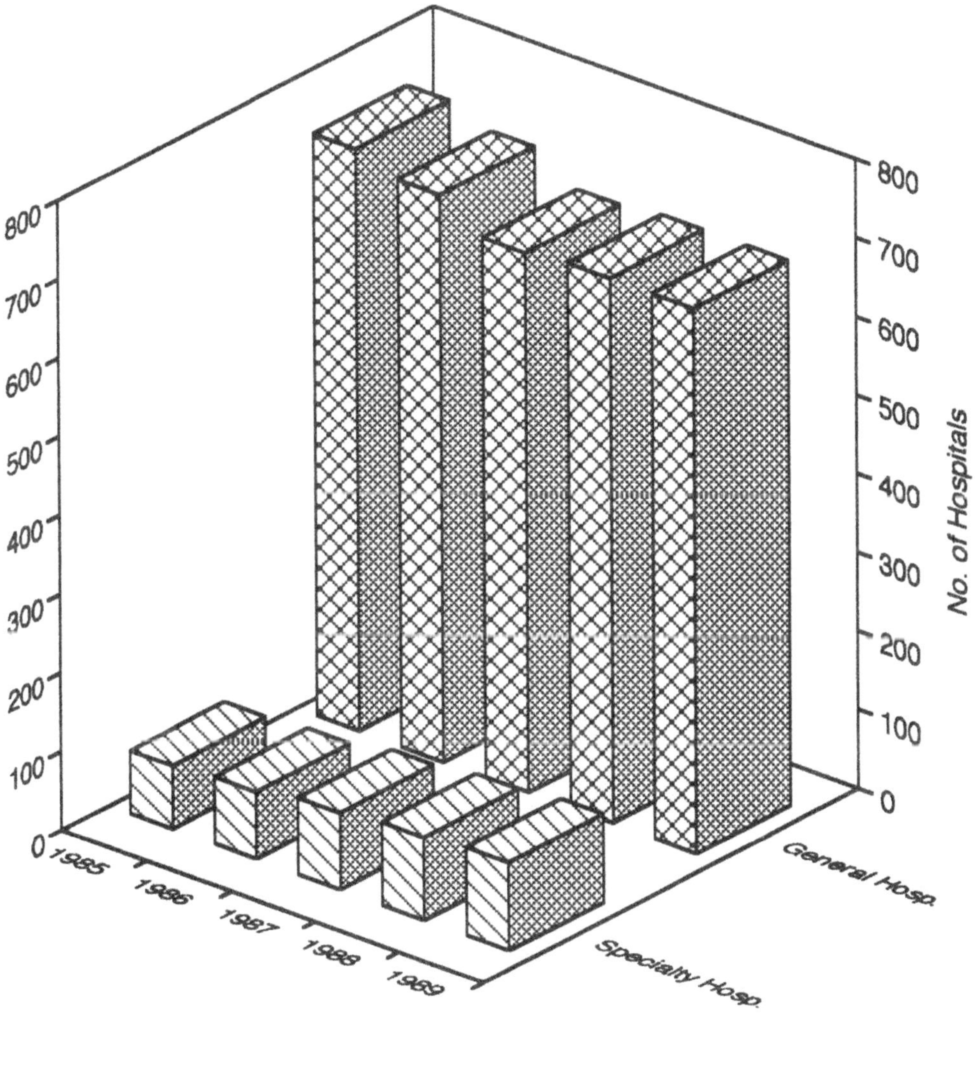

SOURCE: Anuarios Estadisticos, 1988 - 1991.

Table 6.5 Children Receiving No Weekly Meat or Eggs, 1980

No.	State	Population Receiving No Meat or Eggs	Total Population Age < 6	Ratio
1	AGUASCALIENTES	14,205	81,668	0.1739
2	BAJA CALIFORNIA	6,398	157,635	0.0406
3	BAJA CALIFORNIA SUR	1,585	32,143	0.0493
4	CAMPECHE	3,800	62,398	0.0609
5	COAHUILA	14,232	225,148	0.0632
6	COLIMA	5,067	54,166	0.0935
7	CHIAPAS	32,219	289,434	0.1113
8	CHIHUAHUA	23,371	271,103	0.0862
9	DISTRITO FEDERAL	40,038	1,190,698	0.0336
10	DURANGO	19,645	168,709	0.1164
11	GUANAJUATO	89,504	438,715	0.2040
12	GUERRERO	43,053	297,307	0.1448
13	HIDALGO	32,410	226,013	0.1434
14	JALISCO	69,144	621,972	0.1112
15	MEXICO	75,583	1,166,423	0.0648
16	MICHOACAN	59,618	414,085	0.1440
17	MORELOS	9,674	132,497	0.0730
18	NAYARIT	12,711	120,177	0.1058
19	NUEVO LEON	20,216	357,662	0.0565
20	OAXACA	43,206	305,736	0.1413
21	PUEBLA	77,977	476,210	0.1637
22	QUERETARO	26,233	130,517	0.2010
23	QUINTANA ROO	2,778	36,524	0.0761
24	SAN LUIS POTOSI	41,648	245,170	0.1699
25	SINALOA	17,039	275,583	0.0618
26	SONORA	11,440	216,222	0.0529
27	TABASCO	10,819	165,939	0.0652
28	TAMAULIPAS	16,779	267,300	0.0628
29	TLAXCALA	11,461	77,168	0.1485
30	VERACRUZ	70,619	713,803	0.0989
31	YUCATAN	10,160	129,846	0.0782
32	ZACATECAS	46,468	198,648	0.2339
	National Total	959,100	9,546,619	0.1005
	Mean	29,972	298,332	0.1072
	Median	19,931	225,581	0.0962
	S.D.	25,093	281,037	0.0530
	C.V.	83.72	94.20	49.40
	Minimum	1,585	32,143	0.0336
	Maximum	89,504	1,190,698	0.2339

DEFINITION: Ratio is the population specifying receiving no weekly meat or eggs age < 6 to the total population age < 6. Note that the population not providing a response to these questions are not included in the values shown.

SOURCE: 1980 Mexican Census of Population, Volume 1, Table 17.

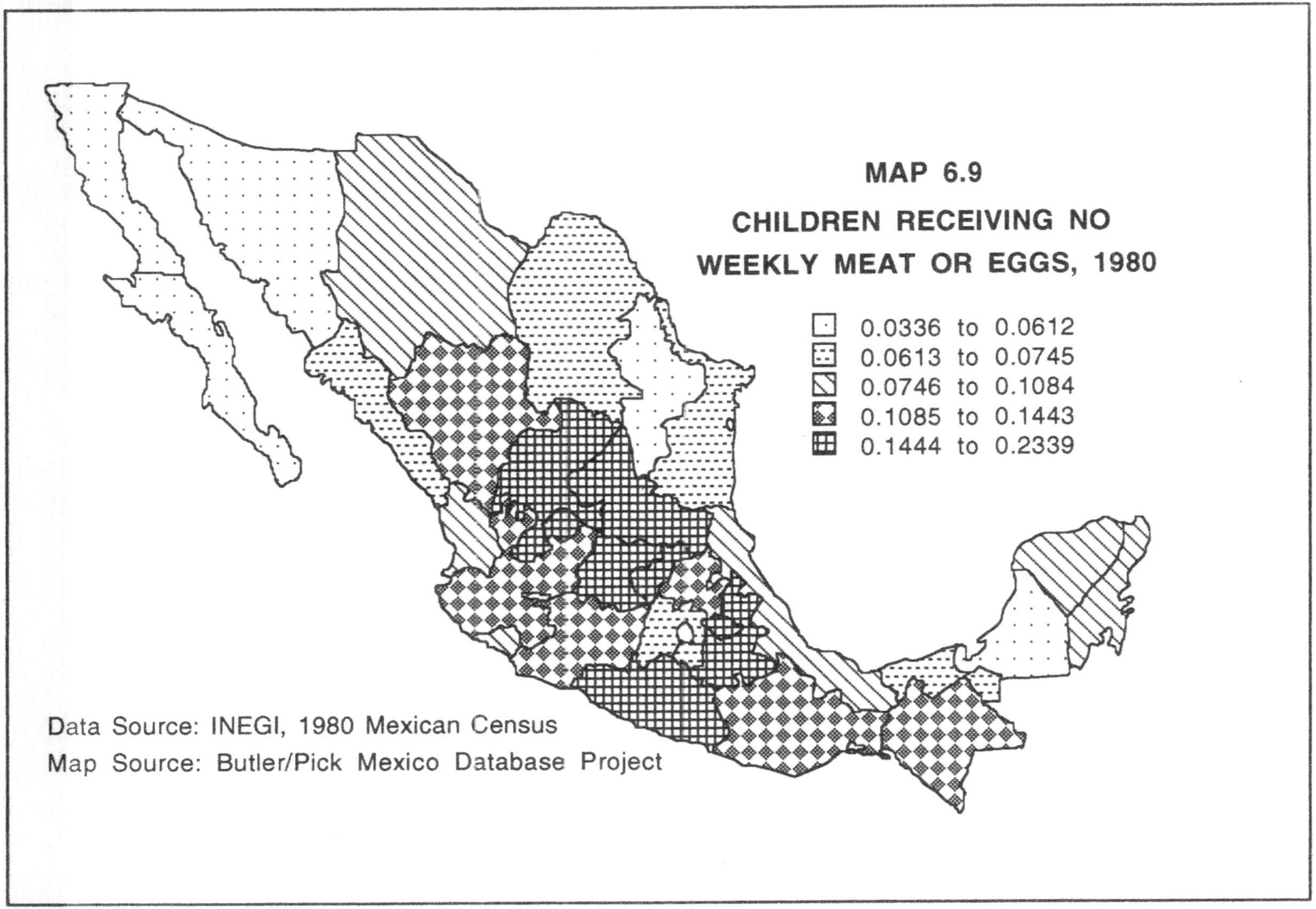

MAP 6.9
CHILDREN RECEIVING NO WEEKLY MEAT OR EGGS, 1980

Housing

Number of Persons Per Housing Unit, 1990

The number of persons per housing unit is one indicator of household crowding. The number of housing units in Mexico in 1990 was 16,035,233, an increase of about 4 million units since 1980. In 1990, there was a national average of 5.07 persons per housing unit, a fall of nine percent from the level of 5.55 in 1980. The decrease in density is partly due to the lowering in fertility in Mexico that started in the mid 70s and continued in the 80s (see Chapter 4 discussion on Total Fertility Rate). There is very low variation in housing density (CV = 6).

As shown in Table 6.6, densities are highest in the central and western states of Guanajuato (5.8), Tlaxcala and Aguascalientes (both 5.5), and Querataro (5.4). Although these states had moderate to high fertility (see Maps 4.6 through 4.10), the highest fertility generally is in the south region. Another possible cause of the higher housing density in these states is that most of them are less prosperous, resulting in reduced spending and hence fewer housing units. The states with the lowest housing densities are Baja California and Baja Sur, Chihuahua, Tamaulipas, the Federal District, and Quintana Roo. These states all have relatively low fertility and high economic prosperity. An exception is Quintana Roo, which has high fertility. However, Quintana Roo was Mexico's most rapidly growing state in the 80s (see Chapter 2). During the decade, it had a housing boom, with units increasing by 131 percent. This very rapid growth in housing has tended to lower housing densities.

Viewed regionally, the pattern of housing density in 1990 reflects high values in the central north-south axis of the nation, including the central region, except for the Federal District and Morelos (see Map 6.10). The border region is generally low, except for Coahuila. Otherwise, there is not correspondence with standard regions. The geographical pattern for 1990 closely resembles that for 1980 (see Map 6.7A in Pick et al. 1989a), with, however, the notable shifts of increased housing density in Coahuila and reduced density in Durango.

Housing density has a significant correlation with crowding (.37), although it is lower than many other correlations. Housing density varies directly with young age structure, fertility, and poverty indicators, and inversely with economic activity, working age population, lifetime inmigration, and indicators of economic and business prosperity. It has especially strong relationships with population age 0–17 (.66), population 18–64 (- .61), economic activity (- .65), and cumulative fertility to women age 45–49 (- .67), i.e., with age structural and demographic variables. This reflects that fact that the age structure has a major impact in determining the numbers of persons resident in households and hence in housing units. Further, economically prosperous states are able to afford a large housing stock.

Crowding, 1990

Crowding measures the ratio of individual housing units having three or fewer rooms and six or more occupants to total housing units. Crowding differs from housing density by considering the average of *micro* effects of high density for individual units, rather than an overall *macro* level state average of people relative to housing units. This differs somewhat from the crowding measure from *Atlas of Mexico,* which included in the ratio's denominator only those housing units having three or fewer rooms.

The national crowding ratio is .1891, which implies that about one in five housing units is crowded. Table 6.7 shows that there is a moderate coefficient of variation of 32, which, however, is much higher than for housing density. The range of crowding is over threefold, from the most crowded state of Chiapas with one third crowded units to a low of only ten percent crowded units for the Federal District. Other states with high crowding of over 25 percent include Guerrero, Oaxaca, Puebla, Tlaxcala, Yucatan, and Campeche. They are all in the southern part of the nation. States besides the Federal District, with low crowding of under one eighth, include Nuevo Leon, Chihuahua, and Baja Sur.

The geographic pattern in Map 6.11 shows a distinctive north to south gradation, with the border region in the north having the lowest values and the pacific south having the highest level. As is the case with other typical north-south gradations such as urbanization, the Federal District punctuates the pattern with a very low value.

Crowding shows many strong associations with other attributes. Its strongest linkage is with literacy (- .93). It also has very strong associations with urbanization (- .74) population age 0–17, (- .74), and standardized fertility (- .83). The opposite relationships with fertility and young age structure reflect the presence of larger families in housing units. It is interesting that more urban areas are associated with lower crowding. This may indicate that urban areas tend to have lower fertility, older age structure and greater prosperity. There are very strong relationships with occupational and industrial attributes, in particular direct relationship with agriculture and inverse ones with professional, managerial, and service occupations and commercial, manufacturing, personal service and social service industries. Crowding varies opposite from cancer and cardiovascular mortality, although this relationship is certainly a proxy for other linkages. There are many other relationships with attributes of economic prosperity (positive) and economic poverty (negative).

Crowding, Federal District, 1990

Crowding in the Federal District averages .1074, which implies one in ten housing units are crowded (see Map 6.12). There is considerable variation, with a coefficient of variation of 67, about double that for state crowding (see Table 6.8). The most crowded delegacion is Milpa Alta, a largely slum area located in the southeast of the District bordering the southern mountains. It is important to note that, even in this impoverished part of the District, the crowding apparent for one fifth of housing units is equivalent to the average crowding at the statewide level.

However, Milpa Alta's apparent moderate crowding level, compared with state levels, should not belie other housing indicators that reflect deteriorated conditions (see Garza 1987). The District's general lower level of fertility may partly account for the disparity. The next most crowded area is Tlalhac, having one sixth of housing units crowded. This area has a moderate level of prosperity. The cause of high crowding may partly relate to the older housing stock in this zone.

The District's lowest crowding is for Benito Juarez in the north center. In this prosperous area, only one in 38 housing units is crowded. The next uncrowded area is Coyoacan, with crowding in one in every 18 housing units. Both these areas are prosperous, with a high prevalence of middle class residents. Crowding in the Federal District is not strongly related to population density (compare Map 6.12 with Map 3.6). This differs from the significant positive association between the two characteristics at the state level. By contrast, there is a strong opposite association with professional/technical occupations (see Map 9.9). This association parallels a highly significant opposite association between these two attributes at the state level. This may be the result of both attributes being influenced by the level of economic prosperity.

Table 6.6 Number of Persons Per Housing Unit, 1990

No.	State	Number of Persons Per Housing Unit	Total Number of Dwellings
1	AGUASCALIENTES	5.5421	129,853
2	BAJA CALIFORNIA	4.5788	362,727
3	BAJA CALIFORNIA SUR	4.7213	67,304
4	CAMPECHE	4.9603	107,894
5	COAHUILA	4.8737	404,691
6	COLIMA	4.8350	88,627
7	CHIAPAS	5.4046	594,025
8	CHIHUAHUA	4.6091	529,799
9	DISTRITO FEDERAL	4.6031	1,789,171
10	DURANGO	5.1471	262,164
11	GUANAJUATO	5.7959	687,136
12	GUERRERO	5.2233	501,725
13	HIDALGO	5.2031	362,933
14	JALISCO	5.1524	1,029,178
15	MEXICO	5.2308	1,876,545
16	MICHOACAN	5.3477	663,496
17	MORELOS	4.8786	244,958
18	NAYARIT	4.8954	168,451
19	NUEVO LEON	4.8245	642,298
20	OAXACA	5.1429	587,131
21	PUEBLA	5.3415	772,461
22	QUERETARO	5.4346	193,434
23	QUINTANA ROO	4.7957	102,859
24	SAN LUIS POTOSI	5.2808	379,336
25	SINALOA	5.2199	422,242
26	SONORA	4.8169	378,587
27	TABASCO	5.2634	285,319
28	TAMAULIPAS	4.6050	488,508
29	TLAXCALA	5.5513	137,135
30	VERACRUZ	4.9332	1,262,509
31	YUCATAN	4.9750	273,958
32	ZACATECAS	5.3452	238,779
	National Total	5.0670	16,035,233
	Mean	5.0791	501,101
	Median	5.1450	378,962
	S.D.	0.3136	443,648
	C.V.	6.18	88.53
	Minimum	4.5788	67,304
	Maximum	5.7959	1,876,545

DEFINITION: Number of Persons Per Housing Unit is the ratio of the 1990 total population to the total number of dwellings.

SOURCE: 1990 Anuario Estadistico, Table 2.4.2.

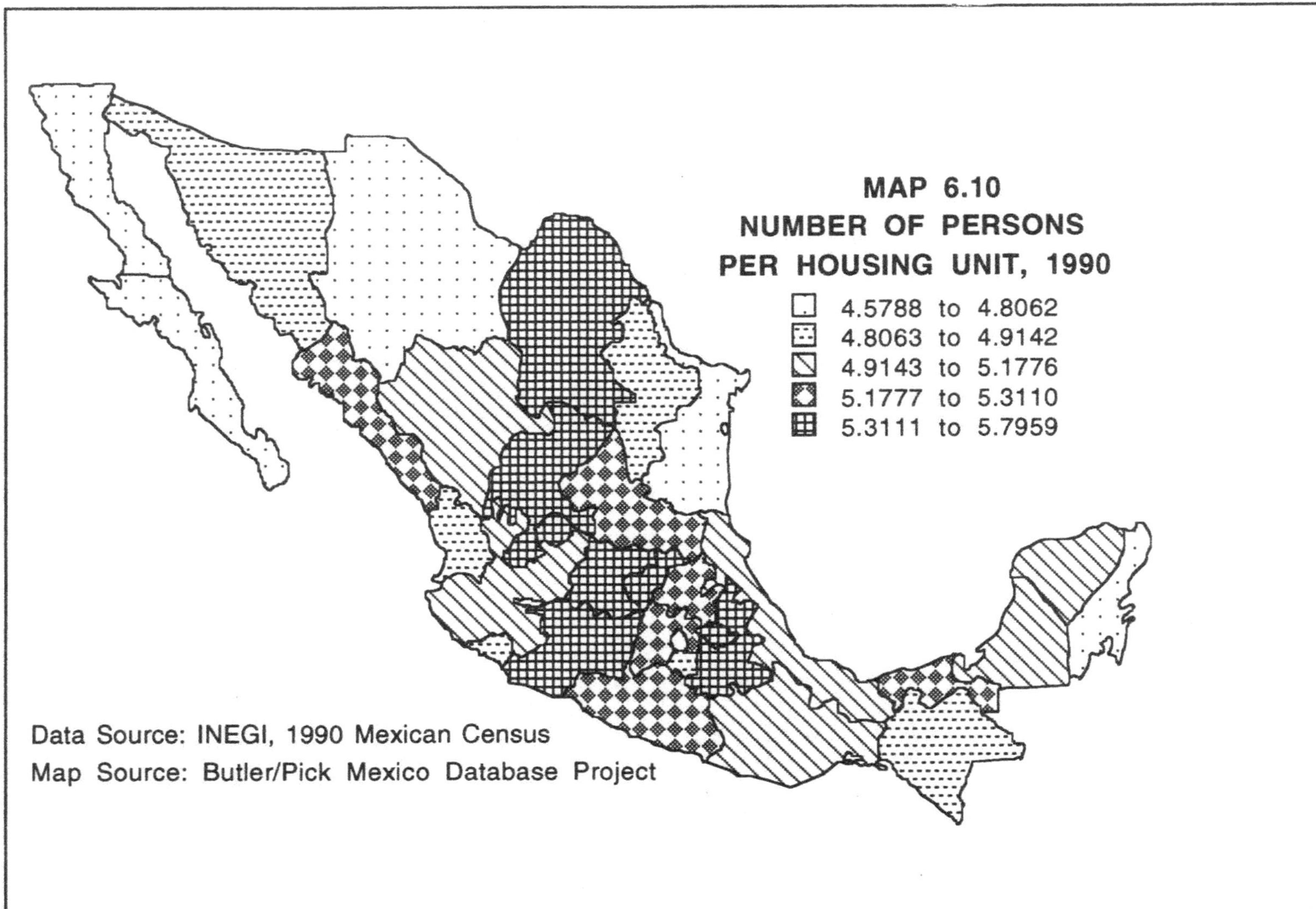

MAP 6.10
NUMBER OF PERSONS
PER HOUSING UNIT, 1990

Table 6.7 Crowding, 1990

No.	State	Crowded Housing Units	Total Housing Units	Ratio
1	AGUASCALIENTES	19,829	129,853	0.1527
2	BAJA CALIFORNIA	33,751	362,727	0.0930
3	BAJA CALIFORNIA SUR	7,898	67,304	0.1173
4	CAMPECHE	27,020	107,894	0.2504
5	COAHUILA	52,344	404,691	0.1293
6	COLIMA	16,814	88,627	0.1897
7	CHIAPAS	198,210	594,025	0.3337
8	CHIHUAHUA	60,564	529,799	0.1143
9	DISTRITO FEDERAL	172,434	1,789,171	0.0964
10	DURANGO	42,887	262,164	0.1636
11	GUANAJUATO	152,921	687,136	0.2225
12	GUERRERO	159,769	501,725	0.3184
13	HIDALGO	87,506	362,933	0.2411
14	JALISCO	153,140	1,029,178	0.1488
15	MEXICO	324,870	1,876,545	0.1731
16	MICHOACAN	154,553	663,496	0.2329
17	MORELOS	44,478	244,958	0.1816
18	NAYARIT	33,464	168,451	0.1987
19	NUEVO LEON	70,769	642,298	0.1102
20	OAXACA	178,631	587,131	0.3042
21	PUEBLA	202,909	772,461	0.2627
22	QUERETARO	40,398	193,434	0.2088
23	QUINTANA ROO	22,503	102,859	0.2188
24	SAN LUIS POTOSI	80,318	379,336	0.2117
25	SINALOA	77,837	422,242	0.1843
26	SONORA	49,941	378,587	0.1319
27	TABASCO	65,410	285,319	0.2293
28	TAMAULIPAS	72,369	488,508	0.1481
29	TLAXCALA	35,474	137,135	0.2587
30	VERACRUZ	280,096	1,262,509	0.2219
31	YUCATAN	68,858	273,958	0.2513
32	ZACATECAS	44,548	238,779	0.1866
	National Total	3,032,513	16,035,233	0.1891
	Mean	94,766	501,101	0.1964
	Median	67,134	378,962	0.1942
	S.D.	79,561	443,648	0.0634
	C.V.	83.95	88.53	32.27
	Minimum	7,898	67,304	0.0930
	Maximum	324,870	1,876,545	0.3337

DEFINITION: Crowded Housing Units are the number of individual housing units with 3 or fewer rooms and 6 or more occupants. Total Housing Units are the total number of housing units. The Ratio is the number of Crowded Housing Units to Total Housing Units.

SOURCE: 1990 Anuario Estadistico, Table 2.4.2.

MAP 6.11
CROWDING, 1990

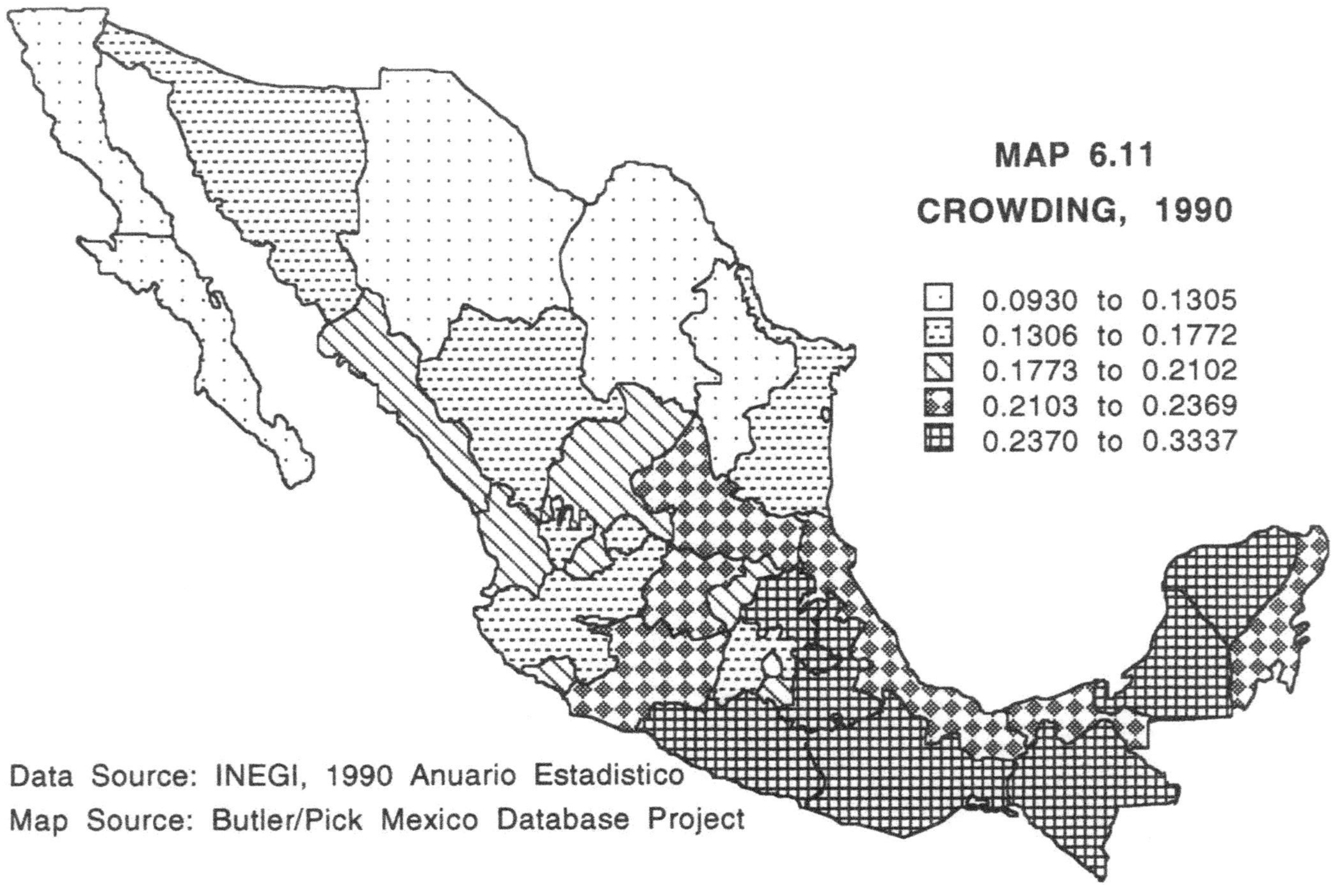

Data Source: INEGI, 1990 Anuario Estadistico
Map Source: Butler/Pick Mexico Database Project

Table 6.8 Crowding, Federal District, 1990

No.	State	Crowded Housing Units	Total Housing Units	Ratio
1	ALVARO OBREGON	15,033	133,937	0.1122
2	AZCAPOTZALCO	8,864	103,130	0.0859
3	BENITO JUAREZ	2,987	114,002	0.0262
4	COYOACAN	7,841	142,533	0.0550
5	CUAJIMALPA	3,348	23,422	0.1429
6	CUAUHTEMOC	11,951	157,079	0.0761
7	GUSTAVO A. MADERO	24,418	262,905	0.0929
8	IZTACALCO	8,458	93,815	0.0902
9	IZTAPALAPA	38,187	294,738	0.1296
10	MAGDALENA CONTRER	4,828	40,247	0.1200
11	MIGUEL HIDALGO	7,141	98,051	0.0728
12	MILPA ALTA	2,399	12,258	0.1957
13	TLAHUAC	6,524	39,311	0.1660
14	TLALPAN	10,817	103,137	0.1049
15	VENUSTIANO CARRANZ	11,753	117,640	0.0999
16	XOCHIMILCO	7,885	52,966	0.1489
	District Total	172,434	1,789,171	0.0964
	Mean	10,777	111,823	0.1074
	Median	8,172	103,134	0.1024
	S.D.	9,080	78,333	0.0428
	C.V.	84.25	70.05	39.80
	Minimum	2,399	12,258	0.0262
	Maximum	38,187	294,738	0.1957

DEFINITION: Crowded Housing Units are the number of housing units with 3 or fewer rooms and 6 or more occupants. Total Housing Units are the total number of individual housing units. The Ratio is the number of Crowded Housing Units to Total Housing Units.

SOURCE: INEGI, 1990 Mexican Census.

MAP 6.12
CROWDING, FEDERAL DISTRICT
1990

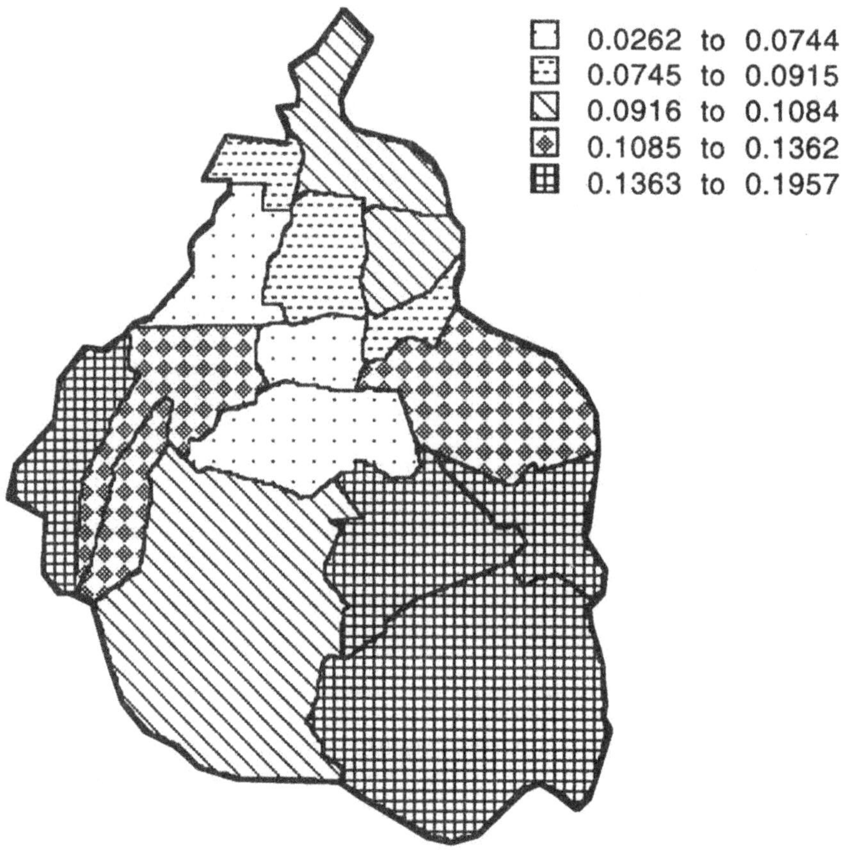

Data Source: INEGI, 1990 Mexican Census

Map Source: Butler/Pick Mexico Database Project

Households with Potable Water, 1990

This attribute measures the proportion of housing units that have a supply of potable water. The national average in 1990 is .794, which is twelve percent higher than the national average of .707 in 1980.

By region, the border region has a generally high proportion (see Table 6.9 and Map 6.13). Baja has a lower proportion, which result from poorer zones of its major cities of Tijuana and Mexicali, that lack adequate plumbing. The other consistent regions are the south and gulf, both of which are very low. Generally, states to the south and east of Mexico City have low proportions of potable water, except for Morelos, Tlaxcala, and Quintana Roo. Southern and southeastern states also tend to be less well off economically (compare with low income in Map 9.19 and corporation value in Map 8.15). The Federal District at .963 has the highest proportion of units with potable water.

Comparing the 1990 geographical distribution with the 1980 pattern of potable water (see Map 6.7C in Pick et al. 1989a) reveals a close correspondence, taking into account the overall increase in households with potable water. There are, however, several notable state changes since the 1980s. Relative to national average for each year, Baja and the state of Mexico have declined in households having potable water, while Quintana Roo has increased. Quintana Roo's increase may be due to that state's growth and economic betterment in the 1980s.

Households with potable water is highly associated with urban and economic prosperity indicators and opposite to rural and marginality indicators. Several examples of these associations are high correlation with urbanization in 1990 (.78), literacy (.81), tertiary sector employment (.67), professional/technical occupation (.74), administrative/managerial occupation (.76), and high monthly income (.71). It is inversely associated with standardized fertility (- .79), dependency ratio (- .60), crowding (- .75), households without electricity (- .49), households without toilet (- .65), low monthly income (- .85), and agricultural occupation (- .81). In general, this attribute is linked to a very large number of other attributes, and can be considered an especially important indicator of quality of life.

Housing Units Using Kitchen as a Bedroom, 1980

This characteristic was available in the 1980 census of population, but was not included in the 1990 census. It is included in this volume, as well as earlier in the *Atlas of Mexico,* because of its unusual nature and usefulness as an indicator of economic marginality. As seen in Table 6.10, an average of one in ten Mexican households in 1980 used the kitchen as a bedroom. There was moderate variation (CV = 37).

There is substantial regional variation (see Map 6.14). The southeast is the only region with consistently high values for all states—Quintana Roo at 20 percent, Campeche at 18 percent and Yucatan at 11 percent. Other states with high rates are Oaxaca and Veracruz in the south and gulf regions, as well as Colima in the west region and the border state of Chihuahua. The largest area of low rates for this variable consists of four states in the northern west and southern north regions, namely Durango, Zacatecas, Aguascalientes, and Jalisco. They all have less than six percent sharing the kitchen as a bedroom. The Federal District has a very low rate (5.3 percent) as does Tlaxcala (5.4 percent), while the state of Mexico is low (7.4 percent).

This 1980 characteristic is associated with several other attributes for 1990. It is directly related to population change 1970–1990, sex ratio, literacy change 1950–1990, indigenous language, male economic activity, hotels/motels, and five star hotels. It varies inversely with percent divorced and non-Catholic population.

Housing Units Without Electricity, 1990

One eighth of Mexican housing units did not have electricity in 1990. This percentage varied considerably by state, from a low of only .74 percent in the Federal District to a high of one third in Chiapas. Other states with over a quarter of non-electricity housing units are San Luis Potosi and Veracruz, while other states with under 5 percent of non-electricity housing are Nuevo Leon, Morelos, and Aguascalientes (see Table 6.11).

Map 6.15 illustrates that from a regional perspective, the south and gulf regions have high values for this attribute, while the Federal District and adjoining states are low and the northwest and west are moderate to low. The border region is highly inconsistent, with very low levels for Chihuahua and Nuevo Leon, very high values for Coahuila and Tamaulipas, and moderate levels for Baja and Sonora.

In very broad view, the east and southeast of the nation tend to be higher and the west and northwest lower. The pattern of lacking electricity housing bears no relationship with installed electrical capacity (see Map 8.14), although it is inversely correlated with crude oil production ($r = -.58$ and see Map 8.1). In the latter case, oil-productive regions may favor petroleum-based methods of household heating and cooking, reducing the need for electrical connections. The attribute is strongly linked to housing without potable water (.75).

The variable is related to several demographic and employment/occupational attributes. It is directly associated with crude fertility, and cumulative fertility for women age 20–29 and inversely related to urbanization, divorce, accounting and information systems employment, professional/technical occupation, and high monthly income. These associations indicate that lack of electricity in housing tends to be in more rural and less prosperous areas.

Households Without Toilet, 1990

This attribute is the percentage of housing units that lacked a toilet in 1990. For the nation, one quarter of housing units did not have a toilet. The coefficient of variation was 54, indicating some differences. Several states have over 45 percent of housing units lacking a toilet (Guerrero, Oaxaca, Chiapas, Hidalgo, and Zacatecas), while several border states (Nuevo Leon, Baja, Sonora, Tamaulipas), Baja Sur, and the Federal District have levels under 10 percent (see Table 6.12).

By region, this characteristic reflects a north-south gradient typical of some key attributes including urbanization (see Map 6.16). In general, the gradient of low levels in the north to high levels in the south is punctuated by low to moderate levels in the Federal District, Mexico, and Morelos. The regions that are distinctive for this attribute are the border and the south regions.

The close inverse relationship with urbanization is reflected in a highly significant correlation of - .80. There are highly significant relationships, also, with nearly all the other housing variables, including housing with potable water (- .65), housing density (.53), crowding (.83), and home ownership (.70). Housing without a toilet is related to economic prosperity attributes (for instance, - .77 with high income) and inversely to poverty and marginality attributes (.81 with no or low income and .70 with no meat and eggs). In general, this variable might serve as a reverse indicator of urbanization and modernization.

Households Without Toilet, Mexico City, 1990

Households without a toilet varied considerably by region in Mexico City. For the conurbated area, the overall mean was .0975, which is higher than the Federal District (.0785) and lower than the state of Mexico (.2173). The areas of lowest level are within the Federal District (Benito Juarez at .0200, Cuauhtemoc at .0362, and Coyoacan at .0579) and just to the north of the District in the municipio of Coacalco at .0179. These are very modernized and economically well off areas where housing standards approach those in some American cities. Generally the Federal District has very low levels (mostly under ten percent). However, the economically impoverished delegacion of Milpa Alta in the southwest of the District has an elevated level of .2190. However, even in this largely slum area, the value for this characteristic is lower than the national average (see Map 6.17). There are also low values for this attribute for a group of ten or so municipios to the north of the District.

Households without a toilet is highest in Mexico City in areas at the border of the metropolis. In the west and southwest, there are six areas with high values including Milpa Alta as well as Texcoco (.2207) and Atenco (.2122). Also in the far northwest, there are high values for a cluster of municipios in the range of .2 to .3. This pattern very much reflects economic patterns. For example, comparison with professional/technical occupations (Map 9.8) reveals a strong opposite relationship. It is also interesting that the more populous areas of the metropolis coincide with areas of high presence of toilets for households (compare with Map 2.3). In the future, as the population of Mexico City likely expands more to the periphery of the metropolis, it is likely that in many of the areas of expansion, there will be greater presence of toilets in households, as is the case currently in most of the urban center. The likely compelling reasons will relate to environment and sanitation.

Home Ownership, 1990

Home ownership represents the proportion of households that are owned. Overall in Mexico in 1990, seventy-eight percent of households are owned, with fourteen percent rented and eight percent other, including cooperatives, etc. There was low variation in this attribute, with a C. V. of only seven, one of the lowest in the book's set of attributes. The lack of variation may relate to national home ownership preferences that are fairly stable around the country. As shown in Table 6.13 and Map 6.18, the highest home ownership, all above 83 percent, is located in the south in the states of Oaxaca, Chiapas, in Yucatan, and in the central state of Hidalgo. These states are perhaps rooted in more family traditions than in some other areas of the country, which may account for somewhat more home ownership. By contrast, the areas with the lowest home ownership, under 71 percent, are the Federal District, Baja, and Jalisco. These states are highly urban, with major cities and may offer more alternatives in owner/rental arrangements, as well as a history of inmigration that favors rentals.

Overall, the geographic pattern resembles closely that for households without toilet (see Map 6.16). This is corroborated by a correlation of .70. Similar to households without toilet, the national pattern for home ownership is characterized by a north south continuum, punctuated most prominently by the Federal District, Mexico, Morelos, and Puebla. It is interesting that Nuevo Leon also varies from this north-south pattern, with a high value of home ownership (.8832).

Home ownership is associated with other variables in a pattern similar to that described for households without toilet. It is inversely associated with indicators of economic prosperity and modernization and positively related to indicators of ruralism and poverty. This pattern is perhaps surprising in cross cultural perspective, since in the United States, home ownership is consistently associated with economic prosperity and middle class status.

Table 6.9 Household Units with Potable Water, 1990

No.	State	Households with Potable Water	Total Housing Units	Potable Water Ratio
1	AGUASCALIENTES	124,116	129,853	0.9558
2	BAJA CALIFORNIA	291,871	362,727	0.8047
3	BAJA CALIFORNIA SUR	59,797	67,304	0.8885
4	CAMPECHE	76,238	107,894	0.7066
5	COAHUILA	371,232	404,691	0.9173
6	COLIMA	82,272	88,627	0.9283
7	CHIAPAS	346,742	594,025	0.5837
8	CHIHUAHUA	464,491	529,799	0.8767
9	DISTRITO FEDERAL	1,722,850	1,789,171	0.9629
10	DURANGO	223,512	262,164	0.8526
11	GUANAJUATO	567,939	687,136	0.8265
12	GUERRERO	285,587	501,725	0.5692
13	HIDALGO	253,883	362,933	0.6995
14	JALISCO	889,874	1,029,178	0.8646
15	MEXICO	1,596,532	1,876,545	0.8508
16	MICHOACAN	522,297	663,496	0.7872
17	MORELOS	216,799	244,958	0.8850
18	NAYARIT	140,634	168,451	0.8349
19	NUEVO LEON	596,390	642,298	0.9285
20	OAXACA	340,872	587,131	0.5806
21	PUEBLA	550,293	772,461	0.7124
22	QUERETARO	161,277	193,434	0.8338
23	QUINTANA ROO	91,089	102,859	0.8856
24	SAN LUIS POTOSI	253,159	379,336	0.6674
25	SINALOA	337,929	422,242	0.8003
26	SONORA	343,191	378,587	0.9065
27	TABASCO	166,438	285,319	0.5833
28	TAMAULIPAS	397,794	488,508	0.8143
29	TLAXCALA	123,906	137,135	0.9035
30	VERACRUZ	755,092	1,262,509	0.5981
31	YUCATAN	195,991	273,958	0.7154
32	ZACATECAS	179,900	238,779	0.7534
	National Total		16,035,233	0.7939
	Mean		501,101	0.7962
	Median		378,962	0.8301
	S.D.		443,648	0.1204
	C.V.		88.53	15.13
	Minimum		67,304	0.5692
	Maximum		1,876,545	0.9629

SOURCE: 1990 Mexican Census, Resumen General, Table 46.

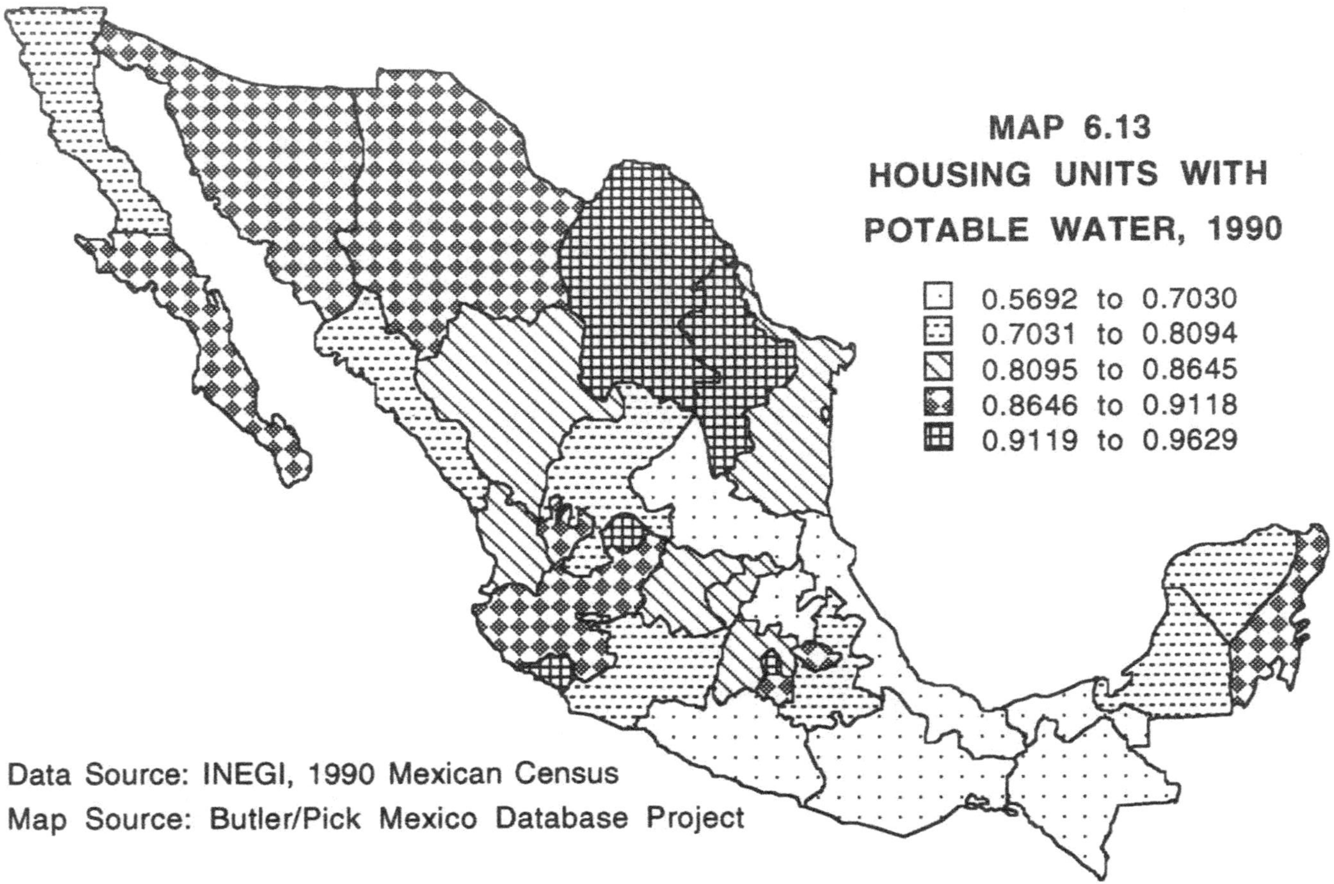

MAP 6.13
HOUSING UNITS WITH
POTABLE WATER, 1990

0.5692 to 0.7030
0.7031 to 0.8094
0.8095 to 0.8645
0.8646 to 0.9118
0.9119 to 0.9629

Data Source: INEGI, 1990 Mexican Census
Map Source: Butler/Pick Mexico Database Project

Table 6.10 Household Characteristics, 1980

No.	State	Number of Hous. Units Total	Hous. Units Potable Water	Potable Water Ratio	Hous. Units Using Kitchen As Bedroom	Kitchen As Bedroom Ratio
1	AGUASCALIENTES	83,791	73,563	0.8779	4,985	0.0595
2	BAJA CALIFORNIA	238,603	186,328	0.7809	15,728	0.0659
3	BAJA CALIFORNIA SUR	39,671	30,597	0.7713	3,012	0.0759
4	CAMPECHE	75,879	45,350	0.5977	13,650	0.1799
5	COAHUILA	282,705	239,904	0.8486	26,996	0.0955
6	COLIMA	64,270	54,186	0.8431	8,117	0.1263
7	CHIAPAS	370,319	161,588	0.4363	33,655	0.0909
8	CHIHUAHUA	391,464	305,452	0.7803	45,918	0.1173
9	DISTRITO FEDERAL	1,747,102	1,628,415	0.9321	92,325	0.0528
10	DURANGO	198,378	145,348	0.7327	12,086	0.0609
11	GUANAJUATO	474,800	324,972	0.6844	33,926	0.0715
12	GUERRERO	377,847	179,927	0.4762	31,891	0.0844
13	HIDALGO	272,162	160,179	0.5885	29,420	0.1081
14	JALISCO	776,809	609,465	0.7846	36,346	0.0468
15	MEXICO	1,281,270	1,044,366	0.8151	94,512	0.0738
16	MICHOACAN	494,638	329,743	0.6666	33,045	0.0668
17	MORELOS	175,397	135,635	0.7733	13,472	0.0768
18	NAYARIT	132,440	94,513	0.7136	13,802	0.1042
19	NUEVO LEON	461,105	403,453	0.875	41,971	0.091
20	OAXACA	448,665	198,276	0.4419	51,054	0.1138
21	PUEBLA	589,485	354,411	0.6012	55,924	0.0949
22	QUERETARO	120,503	79,197	0.6572	12,062	0.1001
23	QUINTANA ROO	44,440	25,765	0.5798	8,753	0.197
24	SAN LUIS POTOSI	283,031	142,118	0.5021	27,827	0.0983
25	SINALOA	319,834	214,237	0.6698	33,037	0.1033
26	SONORA	276,848	229,641	0.8295	27,714	0.1001
27	TABASCO	180,929	75,559	0.4176	13,483	0.0745
28	TAMAULIPAS	379,476	272,143	0.7172	36,956	0.0974
29	TLAXCALA	92,327	65,808	0.7128	4,977	0.0539
30	VERACRUZ	1,015,323	514,507	0.5067	133,329	0.1313
31	YUCATAN	200,966	100,861	0.5019	22,674	0.1128
32	ZACATECAS	184,132	106,654	0.5792	8,290	0.045
	National Total	12,074,609	8,532,164	0.7066	1,020,937	0.0846
	Mean	377,332	266,630	0.6780	31,904	0.0928
	Median	279,777	170,758	0.6986	27,771	0.0930
	S.D.	371,962	321,620	0.1451	28,757	0.0341
	C.V.	98.58	120.62	21.41	90.13	36.68
	Minimum	39,671	25,765	0.4176	3,012	0.0450
	Maximum	1,747,102	1,628,415	0.9321	133,329	0.1970

DEFINITION: Potable Water Ratio is the number of housing units with potable water to the number of housing units. Kitchen As Bedroom Ratio is the number of housing units where the kitchen is used as a bedroom to the total number of housing units.

SOURCE: 1980 Mexican Census of Population, Volume 1, Tables 21 & 22.

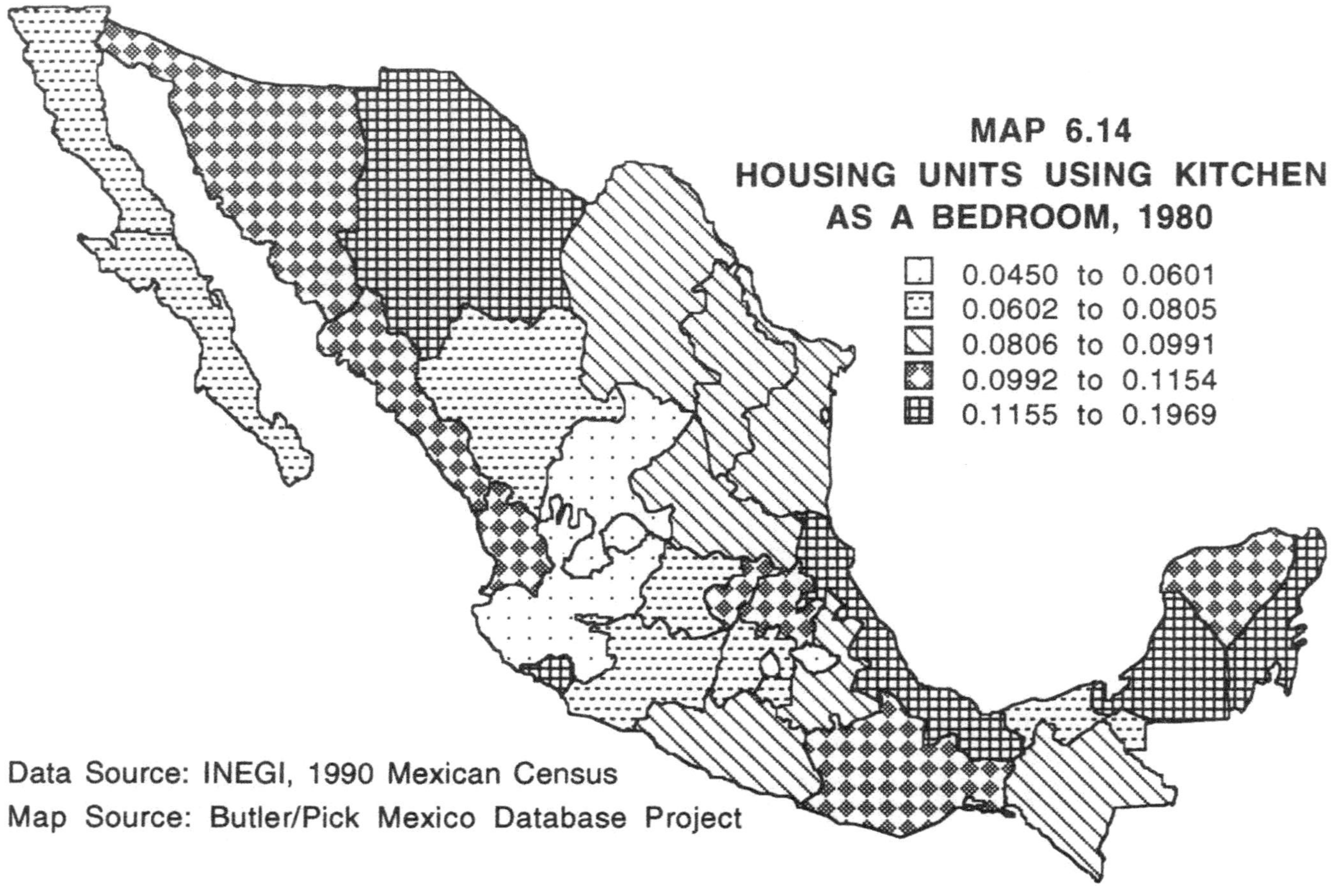

MAP 6.14
HOUSING UNITS USING KITCHEN AS A BEDROOM, 1980

Data Source: INEGI, 1990 Mexican Census
Map Source: Butler/Pick Mexico Database Project

Table 6.11 Housing Units Without Electricity, 1990

No.	State	Housing Units Without Electricity	Total Housing Units	Ratio
1	AGUASCALIENTES	6,427	129,853	0.0495
2	BAJA CALIFORNIA	37,973	362,727	0.1047
3	BAJA CALIFORNIA SUR	7,773	67,304	0.1155
4	CAMPECHE	15,861	107,894	0.1470
5	COAHUILA	22,361	404,691	0.0553
6	COLIMA	5,365	88,627	0.0605
7	CHIAPAS	196,906	594,025	0.3315
8	CHIHUAHUA	68,355	529,799	0.1290
9	DISTRITO FEDERAL	13,316	1,789,171	0.0074
10	DURANGO	34,065	262,164	0.1299
11	GUANAJUATO	85,426	687,136	0.1243
12	GUERRERO	108,373	501,725	0.2160
13	HIDALGO	82,304	362,933	0.2268
14	JALISCO	76,825	1,029,178	0.0746
15	MEXICO	116,491	1,876,545	0.0621
16	MICHOACAN	84,840	663,496	0.1279
17	MORELOS	10,026	244,958	0.0409
18	NAYARIT	14,374	168,451	0.0853
19	NUEVO LEON	24,112	642,298	0.0375
20	OAXACA	140,281	587,131	0.2389
21	PUEBLA	119,902	772,461	0.1552
22	QUERETARO	29,102	193,434	0.1504
23	QUINTANA ROO	15,908	102,859	0.1547
24	SAN LUIS POTOSI	102,388	379,336	0.2699
25	SINALOA	38,563	422,242	0.0913
26	SONORA	36,662	378,587	0.0968
27	TABASCO	42,272	285,319	0.1482
28	TAMAULIPAS	76,270	488,508	0.1561
29	TLAXCALA	8,497	137,135	0.0620
30	VERACRUZ	323,134	1,262,509	0.2559
31	YUCATAN	26,165	273,958	0.0955
32	ZACATECAS	31,122	238,779	0.1303
	National Total	2,001,439	16,035,233	0.1248
	Mean	62,545	501,101	0.1291
	Median	37,318	378,962	0.1261
	S.D.	66,603	443,648	0.0751
	C.V.	106.49	88.53	58.19
	Minimum	5,365	67,304	0.0074
	Maximum	323,134	1,876,545	0.3315

DEFINITION: Total Housing Units are the total number of housing units. The Ratio is the number of Housing Units Without Electricity to Total Housing Units.

SOURCE: 1990 Anuario Estadistico, Table 2.4.3.

Table 6.12 Households Without Toilet, 1990

No.	State	Hous.Units Without Toilet	Total Housing Units	Ratio	Occupants Without Toilet	Total Occupants	Ratio
1	AGUASCALIENTES	19,524	129,853	0.1504	111,460	714,542	0.1560
2	BAJA CALIFORNIA	26,843	362,727	0.0740	107,253	1,615,395	0.0664
3	BAJA CALIFORNIA SUR	6,044	67,304	0.0898	26,061	309,966	0.0841
4	CAMPECHE	28,531	107,894	0.2644	142,733	525,660	0.2715
5	COAHUILA	52,419	404,691	0.1295	253,827	1,955,567	0.1298
6	COLIMA	9,973	88,627	0.1125	46,314	420,397	0.1102
7	CHIAPAS	272,658	594,025	0.4590	1,512,932	3,184,658	0.4751
8	CHIHUAHUA	90,364	529,799	0.1706	403,226	2,398,319	0.1681
9	DISTRITO FEDERAL	140,507	1,789,171	0.0785	602,008	8,163,961	0.0737
10	DURANGO	92,937	262,164	0.3545	490,839	1,342,285	0.3657
11	GUANAJUATO	248,793	687,136	0.3621	1,439,177	3,933,098	0.3659
12	GUERRERO	262,458	501,725	0.5231	1,410,252	2,580,189	0.5466
13	HIDALGO	169,460	362,933	0.4669	892,199	1,869,089	0.4773
14	JALISCO	148,826	1,029,178	0.1446	780,356	5,235,463	0.1491
15	MEXICO	407,740	1,876,545	0.2173	2,174,032	9,758,406	0.2228
16	MICHOACAN	187,215	663,496	0.2822	1,008,881	3,494,088	0.2887
17	MORELOS	59,327	244,958	0.2422	297,856	1,184,235	0.2515
18	NAYARIT	36,840	168,451	0.2187	178,070	807,003	0.2207
19	NUEVO LEON	37,607	642,298	0.0586	167,172	3,075,173	0.0544
20	OAXACA	291,004	587,131	0.4956	1,494,833	2,997,129	0.4988
21	PUEBLA	305,418	772,461	0.3954	1,677,215	4,103,102	0.4088
22	QUERETARO	73,107	193,434	0.3779	417,592	1,041,425	0.4010
23	QUINTANA ROO	22,210	102,859	0.2159	103,868	479,664	0.2165
24	SAN LUIS POTOSI	102,081	379,336	0.2691	555,848	1,990,592	0.2792
25	SINALOA	89,744	422,242	0.2125	459,734	2,173,603	0.2115
26	SONORA	37,584	378,587	0.0993	166,262	1,798,442	0.0924
27	TABASCO	54,525	285,319	0.1911	293,160	1,493,087	0.1963
28	TAMAULIPAS	44,364	488,508	0.0908	188,208	2,221,638	0.0847
29	TLAXCALA	53,864	137,135	0.3928	300,642	758,762	0.3962
30	VERACRUZ	373,859	1,262,509	0.2961	1,886,017	6,183,387	0.3050
31	YUCATAN	86,008	273,958	0.3139	449,902	1,354,285	0.3322
32	ZACATECAS	112,209	238,779	0.4699	617,443	1,271,214	0.4857
	National Total	3,831,834	15,796,454	0.2426	20,037,929	79,162,610	0.2531
	Mean	123,251	501,101	0.2569	645,480	2,513,557	0.2621
	Median	87,876	378,962	0.2304	433,747	1,912,328	0.2372
	S.D.	112,179	443,648	0.1393	604,409	2,200,582	0.1461
	C.V.	91.02	88.53	54.23	93.64	87.55	55.74
	Minimum	6,044	67,304	0.0586	26,061	309,966	0.0544
	Maximum	407,740	1,876,545	0.5231	2,174,032	9,758,406	0.5466

DEFINITION: Total Housing Units are the total number of housing units. The Ratios are the number of Housing Units Without Toilet to Total Housing Units and the number of Occupants Without Toilet to Total Occupants.

SOURCE: 1990 Mexican Census of Population, Resumen General, Table 45.

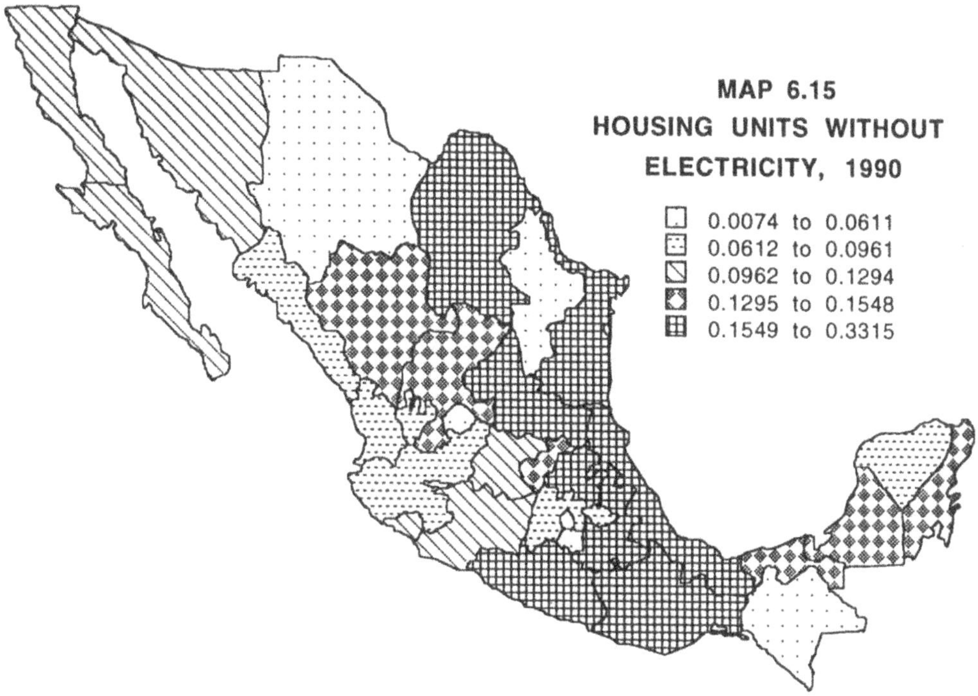

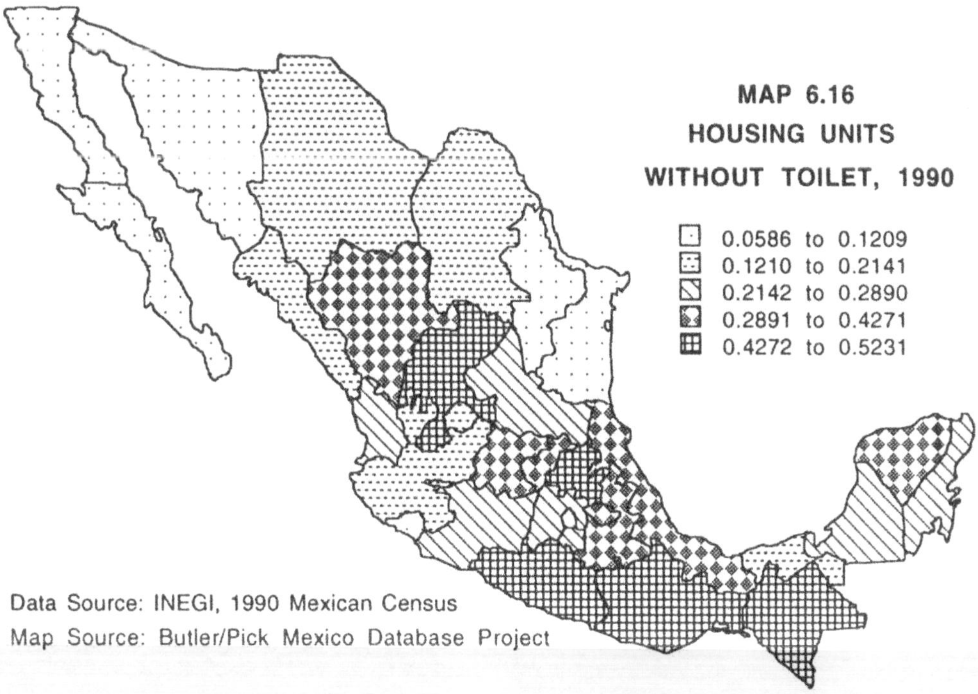

Data Source: INEGI, 1990 Mexican Census

Map Source: Butler/Pick Mexico Database Project

MAP 6.17
HOUSEHOLDS WITHOUT TOILET
MEXICO CITY (CMZ)
1990

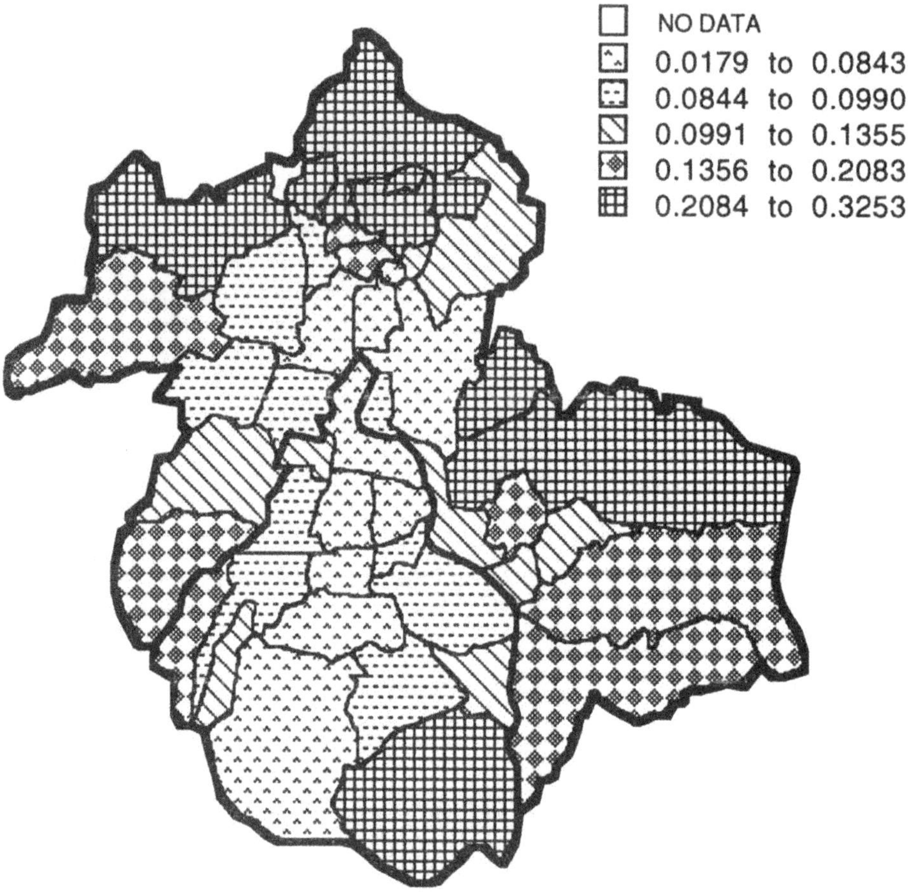

Data Source: INEGI, 1990 Mexican Census

Map Source: Butler/Pick Mexico Database Project

Table 6.13 Home Ownership, 1990

No.	State	Households Owned	Households Rented	Other or Not Specified	Total Households	Ratio
1	AGUASCALIENTES	95,503	21,574	12,776	129,853	0.7355
2	BAJA CALIFORNIA	252,426	79,452	30,849	362,727	0.6959
3	BAJA CALIFORNIA SUR	51,935	8,424	6,945	67,304	0.7716
4	CAMPECHE	89,015	9,516	9,363	107,894	0.8250
5	COAHUILA	307,495	67,726	29,470	404,691	0.7598
6	COLIMA	64,065	16,981	7,581	88,627	0.7229
7	CHIAPAS	495,990	64,330	33,705	594,025	0.8350
8	CHIHUAHUA	411,935	71,550	46,314	529,799	0.7775
9	DISTRITO FEDERAL	1,166,385	458,829	163,957	1,789,171	0.6519
10	DURANGO	218,108	23,248	20,808	262,164	0.8320
11	GUANAJUATO	551,958	79,863	55,315	687,136	0.8033
12	GUERRERO	426,159	48,241	27,325	501,725	0.8494
13	HIDALGO	305,238	37,051	20,644	362,933	0.8410
14	JALISCO	726,244	210,723	92,211	1,029,178	0.7057
15	MEXICO	1,467,827	275,125	133,593	1,876,545	0.7822
16	MICHOACAN	541,945	67,671	53,880	663,496	0.8168
17	MORELOS	188,419	35,032	21,507	244,958	0.7692
18	NAYARIT	139,240	16,996	12,215	168,451	0.8266
19	NUEVO LEON	525,638	77,886	38,774	642,298	0.8184
20	OAXACA	518,542	44,635	23,954	587,131	0.8832
21	PUEBLA	604,115	126,226	42,120	772,461	0.7821
22	QUERETARO	161,344	20,851	11,239	193,434	0.8341
23	QUINTANA ROO	75,925	20,430	6,504	102,859	0.7381
24	SAN LUIS POTOSI	307,483	46,461	25,392	379,336	0.8106
25	SINALOA	357,414	28,564	36,264	422,242	0.8465
26	SONORA	303,715	41,095	33,777	378,587	0.8022
27	TABASCO	225,938	38,509	20,872	285,319	0.7919
28	TAMAULIPAS	358,428	86,439	43,641	488,508	0.7337
29	TLAXCALA	115,049	14,799	7,287	137,135	0.8389
30	VERACRUZ	1,001,504	167,614	93,391	1,262,509	0.7933
31	YUCATAN	236,685	20,148	17,125	273,958	0.8639
32	ZACATECAS	195,231	21,470	22,078	238,779	0.8176
	National Total	12,486,898	2,347,459	1,200,876	16,035,233	0.7787
	Mean	390,216	73,358	37,527	501,101	0.7924
	Median	306,361	42,865	26,359	378,962	0.8028
	S.D.	325,755	92,256	36,288	443,648	0.0531
	C.V.	83.48	125.76	96.70	88.53	6.70
	Minimum	51,935	8,424	6,504	67,304	0.6519
	Maximum	1,467,827	458,829	163,957	1,876,545	0.8832

DEFINITION: Ratio is the number of households owned to the total number of households.

SOURCE: 1990 Mexican Census of Population, Table 48.

MAP 6.18

HOME OWNERSHIP, 1990

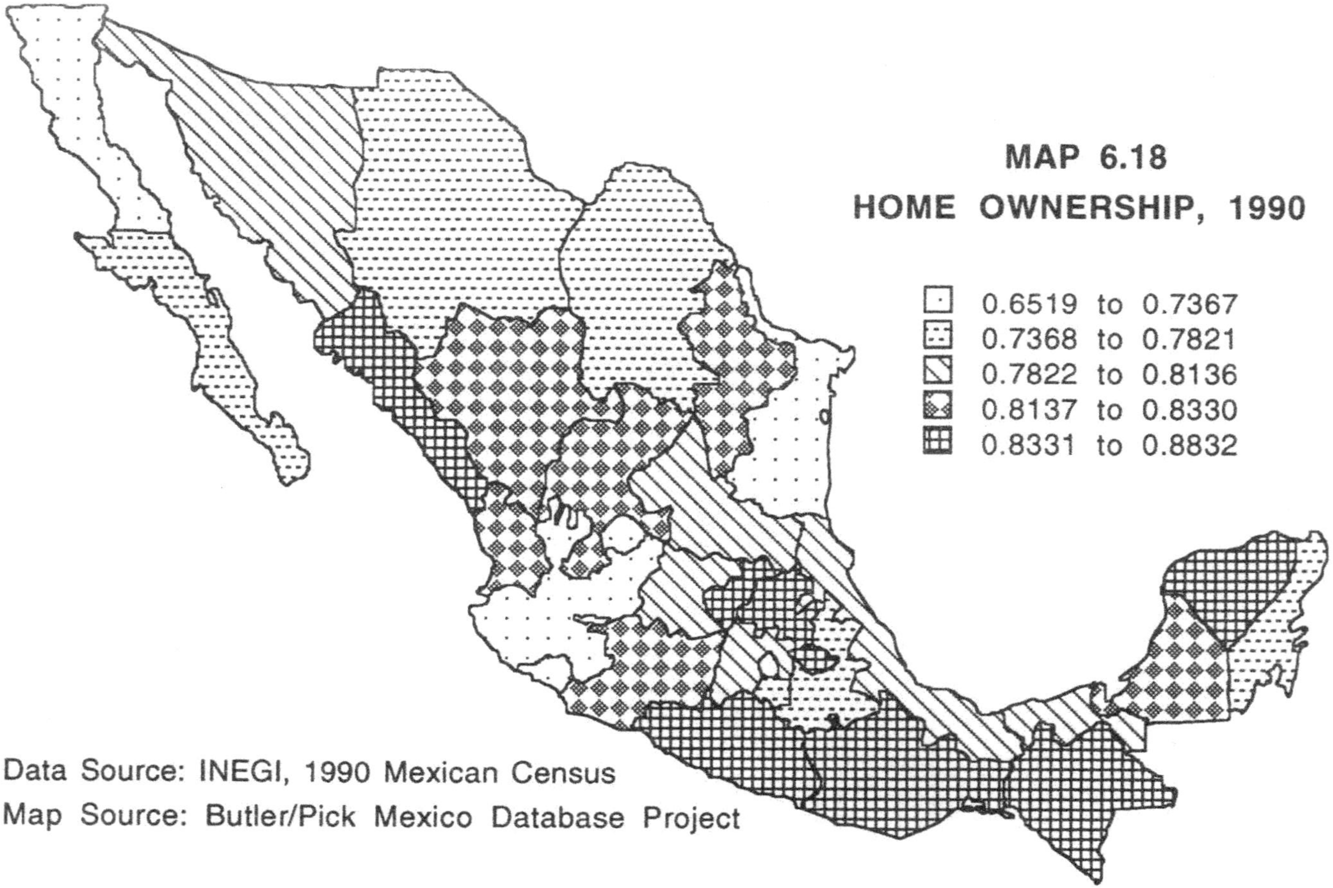

Data Source: INEGI, 1990 Mexican Census

Map Source: Butler/Pick Mexico Database Project

7

Social Characteristics

Introduction

This chapter presents data, maps, and figures on various social characteristics. First there is an emphasis on literacy with information presented for Mexico in 1900, 1930, 1950, 1970, and 1990. Also an analysis is presented of literacy change between 1950 and 1990. Another perspective presents a longitudinal analysis of the proportion of the national population and of the state of Chiapas and the Federal District—the low and high end of the scale—knowing the alphabet between 1900 and 1990. Next the chapter focuses on secondary educational attainment for the population aged 12 and over in 1990 and higher education for the population aged 16 and over in 1990.

Data, maps, and figures are used to illustrate the variety of indigenous languages spoken in Mexico for 1990 and to trace indigenous language for 1900 through 1990. A section on Non-Catholic religion and No Religion in 1990 demonstrates that there is variation among the Mexican states in reported religious affiliation.

A portion of this chapter focuses on the consumption of goods and services including sugar sales, various measures of the national service sector as well as presenting information on various service subsectors. Accounting and information system services and business consulting services show great variation in Mexico by number of establishments, number of employees, and gross revenues per 1,000 population.

The final section of Chapter 7 focuses on crime. At the state level, an analysis of juvenile delinquent sentences for 1988 is reported and penal sentences for 1986 and 1987 are presented. Then, information on murders, robberies, and rapes for the Federal District averaged over the years of 1983–1985 demonstrate that there is substantial variation in the district for these crimes and that these crimes are concentrated in specific areas in the Federal District.

Literacy

Literacy in Mexico for 1900, 1930, 1950, 1970, and 1990 is shown in Table 7.1. Literacy is defined as the literate population to the total population; the age criterion used, however, varied slightly by census year. Map 7.1 illustrates literacy in 1900. In 1900, Guerrero had a literacy rate of just under nine percent while the highest literacy rate of just under 50 percent was in the Federal District. The border region had high literacy rates in the range of 30 to 40 percent, as did Jalisco and Colima. States slightly north of the Federal District and all southern and southeastern states, except Campeche, had low rates of literacy.

Map 7.2 shows the literacy rate in 1990. What is striking is that while the mean literacy rate between 1900 increased from .24 to .87 by 1990, the relative standing of states remained virtually the same. That is, the northern border states had the highest literacy rates as did the Federal District. The major change was that the state of Mexico substantially increased while Campeche declined relatively compared to the national average. In 1990, the state with the maximum literacy rate was the same one as in 1900—the Federal District. The state with the lowest rate in 1990 was Chiapas that also had an extremely low literacy rate in 1900.

Literacy change between 1950 and 1990 is shown on Map 7.3. Table 7.2 reports that the literacy rate in Mexico increased almost 30 percent between 1950 and 1990. The largest increase took place in Queretaro (49 percent) and in other states in the mid-section of the country and states surrounding the Federal District. The Yucatan states and Campeche had low rates in the 1950 and continued to lag in 1990. However, Oaxaca and Chiapas in the south had relatively large increases in literacy between 1950 and 1990.

Figure 7.1 presents a slightly different view of literacy in Mexico by illustrating the proportion of the national population that Knows the Alphabet from 1900 through 1990. The Federal District in all census years had the highest proportion of the population knowing the alphabet and Chiapas had the lowest or near lowest proportion; thus they also are included in Figure 7.1 for comparison purposes. The national, Federal District, and Chiapas rates have all steadily increased over the years; however, the relative differences have remained substantially the same. That is, the Federal District always had higher rates than the rest of Mexico and Chiapas consistently had a much lower rate than the nation and substantially lower rate than the Federal District.

Table 7.1 Literacy, 1900-1990

No.	State	1900		1930		1950		1970		1990	
		Lit. Pop. Age 10+	Ratio	Lit. Pop. Age 10+	Ratio	Lit. Pop. Age 6+	Ratio	Lit. Pop. Age 10+	Ratio	Lit. Pop. Age 10+	Ratio
1	AGUASCALIENTES	16,820	0.2141	45,161	0.4708	104,608	0.6903	189,808	0.8532	395,790	0.5500
2	BAJA CALIFORNIA	14,344	0.4116	27,580	0.7730	149,309	0.8125	513,750	0.8824	1,007,665	0.6067
3	BAJA CALIFORNIA SUR			21,003	0.6214	38,069	0.7732	74,526	0.8764	187,036	0.5886
4	CAMPECHE	15,909	0.2485	26,291	0.4393	61,398	0.6207	131,846	0.7718	266,668	0.4983
5	COAHUILA	74,265	0.3417	170,719	0.5448	428,459	0.7405	658,769	0.8759	1,173,503	0.5950
6	COLIMA	16,025	0.3252	24,694	0.5314	59,208	0.6673	128,521	0.8013	237,203	0.5536
7	CHIAPAS	32,046	0.1309	76,317	0.2105	245,591	0.3463	587,637	0.5673	1,238,682	0.3858
8	CHIHUAHUA	75,388	0.3143	194,797	0.5594	498,413	0.7285	938,465	0.8707	1,453,411	0.5952
9	DISTRITO FEDERAL	208,742	0.4948	702,459	0.7513	2,067,970	0.8174	4,417,195	0.9091	5,462,684	0.6633
10	DURANGO	58,688	0.2147	124,502	0.4365	346,924	0.6859	523,409	0.8567	740,130	0.5485
11	GUANAJUATO	129,467	0.1634	190,874	0.2747	466,282	0.4428	963,024	0.6470	1,910,604	0.4797
12	GUERRERO	29,244	0.0892	80,315	0.1804	233,976	0.3200	580,506	0.5540	1,013,014	0.3866
13	HIDALGO	90,936	0.2174	124,300	0.2652	271,039	0.4053	493,692	0.6213	869,884	0.4607
14	JALISCO	242,253	0.2821	396,106	0.4312	856,753	0.6118	1,775,358	0.8063	2,917,323	0.5502
15	MEXICO	124,621	0.1899	192,022	0.2826	532,035	0.4805	1,856,916	0.7506	5,478,799	0.5582
16	MICHOACAN	120,979	0.1770	223,220	0.3016	515,628	0.4571	1,012,136	0.6622	1,687,462	0.4756
17	MORELOS	30,849	0.2605	34,265	0.3685	129,267	0.5878	308,965	0.7462	653,431	0.5468
18	NAYARIT	25,807	0.2290	52,425	0.4221	141,018	0.6161	282,264	0.7854	432,194	0.5241
19	NUEVO LEON	78,871	0.3330	183,117	0.6045	473,758	0.7846	1,028,031	0.8934	1,933,702	0.6240
20	OAXACA	74,098	0.1108	154,979	0.2017	421,289	0.3705	791,099	0.5802	1,249,297	0.4137
21	PUEBLA	151,778	0.2088	242,569	0.2991	584,362	0.4490	1,131,943	0.6678	1,943,675	0.4711
22	QUERETARO	27,943	0.1642	37,552	0.2267	81,274	0.3619	196,385	0.6205	513,609	0.4886
23	QUINTANA ROO			4,011	0.5144	13,222	0.6289	43,289	0.7619	251,742	0.5103
24	SAN LUIS POTOSI	72,601	0.1738	121,670	0.3042	334,430	0.4873	602,932	0.7095	996,753	0.4976
25	SINALOA	53,824	0.2471	121,009	0.4204	297,308	0.5819	658,493	0.7874	1,209,781	0.5489

26 SONORA	59,263	0.3672	134,595	0.5865	301,443	0.7278	643,045	0.8644	1,088,944	0.5971
27 TABASCO	22,471	0.2094	48,059	0.3271	165,091	0.5774	375,882	0.7616	754,206	0.5022
28 TAMAULIPAS	51,153	0.3229	142,398	0.5795	434,910	0.7423	842,590	0.8567	1,344,595	0.5977
29 TLAXCALA	24,372	0.2005	54,533	0.3817	124,540	0.5499	213,999	0.7666	399,891	0.5253
30 VERACRUZ	139,167	0.2071	310,988	0.3248	801,184	0.4892	1,811,202	0.7056	3,106,903	0.4988
31 YUCATAN	51,397	0.2281	138,601	0.4853	266,295	0.6409	391,842	0.7378	709,699	0.5207
32 ZACATECAS	72,482	0.2096	123,914	0.3910	313,093	0.5915	490,140	0.8123	665,787	0.5216
National Total	2,185,803	0.2226	4,525,045	0.3851	11,758,146	0.5682	24,657,659	0.7626	43,294,067	
Mean	72,860	0.2429	141,408	0.4222	367,442	0.5871	770,552	0.7614	1,352,940	0.5276
Median	58,976	0.2161	124,107	0.4213	299,376	0.6017	584,072	0.7692	1,010,340	0.5247
S.D.	57,394	0.0896	136,146	0.1546	375,023	0.1446	820,681	0.1029	1,292,405	0.0651
C.V.	78.77	36.87	96.28	36.61	102.06	24.63	106.51	13.52	95.53	12.33
Minimum	14,344	0.0892	4,011	0.1804	13,222	0.3200	43,289	0.5540	187,036	0.3858
Maximum	242,253	0.4948	702,459	0.7730	2,067,970	0.8174	4,417,195	0.9091	5,478,799	0.6633

DEFINITION: The literacy ratios are the literate population to the total population of the specified age group for each year shown.

NOTE: For 1900, data for Baja Sur are included with Baja California and data for Quintana Roc are included with Yucatan.

SOURCE: 1900, 1930, 1950, 1970 and 1990 Mexican Census of Population; Estadisticas Historicas de Mexico, 1985.

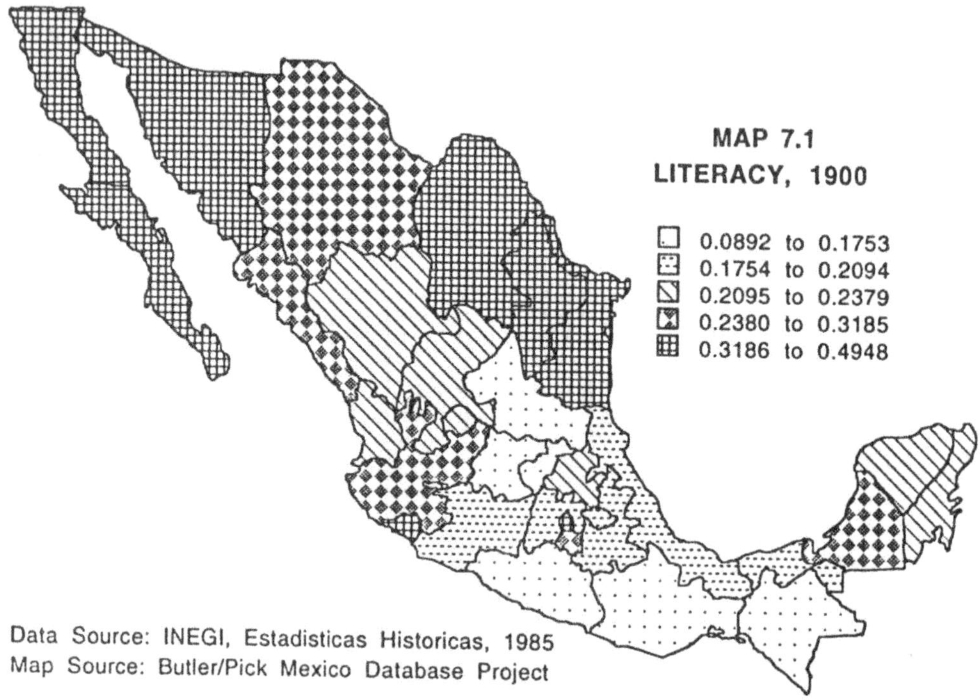
MAP 7.1
LITERACY, 1900
0.0892 to 0.1753
0.1754 to 0.2094
0.2095 to 0.2379
0.2380 to 0.3185
0.3186 to 0.4948
Data Source: INEGI, Estadisticas Historicas, 1985
Map Source: Butler/Pick Mexico Database Project

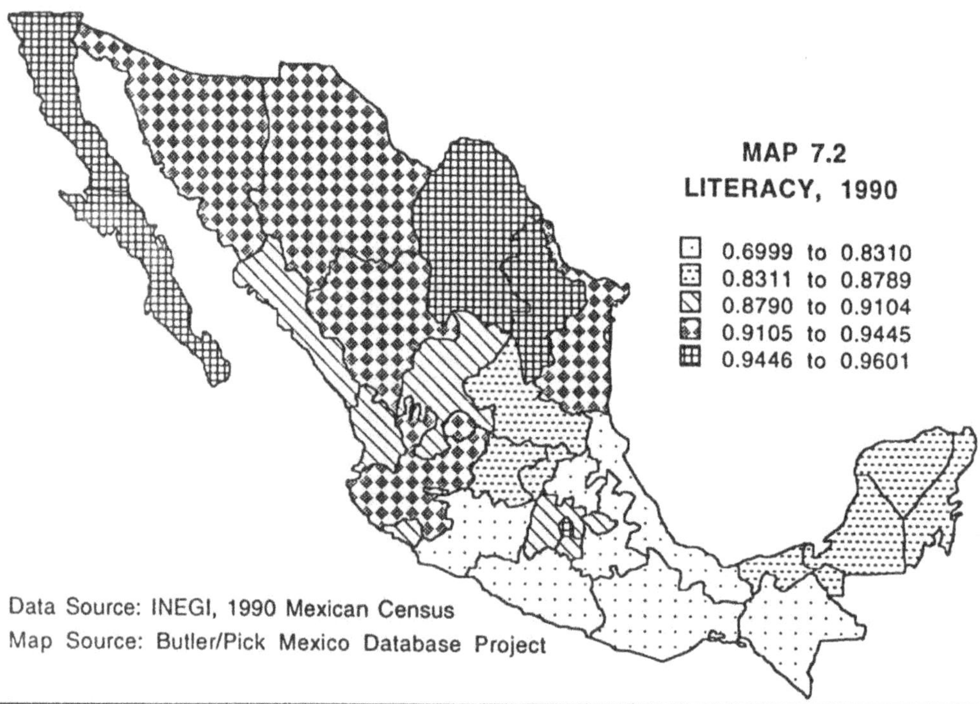
MAP 7.2
LITERACY, 1990
0.6999 to 0.8310
0.8311 to 0.8789
0.8790 to 0.9104
0.9105 to 0.9445
0.9446 to 0.9601
Data Source: INEGI, 1990 Mexican Census
Map Source: Butler/Pick Mexico Database Project

MAP 7.3

LITERACY CHANGE, 1950 - 1990

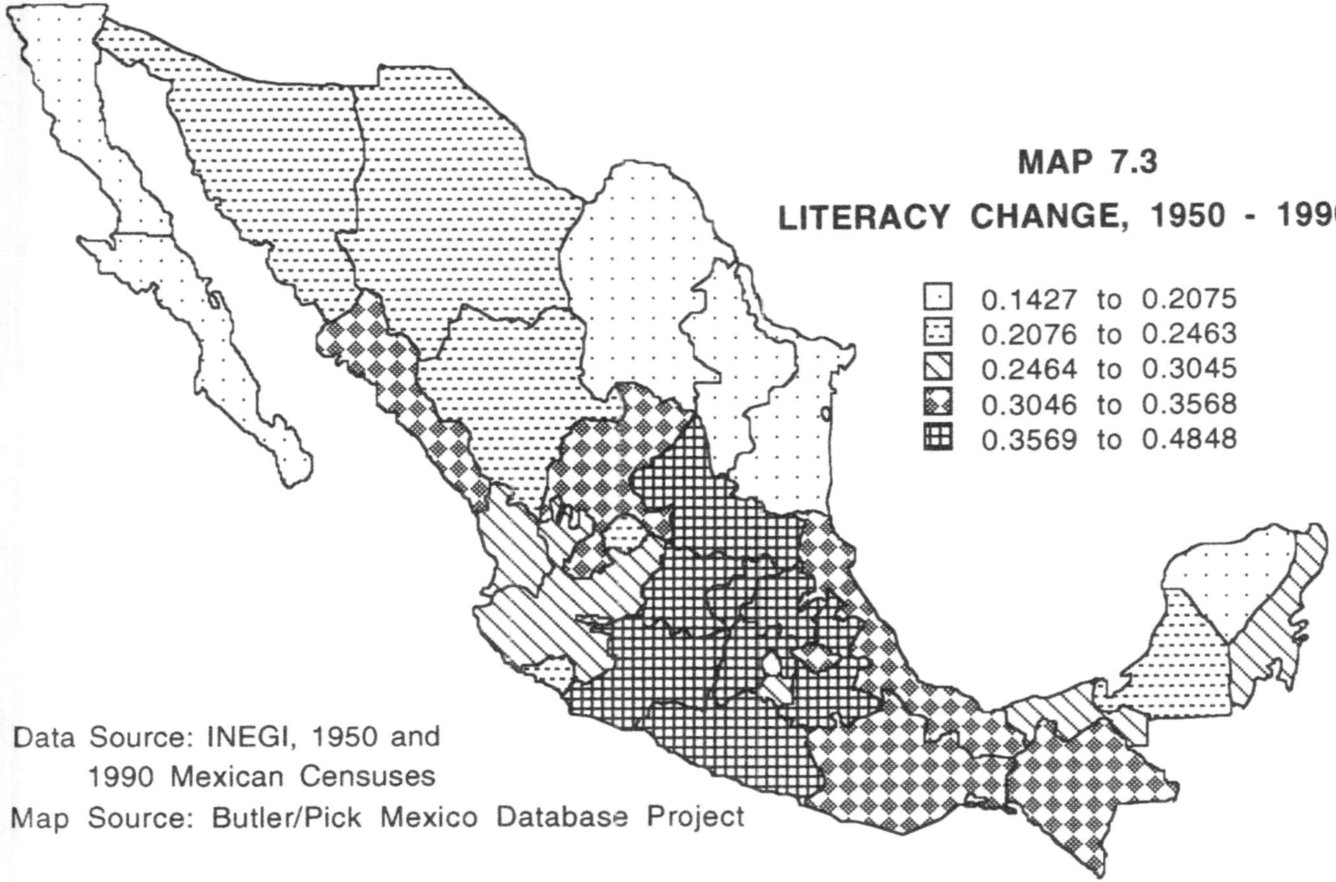

Data Source: INEGI, 1950 and
1990 Mexican Censuses
Map Source: Butler/Pick Mexico Database Project

Table 7.2 Literacy Change, 1950 - 1990

No.	State	Literacy Ratio 1950	Literacy Ratio 1990	Literacy Change 1950 - 1990
1	AGUASCALIENTES	0.6903	0.9295	0.2392
2	BAJA CALIFORNIA	0.8125	0.9534	0.1409
3	BAJA CALIFORNIA SUR	0.7732	0.9463	0.1731
4	CAMPECHE	0.6207	0.8464	0.2257
5	COAHUILA	0.7405	0.9453	0.2048
6	COLIMA	0.6673	0.9071	0.2398
7	CHIAPAS	0.3463	0.6999	0.3536
8	CHIHUAHUA	0.7285	0.9389	0.2104
9	DISTRITO FEDERAL	0.8174	0.9601	0.1427
10	DURANGO	0.6859	0.9302	0.2443
11	GUANAJUATO	0.4428	0.8348	0.3920
12	GUERRERO	0.3200	0.7318	0.4118
13	HIDALGO	0.4053	0.7935	0.3882
14	JALISCO	0.6118	0.9112	0.2994
15	MEXICO	0.4805	0.9099	0.4294
16	MICHOACAN	0.4571	0.8275	0.3704
17	MORELOS	0.5878	0.8805	0.2927
18	NAYARIT	0.6161	0.8870	0.2709
19	NUEVO LEON	0.7846	0.9535	0.1689
20	OAXACA	0.3705	0.7252	0.3547
21	PUEBLA	0.4490	0.8082	0.3592
22	QUERETARO	0.3619	0.8467	0.4848
23	QUINTANA ROO	0.6289	0.8774	0.2485
24	SAN LUIS POTOSI	0.4873	0.8508	0.3635
25	SINALOA	0.5819	0.9016	0.3197
26	SONORA	0.7278	0.9439	0.2161
27	TABASCO	0.5774	0.8736	0.2962
28	TAMAULIPAS	0.7423	0.9315	0.1892
29	TLAXCALA	0.5499	0.8888	0.3389
30	VERACRUZ	0.4892	0.8177	0.3285
31	YUCATAN	0.6409	0.8416	0.2007
32	ZACATECAS	0.5915	0.9013	0.3098
	National Total	0.5682	0.8739	0.3057
	Mean	0.5871	0.8748	0.2877
	Median	0.6017	0.8879	0.2945
	S.D.	0.1446	0.0691	0.0889
	C.V.	24.63	7.90	30.90
	Minimum	0.3200	0.6999	0.1409
	Maximum	0.8174	0.9601	0.4848

DEFINITION: The literacy ratios are the literate population to the total population.

SOURCE: 1950 and 1990 Mexican Census of Population, Resumen General.

Figure 7.1
Population Knowing Alphabet, Mexico, 1900-1990

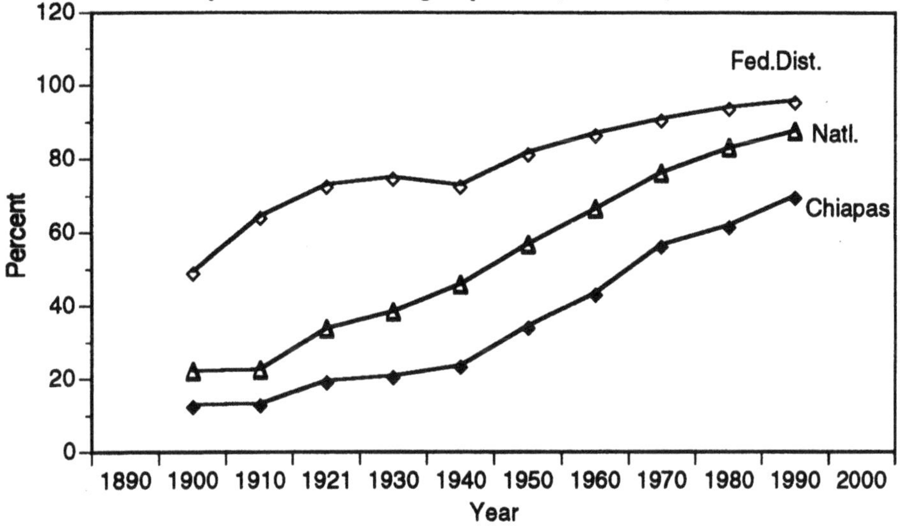

SOURCE: Estadisticas Historicas de Mexico, 1985, Table 2.3; 1990 Mexican Census.

Education

Secondary education attainment for the population age 12 and over in 1990 is reported in Table 7.3. In 1990, over 11 percent of the population age 12 and over had a secondary level education. Variation among states was relatively small. Baja California had the highest percentage (15.66%) and the Federal District (14.43%) and the state of Mexico (14.49%) had high rates. The lowest states were those very same ones that had low literacy rates—Chiapas, Guanajuato, Michoacan, Yucatan, Zacatecas, and Oaxaca. Map 7.4 shows that the border states had relatively high rates as did the Central Metropolitan Zone. The development of tourism in Quintana Roo undoubtedly influenced its higher rate of secondary education, versus its neighbors.

Table 7.3 also reports higher education for the population aged 16 years or older in 1990. Higher education made large strides in the 1980s; the statewide mean rose from 4.8 percent in 1980 to 7.7 percent in 1990. The Federal District had by far the highest rate of higher education (17.12%). Nuevo Leon, Baja California, Coahuila, Sinaloa, and Tamaulipas also had high rates. Again, as with other literacy and educational measures, the border states and the Central Metropolitan Zone outpace the rest of the county. As shown on Map 7.5, as with many other dimensions, the south lags the rest of the country.

Table 7.3 Secondary and Higher Education, 1990

No.	State	Secondary Education			Higher Education		
		With Secondary Education	Population Age 12+	Ratio	With Higher Education	Population Age 16+	Ratio
1	Aguascalientes	50,193	483,625	0.1038	32,803	407,945	0.0804
2	Baja California	183,297	1,170,617	0.1566	103,012	1,021,029	0.1009
3	Baja Sur	27,009	221,997	0.1217	16,467	190,758	0.0863
4	Campeche	29,637	357,088	0.0830	20,122	302,921	0.0664
5	Coahuila	162,826	1,397,353	0.1165	125,250	1,193,020	0.1050
6	Colima	32,818	296,144	0.1108	21,413	250,734	0.0854
7	Chiapas	122,280	2,037,245	0.0600	62,297	1,702,410	0.0366
8	Chihuahua	183,872	1,724,403	0.1066	122,780	1,491,897	0.0823
9	Distrito Federal	897,144	6,217,435	0.1443	943,194	5,509,469	0.1712
10	Durango	84,970	912,568	0.0931	49,321	760,095	0.0649
11	Guanajuato	233,373	2,628,298	0.0888	106,170	2,192,716	0.0484
12	Guerrero	155,353	1,694,344	0.0917	72,653	1,401,753	0.0518
13	Hidalgo	128,027	1,255,410	0.1020	54,535	1,051,977	0.0518
14	Jalisco	395,926	3,621,286	0.1093	266,106	3,073,840	0.0866
15	Mexico	983,903	6,790,192	0.1449	512,718	5,784,180	0.0886
16	Michoacan	199,879	2,352,414	0.0850	114,256	1,954,701	0.0585
17	Morelos	120,837	836,789	0.1444	60,808	711,775	0.0854
18	Nayarit	63,197	558,779	0.1131	34,503	466,979	0.0739
19	Nuevo Leon	345,935	2,256,645	0.1533	253,930	1,954,327	0.1299
20	Oaxaca	137,736	1,977,098	0.0697	59,980	1,653,268	0.0363
21	Puebla	257,875	2,751,729	0.0937	168,881	2,309,307	0.0731
22	Queretaro	72,011	692,601	0.1040	45,365	581,795	0.0780
23	Quintana Roo	39,281	323,021	0.1216	20,656	276,929	0.0746
24	San Luis Potosi	132,689	1,337,312	0.0992	78,213	1,123,332	0.0696
25	Sinaloa	146,204	1,527,508	0.0957	124,342	1,284,864	0.0968
26	Sonora	172,680	1,292,959	0.1336	100,154	1,111,986	0.0901
27	Tabasco	94,877	988,992	0.0959	53,716	828,843	0.0648
28	Tamaulipas	182,411	1,610,246	0.1133	136,283	1,390,081	0.0980
29	Tlaxcala	68,229	513,591	0.1328	28,085	431,338	0.0651
30	Veracruz	374,419	4,285,585	0.0874	229,282	3,657,579	0.0627
31	Yucatan	84,291	948,552	0.0889	51,711	810,876	0.0638
32	Zacatecas	66,326	852,021	0.0778	35,299	704,420	0.0501
National Total		6,229,505	55,913,847	0.1114	4,104,305	47,587,144	0.0862
Mean		194,672	1,747,308	0.1076	128,260	1,487,098	0.0774
Median		135,213	1,315,136	0.1039	67,475	1,117,659	0.0742
S.D.		217,842	1,572,289	0.0243	179,037	1,358,721	0.0266
C.V.		111.90	89.98	22.60	139.59	91.37	34.39
Minimum		27,009	221,997	0.0600	16,467	190,758	0.0363
Maximum		983,903	6,790,192	0.1566	943,194	5,784,180	0.1712

DEFINITION: Secondary Education Ratio is the population age 12+ with third level secondary education to total population age 12+. Higher Education Ratio is the population age 16+ with higher education ("con instruccion superior") to total population age 16+.

SOURCE: INEGI, 1990 Mexican Census of Population, Resumen General, Tables 16 and 17.

MAP 7.4
SECONDARY EDUCATION FOR POPULATION 12 YEARS OR OLDER, 1990

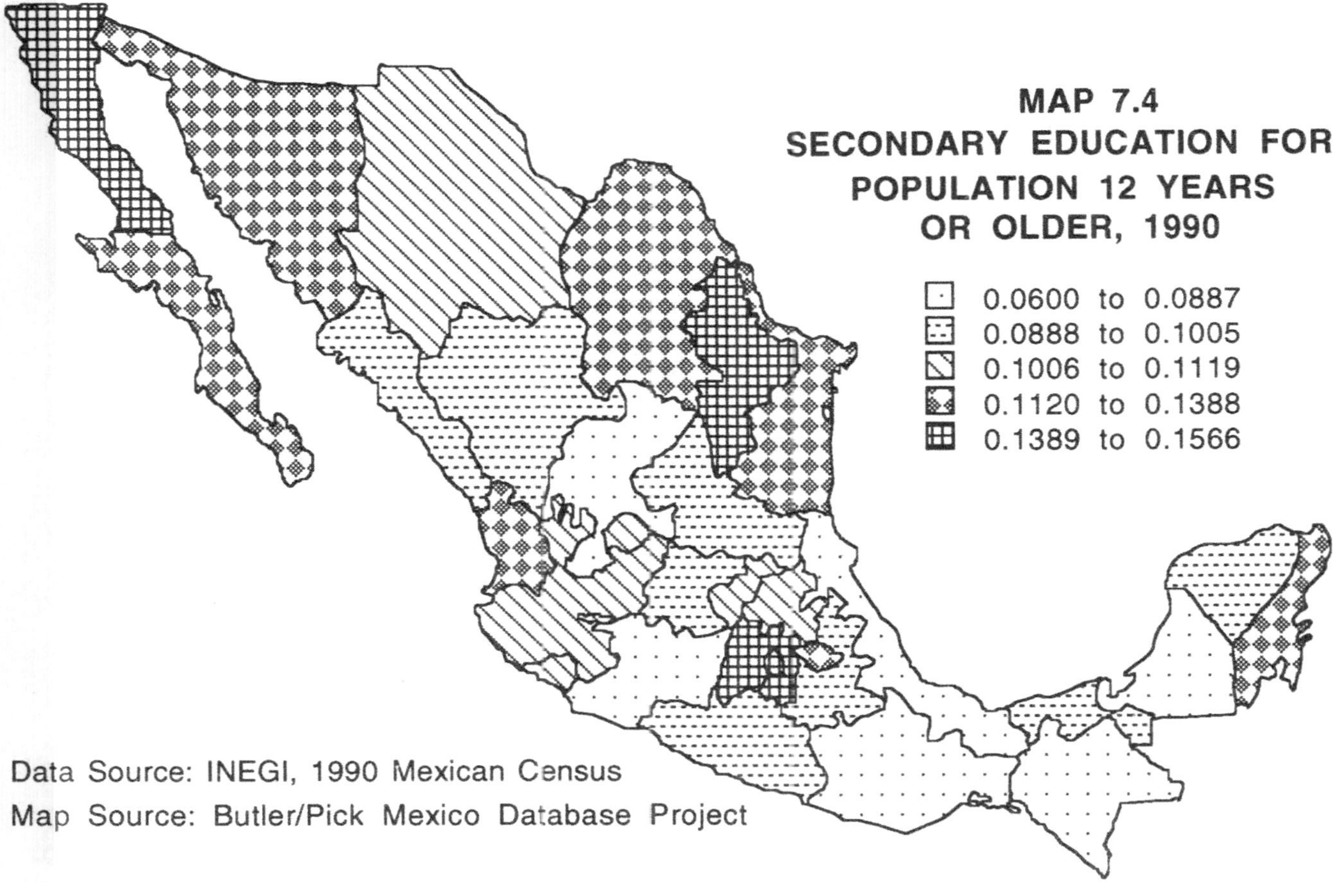

Data Source: INEGI, 1990 Mexican Census
Map Source: Butler/Pick Mexico Database Project

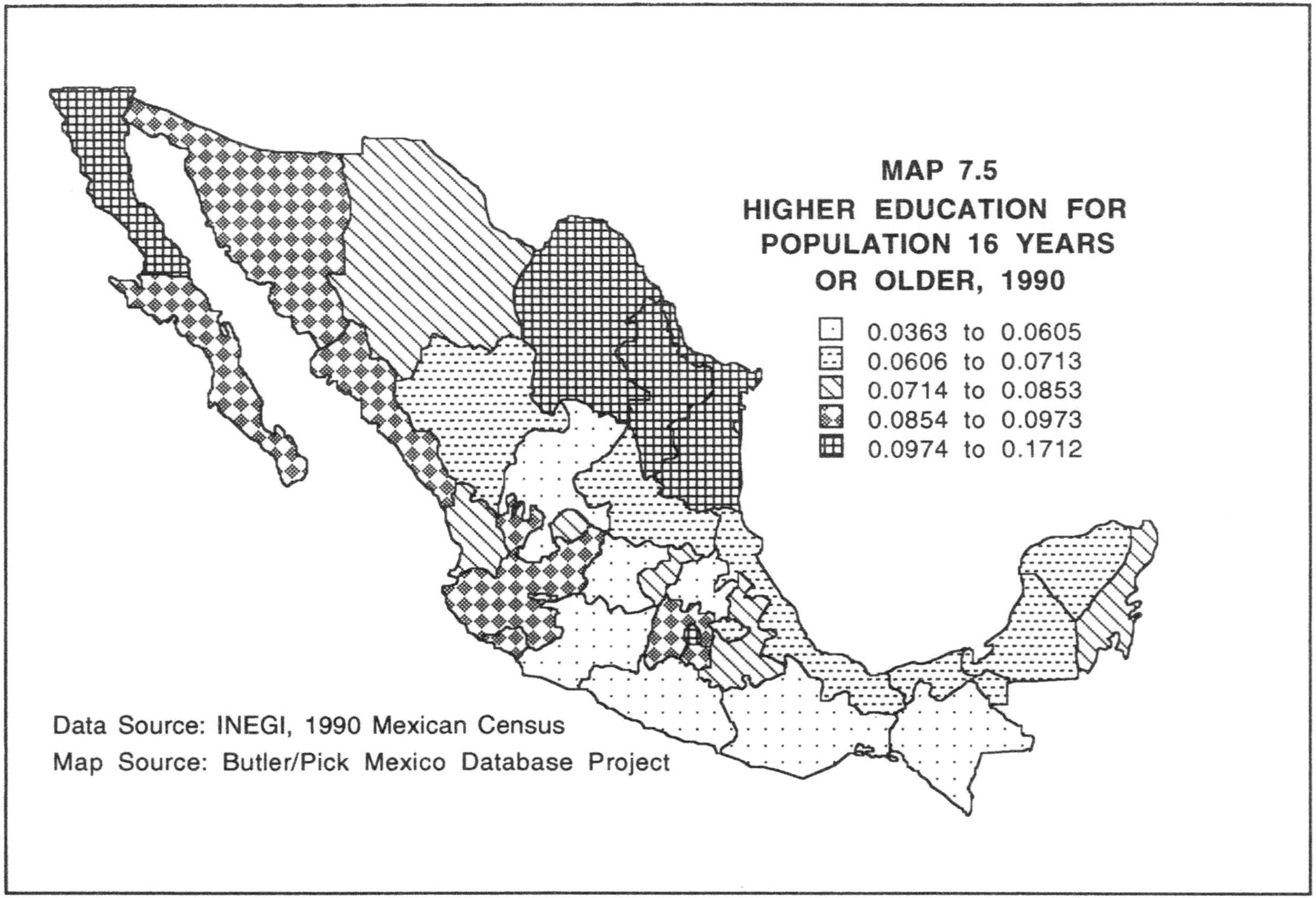

MAP 7.5
HIGHER EDUCATION FOR POPULATION 16 YEARS OR OLDER, 1990

Indigenous Language

The variety of indigenous languages spoken in Mexico varies by state and within states. The Mexican census of 1900 reported that 2,078,914 people, or 15.28 percent of the total population spoke an indigenous language (see Table 7.4). As shown on Map 7.6, in 1900 the major indigenous speaking states were located in the southern and southeastern regions of the country. The only major exception was the border state of Sonora. Aguascalientes, Colima, Nuevo Leon, and Tamaulipas reported no persons speaking a native language.

Figure 7.2 traces the population speaking a native language between 1900 and 1990. The definition varies slightly by census year but generally the population base is for persons 5 years of age and older. The highest percentage of indigenous speakers was in 1900. There was a slight decrease reported by the 1910 and 1921 censuses and then a decline through 1950. However, between 1950 and 1960 an increase took place continued in the 60s and 70s, dropping slightly in the 80s.

In 1990, the number of persons aged 5 years older speaking an indigenous language was over double the number that spoke a native language in 1900; however, the percentage of the population speaking an indigenous language declined from 15.28 percent in 1900 to 7.49 percent in 1990. In comparing the 1900 and 1990 maps, it is readily apparent that the states that had the highest percentage speaking an indigenous language in 1900 were virtually the same states in 1990 (see Map 7.7); the major exception being Sonora that declined in relative proportion of native speakers, although the absolute number had almost doubled (see Table 7.4).

In 1990, Oaxaca had over one million persons who spoke a native language. Chiapas had over 700,000 indigenous speakers and Veracruz and Yucatan over 500,000. On the other hand, Aguascalientes and Zacatecas together had under 1,482 indigenous language speakers. Other states with few native speakers were Baja California Sur, Coahuila, Colima, and Nuevo Leon.

Figure 7.2
Population Speaking Native Language
Mexico: 1900-1990

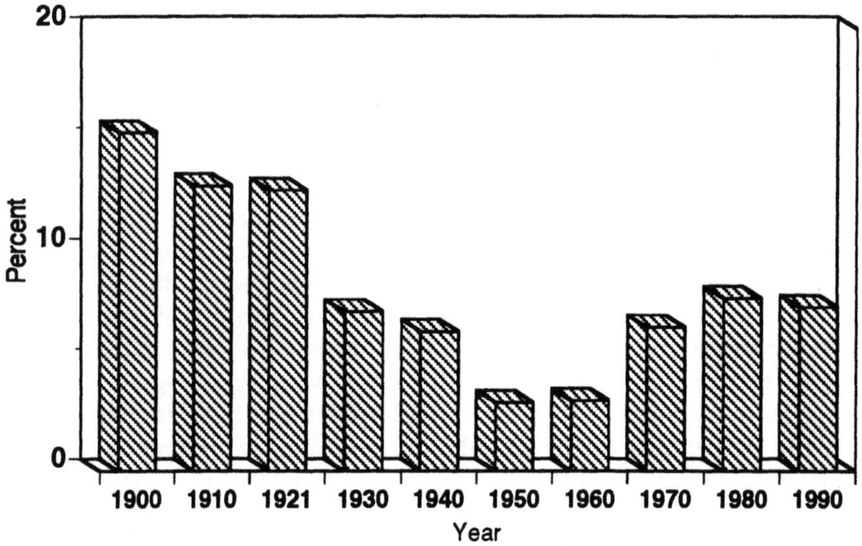

DEFINITION: Population 5 years of age and more who speak a native language.

SOURCE: Estadisticas Historicas de Mexico, 1985; Mexican Census of Population, 1990.

Table 7.4 Population Speaking Indigenous Language, 1900 and 1990

No.	State	Indigenous Speaking Population	Total Population 1900	Ratio	Indigenous Speaking Population	Population Age 5+ 1990	Ratio
1	AGUASCALIENTES	0	102,416	0.0000	599	619,401	0.0010
2	BAJA CALIFORNIA	1,111	47,624	0.0233	18,177	1,425,801	0.0127
3	BAJA CALIFORNIA SUR				2,749	275,985	0.0100
4	CAMPECHE	35,977	86,542	0.4157	86,676	456,452	0.1899
5	COAHUILA	55	296,938	0.0002	3,821	1,730,829	0.0022
6	COLIMA	0	65,115	0.0000	1,481	371,876	0.0040
7	CHIAPAS	129,843	360,799	0.3599	716,012	2,710,283	0.2642
8	CHIHUAHUA	22,025	327,784	0.0672	61,504	2,118,557	0.0290
9	DISTRITO FEDERAL	9,494	541,516	0.0175	111,552	7,373,239	0.0151
10	DURANGO	3,847	370,294	0.0104	18,125	1,169,332	0.0155
11	GUANAJUATO	12,188	1,061,724	0.0115	8,966	3,396,283	0.0026
12	GUERRERO	117,735	479,205	0.2457	298,532	2,228,077	0.1340
13	HIDALGO	177,806	605,051	0.2939	317,838	1,628,542	0.1952
14	JALISCO	3,918	1,153,891	0.0034	24,914	4,584,728	0.0054
15	MEXICO	121,288	934,463	0.1298	312,595	8,563,538	0.0365
16	MICHOACAN	50,063	935,808	0.0535	105,578	3,037,340	0.0348
17	MORELOS	26,983	160,115	0.1685	19,940	1,048,065	0.0190
18	NAYARIT	4,166	150,098	0.0278	24,157	711,691	0.0339
19	NUEVO LEON	0	327,937	0.0000	4,852	2,750,624	0.0018
20	OAXACA	495,698	948,633	0.5225	1,018,106	2,602,479	0.3912
21	PUEBLA	325,124	1,021,133	0.3184	503,277	3,565,924	0.1411
22	QUERETARO	24,213	232,389	0.1042	20,392	898,199	0.0227
23	QUINTANA ROO				133,081	412,868	0.3223
24	SAN LUIS POTOSI	31,937	575,432	0.0555	204,328	1,723,605	0.1185
25	SINALOA	7,823	296,701	0.0264	31,390	1,923,515	0.0163
26	SONORA	25,894	221,682	0.1168	47,913	1,596,063	0.0300
27	TABASCO	14,292	159,834	0.0894	47,967	1,288,222	0.0372
28	TAMAULIPAS	0	218,948	0.0000	8,509	1,974,755	0.0043
29	TLAXCALA	26,774	172,315	0.1554	22,783	662,426	0.0344
30	VERACRUZ	196,466	981,030	0.2003	580,386	5,424,172	0.1070
31	YUCATAN	213,936	309,652	0.6909	525,264	1,188,433	0.4420
32	ZACATECAS	258	462,190	0.0006	883	1,100,898	0.0008
	National Total	2,078,914	13,607,259	0.1528	5,282,347	70,562,202	0.0749
	Mean	69,297	453,575	0.1370	165,073	2,205,069	0.0836
	Median	23,119	327,861	0.0614	39,652	1,676,074	0.0295
	S.D.	114,068	342,800	0.1755	249,804	1,946,345	0.1199
	C.V.	164.61	75.58	128.14	151.33	88.27	143.49
	Minimum	0	47,624	0.0000	599	275,985	0.0008
	Maximum	495,698	1,153,891	0.6909	1,018,106	8,563,538	0.4420

NOTE: For 1900, data for Baja Sur are included with Baja California and data for Quintana Roo are included with Yucatan.

DEFINITION: 1990 Ratio of population age 5+ speaking an indigenous language to population 5+. Those not specifying age are excluded, those speaking an indigenous language include those that do and those that do not speak Spanish also.

DEFINITION: 1900 Ratio of Population speaking an indigenous language to total population. The 1900 Census does not specify whether these people also speak Spanish. Therefore, this numerator may include those exclusively speaking an indigenous language or it may include all indigenous speakers regardless of proficiency in Spanish, as the 1990 variable does. No determination can be made from the data source.

SOURCE: SPP, 1900 Mexican Census of Population; INEGI, 1990 Mexican Census of Population, Table 6.

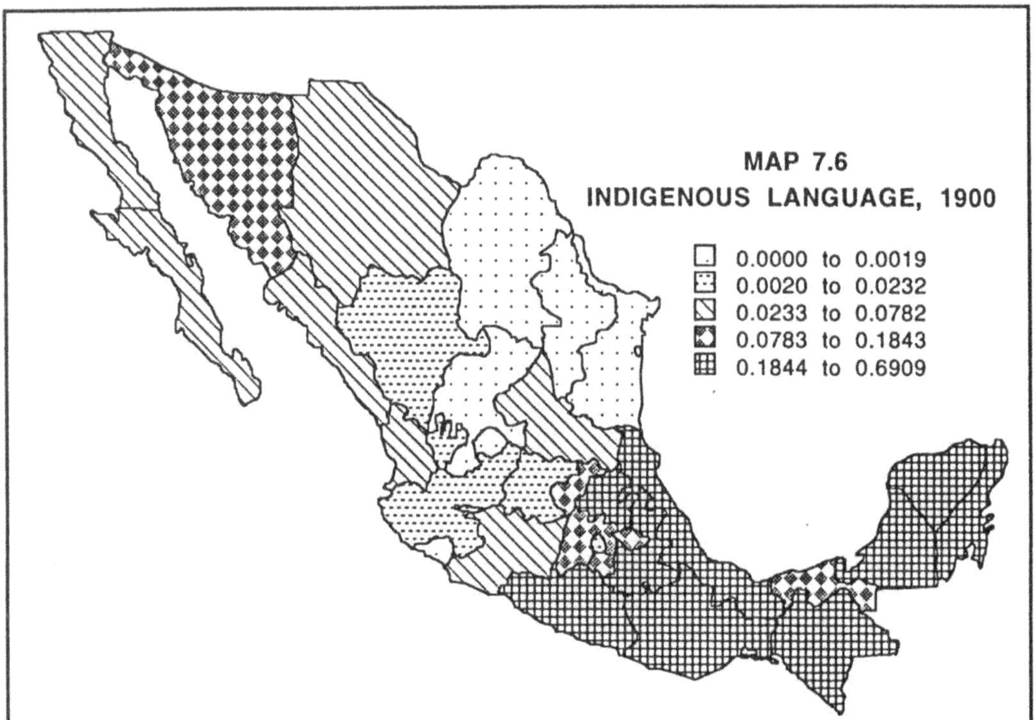
MAP 7.6
INDIGENOUS LANGUAGE, 1900
0.0000 to 0.0019
0.0020 to 0.0232
0.0233 to 0.0782
0.0783 to 0.1843
0.1844 to 0.6909

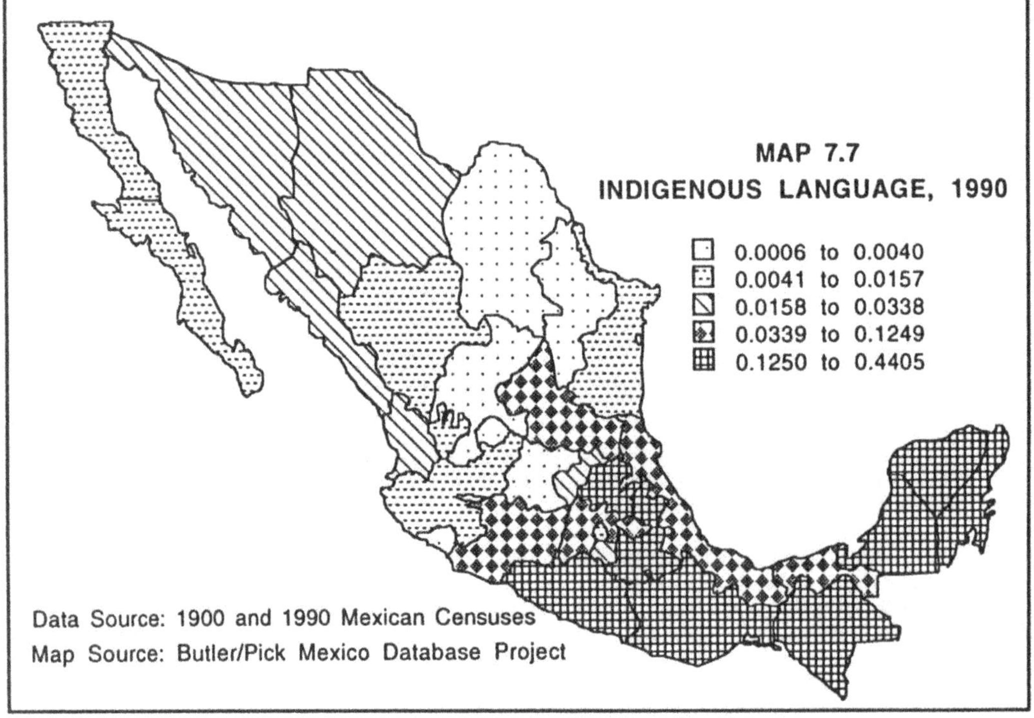
MAP 7.7
INDIGENOUS LANGUAGE, 1990
0.0006 to 0.0040
0.0041 to 0.0157
0.0158 to 0.0338
0.0339 to 0.1249
0.1250 to 0.4405
Data Source: 1900 and 1990 Mexican Censuses
Map Source: Butler/Pick Mexico Database Project

Religious Affiliation

Table 7.5 presents information on religion in Mexico. All data are based upon the population 5 years of age and older. The Non-Catholic column includes those persons *specifying* a religion other than being Catholic; this includes those who are Protestant or evangelical, Jewish, or another specified religion. The column designated No Religion consists of those replying that they had no religion. In addition, the census also reports a category of persons who did respond to this question; these persons are excluded from Table 7.5 and Map 7.8.

In 1990, 6.4 percent of the population specified that they had a Non-Catholic religion and 3.2 percent reported that they did not have a religion. In general, the male and female distribution was about equal. Map 7.8 shows the ratio of Non-Catholics by state. In contrast to many other dimensions in Mexico, the southern and border regions are similar in that they have the highest ratios of Non-Catholics. States with the highest ratios of Non-Catholics are Chiapas, Tabasco, Campeche, and Quintana Roo. States with the lowest proportions of Non-Catholics are Aguascalientes, Colima, Guanajuato, Jalisco, Michoacan, Queretaro, and Zacatecas. Thus, the west, southern north, and southern northwest regions have a lower proportion of Non-Catholics than the remainder of the country.

Table 7.4 shows the No Religion population as reported by the 1990 Mexican census. The three states with the highest proportion of No Religion persons of Campeche, Chiapas, and Tabasco also are states with high proportions of Non-Catholic religion adherents. In addition, Sinaloa had a high ratio of No Religion persons.

Table 7.5 Population Having Non-Catholic Religion, 1990

No.	State	Population Age 5+	Non-Catholic Pop.	Non-Catholic Ratio	No Relig. Pop.	No Relig. Ratio
1	AGUASCALIENTES	619,401	10,159	0.0164	4,831	0.0078
2	BAJA CALIFORNIA	1,425,801	122,174	0.0857	64,343	0.0451
3	BAJA CALIFORNIA SUR	275,985	11,877	0.0430	7,183	0.0260
4	CAMPECHE	456,452	72,176	0.1581	32,573	0.0714
5	COAHUILA	1,730,829	139,308	0.0805	53,379	0.0308
6	COLIMA	371,876	11,613	0.0312	4,957	0.0133
7	CHIAPAS	2,710,283	493,175	0.1820	344,896	0.1273
8	CHIHUAHUA	2,118,557	176,263	0.0832	83,293	0.0393
9	DISTRITO FEDERAL	7,373,239	371,715	0.0504	160,363	0.0217
10	DURANGO	1,169,332	57,775	0.0494	30,136	0.0258
11	GUANAJUATO	3,396,283	53,613	0.0158	34,518	0.0102
12	GUERRERO	2,228,077	121,624	0.0546	76,914	0.0345
13	HIDALGO	1,628,542	94,102	0.0578	27,354	0.0168
14	JALISCO	4,584,728	100,589	0.0219	37,097	0.0081
15	MEXICO	8,563,538	449,036	0.0524	123,992	0.0145
16	MICHOACAN	3,037,340	73,945	0.0243	57,893	0.0191
17	MORELOS	1,048,065	101,888	0.0972	35,148	0.0335
18	NAYARIT	711,691	24,951	0.0351	16,586	0.0233
19	NUEVO LEON	2,750,624	212,536	0.0773	61,158	0.0222
20	OAXACA	2,602,479	212,422	0.0816	104,467	0.0401
21	PUEBLA	3,565,924	191,783	0.0538	56,509	0.0158
22	QUERETARO	898,199	18,087	0.0201	7,842	0.0087
23	QUINTANA ROO	412,868	60,958	0.1476	26,468	0.0641
24	SAN LUIS POTOSI	1,723,605	87,443	0.0507	32,300	0.0187
25	SINALOA	1,923,515	77,562	0.0403	155,679	0.0809
26	SONORA	1,596,063	86,824	0.0544	58,506	0.0367
27	TABASCO	1,288,222	222,283	0.1726	124,162	0.0964
28	TAMAULIPAS	1,974,755	193,250	0.0979	72,881	0.0369
29	TLAXCALA	662,426	29,365	0.0443	6,424	0.0097
30	VERACRUZ	5,424,172	494,773	0.0912	336,080	0.0620
31	YUCATAN	1,188,433	125,771	0.1058	36,146	0.0304
32	ZACATECAS	1,100,898	27,711	0.0252	14,156	0.0129
	National Total	70,562,202	4,526,751	0.0642	2,288,234	0.0324
	Mean	2,205,069	141,461	0.0688	71,507	0.0345
	Median	1,676,074	97,346	0.0541	45,238	0.0259
	S.D.	1,946,345	135,769	0.0450	82,118	0.0279
	C.V.	88.27	95.98	65.43	114.84	80.84
	Minimum	275,985	10,159	0.0158	4,831	0.0078
	Maximum	8,563,538	494,773	0.1820	344,896	0.1273

DEFINITION: Non-Catholic Ratio is the population specifying a non-Catholic religion to the total population age 5+. No Religion Ratio is the population specifying no religion ("no tiene religion") to the total population age 5+. These figures exclude an additional category of persons who did not specify a religious preference.

SOURCE: INEGI, 1990 Annuario Estadistico, Table 3.1.4.

MAP 7.8
POPULATION HAVING
NON-CATHOLIC RELIGION, 1990

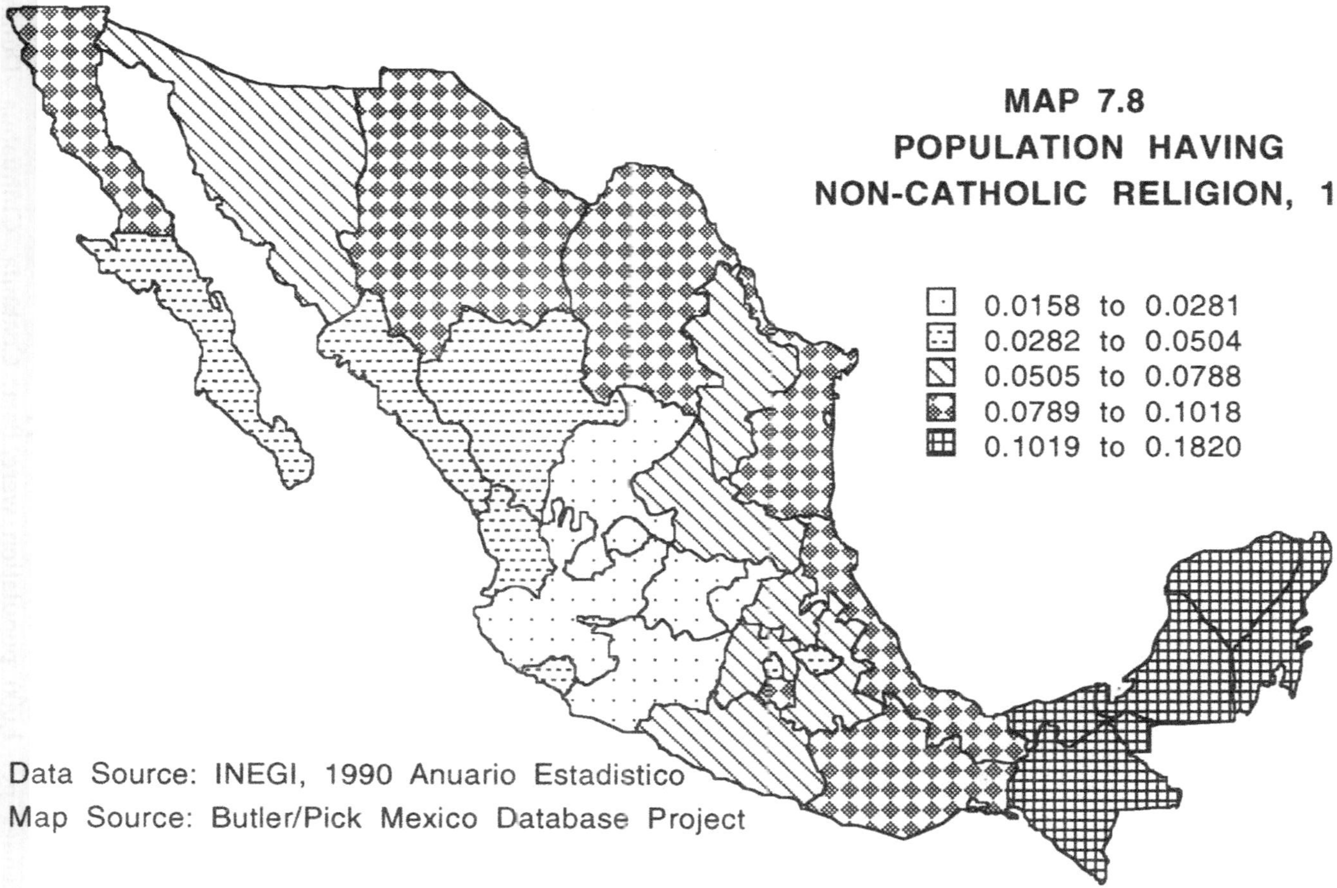

Data Source: INEGI, 1990 Anuario Estadistico
Map Source: Butler/Pick Mexico Database Project

Consumption of Goods and Services

Sugar sales in tons per capita are reported in Table 7.6 and shown on Map 7.9. Sugar sales are highly variable and apparently have no regional consistency. The highest ratios reported for 1989 were in the states of Aguascalientes, Colima, the Federal District, Hidalgo, and Nayarit—a disparate listing of states. A number of states had low ratios with the state of Mexico having the lowest. The only regional variation appeared to be that all of the border states had medium or higher ratios and the south generally had lower ratios, except for Yucatan, Campeche, and Tabasco.

Information on the national service sector for 1985 on Number of Establishments, Number of Employees, Gross Revenues, Gross Expenses, and Fixed Assets are shown in Table 7.7. The average number of employees per establishment in 1985 was 4.11; however, there was great variation among service subsectors. For example, the average number of employees for private entertainment services was the lowest among sectors at 2.48.

On the other hand, private education services had a high rate of employees of 14.39 per establishment and hotels and temporary lodging had an average number of employees of 14.24 per establishment. Figure 7.3 reports the gross revenues and gross expenses by various service sector categories. Gross revenues were greater in every category except for Hotels that had greater expenses than revenues. Figure 7.4 reports on the number of establishments and employees across service subsectors.

Industrial machinery and equipment rental services for 1985 are shown in Table 7.8; the table lists the number of establishments, number of employees, gross revenues and gross revenues per 1,000 population as defined by the average of the 1980 and 1990 population. States with highest gross revenues per 1,000 population in 1985 were the Federal District, Tamaulipas, Mexico, and Nuevo Leon.

Map 7.10 illustrates the variation in industrial and machinery equipment rental services for 1985. There was substantial variation in 1985 with gross revenues by state ranging from virtually no revenues to substantial revenues in the Federal District, the state of Mexico, Nuevo Leon, and Tamaulipas, the most industrialized states in Mexico. The south either reported no data or had low gross revenues while all of the border states reported medium—Sonora, Chihuahua, Coahuila—or the highest gross revenues—Baja California, Nuevo Leon, Tamaulipas.

The number of establishments, number of employees, and gross Revenues per 1,000 population for Accounting and Information Systems Services in 1985 is reported in Table 7.9. As shown in Figure 7.5, five states contained almost two-thirds of the number of accounting and information system services employees—the Federal District, Nuevo Leon, Jalisco, Coahuila, and Chihuahua. However, Table 7.9 shows clearly that the Federal District and Nuevo Leon dominated the gross revenues per 1,000 population derived from accounting and information system services. The heavy concentration of corporate headquarters, assets, and operations in these two states (see Chapter 8) contributes to the need for accounting and information systems services and support. Other states with relatively high revenues per 1,000 population were Baja, Coahuila, Chihuahua, Durango, Morelos, Quintana Roo, and Sinaloa. Thus all border states had high gross revenues except Tamaulipas. The lowest revenue states were Hidalgo, Michoacan, Oaxaca, and Zacatacas (see Map 7.11).

Table 7.10 reports for Business Consulting Services the number of Establishments, number of Employees, and Gross Revenues Per 1,000 Population. Gross Revenues shown are in millions of pesos for the economic census categories of 84,003 and 840,004.

Figure 7.6 illustrates that almost two-thirds of business consulting employees in 1985 were in the Federal District, with Sonora, Guanajuato, and Nuevo Leon having about as many business consulting employees as all of the remaining states. Table 7.10 indicates that Gross Revenues for business consulting services in 1985 had a somewhat different distribution with the Federal District dwarfing all of the other states including Sonora and Nuevo Leon, who, in turn, have substantially larger gross revenues per 1,000 population that all other the other states. Again, the corporate concentration in the Federal District and Nuevo Leon implies leading markets for business consultants.

Table 7.6 Sugar Sales, 1988-1989

No.	State	Sugar Sales 1988	Sugar Sales 1989	Total Population 1990	Ratio
1	AGUASCALIENTES	38,816	40,246	719,659	0.0549
2	BAJA CALIFORNIA	66,128	59,684	1,660,855	0.0379
3	BAJA CALIFORNIA SUR	ND	11,593	317,764	ND
4	CAMPECHE	22,925	25,151	535,185	0.0449
5	COAHUILA	87,944	93,644	1,972,340	0.0460
6	COLIMA	22,315	23,083	428,510	0.0530
7	CHIAPAS	90,122	94,939	3,210,496	0.0288
8	CHIHUAHUA	96,312	95,665	2,441,873	0.0393
9	DISTRITO FEDERAL	877,478	821,445	8,235,744	0.1031
10	DURANGO	30,902	29,914	1,349,378	0.0225
11	GUANAJUATO	142,684	148,368	3,982,593	0.0365
12	GUERRERO	70,965	72,821	2,620,637	0.0274
13	HIDALGO	48,277	48,148	1,888,366	0.0255
14	JALISCO	314,777	337,066	5,302,689	0.0615
15	MEXICO	109,042	134,952	9,815,795	0.0124
16	MICHOACAN	133,060	138,801	3,548,199	0.0383
17	MORELOS	77,737	85,316	1,195,059	0.0682
18	NAYARIT	26,522	27,039	824,643	0.0325
19	NUEVO LEON	164,825	165,047	3,098,736	0.0532
20	OAXACA	83,939	87,347	3,019,560	0.0284
21	PUEBLA	144,637	159,886	4,126,101	0.0369
22	QUERETARO	61,426	66,223	1,051,235	0.0607
23	QUINTANA ROO	14,012	14,787	493,277	0.0292
24	SAN LUIS POTOSI	77,461	91,437	2,003,187	0.0422
25	SINALOA	75,928	83,457	2,204,054	0.0362
26	SONORA	79,349	76,985	1,823,606	0.0429
27	TABASCO	70,499	68,390	1,501,744	0.0462
28	TAMAULIPAS	91,843	100,376	2,249,581	0.0427
29	TLAXCALA	52,793	49,681	761,277	0.0673
30	VERACRUZ	243,669	257,204	6,228,239	0.0402
31	YUCATAN	60,405	63,725	1,362,940	0.0455
32	ZACATECAS	33,980	36,352	1,276,323	0.0276
	National Total	3,510,772	3,608,772	81,249,645	0.0247
	Mean	113,251	112,774	2,539,051	0.0430
	Median	77,461	80,221	1,930,353	0.0402
	S.D.	155,568	146,562	2,216,375	0.0173
	C.V.	137.37	129.96	87.29	40.14
	Minimum	14,012	11,593	317,764	0.0124
	Maximum	877,478	821,445	9,815,795	0.1031

DEFINITION: Sugar Sales figures are shown in tons per capita.

NOTE: ND = no data.

SOURCE: INEGI, 1990 Anuario Estadistico, Table 4.3.7.

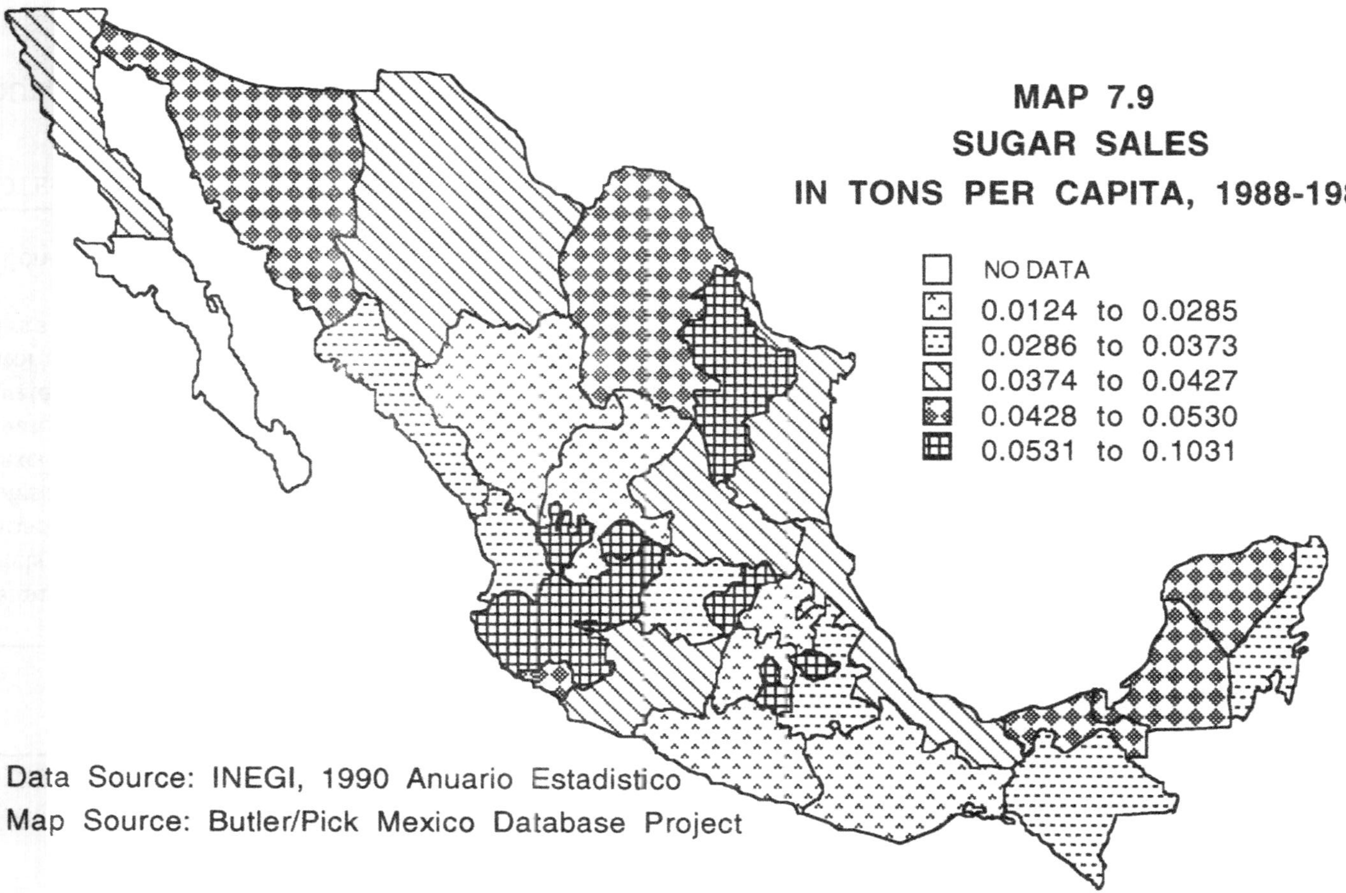

MAP 7.9
SUGAR SALES
IN TONS PER CAPITA, 1988-1989

Data Source: INEGI, 1990 Anuario Estadistico
Map Source: Butler/Pick Mexico Database Project

Table 7.7 National Service Sector, 1985

Service Subsector	Number of Establishments	Number of Employees	Gross Revenues*	Gross Expenses*	Fixed Assets*
Restaurants, bars, and nightclubs	110,214	347,091	643,519	557,390	187,015
Hotels and temporary lodging	8,050	114,691	323,198	368,066	486,561
Transport services	4,026	48,842	237,430	213,818	451,058
Professional and technical services, except agriculture and forestry	21,895	199,944	743,638	686,014	420,630
Private education services	8,450	121,619	171,111	144,561	140,909
Private entertainment services **	38,755	96,416	156,496	114,515	152,011
Automobile repair and maintenance	57,072	152,058	216,728	177,859	103,008
Others	102,321	359,898	1,347,170	1,137,473	1,163,430
National Total	350,783	1,440,559	3,839,290	3,399,696	3,104,622

NOTE: * in millions of pesos.
** includes cinema, theatre, radio/TV, writers, composers, and artists.

SOURCE: INEGI, 1986 Censo de Servicios.

Figure 7.3
National Service Sector, 1985
(in millions)

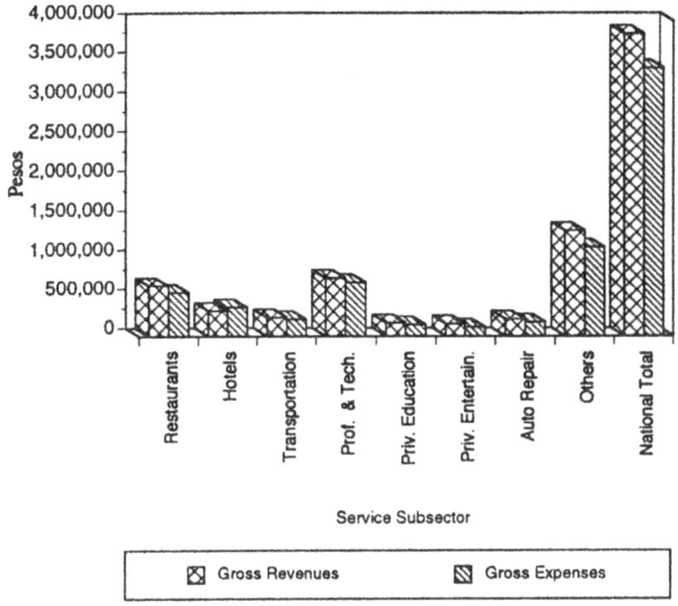

Figure 7.4
National Service Sector, 1985

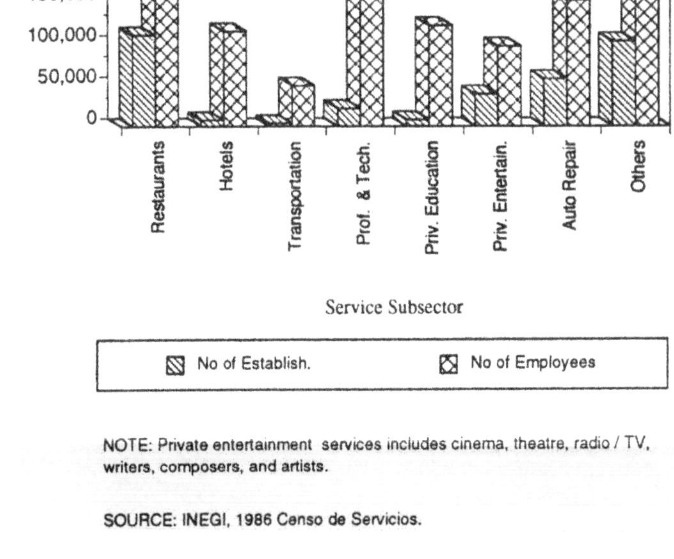

NOTE: Private entertainment services includes cinema, theatre, radio / TV, writers, composers, and artists.

SOURCE: INEGI, 1986 Censo de Servicios.

Table 7.8 Industrial Machinery and Equipment Rental Services, 1985

No.	State	Number of Establishments	Number of Employees	Gross Revenues	Gross Revenues Per 1000 Population
1	AGUASCALIENTES	4	15	24	0.0387
2	BAJA CALIFORNIA	13	103	750	0.5284
3	BAJA CALIFORNIA SUR	ND	ND	ND	ND
4	CAMPECHE	ND	ND	ND	ND
5	COAHUILA	6	168	488	0.2765
6	COLIMA	ND	ND	ND	ND
7	CHIAPAS	ND	ND	ND	ND
8	CHIHUAHUA	6	82	354	0.1592
9	DISTRITO FEDERAL	89	1,096	11,793	1.3820
10	DURANGO	ND	ND	ND	ND
11	GUANAJUATO	8	228	440	0.1259
12	GUERRERO	5	53	208	0.0879
13	HIDALGO	ND	ND	ND	ND
14	JALISCO	21	216	1,364	0.2820
15	MEXICO	39	888	7,202	0.8288
16	MICHOACAN	3	10	21	0.0065
17	MORELOS	5	17	68	0.0635
18	NAYARIT	ND	ND	ND	ND
19	NUEVO LEON	46	471	2,068	0.7370
20	OAXACA	ND	ND	ND	ND
21	PUEBLA	17	122	647	0.1731
22	QUERETARO	4	62	392	0.4378
23	QUINTANA ROO	ND	ND	ND	ND
24	SAN LUIS POTOSI	7	44	57	0.0310
25	SINALOA	7	62	67	0.0331
26	SONORA	8	89	334	0.2002
27	TABASCO	ND	ND	ND	ND
28	TAMAULIPAS	12	101	1,970	0.9439
29	TLAXCALA	ND	ND	ND	ND
30	VERACRUZ	11	220	1,981	0.3411
31	YUCATAN	6	28	60	0.0495
32	ZACATECAS	ND	ND	ND	ND
	National Total	317	4,075	30,288	
	Mean	16	204	1,514	0.3363
	Median	8	95	416	0.1867
	S.D.	21	292	2,910	0.3728
	C.V.	130.45	143.35	192.15	110.86
	Minimum	3	10	21	0.0065
	Maximum	89	1,096	11,793	1.3820

DEFINITION: Gross revenues per 1000 population is the ratio of gross revenues to the average of 1980 and 1990 total population multiplied by 1000.

NOTE: ND = no data.

SOURCE: INEGI, IX Censo de Servicios, 1986, Table 16.

MAP 7.10
INDUSTRIAL MACHINERY AND EQUIPMENT RENTAL SERVICES
1985

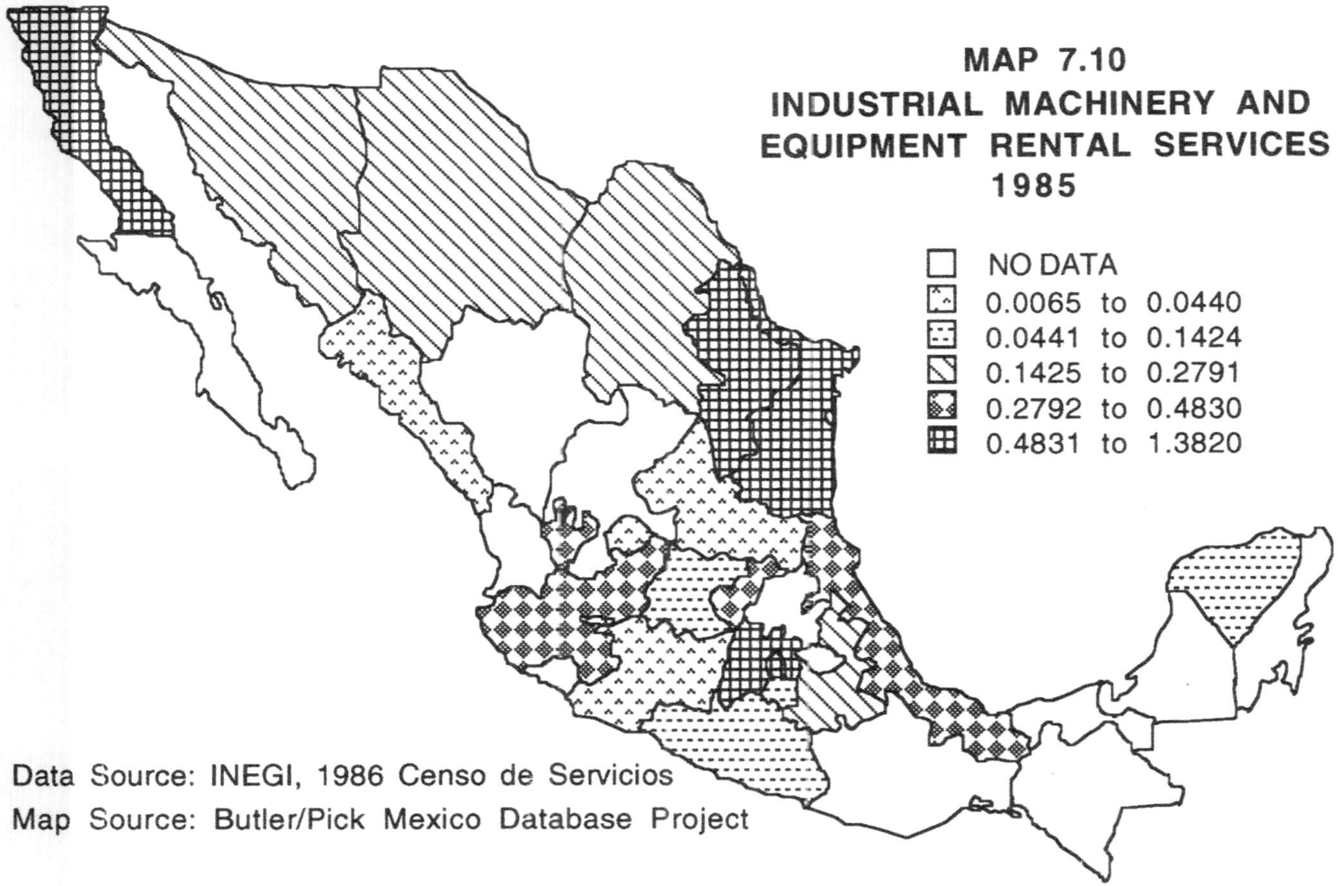

Data Source: INEGI, 1986 Censo de Servicios
Map Source: Butler/Pick Mexico Database Project

Table 7.9 Accounting and Information Systems Services, 1985

No.	State	Number of Establishments	Number of Employees	Gross Revenues Per 1000 Population
1	AGUASCALIENTES	56	388	0.8712
2	BAJA CALIFORNIA	253	1,439	2.6775
3	BAJA CALIFORNIA SUR	35	141	0.8780
4	CAMPECHE	33	119	0.1981
5	COAHUILA	199	2,509	1.6706
6	COLIMA	19	70	0.1634
7	CHIAPAS	76	352	0.1012
8	CHIHUAHUA	160	4,943	1.7822
9	DISTRITO FEDERAL	1,002	12,064	4.6550
10	DURANGO	32	1,174	1.8475
11	GUANAJUATO	204	881	0.2970
12	GUERRERO	63	252	0.1110
13	HIDALGO	33	103	0.0450
14	JALISCO	333	1,939	2.7467
15	MEXICO	146	835	0.1930
16	MICHOACAN	127	369	0.0885
17	MORELOS	71	363	1.0912
18	NAYARIT	22	130	0.5978
19	NUEVO LEON	288	3,175	5.2166
20	OAXACA	52	210	0.0669
21	PUEBLA	181	1,318	0.7797
22	QUERETARO	57	217	0.3777
23	QUINTANA ROO	30	227	1.1069
24	SAN LUIS POTOSI	100	329	0.1992
25	SINALOA	143	923	1.2155
26	SONORA	167	917	0.6558
27	TABASCO	36	121	0.1512
28	TAMAULIPAS	168	905	0.5934
29	TLAXCALA	10	46	0.9287
30	VERACRUZ	262	1,451	0.2262
31	YUCATAN	112	714	0.7946
32	ZACATECAS	21	78	0.0556
	National Total	4,491	38,702	
	Mean	140	1,209	1.0120
	Median	88	379	0.6268
	S.D.	180	2,244	1.2618
	C.V.	128.50	185.50	124.69
	Minimum	10	46	0.0450
	Maximum	1,002	12,064	5.2166

DEFINITION: Gross revenues, shown in millions of pesos, are for economic census categories 840003 and 840004.

SOURCE: IX Censo de Servicios de 1986, INEGI, 1991, Vol.1, Tables 9 and 16.

Figure 7.5
Accounting and Information Systems Services
Number of Employees, 1985

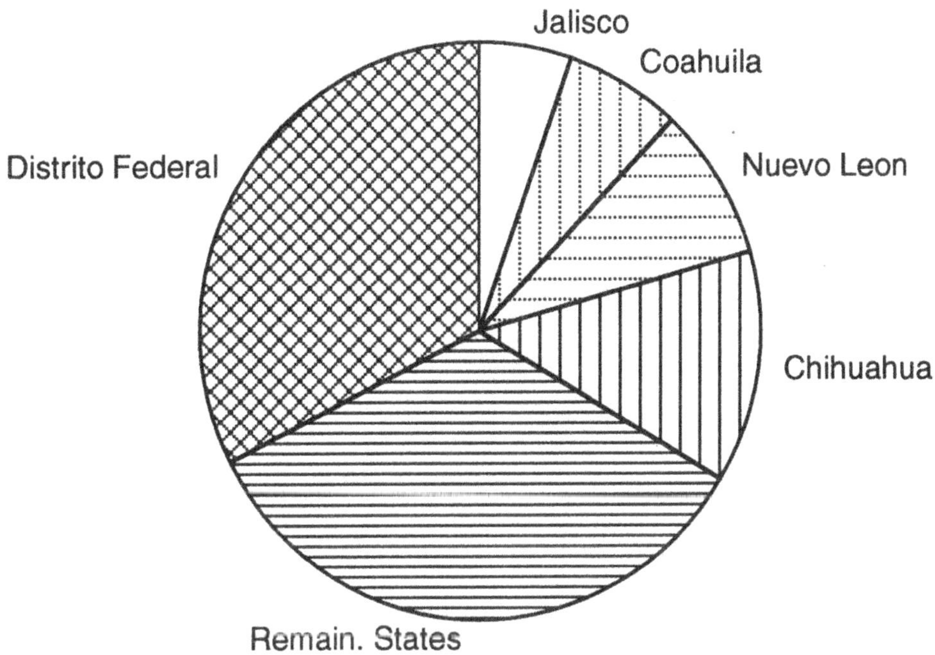

Data Source: IX Censo de Servicios de 1986, INEGI, 1991, Vol.1, Tables 9 and 16.

MAP 7.11
ACCOUNTING AND INFORMATION SYSTEMS SERVICES, GROSS REVENUES PER 1000 POPULATION, 1985

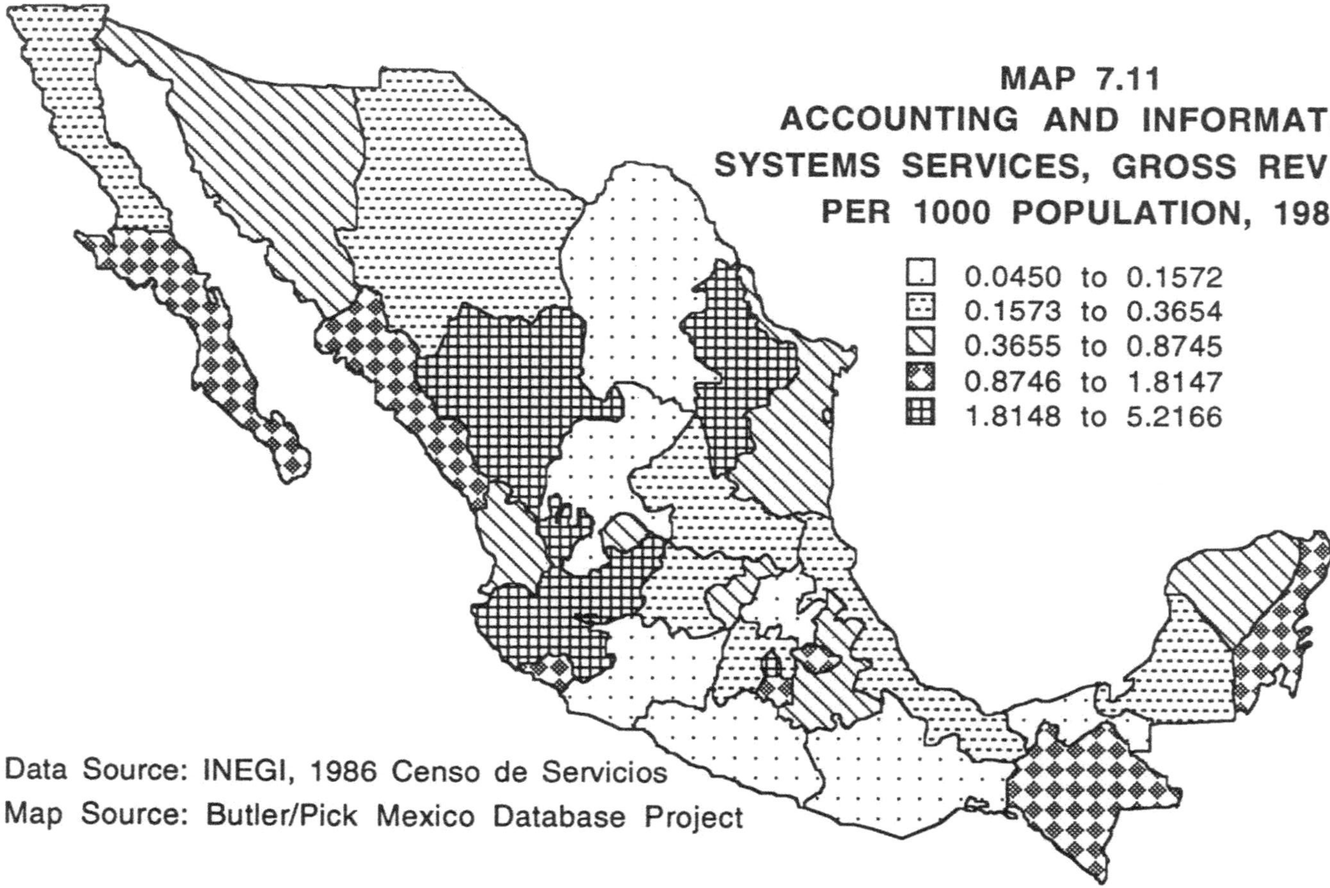

Data Source: INEGI, 1986 Censo de Servicios
Map Source: Butler/Pick Mexico Database Project

Table 7.10 Business Consulting Services, 1985

No.	State	Number of Establishments	Number of Employees	Gross Revenues Per 1000 Population
1	AGUASCALIENTES	24	298	0.9602
2	BAJA CALIFORNIA	29	491	1.0970
3	BAJA CALIFORNIA SUR	0	0	0.0000
4	CAMPECHE	3	27	0.1663
5	COAHUILA	29	704	2.2947
6	COLIMA	0	0	0.0000
7	CHIAPAS	18	97	0.0540
8	CHIHUAHUA	52	869	0.6921
9	DISTRITO FEDERAL	838	26,455	20.2019
10	DURANGO	31	538	0.5425
11	GUANAJUATO	85	2,338	1.2992
12	GUERRERO	3	19	0.0179
13	HIDALGO	8	105	0.0583
14	JALISCO	116	1,642	1.0236
15	MEXICO	61	1,481	0.8945
16	MICHOACAN	24	264	0.5110
17	MORELOS	11	74	0.1264
18	NAYARIT	5	31	0.0570
19	NUEVO LEON	127	3,819	8.3176
20	OAXACA	7	123	0.0553
21	PUEBLA	31	653	0.2787
22	QUERETARO	12	99	0.1608
23	QUINTANA ROO	6	34	0.7825
24	SAN LUIS POTOSI	27	396	0.2786
25	SINALOA	20	123	0.0817
26	SONORA	119	1,920	11.3352
27	TABASCO	5	45	0.0413
28	TAMAULIPAS	41	735	3.7065
29	TLAXCALA	0	0	0.0000
30	VERACRUZ	36	532	0.2306
31	YUCATAN	39	1,498	3.6311
32	ZACATECAS	0	0	0.0000
	National Total	1,807	45,410	
	Mean	56	1,419	1.8405
	Median	24	281	0.2787
	S.D.	147	4,648	4.1627
	C.V.	260.11	327.54	226.17
	Minimum	0	0	0.0000
	Maximum	838	26,455	20.2019

DEFINITION: Business consulting is for economic census category 840010. Gross revenues, shown in millions of pesos, are for economic census categories 840003 and 840004.

SOURCE: IX Censo de Servicios de 1986, INEGI, 1991, Vol.1, Tables 9 and 16.

Figure 7.6
Business Consulting
Number of Employees, 1985

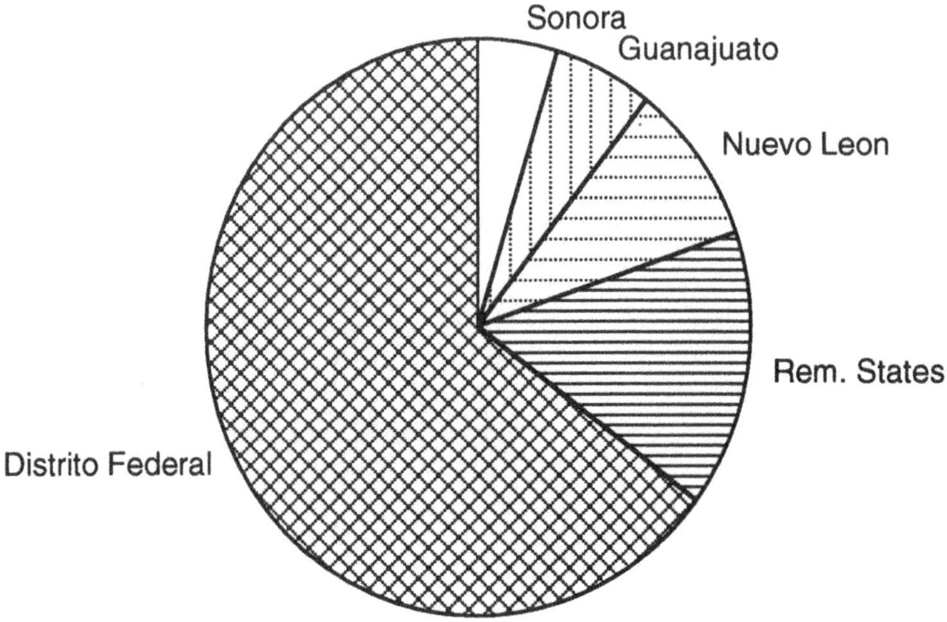

Data Source: IX Censo de Servicios de 1986, INEGI, 1991, Vol.1, Tables 9 and 16.

MAP 7.12
BUSINESS CONSULTING SERVICES GROSS REVENUES PER 1000 POPULATION, 1985

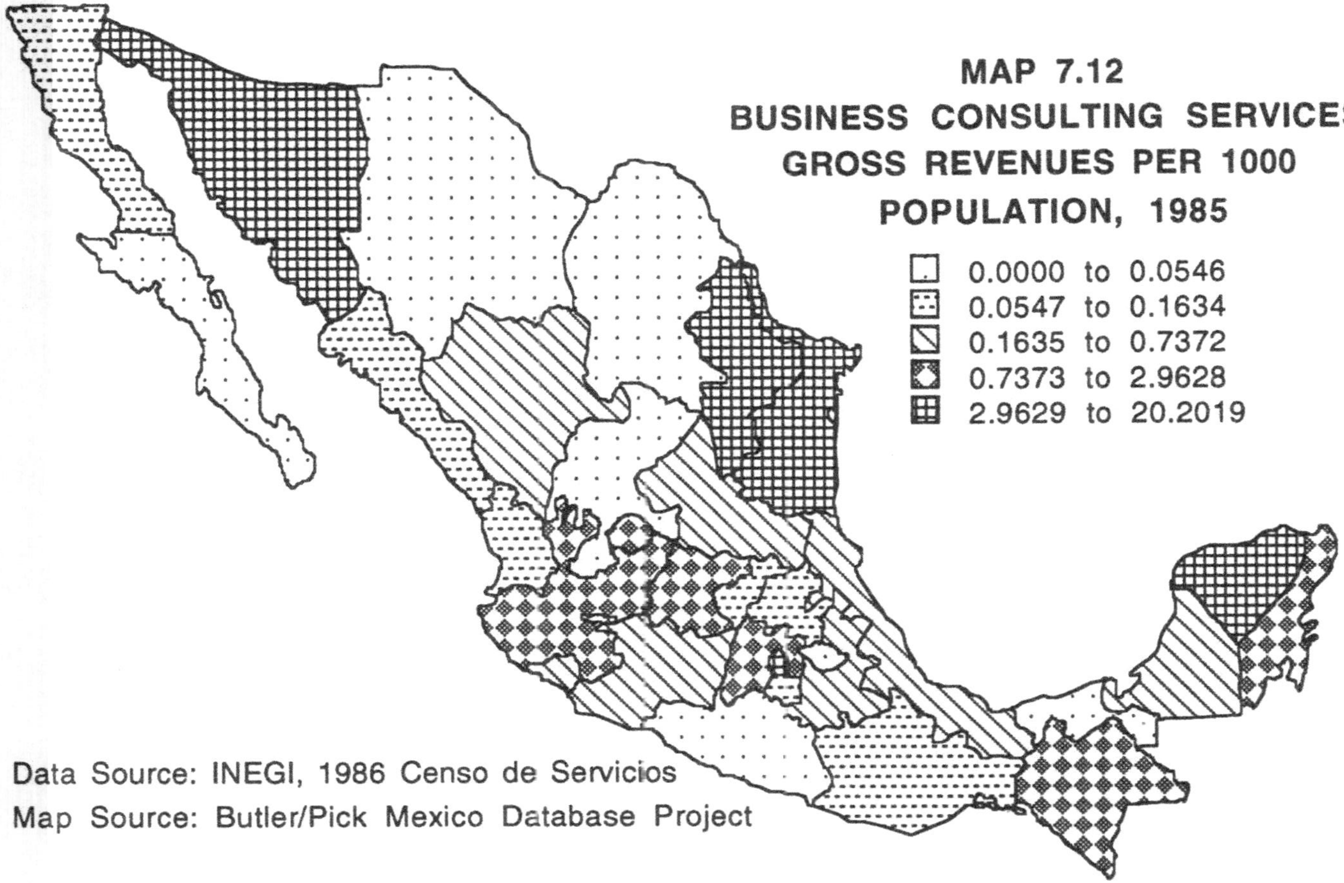

Data Source: INEGI, 1986 Censo de Servicios
Map Source: Butler/Pick Mexico Database Project

Crime

As shown in Table 7.11, there was relatively little variation in Juvenile Delinquent Sentences in 1988 by state, except Tabasco, Nayarit, and Tamaulipas had much higher rates of sentences than other states. As Map 7.13 also illustrates, there is little regional variation in juvenile sentences.

There is even less variation for Penal Sentences in 1986 and 1987 than there was for juvenile delinquent sentences (see Table 7.12). In 1986, states with the highest ratios were Baja California, Colima, the Federal District, Queretaro, and Tabasco. In 1987, all of these states except Baja also had high rates. In addition, rates increased between 1986 and 1987 in Aguascalientes and Sonora. In both years, the highest rate of penal sentences were in Tabasco, a state that also had a higher rate of juvenile delinquency sentences in 1988. As Map 7.14 shows, there is no systematic regional variation in penal sentences, although the three western border states have higher than average rates as does the mid-section of the country.

Maps 7.15, 7.16, and 7.17 illustrate the Murders, Robberies, and Rapes per 100 population for the Federal District averaged over the years of 1983–1985 for each of the *delagaciones*. As shown in Table 7.13, while there is variation, Cuauhtemoc and Benito Juarez have high rates for all three indicators and Miguel Hidalgo also has high rates for murders and robberies. Rape is also elevated in Iztapalapa, Milpa Alpa, and Tlalpan.

Table 7.11 Juvenile Delinquent Sentences, 1988

No.	State	Delinquents Charged	Total Population	Delinquents Sentenced			
				Total Sent.	No. Sent. Per Capita	Males	Females
1	AGUASCALIENTES	281	719,659	195	0.2710	180	14
2	BAJA CALIFORNIA	336	1,660,855	256	0.1541	241	14
3	BAJA CALIFORNIA SUR	145	317,764	82	0.2581	76	6
4	CAMPECHE	113	535,185	28	0.0523	28	0
5	COAHUILA	436	1,972,340	107	0.0543	103	4
6	COLIMA	171	428,510	107	0.2497	103	4
7	CHIAPAS	425	3,210,496	275	0.0857	235	40
8	CHIHUAHUA	755	2,441,873	513	0.2101	493	17
9	DISTRITO FEDERAL	2,732	8,235,744	1,599	0.1942	1,477	121
10	DURANGO	140	1,349,378	65	0.0482	63	2
11	GUANAJUATO	1,017	3,982,593	886	0.2225	836	48
12	GUERRERO	355	2,620,637	242	0.0923	228	13
13	HIDALGO	166	1,888,366	73	0.0387	69	4
14	JALISCO	1,811	5,302,689	1,102	0.2078	1,057	45
15	MEXICO	1,345	9,815,795	1,239	0.1262	1,170	67
16	MICHOACAN	696	3,548,199	596	0.1680	560	33
17	MORELOS	200	1,195,059	77	0.0644	76	1
18	NAYARIT	389	824,643	296	0.3589	282	11
19	NUEVO LEON	848	3,098,736	394	0.1271	382	12
20	OAXACA	465	3,019,560	262	0.0868	233	29
21	PUEBLA	689	4,126,101	337	0.0817	322	14
22	QUERETARO	287	1,051,235	246	0.2340	227	19
23	QUINTANA ROO	235	493,277	87	0.1764	86	1
24	SAN LUIS POTOSI	864	2,003,187	550	0.2746	513	34
25	SINALOA	368	2,204,054	202	0.0916	197	5
26	SONORA	534	1,823,606	483	0.2649	470	12
27	TABASCO	772	1,501,744	750	0.4994	702	46
28	TAMAULIPAS	739	2,249,581	764	0.3396	731	33
29	TLAXCALA	67	761,277	29	0.0381	27	2
30	VERACRUZ	1,360	6,228,239	904	0.1451	842	61
31	YUCATAN	493	1,362,940	160	0.1174	155	5
32	ZACATECAS	345	1,276,323	296	0.2319	287	9
	National Total	19,579	81,249,645	13,202	0.1625	12,451	726
	Mean	612	2,539,051	413	0.1739	389	23
	Median	431	1,930,353	269	0.1611	238	14
	S.D.	560	2,216,375	389	0.1078	365	26
	C.V.	91.54	87.29	94.32	62.00	93.77	113.74
	Minimum	67	317,764	28	0.0381	27	0
	Maximum	2,732	9,815,795	1,599	0.4994	1,477	121

DEFINITION: The number sentenced per capita is the ratio of the total sentenced 1988 per 1,000 population in 1990.

SOURCE: INEGI, 1990 Anuario Estadistico, Table 3.5.2.

Table 7.12 Penal Sentences, 1986 and 1987

No.	State	1986 Persons Sentenced	1986 Ratio	1987 Persons Sentenced	1987 Ratio
1	AGUASCALIENTES	835	0.0012	1,413	0.0020
2	BAJA CALIFORNIA	2,234	0.0013	2,292	0.0014
3	BAJA CALIFORNIA SUR	542	0.0017	360	0.0011
4	CAMPECHE	377	0.0007	459	0.0009
5	COAHUILA	840	0.0004	803	0.0004
6	COLIMA	731	0.0017	861	0.0020
7	CHIAPAS	3,098	0.0010	2,986	0.0009
8	CHIHUAHUA	3,251	0.0013	2,633	0.0011
9	DISTRITO FEDERAL	14,304	0.0017	12,801	0.0016
10	DURANGO	657	0.0005	532	0.0004
11	GUANAJUATO	4,973	0.0012	5,357	0.0013
12	GUERRERO	2,776	0.0011	2,550	0.0010
13	HIDALGO	1,066	0.0006	1,034	0.0005
14	JALISCO	6,436	0.0012	7,976	0.0015
15	MEXICO	10,794	0.0011	11,064	0.0011
16	MICHOACAN	4,130	0.0012	4,850	0.0014
17	MORELOS	799	0.0007	800	0.0007
18	NAYARIT	789	0.0010	956	0.0012
19	NUEVO LEON	2,922	0.0009	2,977	0.0010
20	OAXACA	2,126	0.0007	2,058	0.0007
21	PUEBLA	2,589	0.0006	2,574	0.0006
22	QUERETARO	1,654	0.0016	2,098	0.0020
23	QUINTANA ROO	540	0.0011	402	0.0008
24	SAN LUIS POTOSI	2,325	0.0012	2,671	0.0013
25	SINALOA	1,694	0.0008	2,104	0.0010
26	SONORA	2,557	0.0014	2,984	0.0016
27	TABASCO	5,236	0.0035	5,618	0.0037
28	TAMAULIPAS	3,220	0.0014	3,818	0.0017
29	TLAXCALA	591	0.0008	534	0.0007
30	VERACRUZ	4,567	0.0007	5,271	0.0008
31	YUCATAN	539	0.0004	884	0.0006
32	ZACATECAS	1,859	0.0015	1,936	0.0015
National Total		91,051	0.0011	95,656	0.0012
Mean		2,845	0.0011	2,989	0.0012
Median		2,180	0.0011	2,198	0.0011
S.D.		3,025	0.0006	2,972	0.0006
C.V.		106.31	51.03	99.44	53.71
Minimum		377	0.0004	360	0.0004
Maximum		14,304	0.0035	12,801	0.0037

DEFINITION: Ratio is the number of persons sentenced in 1986 or 1987 per 1,000 population in 1990.

SOURCE: INEGI, 1988–89 Anuario Estadistico, Table 3.5.1.

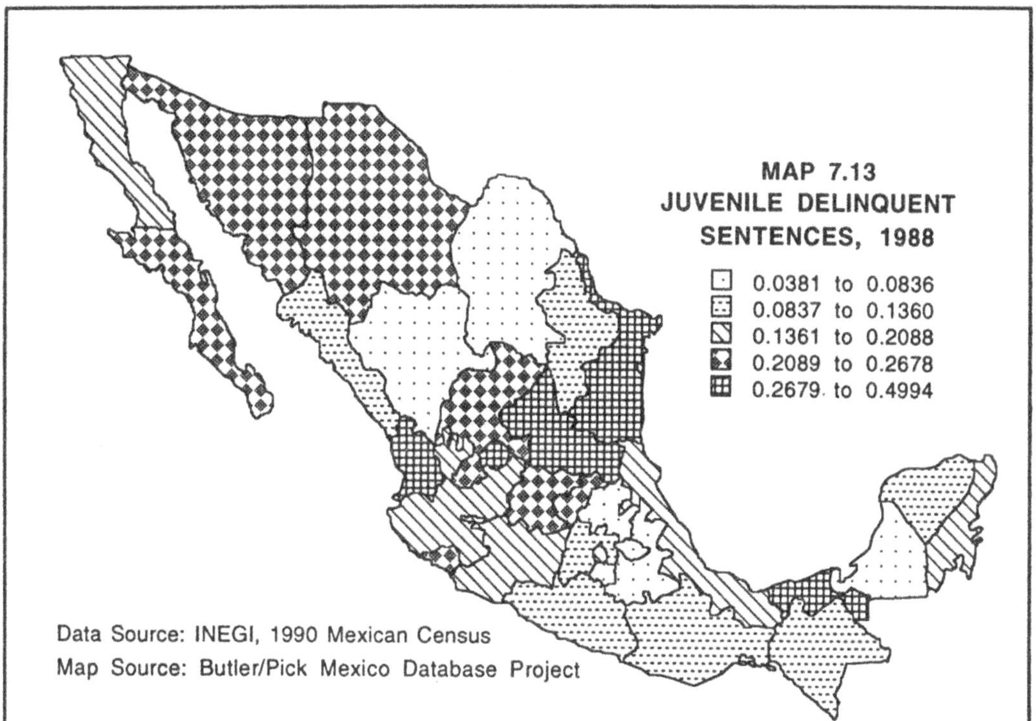
MAP 7.13
JUVENILE DELINQUENT
SENTENCES, 1988
0.0381 to 0.0836
0.0837 to 0.1360
0.1361 to 0.2088
0.2089 to 0.2678
0.2679 to 0.4994
Data Source: INEGI, 1990 Mexican Census
Map Source: Butler/Pick Mexico Database Project

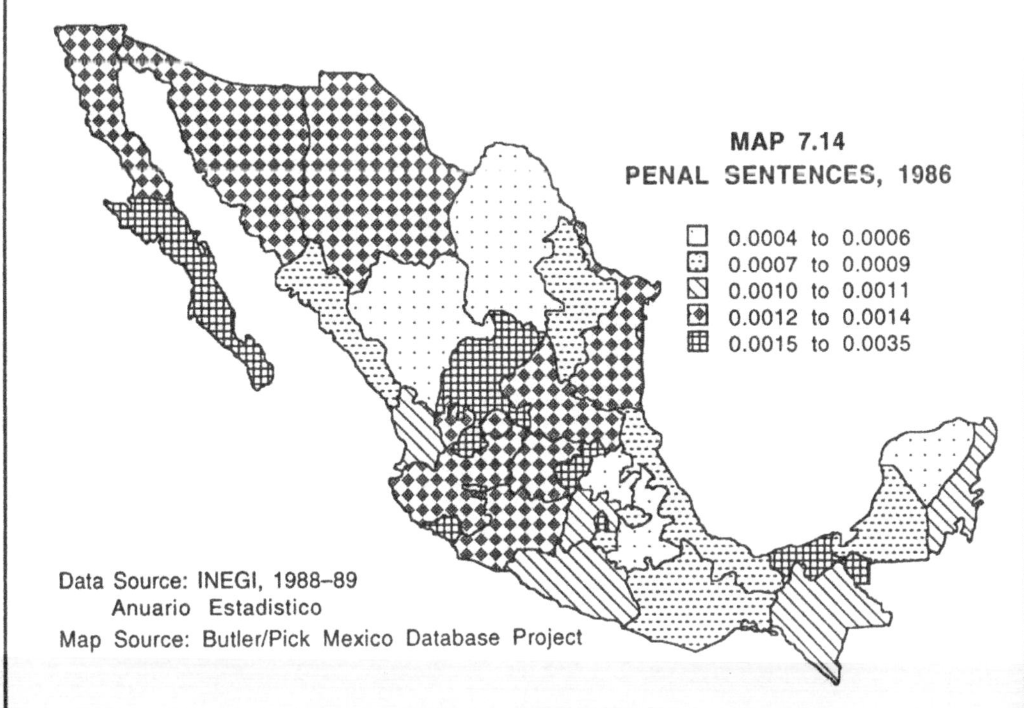
MAP 7.14
PENAL SENTENCES, 1986
0.0004 to 0.0006
0.0007 to 0.0009
0.0010 to 0.0011
0.0012 to 0.0014
0.0015 to 0.0035
Data Source: INEGI, 1988–89
Anuario Estadistico
Map Source: Butler/Pick Mexico Database Project

Table 7.13 Crime in the Federal District, 1983–1985

No.	State	Robberies per 100 Population	Murders per 100 Population	Rapes per 100 Population
1	ALVARO OBREGON	0.5137	0.0419	0.0111
2	AZCAPOTZALCO	0.5321	0.0329	0.0089
3	BENITO JUAREZ	1.7196	0.0592	0.0134
4	COYOACAN	0.8999	0.0398	0.0119
5	CUAJIMALPA	0.2795	0.0785	0.0091
6	CUAUHTEMOC	1.5923	0.0927	0.0217
7	GUSTAVO A. MADERO	0.6260	0.0388	0.0113
8	IZTACALCO	0.5237	0.0307	0.0109
9	IZTAPALAPA	0.4930	0.0406	0.0135
10	MAGDALENA CONTRERAS	0.3126	0.0276	0.0113
11	MIGUEL HIDALGO	1.2859	0.0520	0.0128
12	MILPA ALTA	0.1855	0.0419	0.0138
13	TLAHUAC	0.3269	0.0431	0.0196
14	TLALPAN	0.6276	0.0445	0.0132
15	VENUSTIANO CARRANZA	0.4554	0.0320	0.0057
16	XOCHIMILCO	0.3249	0.0485	0.0150
National Total		10.6987	0.7446	0.2030
Mean		0.6687	0.0465	0.0127
Median		0.5187	0.0419	0.0123
S.D.		0.4678	0.0174	0.0039
C.V.		69.96	37.44	30.48
Minimum		0.1855	0.0276	0.0057
Maximum		1.7196	0.0927	0.0217

DEFINITION: Each catagory is the ratio of crimes to 100 Population.

SOURCE: Garza, 1987.

MAP 7.15

MURDERS PER 100 POPULATION IN FEDERAL DISTRICT, 1983 - 1985

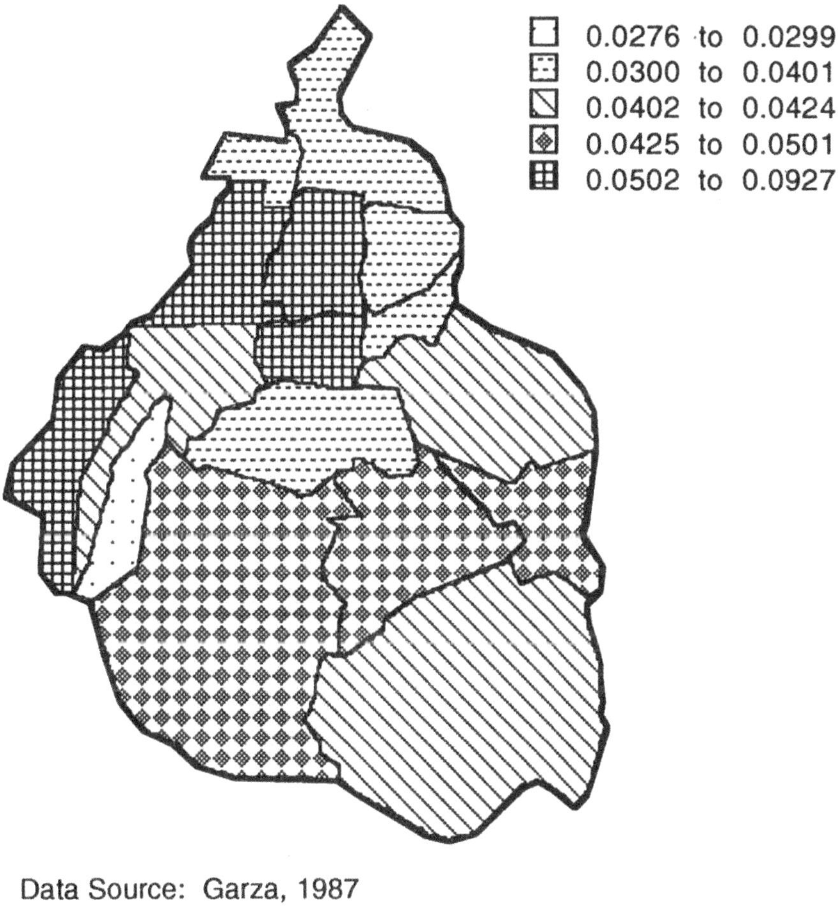

Data Source: Garza, 1987

Map Source: Butler/Pick Mexico Database Project

MAP 7.16
ROBBERIES PER 100 POPULATION IN
FEDERAL DISTRICT, 1983 - 1985

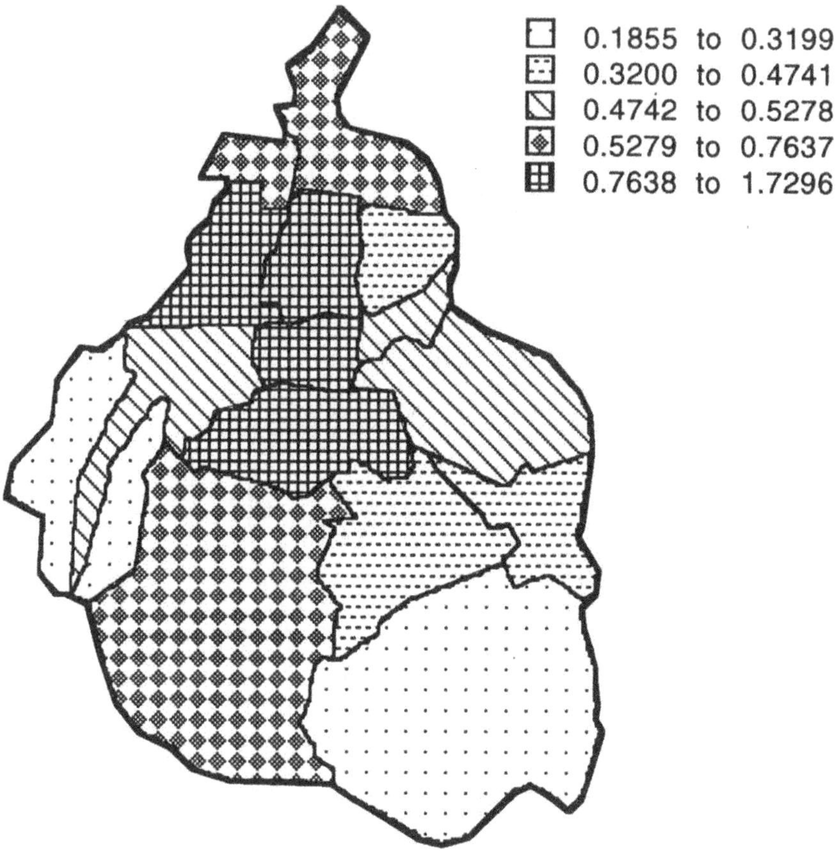

Data Source: Garza, 1987
Map Source: Butler/Pick Mexico Database Project

MAP 7.17
RAPES PER 100 POPULATION IN FEDERAL DISTRICT, 1983 - 1985

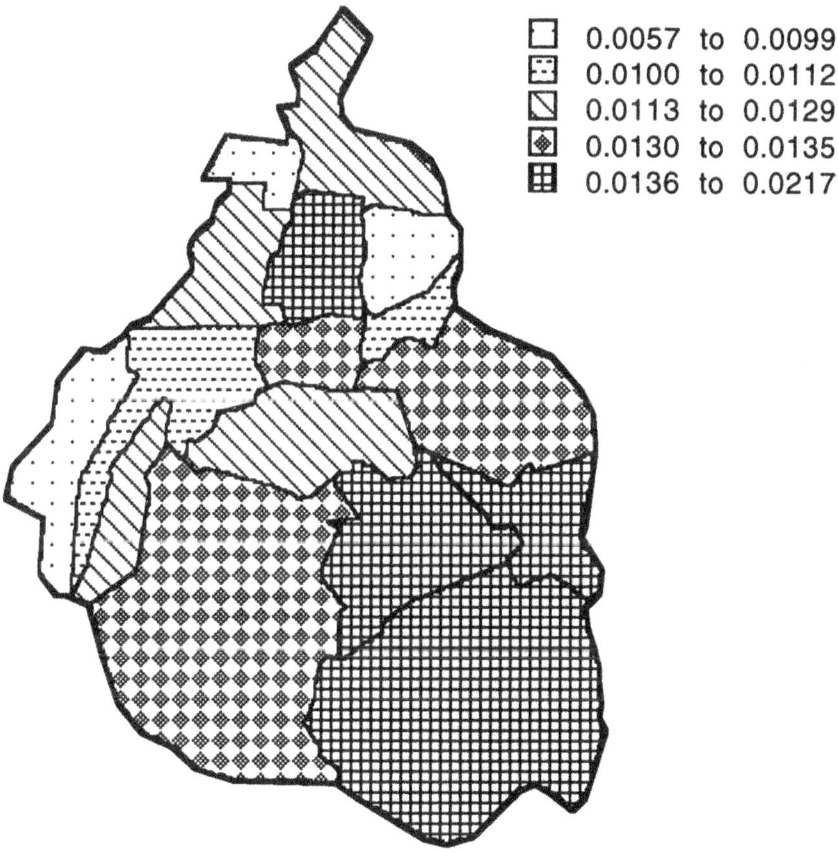

Data Source: Garza, 1987

Map Source: Butler/Pick Mexico Database Project

8

The Economy

- Introduction
- Currency
- Natural Resource Production
- Agricultural Production
- Manufacturing Production
- Installed Electrical Energy Capacity
- Corporations
- Communications/Transport
- Economic Development
- Mexican–United States Balance of Trade, 1960–1990

Introduction

There are extensive data available to analyze various aspects of the Mexican economy. This chapter focuses on a variety of dimensions related to the economy, including (1) Currency, (2) Natural Resource Production, (3) Agricultural Production, (4) Manufacturing Production, (5) Installed Electrical Energy Capacity, (6) Corporations, (7) Communications/Transport Sector, and (8) Economic Development and Mexican-United States Trade. Information included in this chapter is from a variety of sources including the 1989 *Censos Economicos,* the 1990 Population and Housing Census, the 1990 *Anuario Estadistico,* several years of the *International Financial Statistics Yearbook* and of the *Direction of Trade Statistics.* All maps and tables in this chapter report information at the state level.

The Currency section of the chapter examines peso devaluation for the period of 1960–1990, with both a standard and log scale. The Natural Resource Production division focuses on crude oil, natural gas, copper, and timber production. Corn, beans, fish, beef and pork, and irrigated land are reported in the Agricultural Production section. Productions of cement, beverages, paper, and automobiles are presented in the manufacturing part of the chapter.

Installed Electrical Energy Capacity covers the years from 1920 through 1989 and shows that electrical capacity has grown rapidly during the twentieth century. The following section then focuses on the value and number of corporations per capita. There also is a brief description of the 500 major Mexican corporations and their locations. Communications/Transport examines telephones, radio and television stations, and vehicle ownership. The Economic Development division presents information on gross state revenues, public investment, value of new mortgages, and taxes and duties collected. The Trade section includes a longitudinal examination of trade between Mexico and the United States between 1960 and 1990, and information on imports and exports with the U.S. and several other industrialized nations.

As with all previous chapters, this one contains only a few of the vast variety of dimensions that are available from multifarious sources. All data included in this chapter are included on the *Handbook of Mexico* diskette.

Currency

The value of the Mexican peso, relative to the U.S. dollar, is shown in Table 8.1 and Figures 8.1 and 8.2 for the period 1960 to 1990. Figure 8.2 presents information using a logarithmic scale. The log analysis presented in Figure 8.2 controls for the large devaluations that have taken place since 1982, as shown in Table 8.1. Figure 8.1 is presented for comparison with the log scale. Note that the peso was recently standardized so that while it was ca. 3,000 pesos to the dollar for the time period in the table, is now ca. 3.0 to the dollar. However, this does not alter the inherent value relationship between the Mexican peso and the U.S. dollar.

Statistics were drawn from the International Monetary Fund's *International Financial Yearbook,* 1979 and 1991 (IMF 1979, 1991). The Mexican peso was relatively stable for the period 1937 to 1948, but still increased by 54 percent. However, in the single year of 1948-49, it underwent devaluation and gained by 44 percent. It remained relatively stable until 1954, when it increased by 50 percent to 12.5 per dollar. By 1977 the rate was about 23 pesos per dollar. The 23 rate lasted for over 20 years until 1980.

Over the period of 1982-1988 term of De La Madrid's administration, a drop in oil price and large loans from major U.S. banks resulted in a major debt crisis and general financial instability in Mexico. The peso lost much of its value, relative to the dollar during this period, rising from 56 in 1982 to 2,273 in July 1988, a 40 fold relative devaluation. Between 1988 and 1990, the peso continued to lose value but at a slower rate, going from 2,273 in 1988 to slightly over 2,800 in 1990. It has remained relatively stable so far during the Salinas administration, compared to earlier administrations.

Table 8.1 Value of Peso in U.S. Dollars, 1960-1990

Year	Peso Value
1960-75	12.5
1976	15.4
1977	22.6
1978	22.8
1979	22.8
1980	23.0
1981	24.5
1982	56.4
1983	120.1
1984	167.8
1985	256.9
1986	611.8
1987	1378.2
1988	2273.1
1989	2461.5
1990	2812.6

NOTE: The series refers to period averages of the market rate/par value.

SOURCE: IMF, International Financial Statistics Yearbook, 1979, 1991.

Figure 8.1
Peso Devaluation, Mexico, 1937–1991
(Log Scale)

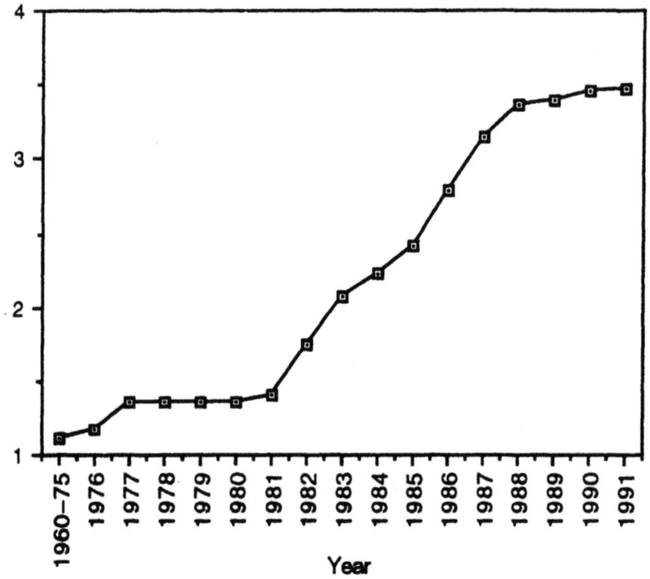

Figure 8.2
Peso Devaluation, Mexico, 1937–1991

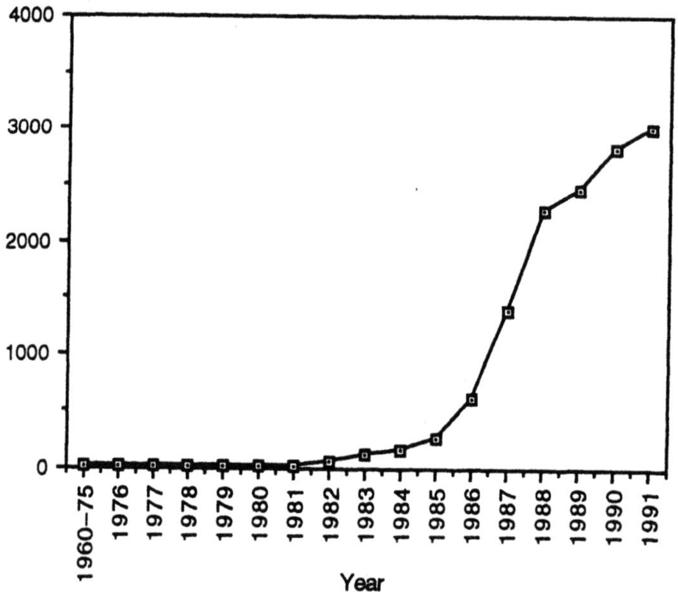

SOURCE: IMF, International Financial Statistics.

Natural Resource Production

Crude Oil and Natural Gas Production, 1988

In 1991, Mexico's oil production was 6th in the world at 2,676,000 barrels of oil daily. It was ninth in natural gas production at 3,633,000 million cubic feet of natural gas daily (PEMEX 1992). Mexico also has very large proven reserves of oil and natural gas. In 1991, it ranked eighth worldwide in proven reserves of oil at 50.9 billion barrels, compared to 257.8 billion barrels for the leading nation of Saudi Arabia and 26.2 billion barrels for the U.S. It ranked twelfth in natural gas reserves at 71 billion cubic feet, versus 1,750 billion cubic feet for the leader, Russia, and 169 billion cubic feet for the U.S. (PEMEX 1992). Overall among nations in the Western Hemisphere, Mexico shares petroleum reserve leadership with Venezuela and the U.S., but far exceeds other nations (PEMEX 1992, page 21).

Crude oil and natural gas production for 1988 is shown in Figure 8.3 and Table 8.2. Map 8.1 illustrates that the major oil and natural production states are located in the Gulf of Mexico regions. The major oil producing state is Campeche with over two-thirds of the total production in 1988. Tabasco produced over 25 percent with Tamaulipas, Veracruz, and San Luis Potosi accounting for nearly all of the remainder of production. Thus, the major oil and gas production region is along the Gulf of Mexico and adjacent states.

In 1991, Mexico's exports totaled 1,468,000 barrels daily, including 1,368,600 barrels of crude oil, no natural gas, and 99,400 barrels of refined products (PEMEX 1992). On the other hand, it imported 160,800 barrels daily, consisting of 24,100 barrels of natural gas, and 136,700 barrels of refined products.

Mexico's crude oil exports by trading partner for 1991 are presented below.

Nation	Volume	Percent
United States	771.7	56.4
Spain	247.1	18.0
Japan	144.6	10.6
Nations of San Jose Agreement	44.2	3.2
Others	161.0	11.8
TOTAL	1,368.6	100.0

NOTE: Figures are in thousands of barrels daily.
SOURCE: PEMEX, 1992.

Clearly, the industrialized nations of the U.S., Spain, and Japan dominate as Mexico's oil export trading partners. The Spanish alliance underscores Mexico's continuing economic ties, at least in petroleum, with its historical colonial roots.

Figure 8.3
Crude Oil and Natural Gas Production, 1988

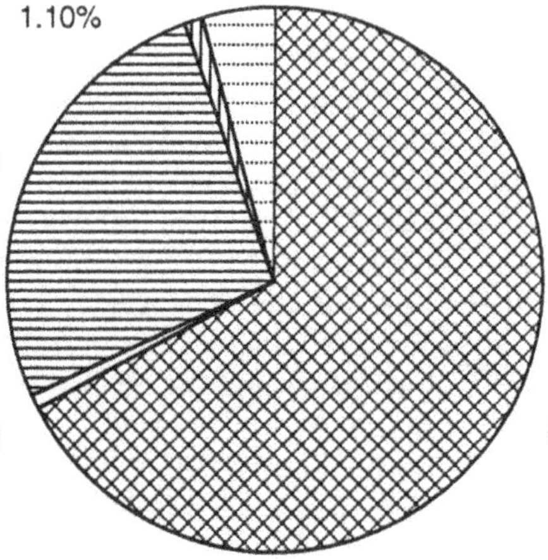

NOTE: The percentages are for volume of production of crude oil and natural gas in 1988.

Table 8.2 Crude Oil and Natural Gas Production, 1988

No	State	Workers	Total Assets	Volume	Percent of Nation
4	CAMPECHE	7,726	20,203,655	15,057,692	67.2732
5	COAHUILA	278	485,231	14,361	0.0642
24	SAN LUIS POTOSI	4,147	1,560,245	160,667	0.7178
27	TABASCO	15,594	15,739,717	5,935,836	26.5195
28	TAMAULIPAS	4,106	4,831,332	240,651	1.0752
30	VERACRUZ	25,371	17,744,764	973,677	4.3501
	National Total	57,222	60,564,944	22,382,883	
	Mean	9,537	10,094,157	3,730,481	16.6667
	Median	5,937	10,285,525	607,164	2.7126
	S.D.	9,327	8,780,234	5,991,683	26.7690
	C.V.	97.80	86.98	160.61	160.61
	Minimum	278	485,231	14,361	0.0642
	Maximum	25,371	20,203,655	15,057,692	67.2732

DEFINITION: The production figures are shown in millions of pesos.

SOURCE: INEGI, 1989 Censos Economicos.

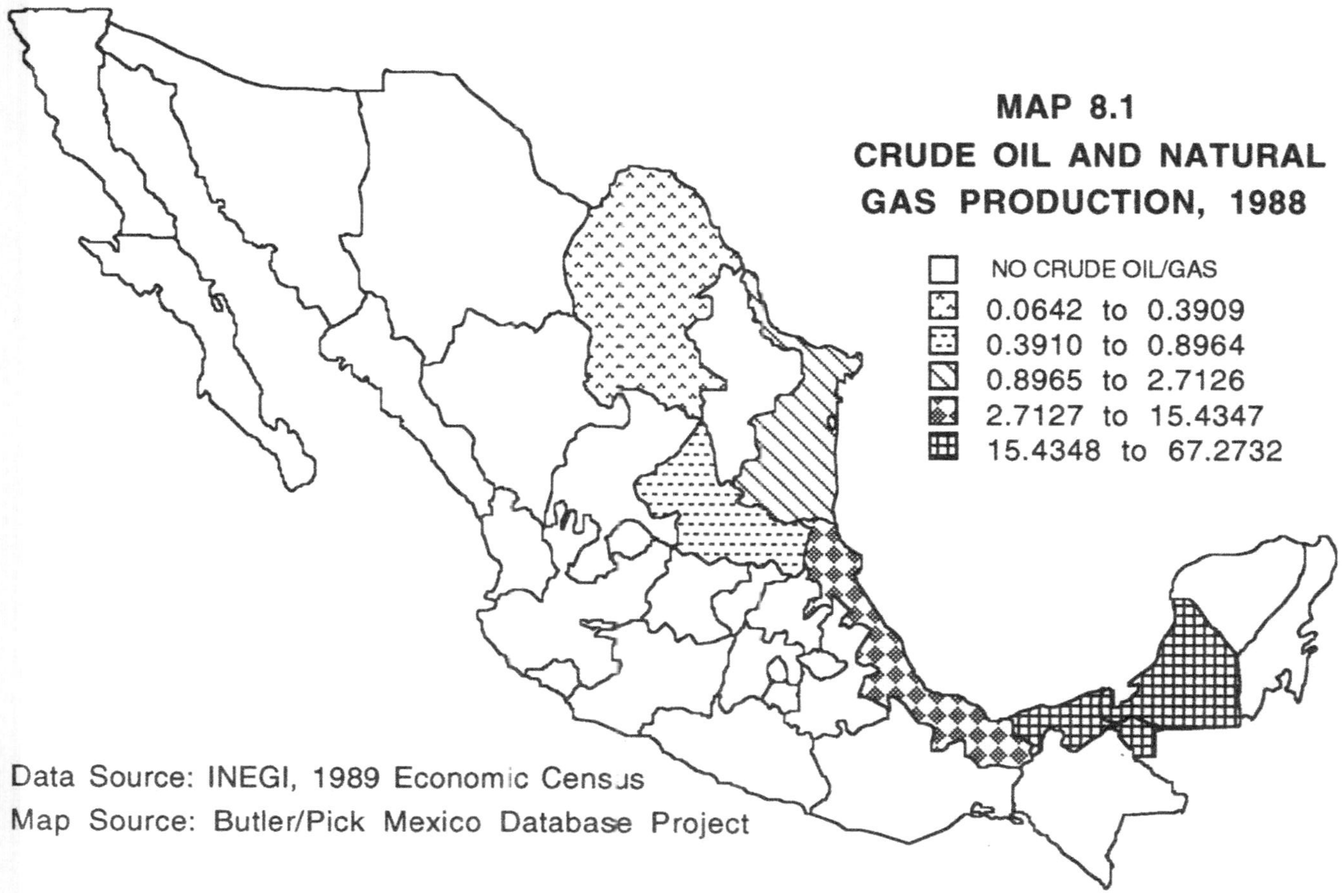

MAP 8.1
CRUDE OIL AND NATURAL GAS PRODUCTION, 1988

Data Source: INEGI, 1989 Economic Census
Map Source: Butler/Pick Mexico Database Project

Copper Production, 1988

Copper is one of the major minerals mined in Mexico. The annual production of copper fluctuated between 1976 and 1980 from just under 90,000 tons to over 175,000 tons in 1980. In 1982, production increased to over 190,000 tons but then decreased to 192,385 tons in 1984 and 184,474 tons in 1985. However, 1988 copper production was 278,135 tons with 90 percent of the production taking place in Sonora, slightly over four percent in Zacatecas, and about three percent in Chihuahua (see Table 8.3 and Map 8.2). Thus, there is a strong concentration of copper production in the north and northwest. Copper production within Sonora is concentrated in Macazari, Cananea, and La Caridad (Tamayo 1985). The geographic concentration of copper production has remained steady over the past several decades and undoubtedly will remain consistent in the future unless new deposits are found.

Timber Production, 1988

Mexico has important forest products, of which the most important is the production of timber. Mexico also produces resins, gums, waxes, etc., but which are substantially less important insofar as generating revenue. Map 8.3 shows the distribution of timber production in Mexico in thousands of cubic meters. The major timber producing states in 1988 were Durango, Chihuahua, Michoacan, and Jalisco. As shown in Table 8.3, these four states account for over 70 percent of the nation's production value. The leading species of timber produced is pine. By topography, timber production is concentrated in the mountain ranges of Sierra Madre Occidental and Corillera Neovolcanica. By region, the most important production areas are the north central and central west. This regional pattern is fairly stable. The future direction of change appears towards a lessening of production in more urbanized states, such as the Federal District and Mexico.

Table 8.3 Copper and Timber Production, 1988

No.	State	Tons of Copper Production	Percent of Nation	Volume of Timber Production	Percent of Nation
1	AGUASCALIENTES	0	0.00	4,282	0.05
2	BAJA CALIFORNIA	0	0.00	7,627	0.08
3	BAJA CALIFORNIA SUR	0	0.00	12,078	0.13
4	CAMPECHE	0	0.00	173,424	1.86
5	COAHUILA	5	0.00	16,931	0.18
6	COLIMA	0	0.00	4,115	0.04
7	CHIAPAS	0	0.00	238,984	2.57
8	CHIHUAHUA	8,213	2.95	1,755,367	18.85
9	DISTRITO FEDERAL	0	0.00	86,074	0.92
10	DURANGO	518	0.19	2,731,251	29.32
11	GUANAJUATO	99	0.04	35,130	0.38
12	GUERRERO	874	0.31	157,788	1.69
13	HIDALGO	1,382	0.50	93,233	1
14	JALISCO	462	0.17	943,426	10.13
15	MEXICO	53	0.02	361,188	3.88
16	MICHOACAN	245	0.09	1,182,050	12.69
17	MORELOS	11	0.00	2,310	0.02
18	NAYARIT	28	0.01	33,893	0.36
19	NUEVO LEON	0	0.00	55,673	0.6
20	OAXACA	52	0.02	461,815	4.96
21	PUEBLA	0	0.00	289,931	3.11
22	QUERETARO	899	0.32	5,814	0.06
23	QUINTANA ROO	0	0.00	99,944	1.07
24	SAN LUIS POTOSI	2,467	0.89	38,687	0.42
25	SINALOA	826	0.30	33,983	0.36
26	SONORA	250,370	90.02	128,174	1.38
27	TABASCO	0	0.00	9,799	0.11
28	TAMAULIPAS	0	0.00	212,938	2.29
29	TLAXCALA	0	0.00	35,290	0.38
30	VERACRUZ	0	0.00	69,864	0.75
31	YUCATAN	0	0.00	10,201	0.11
32	ZACATECAS	11,631	4.18	23,130	0.25
Total National Production		278,135		9,314,394	
Mean		8,692	3.13	291,075	3.13
Median		8	0.00	62,769	0.67
S.D.		44,170	15.88	589,162	6.33
C.V.		508.19	508.19	202.41	202.41
Minimum		0	0.00	2,310	0.02
Maximum		250,370	90.02	2,731,251	29.32

DEFINITION: 1988 copper production figures are shown in tons. 1988 timber production figures are shown in thousands of cubic meters.

SOURCE: INEGI, 1988–1989 Anuario Estadistico, Table 4.2.7 and Table 4.2.3.

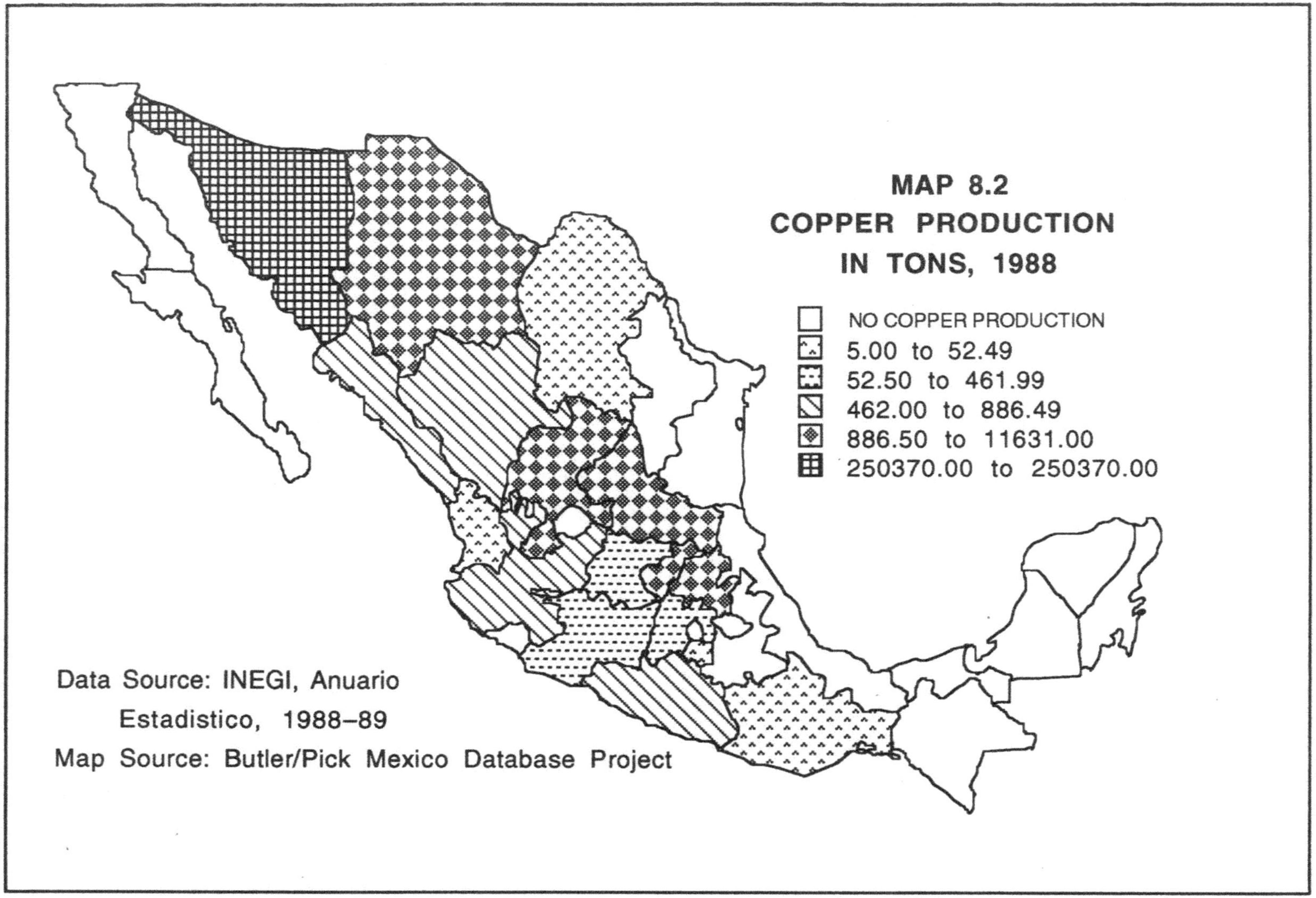
MAP 8.2
COPPER PRODUCTION
IN TONS, 1988
NO COPPER PRODUCTION
5.00 to 52.49
52.50 to 461.99
462.00 to 886.49
886.50 to 11631.00
250370.00 to 250370.00
Data Source: INEGI, Anuario Estadistico, 1988–89
Map Source: Butler/Pick Mexico Database Project

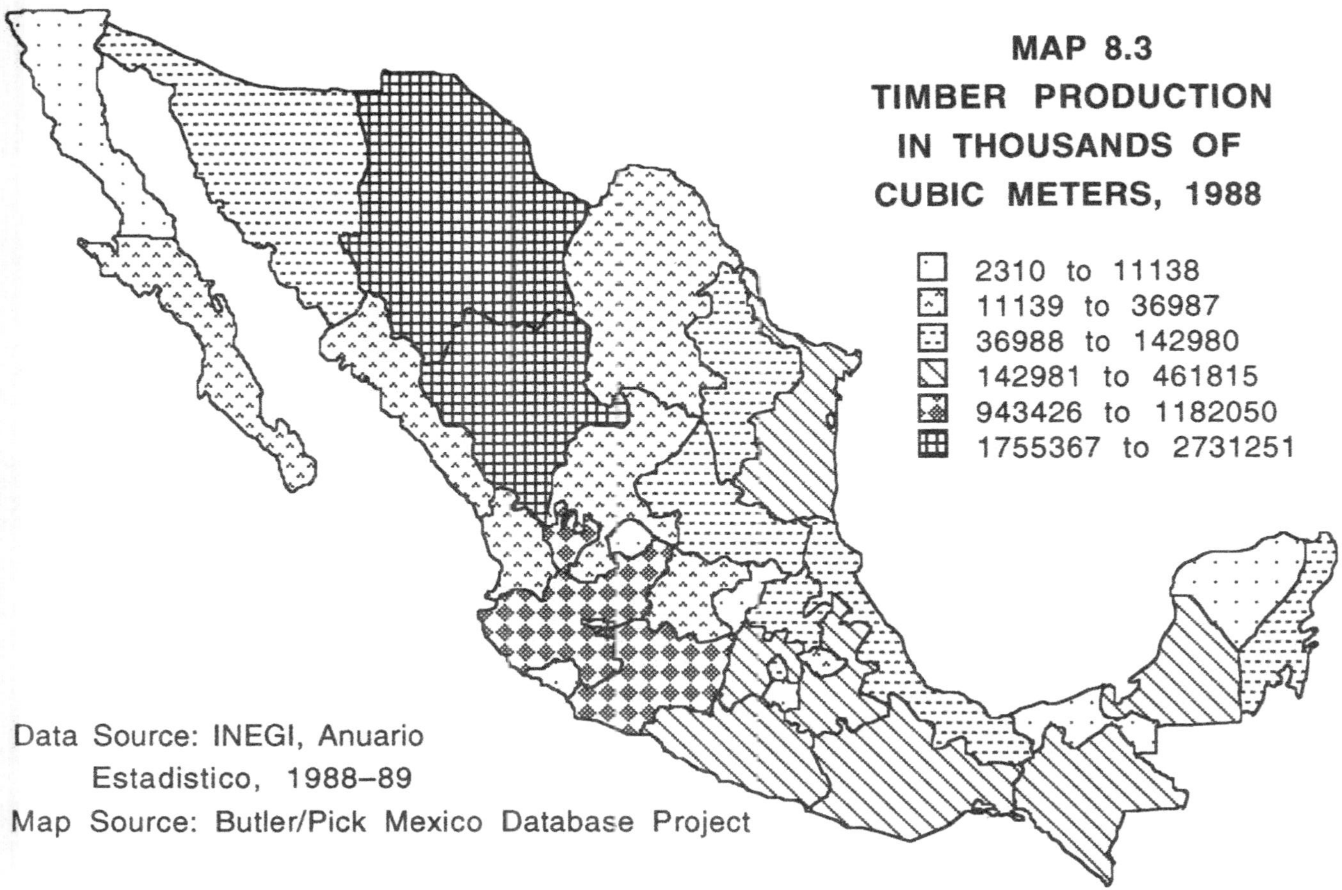

MAP 8.3
TIMBER PRODUCTION IN THOUSANDS OF CUBIC METERS, 1988

Data Source: INEGI, Anuario Estadistico, 1988–89
Map Source: Butler/Pick Mexico Database Project

Agricultural Production

Corn Production, 1985

Mexico is one of the top corn producing countries in the world. Corn (maize) is Mexico's leading agricultural product, with a value of 787.2 billion pesos in 1985. In that year, corn constituted 29 percent in value of Mexico's cultivated crops and fruits. As seen below, of Mexican corn production for 1975–1990, the production volume, cultivated area, and yield grew from 1975 to 1983, but remained steady for the rest of the 1980s.

Year	Value (mil. of pesos)	Production (tons)	Area (hectares)	Yield (tons/hectare)
1975	15,738	8,448,708	6,694,267	0.79
1979	30,031	8,448,795	5,568,831	0.83
1983	272,795	15,918,225	7,420,623	2.15
1985	787,220	14,103,454	7,589,537	1.85
1989/90	NA	14,635,439	7,628,195	1.92

SOURCE: *Anuarios Estadisticos* of 1980, 1986, 1988/89, and 1991.

In 1985, the three states of Chiapas, Jalisco, and Mexico, accounted for 45 percent of the corn production in Mexico (see Table 8.4). The national volume of corn production was 14,103,454 tons in 1985 (*1988–89 Anuario Estadistico*). This volume increased slightly to 14,635,439 tons for the 1989–90 year, i.e., autumn 1989 through summer 1990 (*1991 Anuario Estadistico*).

The major corn producing states are in the central west and the southern state of Chiapas (see Map 8.4). The remaining corn producing states are scattered throughout Mexico with no clear, discernible pattern. While there are major corn producing states, corn is grown so pervasively throughout Mexico that there are few correlations of corn production with other attributes. Those that do exist are an extremely high association with the annual fertility rate (r = .83), households with no electricity (.49), and a negative relationship with crude oil production (- .37). There is a moderate positive association with measures of urbanization (ca. .20), but virtually no association with occupational measures, including agricultural work force, with beef and pork production, and other products.

It is probable that some of domestically-produced corn, especially in the south, is not included in these federal statistics. Thus, the southern states may be producing more corn than shown here since it may be being consumed by those living in the area rather than being exported to other parts of Mexico.

Bean Production, 1985

Beans (Frijol) was Mexico's fifth largest agricultural product in value in 1985 —behind corn, sorghum, coffee, and sugar (INEGI 1992). As shown below, Mexican bean production for 1975–1990 in production volume, cultivated area and yield remained steady over the past two and a half decades.

Year	Value (mil. of pesos)	Production (tons)	Cultivated Area (hectares)	Yield (tons/hectares)
1975	5,404	1,027,303	1,752,632	0.59
1979	6,054	641,287	1,040,910	0.62
1983	39,704	1,281,706	1,996,408	0.64
1985	142,642	911,908	1,782,341	0.51
1989/90	NA	1,286,950	2,182,620	0.59

SOURCE: *Anuarios Estadisticos* of 1980, 1986, 1988/89, and 1991.

Beans are a major constituent of the Mexican diet, with many varieties being produced in Mexico. Although beans are produced in virtually all Mexican states, tropical or temperate climates are more favorable for production. The major bean producing states, by far, are Zacatecas and Durango accounting for almost half of the total value of bean production (see Table 8.4 and Map 8.5). Other significant production occurs in Chiapas, Chihuahua, Guanajuato, and Hidalgo. Referring to regional patterns, bean production is concentrated in five states in the western north and northern west regions.

There is little association between bean production and agricultural occupations and beef and pork production. However, moderate correlations exist between bean production and paper production and gross state revenues (r's = ca. high 40s). There also are moderate correlations between cardiological and nutrition related death rates. Unlike corn, there is only a very small relationship to the annual fertility rate (- .15). There also is a negative relationship to population size (- .39).

Fish Production, 1988

The Mexican government's fish production measures include live weight, i.e., weight when fish are caught, and weight when fish are unloaded ashore. For mapping in this book, the former measure is used. The amount of fish produced varies from year-to-year depending upon world and domestic markets, the fishing industry, and biological supply factors. As seen in the text table presented on the next page, the volume and value of fish production between 1975 and 1990 grew by about 224 percent.

Year	Production (live weight)	Production (fish unloaded ashore)
1975	451,330	NA
1980	1,058,566	NA
1982	1,285,539	NA
1985	1,255,880	1,099,046
1989	1,394,175	1,236,886
1990	1,461,117	1,283,712

SOURCE: SPP and INEGI, *Anuarios Estadisticos* of 1980, 1985, 1988/89, and 1991.

Table 8.5 shows that the three northwestern states of Baja, Sinaloa, and Sonora account for almost 50 percent of the total fish production of Mexico. Other states with higher than average production are Baja California Sur, Campeche, Tamaulipas, and Veracruz (see Map 8.6). Not surprisingly, fish production reveals a coastal pattern. Most ocean states on both coasts of the nation have high fish production, although it moderates in the less populous, smaller states of Colima and Quintana Roo.

Fish production has very strong positive relationships with a number of urban related measures. Fish production also is positively related to the population aged 16-64 (.48) and negatively to the population aged 0-17 (- .48), as well as to the dependency ratio (- .44) and sex ratio (- .36). Two contrasting relationships occur with a negative relationship existing between taxes and duties collected (- .36) but a positive relationship with number of corporations per 1,000 population (.70). Finally, there is a positive correlation between fish production and lifetime outmigration (.44).

Beef and Pork Production, 1989

Beef production is registered at the location of beef processing in tons and represents the concentration of the beef processing industry rather than beef grazing areas. Beef production is one of the leading agricultural products of Mexico, although lower in value than corn production.

Beef and Pork production in tons for 1989 is shown in Table 8.6. The two populous states of Jalisco and Veracruz account for over 25 percent of beef production in 1989 and while Guanajuato, Jalisco, and Sonora produced over 45 percent of the pork in 1989. Map 8.7 illustrates that beef production is not concentrated in the gulf region, as well as four states in the northwest and north regions that have relatively large scale tonnage. Pork production (see Map 8.8) varies greatly but with a somewhat similar distribution to beef production (r = .48). Relative to beef, pork production is concentrated less in northern states and more in the west, central, and south regions. As shown on Table 8.6 and Maps 8.7 and 8.8, Jalisco is both a major beef and pork producing state.

The geographic pattern of beef production compares substantially to the total population (see Map 2.1), except for heightened beef production in the northern border region. This, undoubtedly, is related to the historical tendencies to locate beef processing plants near Mexican centers of population as well as in proximity to the large U.S. market.

Other than beef and pork production being highly correlated with each other, there are few other significant associations. The two major ones are the high association of flights with beef production (.66) and nutritional deaths with pork production (.49).

Irrigated Land Area, 1989

Thousands of hectares of irrigated land area in 1988-1989 are shown on Map 8.9 and reported in Table 8.7. The total amount of land area varied greatly over the three years in the table, from 82,035 hectares in 1987 to 25,629 hectares in 1988 to 53,269 hectares in 1989. Irrigated acreage varies so greatly because it depends on factors of weather, annual crop production, and alternative water uses, which fluctuate greatly from year to year. This variable can also be expected to have errors in measurement.

Over the three years, only twelve of Mexico's 32 federal entities had irrigation, with several more states involved in 1987 and 1989, compared to the low irrigation year of 1988. The top two irrigated states of Tamaulipas and Chiapas are consistent over the three years. Tamaulipas has by far the largest irrigation, accounting for a mean of 43 percent of the national acreage over the three years. Tamaulipas is situated near the Rio Grande River and has a climate and agriculture that is very suitable for irrigation. Likewise, Chiapas averaged 16.1 percent of irrigated land from 1987–1989. It has abundant water resources, as also reflected in its large amount of hydroelectric production. These abundant resources can also be diverted for irrigation. Several other leading states for irrigation include Tabasco, Veracruz, San Luis Potosi, and Sinaloa. These states do not have a common region or agriculture. However, in all cases there is an available water supply and appropriate crops for irrigation. In Map 8.9, there is no regional pattern evident. This implies that irrigation is not a regionally based attribute in Mexico, but rather depends on multiple variables in individual states.

Table 8.4 Corn (Maize) and Bean (Frijol) Production, in Pesos, 1985

No.	State	Value of Maize Prod.	Percent of Nation	Value of Frijol Prod.	Percent of Nation
1	AGUASCALIENTES	2,531,031	0.32	1,070,810	0.76
2	BAJA CALIFORNIA	1,175,037	0.15	0	0.00
3	BAJA CALIFORNIA SUR	411,742	0.05	267,954	0.19
4	CAMPECHE	2,545,149	0.32	8,700	0.01
5	COAHUILA	1,823,122	0.23	756,066	0.54
6	COLIMA	3,451,273	0.44	0	0.00
7	CHIAPAS	124,497,541	15.81	8,232,299	5.85
8	CHIHUAHUA	19,154,783	2.43	10,294,170	7.32
9	DISTRITO FEDERAL	1,493,325	0.19	123,000	0.09
10	DURANGO	13,969,605	1.77	21,844,500	15.53
11	GUANAJUATO	26,125,474	3.32	9,030,373	6.42
12	GUERRERO	42,916,068	5.45	1,176,557	0.84
13	HIDALGO	22,431,909	2.85	7,163,047	5.09
14	JALISCO	109,406,564	13.90	4,899,300	3.48
15	MEXICO	123,163,326	15.65	2,483,119	1.77
16	MICHOACAN	46,588,066	5.92	2,888,671	2.05
17	MORELOS	3,735,130	0.47	469,237	0.33
18	NAYARIT	7,852,771	1.00	3,280,538	2.33
19	NUEVO LEON	2,484,971	0.32	163,100	0.12
20	OAXACA	26,142,332	3.32	3,550,370	2.52
21	PUEBLA	54,590,590	6.93	4,646,612	3.30
22	QUERETARO	7,377,167	0.94	1,968,622	1.40
23	QUINTANA ROO	446,587	0.06	105,275	0.07
24	SAN LUIS POTOSI	8,681,083	1.10	2,438,378	1.73
25	SINALOA	8,245,598	1.05	3,290,639	2.34
26	SONORA	9,915,908	1.26	0	0.00
27	TABASCO	5,309,484	0.67	0	0.00
28	TAMAULIPAS	33,719,307	4.28	1,565,837	1.10
29	TLAXCALA	17,995,359	2.29	0	0.00
30	VERACRUZ	38,267,719	4.86	1,203,445	0.86
31	YUCATAN	5,009,167	0.64	922,666	0.66
32	ZACATECAS	15,763,155	2.00	46,841,465	33.30
Total National Production		787,220,343		140,684,750	
Mean		24,600,636	3.13	4,396,398	3.13
Median		9,298,496	1.18	1,384,641	0.98
S.D.		34,234,998	4.35	8,929,321	6.35
C.V.		139.16	139.16	203.11	203.11
Minimum		411,742	0.05	0	0.00
Maximum		124,497,541	15.81	46,841,465	33.30

DEFINITION: 1985 maize production figures are shown in thousands of pesos. Maize for grain and feed are included. 1985 frijol production figures are shown in thousands of pesos.

SOURCE: 1988-1989 Anuario Estadistico, Table 4.2.1.

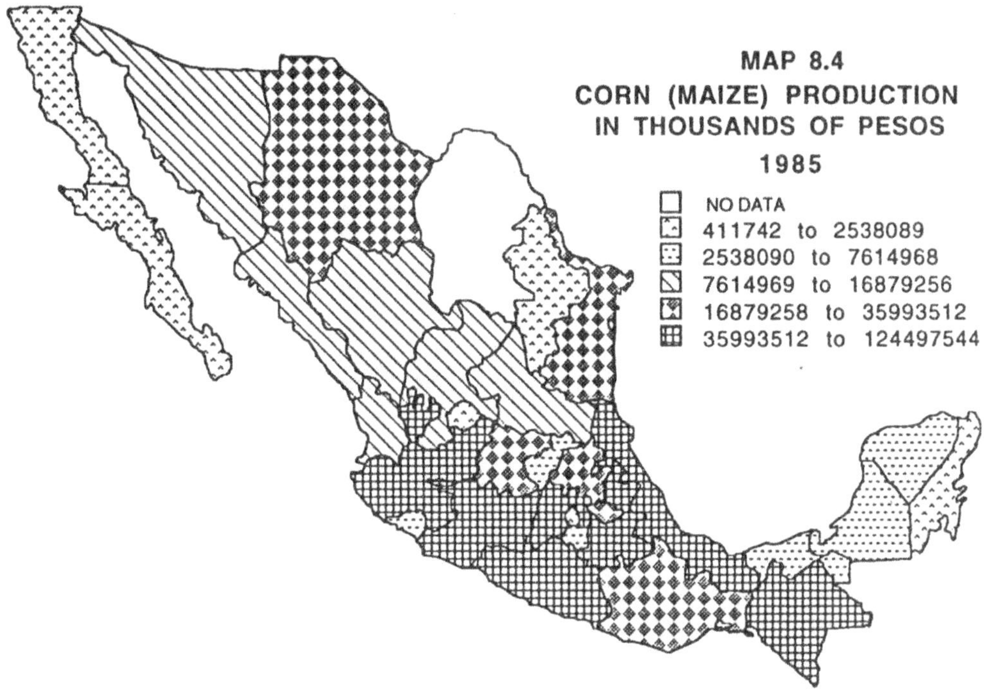

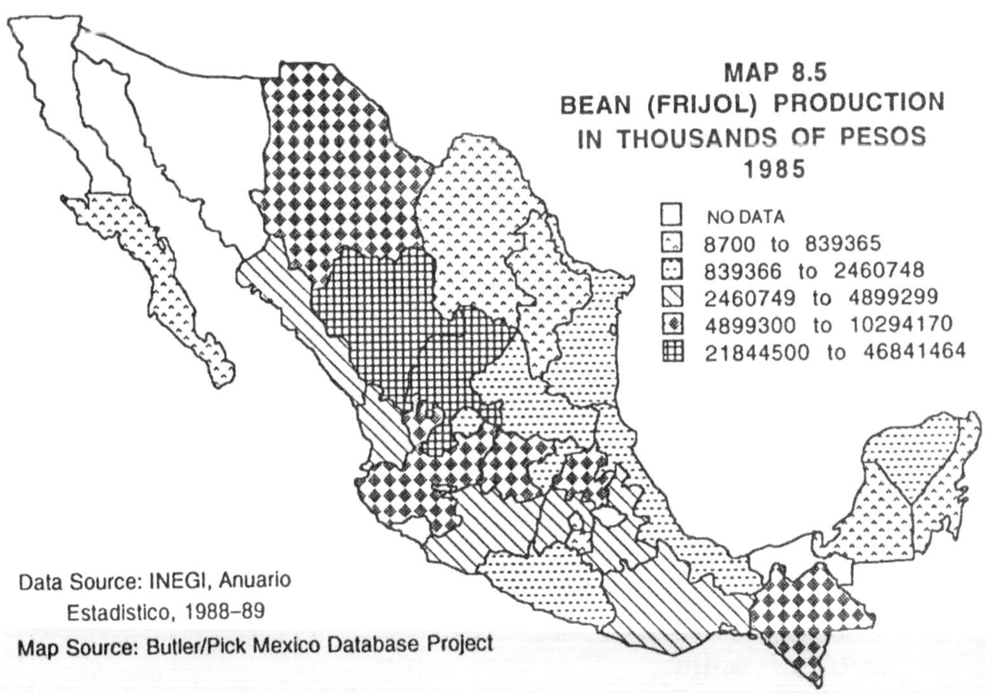

Data Source: INEGI, Anuario Estadistico, 1988–89

Map Source: Butler/Pick Mexico Database Project

Table 8.5 Fish Production, Live Weight in Tons, 1988

No.	State	Tons	Percent of Nation
1	AGUASCALIENTES	1,865	0.13
2	BAJA CALIFORNIA	231,805	16.63
3	BAJA CALIFORNIA SUR	90,281	6.48
4	CAMPECHE	65,942	4.73
5	COAHUILA	2,331	0.17
6	COLIMA	7,418	0.53
7	CHIAPAS	18,942	1.36
8	CHIHUAHUA	698	0.05
9	DISTRITO FEDERAL	ND	ND
10	DURANGO	3,732	0.27
11	GUANAJUATO	6,297	0.45
12	GUERRERO	17,705	1.27
13	HIDALGO	3,821	0.27
14	JALISCO	22,315	1.60
15	MEXICO	12,968	0.93
16	MICHOACAN	41,048	2.94
17	MORELOS	2,813	0.20
18	NAYARIT	15,389	1.10
19	NUEVO LEON	390	0.03
20	OAXACA	14,566	1.04
21	PUEBLA	3,239	0.23
22	QUERETARO	2,408	0.17
23	QUINTANA ROO	4,936	0.35
24	SAN LUIS POTOSI	1,901	0.14
25	SINALOA	141,850	10.17
26	SONORA	437,053	31.35
27	TABASCO	31,093	2.23
28	TAMAULIPAS	54,350	3.90
29	TLAXCALA	1,500	0.11
30	VERACRUZ	119,481	8.57
31	YUCATAN	34,089	2.45
32	ZACATECAS	1,949	0.14
	National Total	1,394,175	
	Mean	44,973	3.23
	Median	12,968	0.93
	S.D.	89,011	6.38
	C.V.	197.92	197.92
	Minimum	390	0.03
	Maximum	437,053	31.35

DEFINITION: 1988 fish production figures are shown in tons. The figures refer to live weight.

NOTE: ND = no data.

SOURCE: 1988-89 Anuario Estadistico, Table 4.2.5.

MAP 8.6
FISH PRODUCTION
LIVE WEIGHT, IN TONS, 1988

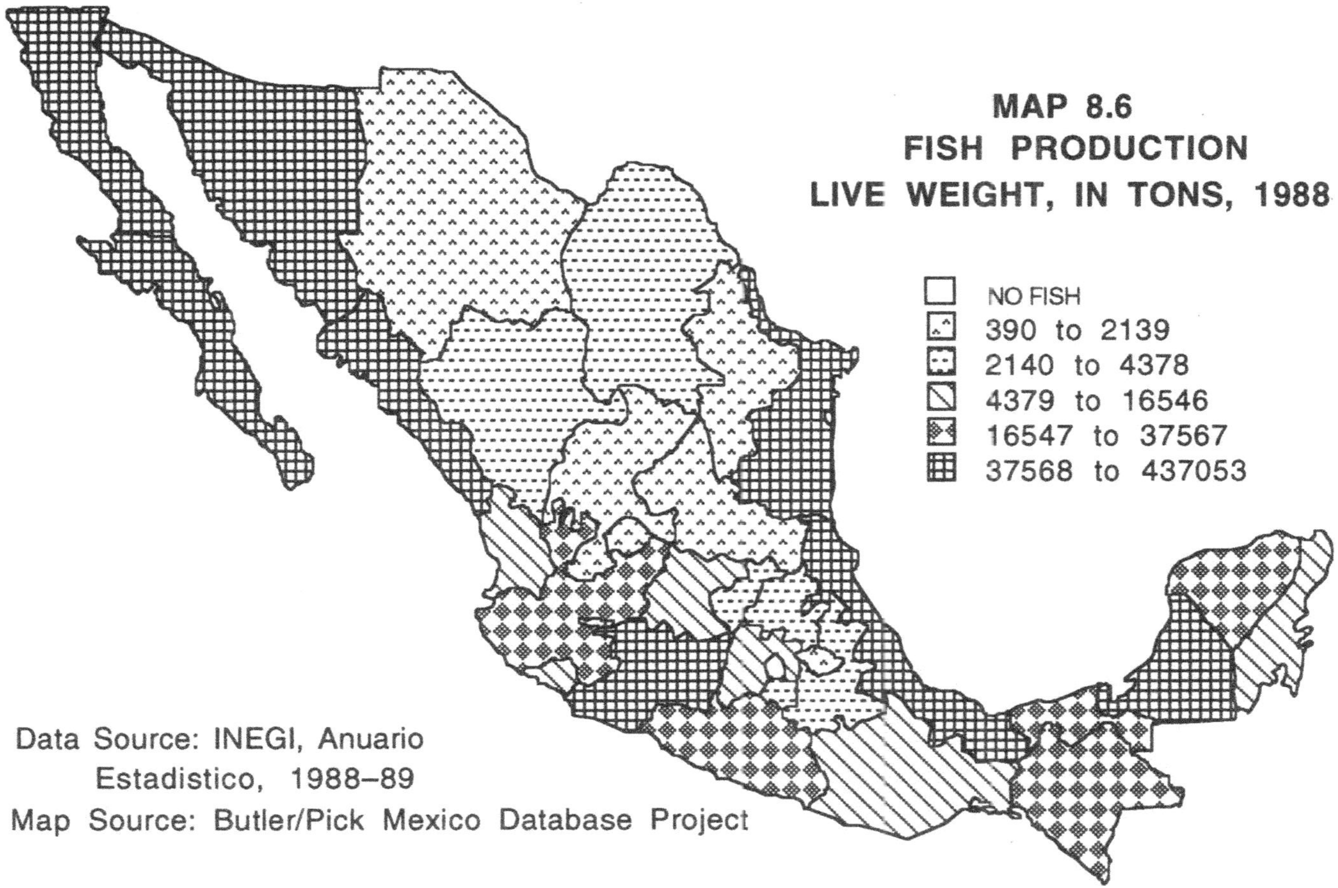

Data Source: INEGI, Anuario Estadistico, 1988–89
Map Source: Butler/Pick Mexico Database Project

Table 8.6 Beef and Pork Production, in Tons, 1989

No.	State	Beef Production			Pork Production		
		Tons	Percent of Nation	Heads	Tons	Percent of Nation	Heads
1	AGUASCALIENTES	6,531	0.56	122,008	4,089	0.56	35,991
2	BAJA CALIFORNIA	45,480	3.91	246,516	6,580	0.91	64,758
3	BAJA CALIFORNIA SUR	5,514	0.47	166,292	850	0.12	13,452
4	CAMPECHE	18,945	1.63	573,462	3,574	0.49	149,612
5	COAHUILA	30,916	2.66	632,285	8,618	1.19	72,213
6	COLIMA	9,995	0.86	272,827	1,718	0.24	82,900
7	CHIAPAS	64,440	5.54	2,128,680	13,741	1.89	1,548,979
8	CHIHUAHUA	60,846	5.23	2,371,287	11,455	1.58	319,103
9	DISTRITO FEDERAL	992	0.09	43,871	4,036	0.56	14,325
10	DURANGO	54,252	4.67	1,307,187	8,871	1.22	213,652
11	GUANAJUATO	33,066	2.84	982,482	85,107	11.71	698,632
12	GUERRERO	29,940	2.57	1,224,824	20,142	2.77	817,147
13	HIDALGO	19,680	1.69	510,529	15,965	2.20	490,584
14	JALISCO	120,224	10.34	2,788,413	138,384	19.04	1,798,937
15	MEXICO	25,598	2.20	1,005,308	36,215	4.98	1,220,222
16	MICHOACAN	34,495	2.97	1,683,144	55,664	7.66	1,589,915
17	MORELOS	6,271	0.54	202,668	1,978	0.27	188,009
18	NAYARIT	14,857	1.28	625,472	3,886	0.53	109,792
19	NUEVO LEON	18,730	1.61	715,837	14,410	1.98	196,763
20	OAXACA	37,294	3.21	1,414,778	27,512	3.79	869,236
21	PUEBLA	28,665	2.47	501,929	37,074	5.10	835,002
22	QUERETARO	9,617	0.83	261,634	5,229	0.72	62,530
23	QUINTANA ROO	1,428	0.12	69,274	4,800	0.66	144,426
24	SAN LUIS POTOSI	22,595	1.94	559,494	5,740	0.79	246,789
25	SINALOA	46,131	3.97	1,517,734	16,597	2.28	369,466
26	SONORA	63,746	5.48	1,719,608	109,729	15.10	1,212,408
27	TABASCO	63,655	5.47	1,737,955	11,389	1.57	446,788
28	TAMAULIPAS	40,111	3.45	1,033,569	3,294	0.45	101,046
29	TLAXCALA	179	0.02	77,509	10,114	1.39	244,914
30	VERACRUZ	187,198	16.10	4,556,712	32,131	4.42	1,286,527
31	YUCATAN	24,743	2.13	881,618	15,461	2.13	292,206
32	ZACATECAS	36,646	3.15	1,133,386	12,317	1.69	420,783
	National Total	1,162,780		33,068,292	726,670		16,157,107
	Mean	36,337	3.12	1,033,384	22,708	3.13	504,910
	Median	29,303	2.52	798,728	11,422	1.57	269,498
	S.D.	37,269	3.21	962,345	32,104	4.42	523,547
	C.V.	102.57	102.57	93.13	141.38	141.38	103.69
	Minimum	179	0.02	43,871	850	0.12	13,452
	Maximum	187,198	16.10	4,556,712	138,384	19.04	1,798,937

DEFINITION: Beef and pork production are in heads.

SOURCE: 1990 Anuario Estadistico, Table 4.2.2.

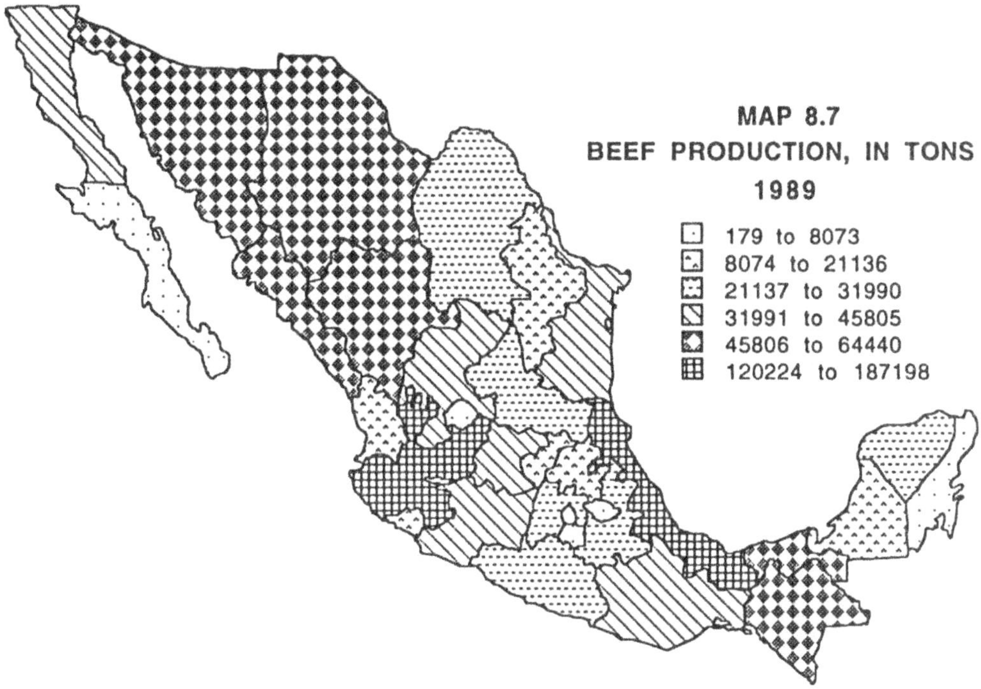

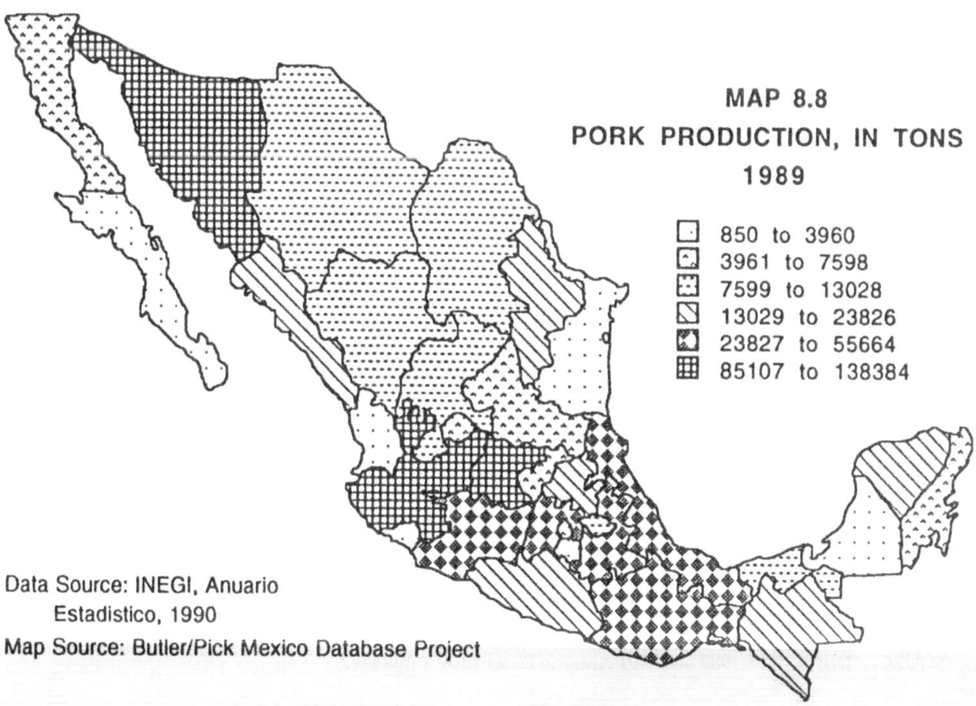

Data Source: INEGI, Anuario Estadistico, 1990

Map Source: Butler/Pick Mexico Database Project

Table 8.7 Irrigated Land Area, 1987–1989

No.	State	1987		1988		1989	
		Irrigated Land Area	Percent	Irrigated Land Area	Percent	Irrigated Land Area	Percent
1	AGUASCALIENTES	0	0.0000	0	0.0000	0	0.0000
2	BAJA CALIFORNIA	0	0.0000	0	0.0000	0	0.0000
3	BAJA CALIFORNIA SUR	0	0.0000	0	0.0000	0	0.0000
4	CAMPECHE	0	0.0000	0	0.0000	0	0.0000
5	COAHUILA	0	0.0000	0	0.0000	0	0.0000
6	COLIMA	927	0.0113	0	0.0000	320	0.0060
7	CHIAPAS	12,706	0.1549	2,430	0.0948	12,400	0.2328
8	CHIHUAHUA	111	0.0014	12	0.0005	448	0.0084
9	DISTRITO FEDERAL	0	0.0000	0	0.0000	0	0.0000
10	DURANGO	0	0.0000	0	0.0000	0	0.0000
11	GUANAJUATO	0	0.0000	0	0.0000	0	0.0000
12	GUERRERO	4,233	0.0516	278	0.0108	460	0.0086
13	HIDALGO	779	0.0095	0	0.0000	1,014	0.0190
14	JALISCO	0	0.0000	0	0.0000	0	0.0000
15	MEXICO	0	0.0000	0	0.0000	0	0.0000
16	MICHOACAN	0	0.0000	0	0.0000	0	0.0000
17	MORELOS	0	0.0000	0	0.0000	0	0.0000
18	NAYARIT	5,800	0.0707	550	0.0215	2,000	0.0375
19	NUEVO LEON	0	0.0000	0	0.0000	0	0.0000
20	OAXACA	300	0.0037	0	0.0000	0	0.0000
21	PUEBLA	0	0.0000	0	0.0000	0	0.0000
22	QUERETARO	0	0.0000	0	0.0000	0	0.0000
23	QUINTANA ROO	0	0.0000	0	0.0000	0	0.0000
24	SAN LUIS POTOSI	4,657	0.0568	100	0.0039	2,366	0.0444
25	SINALOA	6,422	0.0783	2,059	0.0803	3,161	0.0593
26	SONORA	0	0.0000	0	0.0000	0	0.0000
27	TABASCO	1,000	0.0122	100	0.0039	7,100	0.1333
28	TAMAULIPAS	42,100	0.5132	20,000	0.7804	20,000	0.3755
29	TLAXCALA	0	0.0000	0	0.0000	0	0.0000
30	VERACRUZ	3,000	0.0366	100	0.0039	4,000	0.0751
31	YUCATAN	0	0.0000	0	0.0000	0	0.0000
32	ZACATECAS	0	0.0000	0	0.0000	0	0.0000
National Total		82,035		25,629		53,269	
Mean		2,564	0.0313	801	0.0313	1,665	0.0313
Median		0	0.0000	0	0.0000	0	0.0000
S.D.		7,724	0.0942	3,547	0.1384	4,222	0.0793
C.V.		301.31	301.31	442.88	442.88	253.64	253.64
Minimum		0	0.0000	0	0.0000	0	0.0000
Maximum		42,100	0.5132	20,000	0.7804	20,000	0.3755

DEFINITION: Irrigated Land Area is that land having large irrigation works. The Ratio is the percent of irrigated land as a ratio to the total irrigated land.

SOURCE: INEGI, 1988-1989 and 1991 Anuario Estadistico, Table 2.3.2.

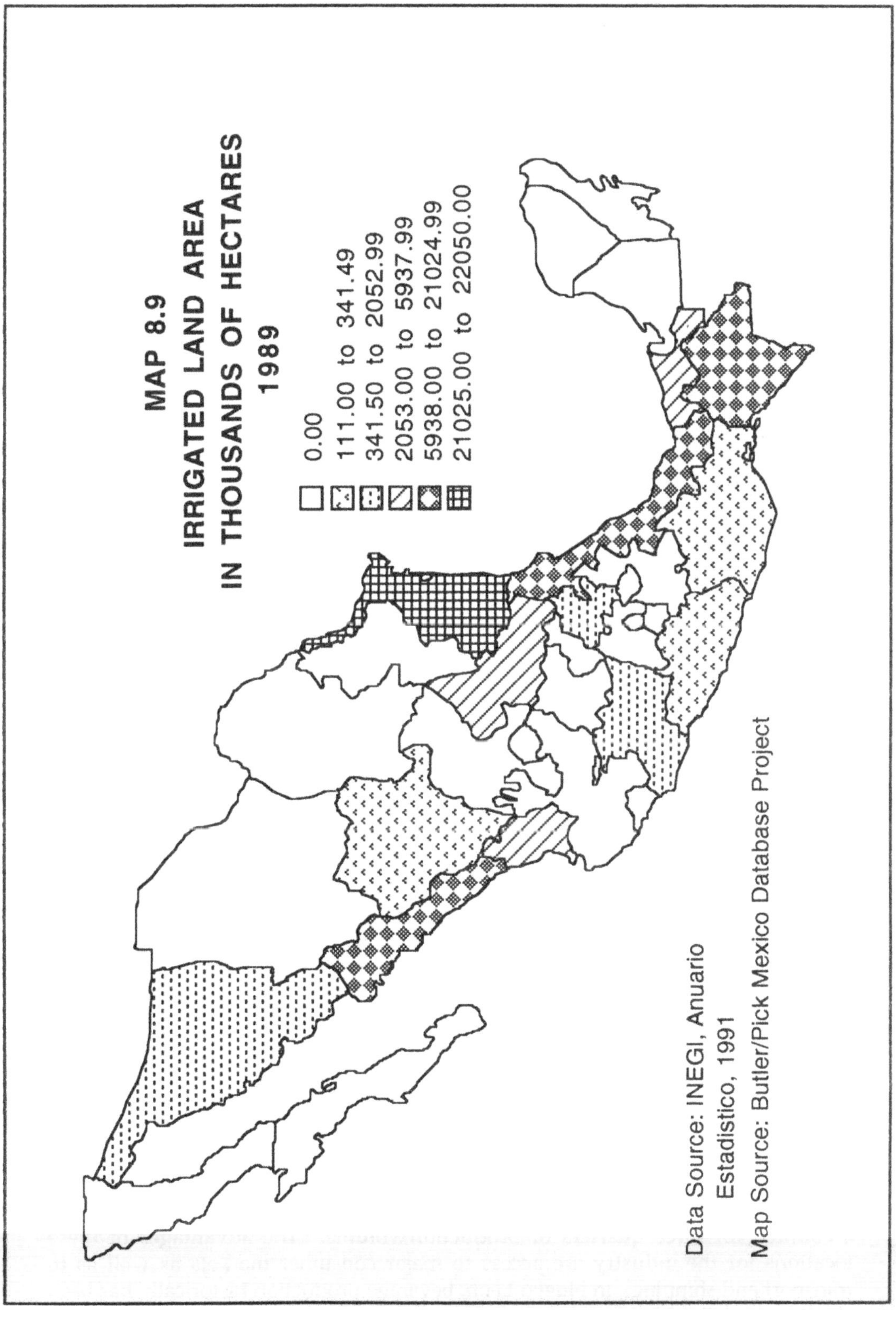
MAP 8.9
IRRIGATED LAND AREA
IN THOUSANDS OF HECTARES
1989
0.00
111.00 to 341.49
341.50 to 2052.99
2053.00 to 5937.99
5938.00 to 21024.99
21025.00 to 22050.00
Data Source: INEGI, Anuario
Estadistico, 1991
Map Source: Butler/Pick Mexico Database Project

Manufacturing Production

Figure 8.4 and Table 8.8 present the production of selected manufactured products for the period of 1950–1990. They illustrate information for textiles and clothing, mechanical equipment, and autos/motors. The production of all three selected product categories increased between 1950 and the early 1980s and almost at about the same pace. However, after around 1981 there was a decrease in these products, and others as well, but with a rather large upswing two years later in the production of autos/motors. Similar trends are apparent for other products. These three product categories may be contrasted with the other categories in Table 8.8. Production in the traditional category of textiles and clothing grew much more slowly than for the heavy durable categories, about fifty percent more rapidly than population. One reason for the slower growth pace in textile and clothing production is that, in contrast to heavy durables, there has been a much lower export component.

Basic chemical production increased rapidly over the four decades—by 22 times. Its growth is tied to the industrialization of modern Mexico as well as to rising export market demand. Auto production grew phenomenally, by 67 fold. This represents maquiladora industry serving both the export (U.S.) and domestic markets.

Cement, Lime, Gypsum, and Other Non-Metallic Mineral Production

Table 8.9 presents the cement, lime, gypsum, and other non-metallic production in Mexico for 1988. The three states of Hidalgo, Nuevo Leon, and Mexico produced about forty percent of the production of these non-metallic minerals in 1988. Other states with relatively high production were Jalisco, San Luis Potosi, Veracruz, Coahuila, and the Federal District. Every Mexican state, however, had some production of these materials. As illustrated by Map 8.10, major production states are located in the central part of the country, with somewhat larger production in the eastern north, northeast, and gulf regions of Mexico. Since these materials are heavily utilized in the building and construction industries, it is not surprising that half of the production is located in the major metropolitan states. This linkage is also reflected is the significant association with urbanization (r = .71).

Beverage Production, 1988

Map 8.11 and Table 8.10 present information on beverage production in Mexico in 1988. The Federal District and Nuevo Leon produced over 60 percent of the nation's beverages in 1988. Jalisco and San Luis Potosi produced over 30 percent of the total output of beverages in 1988. Thus, these four states produced over 90 percent of total beverage production in Mexico. A few other states produced some beverages but most of them had no production. The four major metropolitan states accounted for three quarters of production volume. The advantages of these locations for the industry are access to major consumer markets as well as to transport and shipping. In Nuevo Leon, beverage production historically has been a major specialized industry.

Paper Production, 1988

As with so many other products, paper production in Mexico is highly concentrated in a few states. In 1988, the Federal District and the state of Mexico produced well over half of the paper products in Mexico (see Table 8.11). Nuevo Leon, Veracruz, and Queretaro also produced relatively large quantities of paper products (ca. 25%). As shown on Map 8.12, paper production was concentrated in the Federal District and a few surrounding states. Most high producing states are metropolitan (Federal District, Mexico, Nuevo Leon) or metropolitan-adjacent (Queretaro), implying that they are near the important paper consumer markets. Veracruz's large population also implies a consumer market for paper. There are very few associations with other variables and none that appears meaningful.

Automobile Production, 1988

Map 8.13 shows where the major automobile production facilities in Mexico were located as of 1988. The major production areas were the central border states and the Central Metropolitan Zone and surrounding states. The four border states plus adjacent Durango accounted for 29 percent of production. This production is housed in major maquiladora plant sites (see Chapter 10) and is mostly exported to the U.S. Fifty-two percent of production is located in the central region; it also consists nearly entirely of foreign manufacturing plants, but it involves more domestic consumption rather than export (see Table 8.12). In the future, Aguascalientes will become a more important automobile producing state as the new Nissan factory expands production. There was no automobile production in most of the far south states, the Bajas, and in Zacatecas.

Automobile production is closely associated with gross state revenues per capita (r = .45). This reflects the location of auto production in more economically productive states; in addition, automobiles contribute to state economic product.

Figure 8.4
Production of Selected Products:
1950-1990

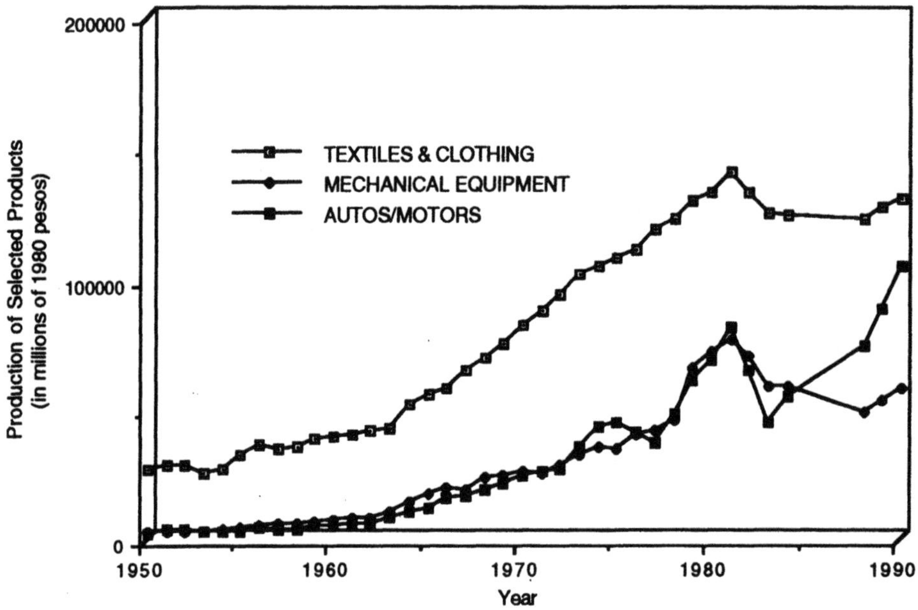

SOURCE: Estadisticas Historicas de Mexico, 1966; Anuario Estadistico, 1991, 1992.

Table 8.8 Production of Manufactured Products, 1950–1990

Year	Textiles and Clothing	Basic Chemicals	Electrical Equipment	Mechanical Equipment	Autos/ Motors
1950	26,662	916	4,321	2,302	1,556
1951	27,831	1,004	3,363	2,625	3,184
1952	26,362	939	5,005	2,596	3,249
1953	25,092	1,205	3,650	2,617	2,524
1954	26,290	1,162	4,339	2,640	2,510
1955	31,754	1,499	6,160	3,571	2,562
1956	35,476	1,513	7,924	4,425	3,650
1957	34,185	1,850	8,613	5,163	3,435
1958	34,787	2,051	10,133	5,199	3,363
1959	37,813	2,137	10,778	5,945	4,374
1960	38,968	2,675	12,606	7,142	4,475
1961	39,420	3,105	13,668	7,924	5,170
1962	41,264	3,363	14,048	7,996	5,601
1963	42,360	3,729	16,702	10,205	7,393
1964	51,611	4,202	19,563	14,041	10,104
1965	55,010	4,697	21,148	17,024	11,510
1966	57,826	5,265	23,973	19,563	15,361
1967	64,332	5,830	25,567	18,882	16,185
1968	69,237	6,796	26,362	23,105	16,552
1969	74,394	8,369	30,736	24,138	21,264
1970	81,730	9,201	33,245	25,852	24,339
1971	86,979	9,975	34,149	24,719	26,003
1972	93,275	10,499	38,366	26,132	26,606
1973	101,472	11,739	41,492	32,041	34,760
1974	104,175	13,066	48,154	34,995	42,482
1975	107,051	12,370	45,494	34,572	44,576
1976	110,694	13,023	47,509	39,750	40,060
1977	118,632	14,127	51,655	41,076	36,560
1978	122,326	13,360	62,375	45,401	47,853
1979	129,200	12,532	58,057	65,235	60,897
1980	132,314	13,578	60,063	71,610	68,466
1981	140,208	14,485	62,177	76,309	81,094
1982	132,146	14,518	56,716	70,243	64,701
1983	124,801	14,493	53,023	68,260	44,170
1984	124,801	15,295	59,713	58,672	54,262
1985					
1986					
1987					
1988	122,497	14,754	66,701	48,063	74,096
1989	126,797	17,495	68,356	53,077	87,940
1990	129,636	20,238	73,439	57,898	104,207
National Total	2,929,408	307,055	1,229,343	1,061,008	1,107,094
Mean	77,090	8,080	32,351	27,921	29,134
Median	71,816	7,583	28,549	23,622	18,908
S.D.	40,611	5,798	22,573	23,603	28,370
C.V.	52.68	71.75	69.77	84.54	97.38
Minimum	25,092	916	3,363	2,302	1,556
Maximum	140,208	20,238	73,439	76,309	104,207

DEFINITION: Values of production are in millions of pesos at 1980 prices.

SOURCE: INEGI, Estadisticas Historicas 1986; 1990 and 1991 Anuarios Estadisticos.

Table 8.9 Cement, Lime, Gypsum, and Other Non-Metallic Mineral Production, 1988

No.	State	Workers	Volume	Total Assets	Percent of Nation
1	AGUASCALIENTES	676	15,995	10,941	0.3677
2	BAJA CALIFORNIA	1,090	139,371	18,655	3.2041
3	BAJA CALIFORNIA SUR	339	28,430	6,600	0.6536
4	CAMPECHE	453	6,578	4,499	0.1512
5	COAHUILA	4,159	208,172	44,037	4.7859
6	COLIMA	239	6,485	3,762	0.1491
7	CHIAPAS	416	9,206	5,044	0.2116
8	CHIHUAHUA	2,133	137,097	458,051	3.1519
9	DISTRITO FEDERAL	3,344	196,570	138,359	4.5191
10	DURANGO	2,198	51,367	35,328	1.1809
11	GUANAJUATO	1,612	92,252	116,534	2.1209
12	GUERRERO	711	29,304	9,628	0.6737
13	HIDALGO	4,319	610,921	547,621	14.0451
14	JALISCO	4,637	247,780	454,258	5.6964
15	MEXICO	9,120	824,182	1,168,048	18.9479
16	MICHOACAN	1,152	32,647	23,523	0.7506
17	MORELOS	1,548	65,202	85,355	1.4990
18	NAYARIT	425	8,569	6,526	0.1970
19	NUEVO LEON	5,753	432,855	226,131	9.9513
20	OAXACA	1,217	82,613	34,294	1.8993
21	PUEBLA	3,459	85,138	79,025	1.9573
22	QUERETARO	471	14,113	12,234	0.3244
23	QUINTANA ROO	666	55,525	23,944	1.2765
24	SAN LUIS POTOSI	2,691	265,573	495,298	6.1055
25	SINALOA	966	48,194	83,059	1.1080
26	SONORA	1,811	141,151	355,168	3.2451
27	TABASCO	892	92,146	529,408	2.1184
28	TAMAULIPAS	3,202	25,591	19,283	0.5883
29	TLAXCALA	700	41,653	6,383	0.9576
30	VERACRUZ	2,784	222,260	556,714	5.1098
31	YUCATAN	2,373	124,196	302,596	2.8553
32	ZACATECAS	657	8,587	6,578	0.1974
	National Total	66,213	4,349,721	5,866,881	
	Mean	2,069	135,929	183,340	3.1250
	Median	1,383	73,907	39,683	1.6991
	S.D.	1,946	182,699	264,519	4.2002
	C.V.	94.05	134.41	144.28	134.41
	Minimum	239	6,485	3,762	0.1491
	Maximum	9,120	824,182	1,168,048	18.9479

DEFINITION: Volume of production in tons. Total assets in millions of pesos. Percent of nation represents the percent of volume.

SOURCE: INEGI, 1989 Censos Economicos.

MAP 8.10
CEMENT, LIME, GYPSUM AND OTHER NON-METALLIC MINERAL PRODUCTION, 1988

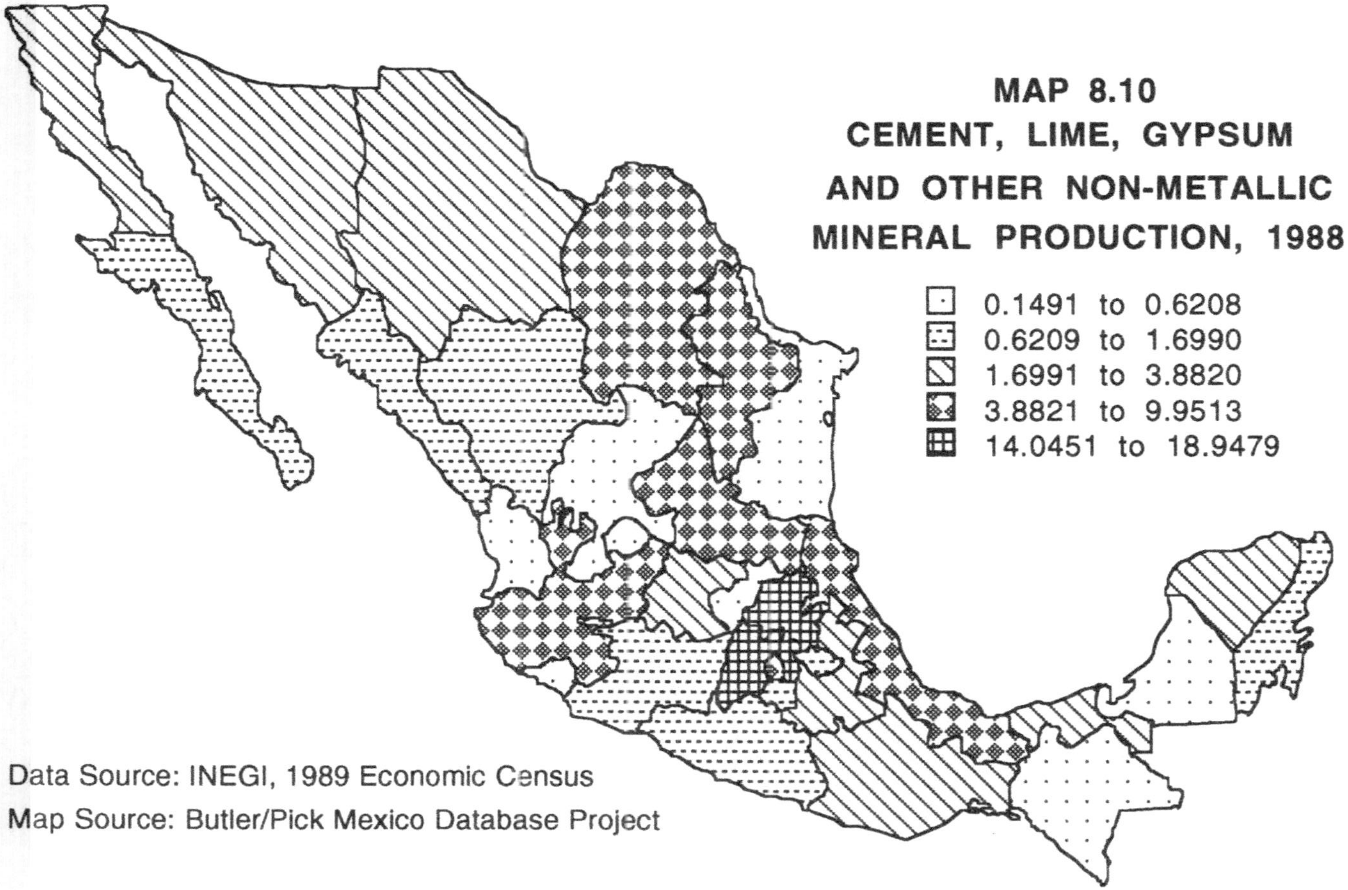

Data Source: INEGI, 1989 Economic Census
Map Source: Butler/Pick Mexico Database Project

Table 8.10 Beverage Production, 1988

No.	State	Workers	Volume	Total Assets	Percent of Nation
1	AGUASCALIENTES	0	0	0	0
2	BAJA CALIFORNIA	0	0	0	0
3	BAJA CALIFORNIA SUR	0	0	0	0
4	CAMPECHE	0	0	0	0
5	COAHUILA	0	0	0	0
6	COLIMA	0	0	0	0
7	CHIAPAS	0	0	0	0
8	CHIHUAHUA	0	0	0	0
9	DISTRITO FEDERAL	1,148	644,999	101,846	31.2489
10	DURANGO	0	0	0	0
11	GUANAJUATO	0	0	0	0
12	GUERRERO	0	0	0	0
13	HIDALGO	0	0	0	0
14	JALISCO	581	250,162	128,770	12.1199
15	MEXICO	529	91,431	159,261	4.4296
16	MICHOACAN	136	10,445	620	0.5060
17	MORELOS	0	0	0	0
18	NAYARIT	2,190	62,283	44,895	3.0175
19	NUEVO LEON	1,546	610,154	240,251	29.5607
20	OAXACA	0	0	0	0
21	PUEBLA	0	0	0	0
22	QUERETARO	0	0	0	0
23	QUINTANA ROO	0	0	0	0
24	SAN LUIS POTOSI	320	378,745	63,129	18.3494
25	SINALOA	0	0	0	0
26	SONORA	0	0	0	0
27	TABASCO	0	0	0	0
28	TAMAULIPAS	0	0	0	0
29	TLAXCALA	0	0	0	0
30	VERACRUZ	1,109	15,852	7,560	0.7680
31	YUCATAN	0	0	0	0
32	ZACATECAS	0	0	0	0
	National Total	7,559	2,064,070	746,331	
	Mean	236	64,502	23,323	3.1250
	Median	0	0	0	0.0000
	S.D.	529	167,890	56,423	8.1339
	C.V.	224.10	260.29	241.92	260.29
	Minimum	0	0	0	0.0000
	Maximum	2,190	644,999	240,251	31.2489

DEFINITION: Total assets in millions of pesos. Percent of nation represents the percent of volume of production.

SOURCE: INEGI, 1989 Censos Economicos.

MAP 8.11
BEVERAGE PRODUCTION, 1988

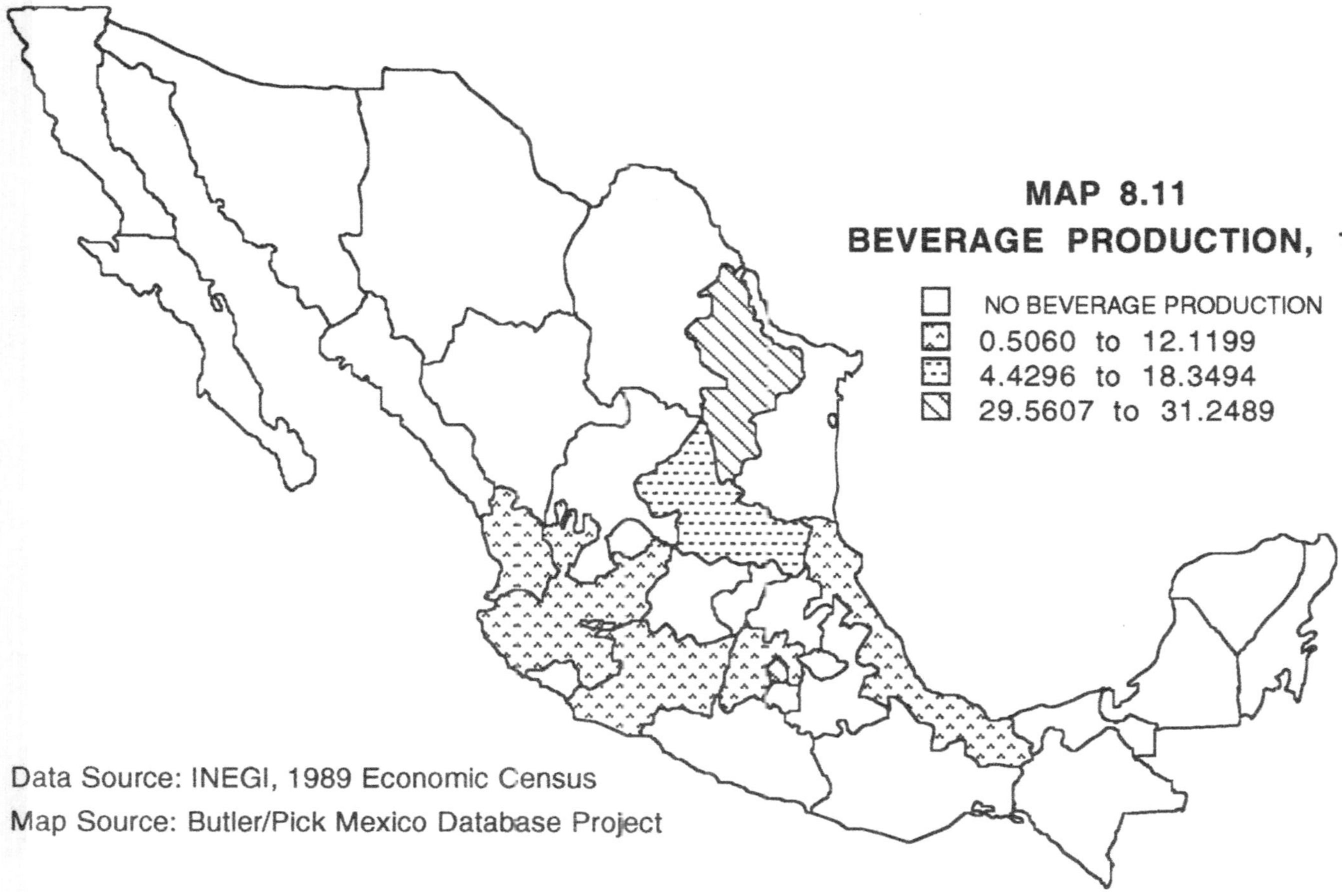

Data Source: INEGI, 1989 Economic Census

Map Source: Butler/Pick Mexico Database Project

Table 8.11 Paper Production, 1988

No.	State	Workers	Volume	Total Assets	Percent of Nation
1	AGUASCALIENTES	24	373	138	0.0060
2	BAJA CALIFORNIA	1,939	87,584	54,781	1.4009
3	BAJA CALIFORNIA SUR	13	228	120	0.0036
4	CAMPECHE	3	12	8	0.0002
5	COAHUILA	29	667	370	0.0107
6	COLIMA	0	0	0	0.0000
7	CHIAPAS	3	5	1	0.0001
8	CHIHUAHUA	1,042	189,864	138,963	3.0368
9	DISTRITO FEDERAL	13,803	1,217,144	870,503	19.4679
10	DURANGO	1,147	94,212	176,072	1.5069
11	GUANAJUATO	1,704	48,387	44,739	0.7739
12	GUERRERO	11	518	255	0.0083
13	HIDALGO	113	4,672	2,815	0.0747
14	JALISCO	2,014	146,168	90,241	2.3379
15	MEXICO	15,454	2,149,234	1,470,968	34.3765
16	MICHOACAN	564	123,499	102,871	1.9753
17	MORELOS	311	46,471	29,841	0.7433
18	NAYARIT	12	150	520	0.0024
19	NUEVO LEON	5,124	587,811	624,826	9.4019
20	OAXACA	1,214	167,773	258,679	2.6835
21	PUEBLA	1,344	122,557	94,381	1.9603
22	QUERETARO	2,087	499,301	462,336	7.9862
23	QUINTANA ROO	4	156	116	0.0025
24	SAN LUIS POTOSI	1,660	144,085	301,533	2.3046
25	SINALOA	227	20,493	6,493	0.3278
26	SONORA	689	36,060	19,402	0.5768
27	TABASCO	0	0	0	0.0000
28	TAMAULIPAS	651	2,496	947	0.0399
29	TLAXCALA	340	32,986	7,007	0.5276
30	VERACRUZ	2,182	527,935	364,903	8.4442
31	YUCATAN	89	1,212	713	0.0194
32	ZACATECAS	0	0	0	0.0000
	National Total	53,797	6,252,050	5,124,541	
	Mean	1,681	195,377	160,142	3.1250
	Median	452	34,523	13,205	0.5522
	S.D.	3,569	436,746	315,223	6.9856
	C.V.	212.31	223.54	196.84	223.54
	Minimum	0	0	0	0.0000
	Maximum	15,454	2,149,234	1,470,968	34.3765

DEFINITION: Volume of production in tons. Total assets in in millions of pesos. Percent of nation represents the percent of volume.

SOURCE: INEGI, 1989 Censos Economicos.

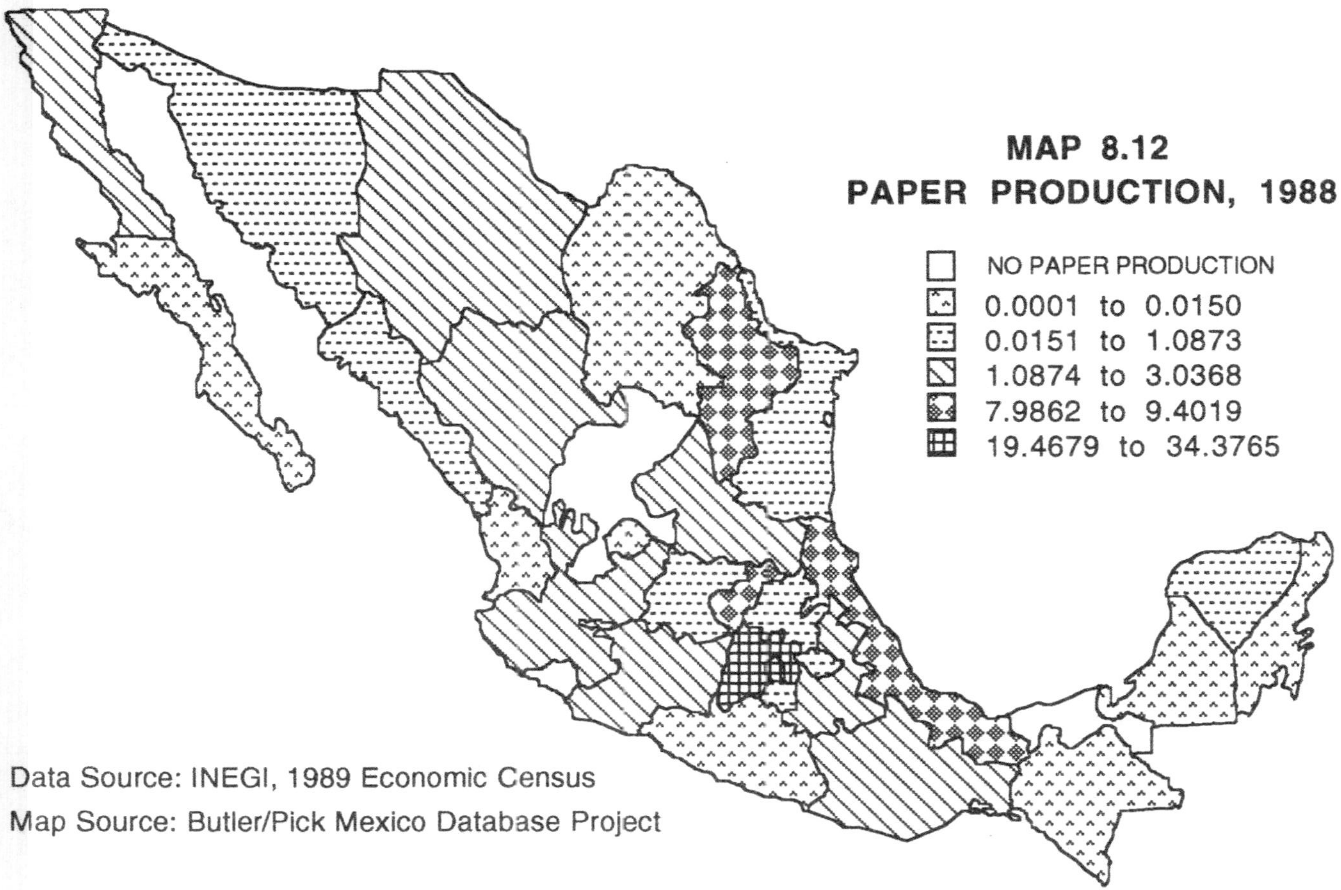

MAP 8.12
PAPER PRODUCTION, 1988

Data Source: INEGI, 1989 Economic Census
Map Source: Butler/Pick Mexico Database Project

Table 8.12 Automobile Production, 1988

No.	State	Workers	Volume	Total Assets	Percent of Nation
1	AGUASCALIENTES	3,150	222,879	422,458	1.1472
2	BAJA CALIFORNIA	2,901	231,831	69,850	1.1932
3	BAJA CALIFORNIA SUR	0	0	0	0.0000
4	CAMPECHE	0	0	0	0.0000
5	COAHUILA	11,260	2,789,768	3,174,914	14.3591
6	COLIMA	22	398	296	0.0020
7	CHIAPAS	0	0	0	0.0000
8	CHIHUAHUA	4,580	792,769	525,593	4.0804
9	DISTRITO FEDERAL	18,683	2,414,223	788,644	12.4261
10	DURANGO	1,021	374,723	38,411	1.9287
11	GUANAJUATO	3,768	303,623	294,864	1.5628
12	GUERRERO	19	513	261	0.0026
13	HIDALGO	3,689	424,213	427,723	2.1834
14	JALISCO	3,343	136,785	126,468	0.7040
15	MEXICO	35,444	5,107,540	4,136,016	26.2888
16	MICHOACAN	272	5,503	4,875	0.0283
17	MORELOS	4,380	1,951,957	555,981	10.0468
18	NAYARIT	23	285	467	0.0015
19	NUEVO LEON	9,554	846,148	823,451	4.3552
20	OAXACA	306	8,217	2,472	0.0423
21	PUEBLA	13,042	1,726,962	3,585,166	8.8888
22	QUERETARO	5,542	515,076	400,728	2.6511
23	QUINTANA ROO	0	0	0	0.0000
24	SAN LUIS POTOSI	2,254	267,363	275,807	1.3761
25	SINALOA	122	4,706	3,543	0.0242
26	SONORA	4,256	1,269,663	324,149	6.5350
27	TABASCO	10	294	112	0.0015
28	TAMAULIPAS	8,460	3,967	63,317	0.0204
29	TLAXCALA	410	21,537	51,457	0.1109
30	VERACRUZ	329	6,753	6,714	0.0348
31	YUCATAN	0	0	0	0.0000
32	ZACATECAS	0	0	0	0.0000
	National Total	136,840	19,427,695	16,103,734	
	Mean	4,276	607,115	503,242	3.1249
	Median	1,638	79,161	57,387	0.4074
	S.D.	7,257	1,114,777	1,057,090	5.7378
	C.V.	169.72	183.62	210.06	183.62
	Minimum	0	0	0	0.0000
	Maximum	35,444	5,107,540	4,136,016	26.2888

DEFINITION: Volume of production and total assets are in millions of pesos. Percent of nation represents the percent of volume.

SOURCE: INEGI, 1989 Censos Economicos.

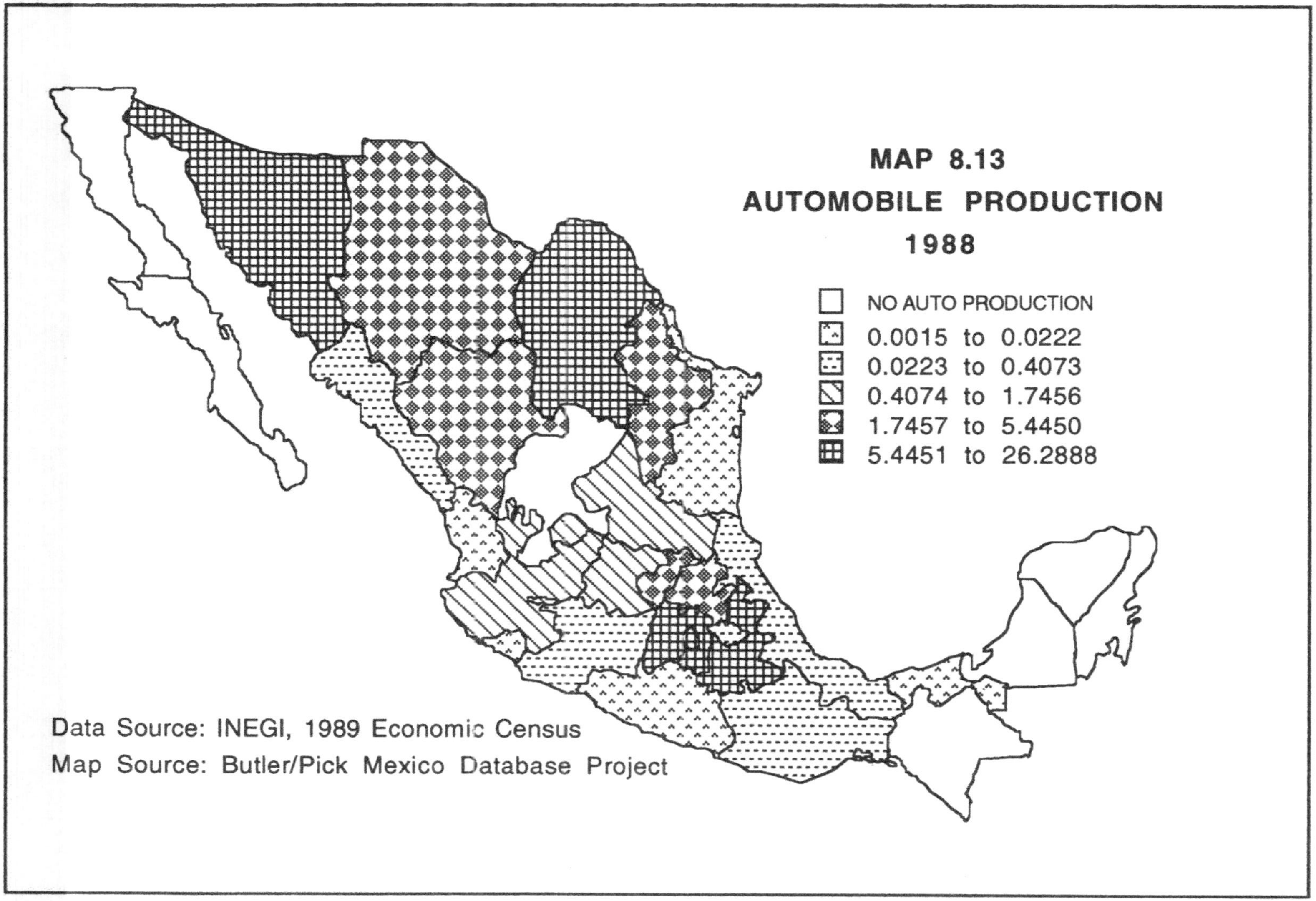
MAP 8.13
AUTOMOBILE PRODUCTION
1988
NO AUTO PRODUCTION
0.0015 to 0.0222
0.0223 to 0.4073
0.4074 to 1.7456
1.7457 to 5.4450
5.4451 to 26.2888
Data Source: INEGI, 1989 Economic Census
Map Source: Butler/Pick Mexico Database Project

Installed Electrical Energy Capacity

Electrical energy is measured in megawatts, or millions of watts. Installed electrical energy capacity for 1920–1989 by hydro and other types is shown in Figure 8.5 and Table 8.13. The other category includes all generating plants except hydro plants (*plantas de vapor* [1955–1966], *plantas de combustion interna* [1965–1976], and *plantas de gas y geotermica* [1965–1976]). Energy capacity remained relatively stable from 1930 through 1950; however, between 1950 and 1960, both hydro and other energy capacity expanded. Since the 1970s energy capacity has greatly expanded but with most of this increase being in the other category—oil and nuclear.

Table 8.13 shows the installed electrical energy capacity, by state, for 1985 and 1989. The per capita measure was determined by the ratio of total state megawattage in 1989 to total state population in 1990.

Map 8.14 illustrates variation in installed electrical energy capacity in 1989. Current electrical capacity is about two thirds thermoelectric, including internal combustion, gas, geothermal, and some nuclear energy. Present electricity is almost entirely produced by the Federal Electrical Commission (*La Comision Federal de Electricidad*).

Average state energy capacity is 762 megawatts. Five states account for 44 percent of the nation's capacity: Chiapas, with 3,929 megawatts of hydroelectric capacity, Guerrero, which is also nearly entirely hydroelectric, and Sonora, Hidalgo, and Mexico, which are largely thermoelectric. The latter two are the most important suppliers of energy to Mexico City. The border region accounts for 30 percent of the national capacity. This is not surprising given the urban and industrialized nature of the border area. Baja California's capacity is over half geothermal. Its geothermal plants constitute the second largest geothermal producing site in North America and one of the largest in the world.

From 1985 to 1989, the national energy capacity grew by 18 percent. Most states gained in energy capacity, although a few had significant lowering. The largest gainers in total capacity were the states of Sonora that gained 1,437 megawatts, Guerrero that gained 581 megawatts, and Chiapas, which increased by 420 megawatts. Sonora's increase was substantial and reflects the influence of increasing industrialization (for instance, note its auto production in Map 8.13). In relative terms, the greatest capacity gains of between two and eight fold growth were in Sonora, Quintana Roo, and Queretaro. As Mexico's premier relative population growth state in the 80s, Quintana Roo needed more energy capacity to support this growth. Queretaro's growth reflects its adjacency to Mexico City, as well as its own demographic growth. As seen in Table 8.13, the states with the highest per capita energy capacity were Colima and Chiapas, both of which grid most of their energy out of state. Other states with high per capita capacity include the high producing states of Guerrero, Hidalgo, and Sonora.

Figure 8.5
Installed Electrical Energy Capacity by Type
Mexico: 1920 - 1989

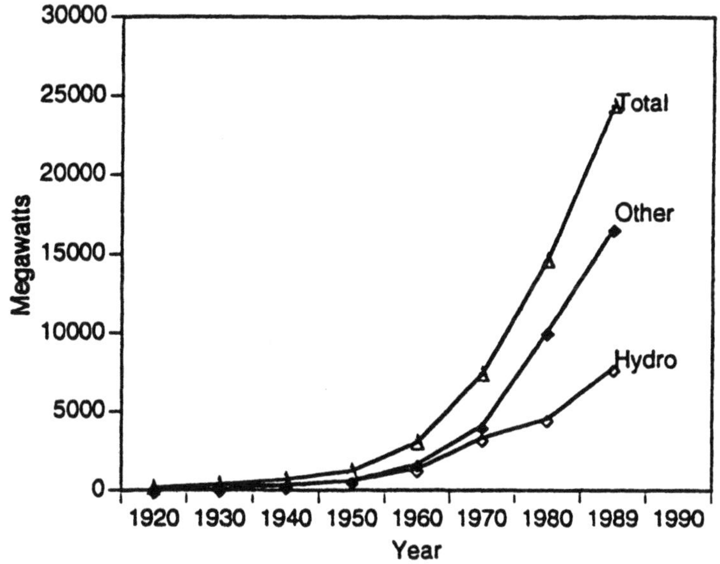

SOURCE: INEGI, Estadisticas Historicas 1986; Anuarios Estadisticos, 1986 and 1989.

Installed Electrical Energy Capacity, by Type, 1900–1989, in Megawatts

Year	Total Capacity	Class of Service			Hydro	Other	Number of Plants/ Plants in Service *
		Public	Private	Mixed			
1900	18				14	4	
1910	99				99		
1920	192				192		
1930	411				304	107	
1940	681	479	148	54	389	292	
1950	1,234	916	223	46	607	628	
1955	1,929	1,458	364	106	922	1,007	2,321
1960	3,048	2,320	561	175	1,357	1,691	2,766
1965	5,238	4,174	887	176	2,214	3,023	1,493
1970	7,413	6,028	1,209	175	3,326	4,087	2,487
1975	11,326	9,946	1,217	162	4,120	7,205	2,643
1980	14,625	14,625			4,541	10,084	
1985	20,807				6,532	14,275	498
1989	24,399				7,761	16,638	543

NOTE: The "other" category includes thermal and other generating plants including "plantas de vapor" (1955–1966), "plantas de combustion interna" (1965–1976), and from 1965–1976 "plantas de gas y geotermica." The figures in the righthand column are number of plants from 1955–1979 and plants in service from 1983–1989.

SOURCE: INEGI, Estadisticas Historicas, 1986; Anuarios Estadisticos, 1986 and 1991.

Table 8.13 Installed Electrical Energy Capacity, 1985-1989

No.	State	1985 Inst. Elect. Energy Cap.		1989 Inst. Elect. Energy Cap.					Capacity Growth, 1985-1989
		Total Capita	% of Nation	Thermo-electric	Hydro-electric	Total Cap.	% of Nation	Per Capita	
1	AGUASCALIENTES								
2	BAJA CALIFORNIA	938	5.00	1,100	0	1,100	4.51	0.0664	14.7
3	BAJA CALIF. SUR	192	1.00	222	0	222	0.91	0.0604	13.5
4	CAMPECHE	181	1.00	168	0	168	0.69	0.0340	-7.7
5	COAHUILA	1,066	5.00	1,291	66	1,357	5.56	0.0735	21.4
6	COLIMA	1,200	6.00	1,900	0	1,900	7.79	0.3617	36.8
7	CHIAPAS	3,509	17.00	0	3,929	3,929	16.10	0.2448	10.7
8	CHIHUAHUA	954	5.00	954	19	973	3.99	0.0401	2.0
9	DISTRITO FEDERAL	148	1.00	148	0	148	0.61	0.0018	0.0
10	DURANGO	415	2.00	415	0	415	1.70	0.0308	0.0
11	GUANAJUATO	907	4.00	907	0	901	3.69	0.0228	-0.7
12	GUERRERO	1,094	5.00	37	1,638	1,675	6.87	0.1260	34.7
13	HIDALGO	1,786	9.00	1,886	4	1,986	8.14	0.1054	10.1
14	JALISCO	217	1.00	62	154	211	0.86	0.0068	-2.8
15	MEXICO	1,497	7.00	1,458	340	1,528	6.26	0.0191	2.0
16	MICHOACAN	482	2.00	80	457	533	2.18	0.0278	9.6
17	MORELOS	0	0.00	0	0	0	0.00	0.0000	0.0
18	NAYARIT	4	0.00	2	2	5	0.02	0.0010	20.0
19	NUEVO LEON	1,078	5.00	1,030	0	1,030	4.22	0.0332	-4.7
20	OAXACA	156	1.00	0	156	156	0.64	0.0103	0.0
21	PUEBLA	460	2.00	38	431	469	1.92	0.0218	1.9
22	QUERETARO	79	0.00	298	2	300	1.23	0.0308	73.7
23	QUINTANA ROO	29	0.00	194	0	194	0.80	0.0262	85.1
24	SAN LUIS POTOSI	821	4.00	729	20	720	2.95	0.0369	-14.0
25	SINALOA	1,193	6.00	656	163	819	3.36	0.0452	-45.7
26	SONORA	164	1.00	1,205	256	1,601	6.56	0.0932	89.8
27	TABASCO	0	0.00	0	0	0	0.00	0.0000	0.0
28	TAMAULIPAS	1,227	6.00	1,197	32	1,198	4.91	0.0547	-2.4
29	TLAXCALA	0	0.00	0	0	0	0.00	0.0000	0.0
30	VERACRUZ	588	3.00	417	92	569	2.33	0.0106	-3.3
31	YUCATAN	261	1.00	227	0	277	1.14	0.0232	5.8
32	ZACATECAS	17	0.00	17	0	15	0.06	0.0012	-13.3
	National Total	20,663		16,638	7,761	24,399			18.1
	Mean	646	3.13	537	250	989	3.00	0.0519	10.9
	Median	438	2.00	227	2	701	2.00	0.0308	1.9
	S.D.	724	3.50	592	749	1,462	5.00	0.0757	28.2
	C.V.	112.14	99.68	110.32	299.28	147.77	166.67	145.86	259.1
	Minimum	4	0.00	0	0	0	0.00	0.0000	-45.7
	Maximum	3,509	17.00	1,900	3,929	7,858	25.00	0.3617	89.8

DEFINITION: Electrical energy capacity values are shown in megawatts. The per capita column is the ratio of the total megawattage in 1989 to total population 1990.

NOTE: National totals exclude mobile plants.

SOURCE: INEGI, 1986 Anuario Estadistico, Table 2.2.5, 1991 Anuario Estadistico, Table 2.3.3.

MAP 8.14
INSTALLED ELECTRICAL ENERGY CAPACITY IN MEGAWATTS, 1989

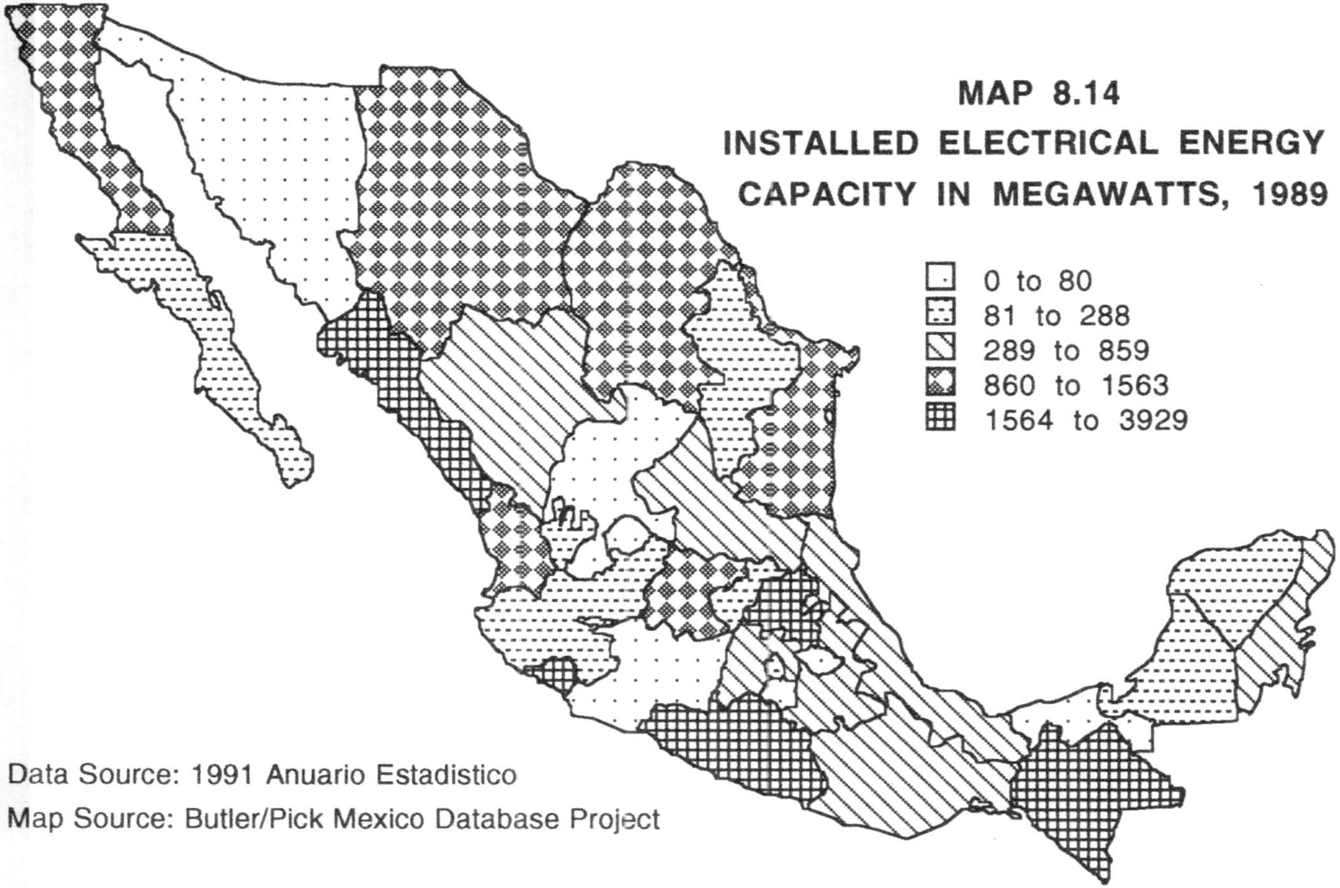

Data Source: 1991 Anuario Estadistico

Map Source: Butler/Pick Mexico Database Project

Corporations

Value of Corporations, 1986

In Mexico, the U.S. concept of a corporation is roughly equivalent to an S.A.C.V. (*Sociedad Anonima Constituida*). The unadjusted corporation value, for Mexico, in thousands of pesos in 1986, is shown in Table 8.14. The total unadjusted corporation value in 1986 was 142.4 billion pesos. It is important to note that this represents accounting or book value rather than market value. Also, many large "corporations" in 1986 such as PEMEX were nationalized and hence not included in this table.

The dominance of the northern border region and the central part of the country is readily apparent. As illustrated by Map 8.15, the only major deviation from this generalization is the state of Yucatan and to some degree Quintana Roo. There is very low corporation value in the pacific south region. Its total corporation value is only 1.25 billion pesos, which is under one percent of the nation!

As reported in Table 8.14, there is variation in state by type of corporation —commercial, industrial, or other. The major states for commercial corporations are Nuevo Leon, Mexico, Jalisco, the Federal District, and Baja California. These are major metropolitan states plus the important border state of Baja. They all are centers for major commercial enterprises and markets. The major state with industrial corporation value is Nuevo Leon that overwhelms the rest of the nation —this single state accounts for 70 percent of industrial corporation value. This reinforces the importance of Monterrey as the headquarters of Mexico's private industry. Coahuila and Chihuahua are in remote second and third place, each having 4–6 percent of the nations' industrial corporation value. The value of 'other' corporations, again, is dominated by Nuevo Leon along with the state of Mexico and the Federal District.

Number of Corporations, 1988

In 1988, there were 20,634 corporations (S.A.C.V.s) in Mexico. The number of corporations increased greatly especially in the Federal District between 1986 and 1988. This may have been the result of the advent of the Salinas administration. The number of corporations per 1,000 persons in 1986 and 1988 is shown on Table 8.15. The number of corporations shows large variation, as shown by a coefficient of variation of 219. In contrast to value of corporations, the Federal District dominates in absolute and per capita number of corporations. Other states with a relatively large ratio of corporations are San Luis Potosi, the Bajas, Nuevo Leon, and Quintana Roo. There are several clearly discernible regional patterns. The border region consistently has a large number of corporations (see Map 8.16). The south region has a very small number of corporations per capita and has only 514 corporations. The gulf region also has a low prevalence of corporations per capita.

Mexican "Fortune" 500 Corporations, 1986

Table 8.16 and Map 8.17 show the states in which Mexico's major 500 corporations were located in 1986 (*Expansion* 1987). Clearly, the Federal District with 149 headquarters dominates, equaling the total number in the state of Mexico (78) and Nuevo Leon (63), which totals 141. Jalisco follows with 36 corporate headquarters. These dominant states are the same as for the value of corporations. There is a substantial drop in number with Chihuahua, Puebla, Queretaro, Coahuila, and Veracruz having a number of headquarters varying from 14-15. A few states have between one and ten, while five states have no headquarters. The latter states comprise the south region plus Campeche and Nayarit.

Within states, there is further concentration within 108 *municipios* but seven of them contain 28 percent of the enterprises. Virtually all major enterprises located in "Mexico City," i.e., the Federal District, are located in two of its sixteen districts. In the state of Mexico, 40 of 78 enterprises are located in two *municipios*. Thus the Mexican 500 is located within a few states, within these states primarily in major cities, and in the major cities in a few concentrated districts (see Butler and Pick 1990).

Ownership of the Mexican 500 is shown in Figure 8.6. Note that this figure illustrates ownership prior to the extensive privatization that began with 1,155 state owned enterprises that was reduced to 737 in 1986 (see Chapter 10). Subsequent reductions to 221 by 1992, of course, alter this picture somewhat further. Over 70 percent of Mexico's 500 major enterprises are owned privately by Mexican citizens. In 1986, about 10 percent still were state owned enterprises. With the de-nationalization of the Salinas era, the proportion of state-owned enterprises has diminished further. The origin of capital for the 500 enterprises (see Figure 8.7) presents a different picture illustrating that capital for these major corporations is from throughout the world.

The principal activities of the 500 major Mexican enterprises in 1986 are shown below:

Principal Activity	Number	Percent
Minerals/Metals	78	18.2
Consumer Products	61	14.2
Food/Beverages	61	14.2
Commercial	60	14.0
Oil/Chemicals	57	13.3
Transportation	41	9.6
Construction	25	5.8
Financial/Professional	24	5.6
Comm. /Electrical	22	5.1
TOTALS	429*	100.0

* The remainder of the 500 did not fit any of these categories.
SOURCE: *Expansion*, 1987.

From an analysis of the value of corporations, the number of corporations per capita, and the 500 major corporations, it clearly appears that each of these is a distinct measure in itself. The major value of corporations was substantially in Nuevo Leon, with some variation in type of corporation. On the other hand, numerically the major 500 corporations were substantially located in Mexico City.

Table 8.14 Unadjusted Corporation Value, 1986

No.	State	Commercial Corps.	Industrial Corps.	Other Corps.	Total	Unadj. Corp. Value Per Capita, 1986
1	AGUASCALIENTES	238,649	264,978	299,094	802,721	1.1154
2	BAJA CALIFORNIA	1,525,949	1,158,171	1,668,272	4,352,392	2.6206
3	BAJA CALIFORNIA SUR	142,289	46,319	162,291	350,899	1.1043
4	CAMPECHE	127,390	99,991	215,254	442,635	0.8271
5	COAHUILA	1,377,279	4,033,782	2,074,153	7,485,214	3.7951
6	COLIMA	149,037	3,428	135,535	288,000	0.6721
7	CHIAPAS	182,972	48,822	114,219	346,013	0.1078
8	CHIHUAHUA	968,057	3,168,894	1,053,703	5,190,654	2.1257
9	DISTRITO FEDERAL	2,003,127	178,404	8,251,423	10,432,954	1.2668
10	DURANGO	268,295	436,892	435,524	1,140,711	0.8454
11	GUANAJUATO	497,430	963,289	1,105,999	2,566,718	0.6445
12	GUERRERO	139,041	51,468	143,484	333,993	0.1274
13	HIDALGO	237,638	141,887	200,079	579,604	0.3069
14	JALISCO	2,252,671	905,449	1,405,637	4,563,757	0.8606
15	MEXICO	2,149,096	2,300,684	14,738,578	19,188,358	1.9548
16	MICHOACAN	162,720	144,318	434,957	741,995	0.2091
17	MORELOS	328,562	154,426	473,804	956,792	0.8006
18	NAYARIT	162,354	404,948	770,044	1,337,346	1.6217
19	NUEVO LEON	3,927,714	46,199,435	10,862,204	60,989,353	19.682
20	OAXACA	203,815	81,013	285,285	570,113	0.1888
21	PUEBLA	837,512	1,036,353	1,033,155	2,907,020	0.7045
22	QUERETARO	627,584	722,391	435,470	1,785,445	1.6984
23	QUINTANA ROO	385,131	86,711	124,521	596,363	1.209
24	SAN LUIS POTOSI	654,048	127,002	1,382,524	2,163,574	1.0801
25	SINALOA	632,474	551,859	1,407,773	2,592,106	1.1761
26	SONORA	926,089	580,291	918,571	2,424,951	1.3298
27	TABASCO	264,045	53,098	533,792	850,935	0.5666
28	TAMAULIPAS	251,491	104,262	222,519	578,272	0.2571
29	TLAXCALA	79,436		26,479	105,915	0.1391
30	VERACRUZ	424,519	206,795	1,103,542	1,734,856	0.2785
31	YUCATAN	499,532	1,897,953	986,881	3,384,366	2.4831
32	ZACATECAS	144,649	41,320	422,568	608,537	0.4768
	National Total	22,770,595	66,194,633	53,427,334	142,392,562	1.7525
	Mean	711,581	2,135,311	1,669,604	4,449,768	1.6336
	Median	356,847	206,795	503,798	1,239,029	0.8530
	S.D.	849,244	8,234,488	3,290,936	10,989,922	3.3991
	C.V.	119.35	385.63	197.11	246.98	208.07
	Minimum	79,436	3,428	26,479	105,915	0.1078
	Maximum	3,927,714	46,199,435	14,738,578	60,989,353	19.6820

DEFINITION: Values shown are in thousands of pesos. The ratios are the total value of corporations to the 1990 total population.

SOURCE: INEGI, 1988-1989 Anuario Estadistico, Table IV.7.1.

Table 8.15 Number of Corporations, per 1000 Population, 1988

No.	State	1986 Number of Corporations	1986 Number of Corporations Per 1,000Persons	1988 Number of Corporations	1988 Number of Corporations Per 1,000Persons
1	AGUASCALIENTES	218	0.3029	184	0.2557
2	BAJA CALIFORNIA	764	0.4600	734	0.4419
3	BAJA CALIFORNIA SUR	92	0.2895	125	0.3934
4	CAMPECHE	42	0.0785	65	0.1215
5	COAHUILA	448	0.2271	452	0.2292
6	COLIMA	85	0.1984	52	0.1214
7	CHIAPAS	26	0.0081	140	0.0436
8	CHIHUAHUA	451	0.1847	478	0.1958
9	DISTRITO FEDERAL	1,591	0.1932	8,021	0.9739
10	DURANGO	181	0.1341	152	0.1126
11	GUANAJUATO	696	0.1748	664	0.1667
12	GUERRERO	123	0.0469	198	0.0756
13	HIDALGO	94	0.0498	146	0.0773
14	JALISCO	746	0.1407	1,590	0.2998
15	MEXICO	1,218	0.1241	1,611	0.1641
16	MICHOACAN	130	0.0366	215	0.0606
17	MORELOS	166	0.1389	198	0.1657
18	NAYARIT	82	0.0994	84	0.1019
19	NUEVO LEON	1,264	0.4079	1,465	0.4728
20	OAXACA	112	0.0371	176	0.0583
21	PUEBLA	583	0.1413	607	0.1471
22	QUERETARO	240	0.2283	275	0.2616
23	QUINTANA ROO	50	0.1014	323	0.6548
24	SAN LUIS POTOSI	243	0.1213	338	0.1687
25	SINALOA	289	0.1311	288	0.1307
26	SONORA	481	0.2638	488	0.2676
27	TABASCO	162	0.1079	159	0.1059
28	TAMAULIPAS	61	0.0271	518	0.2303
29	TLAXCALA	40	0.0525	51	0.0670
30	VERACRUZ	216	0.0347	585	0.0939
31	YUCATAN	310	0.2274	200	0.1467
32	ZACATECAS	73	0.0572	52	0.0407
National Total		11,277	4.8267	20,634	6.8468
Mean		352	0.1508	645	0.2140
Median		199	0.1326	245	0.1556
S.D.		394	0.1092	1,410	0.1964
C.V.		112	72.39	219	91.78
Minimum		26	0.0081	51	0.0407
Maximum		1,591	0.4600	8,021	0.9739

DEFINITION: The number of corporations per 1000 population is the number of corporations to the total population 1990 multiplied by 1000.

SOURCE: INEGI, 1988-1989 Anuario Estadistico, Table IV.7.1.

Table 8.16 Location of Mexico's "Fortune" 500 Corporations, 1986

Location	Number of Corporations
FEDERAL DISTRICT	149
MEXICO STATE	78
NUEVO LEON	63
JALISCO	36
CHIHUAHUA PUEBLA QUERETARO COAHUILA VERACRUZ	14 – 16
AGUASCALIENTES BAJA CALIFORNIA BAJA CALIFORNIA SUR COLIMA DISTRITO FEDERAL DURANGO GUANAJUATO HIDALGO MEXICO MICHOACAN MORELOS QUINTANA ROO SAN LUIS POTOSI SINALOA SONORA TABASCO TAMAULIPAS TLAXCALA YUCATAN ZACATECAS	1 – 10
CAMPECHE CHIAPAS GUERRERO NAYARIT OAXACA	0

DEFINITION: Number and location of "Fortune" 500 Corporations found within primary areas of Mexico City, Mexico State, Nuevo Leon, Jalisco, and three groups of the remaining states.

SOURCE: Expansion, Agosto 17, 1987.

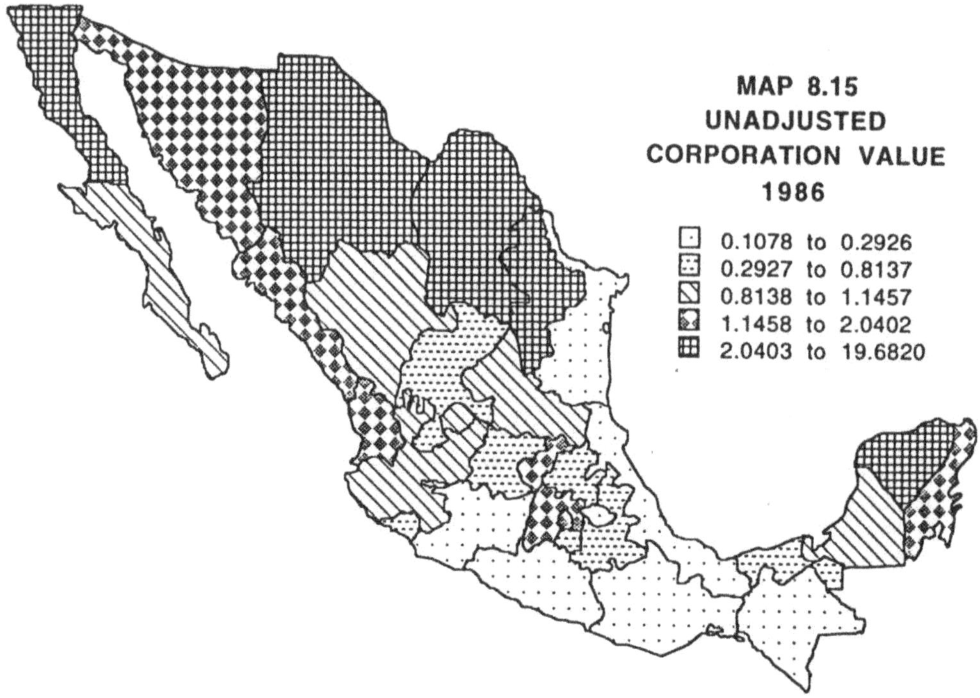

MAP 8.15
UNADJUSTED CORPORATION VALUE
1986

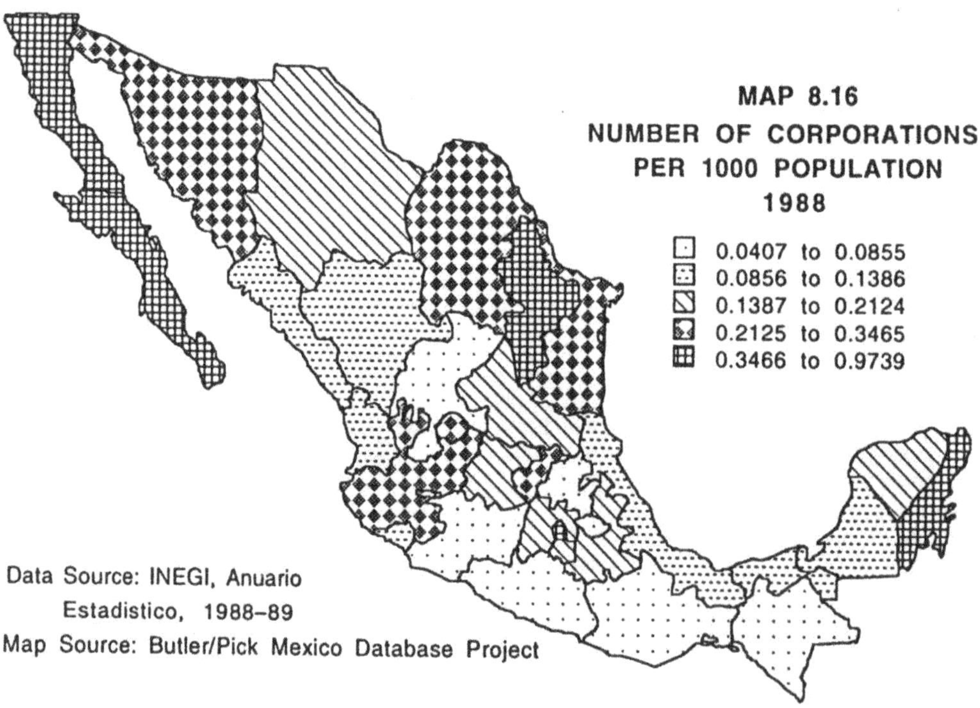

MAP 8.16
NUMBER OF CORPORATIONS PER 1000 POPULATION
1988

Data Source: INEGI, Anuario Estadistico, 1988-89
Map Source: Butler/Pick Mexico Database Project

MAP 8.17
500 MAJOR CORPORATIONS, 1986

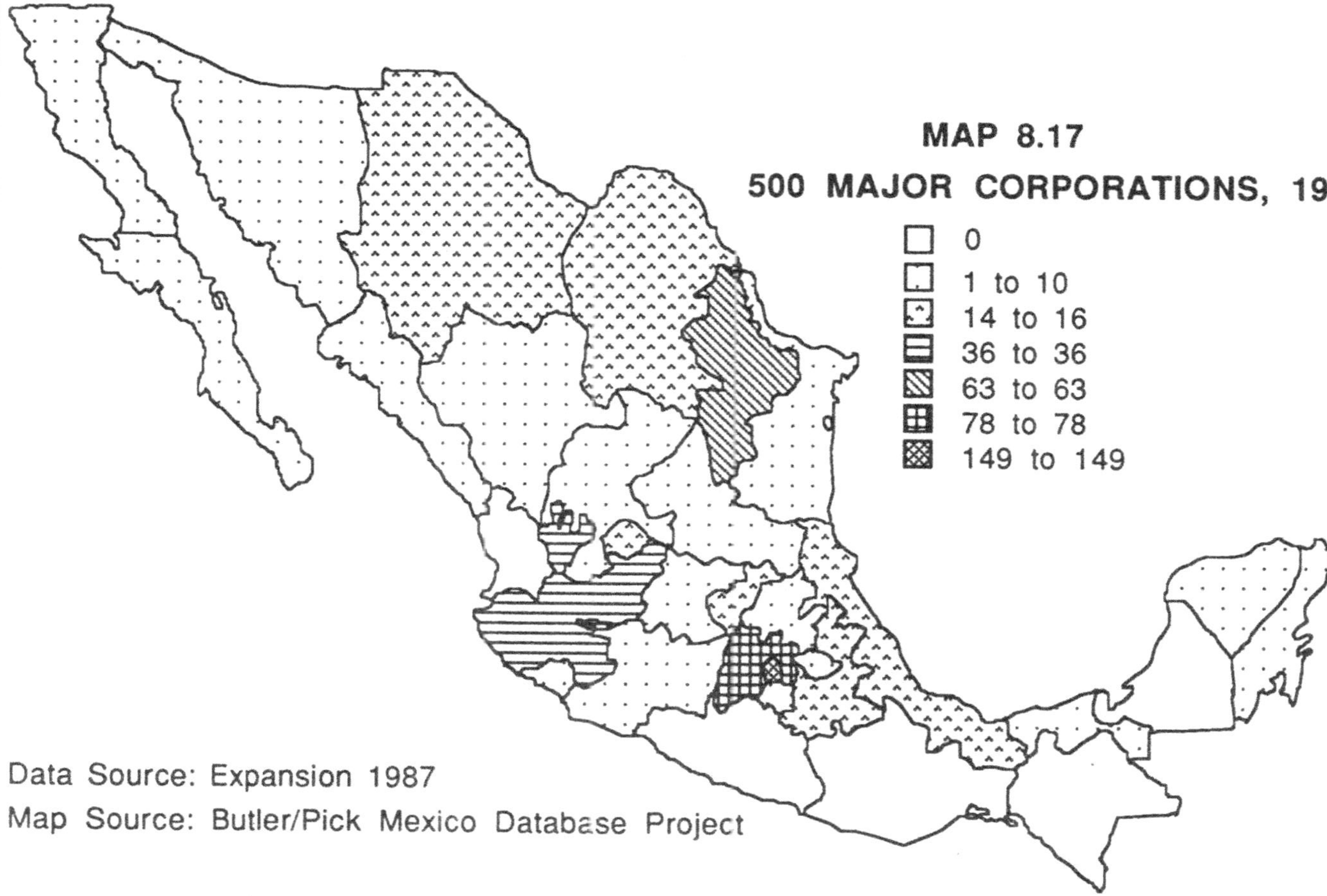

Figure 8.6
Origin of Capital:
Mexican "Fortune" 500 Corporations, 1986

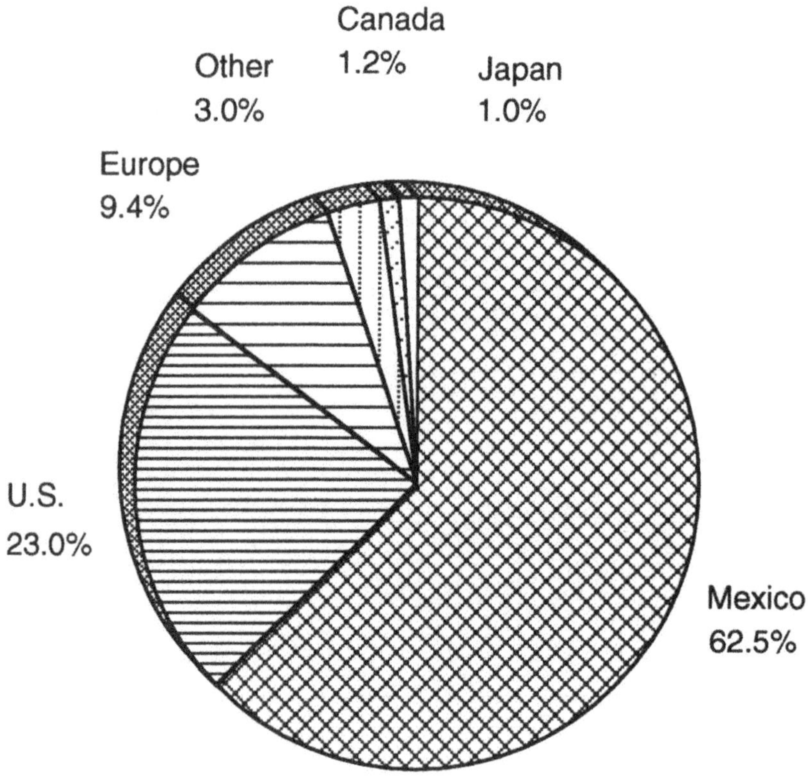

SOURCE: Expansion 1987.

Communications/Transport

Telephones, 1989

Nationally in 1989, there was one phone for about every eight Mexicans. This contrasts with one phone for every 13 Mexicans in 1980 (*Atlas of Mexico*, p. 323). The entire nation, as shown in Table 8.17 (with the exception of Tlaxcala), had per capita increases in telephones between 1988 and 1989. Major increases took place in Aguascalientes, Baja, Colima, Chihuahua, the Federal District, Jalisco, Puebla, Queretaro, San Luis Potosi, and Tabasco. As shown on Map 8.18, in 1989, the Border region clearly stands out as the region with the highest number of telephones per capita while the south has very low ratio of telephones per capita. The Federal District, with three million phones, also has the highest prevalence, with one phone for every three residents. Nuevo Leon and Baja Sur are next in position in per capita phone use. Interestingly, the areas surrounding the Federal District have a very low per capita ratio of telephones.

Telephones clearly are associated with various measures of urbanization, population characteristics such as age 18-64 (r = .83), ages 0-17 (- .85), and the dependency ratio (- .81). Substantial relationships exist between telephones per capita and literacy and measures of educational attainment, e.g., high level educational attainment and telephones (.89), secondary education (.57), etc. Substantial correlations exist also for the economically active population (.60) and the female economically active population (.82). Similarly, all higher level occupations and tertiary occupations are substantially related to telephones per capita, as are gross state revenues (.48) and owner registered vehicles (.78). The death rates for cardiology (.48) and cancer (.62) also are significantly associated with telephones. These are all indicators of modernization.

Radio and Television Stations, 1988

Radio Stations. The number of radio and television stations in the various states is presented in Table 8.18. Virtually all northern border states have a disproportionate number of ratio stations. In addition, Guanajuato, Veracruz, and the Federal District have a substantial number of radio stations. There appears to be little relationship between the number of radio concessions and the number of permits. A few states have very few radio stations and Baja California Sur, Morelos, Nayarit, and Puebla have no permits.

The highest radio stations per capita are in Sonora, Baja California, Coahuila, and Tamaulipas. Stations in those states can broadcast into the U.S. as well as Mexico. Stations per capita are also high in Campeche and Quintana Roo. States with the lowest radio stations per capita are located primarily in the south and central regions (see Map 8.19).

Radio stations per capita are positively associated with a variety of dimensions that are also interrelated: Sex ratio (r = .48), measures of education and literacy (r's = high .40s), labor force and occupational measures, and gross state revenues (.44). High negative correlations exist with lifetime outmigration (- .39), net migration (- .40), measures of density and crowding, low monthly incomes and no meat or eggs, agricultural occupations (- .35), and dependency ratio (- .51). There also is a high negative association with the total economically active population (- .38) but a high association with the percent female economically active (.48).

Television Stations. Radio and television stations are somewhat, but not significantly, correlated (r = .24). The concentration of television concessions is greater than radio concessions with the border states of Chihuahua, Sonora, and Tamaulipas having the greatest number. Several states have extremely few concessions, among them are Aguascalientes, Colima, Guanajuato, Hidalgo, Mexico, Morelos, Nayarit, Puebla, Queretaro, and Tabasco (see Map 8.20).

The total number of television concessions and permits shown in Table 8.18 illustrates that Sonora, Chihuahua, and Durango have the most stations. Television stations per capita, however, are concentrated in Baja California Sur, Durango, Quintana Roo, and Sonora, for the most part not very dense states.

Substantial negative correlations exist between per capita television stations and the elderly population (r = - .38) and, similar to radio stations, with the total economically active population (- .37). Positive association appears for a variety of dimensions including the sex ratio (.60), high monthly incomes (.55), auto production (.44), population growth, inmigration between 1985–1990, and indigenous language (.38), among others.

Registered Personally Owned Automobiles

There were 6.4 million registered personally owned automobiles in 1990. As seen below, this is the largest component of registered motor vehicles.

	Pers. Owned	Rental	Official	Total
Automobiles	6,439,620	282,263	32,213	6,754,096
Motorcycles	229,860	667	976	231,503
Buses	12,690	78,633	2,681	94,004
Trucks	4,759,189	117,182	16,477	4,892,848
TOTAL	11,441,359	478,745	52,347	11,972,451

SOURCE: INEGI,*1991 Anuario Estadistico*, Table 2.2.2.

Clearly, Mexico has an abundance of registered vehicles, in fact more vehicles than telephones (see Tables 8.17 and 8.19). The number of registered personally owned automobiles grew by nearly one sixth between 1988 and 1990, a result indicative of Salinas era prosperity. The largest concentration of 2.6 million automobiles is in the Federal District/Mexico, a small geographic area that accounts for 2/5 of automobiles. The largely uncontrolled emission from this fleet

Mexico City's devastating smog. There are 1.6 million automobiles in the border region—another quarter of the national total.

As seen in Map 8.21, vehicles per capita are concentrated in the border region and Baja Sur, the Federal District and Morelos, and Jalisco and Colima. As usual, the south is disadvantaged and on the lower end of the spectrum as measured by vehicles per capita.

Table 8.17 Telephones, 1988-1989

No.	State	1988 Total Telephones	1988 Telephones Per Capita	1989 Total Telephones	1989 Telephones Per Capita	Per Capita % Change 1988-89
1	AGUASCALIENTES	71,476	0.0993	80,929	0.1125	13.23
2	BAJA CALIFORNIA	179,683	0.1082	207,433	0.1249	15.44
3	BAJA CALIFORNIA SUR	59,200	0.1863	62,657	0.1972	5.84
4	CAMPECHE	28,238	0.0528	30,880	0.0577	9.36
5	COAHUILA	257,493	0.1306	277,208	0.1405	7.66
6	COLIMA	55,216	0.1289	61,582	0.1437	11.53
7	CHIAPAS	96,108	0.0299	100,023	0.0312	4.07
8	CHIHUAHUA	302,585	0.1239	336,107	0.1376	11.08
9	DISTRITO FEDERAL	2,643,869	0.3210	2,998,951	0.3641	13.43
10	DURANGO	92,531	0.0686	101,740	0.0754	9.95
11	GUANAJUATO	265,230	0.0666	286,368	0.0719	7.97
12	GUERRERO	141,151	0.0539	155,192	0.0592	9.95
13	HIDALGO	90,585	0.0480	95,177	0.0504	5.07
14	JALISCO	708,326	0.1336	784,645	0.1480	10.77
15	MEXICO	692,312	0.0705	721,169	0.0735	4.17
16	MICHOACAN	214,609	0.0605	239,990	0.0676	11.83
17	MORELOS	128,570	0.1076	142,339	0.1191	10.71
18	NAYARIT	52,871	0.0641	57,791	0.0701	9.31
19	NUEVO LEON	554,587	0.1790	601,171	0.1940	8.40
20	OAXACA	83,117	0.0275	90,426	0.0299	8.79
21	PUEBLA	281,554	0.0682	320,752	0.0777	13.92
22	QUERETARO	70,370	0.0669	77,708	0.0739	10.43
23	QUINTANA ROO	31,472	0.0638	35,154	0.0713	11.70
24	SAN LUIS POTOSI	128,862	0.0643	152,036	0.0759	17.98
25	SINALOA	207,419	0.0941	230,919	0.1048	11.33
26	SONORA	242,806	0.1331	265,349	0.1455	9.28
27	TABASCO	80,567	0.0536	90,071	0.0600	11.80
28	TAMAULIPAS	260,271	0.1157	283,681	0.1261	8.99
29	TLAXCALA	26,701	0.0351	15,361	0.0202	-42.47
30	VERACRUZ	438,508	0.0704	479,580	0.0770	9.37
31	YUCATAN	130,869	0.0960	141,280	0.1037	7.96
32	ZACATECAS	48,156	0.0377	52,081	0.0408	8.15
	National Total	8,665,312	0.1066	9,575,750	0.1179	10.60
	Mean	270,791	0.0925	299,242	0.1014	8.34
	Median	129,866	0.0695	147,188	0.0764	9.66
	S.D.	468,828	0.0581	529,663	0.0656	9.75
	C.V.	173.13	62.79	177.00	64.68	116.86
	Minimum	26,701	0.0275	15,361	0.0202	-42.47
	Maximum	2,643,869	0.3210	2,998,951	0.3641	17.98

DEFINITION: Per capita values are the number of telephones to the total population of the year shown. Per Capita Percent Change was calculated by subtracting the 1988 Per Capita rate from the 1989 Per Capita rate and dividing by the 1988 Per Capita rate multiplied by 100.

SOURCE: INEGI, 1988-1989 Anuario Estadistico, Table 2.1.11, 1990 Anuario Estadistico, Table 2.1.9.

MAP 8.18

TELEPHONES PER CAPITA, 1989

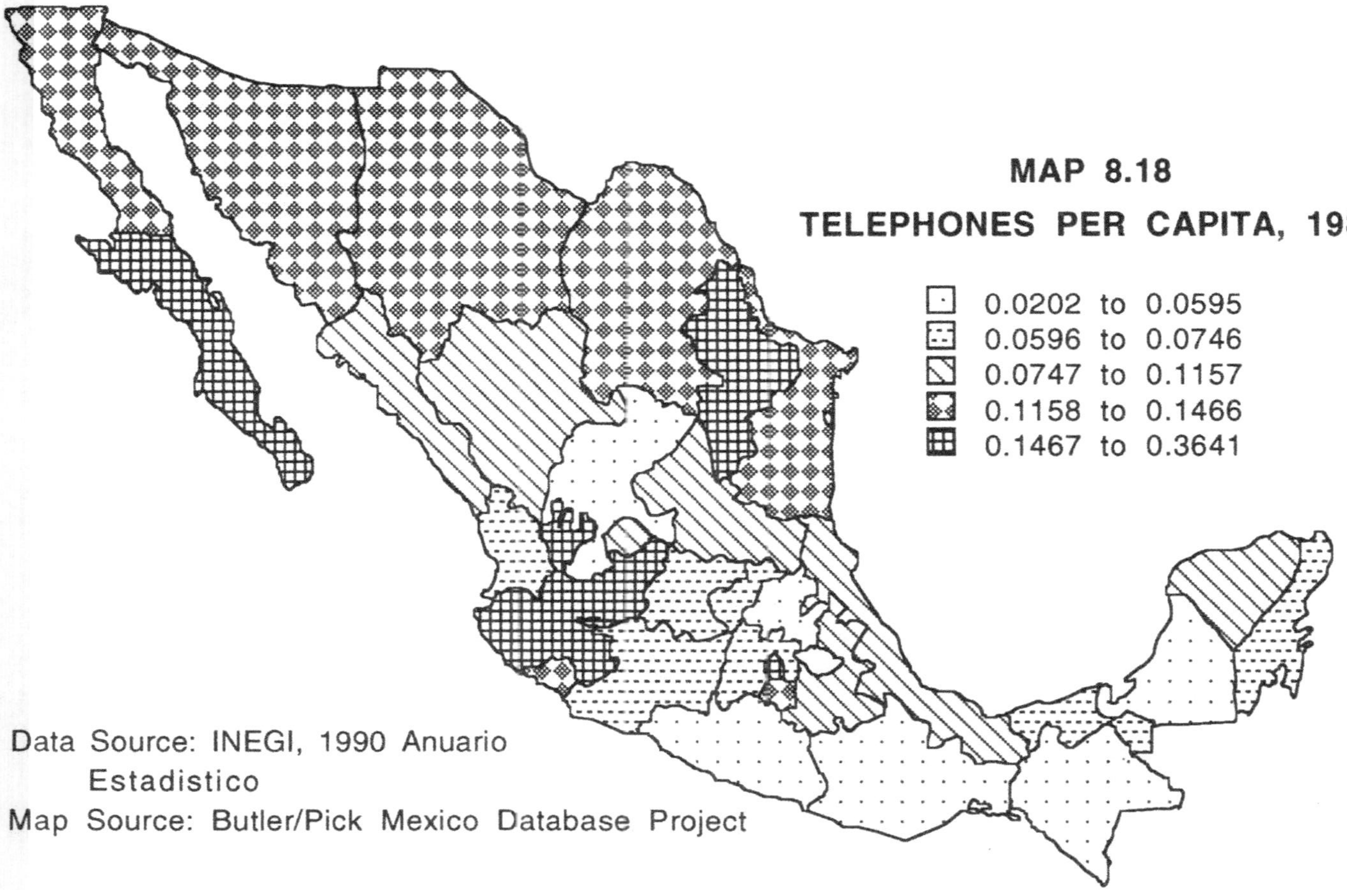

Data Source: INEGI, 1990 Anuario Estadistico

Map Source: Butler/Pick Mexico Database Project

Table 8.18 Radio and Television Stations, 1988

No.	State	Radio Stations: Con-cessions	Radio Stations: Permits	Radio Stations: Per Capita	Radio Stations: Perc. of Nation	TV Stations: Con-cession	TV Stations: Permits	TV Stations: Per Capita	TV Stations: Perc. of Nation
1	AGUASCALIENTES	10	3	0.1810	1.30	2	5	0.0970	1.26
2	BAJA CALIFORNIA	48	2	0.3010	5.00	8	3	0.0660	1.99
3	BAJA CALIFORNIA SUR	6	0	0.1890	0.60	5	22	0.8500	4.87
4	CAMPECHE	10	3	0.2430	1.30	4	3	0.1310	1.26
5	COAHUILA	49	1	0.2540	5.00	12	15	0.1370	4.87
8	COLIMA	7	1	0.1870	0.80	2	4	0.1400	1.08
6	CHIAPAS	28	1	0.0900	2.90	12	15	0.0840	4.87
7	CHIHUAHUA	56	2	0.2380	5.80	18	22	0.1640	7.22
9	DISTRITO FEDERAL	63	10	0.0890	7.30	6	2	0.0100	1.44
10	DURANGO	14	1	0.1110	1.50	4	71	0.5560	13.54
11	GUANAJUATO	47	5	0.1310	5.20	3	8	0.0280	1.99
12	GUERRERO	24	4	0.1070	2.80	10	9	0.0730	3.43
13	HIDALGO	6	4	0.0530	1.00	1	11	0.0640	2.17
14	JALISCO	61	4	0.1230	6.50	10	9	0.0360	3.43
15	MEXICO	10	3	0.0130	1.30	3	9	0.0120	2.17
16	MICHOACAN	35	2	0.1040	3.70	10	13	0.0650	4.15
17	MORELOS	13	0	0.1090	1.30	1	1	0.0170	0.36
18	NAYARIT	14	0	0.1700	1.40	3	3	0.0730	1.08
19	NUEVO LEON	43	7	0.1610	5.00	6	3	0.0290	1.62
20	OAXACA	20	3	0.0760	2.30	10	13	0.0760	4.15
21	PUEBLA	28	0	0.0680	2.80	3	5	0.0190	1.44
22	QUERETARO	14	3	0.1620	1.70	3	4	0.0670	1.26
23	QUINTANA ROO	7	2	0.1820	0.90	4	21	0.5070	4.51
24	SAN LUIS POTOSI	26	2	0.1400	2.80	6	7	0.0650	2.35
25	SINALOA	38	1	0.1770	3.90	8	2	0.0450	1.81
26	SONORA	53	8	0.3350	6.10	17	32	0.2690	8.84
27	TABASCO	15	2	0.1130	1.70	3	8	0.0730	1.99
28	TAMAULIPAS	62	1	0.2800	6.30	16	3	0.0840	3.43
29	TLAXCALA	4	1	0.0660	0.50	0	4	0.0530	0.72
30	VERACRUZ	77	3	0.1280	8.00	9	7	0.0260	2.89
31	YUCATAN	18	2	0.1470	2.00	5	2	0.0510	1.26
32	ZACATECAS	12	1	0.1020	1.30	7	7	0.1100	2.53
National Total		918	82	0.4830		211	343	0.4077	
Mean		28.6875	2.5625	0.1510	3.1250	6.5938	10.7188	0.1270	3.1244
Median		22.0000	2.0000	0.1360	2.5500	5.5000	7.0000	0.0700	2.1700
S.D.		20.9922	2.3132	0.0750	2.2088	4.7305	13.1744	0.1810	2.6846
C.V.		73.18	90.27	496.69	70.68	71.74	122.91	1425.20	85.92
Minimum		4.0000	0.0000	0.0130	0.5000	0.0000	1.0000	0.0100	0.3600
Maximum		77.0000	10.0000	0.3350	8.0000	18.0000	71.0000	0.8500	13.5400

DEFINITION: Per capita values are the number of radio and television stations to the total population of the year 1988.

SOURCE: INEGI, 1988–89 Anuario Estadistico, Table 2.1.13.

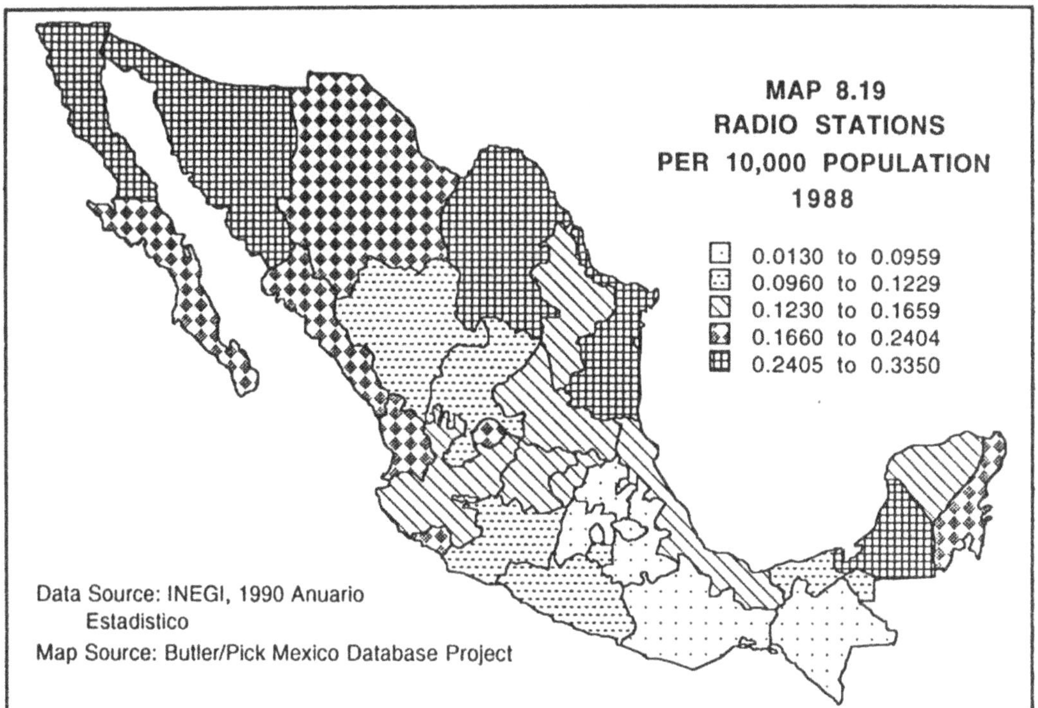
MAP 8.19
RADIO STATIONS
PER 10,000 POPULATION
1988
0.0130 to 0.0959
0.0960 to 0.1229
0.1230 to 0.1659
0.1660 to 0.2404
0.2405 to 0.3350
Data Source: INEGI, 1990 Anuario Estadistico
Map Source: Butler/Pick Mexico Database Project

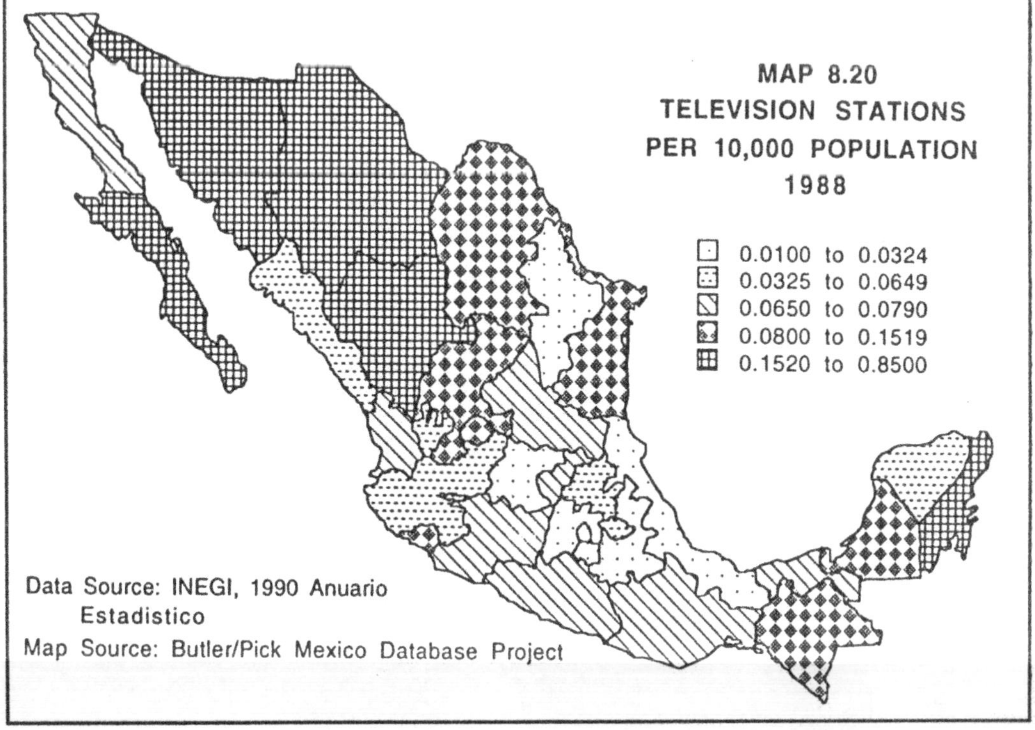
MAP 8.20
TELEVISION STATIONS
PER 10,000 POPULATION
1988
0.0100 to 0.0324
0.0325 to 0.0649
0.0650 to 0.0790
0.0800 to 0.1519
0.1520 to 0.8500
Data Source: INEGI, 1990 Anuario Estadistico
Map Source: Butler/Pick Mexico Database Project

Table 8.19 Registered Personally Owned Automobiles, 1988 and 1990

No.	State	Automobiles 1988	Ratio	Automobiles 1990	Ratio	Ratio % Change 1988-1990
1	AGUASCALIENTES	40,388	0.0561	44,240	0.0005	9.5
2	BAJA CALIFORNIA	365,388	0.2200	395,087	0.0049	8.1
3	BAJA CALIFORNIA SUR	34,796	0.1095	37,668	0.0005	8.3
4	CAMPECHE	23,729	0.0443	30,507	0.0004	28.6
5	COAHUILA	160,376	0.0813	204,353	0.0025	27.4
6	COLIMA	49,257	0.1149	48,343	0.0006	-1.9
7	CHIAPAS	48,238	0.0150	62,435	0.0008	29.4
8	CHIHUAHUA	309,721	0.1268	321,590	0.0040	3.8
9	DISTRITO FEDERAL	1,619,541	0.1966	1,944,479	0.0239	20.1
10	DURANGO	53,159	0.0394	57,295	0.0007	7.8
11	GUANAJUATO	128,495	0.0323	147,301	0.0018	14.6
12	GUERRERO	58,806	0.0224	64,910	0.0008	10.4
13	HIDALGO	56,598	0.0300	74,109	0.0009	30.9
14	JALISCO	363,407	0.0685	409,047	0.0050	12.6
15	MEXICO	557,565	0.0568	671,551	0.0083	20.4
16	MICHOACAN	113,416	0.0320	130,834	0.0016	15.4
17	MORELOS	119,384	0.0999	120,750	0.0015	1.1
18	NAYARIT	25,431	0.0308	26,464	0.0003	4.1
19	NUEVO LEON	271,383	0.0876	303,085	0.0037	11.7
20	OAXACA	38,194	0.0126	46,053	0.0006	20.6
21	PUEBLA	191,450	0.0464	218,640	0.0027	14.2
22	QUERETARO	40,348	0.0384	54,530	0.0007	35.1
23	QUINTANA ROO	16,722	0.0339	22,381	0.0003	33.8
24	SAN LUIS POTOSI	63,380	0.0316	73,422	0.0009	15.8
25	SINALOA	95,668	0.0434	105,511	0.0013	10.3
26	SONORA	123,792	0.0679	149,932	0.0018	21.1
27	TABASCO	47,840	0.0319	56,493	0.0007	18.1
28	TAMAULIPAS	223,771	0.0995	239,634	0.0029	7.1
29	TLAXCALA	23,483	0.0308	28,813	0.0004	22.7
30	VERACRUZ	196,516	0.0316	223,272	0.0027	13.6
31	YUCATAN	77,316	0.0567	86,768	0.0011	12.2
32	ZACATECAS	31,564	0.0247	40,123	0.0005	27.1
	National Total	5,569,122	0.0685	6,439,620	0.0793	15.6
	Mean	174,035	0.0629	201,238	0.0025	16.1
	Median	70,348	0.0439	80,439	0.0010	14.4
	S.D.	292,618	0.0489	349,516	0.0043	9.7
	C.V.	168.14	77.76	174	173.68	60.1
	Minimum	16,722	0.0126	22,381	0.0003	-1.9
	Maximum	1,619,541	0.2200	1,944,479	0.0239	35.1

DEFINITION: Ratio is the number of registered privately owned vehicles 1988 or 1990 to the total population 1990. Ratio percent change was calculated by subtracting the 1990 ratio from the 1988 ratio, multiplying by 100, and dividing by the 1988 ratio.

SOURCE: INEGI, 1988-89 Anuario Estadistico, Table 2.1.18, and 1991 Anuario Estadistico, Table 2.2.2.

MAP 8.21
REGISTERED PERSONALLY OWNED AUTOMOBILES, 1990

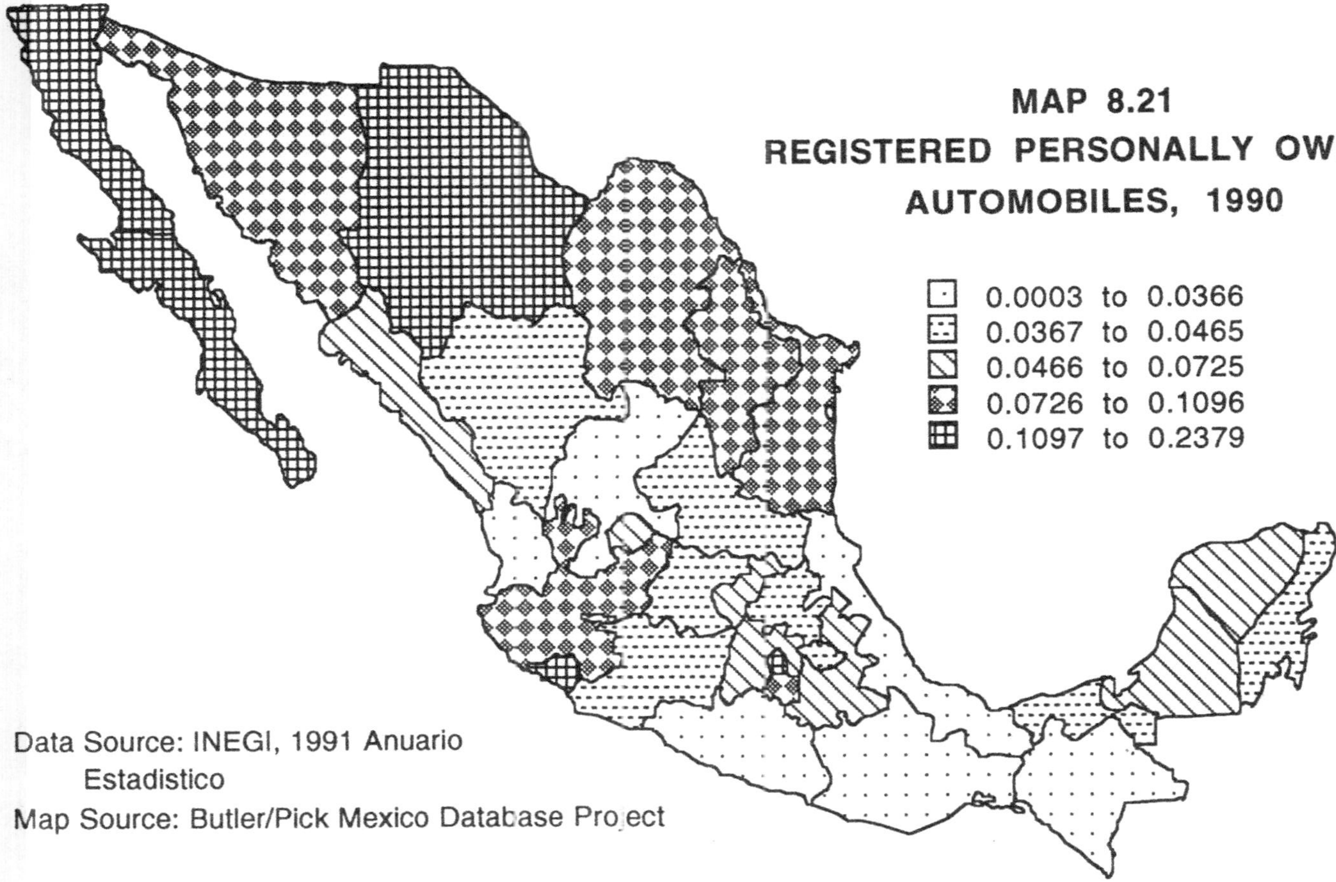

Data Source: INEGI, 1991 Anuario Estadistico
Map Source: Butler/Pick Mexico Database Project

Economic Development

Gross Domestic Product

The Mexican gross domestic product in billions of pesos for the years 1960 through 1989 is shown in Figures 8.7 and 8.8 and Table 8.20. The middle column of the table controls for inflation by evaluating the gross domestic product by standardizing information for the base year of 1985. Figure 8.8 shows the rise in gross domestic product in billions of pesos between 1960 through 1980 and then a slight downturn, a rise, and then another dip. Figure 8.9 presents a different picture by showing the GDP deflator using 1985 as the base year equalling 100. Thus, the major changes took place during the early 1980s and continued until 1986.

Gross State Revenue, 1988

Gross state revenues and gross state revenues per capita are reported in Table 8.21; Map 8.22 shows gross state revenue in thousands of pesos per capita, 1988. This revenue is received by each state government and is equal to state expenditure. In 1988, Nuevo Leon, Baja, Tabasco, and the Federal District had a substantially higher gross state revenue than other states. Baja California, Campeche, Colima, Jalisco, Oaxaca, and Sonora had relatively high gross revenues per capita. Michoacan, by far, had the lowest per capita. Other relatively low per capita states were Guanajuato, Hidalgo, Puebla, and San Luis Potosi. By region, the western border states all had substantial per capita gross state revenues. The lower per capita states were located primarily in the nation's mid-section and slightly north.

Gross state revenues were significantly associated with fertility, migration, and death rates. For standardized fertility rates, there was a negative correlation of - .51. There was a positive association of gross state revenues with lifetime and net migration rates (.37 and .36, respectively). Gross state revenues also were closely tied to the age of the population with a positive association with those aged 18-64 (.53) and negatively with the ages 0-17 (- .51) and those 65 and over (- .23). Thus, it is not too surprising that gross state revenues also were negatively associated with the dependency ratio. Both cancer (.37) and cardiology (.50) death rates were significantly associated with gross state revenues.

Gross state revenues were positively linked with all urban measures (r's = ca. 40s), educational dimensions, high monthly incomes, the economically active population (.48) and the female economically active population (.45). Virtually all higher level labor force and occupations were positively linked to gross state revenues while the agricultural labor force was negatively associated with gross state revenues.

Taxes and Duties Collected as Proportion of State Revenues, 1988

Taxes and duties (*impuestos, participaciones,* and *derechos*) collected in 1988 are shown on Map 8.23 and reported state-by-state in Table 8.21. The characteristic mapped is the ratio of state taxes and duties collected in 1988 to gross state revenues in 1988. The most taxes and duties were collected in the Federal District and the state if Mexico. However, a more useful measure is the ratio. The ratio was calculated by taking the peso value of state taxes and duties collected in 1988 to the gross state revenues in 1988.

While Map 8.23 illustrates differences among the states, the four states of Jalisco, Nuevo Leon, Oaxaca, Baja California, and the Federal District have a relatively low ratio of taxes and duties collected in relationship to their gross state revenues. Three of these states and the Federal District are among the wealthier entities in Mexico with a major exception being Oaxaca. States with an extremely high ratio are Chiapas and Chihuahua, states which on the surface certainly have little in common. There are few correspondences with standard regions. It may be that this ratio is determined based on history and political situations in particular states.

Federal Public Investment, 1990

The total capital investment by the federal government and other entities for 1988-1990 is shown in Table 8.22. The table shows that there was a significant increase in investment nationwide during this period and that foreign investment between 1988 and 1990 increased substantially. Only Michoacan and Sonora had less investment in 1990 than in 1988. Baja California Sur, Coahuila, the Federal District, Durango, San Luis Potosi, and Yucatan had large increases in investment. However, the most remarkable increase in investment took place in Sinaloa. Figure 8.9 illustrates the distribution of the investment in 1990. The major areas of investment were in energy, communications/transport, and social development, including education, health, and regional development.

Total Value of New Mortgages, 1986

The Value of new mortgages was 1.7 billion pesos in 1986. As with so many 'economic' dimensions, there is a substantial north-south axis with the north having substantial more total value of new mortgages than the south. Table 8.23 reports for 1986 total real estate transactions, real estate sales, other real estate fees, the total value of new mortgages, and value of new mortgages per capita. Map 8.24 presents the per capita data by state. Per capita mortgages were highest in the border states of Nuevo Leon, Sonora, and Baja, as well as in Aguascalientes. By region, it is quite evident that the border region has the highest per capita with only Yucatan in the entire southern half of Mexico a relatively high per capita of new mortgages.

Table 8.20 Gross Domestic Product, 1960–1989, in Billions of Pesos

Year	Gross Domestic Product	GDP in 1985 Prices	GDP Deflator (1985+100)
1960	156	11,225	1.40
1961	166	11,830	1.40
1962	180	12,384	1.50
1963	195	13,373	1.50
1964	221	14,939	1.50
1965	252	15,906	1.60
1966	283	17,007	1.70
1967	306	18,078	1.70
1968	339	19,547	1.70
1969	375	20,783	1.80
1970	444	22,222	2.00
1971	490	23,147	2.10
1972	565	25,112	2.20
1973	691	27,223	2.50
1974	900	28,889	3.10
1975	1,110	30,509	3.60
1976	1,371	31,799	4.30
1977	1,849	32,895	5.60
1978	2,337	35,611	6.60
1979	3,068	38,871	7.90
1980	4,276	42,107	10.20
1981	5,874	45,453	12.90
1982	9,417	45,203	20.80
1983	17,142	42,823	40.00
1984	28,749	44,388	64.80
1985	45,588	45,588	100.00
1986	79,443	43,918	180.90
1987	193,462		
1988	395,883		
1989	494,055		
Mean	42,973	28,179	17.9741
Median	1,005	27,223	2.5000
S.D.	116,340	12,085	39.5781
C.V.	270.73	42.89	220.20
Minimum	156	11,225	1.4000
Maximum	494,055	45,588	180.9000

DEFINITION: Gross Domestic Product from 1960 to 1989 in billions of Pesos.

SOURCE: IMF, International Financial Statistics Yearbook, 1979 and 1991.

Figure 8.7
Gross Domestic Product, 1960-1986: 1985 Prices

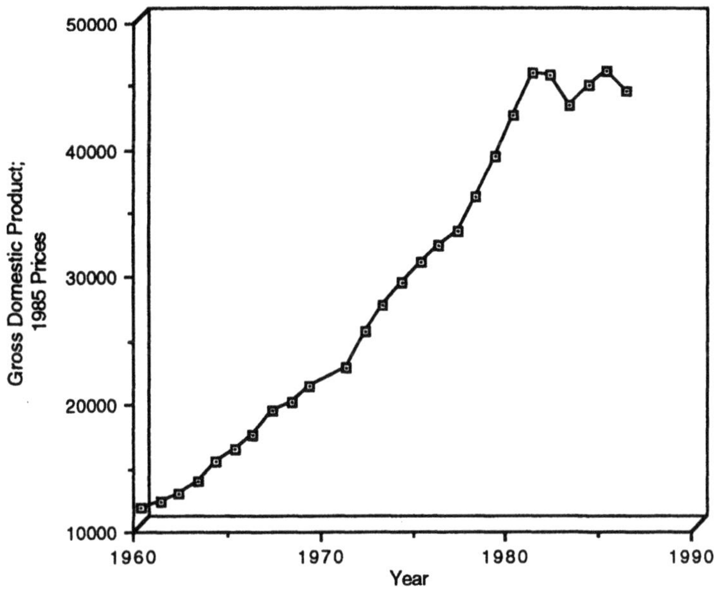

FIGURE 8.8
GROSS DOMESTIC PRODUCT DEFLATOR 1960-1986; 1985 = 100

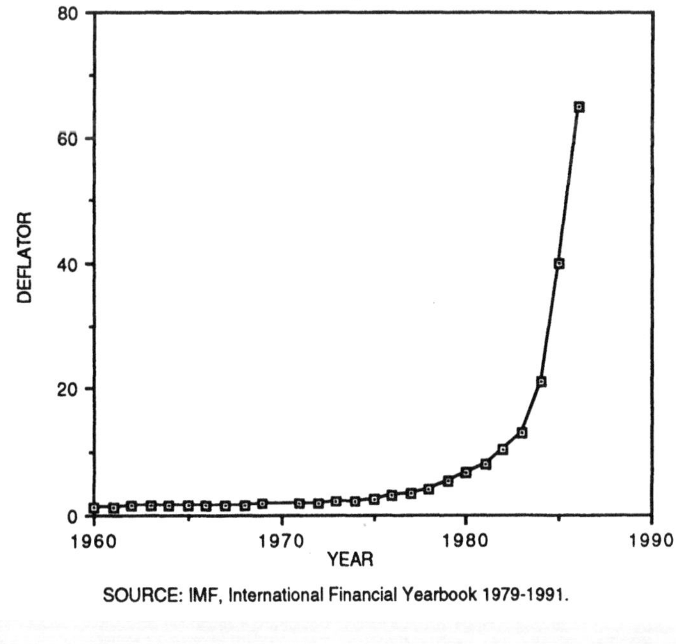

SOURCE: IMF, International Financial Yearbook 1979-1991.

Table 8.21 Gross State Revenue and Taxes/Duties Collected, 1988

No.	State	Gross State Revenue (1)	Gross State Revenue Per Capita	Tax. & Dut. Collected (2)	Tax. & Dut. Collected Per Capita	Ratio of (2) to (1)
1	AGUASCALIENTES	140,384	0.1951	116,652	0.1621	0.8309
2	BAJA CALIFORNIA	1,019,697	0.6140	373,953	0.2252	0.3667
3	BAJA CALIFORNIA SUR	89,365	0.2812	73,736	0.2320	0.8251
4	CAMPECHE	171,365	0.3202	117,433	0.2194	0.6853
5	COAHUILA	315,023	0.1597	285,683	0.1448	0.9069
6	COLIMA	143,019	0.3338	81,097	0.1893	0.5670
7	CHIAPAS	531,219	0.1655	479,346	0.1493	0.9024
8	CHIHUAHUA	373,855	0.1531	352,226	0.1442	0.9421
9	DISTRITO FEDERAL	4,139,976	0.5027	1,246,517	0.1514	0.3011
10	DURANGO	198,669	0.1472	140,871	0.1044	0.7091
11	GUANAJUATO	432,472	0.1086	335,285	0.0842	0.7753
12	GUERRERO	354,870	0.1354	200,299	0.0764	0.5644
13	HIDALGO	200,181	0.1060	151,093	0.0800	0.7548
14	JALISCO	1,581,947	0.2983	692,419	0.1306	0.4377
15	MEXICO	1,378,685	0.1405	1,231,818	0.1255	0.8935
16	MICHOACAN	313,329	0.0883	262,779	0.0741	0.8387
17	MORELOS	147,558	0.1235	131,468	0.1100	0.8910
18	NAYARIT	153,182	0.1858	105,137	0.1275	0.6864
19	NUEVO LEON	2,027,942	0.6544	585,767	0.1890	0.2888
20	OAXACA	907,947	0.3007	137,343	0.0455	0.1513
21	PUEBLA	447,113	0.1084	335,074	0.0812	0.7494
22	QUERETARO	157,185	0.1495	142,656	0.1357	0.9076
23	QUINTANA ROO	112,070	0.2272	68,284	0.1384	0.6093
24	SAN LUIS POTOSI	206,743	0.1032	182,356	0.0910	0.8820
25	SINALOA	395,087	0.1793	343,625	0.1559	0.8697
26	SONORA	508,867	0.2790	438,179	0.2403	0.8611
27	TABASCO	884,252	0.5888	800,931	0.5333	0.9058
28	TAMAULIPAS	476,016	0.2116	422,837	0.1880	0.8883
29	TLAXCALA	168,562	0.2214	104,525	0.1373	0.6201
30	VERACRUZ	861,385	0.1383	733,153	0.1177	0.8511
31	YUCATAN	175,605	0.1288	150,691	0.1106	0.8581
32	ZACATECAS	156,525	0.1226	118,855	0.0931	0.7593
	National Total	19,170,095		10,942,088		0.5708
	Mean	599,065	0.2335	341,940	0.1496	0.7213
	Median	334,947	0.1724	231,539	0.1365	0.8002
	S.D.	797,154	0.1543	309,242	0.0858	0.2114
	C.V.	133.07	66.07	90.44	57.33	29.31
	Minimum	89,365	0.0883	68,284	0.0455	0.1513
	Maximum	4,139,976	0.6544	1,246,517	0.5333	0.9421

DEFINITION: Values shown are in millions of pesos. The ratios are the state income to the total population of the corresponding year.

SOURCE: INEGI, 1990 Anuario Estadistico, Table 4.8.10.

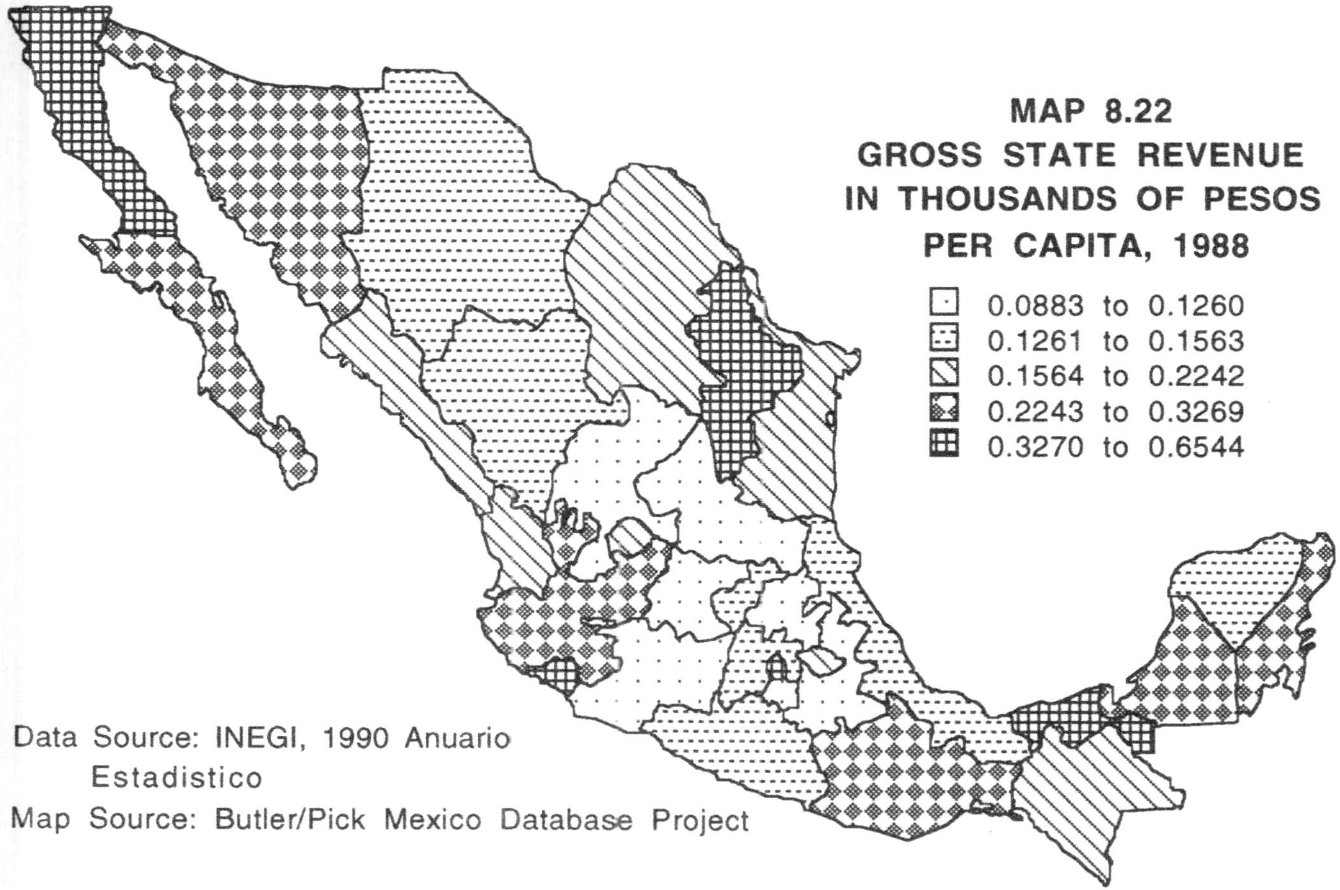

MAP 8.22
GROSS STATE REVENUE
IN THOUSANDS OF PESOS
PER CAPITA, 1988

Data Source: INEGI, 1990 Anuario Estadistico
Map Source: Butler/Pick Mexico Database Project

MAP 8.23
TAXES AND DUTIES COLLECTED AS PROPORTION OF STATE REVENUES, 1988

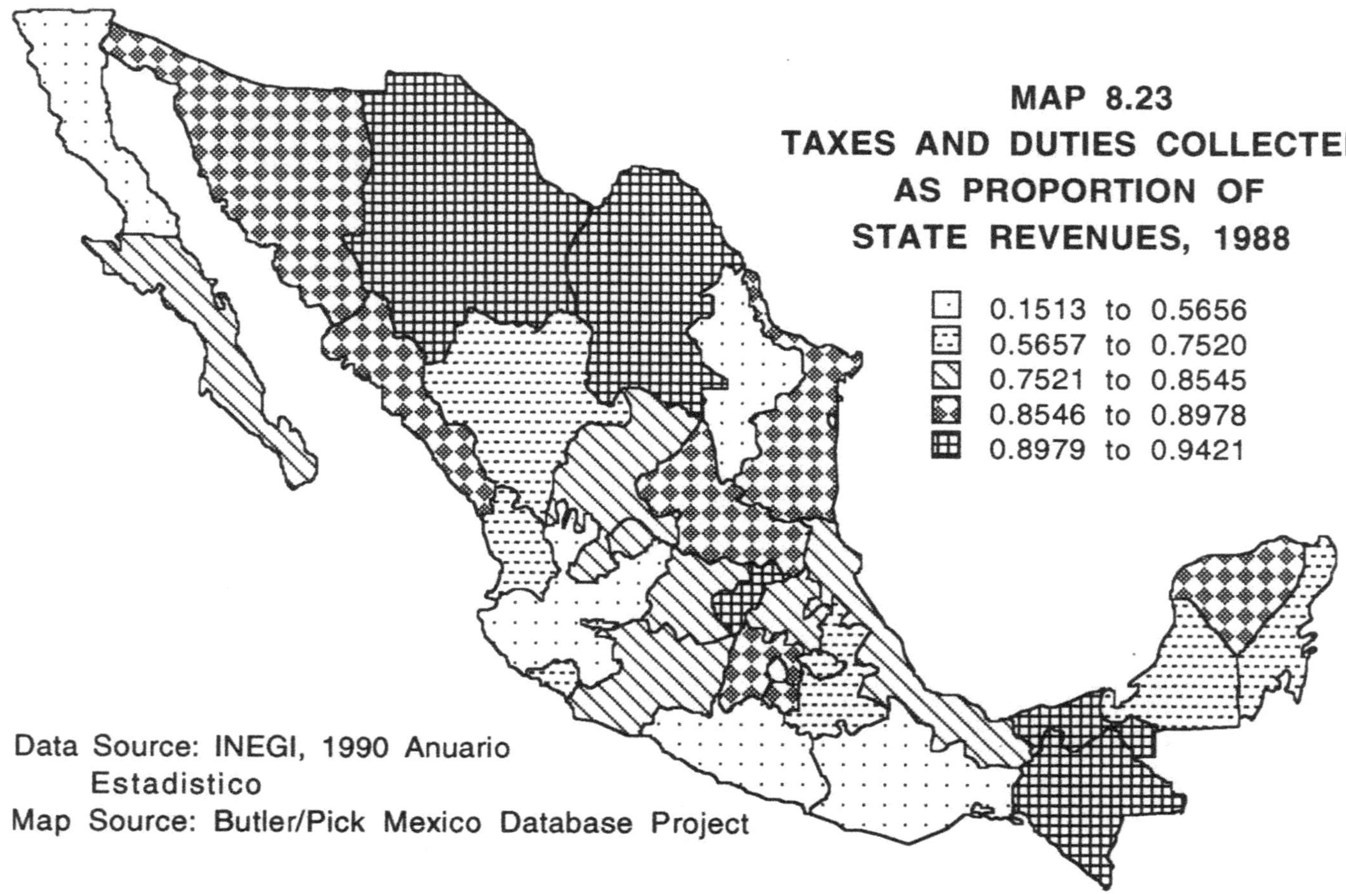

Data Source: INEGI, 1990 Anuario Estadistico
Map Source: Butler/Pick Mexico Database Project

Table 8.22 Federal Government Public Investment, in Millions of Pesos, 1990

No.	State	Millons of Pesos Invested	Ratio per 1990 Capita
1	AGUASCALIENTES	219,154.5	0.3045
2	BAJA CALIFORNIA	568,125.7	0.3421
3	BAJA CALIFORNIA SUR	485,677.2	1.5284
4	CAMPECHE	1,343,662.5	2.5107
5	COAHUILA	903,543.2	0.4581
6	COLIMA	190,119.8	0.4437
7	CHIAPAS	455,110.5	0.1418
8	CHIHUAHUA	568,678.0	0.2329
9	DISTRITO FEDERAL	10,334,435.7	1.2548
10	DURANGO	347,324.5	0.2574
11	GUANAJUATO	435,540.2	0.1094
12	GUERRERO	811,156.6	0.3095
13	HIDALGO	655,473.0	0.3471
14	JALISCO	841,589.3	0.1587
15	MEXICO	1,279,150.8	0.1303
16	MICHOACAN	1,026,910.9	0.2894
17	MORELOS	275,308.0	0.2304
18	NAYARIT	345,561.4	0.4190
19	NUEVO LEON	616,876.4	0.1991
20	OAXACA	1,016,779.2	0.3367
21	PUEBLA	460,525.7	0.1116
22	QUERETARO	236,182.1	0.2247
23	QUINTANA ROO	327,062.8	0.6630
24	SAN LUIS POTOSI	777,289.9	0.3880
25	SINALOA	1,211,413.9	0.5496
26	SONORA	535,786.6	0.2938
27	TABASCO	5,744,352.3	3.8251
28	TAMAULIPAS	525,837.4	0.2337
29	TLAXCALA	155,346.9	0.2041
30	VERACRUZ	3,090,348.3	0.4962
31	YUCATAN	556,911.3	0.4086
32	ZACATECAS	241,691.6	0.1894
National Total		36,582,926	0.4503
Mean		1,143,216.4438	0.5497
Median		562,518.5000	0.3070
S.D.		1,976,725.4185	0.7674
C.V.		172.91	139.59
Minimum		155346.9	0.1094
Maximum		10334435.7	3.8251

DEFINITION: The Millions of Pesos Invested are the public federal government investments in million of pesos for 1990. The Ration per Capita are the Million of Pesos Invested divided by the total population of the corresponding year.

SOURCE: INEGI, Anuario Estadistico, 1992.

Figure 8.9
Federal Public Investment by Sector
1990

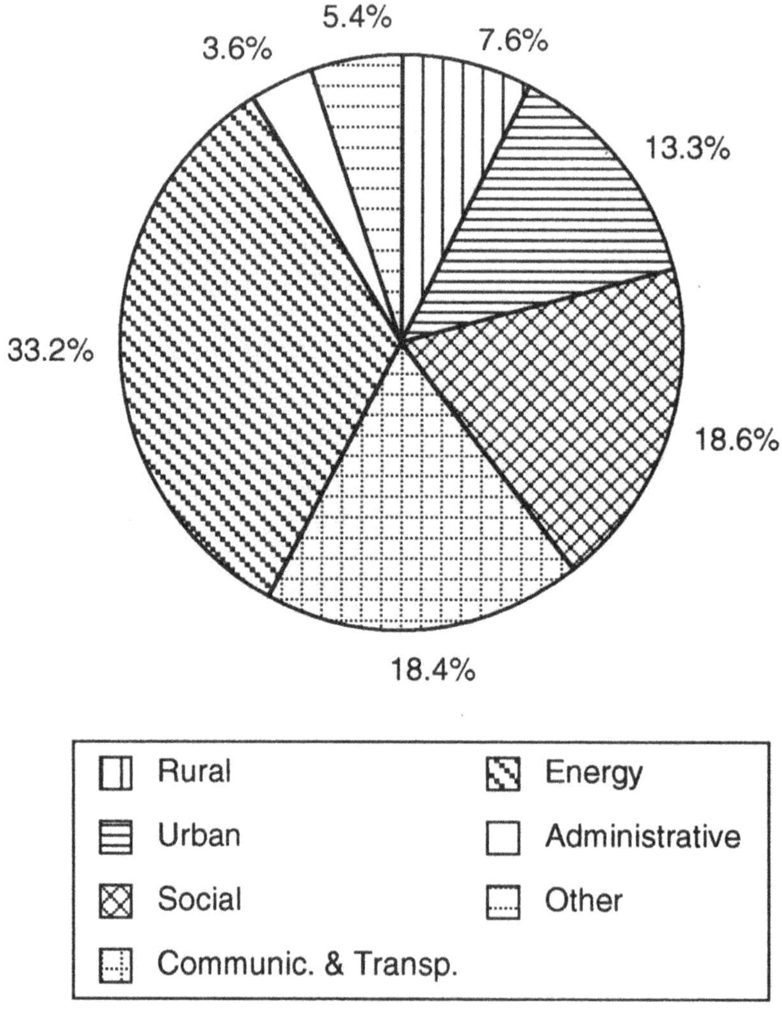

SOURCE: INEGI, Anuario Estadistico, 1992.

Table 8.23 Total Value of New Mortgages, 1986

No.	State	Total Real Estate Transactions	Real Estate Sales	Other Real Estate Fees	Value of New Mortgages Total	Value of New Mortgages Per Capita
1	AGUASCALIENTES	32,189,771	5,150,363	70,818	26,962,152	37.47
2	BAJA CALIFORNIA	119,660,011	19,815,698	2,405,166	56,563,287	34.06
3	BAJA CALIFORNIA SUR	11,016,323	3,651,911	1,054,262	3,429,381	10.79
4	CAMPECHE	14,877,204	996,773	47,607	6,542,994	12.23
5	COAHUILA	94,180,974	20,230,073	2,279,180	27,105,284	13.74
6	COLIMA	14,446,604	2,289,787	254,260	11,742,200	27.40
7	CHIAPAS	71,311,844	23,896,599	877,136	15,317,784	4.77
8	CHIHUAHUA	170,455,083	36,784,207	1,909,097	65,352,479	26.76
9	DISTRITO FEDERAL	486,346,970	283,977,996	40,415,433	153,831,547	18.68
10	DURANGO	77,100,950	7,964,528	316,114	36,515,010	27.06
11	GUANAJUATO	267,768,737	42,602,006	4,498,515	85,793,103	21.54
12	GUERRERO	40,296,020	10,460,847	350,575	6,668,991	2.54
13	HIDALGO	39,323,437	9,123,038	1,340,929	20,361,676	10.78
14	JALISCO	241,292,579	51,491,836	4,319,137	141,566,356	26.70
15	MEXICO	551,591,268	168,455,974	9,652,847	160,182,104	16.32
16	MICHOACAN	136,588,134	26,252,240	1,447,834	30,281,589	8.53
17	MORELOS	25,328,991	8,887,943	1,041,022	6,919,880	5.79
18	NAYARIT	12,095,181	3,464,060	81,038	5,094,490	6.18
19	NUEVO LEON	724,879,495	152,152,206	25,225,807	239,137,745	77.17
20	OAXACA	32,070,262	4,909,957	269,390	7,921,355	2.62
21	PUEBLA	146,403,062	50,304,092	12,180,735	59,015,074	14.30
22	QUERETARO	43,286,133	14,271,438	731,536	16,509,331	15.70
23	QUINTANA ROO	16,162,298	2,107,564	48,487	7,943,769	16.10
24	SAN LUIS POTOSI	105,080,085	26,921,518	640,989	48,189,727	24.06
25	SINALOA	166,029,998	26,730,830	2,922,128	37,157,513	16.86
26	SONORA	186,484,105	18,200,849	1,062,959	134,231,259	73.61
27	TABASCO	52,526,691	9,896,029	3,156,854	7,695,160	5.12
28	TAMAULIPAS	217,102,081	43,138,184	434,204	76,506,773	34.01
29	TLAXCALA	5,149,894	1,827,182	200,331	2,665,585	3.50
30	VERACRUZ	172,763,305	28,212,248	4,129,043	80,715,016	12.96
31	YUCATAN	114,908,250	36,552,314	287,271	33,013,140	24.22
32	ZACATECAS	101,011,235	5,596,022	1,232,337	62,384,539	48.88
	National Total	4,489,726,975	1,146,316,312	124,883,041	1,673,316,293	
	Mean	140,303,968	35,822,385	3,902,595	52,291,134	21.26
	Median	97,596,105	19,008,274	1,058,611	31,647,365	16.21
	S.D.	166,060,829	59,035,520	8,277,717	57,240,829	18.07
	C.V.	118.36	164.80	212.11	109.47	84.98
	Minimum	5,149,894	996,773	47,607	2,665,585	2.54
	Maximum	724,879,495	283,977,996	40,415,433	239,137,745	77.17

DEFINITION: Other Real Estate Fees include legal, administrative, and estate fees.

SOURCE: INEGI, 1988-1989 Anuario Estadistico, Table 4.7.7.

MAP 8.24
TOTAL VALUE OF
NEW MORTGAGES, 1986

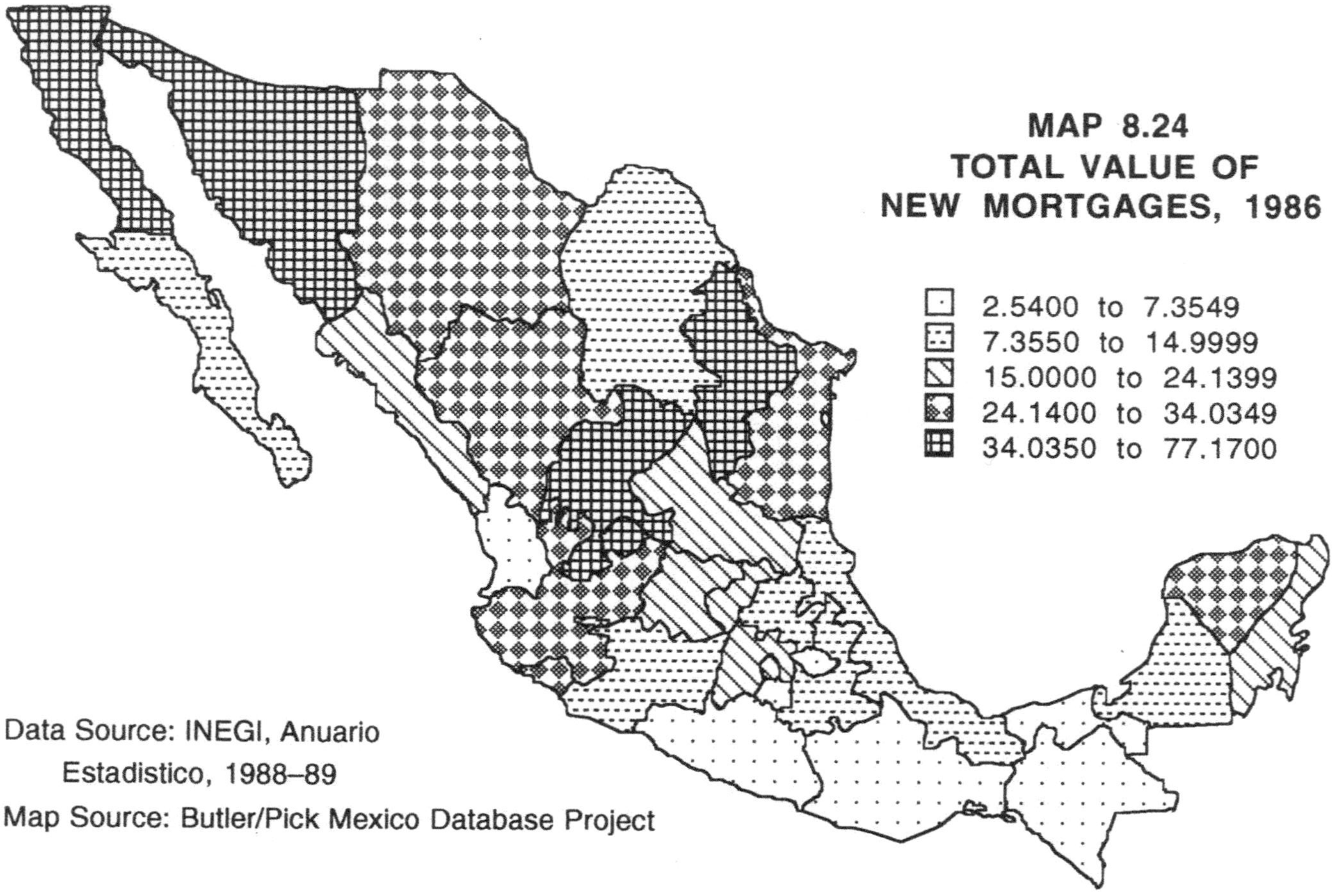

Data Source: INEGI, Anuario
Estadistico, 1988–89
Map Source: Butler/Pick Mexico Database Project

Mexican–United States Balance of Trade, 1960–1990

As shown in Table 8.24, the balance of trade between Mexico and the United States was on the negative side of Mexico from 1960 through 1982. Beginning in 1973 through 1981 this balance of trade was severe and especially so in 1974, 1975, 1979, 1980, and 1981. Figure 8.10 shows that beginning in 1982, there was a severe reversal of form and the balance of trade shifted to a positive side for Mexico. This favorable balance of trade for Mexico continued through 1988, with substantial surpluses between 1982-1988. These surpluses stemmed largely from Mexico's mid 80s boom in oil production, leading to oil surpluses for export. However, in 1989 the balance of trade again reversed with Mexico having a negative balance with the U.S.

Table 8.25 and Figure 8.11 illustrate Mexican trade exports between 1973-1990 to a variety of industrial countries. Exports from Mexico historically have been directed toward the United States and the U.S. dominated Mexican exports during this time period with substantial increases beginning in the 1980s. Table 8.25 and Figure 8.11 demonstrate that exports from the Mexico to the U.S. not only have outpaced exports to other countries but also that the rate of exports to the U.S. is accelerating.

Imports to Mexico during the same time period demonstrate that there was a strong parallel between imports and exports but with substantial imports beginning several years prior to expanded exports. Table 8.25 and Figure 8.12 present information on imports from the major industrial countries of the U.S., Canada, Germany, and Japan. As both the table and figure illustrate, the U.S. proportion of Mexican imports has grown each year except during the early 1980s when there was an overall reduction of imports into Mexico.

Figure 8.10
Mexican - U.S. Balance Of Trade, 1960–1990
(in millions)

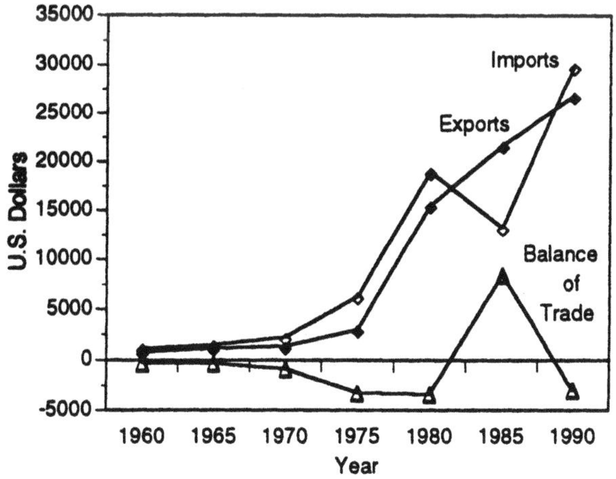

SOURCE: IMF, International Financial Statistics Yearbook, 1979, 1991

Table 8.24 Mexican-U.S. Balance of Trade, 1960–1990, in Millions of U.S. Dollars

Year	Exports fob	Imports fob	Balance of Trade: Mexico
1960	778	1,132	-354.00
1961	826	1,086	-260.00
1962	930	1,097	-167.00
1963	985	1,186	-201.00
1964	1,054	1,424	-370.00
1965	1,146	1,498	-352.00
1966	1,244	1,571	-327.00
1967	1,152	1,760	-608.00
1968	1,258	1,892	-634.00
1969	1,454	1,983	-529.00
1970	1,348	2,236	-888.00
1971	1,409	2,158	-749.00
1972	1,717	2,610	-893.00
1973	2,141	3,656	-1515.00
1974	2,999	5,791	-2792.00
1975	3,007	6,278	-3271.00
1976	3,475	5,771	-2296.00
1977	4,604	5,625	-1021.00
1978	6,246	7,992	-1746.00
1979	9,301	12,131	-2830.00
1980	15,511	18,896	-3385.00
1981	20,102	23,948	-3846.00
1982	21,230	14,435	6795.00
1983	22,312	8,550	13762.00
1984	24,196	11,255	12941.00
1985	21,663	13,212	8451.00
1986	16,031	11,432	4599.00
1987	20,655	12,222	8433.00
1988	20,566	18,898	1668.00
1989	22,765	23,410	-645.00
1990	26,773	29,799	-3026.00

SOURCE: IMF, International Financial Statistics Yearbook, 1979 and 1991.

Table 8.25 Mexican Trade, Imports and Exports 1973–1990, in millions of U.S. dollars

Imports

Year	World Total	Industrial Countries: Total	United States	Canada	Japan	Germany	Western Hemisphere	Other
1973	3,813	3,431	2,277	85	178	269	202	180
1974	6,059	5,515	3,779	146	224	476	268	276
1975	6,581	5,936	4,113	146	299	481	459	186
1976	6,036	5,494	3,773	141	307	424	384	158
1977	5,486	5,092	3,493	166	296	312	294	100
1978	7,560	7,038	4,564	126	609	536	343	179
1979	10,987	10,103	6,876	180	718	346	608	276
1980	17,687	15,171	10,890	321	899	473	749	1,767
1981	21,933	19,223	13,998	405	1,095	534	1,075	1,635
1982	13,687	12,058	8,188	291	777	318	635	994
1983	8,200	6,897	4,958	203	320	327	261	1,042
1984	10,327	8,875	6,440	207	457	440	446	1,006
1985	13,441	12,104	8,954	235	723	536	630	707
1986	11,507	10,609	7,574	214	698	672	400	498
1987	12,758	11,901	8,252	375	837	859	387	470
1988	18,711	17,468	12,102	549	1,228	1,260	567	676
1989	22,084	20,153	15,553	359	818	919	965	966
1990	32,687	30,322	23,144	414	1,682	1,483	1,093	1,272

Exports

Year	World Total	Industrial Countries: Total	United States	Canada	Japan	Germany	Western Hemisphere	Other
1973	2,262	1,742	1,318	30	147	59	217	303
1974	2,993	2,369	1,703	64	142	110	373	251
1975	2,916	2,142	1,668	43	109	87	361	413
1976	3,469	2,728	2,111	48	177	89	416	325
1977	4,171	3,328	2,738	45	129	92	450	393
1978	5,954	4,866	4,057	62	200	115	448	640
1979	8,983	7,598	6,876	75	248	213	615	770
1980	15,557	13,279	10,890	117	671	257	1,068	1,210
1981	19,381	1,617	13,998	661	1,157	212	1,905	1,305
1982	21,209	17,682	8,188	584	1,450	240	1,858	1,669
1983	22,313	19,080	4,958	467	1,512	270	1,665	1,568
1984	24,382	21,082	6,440	495	1,868	231	1,552	1,748
1985	22,105	19,569	8,954	393	1,709		1,199	1,337
1986	16,120	14,150	7,574	224	1,115		1,073	897
1987	20,526	18,062	8,252	312	1,347		1,599	865
1988	20,765	18,272	12,102	316	1,362		1,618	875
1989	22,975	20,503	15,553	272	1,311		1,645	827
1990	29,982	27,508	23,144	725	1,610		1,620	854

DEFINITION: Mexican trade imports and exports 1973–1990 in millions of U.S. dollars. Other includes other countries and country/area not specified. World Total is Direction of Trade Statistics Total.

SOURCE: IMF, Direction of Trade Statistics Yearbook, 1986 and 1991.

Figure 8.11 Mexican Trade, Exports 1975 - 1990
(in millions)

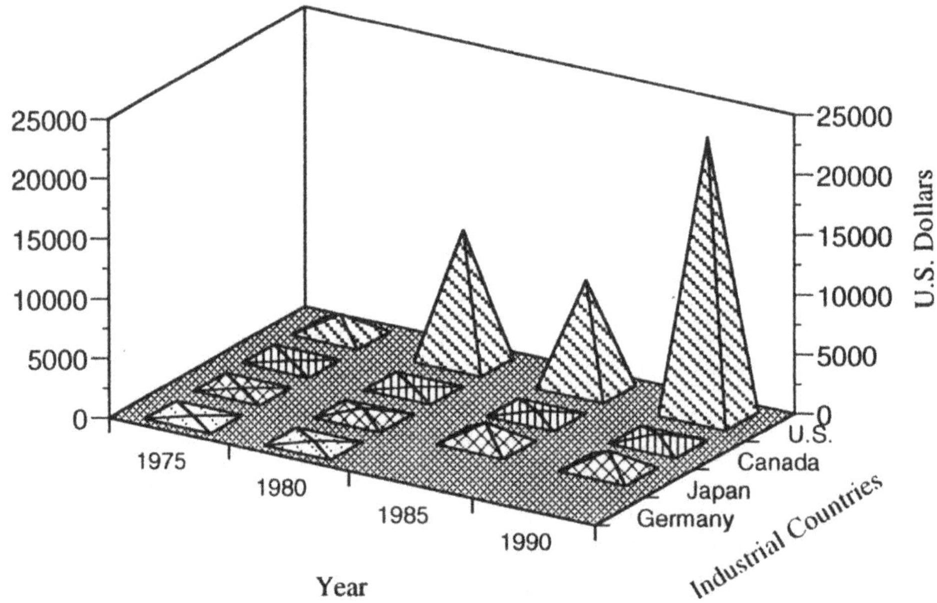

Figure 8.12 Mexican Trade, Imports, 1975 - 1990
(in millions)

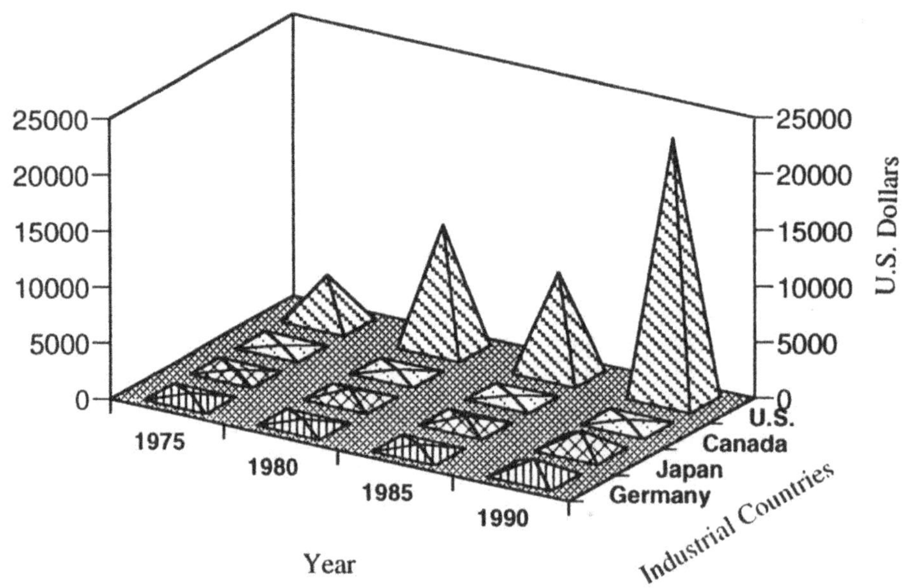

SOURCE: IMF, Direction Of Trade Statistics Yearbook, 1986, 1991.

9

Labor Force

- Introduction
- Economically Active Population
- Underemployment and Unemployment
- Occupations
- Labor Force by Industry
- Income
- Projected Eligible Work Force

Introduction

Chapter 9 expands information presented in Chapter 8. There are six major divisions in this chapter: (1) The economically active population focusing on its male and female components, the economically active population of the Central Metropolitan Zone, and tertiary occupations; (2) a presentation on underemployment and unemployment; (3) a discussion of a variety of occupational categories, including professional and technical, administrative and managerial for the states and for the Central Metropolitan Zone, service and support, agricultural, and others; (4) the work force by a variety of industries—agriculture, commerce, construction, manufacturing, personal services, and community and social services; (5) income focusing on the high and the no or very low levels, and (6) projections of the labor force to the year 2005, with a discussion of labor force implications of millions of new eligible workers.

The information presented in this chapter is primarily from the 1990 Mexican census, mainly at the state level, but with some description of the labor force dimensions for the Central Metropolitan Zone and some data from other publications. As with all other topics presented in this *Handbook*, this chapter includes only a few dimensions available from the 1990 census and other official and non-official Mexican publications.

Economically Active Population

The economically active population was determined by an analysis of 1990 Mexican census data. Census figures are for the economically active population of persons 12 years of age and older. Rates were determined by dividing the economically active population by the total population 12 years of age and over.

The Total Economically Active Population, 1990

The Mexican economically active population more than tripled between 1950 and 1990 (see Alba 1984 and Pick et al. 1993 in press). In 1990, there were 24,063,283 persons economically active (EAP) in Mexico, of whom 18,418,695 were male. In 1980, variations described in the economically active population by state were relatively minor (Pick et al. 1989a). This remained substantially true in 1990 as shown in Table 9.1 and Map 9.1. However, by region between 1980 and 1990 some changes occurred. For example, in 1980 the highest percentage of the economically active population was in the pacific south. In 1990, the highest percentage of economically active population was in the border states, except for Coahuila, and in Quintana Roo, Colima, and Jalisco. The Federal District and the state of Mexico also had high rates.

Several states that in 1980 had a relatively lower percentage of an economically active population in 1990 had a substantially larger percentage economically active. These differences from 1980 may reflect actual change or, more likely, they may be a result of a more accurate 1990 census (see Rendon and Salas 1986).

Relatively few dimensions were systematically associated with the economically active population per capita. Population size had a high correlation as did population density (r = .62). The population aged 18–64, not too surprisingly had a correlation of .38 with EAP and the population aged 0–17 had a negative correlation (- .35). There was no relationship between EAP and the elderly.

Economically Active Males, 1990

Male economic activity is defined as the proportion of the male economically active population age 12+ to the total male population age 12+. This proportion is shown in Table 9.1 as "proport. EA male pop. 12+" and displayed in Map 9.2. In Table 9.1, an alternative measure of male economic activity, the ratio of male economically active population is also shown. This is defined as the ratio of the male economically active population 12+ to total economically active population age 12+. Table 9.1 and Map 9.2 report variation among the states for economically active males. Map 9.2 show that the highest percentages of an economically active male population were in the Bajas, Colima, and Chiapas. States with the lowest economically active males were scattered through the mid-section of the country, Michoacan, Oaxaca, and Guerrero.

The male economically active population in 1990 was significantly correlated with the total economically active population (r = .72) and with the female economically active population (.85). Other important positive relationships existed with various measures of inmigration, including predictions of future migration. There also was a strong negative correlation with lifetime outmigration (- .66). Further, positive associations exist between male economically active population and what might be labeled as higher quality of life variables, e.g., housing and other dimensions. Male economic activity was negatively associated with unemployment (- .76) but only moderately so with underemployment
(- .31). Finally, there is a negative association with population age 65 and over (- .55).

Economically Active Females, 1990

Over the past fifty years, the sex composition of the labor force has changed, with the proportion female rising from one fourteenth of workers in 1940 to one fourth in 1990. The increasing proportion female in the labor force stems from female educational advances and cultural changes that encourage greater work involvement for women (Garcia 1988). The half century of change for female economic activity in Mexico is portrayed in the text table below.

	1940 Census	1970 Census	1990 Census	1988 Household Survey *	1990 I.L.O. Projection**
Females Econ. Active	432	2,108	5,645	9,050	8,261
Total Econ. Active	5,858	11,253	24,064	28,852	30,487
Percent Female	7.4	17.9	23.5	31.4	27.1
Female Econ. Act. Rate***	4.3	9.8	13.6	22.8	18.6

* Mexican federal government household survey (cited in Garcia, 1993).
** Projection of International Labor Organization (1986).
*** Ratio of females economically active to total female population.
NOTE: The economically active population is in thousands.

Although 1990 census statistics indicate an increase in rates from 1970, they likely represent a substantial undercount in female economic activity, which has been noted for the 1990 Census (Corona 1991; Garcia 1993). Both the 1988 federal government survey data and the I.L.O. projections point to higher female economic activity rates for 1990 (Garcia 1993; International Labor Organization 1986).

In 1990, the census counted 5,644,588 economically active females in Mexico, or about 22 percent of women aged 12 and over. The distribution of economically active females shown on Map 9.3 varies somewhat from that of economically active males. While the border states are similar in relative economic activity, the gulf, south, and southeast regions, with the exception of Quintana Roo, have lower rates of females economically active (see Map 9.3 and column on Table 9.1 labelled "proport. EA female pop. 12+"). The CV of 25 for proportion of economically active females is nearly sixfold that for males.

In contrast to the male economically active population, the female economically active population is associated with many dimensions; the female economically population is highly correlated with the total EA population (r = .85). Both male (.42) and female (.52) economically active were correlated with the divorce rate. As with males, the female EA population is closely related to many migration variables; also, the female EA population is highly correlated with urban dimensions (.87), the population aged 18–64 (.38), various measures of literacy and education, and various improvements in housing, lifestyle, and higher level incomes (.86), and negatively associated with the dependency ratio (.87) In addition, the female EA population is associated with higher gross state revenues (.45) and various other measures of higher level occupations (r's = higher .80s). Female EA is negatively associated with underemployment (- .36) and unemployment (- .40). Cancer (.63) and cardiology death rates (.49) are linked to EA. Finally, as might be anticipated, female EA and the standardized fertility rate are negatively linked (- .78).

Economically Active Population, Mexico City, 1990

The 1990 economically active population in the Central Metropolitan Zone (CMZ) is shown on Map 9.4. Variation by delegation (Federal District) and municipio (state of Mexico) ranges from a low of 37.6 percent to a high of 52.0 percent. The highest proportions of economically active population are in the older sections of the Federal District and adjoining areas to the east and south.

Tertiary Employment, 1990

The Mexican census divides occupations into *primary*—agriculture, livestock-raising, mining, hunting and fishing; *secondary*—extraction of minerals, oil and gas, industrial manufacturing, and construction; and the *tertiary* — commerce and services. Employment in the tertiary sector for 1990 by state, as illustrated on Map 9.5 and reported in Table 9.2, is highly variable.

Four border states are in the highest two categories of tertiary employment with only Coahuila and Chihuahua having average levels. southern states, except for Quintana Roo, have relatively low levels of persons in the tertiary employment sector. The state of Mexico and the Federal District, as might be anticipated, have relatively high rates of tertiary employment.

In 1990, the Mexican census reported 23,403,413 men working in the labor force and 5,521,271 women. As shown on Figure 9.1, of the employed population, 46.1

percent are in the tertiary sector. However, 70.3 percent of employed women as opposed to 38.6 percent of men work in the tertiary sector. This may partly reflect the much higher proportion of males in agricultural occupations. In particular, the ratio of male to female agricultural employees is 27 to 1.

Table 9.1 Economically Active Population, 1990

No.	State	Total Econ. Active Pop. 12+	EA Male Pop. 12+	Ratio EA Male Pop. 12+	Proport. EA Male Pop. 12+	EA Female Pop. 12+	Ratio EA Fem. Pop. 12+	Proport. EA Fem. Pop. 12+
1	AGUASCALIENTES	217,092	160,133	0.7376	0.6938	56,959	0.2624	0.2253
2	BAJA CALIFORNIA	578,395	417,576	0.7220	0.7155	160,819	0.2780	0.2740
3	BAJA CALIFORNIA SUR	104,980	80,351	0.7654	0.7112	24,629	0.2346	0.2259
4	CAMPECHE	152,902	124,555	0.8146	0.6961	28,347	0.1854	0.1591
5	COAHUILA	605,251	460,083	0.7602	0.6691	145,168	0.2398	0.2045
6	COLIMA	136,046	103,146	0.7582	0.7089	32,900	0.2418	0.2184
7	CHIAPAS	874,267	754,229	0.8627	0.7449	120,038	0.1373	0.1171
8	CHIHUAHUA	797,051	591,499	0.7421	0.6964	205,552	0.2579	0.2349
9	DISTRITO FEDERAL	2,961,270	1,949,697	0.6584	0.6681	1,011,573	0.3416	0.3066
10	DURANGO	359,994	285,676	0.7936	0.6442	74,318	0.2064	0.1584
11	GUANAJUATO	1,063,208	828,232	0.7790	0.6656	234,976	0.2210	0.1698
12	GUERRERO	636,938	506,697	0.7955	0.6221	130,241	0.2045	0.1480
13	HIDALGO	508,551	412,959	0.8120	0.6769	95,592	0.1880	0.1481
14	JALISCO	1,588,190	1,180,187	0.7431	0.6882	408,003	0.2569	0.2140
15	MEXICO	2,948,159	2,225,835	0.7550	0.6732	722,324	0.2450	0.2073
16	MICHOACAN	920,154	739,697	0.8039	0.6630	180,457	0.1961	0.1459
17	MORELOS	359,813	269,715	0.7496	0.6712	90,098	0.2504	0.2072
18	NAYARIT	238,079	188,779	0.7929	0.6836	49,300	0.2071	0.1744
19	NUEVO LEON	1,036,770	766,781	0.7396	0.6879	269,989	0.2604	0.2364
20	OAXACA	775,844	649,360	0.8370	0.6828	126,484	0.1630	0.1233
21	PUEBLA	1,110,489	894,040	0.8051	0.6793	216,449	0.1949	0.1508
22	QUERETARO	298,222	225,088	0.7548	0.6707	73,134	0.2452	0.2049
23	QUINTANA ROO	165,424	129,944	0.7855	0.7715	35,480	0.2145	0.2295
24	SAN LUIS POTOSI	541,908	433,337	0.7997	0.6658	108,571	0.2003	0.1582
25	SINALOA	674,431	514,425	0.7628	0.6777	160,006	0.2372	0.2082
26	SONORA	577,205	439,143	0.7608	0.6792	138,062	0.2392	0.2136
27	TABASCO	406,096	339,710	0.8365	0.6913	66,386	0.1635	0.1334
28	TAMAULIPAS	710,047	526,762	0.7419	0.6691	183,285	0.2581	0.2227
29	TLAXCALA	203,908	164,020	0.8044	0.6564	39,888	0.1956	0.1513
30	VERACRUZ	1,792,272	1,474,625	0.8228	0.7044	317,647	0.1772	0.1449
31	YUCATAN	413,593	325,506	0.7870	0.7012	88,087	0.2130	0.1819
32	ZACATECAS	306,734	256,908	0.8376	0.6284	49,826	0.1624	0.1124
	National Total	24,063,283	18,418,695	0.7654	0.6801	5,644,588	0.2346	0.1958
	Mean	751,978	575,584	0.7788	0.6831	176,393	0.2212	0.1878
	Median	577,800	436,240	0.7823	0.6793	123,261	0.2177	0.1932
	S.D.	703,489	509,535	0.0414	0.0293	205,147	0.0414	0.0463
	C.V.	94	88.52	5.32	4.28	116.30	18.73	24.63
	Minimum	104,980	80,351	0.6584	0.6221	24,629	0.1373	0.1124
	Maximum	2,961,270	2,225,835	0.8627	0.7715	1,011,573	0.3416	0.3066

DEFINITION: Ratios are the economically active male population age 12+ to total economically active population, age 12+ ; the economically active male population age 12+ to total male population age 12+; the economically active female population age 12+ to total economically active population age 12+; and the economically active female population age 12+ to total female population age 12+. Maps 9.2 and 9.3 show the "proportion EA Male 12+" and "proportion EA Female 12+".

SOURCE: INEGI, 1990 Mexican Census of Population, Resumen General, Table 26.

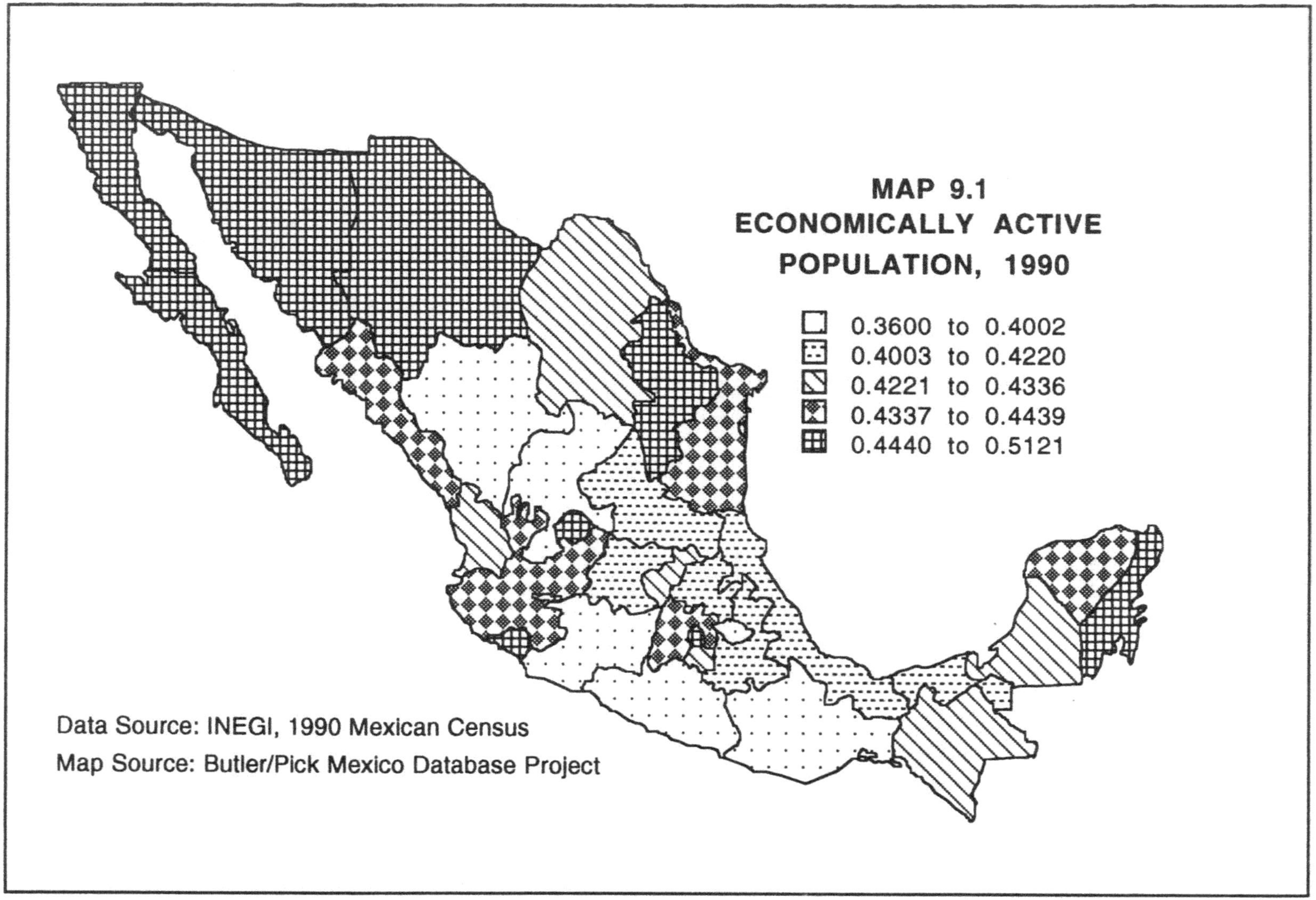
MAP 9.1
ECONOMICALLY ACTIVE
POPULATION, 1990
0.3600 to 0.4002
0.4003 to 0.4220
0.4221 to 0.4336
0.4337 to 0.4439
0.4440 to 0.5121
Data Source: INEGI, 1990 Mexican Census
Map Source: Butler/Pick Mexico Database Project

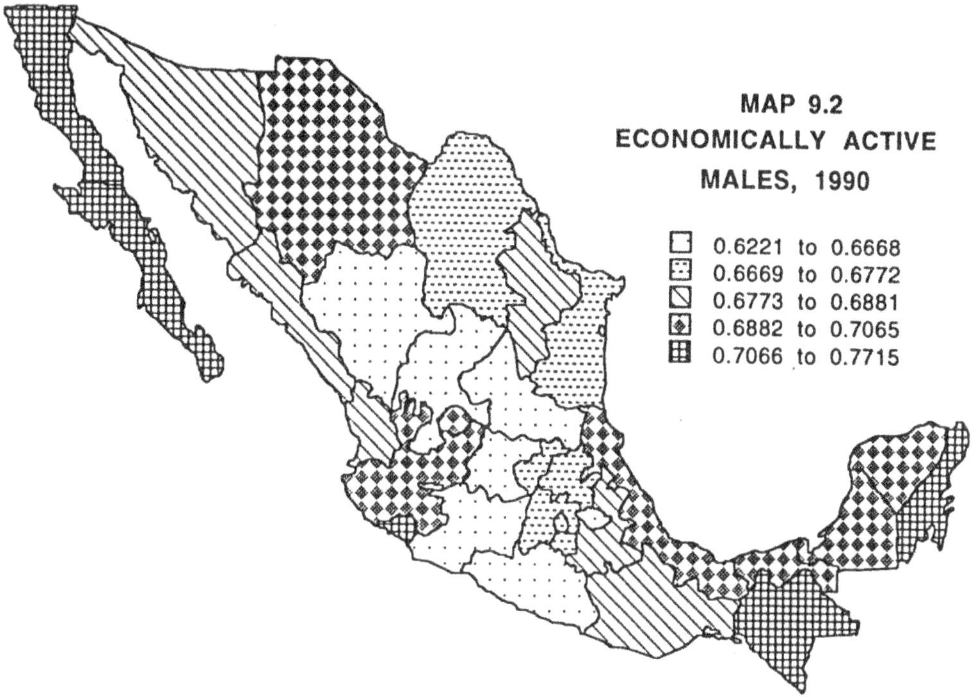

MAP 9.2
ECONOMICALLY ACTIVE MALES, 1990

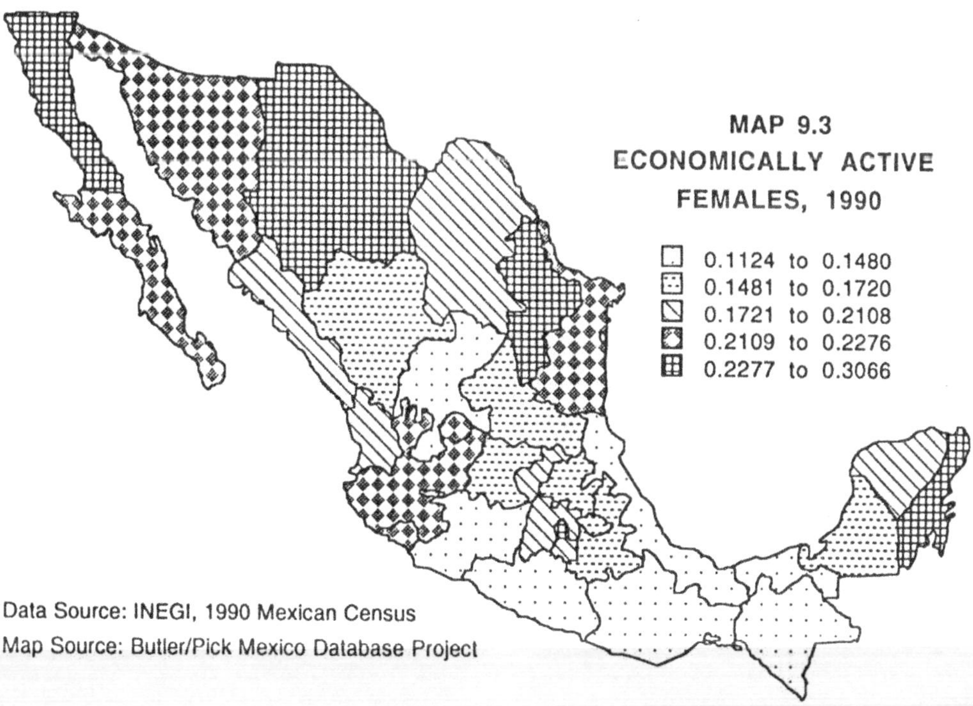

MAP 9.3
ECONOMICALLY ACTIVE FEMALES, 1990

Data Source: INEGI, 1990 Mexican Census
Map Source: Butler/Pick Mexico Database Project

MAP 9.4
ECONOMICALLY ACTIVE POPULATION
MEXICO CITY, 1990

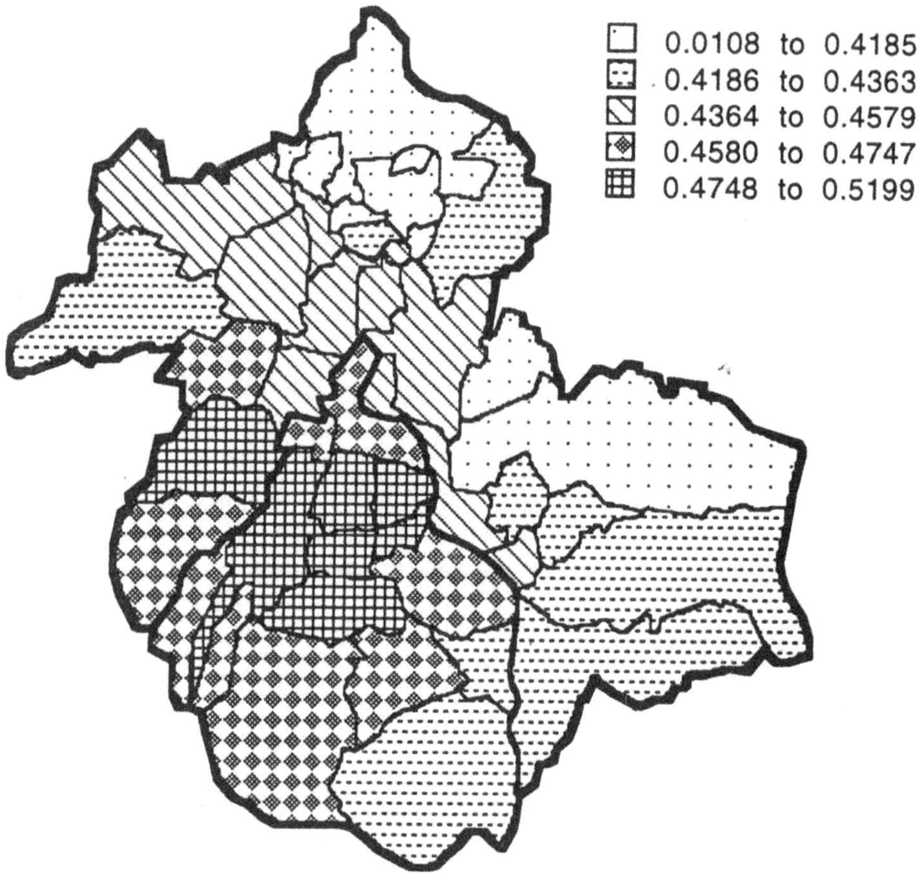

Data Source: INEGI, 1990 Mexican Census
Map Source: Butler/Pick Mexico Database Project

Table 9.2 Employment by Sector of Activity, 1990

No.	State	Employed Population	Sector of Activity: Primary	%	Secondary	%	Tertiary	%	Not Specified	%
1	AGUASCALIENTES	212,365	31,766	15.0	72,662	34.2	103,866	48.9	4,071	1.9
2	BAJA CALIFORNIA	565,471	58,584	10.4	179,527	31.7	305,382	54.0	21,978	3.9
3	BAJA CALIF. SUR	102,763	18,820	18.3	19,318	18.8	61,118	59.4	3,507	3.4
4	CAMPECHE	149,983	51,439	34.3	29,154	19.4	63,362	42.2	6,028	4.0
5	COAHUILA	586,165	71,137	12.1	220,744	37.7	277,037	47.3	17,247	2.9
6	COLIMA	133,474	32,011	24.0	28,547	21.4	68,923	51.6	3,993	3.0
7	CHIAPAS	854,159	498,320	58.3	95,039	11.1	234,273	27.4	26,527	3.1
8	CHIHUAHUA	773,100	131,610	17.0	277,662	35.9	334,376	43.2	29,452	3.8
9	DISTRITO FEDERAL	2,884,807	19,145	0.7	778,444	27.0	1,971,646	68.3	115,572	4.0
10	DURANGO	347,275	99,205	28.6	92,246	26.6	146,379	42.1	9,445	2.7
11	GUANAJUATO	1,030,160	236,713	23.0	360,362	35.0	398,590	38.7	34,495	3.3
12	GUERRERO	611,755	222,670	36.4	103,128	16.9	260,760	42.6	25,197	4.1
13	HIDALGO	493,315	182,684	37.0	124,505	25.2	167,712	34.0	18,414	3.7
14	JALISCO	1,553,202	234,016	15.1	508,679	32.7	757,453	48.8	53,054	3.4
15	MEXICO	2,860,976	248,140	8.7	1,053,808	36.8	1,456,246	50.9	102,782	3.6
16	MICHOACAN	891,873	303,224	34.0	206,491	23.2	333,788	37.4	48,370	5.4
17	MORELOS	348,357	70,887	20.3	97,175	27.9	172,143	49.4	8,152	2.3
18	NAYARIT	233,000	89,081	38.2	41,086	17.6	93,131	40.0	9,702	4.2
19	NUEVO LEON	1,009,584	61,835	6.1	405,771	40.2	509,469	50.5	32,509	3.2
20	OAXACA	754,305	398,848	52.9	123,805	16.4	213,819	28.3	17,833	2.4
21	PUEBLA	1,084,316	400,369	36.9	269,963	24.9	381,055	35.1	32,929	3.0
22	QUERETARO	288,994	51,771	17.9	107,762	37.3	120,738	41.8	8,723	3.0
23	QUINTANA ROO	163,190	32,013	19.6	25,347	15.5	95,939	58.8	9,891	6.1
24	SAN LUIS POTOSI	529,016	164,682	31.1	137,601	26.0	209,182	39.5	17,551	3.3
25	SINALOA	660,905	242,710	36.7	113,496	17.2	280,139	42.4	24,560	3.7
26	SONORA	562,386	127,900	22.7	142,908	25.4	275,821	49.0	15,757	2.8
27	TABASCO	393,434	140,093	35.6	80,680	20.5	155,584	39.5	17,077	4.3
28	TAMAULIPAS	684,550	111,400	16.3	208,863	30.5	342,425	50.0	21,862	3.2
29	TLAXCALA	196,609	56,150	28.5	66,662	33.9	70,109	35.6	3,688	1.9
30	VERACRUZ	1,742,129	685,647	39.4	368,639	21.2	641,828	36.8	46,015	2.6
31	YUCATAN	407,337	110,057	27.0	99,896	24.5	189,334	46.5	8,050	2.0
32	ZACATECAS	294,458	117,187	39.8	63,254	21.5	104,576	35.5	9,441	3.2
	National Total	23,403,413	5,300,114	22.7	6,503,224	27.8	10,796,203	46.1	803,872	3.4
	Mean	731,357	165,629	26.3	203,226	26.1	337,381	44.2	25,121	3.4
	Median	563,929	114,294	25.5	118,651	25.3	224,046	42.5	17,692	3.3
	S.D.	684,325	153,685	13.2	224,909	7.7	401,736	9.0	25,762	0.9
	C.V.	93.57	92.79	50.3	111	29.7	119.07	20.3	102.55	27.1
	Minimum	102,763	18,820	0.7	19,318	11.1	61,118	27.4	3,507	1.9
	Maximum	2,884,807	685,647	58.3	1,053,808	40.2	1,971,646	68.3	115,572	6.1

SOURCE: INEGI, Perfil Sociodemografico, 1992, Table 15.3.

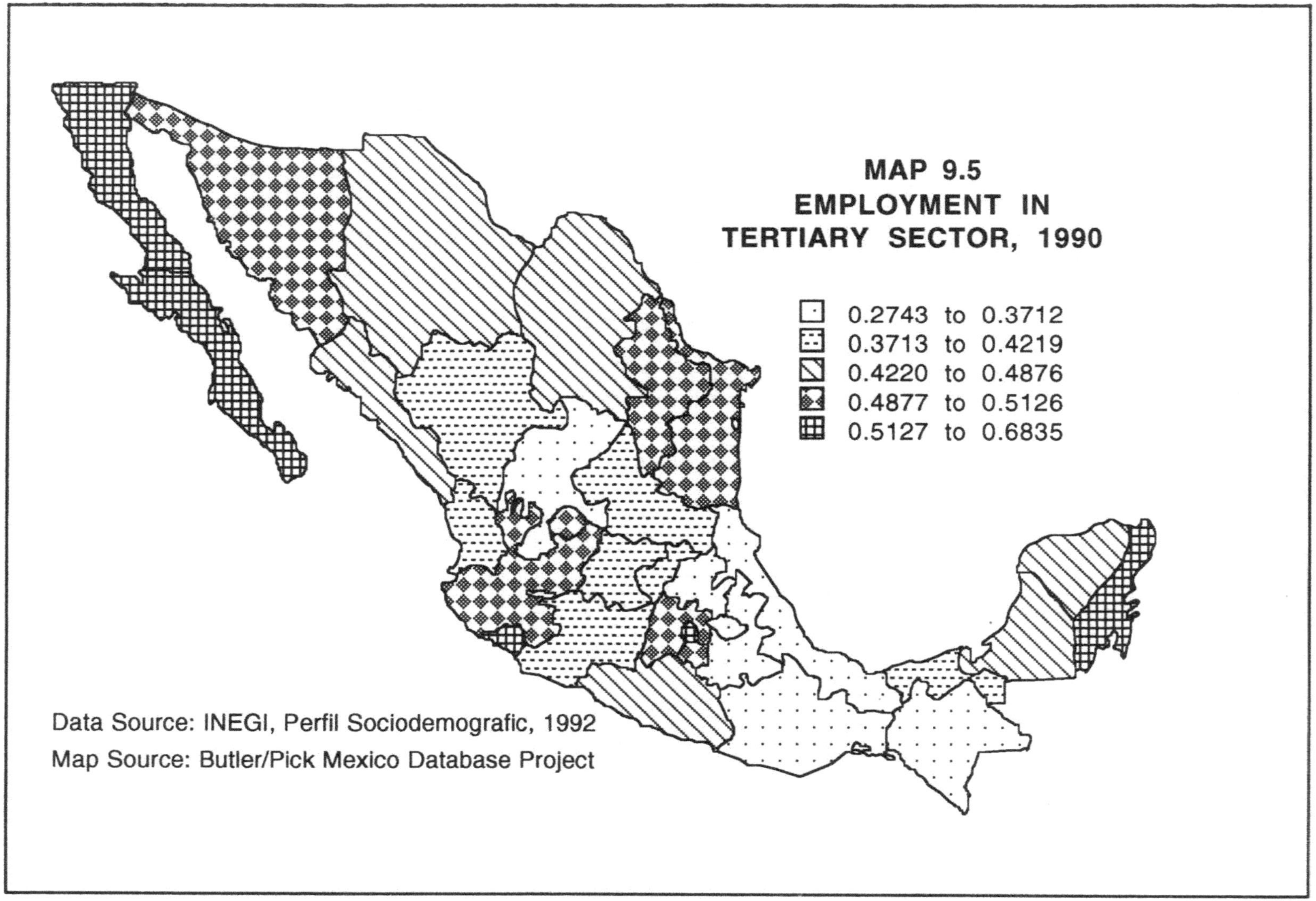
MAP 9.5
EMPLOYMENT IN
TERTIARY SECTOR, 1990
0.2743 to 0.3712
0.3713 to 0.4219
0.4220 to 0.4876
0.4877 to 0.5126
0.5127 to 0.6835
Data Source: INEGI, Perfil Sociodemografic, 1992
Map Source: Butler/Pick Mexico Database Project

Figure 9.1
Employed Population by Sector of Activity and Sex, 1990

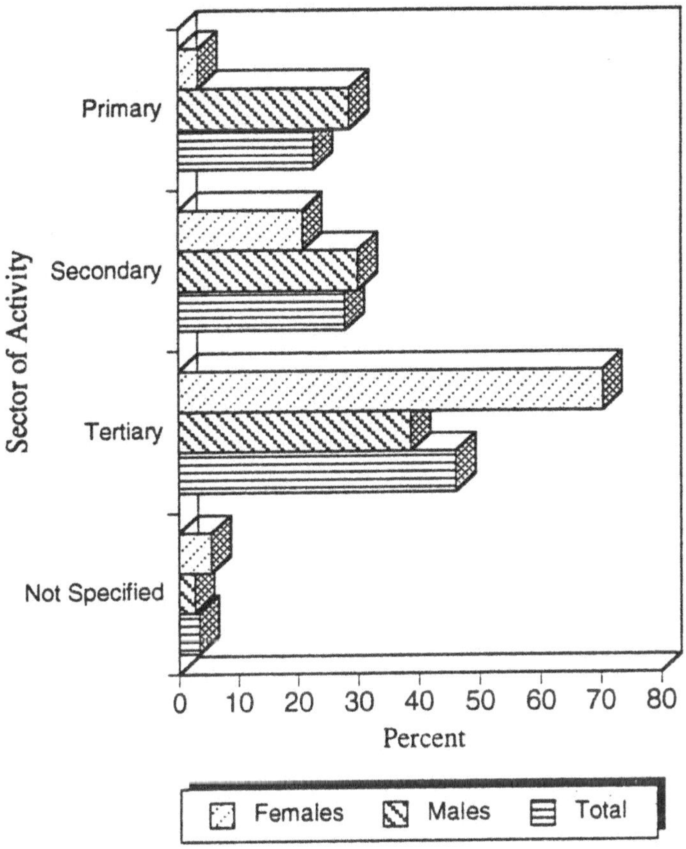

Supporting Data

Sector of Activity	Employed Population 1970	Employed Population 1990		
		Total	Males	Females
Primary	5,103,519	5,300,114	5,110,964	189,150
Secondary	2,973,540	6,503,224	5,355,769	1,147,455
Tertiary	4,130,473	10,796,203	6,916,319	3,879,884
Not Specified	747,525	803,872	499,090	304,782
TOTAL	12,955,057	23,403,413	17,882,142	5,521,271

NOTE: Primary sector consists of agriculture, forest, livestock, and fish industries. Secondary sector consists of mining, petroleum, manufacturing, energy production, and construction industries. Tertiary sector consists of commercial and service industries.

SOURCE: INEGI, Perfil Sociodemografico, 1992, Tables 15.1 and 15.2.

Underemployment and Unemployment

Underemployment, 1990

One measure of underemployment is of persons working full time but not making a living wage given some criterion of poverty level. However, we define underemployment as that population working less than 1 to 16 hours per week.

The table below presents unemployment and underemployment for the economically active population by gender in Mexico for 1990.

	No. of Males	Percent of Males	No. of Fem.	Percent of Fem.	Total No.	Total Percent
Unemployed	384	2.15	94	1.70	478	2.04
Under-employed						
0-8 hours	366	2.05	137	2.48	503	2.15
9-16 hours	411	2.30	194	3.51	605	2.59
Employed						
17-32 hours	1,596	8.93	891	16.14	2,487	10.63
33-40 hours	3,564	19.93	1,504	27.24	5,068	21.66
41-48 hours	6,273	35.08	1,457	26.39	7,730	33.03
49+ hours	4,706	26.32	1,051	19.04	5,757	24.60
Not Specif.	582	3.25	193	3.50	775	3.31
TOTAL	17,882		5,521		23,403	

NOTE: The figures are for population age 12+. Population numbers are in thousands.
SOURCE: INEGI, *1990 Mexican Census of Population,* Resumen General, Table 33.

The rate of unemployment is about 2 percent, with somewhat higher level for males. However, the underemployment rate of 4.7 percent is over one-third higher for females. Overall, the distribution is skewed towards males working longer hours than females. The skewing is more pronounced in 1990 than it was for 1980, although the 1980 figures had very high unspecified (see *Atlas of Mexico,* page 285). The 1980 underemployment rate was 8.5 percent.

According to the 1990 census, the statewide range of underemployment was from a little over three percent to nearly seven percent. As illustrated on Map 9.6 and data included in Table 9.3, there is a regional pattern of high underemployment in the west region and low underemployment in the central region. The west continued the very high underemployment in 1980 (see Map 8.3A in *Atlas of Mexico*). However, the central region in 1980 was low in the Federal District but high in the outlying states. This shift in the central region may reflect Salinas-era improvements in the prosperity of the state of Mexico and other outlying states. States with the highest rates of underemployment are Yucatan, Tabasco, Nuevo Leon, and several mid-pacific states. Underemployment is negatively, significantly correlated with the population aged 18–64 (r = - .39), accounting and information labor force (- .42), administrative and management occupations (- .55), the manufacturing work force (- .41), and positively associated with the agricultural work force characteristics (.38).

Unemployment, 1990

Unemployment is defined as the proportion of persons age 12 or older working zero hours per week. The Mexican Census provides an alternative definition of unemployment, "desocupados", which is not included due to space in the *Handbook* (*1990 Mexican Census of Population*, Resumen General, Table 25). The 2.0 percent unemployment rate compares to a 7.2 percent rate in 1980. The sharp drop is ascribed partly to economic improvements in the Salinas era although comparative censuses and census definitions of unemployment may be involved (Corona 1991; Rendon and Salas 1986). Underemployment and unemployment are positively correlated. There is, thus, some correspondence between under- and unemployment, but the relationship is not statistically significant.

Unemployment's geographical distribution very closely resembles that for 1980 (see *Atlas of Mexico*, Map 8.3B). As noted on Map 9.7 and Table 9.3, unemployment has a somewhat different distribution than underemployment. Unemployment was the highest at over 2.4 percent in Guerrero, Zacatecas and Oaxaca and high in Michoacan, Durango, and Chihuahua. These states have had weak economies in recent years. The lowest unemployment states were the Federal District, Nuevo Leon, Colima, and Yucatan at about 1.6–1.7 percent. Unemployment is negatively associated with the percentage of economically active and of the labor force in administrative and management positions. Among other important negative correlations is that with population growth between 1970 and 1990.

Table 9.3 Underemployment and Unemployment, 1990

No.	State	Econ.Act. Pop. Age 12+	Underempl. Pop. Age 12+	Ratio	Unempl. Pop. Age 12+	Ratio
1	AGUASCALIENTES	217,092	8,700	0.0401	3,837	0.0177
2	BAJA CALIFORNIA	578,395	28,307	0.0489	12,441	0.0215
3	BAJA CALIFORNIA SUR	104,980	4,853	0.0462	2,363	0.0225
4	CAMPECHE	152,902	7,132	0.0466	3,268	0.0214
5	COAHUILA	605,251	25,321	0.0418	10,851	0.0179
6	COLIMA	136,046	7,423	0.0546	2,285	0.0168
7	CHIAPAS	874,267	34,242	0.0392	16,329	0.0187
8	CHIHUAHUA	797,051	36,608	0.0459	19,005	0.0238
9	DISTRITO FEDERAL	2,961,270	103,317	0.0349	48,575	0.0164
10	DURANGO	359,994	16,129	0.0448	8,356	0.0232
11	GUANAJUATO	1,063,208	56,058	0.0527	21,464	0.0202
12	GUERRERO	636,938	39,136	0.0614	19,106	0.0300
13	HIDALGO	508,551	20,800	0.0409	10,654	0.0209
14	JALISCO	1,588,190	79,501	0.0501	28,520	0.0180
15	MEXICO	2,948,159	125,862	0.0427	55,582	0.0189
16	MICHOACAN	920,154	63,346	0.0688	21,493	0.0234
17	MORELOS	359,813	17,477	0.0486	7,572	0.0210
18	NAYARIT	238,079	16,019	0.0673	4,613	0.0194
19	NUEVO LEON	1,036,770	34,988	0.0337	16,450	0.0159
20	OAXACA	775,844	35,129	0.0453	18,699	0.0241
21	PUEBLA	1,110,489	49,607	0.0447	23,359	0.0210
22	QUERETARO	298,222	10,961	0.0368	4,835	0.0162
23	QUINTANA ROO	165,424	6,275	0.0379	2,958	0.0179
24	SAN LUIS POTOSI	541,908	25,334	0.0467	10,979	0.0203
25	SINALOA	674,431	39,190	0.0581	13,133	0.0195
26	SONORA	577,205	25,530	0.0442	12,318	0.0213
27	TABASCO	406,096	22,847	0.0563	7,311	0.0180
28	TAMAULIPAS	710,047	34,901	0.0492	15,631	0.0220
29	TLAXCALA	203,908	8,758	0.0430	4,055	0.0199
30	VERACRUZ	1,792,272	86,541	0.0483	36,928	0.0206
31	YUCATAN	413,593	21,252	0.0514	7,053	0.0171
32	ZACATECAS	306,734	17,519	0.0571	7,682	0.0250
National Total		24,063,283	1,109,063	0.0461	477,705	0.0199
Mean		751,978	34,658	0.0478	14,928	0.0203
Median		577,800	25,432	0.0464	11,649	0.0203
S.D.		703,489	29,223	0.0085	12,759	0.0030
C.V.		93.55	84.32	17.89	85.47	14.85
Minimum		104,980	4,853	0.0337	2,285	0.0159
Maximum		2,961,270	125,862	0.0688	55,582	0.0300

DEFINITION: Underemployed population consists of population working less than 1 to 16 hours per week. The ratio represents column 2 divided by column 1. Note that these figures exclude those not specifying age. Unemployed population consists of persons age 12+ working 0 hours per week. The ratio represents column 4 divided by column 1. Note that these figures exclude those not specifying age.

SOURCE: INEGI, 1990 Mexican Census of Population, Table 33.

MAP 9.6

UNDEREMPLOYMENT, 1990

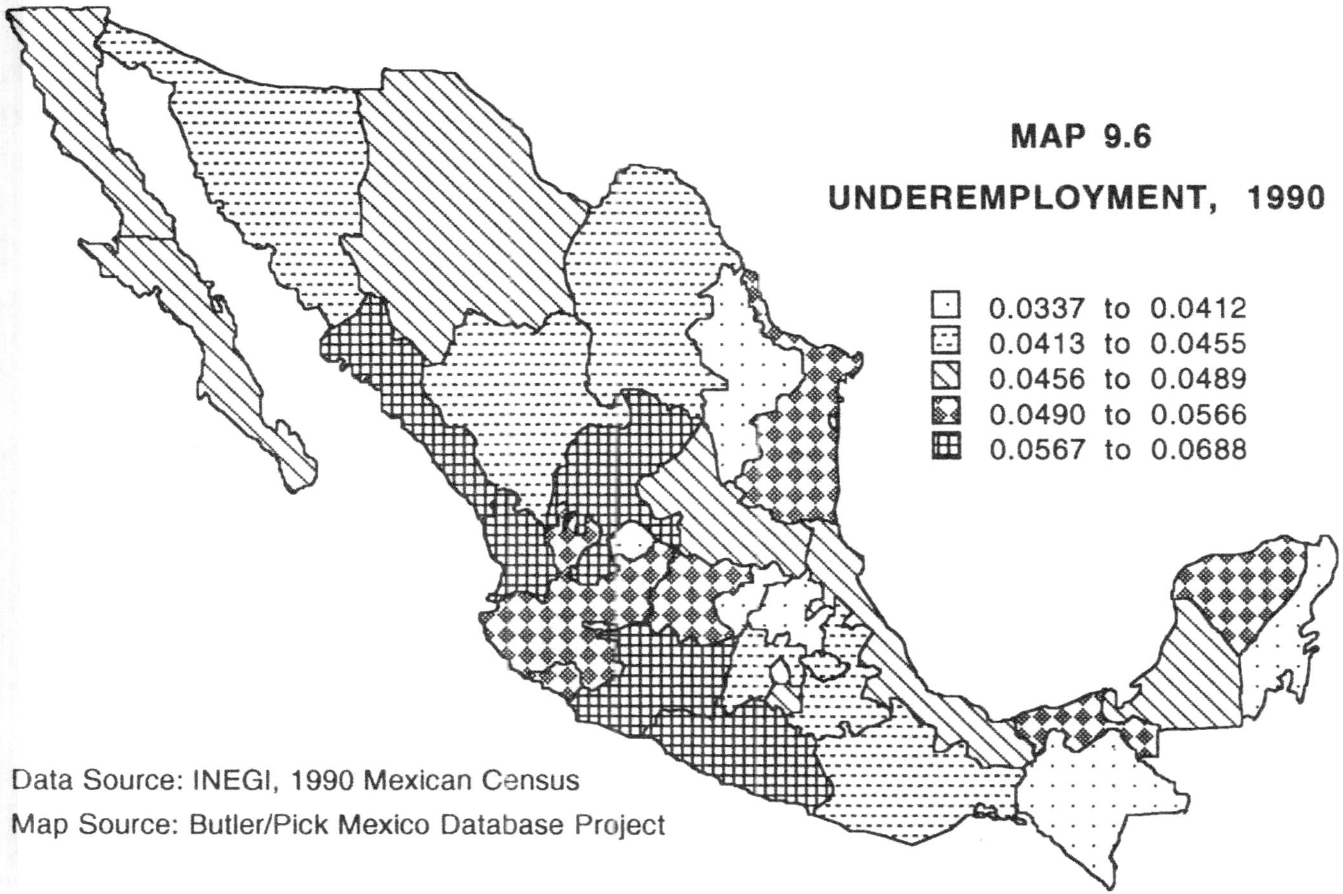

Data Source: INEGI, 1990 Mexican Census

Map Source: Butler/Pick Mexico Database Project

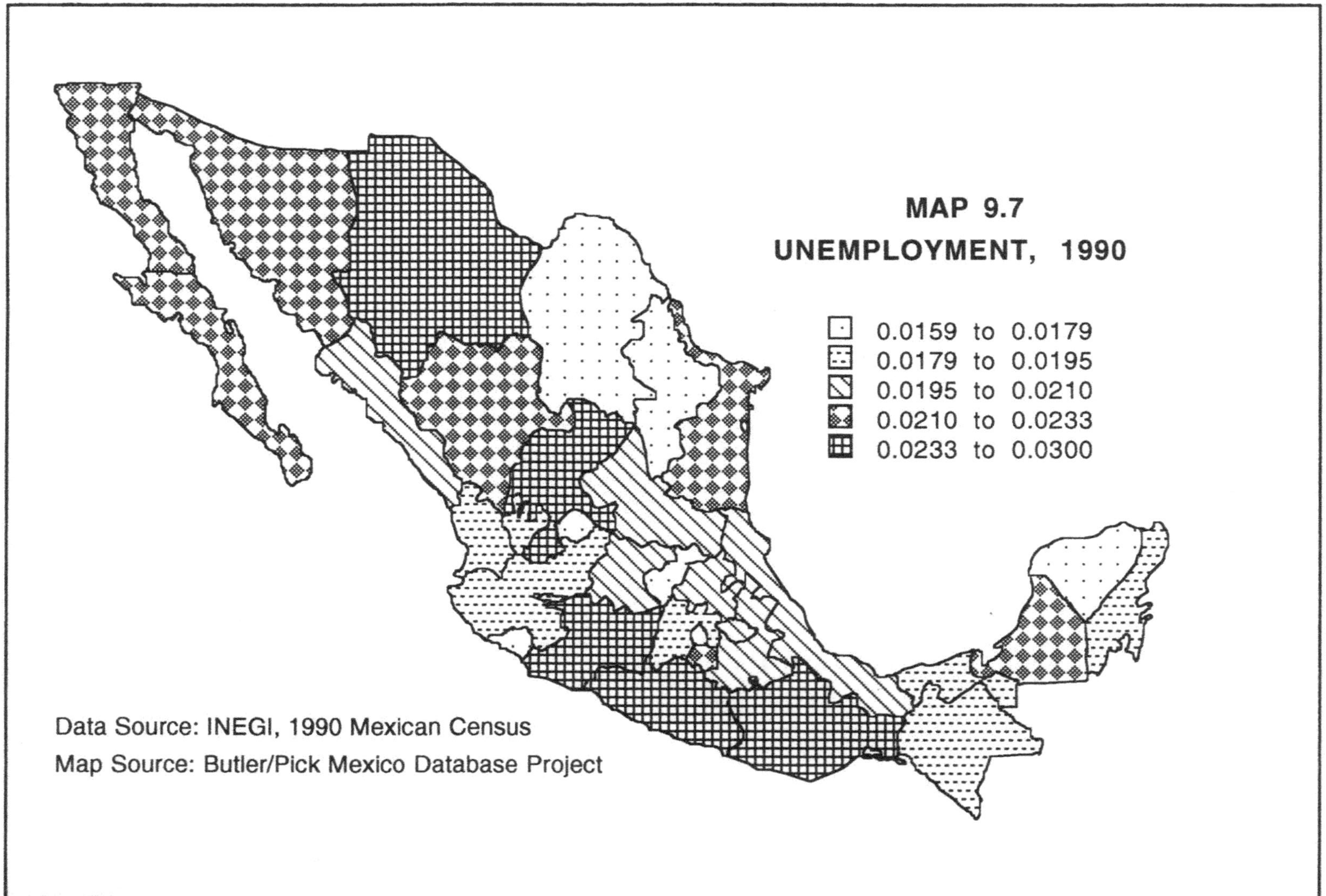
MAP 9.7
UNEMPLOYMENT, 1990
0.0159 to 0.0179
0.0179 to 0.0195
0.0195 to 0.0210
0.0210 to 0.0233
0.0233 to 0.0300
Data Source: INEGI, 1990 Mexican Census
Map Source: Butler/Pick Mexico Database Project

Occupations

There were 23,403,413 employed workers in Mexico in 1990. This was an increase of 81 percent from the 1970 total of 12,955,057 employed. These workers were divided into major occupational groups shown in the text table below for 1990.

Category	Number	Percent
Professional and Technical	1,398,618	6.0
Administ. and Managerial	958,109	4.1
Service and Support	7,524,060	32.1
Other	7,844,401	33.5
Agricultural	5,173,725	22.1
Not Specified	504,500	2.2
TOTAL	23,403,413	100.0

SOURCE: INEGI,*1990 Mexican Census of Population*, Resumen General, Table 32.

The biggest change in the occupational composition during the 80s is the sharp drop in agricultural from 29 percent in 1980 to 22 percent in 1990. Compared to about 3 percent in agricultural occupations in the United States in 1990, there is still a much higher proportion in agriculture, as well as lower proportions in professional/technical, administrative/managerial, and service/support occupations (see Figure 9.2).

Professional and Technical Occupations, 1990

State by state distribution of professional and technical occupations for 1990 is shown on Map 9.8 and Table 9.4. The range is from a low of 3.0 in Chiapas to a high of 10.6 percent in the Federal District. States with the highest ratio of professional and technical occupations are the Federal District, the Bajas, and Nuevo Leon. By region, all border states except Chihuahua are above average. States with the fewest professional and technical workers are other southern states in addition to Chiapas and several in the mid-section of the country north of the Federal District, Tlaxcala, Hidalgo, Guanajuato, and Zacatecas. With the exception of the Federal District and the state of Mexico, there is a substantial north to south axis with northern states, in general, having higher ratios of professional and technical occupations than southern states.

Professional and technical occupations, perhaps not too surprisingly, are concentrated with urbanization (r = .84) and higher population densities (r = .63). Professional and technical occupations also are positively associated with lifetime inmigration (r = .52) and negatively with the total fertility rate (r = - .57), the sex ratio (r = - 45), the dependency ratio (r = - .90), and population aged 0–17 (r = - .90). There are also substantial relationships of professional and technical occupations to the total economically active (r = .70) and female economically active populations (r = .87), population aged 18–64 (r = .91), and all educational measures (e.g., higher level education, r = .93). In addition, there is a substantial relationship with higher level incomes (r = .71) and management and service occupations (r = .82 and .90, respectively).

Professional and Technical Occupations, Central Metropolitan Zone, 1990

The distribution of professional and technical occupations in the Central Metropolitan Zone of Mexico City is shown on Map 9.9. The highest percentages are in the Federal District, with the exception of one state of Mexico municipio immediately north and adjacent to the district. Within the Federal District, there is a ring of areas surrounding the oldest sections that claim a high percentage of professional and technical occupations. In essence, there is somewhat of an appearance of concentric zones with some sectorization.

Thus, most peripheral areas outside of the Federal District have the lowest proportion of the labor force claiming a professional or technical occupation. The impoverished and populous Chalco in the southeast has among the lowest rates. There is a strong association between professional/technical occupations and economically active population (compare with Map 9.4). It is plausible that professional and technical workers would reside in zones of high economic activity.

Administrative and Managerial Occupations, 1990

The state-wide distribution of administrative and managerial occupations is highly correlated with professional and technical occupations (r = .82). Map 9.10 illustrates that all border states have higher than average ratios of persons in these occupations. As with professions and technical occupations, with the exception of the Federal District and the state of Mexico, there is a north-south axis with higher ratios in the north (see Table 9.4). Nuevo Leon has the largest percentage of administrative and managerial labor force. Similar to professionals and technical occupations, the Federal District and state of Mexico also have a substantial labor force in administrative and managerial positions. The Federal District has the largest number of administrators and managers, nearly 200,000. The concentration of one-third of the nation's managers in the CMZ underscores its primacy as the national corporate hub (see section 8.6) as well as government center. Oaxaca and Chiapas have the lowest proportion of their labor force in administrative and managerial occupations, 1.4 percent.

Service and Support Occupations, 1990

Service and support workers, not too surprisingly, are scattered throughout the states of Mexico with the largest ratio of 46.0 percent in the Federal District. Service and support occupations also are concentrated heavily in the Bajas, Nuevo Leon, and in the tourist state of Quintana Roo. Above average ratios also exist for Coahuila, Jalisco, and the state of Mexico (see Table 9.5 and Map 9.11). The contiguous area of lowest service/support is located in the parts of the south, gulf, and eastern central region. This six-state area only includes one city over 1/2 million —Puebla—and only five other cities over 200,000 (see Map 3.5). Comparing the states of Puebla and Nuevo Leon, which both contain million plus cities, Nuevo Leon has 110,000 more service and support workers. This reflects partly the much more advanced economy of Monterrey and the border region, relative to Puebla.

Correlations demonstrate high positive relationships with the total and female economically active population (r = .74 and .90, respectively). There is almost a perfect correlation with tertiary occupations (r = .99) and professional and managerial occupations. Strong negative relationships exist with the dependency ratio (r = - .81), agricultural occupations (r = - .88), several fertility measures, and with indicators of extreme poverty— having no electricity, no meat or eggs in diet, crowding, and no or low monthly income (r's range from .57–.74).

Agricultural Occupations, 1990

In contrast to other occupations, agricultural occupational rates in 1990 were highest in the states of Chiapas, Veracruz, Nayarit, and Zacatecas, with Oaxaca having over 44 percent of its labor force engaged in agricultural occupations.

By volume, about half of Mexico's agricultural occupational work force is located in the six states of Veracruz, Oaxaca, Puebla, Chiapas, Mexico, and Michoacan. These states differ in their metropolitan concentrations. In the case of Mexico, the metropolitan expansion continues to reduce a rich agricultural resource. For instance in 1950, the state of Mexico had 73 percent of work force engaged in agricultural occupations—above the national average. By 1990, that proportion was reduced to only 8 percent. As shown on Map 9.13 and reported in Table 9.6, states with the lowest proportion of agricultural labor force are Baja California, Coahuila, Tamaulipas, the state of Mexico, and the Federal District that has only 1.8 percent.

In 1990, agricultural occupations were associated with the fertility rate (r = .61),the young ages of 0–17 (.74), dependency (.78), population with no or low monthly income (.67), and several housing and poverty related dimensions (r ranges from .67 - 83). In addition, there was a somewhat unexpected relationship between not having available meat/eggs by agricultural occupation (.39). Substantial negative relationships, of course, existed with urban-dimensions, education and literacy variables, and higher level occupations.

Table 9.6 also presents information on the agricultural labor force for 1900, 1930, 1950, and 1970. It is readily apparent that nearly all states in Mexico had substantial declines in agricultural occupations as Mexico has increasingly urbanized. It is remarkable that Oaxaca and Chiapas both *increased* in ratio by about one half and one sixth respectively over the nine decades. These states have strong agricultural-based traditions and indigenous groups as well as lack of metropolitan development.

Other Occupations, 1990

Other occupations consist of artists, artisans and laborers, machinery operators, transport operators and ambulant workers. Other occupations are reported in Table 9.5 and shown on Map 9.12. The labor force in other occupations is concentrated in the states just north of the Federal District and most border states. States with the labor force in other occupations tend to be the more industrialized and urban states, such as state of Mexico, Nuevo Leon, and the other border states.

Besides a high correlation with the urban dimensions (r = .66), there are strong positive associations with all of the education and literacy variables (r ranges from .46–.64), with higher level occupations, and higher monthly incomes. There are substantial negative correlations with agricultural occupations and work force (- .85), with (- .50), and crowding.

MAP 9.8
PROFESSIONAL AND TECHNICAL OCCUPATIONS
MEXICO CITY (CMZ), 1990

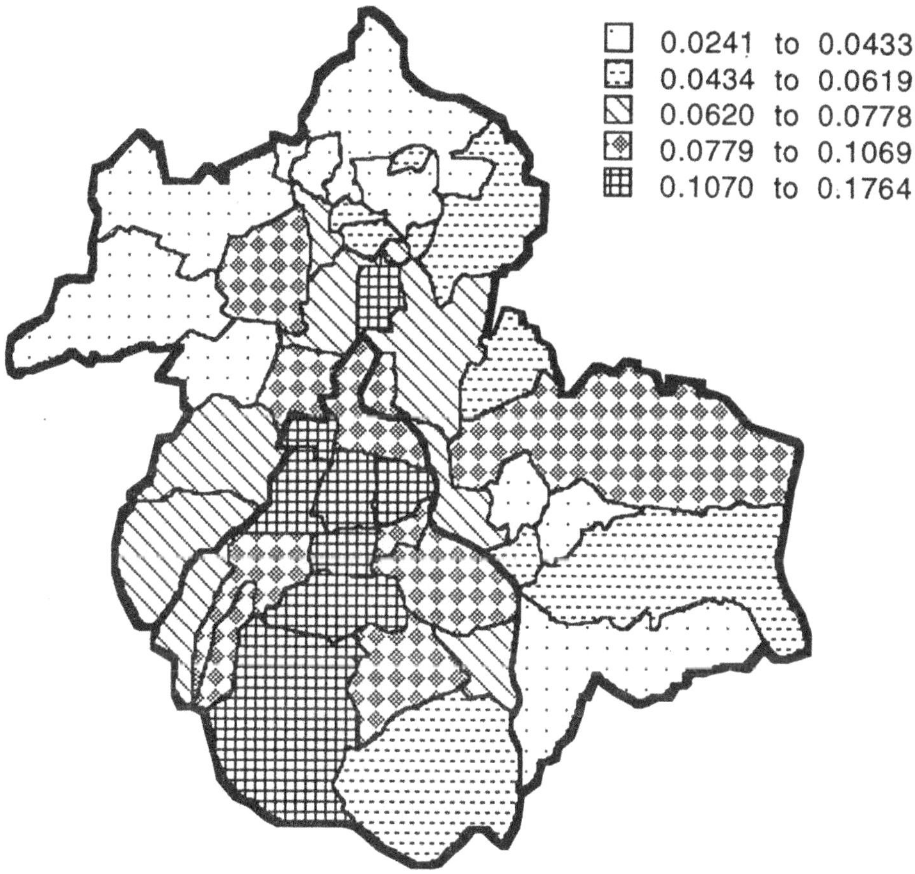

Data Source: INEGI, 1990 Mexican Census

Map Source: Butler/Pick Mexico Database Project

Table 9.4 Professional, Technical, Administrative, and Managerial Occupations, 1990

No.	State	Total Econ. Active Population	Professional & Technical Occupation	Ratio	Admin./ Managerial Occupations	Ratio
1	AGUASCALIENTES	217,092	11,306	0.0521	10,360	0.0477
2	BAJA CALIFORNIA	578,395	40,418	0.0699	32,337	0.0559
3	BAJA CALIFORNIA SUR	104,980	7,252	0.0691	4,668	0.0445
4	CAMPECHE	152,902	8,044	0.0526	3,975	0.0260
5	COAHUILA	605,251	38,451	0.0635	33,068	0.0546
6	COLIMA	136,046	8,114	0.0596	4,486	0.0330
7	CHIAPAS	874,267	26,031	0.0298	12,152	0.0139
8	CHIHUAHUA	797,051	44,694	0.0561	44,359	0.0557
9	DISTRITO FEDERAL	2,961,270	313,564	0.1059	195,505	0.0660
10	DURANGO	359,994	16,894	0.0469	11,613	0.0323
11	GUANAJUATO	1,063,208	41,375	0.0389	32,375	0.0305
12	GUERRERO	636,938	24,134	0.0379	10,500	0.0165
13	HIDALGO	508,551	18,189	0.0358	12,323	0.0242
14	JALISCO	1,588,190	96,431	0.0607	68,129	0.0429
15	MEXICO	2,948,159	179,431	0.0609	136,768	0.0464
16	MICHOACAN	920,154	37,581	0.0408	18,694	0.0203
17	MORELOS	359,813	20,899	0.0581	11,979	0.0333
18	NAYARIT	238,079	10,650	0.0447	5,478	0.0230
19	NUEVO LEON	1,036,770	75,683	0.0730	71,407	0.0689
20	OAXACA	775,844	23,204	0.0299	10,753	0.0139
21	PUEBLA	1,110,489	47,769	0.0430	31,514	0.0284
22	QUERETARO	298,222	14,977	0.0502	15,494	0.0520
23	QUINTANA ROO	165,424	8,715	0.0527	6,692	0.0405
24	SAN LUIS POTOSI	541,908	22,457	0.0414	18,374	0.0339
25	SINALOA	674,431	36,219	0.0537	18,271	0.0271
26	SONORA	577,205	38,727	0.0671	25,454	0.0441
27	TABASCO	406,096	23,026	0.0567	11,587	0.0285
28	TAMAULIPAS	710,047	44,064	0.0621	31,734	0.0447
29	TLAXCALA	203,908	7,735	0.0379	5,164	0.0253
30	VERACRUZ	1,792,272	78,446	0.0438	43,683	0.0244
31	YUCATAN	413,593	23,339	0.0564	13,300	0.0322
32	ZACATECAS	306,734	10,799	0.0352	5,913	0.0193
	National Total	24,063,283	1,398,618	0.0581	958,109	0.0398
	Mean	751,978	43,707	0.0527	29,941	0.0359
	Median	577,800	23,737	0.0526	14,397	0.0327
	S.D.	703,489	59,884	0.0153	40,309	0.0147
	C.V.	93.55	137.01	29.07	134.63	40.93
	Minimum	104,980	7,252	0.0298	3,975	0.0139
	Maximum	2,961,270	313,564	0.1059	195,505	0.0689

DEFINITION: Ratios are the population with professional and technical occupations age 12+ to the economically active population age 12+, and the population with administrative / managerial occupations age 12+ to the economically active population age 12+. Professional/technical includes the categories profesionales and technicos. Administrative/managerial includes the categories funcionarios y directivos and inspectores y supervisores.

SOURCE: INEGI, 1990 Mexican Census of Population, Table No. 32.

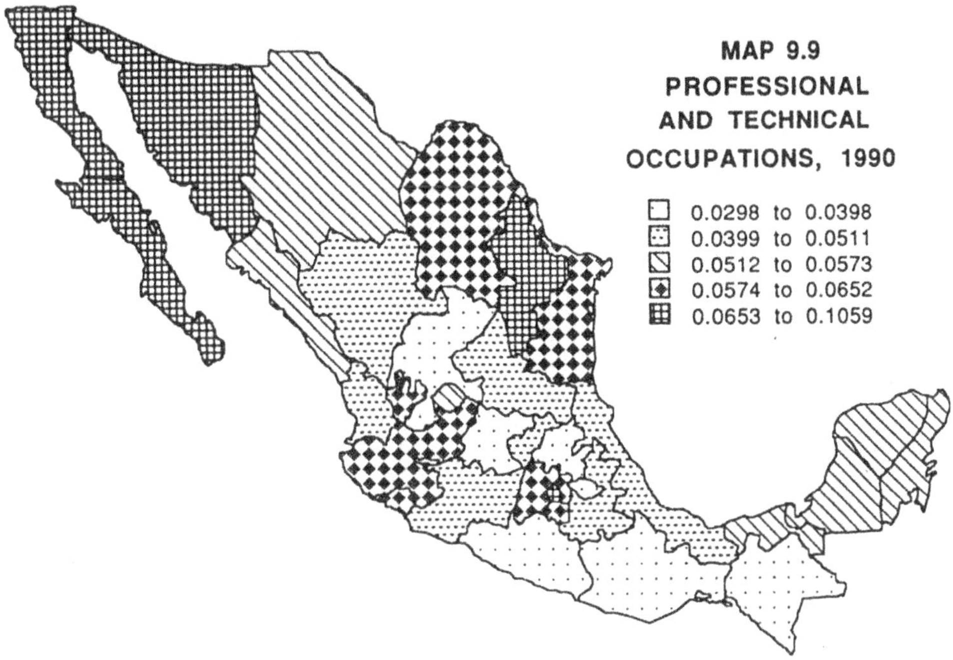

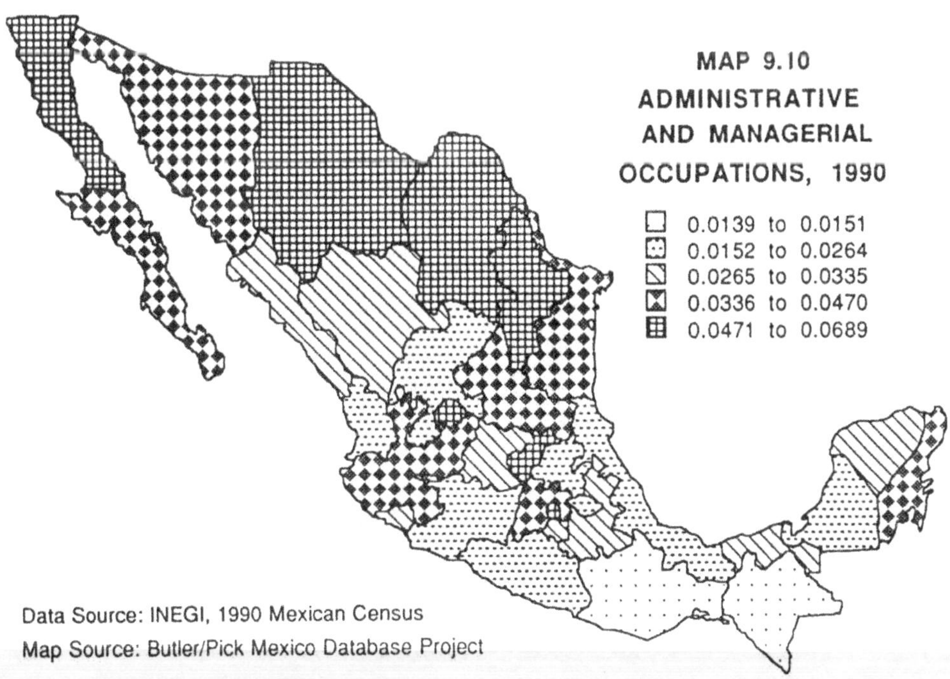

Data Source: INEGI, 1990 Mexican Census

Map Source: Butler/Pick Mexico Database Project

Table 9.5 Service, Support, and Other Occupations, 1990

No.	State	Econ. Active Population	Serv./Support Occupations	Ratio	Other Occupations	Ratio
1	AGUASCALIENTES	217,092	72,861	0.3356	85,359	0.3932
2	BAJA CALIFORNIA	578,395	204,338	0.3533	221,464	0.3829
3	BAJA CALIFORNIA SUR	104,980	40,286	0.3837	31,172	0.2969
4	CAMPECHE	152,902	44,317	0.2898	39,735	0.2599
5	COAHUILA	605,251	201,270	0.3325	232,008	0.3833
6	COLIMA	136,046	46,446	0.3414	41,038	0.3016
7	CHIAPAS	874,267	160,597	0.1837	140,053	0.1602
8	CHIHUAHUA	797,051	238,079	0.2987	299,234	0.3754
9	DISTRITO FEDERAL	2,961,270	1,363,343	0.4604	958,055	0.3235
10	DURANGO	359,994	104,969	0.2916	113,078	0.3141
11	GUANAJUATO	1,063,208	288,995	0.2718	415,675	0.3910
12	GUERRERO	636,938	181,200	0.2845	156,803	0.2462
13	HIDALGO	508,551	116,552	0.2292	151,510	0.2979
14	JALISCO	1,588,190	527,399	0.3321	601,124	0.3785
15	MEXICO	2,948,159	1,027,145	0.3484	1,216,780	0.4127
16	MICHOACAN	920,154	230,116	0.2501	267,506	0.2907
17	MORELOS	359,813	120,815	0.3358	121,118	0.3366
18	NAYARIT	238,079	62,887	0.2641	59,064	0.2481
19	NUEVO LEON	1,036,770	372,035	0.3588	412,836	0.3982
20	OAXACA	775,844	146,456	0.1888	160,371	0.2067
21	PUEBLA	1,110,489	261,367	0.2354	325,357	0.2930
22	QUERETARO	298,222	89,456	0.3000	114,842	0.3851
23	QUINTANA ROO	165,424	63,273	0.3825	46,582	0.2816
24	SAN LUIS POTOSI	541,908	148,322	0.2737	160,346	0.2959
25	SINALOA	674,431	189,631	0.2812	167,409	0.2482
26	SONORA	577,205	184,292	0.3193	190,151	0.3294
27	TABASCO	406,096	108,038	0.2660	103,635	0.2552
28	TAMAULIPAS	710,047	235,167	0.3312	253,112	0.3565
29	TLAXCALA	203,908	47,478	0.2328	78,380	0.3844
30	VERACRUZ	1,792,272	440,956	0.2460	474,635	0.2648
31	YUCATAN	413,593	132,392	0.3201	124,786	0.3017
32	ZACATECAS	306,734	73,582	0.2399	81,183	0.2647
	National Total	24,063,283	7,524,060	0.3127	7,844,401	0.3260
	Mean	751,978	235,127	0.2988	245,138	0.3143
	Median	577,800	154,460	0.2951	158,575	0.3017
	S.D.	703,489	279,962	0.0594	261,438	0.0627
	C.V.	93.55	119.07	19.89	106.65	19.96
	Minimum	104,980	40,286	0.1837	31,172	0.1602
	Maximum	2,961,270	1,363,343	0.4604	1,216,780	0.4127

DEFINITION: Ratio of population in service or support occupations age 12+ to population economically active age 12+, and ratio of the population with other occupations to the economically active population age 12+. Service/support includes the categories trabajadores de la educacion, ofinistas, comerciantes y dependientes, servicios publicos, trabajadores domesticos, and proteccion y vigilancia. Other occupations consists of the categories trabajadores del arte, artesanos y obreros, operadores de maquinaria fija, operadores de transporte, and trabajadores ambulantes.

SOURCE: INEGI, 1990 Mexican Census of Population, Table No. 32.

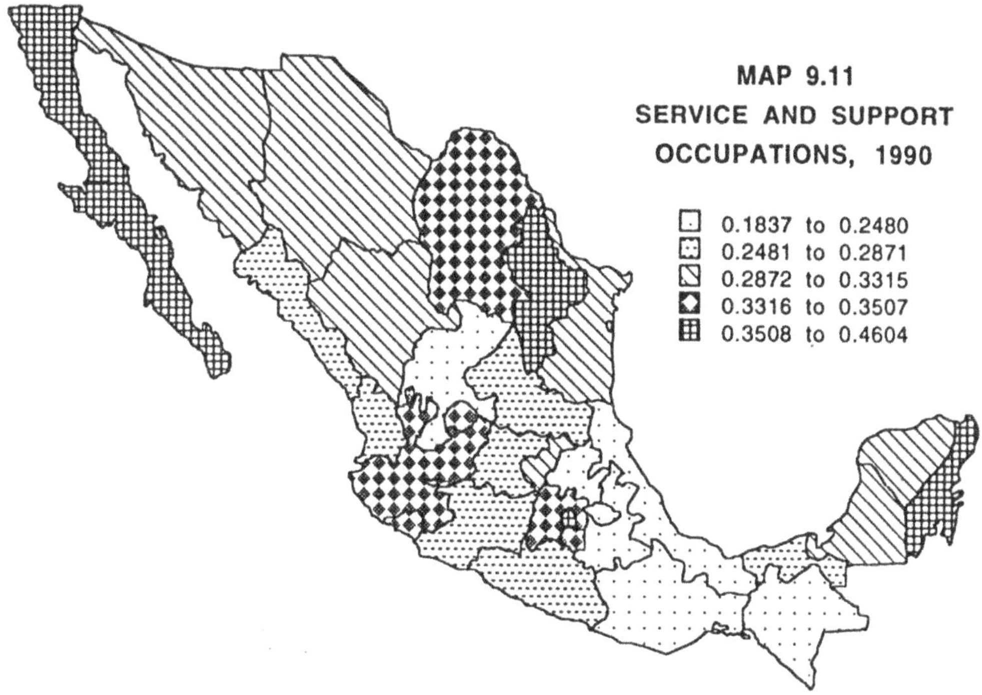

MAP 9.11
SERVICE AND SUPPORT OCCUPATIONS, 1990

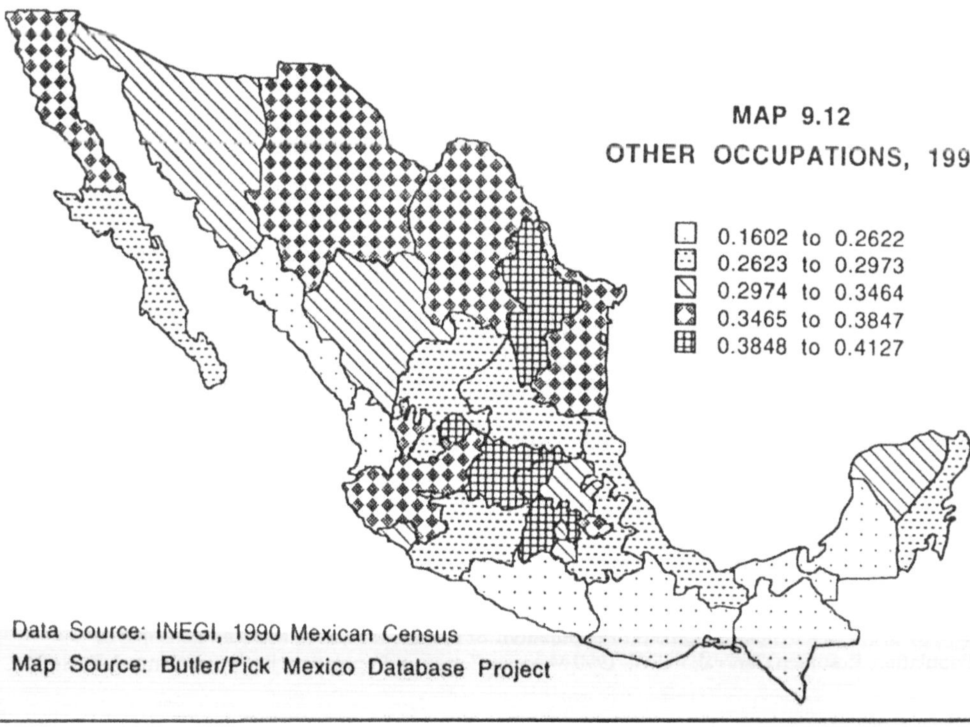

MAP 9.12
OTHER OCCUPATIONS, 1990

Data Source: INEGI, 1990 Mexican Census
Map Source: Butler/Pick Mexico Database Project

Table 9.6 Agricultural Occupations, 1900-1990

No.	State	1900 Agricult. Occup.	1900 Econ. Active	1900 Ratio	1930 Agricult. Occup.	1930 Econ. Active	1930 Ratio
1	AGUASCALIENTES	22,077	51,982	0.4247	22,729	39,495	0.5755
2	BAJA CALIFORNIA	10,246	24,180	0.4237	11,704	19,568	0.5981
3	BAJA CALIFORNIA SUR				7,345	14,809	0.4960
4	CAMPECHE	21,203	39,906	0.5313	17,479	26,059	0.6707
5	COAHUILA	58,149	155,617	0.3737	82,587	137,979	0.5985
6	COLIMA	16,801	28,545	0.5886	12,902	20,002	0.6450
7	CHIAPAS	91,994	254,504	0.3615	134,772	166,746	0.8082
8	CHIHUAHUA	78,818	124,385	0.6337	102,413	149,794	0.6837
9	DISTRITO FEDERAL				42,465	394,097	0.1078
10	DURANGO	71,586	122,287	0.5854	99,313	129,999	0.7640
11	GUANAJUATO	241,455	443,363	0.5446	226,932	306,220	0.7411
12	GUERRERO	120,922	172,194	0.7022	175,960	196,661	0.8947
13	HIDALGO	136,415	287,548	0.4744	167,169	209,213	0.7990
14	JALISCO	275,564	589,742	0.4673	283,869	391,637	0.7248
15	MEXICO	225,170	341,403	0.6595	239,357	302,754	0.7906
16	MICHOACAN	241,620	346,096	0.6981	259,868	327,996	0.7923
17	MORELOS	42,880	59,031	0.7264	36,059	43,866	0.8220
18	NAYARIT	37,785	60,673	0.6228	41,379	55,645	0.7436
19	NUEVO LEON	54,098	140,746	0.3844	79,153	132,081	0.5993
20	OAXACA	256,954	580,746	0.4425	289,626	337,438	0.8583
21	PUEBLA	235,902	377,897	0.6242	261,120	348,527	0.7492
22	QUERETARO	61,481	93,325	0.6588	60,142	76,951	0.7816
23	QUINTANA ROO				2,342	4,118	0.5687
24	SAN LUIS POTOSI	139,121	233,322	0.5963	130,800	178,114	0.7344
25	SINALOA	68,051	169,603	0.4012	94,913	126,209	0.7520
26	SONORA	51,818	91,672	0.5653	64,112	99,951	0.6414
27	TABASCO	38,375	62,622	0.6128	52,916	63,337	0.8355
28	TAMAULIPAS	54,512	135,458	0.4024	63,316	108,236	0.5850
29	TLAXCALA	37,428	91,030	0.4112	47,807	64,264	0.7439
30	VERACRUZ	244,492	333,574	0.7329	325,996	430,258	0.7577
31	YUCATAN	81,498	119,390	0.6826	81,211	124,417	0.6527
32	ZACATECAS	99,143	158,791	0.6244	108,522	139,262	0.7793
	National Total	3,115,558	5,689,632	0.5476	3,626,278	5,165,703	0.7020
	Mean	107,433	196,194	0.5502	113,321	161,428	0.6967
	Median	71,586	140,746	0.5854	81,899	131,040	0.7423
	S.D.	85,930	157,042	0.1191	95,399	127,116	0.1443
	C.V.	79.98	80.04	21.64	84.18	78.74	20.72
	Minimum	10,246	24,180	0.3615	2,342	4,118	0.1078
	Maximum	275,564	589,742	0.7329	325,996	430,258	0.8947

DEFINITION: Ratio of the population with agricultural occupations to the economically active population for the same year.

NOTE: For 1900, data for Baja Sur are included with Baja California and data for Quintana Roo are included withYucatan.

SOURCE: SPP, 1900 Mexican Census of Population; SPP, 1930, 1950, 1970 Mexican Censuses of Population, Resumen General; INEGI, 1990 Mexican Census of Population, Resumen General, Table 32.

Table 9.6 Agricultural Occupations, 1900-1990(Continued)

No.	1950 Agricult. Occup.	1950 Econ. Active	1950 Ratio	1970 Agricult. Occup.	1970 Econ. Active	1970 Ratio	1990 Agricult. Occup.	1990 Econ. Active	1990 Ratio
1	28,095	56,344	0.4986	32,095	86,332	0.3718	29,636	217,092	0.1365
2	34,567	77,424	0.4465	49,440	221,779	0.2229	53,448	578,395	0.0924
3	9,560	18,809	0.5083	12,035	34,292	0.3510	17,278	104,980	0.1646
4	22,248	38,967	0.5709	32,785	71,681	0.4574	49,879	152,902	0.3262
5	109,839	226,769	0.4844	85,760	283,351	0.3027	67,522	605,251	0.1116
6	21,930	37,363	0.5869	29,925	68,122	0.4393	31,550	136,046	0.2319
7	223,965	288,468	0.7764	293,152	413,294	0.7093	496,436	874,267	0.5678
8	141,920	264,016	0.5375	151,498	416,852	0.3634	124,247	797,051	0.1559
9	51,006	1,108,024	0.0460	49,164	2,189,521	0.0225	17,187	2,961,270	0.0058
10	136,854	195,203	0.7011	123,694	227,241	0.5443	93,276	359,994	0.2591
11	279,088	419,644	0.6651	275,644	567,774	0.4855	223,993	1,063,208	0.2107
12	232,195	291,080	0.7977	238,314	372,477	0.6398	221,065	636,938	0.3471
13	192,728	261,995	0.7356	184,941	307,810	0.6008	180,701	508,551	0.3553
14	324,660	555,713	0.5842	306,299	888,468	0.3447	229,499	1,588,190	0.1445
15	316,890	435,840	0.7271	300,296	965,625	0.3110	242,096	2,948,159	0.0821
16	319,535	439,421	0.7272	320,670	553,778	0.5791	300,400	920,154	0.3265
17	60,510	91,050	0.6646	73,545	166,251	0.4424	68,997	359,813	0.1918
18	65,302	93,711	0.6968	87,445	329,026	0.2658	88,083	238,079	0.3700
19	97,680	239,558	0.4078	85,149	1,060,279	0.0803	58,292	1,036,770	0.0562
20	358,349	470,915	0.7610	372,950	1,252,169	0.2978	400,131	775,844	0.5157
21	363,247	542,150	0.6700	380,396	1,558,904	0.2440	395,518	1,110,489	0.3562
22	63,576	90,564	0.7020	61,549	289,815	0.2124	47,581	298,222	0.1595
23	5,470	8,600	0.6360	13,374	25,262	0.5294	31,264	165,424	0.1890
24	186,040	270,486	0.6878	175,113	331,888	0.5276	165,058	541,908	0.3046
25	131,637	195,148	0.6745	177,691	343,947	0.5166	232,410	674,431	0.3446
26	88,927	164,281	0.5413	109,377	289,799	0.3774	113,737	577,205	0.1970
27	79,785	105,400	0.7570	116,147	200,232	0.5801	137,898	406,096	0.3396
28	122,640	234,121	0.5238	126,346	383,380	0.3296	102,629	710,047	0.1445
29	63,435	90,327	0.7023	58,023	104,455	0.5555	55,421	203,908	0.2718
30	434,878	651,872	0.6671	530,800	1,004,809	0.5283	675,405	1,792,272	0.3768
31	100,168	167,762	0.5971	111,076	207,538	0.5352	108,539	413,593	0.2624
32	157,069	199,842	0.7860	138,826	223,278	0.6218	114,549	306,734	0.3734
	4,823,793	8,330,867	0.5790	5,103,519	15,439,429	0.3306	5,173,725	24,063,283	0.0215
	150,744	260,340	0.6209	159,485	482,482	0.4184	161,679	751,978	0.2491
	116,240	213,306	0.6661	119,921	318,418	0.4408	111,138	577,800	0.2455
	120,144	229,925	0.1480	127,995	489,535	0.1637	152,747	703,489	0.1298
	79.70	88.32	23.83	80.26	101.46	39.13	94.48	93.55	52.10
	5,470	8,600	0.0460	12,035	25,262	0.0225	17,187	104,980	0.0058
	434,878	1,108,024	0.7977	530,800	2,189,521	0.7093	675,405	2,961,270	0.5678

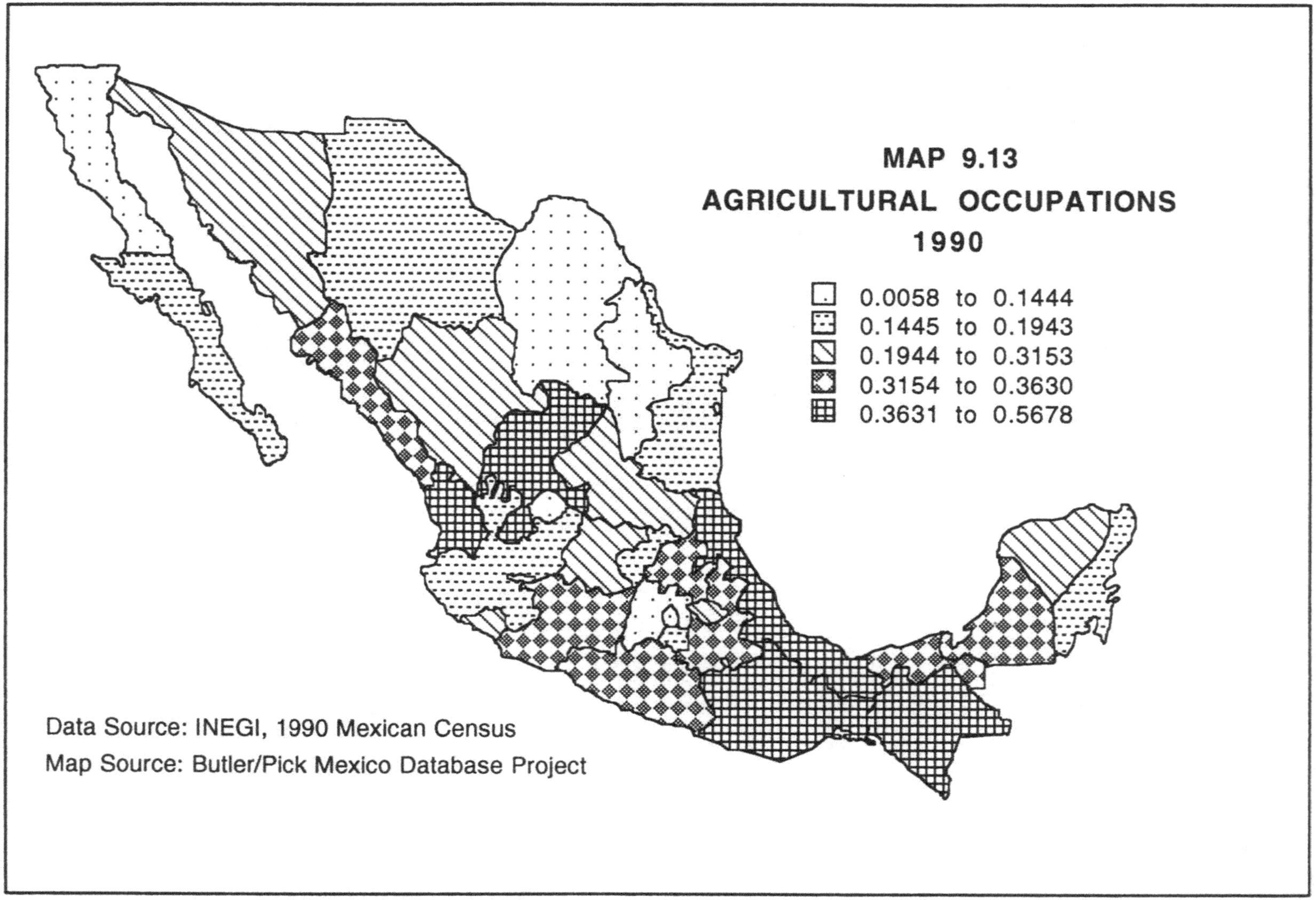
MAP 9.13
AGRICULTURAL OCCUPATIONS
1990
0.0058 to 0.1444
0.1445 to 0.1943
0.1944 to 0.3153
0.3154 to 0.3630
0.3631 to 0.5678
Data Source: INEGI, 1990 Mexican Census
Map Source: Butler/Pick Mexico Database Project

Labor Force by Industry

The work force by industry, except for agriculture, is somewhat a different categorization of work in Mexico. Labor force categories described in this section are the agricultural, commerce, construction, manufacturing, personal services, and community and social services.

The labor force is the economically active population age 12 and older. Shifts in the labor force during the twentieth century are shown in Figure 9.2. The primary category consists over 95 percent of agricultural workers, but also includes mining and resource extraction. It dropped dramatically from 64 percent at the start of the century to 24 percent in 1990. Although the decline has been great, the U.S. decline in primary work force has been much greater (Bogue 1985). Paralleling this drop has been a tripling in the service category to one third of the labor force in 1990. Commerce has grown rapidly during the century, including a 43 percent increase from 1970–1990. On the other hand, manufacturing labor force has grown slowly— by only fifteen percent over the past two decades.

Agricultural Work Force, 1990

In essence, the agricultural work force was described under occupations. The correlation between the two classifications is 1.00. Thus, all the dimensions associated with agricultural occupations described earlier also describe the relationship of the agricultural work force to the same dimensions (see Table 9.6). Because of the nearly exact correspondence, the map for agricultural work force is excluded. For agricultural work force, the reader is referred to Map 9.13 for agricultural occupations. The geographical *pattern* is identical to that for agricultural work force, although the values are slightly different.

Commerce Work Force, 1990

There is considerable range in commerce work force (see Table 9.7 and Map 9.14). As might be expected the areas of high commercial work force correspond to areas with substantial metropolitan population, including the CMZ, Jalisco, Baja, and Nuevo Leon (compare with the metropolitan areas in Map 3.5). At the extreme, in the Federal District, one in six workers is in commerce. There are also elevated commerce work forces in the tourism states of Baja Sur and Quintana Roo. On the other hand, the states with the lowest commerce work force tend to be less urban and metropolitan (e.g. Zacatecas, Hidalgo, Tlaxcala, Tabasco, Oaxaca, Chiapas).

The commerce work force is highly correlated with urban (r = .86), total and female economically active populations (r = .68 and .87, respectively), and with the major education and literacy variables (r's range from .71 to .78). There also are substantial positive correlations with virtually all occupational categories except agriculture (r = - .90). Substantial negative associations exist with the population, aged 0–17 (- .77) and the dependency ratio (- .78). There also are strong negative correlations with poor housing characteristics.

Construction Work Force, 1990

Construction constitutes seven percent of the national work force, slightly more than in 1980. The variation does not correspond to standard regions in the construction work force. Variation by state is between slightly over four and ten percent. Queretaro has the highest percentage of 10.4. Other states with a high percentage are Aguascalientes, Colima, Nuevo Leon, Quintana Roo, and Yucatan. The lowest states are the poorer southern state of Chiapas and Oaxaca and in strong contrast on many other dimensions, the Federal District (Table 9.8 and Map 9.15).

The relationship of various dimensions to the construction work force is somewhat unusual. First, there is a positive association with air flights (r = .42), the currently married population (.38), and several housing variables. On the other hand, negative relationships exist between the construction work force and population density (- .36), the economically active population (- .42), and all years examined of state population size (for 1990, r = - .43). Also, there is a substantial negative correlation with the agriculture work force.

Manufacturing Work Force, 1990

The proportion of the manufacturing work force in Mexico ranges from a low of 5.8 in Chiapas to a high of 29.0 in Nuevo Leon (see Table 9.9 and Map 9.16). Other states with a low percentage of under ten percent in the manufacturing work force are Baja California Sur, Campeche, Guerrero, Nayarit, Oaxaca, Quintana Roo, Tabasco, and Zacatecas. On the other hand, the following states approximate Nuevo Leon's high percentage of manufacturing work force, that is 25 percent and over: Coahuila, the State of Mexico, Tlaxcala, Queretaro, and Veracruz. In addition, the following states have between 21 and 24 percent in the manufacturing work force: Aguascalientes, Baja, Chihuahua, the Federal District, Guanajuato, and Jalisco. There is a clear dichotomy between manufacturing states and those without much manufacturing.

The border region has moderate to high rates, which is not surprising given its urban nature and the presence of the preponderance of Mexico's maquiladora manufacturing industry (see Map 10.6). The mid-section around Mexico city and stretching to the west also contains high rates. This area has a concentration of large cities (see Map 3.5), which support manufacturing. The heavily agricultural southern portion of Mexico has very low rates.

An interesting phenomenon is that there are high correlations with the total and female economically active populations (r = .37 and .47, respectively), but a negative association with males economically active (- .24). Also, there is a positive correlation of the manufacturing work force with mortality (.36) and negative association with fertility (- .38).

Several other substantial positive relationships exist between the population aged 18–64 and education and literacy dimensions. In addition, substantial correlations exist between the manufacturing work force and the production of such varied commodities as cement and beverages (r's = .44 and .36, respectively), and several other occupational categories. Negative associations are with hotels and automobile ownership, crowding, the dependency ratio, and the sex ratio.

Personal Services Work Force, 1990

The personal services work force consists of those persons involved in a variety of personal services and maintenance (see Table 9.10 and Map 9.17). The personal services work force ranges from a low of 4.68 percent in Oaxaca to a high of 12.52 in the Federal District. Other states with a personal services work force percentage of 10 or higher are Baja, Jalisco, the state of Mexico, Morelos, Nuevo Leon, Sonora, Tamaulipas, and Yucatan. The lowest states are located primarily in the pacific-south region.

Personal services is highly correlated with the population 18–64 (r = .81) and negatively associated with the population aged 0–17 (- .79). As with many other relationships, there is a strong association between the total and economically active female populations and services (r = .68 and .86, respectively). There are strong positive relations with literacy and educational measures, high monthly incomes, and tertiary, professional, technical, and management occupations (r ranges from the .8s and .9s). A strong negative association exists with agriculture (- .85) and with fertility.

Community and Social Services Work Force, 1990

There is high variation among the states in the community and social services work force measure (see Table 9.11 and Map 9.18). The highest percentage in this work force category is in the Federal District (12.56%) while the lowest is in Chiapas (5.22%). Other states with a relatively high community and social services work forces are Aguascalientes, Baja California Sur, Coahuila, Colima, Durango, Morelos, Nuevo Leon, Tamaulipas, and Tlaxcala. Low states are Guerrero, Oaxaca, Quintana Roo, and Veracruz. The major regional trends are that the south has low rates while all the middle states and northern states have average or higher rates of a community and social services work force.

The community and social services work force is positively correlated with urban (r = .58), density (.56), the population aged 16–64 (.80), and the economically active population (.53). This work force also is highly associated with higher level occupations and the tertiary labor force (.65). In addition, education and literacy dimensions are highly correlated with the community and social services work force. Important negative relationships are with the population aged 0–17, the dependency ratio, and fertility (r's all in the .5 range).

Figure 9.2
Work Force By Industry, Mexico

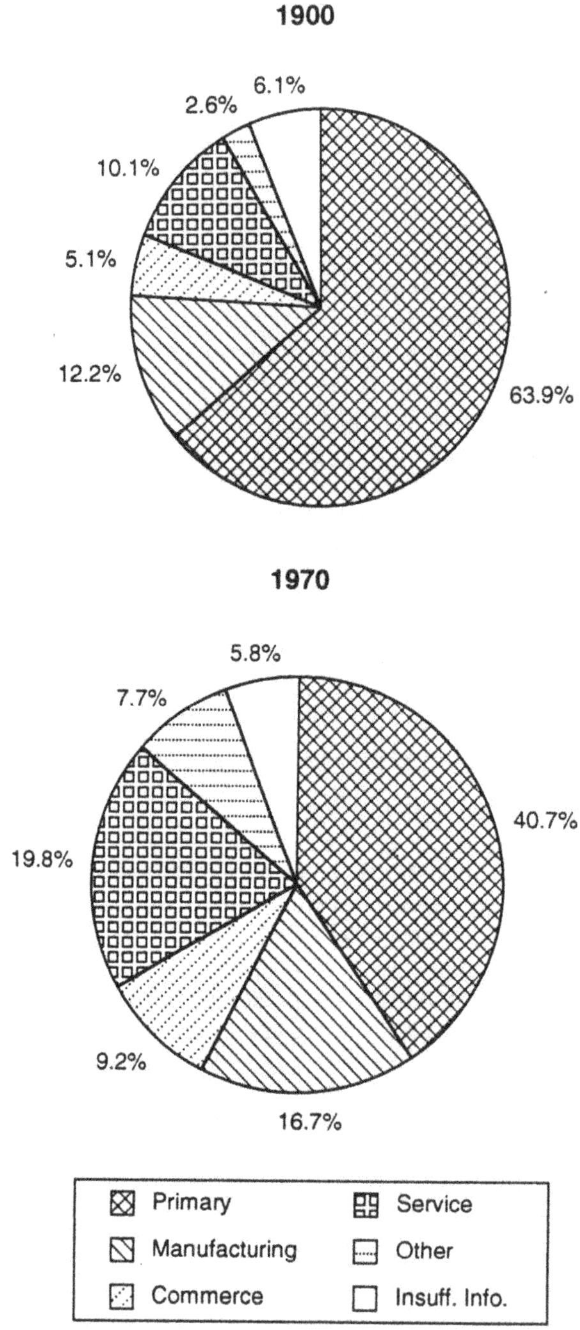

SOURCES: Estadisticas Historicas de Mexico, 1985; Mexican Census of Population, 1990.

Figure 9.2 Continued
Work Force By Industry, Mexico

1990

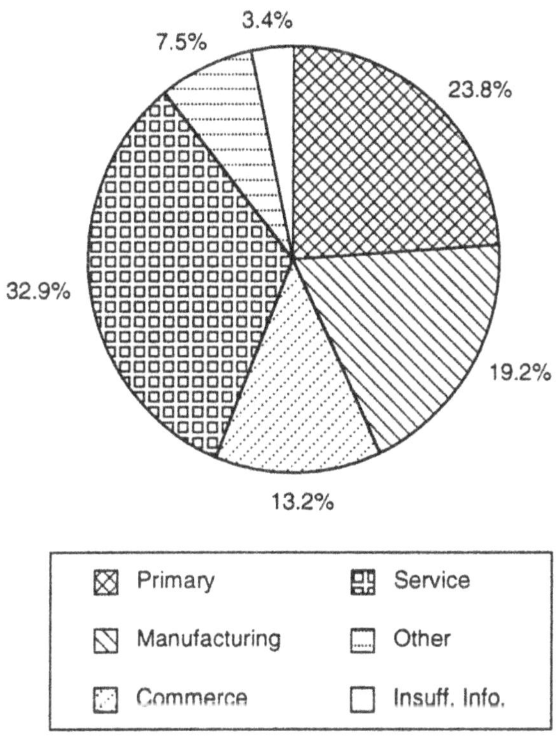

Supporting Data

	1900	1970	1990
Primary	63.9	40.7	23.8
Manufacturing	12.2	16.7	19.2
Commerce	5.1	9.2	13.2
Service	10.1	19.8	32.9
Other	2.6	7.7	7.5
Insuff. Specified	6.1	5.8	3.4
TOTAL	100.0	99.9	100.0

SOURCE: INEGI, Estadisticas Historicas de Mexico, 1985; Mexican Census of Population, 1990.

Table 9.7 Commerce and Agricultural Industry Work Forces, 1990

No.	State	Econ. Active Population	Commerce Industry Workers	Ratio	Agricultural Industry Workers	Ratio
1	AGUASCALIENTES	217,092	30,235	0.1393	31,766	0.1463
2	BAJA CALIFORNIA	578,395	92,887	0.1606	58,584	0.1013
3	BAJA CALIFORNIA SUR	104,980	15,003	0.1429	18,820	0.1793
4	CAMPECHE	152,902	16,459	0.1076	51,439	0.3364
5	COAHUILA	605,251	78,003	0.1289	71,137	0.1175
6	COLIMA	136,046	16,072	0.1181	32,011	0.2353
7	CHIAPAS	874,267	65,028	0.0744	498,320	0.5700
8	CHIHUAHUA	797,051	100,845	0.1265	131,610	0.1651
9	DISTRITO FEDERAL	2,961,270	494,797	0.1671	19,145	0.0065
10	DURANGO	359,994	40,571	0.1127	99,205	0.2756
11	GUANAJUATO	1,063,208	137,597	0.1294	236,713	0.2226
12	GUERRERO	636,938	62,890	0.0987	222,670	0.3496
13	HIDALGO	508,551	49,026	0.0964	182,684	0.3592
14	JALISCO	1,588,190	242,790	0.1529	234,016	0.1473
15	MEXICO	2,948,159	444,467	0.1508	248,140	0.0842
16	MICHOACAN	920,154	112,515	0.1223	303,224	0.3295
17	MORELOS	359,813	46,213	0.1284	70,887	0.1970
18	NAYARIT	238,079	24,800	0.1042	89,081	0.3742
19	NUEVO LEON	1,036,770	147,565	0.1423	61,835	0.0596
20	OAXACA	775,844	56,367	0.0727	398,848	0.5141
21	PUEBLA	1,110,489	125,574	0.1131	400,369	0.3605
22	QUERETARO	298,222	34,041	0.1141	51,771	0.1736
23	QUINTANA ROO	165,424	22,279	0.1347	32,013	0.1935
24	SAN LUIS POTOSI	541,908	61,544	0.1136	164,682	0.3039
25	SINALOA	674,431	80,257	0.1190	242,710	0.3599
26	SONORA	577,205	79,812	0.1383	127,900	0.2216
27	TABASCO	406,096	39,435	0.0971	140,093	0.3450
28	TAMAULIPAS	710,047	95,004	0.1338	111,400	0.1569
29	TLAXCALA	203,908	19,164	0.0940	56,150	0.2754
30	VERACRUZ	1,792,272	191,160	0.1067	685,647	0.3826
31	YUCATAN	413,593	56,103	0.1356	110,057	0.2661
32	ZACATECAS	306,734	29,625	0.0966	117,187	0.3820
	National Total	24,063,283	3,108,128	0.1292	5,300,114	0.2203
	Mean	751,978	97,129	0.1210	165,629	0.2560
	Median	577,800	62,217	0.1206	114,294	0.2507
	S.D.	703,489	111,160	0.0230	153,685	0.1287
	C.V.	93.55	114.45	18.99	92.79	50.27
	Minimum	104,980	15,003	0.0727	18,820	0.0065
	Maximum	2,961,270	494,797	0.1671	685,647	0.5700

DEFINITION: Ratio is the population in commerce industries to population economically active age 12+. This category includes the census designations, commerce and lodging services.

SOURCE: INEGI, 1990 Mexican Census of Population, Table 32.

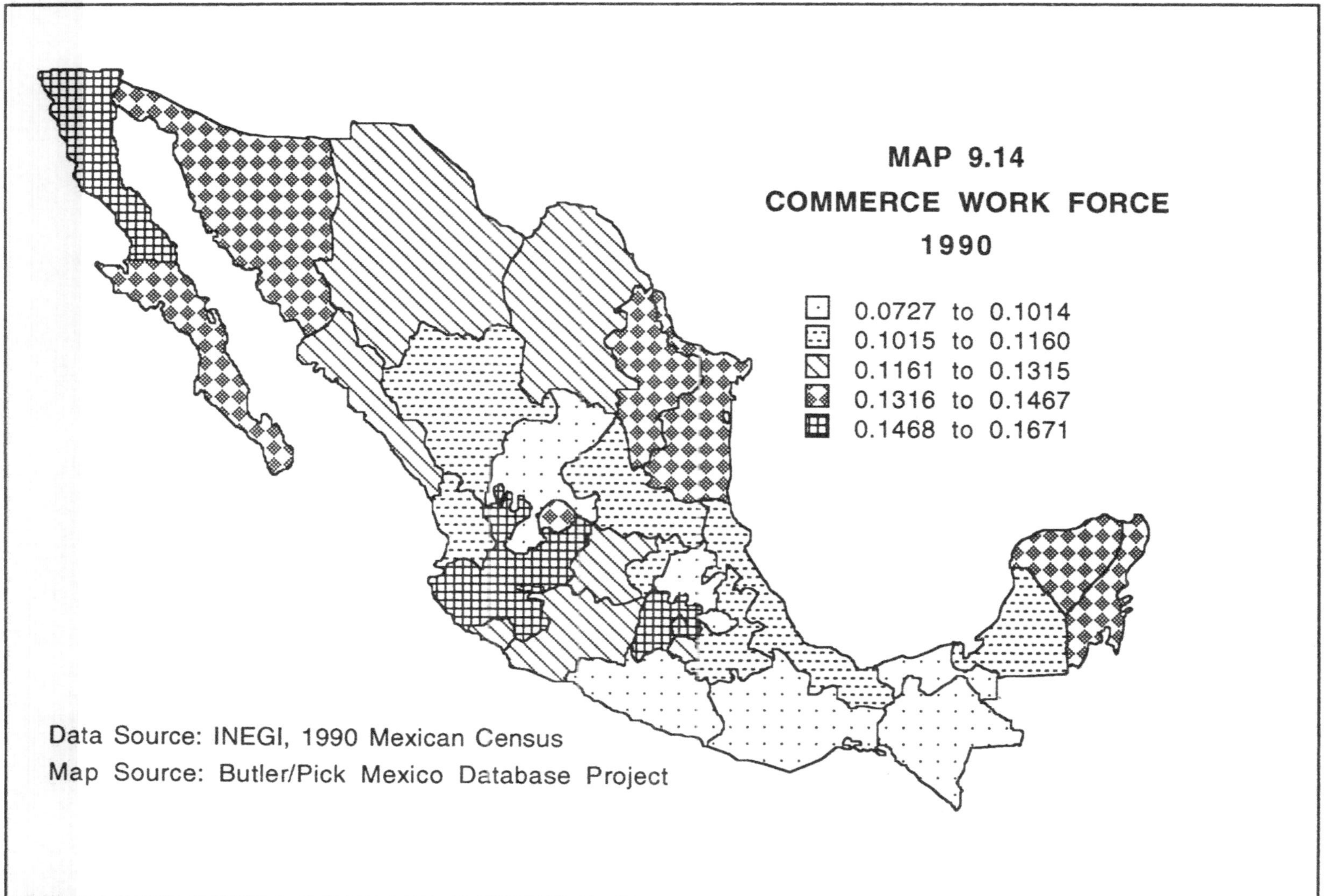
MAP 9.14
COMMERCE WORK FORCE
1990
0.0727 to 0.1014
0.1015 to 0.1160
0.1161 to 0.1315
0.1316 to 0.1467
0.1468 to 0.1671
Data Source: INEGI, 1990 Mexican Census
Map Source: Butler/Pick Mexico Database Project

Table 9.8 Construction Work Force, 1990

No.	State	Construction Industry Workers	Economically Active Population	Ratio
1	AGUASCALIENTES	18,230	217,092	0.0840
2	BAJA CALIFORNIA	42,446	578,395	0.0734
3	BAJA CALIFORNIA SUR	7,935	104,980	0.0756
4	CAMPECHE	10,525	152,902	0.0688
5	COAHUILA	47,998	605,251	0.0793
6	COLIMA	11,076	136,046	0.0814
7	CHIAPAS	38,191	874,267	0.0437
8	CHIHUAHUA	58,608	797,051	0.0735
9	DISTRITO FEDERAL	123,205	2,961,270	0.0416
10	DURANGO	24,349	359,994	0.0676
11	GUANAJUATO	84,792	1,063,208	0.0798
12	GUERRERO	40,779	636,938	0.0640
13	HIDALGO	35,870	508,551	0.0705
14	JALISCO	124,512	1,588,190	0.0784
15	MEXICO	204,210	2,948,159	0.0693
16	MICHOACAN	64,668	920,154	0.0703
17	MORELOS	37,070	359,813	0.1030
18	NAYARIT	15,766	238,079	0.0662
19	NUEVO LEON	90,180	1,036,770	0.0870
20	OAXACA	36,174	775,844	0.0466
21	PUEBLA	66,527	1,110,489	0.0599
22	QUERETARO	30,925	298,222	0.1037
23	QUINTANA ROO	13,596	165,424	0.0822
24	SAN LUIS POTOSI	36,726	541,908	0.0678
25	SINALOA	37,569	674,431	0.0557
26	SONORA	40,443	577,205	0.0701
27	TABASCO	23,772	406,096	0.0585
28	TAMAULIPAS	52,838	710,047	0.0744
29	TLAXCALA	15,600	203,908	0.0765
30	VERACRUZ	98,631	1,792,272	0.0550
31	YUCATAN	32,866	413,593	0.0795
32	ZACATECAS	28,884	306,734	0.0942
National Total		1,594,961	24,063,283	0.0663
Mean		49,843	751,978	0.0719
Median		37,320	577,800	0.0720
S.D.		41,620	703,489	0.0147
C.V.		83.50	93.55	20.41
Minimum		7,935	104,980	0.0416
Maximum		204,210	2,961,270	0.1037

DEFINITION: Ratio is the population in construction industries to the economically active population age 12+.

SOURCE: INEGI, 1990 Mexican Census of Population, Table 32.

MAP 9.15
CONSTRUCTION WORK FORCE
1990

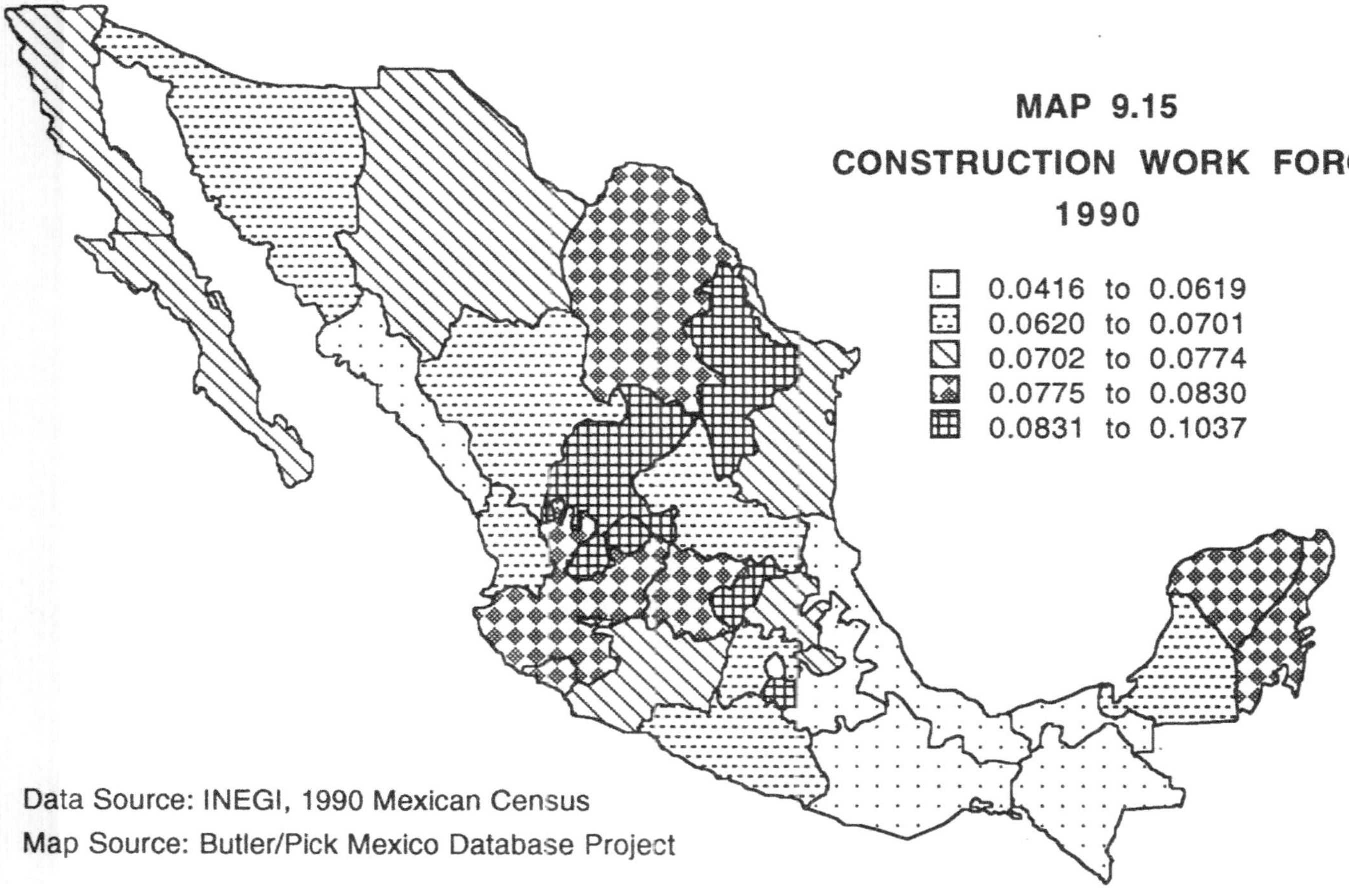

Data Source: INEGI, 1990 Mexican Census
Map Source: Butler/Pick Mexico Database Project

Table 9.9 Manufacturing Work Force, 1990

No.	State	Manufacturing Industry Workers	Economically Active Population	Ratio
1	AGUASCALIENTES	52,496	217,092	0.2418
2	BAJA CALIFORNIA	131,154	578,395	0.2268
3	BAJA CALIFORNIA SUR	8,946	104,980	0.0852
4	CAMPECHE	13,833	152,902	0.0905
5	COAHUILA	150,288	605,251	0.2483
6	COLIMA	13,259	136,046	0.0975
7	CHIAPAS	50,626	874,267	0.0579
8	CHIHUAHUA	203,938	797,051	0.2559
9	DISTRITO FEDERAL	613,685	2,961,270	0.2072
10	DURANGO	58,931	359,994	0.1637
11	GUANAJUATO	257,241	1,063,208	0.2419
12	GUERRERO	56,364	636,938	0.0885
13	HIDALGO	76,044	508,551	0.1495
14	JALISCO	372,498	1,588,190	0.2345
15	MEXICO	811,269	2,948,159	0.2752
16	MICHOACAN	135,880	920,154	0.1477
17	MORELOS	56,378	359,813	0.1567
18	NAYARIT	23,240	238,079	0.0976
19	NUEVO LEON	300,601	1,036,770	0.2899
20	OAXACA	75,921	775,844	0.0979
21	PUEBLA	192,628	1,110,489	0.1735
22	QUERETARO	73,315	298,222	0.2458
23	QUINTANA ROO	10,273	165,424	0.0621
24	SAN LUIS POTOSI	91,595	541,908	0.1690
25	SINALOA	70,247	674,431	0.1042
26	SONORA	90,427	577,205	0.1567
27	TABASCO	33,176	406,096	0.0817
28	TAMAULIPAS	129,792	710,047	0.1828
29	TLAXCALA	50,120	203,908	0.2458
30	VERACRUZ	200,119	1,792,272	0.1117
31	YUCATAN	62,986	413,593	0.1523
32	ZACATECAS	26,009	306,734	0.0848
	National Total	4,493,279	24,063,283	0.1867
	Mean	140,415	751,978	0.1633
	Median	74,618	577,800	0.1567
	S.D.	175,600	703,489	0.0702
	C.V.	125.06	93.55	43.00
	Minimum	8,946	104,980	0.0579
	Maximum	811,269	2,961,270	0.2899

DEFINITION: Ratio is the population in manufacturing industries to economically active population. This category includes the census designations manufacturing (transformation) and refining of petroleum.

SOURCE: INEGI, 1990 Mexican Census of Population, Table No. 32.

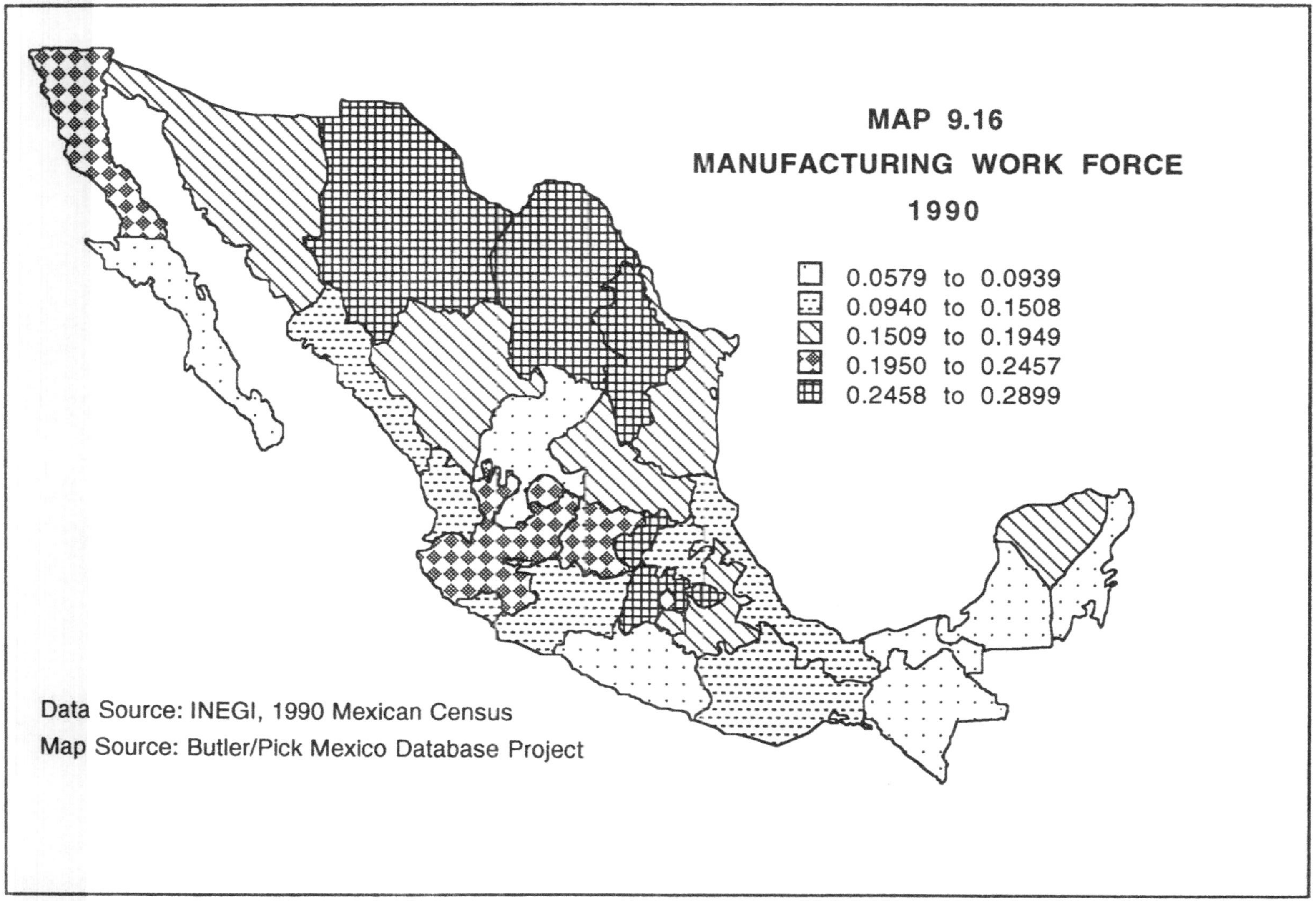
MAP 9.16
MANUFACTURING WORK FORCE
1990
0.0579 to 0.0939
0.0940 to 0.1508
0.1509 to 0.1949
0.1950 to 0.2457
0.2458 to 0.2899
Data Source: INEGI, 1990 Mexican Census
Map Source: Butler/Pick Mexico Database Project

Table 9.10 Personal Services Work Force, 1990

No.	State	Personal Service Industry Workers	Economically Active Population	Ratio
1	AGUASCALIENTES	19,326	217,092	0.0890
2	BAJA CALIFORNIA	63,547	578,395	0.1099
3	BAJA CALIFORNIA SUR	9,842	104,980	0.0938
4	CAMPECHE	12,267	152,902	0.0802
5	COAHUILA	54,442	605,251	0.0899
6	COLIMA	13,300	136,046	0.0978
7	CHIAPAS	45,622	874,267	0.0522
8	CHIHUAHUA	65,228	797,051	0.0818
9	DISTRITO FEDERAL	370,698	2,961,270	0.1252
10	DURANGO	28,174	359,994	0.0783
11	GUANAJUATO	84,371	1,063,208	0.0794
12	GUERRERO	44,172	636,938	0.0694
13	HIDALGO	33,662	508,551	0.0662
14	JALISCO	158,943	1,588,190	0.1001
15	MEXICO	286,437	2,948,159	0.0972
16	MICHOACAN	65,279	920,154	0.0709
17	MORELOS	41,867	359,813	0.1164
18	NAYARIT	16,759	238,079	0.0704
19	NUEVO LEON	108,749	1,036,770	0.1049
20	OAXACA	36,334	775,844	0.0468
21	PUEBLA	72,814	1,110,489	0.0656
22	QUERETARO	27,273	298,222	0.0915
23	QUINTANA ROO	15,103	165,424	0.0913
24	SAN LUIS POTOSI	41,397	541,908	0.0764
25	SINALOA	53,484	674,431	0.0793
26	SONORA	55,809	577,205	0.0967
27	TABASCO	31,763	406,096	0.0782
28	TAMAULIPAS	70,762	710,047	0.0997
29	TLAXCALA	12,248	203,908	0.0601
30	VERACRUZ	135,269	1,792,272	0.0755
31	YUCATAN	43,552	413,593	0.1053
32	ZACATECAS	19,343	306,734	0.0631
	National Total	2,137,836	24,063,283	0.0888
	Mean	66,807	751,978	0.0844
	Median	43,862	577,800	0.0810
	S.D.	77,704	703,489	0.0184
	C.V.	116.31	93.55	21.77
	Minimum	9,842	104,980	0.0468
	Maximum	370,698	2,961,270	0.1252

DEFINITION: Ratio is the population in personal service industries to the economically active population, age 12+. This category includes the census designations, personal services, and maintenance.

SOURCE: INEGI, 1990 Mexican Census of Population, Table No. 32.

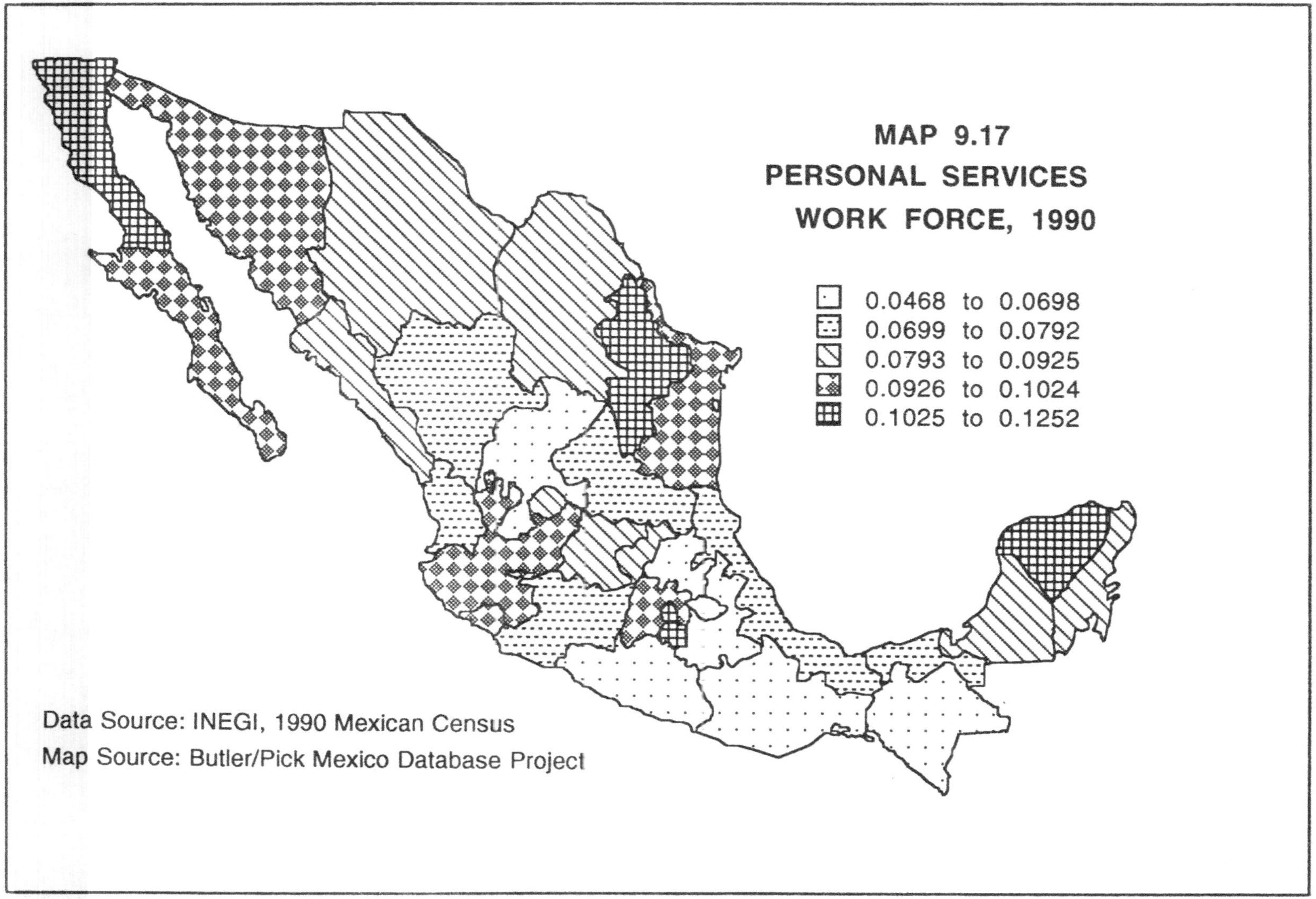
MAP 9.17
PERSONAL SERVICES
WORK FORCE, 1990
0.0468 to 0.0698
0.0699 to 0.0792
0.0793 to 0.0925
0.0926 to 0.1024
0.1025 to 0.1252
Data Source: INEGI, 1990 Mexican Census
Map Source: Butler/Pick Mexico Database Project

Table 9.11 Community and Social Services Work Force, 1990

No.	State	Community & Social Services Workers	Economically Active Population	Ratio
1	AGUASCALIENTES	19,567	217,092	0.0901
2	BAJA CALIFORNIA	47,345	578,395	0.0819
3	BAJA CALIFORNIA SUR	10,860	104,980	0.1034
4	CAMPECHE	12,267	152,902	0.0802
5	COAHUILA	60,325	605,251	0.0997
6	COLIMA	12,782	136,046	0.0940
7	CHIAPAS	45,622	874,267	0.0522
8	CHIHUAHUA	58,600	797,051	0.0735
9	DISTRITO FEDERAL	371,843	2,961,270	0.1256
10	DURANGO	34,430	359,994	0.0956
11	GUANAJUATO	67,895	1,063,208	0.0639
12	GUERRERO	54,230	636,938	0.0851
13	HIDALGO	38,876	508,551	0.0764
14	JALISCO	121,707	1,588,190	0.0766
15	MEXICO	227,173	2,948,159	0.0771
16	MICHOACAN	64,749	920,154	0.0704
17	MORELOS	34,826	359,813	0.0968
18	NAYARIT	21,158	238,079	0.0889
19	NUEVO LEON	95,759	1,036,770	0.0924
20	OAXACA	53,469	775,844	0.0689
21	PUEBLA	78,192	1,110,489	0.0704
22	QUERETARO	22,225	298,222	0.0745
23	QUINTANA ROO	10,853	165,424	0.0656
24	SAN LUIS POTOSI	45,192	541,908	0.0834
25	SINALOA	52,959	674,431	0.0785
26	SONORA	46,882	577,205	0.0812
27	TABASCO	33,064	406,096	0.0814
28	TAMAULIPAS	63,240	710,047	0.0891
29	TLAXCALA	18,262	203,908	0.0896
30	VERACRUZ	121,821	1,792,272	0.0680
31	YUCATAN	35,896	413,593	0.0868
32	ZACATECAS	25,836	306,734	0.0842
	National Total	2,007,905	24,063,283	0.0834
	Mean	62,747	751,978	0.0827
	Median	46,252	577,800	0.0816
	S.D.	70,718	703,489	0.0138
	C.V.	112.70	93.55	16.72
	Minimum	10,853	104,980	0.0522
	Maximum	371,843	2,961,270	0.1256

DEFINITION: Ratio is the population in community and social service industries to the economically active population, age 12+.

SOURCE: INEGI, 1990 Mexican Census of Population, Table No. 32.

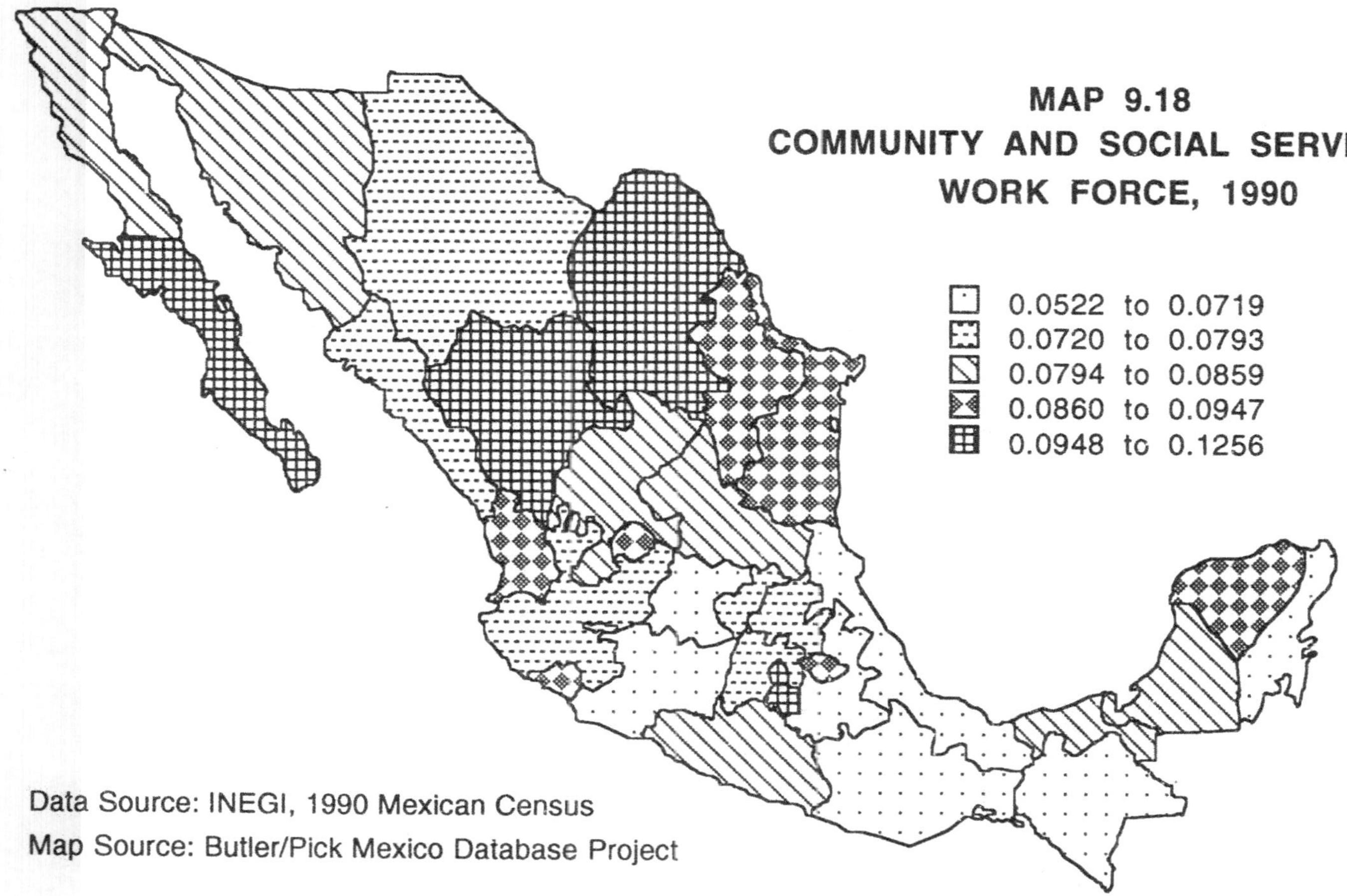

MAP 9.18
COMMUNITY AND SOCIAL SERVICES WORK FORCE, 1990

Data Source: INEGI, 1990 Mexican Census

Map Source: Butler/Pick Mexico Database Project

Income

Figure 9.3 illustrates the income of the employed population by sex. The male population employed is substantially greater than the female population employed, with over 17,882,142 males employed and 5,521,271 females being employed. Despite this disparity in male and female employment, income distribution by gender shows relatively little variation. Thus, the sex difference is not in income level but the proportion of men and women working.

No or Low Monthly Income, 1990

The Mexican census definition of the low income population consists of persons age 12+ with no income or a monthly income less than the minimum wage. Persons not specifying their age or income were excluded. Figure 9.3 illustrates income by sex for 1990. Over seven percent of the population does not receive an income, with 8.6 percent of males and 2.8 percent of females not receiving an income. For the total population, 19.3 percent received less than the minimum wage salary. The minimum wage was approximately $3.90 in U.S. dollars in 1991 (Barry 1992). Table 9.12 reports the population with no and the minimum monthly wage combined into a low monthly income category (also see Map 9.19).

Chiapas (58.9%) and Oaxaca (55.4%) had over half of their population with no or low monthly income. A substantial number of other states had around 30 percent or higher with no or low monthly incomes. As shown on Map 9.19, there is a north-south axis, with the exception of the state of Mexico and the Federal District, with the poorer states being located in the south. The only exception in the far south is Quintana Roo that has an average percentage in the low wage category. This relates to Quintana Roo's position as a population and economic growth state.

There is a small negative relationship between unemployment and low monthly income (r = - .10), while underemployment is positively associated with low monthly income (.26). There are high positive correlations between low monthly income and the population aged 0–17 (.67), the dependency ratio (.72), annual fertility (.66), crowding (.85), and having no electricity (.76). On the other hand, there are substantial negative correlations between low monthly income and the urban and population aged 18–64. Strong negative associations also exist between low monthly income and the total economically active population (- .64), the economically active female population (- .82), and those employed in tertiary activities (- .75). There also are strong negative relationships between all educational and literacy dimensions (r's range from - .70 to - .85) and with upper level occupations (- .69 to - .75). As expected, there is an extremely negative correlation with high monthly incomes (- .87).

High Monthly Income, 1990

High monthly income is defined as receiving five times or more than the minimum salary, i.e., more than $19.50 in U.S. dollars in 1991 (Barry 1992). Thus defined, 7.3 percent of the population, 8.4 percent of males, and 5.0 percent of females are so classified. As reported in Table 9.13 and Map 9.20, Baja California has the highest percentage of high monthly income recipients (13.95%). Also, the three border states Chihuahua, Sonora, and Nuevo Leon have over 10 percent of the population in the high income category. Thus, four of the six states with the high income population are on the U.S. border. The Federal District and the tourist state of Quintana Roo are the two remaining states with high monthly income populations.

States with the lowest percentage of higher level incomes are Oaxaca, with the lowest (3.20%), Chiapas (3.58%), and Guerrero, Hidalgo, Tlaxcala, Veracruz, Yucatan, and Zacatecas, all with under five percent of high income recipients. Again, as with low monthly income, there is a substantial gradient of higher incomes in the north to lower incomes in the south, with the exception of the Federal District and Quintana Roo.

High incomes are associated with the population aged 18–64 (r = .72), inmigration (.67), and with the total and economically active female population (.77 and .86, respectively). There are strong relationships with all the educational and literacy variables (ca. .71) and with higher level occupational categories, especially management (.80). Inverse relationships exist with the population aged 0–17 (- .68), the dependency ratio (- .74), fertility (- .45), crowding (- .79), and measures of agricultural occupations (- .77).

Figure 9.3
Employed Population by Income and Sex, 1990

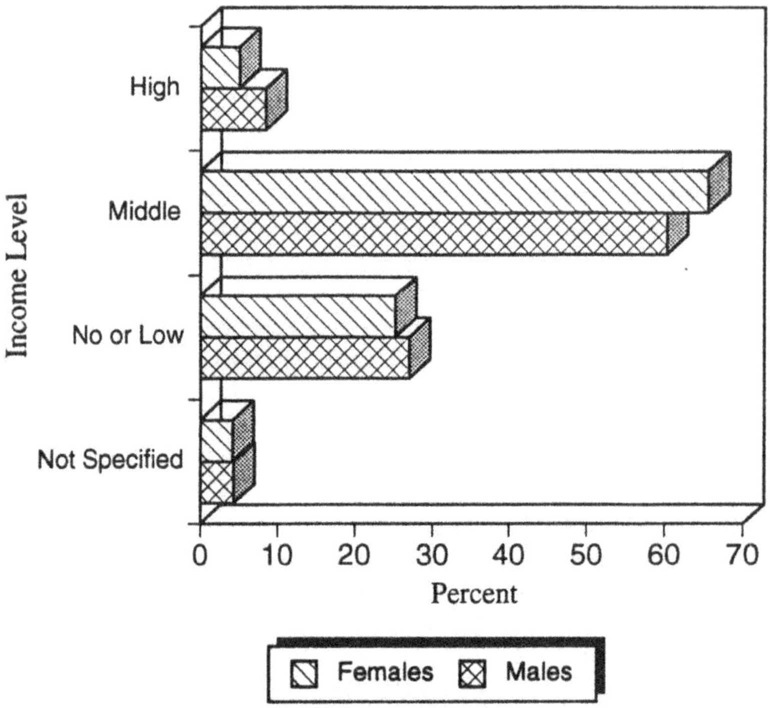

Supporting Data

Level of Monthly Income	Employed Population	Percentage Distrib. Males	Percentage Distrib. Females
High Income *	1,780,769	8.4	5.0
Middle Income **	14,414,191	60.3	65.6
Low Income ***	4,518,090	18.4	22.4
No Income	1,690,126	8.6	2.8
Not Specified	1,000,237	4.3	4.2
Total	23,403,413	100.0	100.0

* More than 5 times the minimum wage.
** From 1 to 5 times the minimum wage.
*** Less than the minimum wage.

NOTE: The minimum wage was 3.90 U.S. dollars in 1991.

SOURCE: INEGI, Perfil Sociodemografico, 1992.

Table 9.12 Population with No or Low Income, 1990

No.	State	Population with No Income	Population with Low Income	Employed Population	Ratio
1	AGUASCALIENTES	8,575	30,486	212,365	0.1839
2	BAJA CALIFORNIA	7,278	45,920	565,471	0.0941
3	BAJA CALIFORNIA SUR	2,773	13,240	102,763	0.1558
4	CAMPECHE	12,553	37,356	149,983	0.3328
5	COAHUILA	14,441	92,616	586,165	0.1826
6	COLIMA	4,950	14,092	133,474	0.1427
7	CHIAPAS	162,323	340,669	854,159	0.5889
8	CHIHUAHUA	42,673	71,451	773,100	0.1476
9	DISTRITO FEDERAL	30,424	545,441	2,884,807	0.1996
10	DURANGO	40,572	61,539	347,275	0.2940
11	GUANAJUATO	81,976	181,038	1,030,160	0.2553
12	GUERRERO	89,965	141,997	611,755	0.3792
13	HIDALGO	44,080	149,579	493,315	0.3926
14	JALISCO	83,242	213,838	1,553,202	0.1913
15	MEXICO	105,295	463,209	2,860,976	0.1987
16	MICHOACAN	104,533	151,798	891,873	0.2874
17	MORELOS	18,013	44,652	348,357	0.1799
18	NAYARIT	19,878	30,322	233,000	0.2155
19	NUEVO LEON	21,691	135,621	1,009,584	0.1558
20	OAXACA	187,020	213,011	754,305	0.5536
21	PUEBLA	136,516	281,079	1,084,316	0.3851
22	QUERETARO	22,152	46,273	288,994	0.2368
23	QUINTANA ROO	12,589	22,838	163,190	0.2171
24	SAN LUIS POTOSI	57,502	133,516	529,016	0.3611
25	SINALOA	29,727	70,665	660,905	0.1519
26	SONORA	10,434	56,387	562,386	0.1188
27	TABASCO	42,567	99,965	393,434	0.3623
28	TAMAULIPAS	23,456	134,670	684,550	0.2310
29	TLAXCALA	17,691	44,512	196,609	0.3164
30	VERACRUZ	179,073	455,257	1,742,129	0.3641
31	YUCATAN	24,367	133,522	407,337	0.3876
32	ZACATECAS	51,797	61,531	294,458	0.3849
National Total		1,690,126	4,518,090	23,403,413	0.2653
Mean		52,816	141,190	731,357	0.2703
Median		30,076	96,291	563,929	0.2339
S.D.		52,508	137,946	684,325	0.1212
C.V.		99.42	97.70	93.57	44.83
Minimum		2,773	13,240	102,763	0.0941
Maximum		187,020	545,441	2,884,807	0.5889

DEFINITION: Low income population consists of persons age 12+ with no income or income less than the Minimum Wage. Ratio is the no income and low income population to the employed population. Note that persons not specifying age or income are excluded from these figures.

SOURCE: INEGI, Perfil Sociodemographico, Table 16.1, 1992.

Table 9.13 Population with High Income, 1990

No.	State	Population with High Income	Employed Population	Ratio
1	AGUASCALIENTES	15,620	212,365	0.0736
2	BAJA CALIFORNIA	78,870	565,471	0.1395
3	BAJA CALIFORNIA SUR	8,145	102,763	0.0793
4	CAMPECHE	7,947	149,983	0.0530
5	COAHUILA	47,421	586,165	0.0809
6	COLIMA	12,177	133,474	0.0912
7	CHIAPAS	30,586	854,159	0.0358
8	CHIHUAHUA	84,071	773,100	0.1087
9	DISTRITO FEDERAL	292,270	2,884,807	0.1013
10	DURANGO	20,196	347,275	0.0582
11	GUANAJUATO	77,462	1,030,160	0.0752
12	GUERRERO	27,635	611,755	0.0452
13	HIDALGO	20,132	493,315	0.0408
14	JALISCO	145,276	1,553,202	0.0935
15	MEXICO	232,385	2,860,976	0.0812
16	MICHOACAN	60,785	891,873	0.0682
17	MORELOS	26,803	348,357	0.0769
18	NAYARIT	16,684	233,000	0.0716
19	NUEVO LEON	108,728	1,009,584	0.1077
20	OAXACA	24,132	754,305	0.0320
21	PUEBLA	58,357	1,084,316	0.0538
22	QUERETARO	27,278	288,994	0.0944
23	QUINTANA ROO	16,688	163,190	0.1023
24	SAN LUIS POTOSI	28,501	529,016	0.0539
25	SINALOA	56,423	660,905	0.0854
26	SONORA	59,950	562,386	0.1066
27	TABASCO	25,092	393,434	0.0638
28	TAMAULIPAS	45,874	684,550	0.0670
29	TLAXCALA	8,322	196,609	0.0423
30	VERACRUZ	84,182	1,742,129	0.0483
31	YUCATAN	19,333	407,337	0.0475
32	ZACATECAS	13,444	294,458	0.0457
	National Total	1,780,769	23,403,413	0.0761
	Mean	55,649	731,357	0.0726
	Median	28,068	563,929	0.0726
	S.D.	63,642	684,325	0.0258
	C.V.	114.36	93.57	35.45
	Minimum	7,947	102,763	0.0320
	Maximum	292,270	2,884,807	0.1395

DEFINITION: High income population consists of persons 12+ with income more than five times the minimum wage. Ratio is the high income population to the employed population. Note that persons not specifying age or income are excluded from these figures.

SOURCE: INEGI, Perfil Sociodemografico, Table 16.1, 1992.

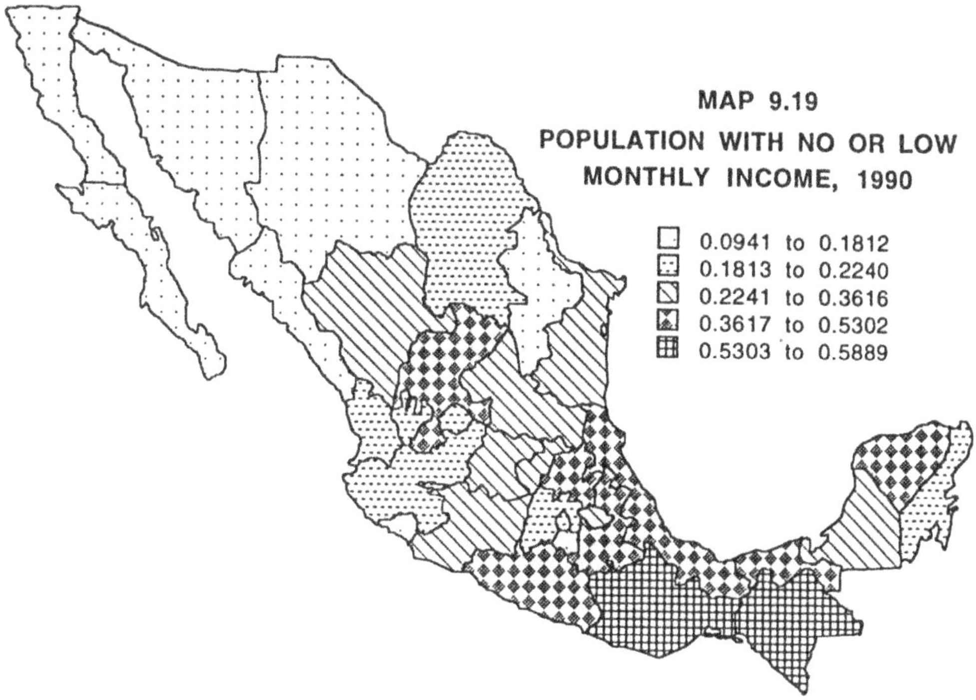

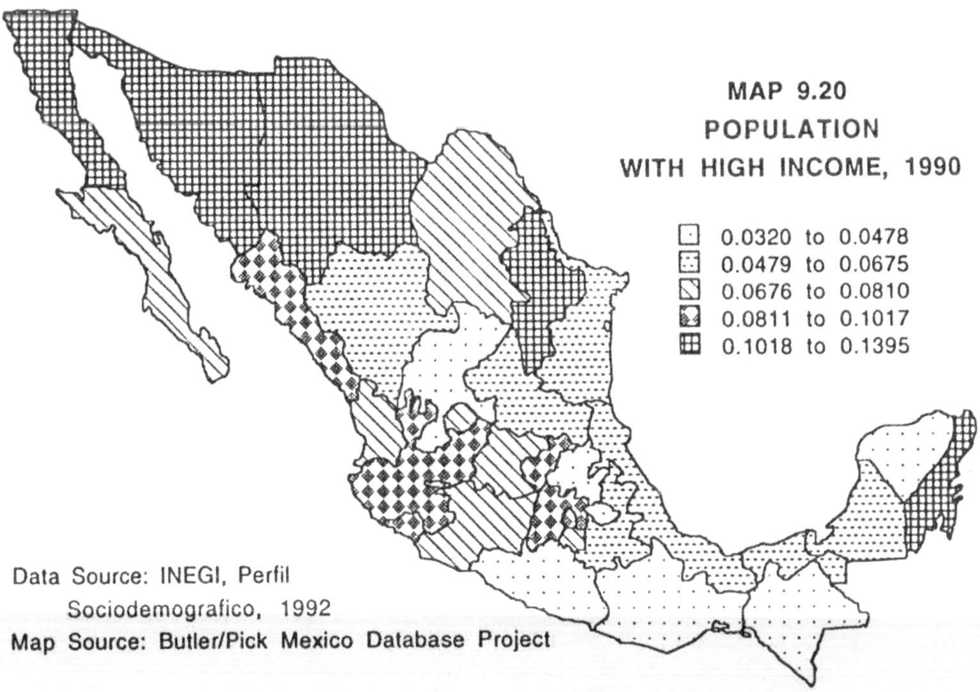

Data Source: INEGI, Perfil Sociodemografico, 1992
Map Source: Butler/Pick Mexico Database Project

Projected Eligible Work Force

Mexico has a large and rapidly growing eligible work force. Elsewhere, we have projected the potential Mexican work force to the year 2005 with varying assumptions of vital rates, economic activity, and international migration (Pick et al. forthcoming). We also divided projections into rural and urban components. The overall projections imply an expanded potential work force increasing at an annual rate of 900,000 to almost 1,200,000 eligible workers. There also was a possibility that the work force will have an increasing number of females which would increase the eligible work force. Thus, the potential Mexican national labor force will increase substantially over the 1990–2005 period between 41 and 49 percent, or *approximately one million potentially new economically active population per year.*

Historically, the Mexican work force has increased roughly at a rate proportional to the population increase. However, since 1980 the Mexican economy has had less success in absorbing eligible persons into the active work force. One indicator of an over supply of potential workers has been the flow of undocumented migrants to the United States. Another indicator of an over supply of potential workers is the increase in the informal labor market in Mexico. Without substantial increases in the rate of job generation in the Mexican economy, it is highly unlikely that there will be enough jobs for this large scale increase—e.g., estimated between 1990 and 2005 at 13 to 16 million potential workers.

The size range of the projected Mexican national labor force for 2005 is between 45 and 48 million (see Figure 9.4). This compares to an economically active population in 1990 of 32 million persons. The 2005 projection could be an underestimate if more than expected females of working age become economically active. Well over two-thirds of the eligible work force is expected to be in urban areas.

Unless some catastrophic occurrence takes place, these estimates are substantially accurate since most of those eligible for the work force by 2005 have already been born. Thus, international migration, and proportion of females who become economically active are the most important variable parameters in these projections. Projections beyond 2005 also depend heavily upon fertility.

FIGURE 9.4
PROJECTED NATIONAL LABOR FORCE:
MEXICO, 1980-2005

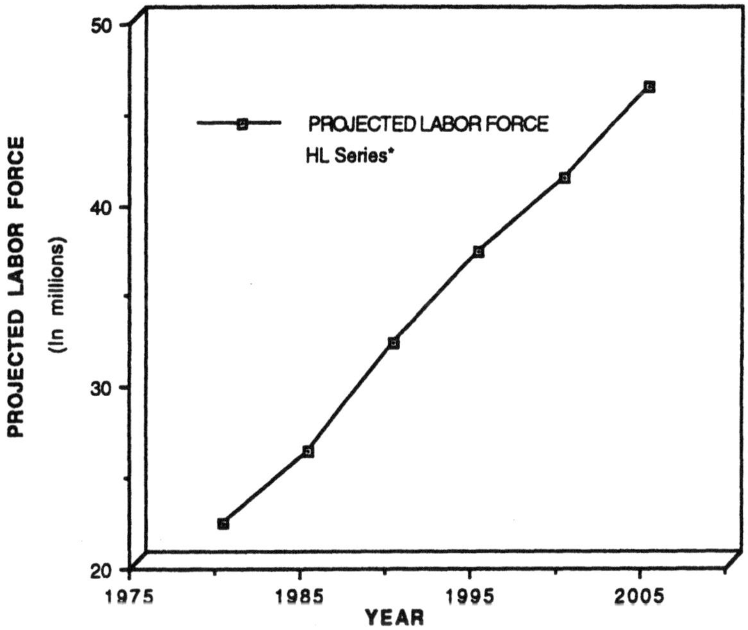

Supporting Data
Alternative Projections

Projection	1980 Labor Force	1990 Labor Force	2005 Labor
Pick et. al. HL Series *	22,552,000	32,283,000	48,089,000
Pick et. al. LH Series **	22,552,000	32,148,000	45,221,000
I.L.O. ***	22,248,000	30,487,000	45,728,000

* Pick et al., in press. HL assumes high fertility and low international outmigration.
** Pick et al., in press. LH assumes low fertility and high international outmigration.
*** International Labor Office, 1986.

10

Development

Introduction

Chapter 10 has five major divisions. The first section focuses on the Economic Plan of the Salinas administration as explicated in the State of the Nation addresses. The next division in the chapter emphasizes both foreign and national tourism, primarily for 1990. The third part of this development chapter then examines the number of five star hotels and the number of five star hotel rooms in 1985, hotel and motel services gross revenues per capita in 1985, the number of hotel and motel services in 1985, and finally the fixed assets of hotel and motel services in 1985. The fourth part of this chapter explores commercial air flights for 1989. The final section presents information on maquiladoras.

Economic Plan of the Salinas Administration

The economic plan of the Salinas administration for Mexico clearly specifies that the country must be reformed. "We will do so, keeping what is important for Mexico clearly in view" (Salinas 1989: 3). President Salinas also notes that the most fundamental factor is maintaining Mexico's sovereignty. Modernization of Mexico, the cornerstone of his approach, involves three national agreements: (1) to broaden democratic life, (2) economic recovery and price stability, and (3) improvement in living standards.

One aspect of the Salinas plan was to develop large consortiums to compete with major transnational companies. He suggests that a 'mixed economy' is necessary, a balance between public and private means of production. He also specifically stated that when public production facilities are sold that the workers should receive a share in the ownership of the companies and benefit from their expansion (Salinas 1989: 11).

The President believed that there had to be economic stability in Mexico so that economic development and modernization of production plants could proceed. His goal was to reach an annual growth of six percent by 1994. As we have noted in earlier chapters, Salinas, and Mexico, face pressures of high population growth with an increasing eligible workforce. The need for increased agricultural production is handicapped by small plots and, as he has noted, "peasants must work harder to produce less. There is still a great deal of poverty in our countryside" (Salinas 1991: 62).

New jobs must be created and productivity increased. He argued that subsidies for the private sector were a heavy burden on the federal budget, especially when production was remaining stagnant. Without question both the internal and external debts had to be overcome. The total net public debt had been reduced from 62.4 percent of GDP in 1988 to 28.4 percent in mid June 1992 (Salinas 1992: 19).

Salinas also had a vision of divesting many public enterprises and developing other means of paying for improvements. The major arguments for divestment were that it would improve the lot of the workers, increase research and development, and modernize facilities. While divestment has been increased, PEMEX, the major corporate enterprise in Mexico, apparently remains inviolate. It has been divided into four main areas of endeavor: (1) exploration and production, (2) refining, (3) gas and basic petrochemicals, and (4) secondary petrochemicals. However, the telephone company, one of the top five corporate entities in Mexico, has become privatized, as have the airlines and banks.

One improvement in the transportation system was to be the development of toll highways by private enterprise that purportedly would pay for themselves and then revert to government ownership. According to Salinas these activities would engender 460,000 jobs. The extent of divestment in Mexico during the Salinas regime declined substantially. In 1982 there were 1,155 state-owned enterprises that had decreased to 221 by mid-June 1992. Revenues from the sale of these enterprises increased the government's coffers, especially beginning in 1989, and amounted to over one billion U.S. dollars in 1991 alone (Mexico 1992).

President Salinas also wanted to increase foreign tourism because he believed that it would generate employment, regional development, and foreign currency flow into the country.

Perhaps because of charges of election fraud in past Mexican elections, Salinas also proposed, and put into action, a National Registry of Citizens and a related identification card.

In summary, the Salinas view of Mexican development includes maintaining PEMEX as a state-owned enterprise but revitalizing it by dividing it into four divisions, divestment of some government owned corporations, restructuring the national debt, expanding foreign tourism, continuing the maquiladora program, and opening up common markets via NAFTA and other such agreements. By most objective observers, many of these goals have been met.

Tourism, 1990

The number of foreign tourists entering Mexico continues to increase. However, in 1984, 29 percent of tourists were foreigners compared to 26.9 percent in 1990. Table 10.1 shows the increase in number of foreign tourists from 1984 through 1990. As reported in Table 10.1, the U.S. is the main source of both tourists entering and leaving Mexico.

Table 10.2 classifies the major tourist centers of Mexico into five different types: (1) planned tourist centers, (2) traditional, (3) grand cities, (4) interior tourist centers, and (5) frontier centers. Map 10.1 locates each of the these major tourist locations.

Map 10.1 illustrates that the planned tourist centers of Cancun, Quintana Roo; Ixtapa/Zihuataneo, Guerrero; Loreto and Los Cabos, Baja California Sur; and Bahias de Huatulco, Oaxaca all are ocean front destinations and most of these locations had a low population and development before tourism development. The key for Map 10.1 appears in Table 10.2. All traditional tourist centers, such as Acapulco and Puerto Vallarta, also are ocean front destinations. On the other hand, all three of the 'grand city' locations are in the interior—the Federal District, Guadalajara, and Monterrey. As suggested by their name, interior tourist centers are located in the interior of the country and most of them are cities that existed in pre-colonial times. Included in this category are Guanajuato, Merida, Morelia, Oaxaca, and Zacatecas. Frontier tourist centers are all located in the northern frontier along the U.S.-Mexico border—Tijuana, Juarez, and Reynosa (see Map 10.1).

There is substantial variation in foreign and national visitors to the various tourist destinations. Table 10.2 shows that the three planned tourist centers of Cancun, Loreto, and Los Cabos are substantially foreign resorts while Ixtapa and Bahias de Huatulco are more likely destinations for Mexican than foreign tourists. Of the traditional centers, La Paz is a more likely tourist destination for national than foreign visitors in contrast to not too far away Los Cabos that is a foreign tourist resort region. Of the traditional centers, only Cozumel draws more foreigners than Mexican tourists. Similarly, the grand cities are a more likely tourist destination for Mexicans than for foreign tourists. All interior cities also draw more Mexican nationals than foreign visitors. Overwhelmingly, frontier tourist centers are visited by foreigners rather than by Mexicans.

Figure 10.1 illustrates for 1990 the volume of visitors by type of tourist center and foreign and national tourists. Thus, only planned tourist areas attract more foreign visitors than the other types of tourist locations that are more likely to appeal to Mexican nationals.

Table 10.1 Tourists Entering and Leaving Mexico by Place of Origin and Destination

Tourists Entering Mexico by Place of Origin

Year	1985	1986	1987	1988	1989	1990
UNITED STATES	3,541	3,895	4,620	5,016	5,385	5,598
CANADA	193	247	336	313	361	294
EUROPE	146	149	219	112	157	189
LATIN AMERICA	301	318	205	225	261	276
OTHER	26	16	27	26	22	36
Total	4,207	4,625	5,407	5,692	6,186	6,393

Tourists Leaving Mexico by Place of Destination

Year	1985	1986	1987	1988	1989	1990
UNITED STATES	2,542	2,303	2,687	3,116	3,587	4,005
CANADA	10	9	11	12	14	17
CENTRAL AMERICA	41	34	39	45	51	59
SOUTH AMERICA	16	14	16	21	25	28
EUROPE	102	91	106	130	154	176
ASIA	7	6	8	8	10	11
OTHER	13	13	15	19	22	25
Total	2,731	2,470	2,882	3,351	3,863	4,321

DEFINITION: Tourists Entering Mexico are classified by their place of origin and place of destination in thousands of persons.

SOURCE: Secretaria de Turismo, Banco de Mexico, 1992.

Table 10.2 Tourist Activity in Major Tourist Centers, 1990

	Key No. *	Number of Rooms	Tourist Visits (1000s)		
			Total	National	Foreign
Total		126,582	17,134.2	12,519.9	4,614.0
Planned Tourist Centers		25,935	2,289.4	703.7	1,585.6
Cancun, Quintana Roo	3	17,470	1,575.7	395.2	1,180.5
Ixtapa Zihuatanejo, Guerrero	16	4,169	300.9	191.5	109.3
Loreto, Baja Sur	23	455	38.1	12.0	26.1
Los Cabos, Baja Sur	19	2,531	255.7	27.7	228.0
Bahias de Huatulco, Oaxaca	22	1,310	119.0	77.3	41.7
Traditional		45,125	4,641.2	3,386.9	1,254.3
Acapulco, Guerrero	4	17,001	1,466.3	1,049.2	417.1
Cozumel, Quintana Roo	21	2,875	218.3	48.0	170.3
La Paz, Baja Sur	20	1,412	224.9	179.0	45.9
Manzanillo, Colima	14	2,987	338.2	288.0	50.2
Mazatian, Sinola	6	7,935	876.1	632.2	243.9
Puerto Vallarta, Jalisco	10	8,646	687.9	380.8	307.1
Veracruz, Veracruz	9	4,269	829.5	809.7	19.8
Grand Cities		35,218	5,525.8	44,777.0	1,048.1
Distrito Federal	1	18,138	2,424.1	1,630.3	793.8
Guadalajara, Jalisco	2	13,092	2,271.1	2,113.8	157.3
Monterrey, Nuevo Leon	8	3,988	830.6	733.6	97.0
Interior		11,286	2,153.8	1,822.6	331.2
Guanajuato, Guanajuato	15	1,717	323.6	296.3	27.3
Merida, Yucatan	12	3,188	469.7	305.7	164.0
Morelia, Michoacan	11	2,678	647.2	629.8	17.3
Oaxaca, Oaxaca	13	2,672	453.3	342.8	110.5
Zacatecas, Zacatecas	18	1,031	260.0	248.0	12.1
Border		9,018	2,524.0	2,129.0	394.8
Tijuana, Baja California	5	4,733	1,396.2	1,080.9	315.2
Ciudad Juarez, Chihuahua	7	2,794	865.6	793.1	72.4
Reynosa, Tamaulipas	17	1,491	262.2	255.0	7.2

DEFINITION: Tourists Visits are of National and Foreign Visitors in thousands.

NOTE: * Key numbers are in descending number order for size and correspond to numbers in Map 10.1.

SOURCE: Secretaria de Tourismo, Fondo Nacional de Fomento al Turismo(FONATUR), Aeropuertos y Servicios Auxiliares (ASA).

MAP 10.1

MAJOR TOURIST CENTERS, BY TYPE, 1990

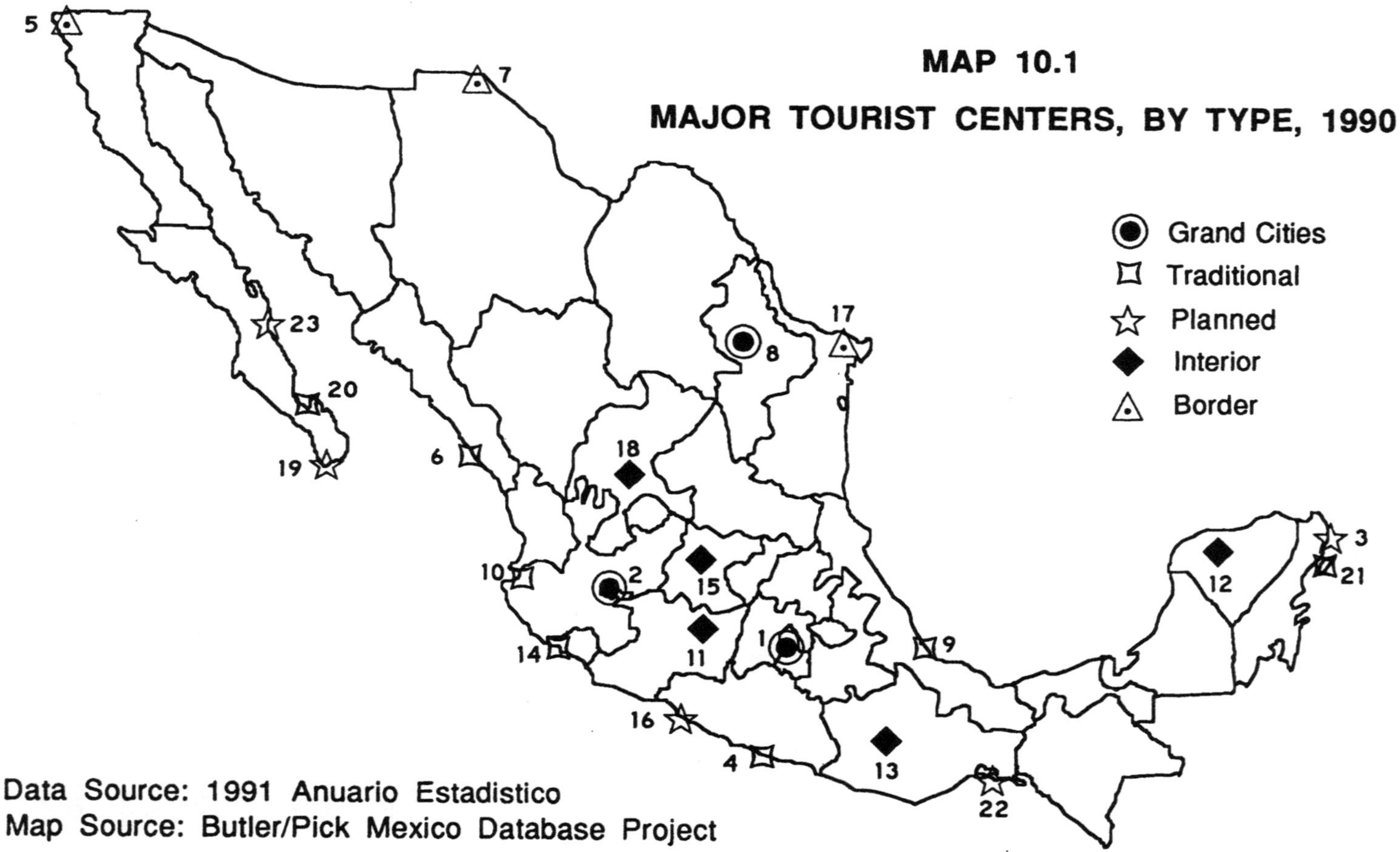

Data Source: 1991 Anuario Estadistico
Map Source: Butler/Pick Mexico Database Project

Figure 10.1
Type of Tourist Center and National and Foreign Tourists, 1990

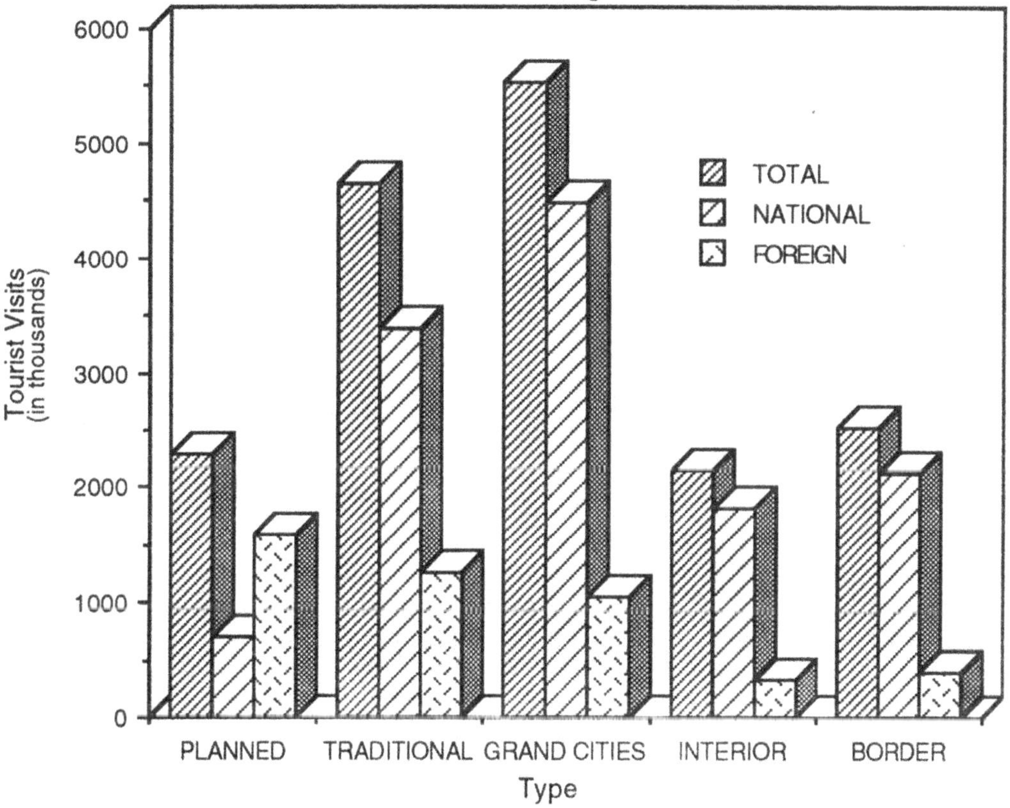

SOURCE: Secretaria de Turismo.

Hotels

Number of Hotels, 1989

The number of hotels per capita, as defined as the number of hotels in 1989 to the 1990 population of the state multiplied by 100, is shown in Table 10.3. The range in per capita hotels is relatively small; the Bajas, Colima, Nayarit, and Quintana Roo have the highest hotels per capita. Except for Nayarit, these states can be considered as tourist destinations. Nayarit is located on the Pan American Highway and this possibly may explain its relatively high ratio per capita. By far, the state with the fewest hotels per capita is Queretaro. As might be expected, states catering to tourists have higher hotels per capita than non-tourist oriented states. Map 10.2, however, illustrates that there is moderate variation (CV = 74) and little correspondence with standard regions.

Five Star Hotels, 1989

While there is moderate variation in the number of hotels per capita, the number of five star hotels, number of five star rooms, and per capita of five star hotel rooms reported in Table 10.4 and Map 10.4 demonstrates that there is great regional variation in the location of five star hotels—many mega-hotels and in resort locations. Four states have between 16–22 five star hotels and thus dominate the five star category of hotels in Mexico. However, except for Mexico City five star hotels, the remainder of the major states contain a large metropolis (Guadalajara) or are located on the ocean front. Not too surprisingly, each of these states emphasize tourism. Quintana Roo, with its major resort areas of Cancun and Cozumel, has the most five star hotels (N = 22). While the Federal District has seventeen, both Jalisco and Guerrero have sixteen each. The states of Durango, Hidalgo, and Tlaxcala contain no five star hotels (see Map 10.3).

Gross Revenues of Hotel and Motel Services, 1985

There is great variation among states insofar as the number of employees and gross revenues per 1000 population (see Table 10.5). The largest number of employees in hotel and motel services are in the same states as major concentration of five star hotels—the Federal District, Guerrero, Jalisco, and Quintana Roo. Thus, there is a high correlation between tourism and hotel employees per capita. Table 10.5 and Figure 10.2 show that six states had over fifty percent of the total hotel and motel service employees in 1985.

Gross revenues per capita, however, show a somewhat different pattern. By far, the highest per capita revenues from hotels and motels are reported for Quintana Roo (89.93). Then still much larger than the other states are Baja California Sur (26.61) and Guerrero (25.09). Several other states have relatively higher per capita revenues compared to the remaining states—Baja (7.33), Colima (11.18), Jalisco (6.02), Sinaloa (6.87), and Yucatan (4.00). Fixed assets of hotel and motel services again demonstrate that a few states dominate. As Figure 10.3 illustrates, the major foreign tourism state of Guerrero leads on fixed assets, followed by Jalisco and the Federal District, which are more representative of national tourism as well as business travel.

Table 10.3 Number of Hotels per Capita, 1989

No.	State	No. Hotels	No. Hotel Rooms	No. Hotels /Capita
1	AGUASCALIENTES	58	2,201	0.0001
2	BAJA CALIFORNIA	376	16,470	0.0002
3	BAJA CALIFORNIA SUR	126	6,279	0.0004
4	CAMPECHE	75	2,199	0.0001
5	COAHUILA	145	5,210	0.0001
6	COLIMA	123	4,989	0.0003
7	CHIAPAS	232	6,177	0.0001
8	CHIHUAHUA	275	9,448	0.0001
9	DISTRITO FEDERAL	597	40,724	0.0001
10	DURANGO	125	3,262	0.0001
11	GUANAJUATO	272	10,233	0.0001
12	GUERRERO	495	28,241	0.0002
13	HIDALGO	136	3,712	0.0001
14	JALISCO	664	32,815	0.0001
15	MEXICO	231	8,674	0.0000
16	MICHOACAN	373	11,468	0.0001
17	MORELOS	200	5,857	0.0002
18	NAYARIT	217	5,590	0.0003
19	NUEVO LEON	71	4,736	0.0000
20	OAXACA	258	9,270	0.0001
21	PUEBLA	210	7,235	0.0001
22	QUERETARO	106	4,442	0.0001
23	QUINTANA ROO	230	19,730	0.0005
24	SAN LUIS POTOSI	156	5,188	0.0001
25	SINALOA	249	12,388	0.0001
26	SONORA	203	8,368	0.0001
27	TABASCO	103	3,694	0.0001
28	TAMAULIPAS	332	10,914	0.0001
29	TLAXCALA	45	1,051	0.0001
30	VERACRUZ	760	22,212	0.0001
31	YUCATAN	156	5,568	0.0001
32	ZACATECAS	122	3,420	0.0001
National Total		7,721	321,765	0.0044
Mean		241	10,055	0.0001
Median		207	6,228	0.0001
S.D.		175	9,313	0.0001
C.V.		72.40	92.62	75.60
Minimum		45	1,051	0.0000
Maximum		760	40,724	0.0005

DEFINITION: The number of hotels per capita is the ratio of the number of hotels to the 1990 population multiplied by 100.

SOURCE: INEGI, 1990 Anuario Estadistico, Table No. 4.4.1.

MAP 10.2
NUMBER OF HOTELS PER CAPITA, 1989

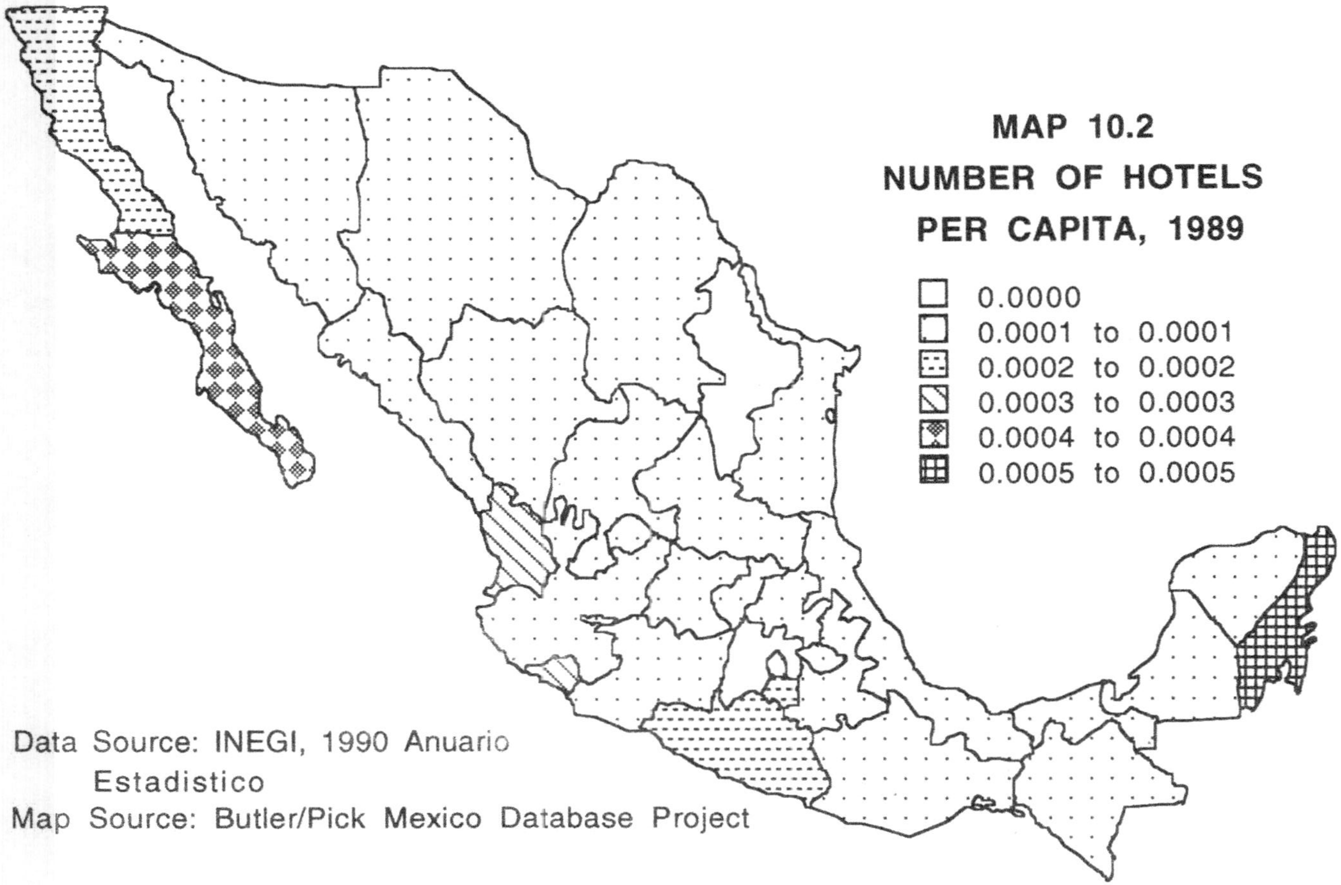

Data Source: INEGI, 1990 Anuario Estadistico
Map Source: Butler/Pick Mexico Database Project

Table 10.4 Five Star Hotel Rooms per Capita, 1989

No.	State	No. Five Star Hotels	No. Five Star Hotel Rooms	No. Five Star Hotel Rooms/Capita
1	AGUASCALIENTES	1	160	0.0222
2	BAJA CALIFORNIA	1	49	0.0030
3	BAJA CALIFORNIA SUR	4	940	0.2958
4	CAMPECHE	1	92	0.0172
5	COAHUILA	6	776	0.0393
6	COLIMA	2	257	0.0600
7	CHIAPAS	1	112	0.0035
8	CHIHUAHUA	4	591	0.0242
9	DISTRITO FEDERAL	17	5,469	0.0664
10	DURANGO	0	0	0.0000
11	GUANAJUATO	2	304	0.0076
12	GUERRERO	16	5,458	0.2083
13	HIDALGO	0	0	0.0000
14	JALISCO	16	5,164	0.0974
15	MEXICO	3	807	0.0082
16	MICHOACAN	2	379	0.0107
17	MORELOS	3	418	0.0350
18	NAYARIT	0	0	0.0000
19	NUEVO LEON	5	1,306	0.0421
20	OAXACA	2	648	0.0215
21	PUEBLA	5	784	0.0190
22	QUERETARO	1	175	0.0166
23	QUINTANA ROO	22	5,628	1.1409
24	SAN LUIS POTOSI	3	603	0.0301
25	SINALOA	5	1,525	0.0692
26	SONORA	1	218	0.0120
27	TABASCO	2	260	0.0173
28	TAMAULIPAS	2	243	0.0108
29	TLAXCALA	0	0	0.0000
30	VERACRUZ	1	195	0.0031
31	YUCATAN	3	457	0.0335
32	ZACATECAS	1	49	0.0000
	National Total	132	33,067	0.0407
	Mean	4	1,033	0.0723
	Median	2	342	0.0182
	S.D.	6	1,730	0.2046
	C.V.	134.31	167.41	282.78
	Minimum	0	0	0.0000
	Maximum	22	5,628	1.1409

DEFINITION: The number of five star hotel rooms per capita is the ratio of the number of five star hotels to the 1990 population multiplied by 100.

SOURCE: INEGI, 1990 Anuario Estadistico, Table No. 4.4.1.

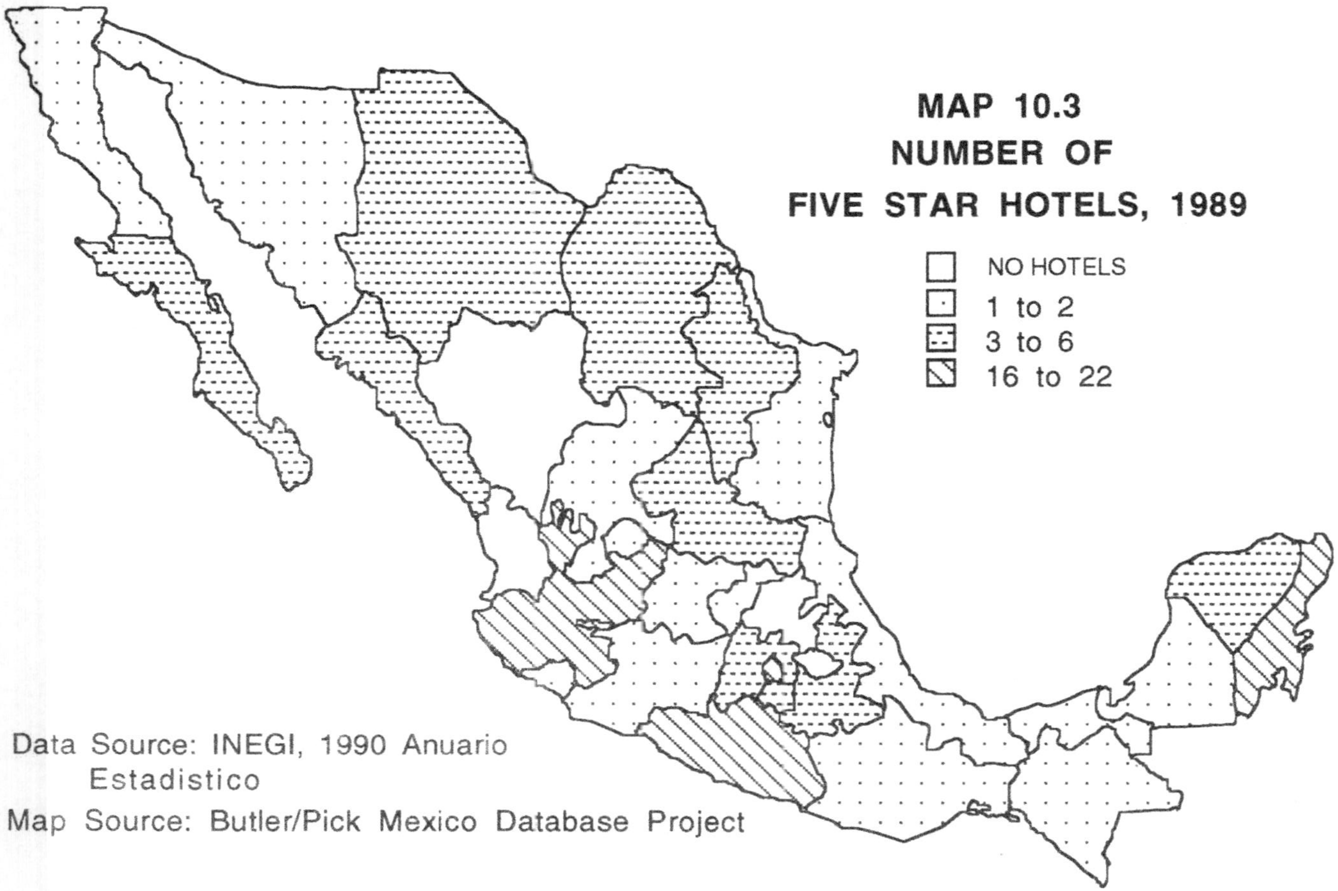

**MAP 10.3
NUMBER OF
FIVE STAR HOTELS, 1989**

Data Source: INEGI, 1990 Anuario Estadistico

Map Source: Butler/Pick Mexico Database Project

Table 10.5 Hotel and Motel Services, 1985

No.	State	Number of Establishments	Number of Employees	Gross Revenues Per 1000 Population
1	AGUASCALIENTES	64	898	2.0093
2	BAJA CALIFORNIA	315	4,359	7.3312
3	BAJA CALIFORNIA SUR	139	4,142	26.6078
4	CAMPECHE	105	769	2.5617
5	COAHUILA	176	1,673	1.5798
6	COLIMA	108	1,824	11.1783
7	CHIAPAS	315	1,910	0.8485
8	CHIHUAHUA	381	3,379	3.1758
9	DISTRITO FEDERAL	562	10,538	4.4701
10	DURANGO	155	1,046	1.2687
11	GUANAJUATO	285	2,978	1.3092
12	GUERRERO	474	18,945	25.0863
13	HIDALGO	97	574	0.2817
14	JALISCO	573	13,308	6.0247
15	MEXICO	251	2,484	0.4202
16	MICHOACAN	391	3,660	1.3584
17	MORELOS	149	1,411	2.6492
18	NAYARIT	168	750	1.1496
19	NUEVO LEON	214	2,165	1.7236
20	OAXACA	330	2,461	1.1068
21	PUEBLA	271	2,116	0.8759
22	QUERETARO	85	1,459	2.6340
23	QUINTANA ROO	230	9,602	80.9282
24	SAN LUIS POTOSI	143	1,368	1.1711
25	SINALOA	260	6,308	6.8701
26	SONORA	233	2,485	3.4064
27	TABASCO	199	2,778	3.8275
28	TAMAULIPAS	274	2,609	2.3044
29	TLAXCALA	112	1,304	2.6692
30	VERACRUZ	693	5,608	1.4039
31	YUCATAN	169	2,255	3.9980
32	ZACATECAS	97	756	0.8266
	National Total	8,018	117,922	213.0562
	Mean	251	3,685	6.6580
	Median	222	2,358	2.4331
	S.D.	154	4,073	14.8743
	C.V.	61.56	110.54	223.40
	Minimum	64	574	0.2817
	Maximum	693	18,945	80.9282

SOURCE: IX Censo de Servicios de 1986, INEGI, 1991, Vol.1, Tables 9, 13, and 16.

MAP 10.4
HOTEL AND MOTEL SERVICES GROSS REVENUES PER 1000 POPULATION, 1985

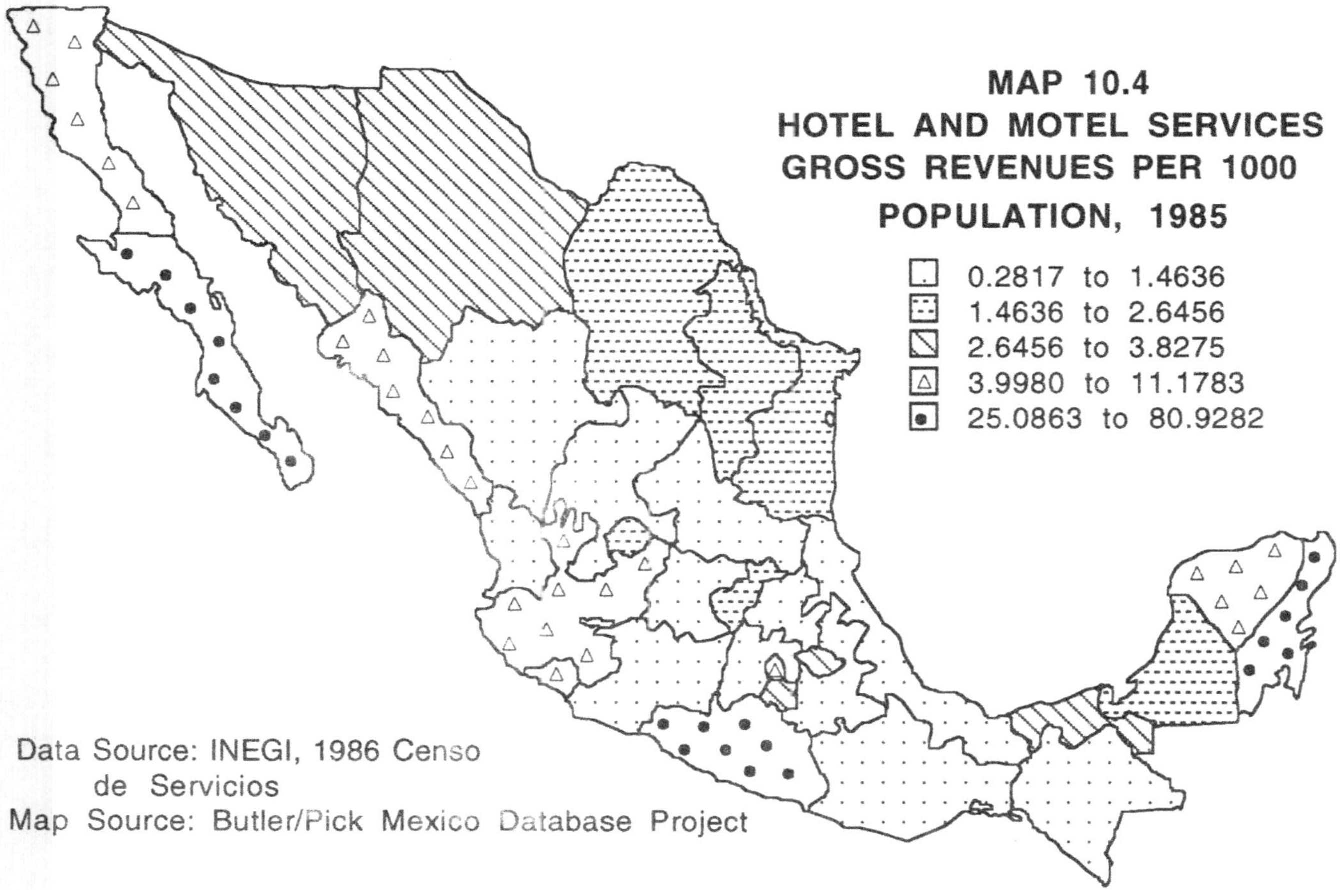

Data Source: INEGI, 1986 Censo de Servicios
Map Source: Butler/Pick Mexico Database Project

Figure 10.2
Hotel and Motel Services
Number of Employees, 1985

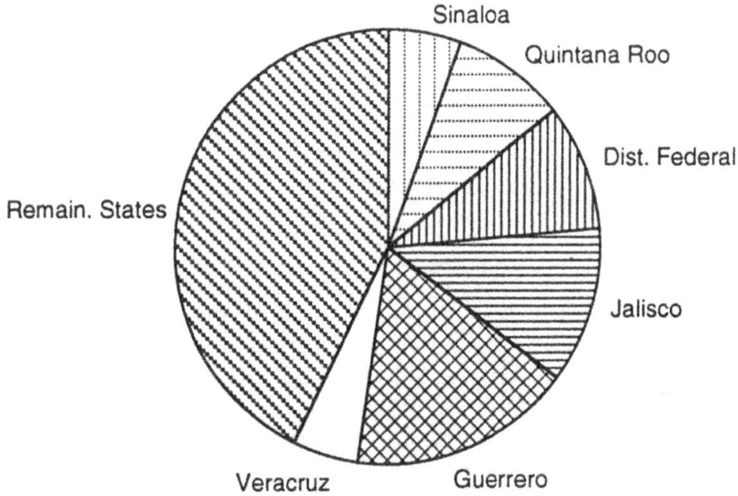

Figure 10.3
Hotel and Motel Services
Fixed Assets, 1985

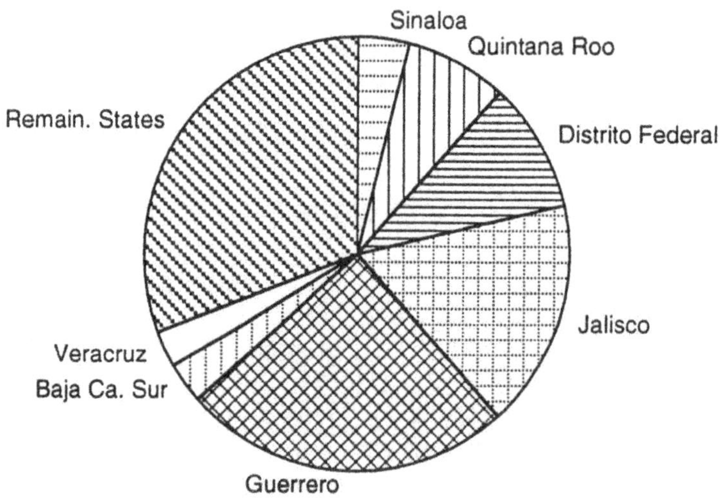

Data Source: IX Censo de Servicios de 1986, INEGI, 1991, Vol. 1, Tables 9, 13, and 16.

Commercial Air Flights, 1989

Table 10.6 reports data on commercial air flights for 1989. Hidalgo, Morelos, Queretaro, and Tlaxcala had no commercial air flights in 1989. The Federal District had 7,571,695 passengers in 1989, or 48.9 percent of the total passengers for the country. The two other major passenger states were Jalisco and Nuevo Leon, which with the addition of the Federal District, had 70 percent of the total commercial air passengers in 1989. Map 10.5 shows air passengers on a per capita basis; however, Quintana Roo (1.03) and Baja California Sur (.99) had a higher per capita than the Federal District (.91). After these three states there was a large drop in per capita commercial air passengers to Jalisco's (.42). Of those states in the intermediate per capita range, most are tourist destinations except for Aguascalientes that is now emerging as an important governmental center, e.g., the location of INEGI headquarters and of the new large Nissan factory, and Campeche that may be oil-related. The total number of airports was not related either to passengers, passengers per capita, total flights, or airports per 10,000 population.

There are distinctive regional patterns. The west and southeast have quite high levels of commercial air flights. This is due partly to tourism-related traffic, especially in the southeast. The central region is a contrast with a large amount of air flights in the Federal District and Puebla but reduced elsewhere. The border region has a moderate amount of commercial air flights.

Table 10.6 Commercial Air Flights, 1989

No.	State	Total Passengers	Passengers Per Capita	Total Flights	Flights Per 10,000 Pop.	Total Airports	Airports Per 10,000 Pop.
1	AGUASCALIENTES	200,912	0.2792	4,397	0.0061	1	0.0139
2	BAJA CALIFORNIA	146,262	0.0881	1,874	0.0011	5	0.0301
3	BAJA CALIFORNIA SUR	314,928	0.9911	9,673	0.0304	6	0.1888
4	CAMPECHE	155,639	0.2908	15,282	0.0286	2	0.0374
5	COAHUILA	172,200	0.0873	5,757	0.0029	5	0.0254
6	COLIMA	54,747	0.1278	2,073	0.0048	2	0.0467
7	CHIAPAS	125,340	0.0390	1,396	0.0004	3	0.0093
8	CHIHUAHUA	255,219	0.1045	8,468	0.0035	2	0.0082
9	DISTRITO FEDERAL	7,571,695	0.9194	77,359	0.0094	1	0.0012
10	DURANGO	155,792	0.1155	8,857	0.0066	1	0.0074
11	GUANAJUATO	143,280	0.0360	3,964	0.0010	3	0.0075
12	GUERRERO	758,372	0.2894	13,866	0.0053	2	0.0076
13	HIDALGO	0	0.0000	0	0.0000	1	0.0053
14	JALISCO	2,249,135	0.4241	40,213	0.0076	3	0.0057
15	MEXICO	2,427	0.0002	1,323	0.0001	3	0.0031
16	MICHOACAN	55,246	0.0156	3,733	0.0011	4	0.0113
17	MORELOS	0	0.0000	0	0.0000	1	0.0084
18	NAYARIT	48,861	0.0593	5,670	0.0069	1	0.0121
19	NUEVO LEON	1,011,023	0.3263	11,500	0.0037	2	0.0065
20	OAXACA	112,745	0.0373	1,366	0.0005	4	0.0132
21	PUEBLA	590	0.0001	96	2.3267	2	0.0048
22	QUERETARO	0	0.0000	0	0.0000	1	0.0095
23	QUINTANA ROO	512,946	1.0399	11,027	0.0224	4	0.0811
24	SAN LUIS POTOSI	90,001	0.0449	3,886	0.0019	2	0.0100
25	SINALOA	257,953	0.1170	13,817	0.0063	3	0.0136
26	SONORA	108,400	0.0594	3,875	0.0021	5	0.0274
27	TABASCO	315,157	0.2099	6,591	0.0044	1	0.0067
28	TAMAULIPAS	24,801	0.0110	1,135	0.0005	5	0.0222
29	TLAXCALA	0	0.0000	0	0.0000	1	0.0131
30	VERACRUZ	817	0.0001	301	4.8328	5	0.0080
31	YUCATAN	431,425	0.3165	8,695	0.0064	1	0.0073
32	ZACATECAS	199,573	0.1564	2,784	0.0022	1	0.0078
National Total		15,475,486	0.1905	268,978	0.0033	83	0.0000
Mean		483,609	0.1933	8,406	0.2289	3	0.0206
Median		144,771	0.0877	3,925	0.0036	2	0.0094
S.D.		1,362,391	0.2838	14,746	0.9349	2	0.0345
C.V.		281.71	146.83	175.43	408.39	61.05	167.10
Minimum		0	0.0000	0	0.0000	1	0.0012
Maximum		7,571,695	1.0399	77,359	4.8328	6	0.1888

DEFINITION: Per capita values were calculated per 10,000 1990 total population. Flight and passenger values include both arrivals and departures. National and International airports are both included in the airport total.

SOURCE: INEGI, 1990 Anuario Estadistico, Tables 2.2.22 and 2.2.24.

MAP 10.5
COMMERCIAL AIR FLIGHTS PER 10,000 POPULATION, 1989

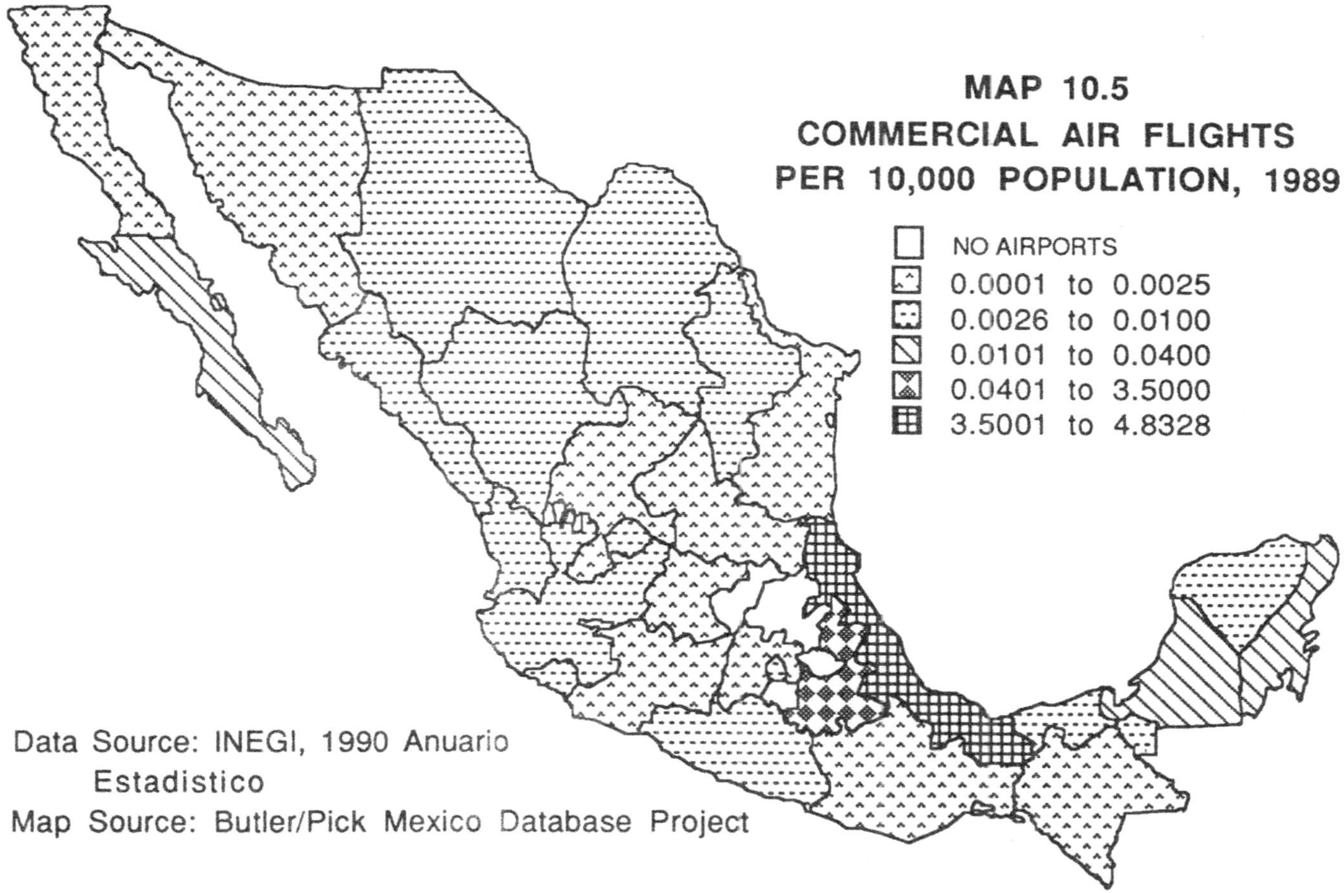

Data Source: INEGI, 1990 Anuario Estadistico
Map Source: Butler/Pick Mexico Database Project

Maquiladoras

Maquiladoras (Border In-Bond Production) in Mexico are a relatively recent phenomenon. Maquiladora production could have been described in Chapter 8 on the economy and economic development. However, maquiladoras are essentially a foreign impact upon Mexico and are described here instead.

Between 1979 and 1989, the number of maquiladora employees increased from 111,365 to 429,725, or a 286 percent increase! As Figure 10.4 and Table 10.7 illustrate via sex ratios, females dominated the maquila workforce until about 1985. Since that time there has been an increasing proportion of the employees who are male. Figure 10.6 shows that the national sex ratio is less than the Tijuana and Ciudad Juarez sex ratios. In essence this means that there is a larger proportion of male workers in these two cities than in maquiladoras elsewhere in Mexico. Laborers make up 81.4 percent of the maquiladora labor force, although as Figures 10.5 and 10.6 illustrate, over time managers have increasingly become a larger part of the maquiladora labor force. Table 10.7 shows the impact that maquiladoras have had upon Mexico and the two leading maquiladora cities—Tijuana and Ciudad Juarez. The growth in maquila employees in Tijuana was even greater than the national average, 433 percent, while the growth in Juarez was somewhat less than the national average. Tijuana and Juarez accounted for 41.6 percent of maquiladora establishments but 61.2 percent of maquila employees, indicating that plants located in these two cities in general are larger than those located in other cities.

Other Mexican cities along the U.S. border also contain maquilas. Table 10.8 reports more detailed information on these cities and presents data on level of work, maquiladora workers per capita, salaries received, the extent of which the components were foreign imports or domestically produced. Components utilized in maquiladoras are primarily foreign imports (87.3 percent) rather than being produced in Mexico. Value added annually to selected border municipios by the maquiladora industry is shown on Map 10.6.

Figure 10.4
Maquiladora Sex Ratio: National, Tijuana, and Ciudad Juarez, 1979-1989

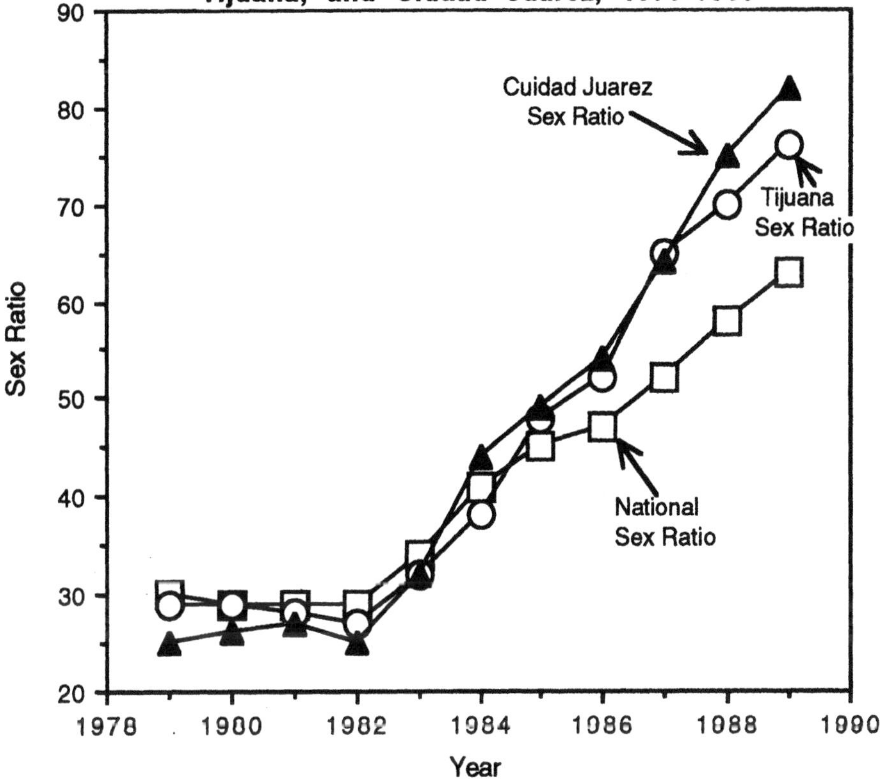

Supporting Data

	Sex Ratio		
	Nation	Tijuana	Ciudad Juarez
1979	30	29	25
1980	29	29	26
1981	29	28	27
1982	29	27	25
1983	34	32	32
1984	41	38	44
1985	45	48	49
1986	47	52	54
1987	52	65	64
1988	58	70	75
1989	63	76	82

SOURCE: INEGI, 1992.

Table 10.7 Maquiladora Employment, Nation and Leading Cities, 1979–1989

	Nation			Tijuana			Ciudad Juarez		
		Laborers			Laborers			Laborers	
Year	Total No. of Employees	No.	Sex Ratio	Total No. of Employees	No.	Sex Ratio	Total No. of Employees	No.	Sex Ratio
1979	111,365	95,818	30	10,889	9,738	29	36,206	31,140	25
1980	119,546	102,020	29	12,343	10,841	29	39,402	336,648	26
1981	130,973	110,684	29	14,482	12,332	28	43,994	37,498	27
1982	127,048	105,383	29	14,959	12,645	27	426,995	35,304	25
1983	150,867	125,278	34	17,423	14,664	32	54,073	44,639	32
1984	199,684	165,505	41	23,047	19,329	38	72,495	59,193	44
1985	211,968	173,874	45	25,913	21,578	48	77,592	62,365	49
1986	249,833	203,894	47	30,248	25,247	52	86,526	69,172	54
1987	305,253	248,638	52	38,575	32,259	65	97,800	78,494	64
1988	369,489	301,379	58	49,779	41,641	70	110,999	88,825	75
1989	429,725	349,602	63	58,029	48,122	76	124,386	99,741	82
				Percent Changes, 1979–1989					
	286	265	112	433	394	163	244	220	227
				Annual Growth Rates, 1979–1989					
	0.053	0.051		0.066	0.063		0.049	0.046	

DEFINITION: Data are numbers of Maquiladora population employed for Nation and Leading Municipios in 1989.

SOURCE: Estadistica de la Industria Maquiladora 1991.

Figure 10.5
Maquiladora Managers and Laborers, 1979-1989

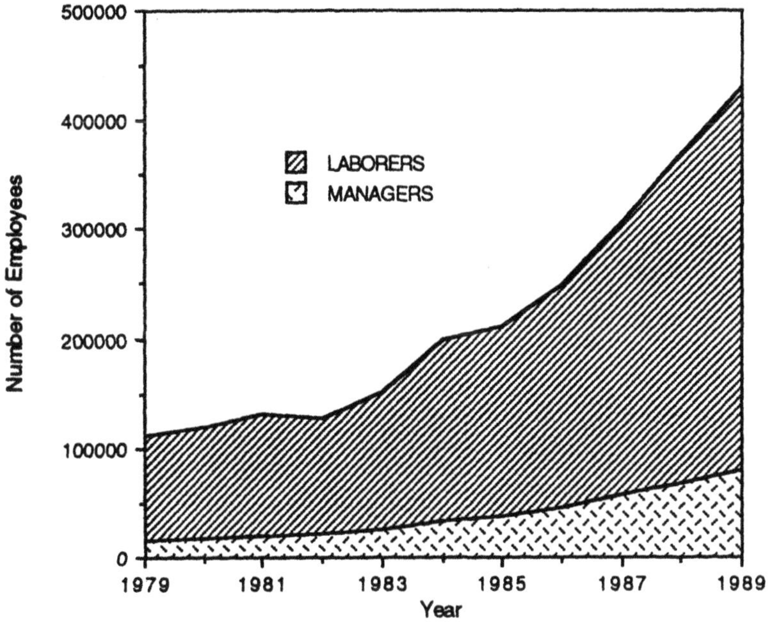

Figure 10.6
Managers as Percent of Maquiladora Work Force, 1979-1989

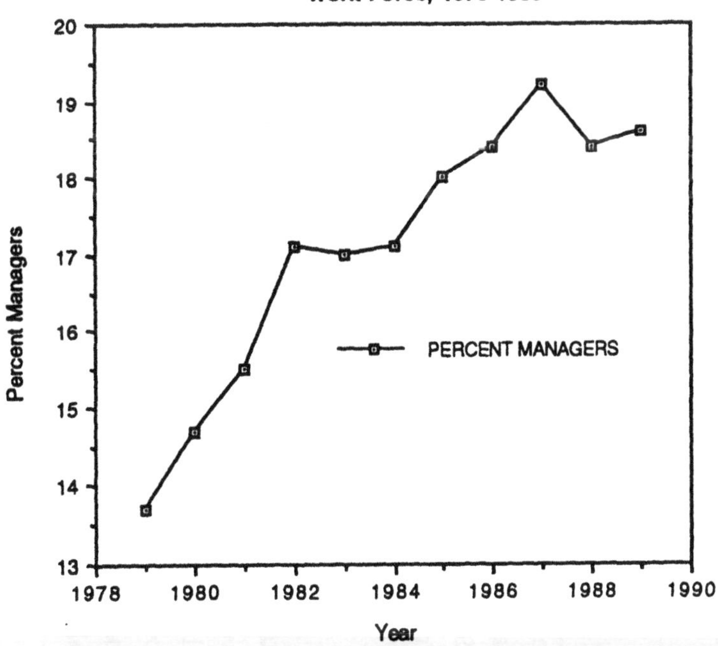

SOURCE: Estadistica de la Industria Maquiladora, 1991.

Table 10.8 Maquiladora Statistics for Nation and Leading Municipios, 1989

	Nation	Mexicali Baja Ca.	Tecate Baja Ca.	Tijuana Baja Ca.	Ciudad Acuna Coah-uila	Piedras Negras Coah-uila	Ciudad Juarez Chihua-hua
Maquiladora Employees	429,725	21,374	4,640	58,029	13,173	8,051	124,386
Laborers	349,602	16,782	3,817	48,122	10,928	6,757	99,741
Sex Ratio of Laborers	63	57	75	76	82	70	82
Production Technicians	50,921	2,890	2,890	50,921	1,638	951	15,713
White Collar Workers	29,202	1,702	1,702	29,202	607	343	8,932
Number of Establishments	1,655	147	71	438	38	39	252
Average Person Hours Worked	65,495	3,140	751	9,564	2,042	1,425	18,073
Salaries *	3,811,892	213,770	34,446	550,676	94,505	49,482	1,177,067
Components - Foreign Imports *	23,177,315	1,345,763	232,770	4,031,353	603,814	148,763	5,994,426
Components - Domestic *	372,520	24,752	627	22,585	508	1,962	62,131
Value Added *	7,499,322	446,423	85,747	1,007,913	147,975	92,357	2,197,102

Table 10.8 Maquiladora Statistics for Nation and Leading Municipios, 1989 (Continued)

	Agua Prieta Sonora	Nogales Sonora	Matamoros Tamaul-ipas	Nuevo Laredo Tamaul-ipas	Reynosa Tamaul-ipas	Other States
Maquiladora Employees	6,806	22,635	38,132	14,747	23,938	93,814
Laborers	5,236	18,089	32,362	12,097	18,660	77,011
Sex Ratio of Laborers	87	99	40	70	58	38
Production Technicians	1,211	3,288	3,852	1,890	28,854	9,941
White Collar Workers	359	1,258	1,918	760	2,424	6,862
Municipio Pop. Maquilad.						
Employees Per Capita						
Number of Establishments	27	68	88	56	60	373
Average Person Hours Worked	1,138	3,625	5,507	2,134	4,089	14,007
Salaries	58,777	215,932	388,052	129,432	211,711	688,039
Components - Foreign Imports	343,626	1,358,878	2,989,486	935,145	1,882,482	4,717,304
Components - Domestic	627	13,733	34,959	3,044	35,249	196,721
Value Added	92,881	347,177	735,411	279,767	441,499	1,625,070

DEFINITION: * in thousands of pesos.

SOURCE: Estadistica de la Industria Maquiladora 1991; INEGI, 1992.

MAP 10.6
MAQUILADORA INDUSTRY, VALUE ADDED, 1990

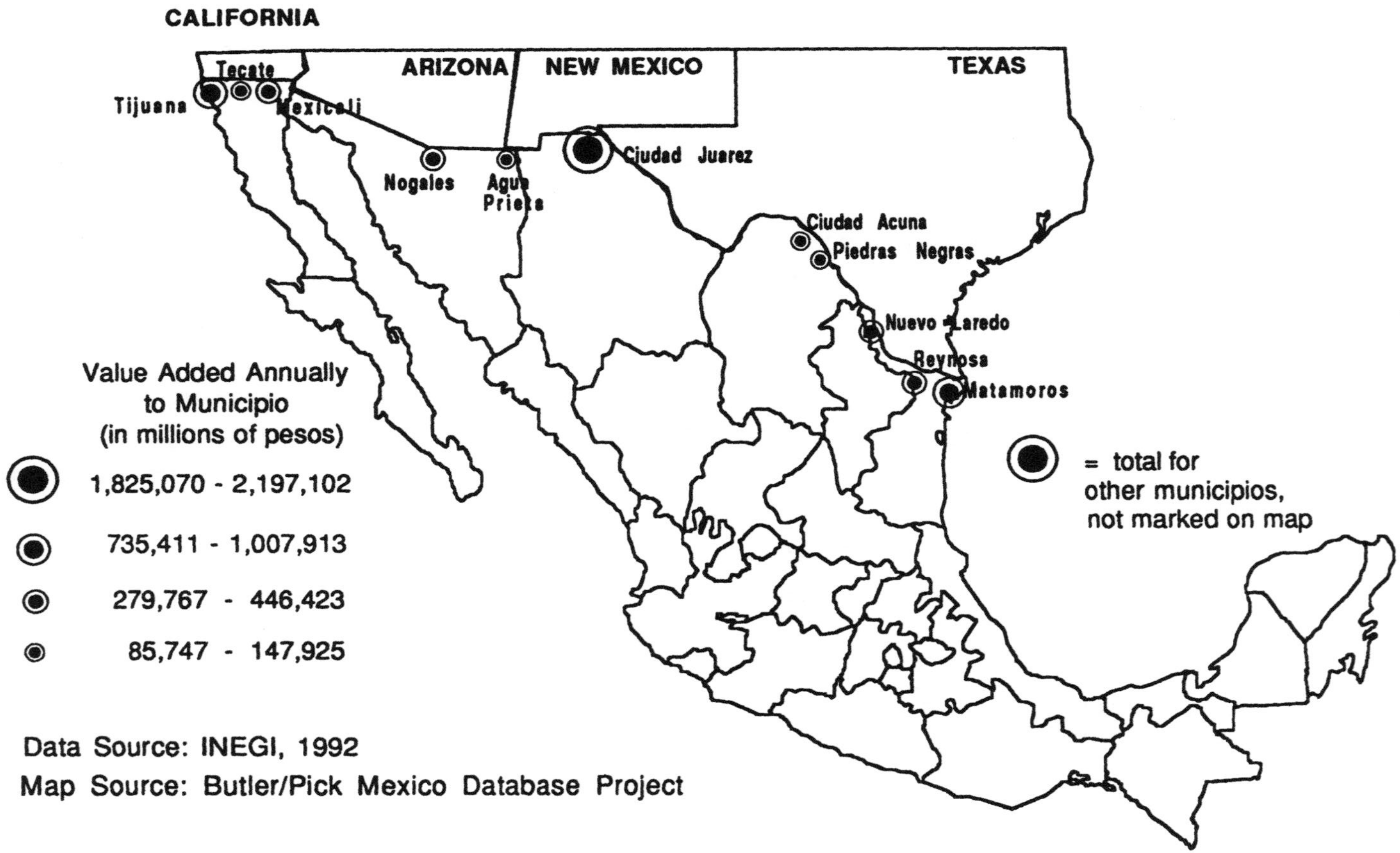

Data Source: INEGI, 1992

Map Source: Butler/Pick Mexico Database Project

11

Politics

- Introduction
- PRI and Opposition Vote: 1934–1988
- Presidential Election, 1988
- Congressional Elections, 1991
- Projected Presidential Election, 1994

Introduction

From a political view, Mexico remained relatively stable between 1934 and 1988. However, in the 1988 presidential election for the first time in anyone's memory the ruling party was seriously challenged. In fact, some argued that the PRI (Institutional Revolutionary Party) only 'won' the election by fraud (Barberan et al. 1988; PAN 1988). In 1986 a small number of persons within the PRI attempted to revise the party by developing what they called the *Democratic Current*. These dissidents may have had enough influence so that the 1988 presidential election was barely won by the ruling party; this time was viewed as being when the political system in Mexico was weakening (Reyna and Butler 1993:189). Neo-Cardenismo, which had largely been unanticipated until 1988, became the byword of the day and the new party made up of Cardenismos (FDN) replaced PAN (National Action Party) as the second-most vote gathering political party in Mexico. It remains to be seen, however, whether the Cardenismos party (now the PRD) will be able to maintain their party as a political force.

This chapter presents information on presidential elections between 1934 and 1988 with an emphasis on political opposition states prior to 1988. Then, information on the 1988 Mexican presidential election is presented. President Carlos Salinas de Gotari who was elected president in 1988 will remain president until 1994 at which time he cannot be re-elected. Thus, in a subsequent part of this chapter, projections are made for the 1994 presidential election. These projections rely primarily upon past election results and the anticipated inability of the PRD to maintain itself as a major political force and the PAN continuing its minority party status. An analysis also is presented of the 1991 congressional elections.

PRI and Opposition Vote, 1934–1988

Support for opposition parties in the 1988 presidential election came primarily from areas and regions in which the PRI's strength was already in decline (Middlebrook 1986; Butler et al. 1991). Table 11.1 shows that, beginning in 1934, states voting in opposition to the PRI could have been identified as early as 1940. While the magnitude of opposition varied between the PRI and opposition, opposition states remained remarkably similar for almost 50 years. Figure 11.1 illustrates the extent of opposition between 1934 and 1988. While information is reported for 1934, there was very little opposition in that election and it appears to have been an anomaly. Figure 11.2 shows opposition vote between 1934 and 1988 for five states—Baja California, Mexico, Michoacan, Morelos, and the Federal District—which over the years have been the states most likely to vote in opposition to the PRI. Table 11.2 shows the non-PRI vote for these states for all presidential elections between 1934 and 1988.

Historically, except for the 1934 presidential election, there are significant correlations between voting for the PRI and all election years and voting for the PRI in the 1988 presidential election (see Butler et al. 1991). Shown below are the correlations between earlier years' elections and 1988 PRI election results.

Election Year	Correlation Between Earlier Years and 1988 PRI Results
1934	-16
1940	36
1946	52
1952	67
1958	28
1964	47
1970	55
1976	41
1982	69

SOURCE: Butler et al. 1991: 35–37.

Variation in the strength of these relationships can be attributed to circumstances of particular elections, including the extent of party competition (1940 and 1952), the personalities involved (1946 and 1952), and structural electoral reforms (1982).

Table 11.1 PRI Presidential Election Results: 1934–1982

No.	State	1934	1940	1946	1952	1958	1964	1970	1976	1982
1	AGUASCALIENTES	95.96	93.89	70.36	67.92	89.25	91.23	87.38	93.81	75.60
2	BAJA CALIFORNIA	97.18	93.92	63.26	61.74	60.67	81.39	74.35	92.42	56.35
3	BAJA CALIFORNIA SUR	99.59		91.68	82.25	93.42	96.83	68.09	94.23	74.11
4	CAMPECHE	0.00	98.06	75.08	86.98	87.73	95.94	98.07	99.62	90.04
5	COAHUILA	93.54	95.06	81.36	80.79	94.88	93.40	91.20	99.76	68.07
6	COLIMA	94.77	95.33	66.83	80.10	89.66	87.33	90.74	97.29	90.48
7	CHIAPAS	0.00	98.05	87.26	90.53	98.00	98.89	98.91	99.55	92.07
8	CHIHUAHUA	99.82	97.09	75.66	63.86	64.60	78.72	81.10	89.34	65.50
9	DISTRITO FEDERAL	97.32	71.99	57.01	51.39	78.87	74.86	69.25	80.38	52.09
10	DURANGO	99.66	96.75	65.37	65.02	84.73	90.00	86.73	98.79	75.94
11	GUANAJUATO	98.71	95.94	63.96	64.12	89.49	79.60	80.82	97.99	67.29
12	GUERRERO	99.98	95.43	85.06	82.48	98.19	96.95	95.68	98.74	84.17
13	HIDALGO	99.99	99.46	90.35	88.69	98.09	98.36	97.16	96.48	84.49
14	JALISCO	99.09	98.71	78.89	64.70	88.95	87.02	82.76	93.85	59.79
15	MEXICO	99.78	94.86	84.05	81.06	98.92	91.72	84.66	90.57	59.09
16	MICHOACAN	98.83	92.90	67.33	55.37	87.20	86.00	86.77	97.77	78.19
17	MORELOS	99.76	98.13	57.31	68.46	95.83	94.21	90.29	92.21	76.75
18	NAYARIT	99.99	96.98	85.27	97.33	98.68	91.62	96.49	97.06	80.61
19	NUEVO LEON	84.45	89.32	70.40	80.83	90.33	84.26	84.18	90.45	72.66
20	OAXACA	99.95	99.36	90.20	79.76	95.62	96.64	96.57	99.73	84.53
21	PUEBLA	99.26	98.83	81.85	80.87	95.24	93.65	85.50	95.46	83.93
22	QUERETARO		95.72	91.42	95.25	79.88	96.58	98.21	97.65	92.18
23	QUINTANA ROO	99.46	98.75	84.30	82.00	89.50	91.29	90.74	97.07	78.29
24	SAN LUIS POTOSI	99.92	98.18	80.15	88.90	94.33	91.57	90.23	97.76	84.14
25	SINALOA	97.65	89.51	89.89	68.27	98.09	98.07	94.57	97.93	79.23
26	SONORA	99.91	92.42	81.49	81.09	97.28	98.36	93.50	99.55	76.14
27	TABASCO	0.00	99.83	95.58	79.33	98.85	99.33	98.85	99.57	92.57
28	TAMAULIPAS	97.15	88.09	72.41	69.53	94.78	96.51	91.62	96.08	77.64
29	TLAXCALA	99.61	95.64	81.09	81.22	98.39	98.43	94.31	99.98	82.13
30	VERACRUZ	99.06	94.80	90.54	91.53	97.63	96.80	92.67	98.50	83.01
31	YUCATAN	99.39	88.08	75.94	81.48	77.38	85.38	85.27	92.59	80.27
32	ZACATECAS	93.82	94.32	67.63	71.78	91.73	79.48	90.75	98.57	86.16
National Total		98.19	93.89	77.91	74.32	90.56	88.62	85.80	93.60	71.00
Mean		88.50	94.69	78.09	77.02	90.51	91.26	88.98	95.96	77.61
Median		99.09	95.64	80.62	80.81	93.88	92.56	90.74	97.47	78.76
S.D.		29.61	5.34	10.70	11.42	9.46	6.93	8.02	4.19	10.60
C.V.		33.46	5.64	13.70	14.83	10.46	7.59	9.02	4.37	13.66
Minimum		0.00	71.99	57.01	51.39	60.67	74.86	68.09	80.38	52.09
Maximum		99.99	99.83	95.58	97.33	98.92	99.33	98.91	99.98	92.57

DEFINITION: Percent of official vote for the PRI candidate.

SOURCE: Ponce and Alonso, 1987.

FIGURE 11.1
PRI AND NON-PRI VOTE: MEXICAN PRESIDENTIAL ELECTIONS, 1934 - 1988

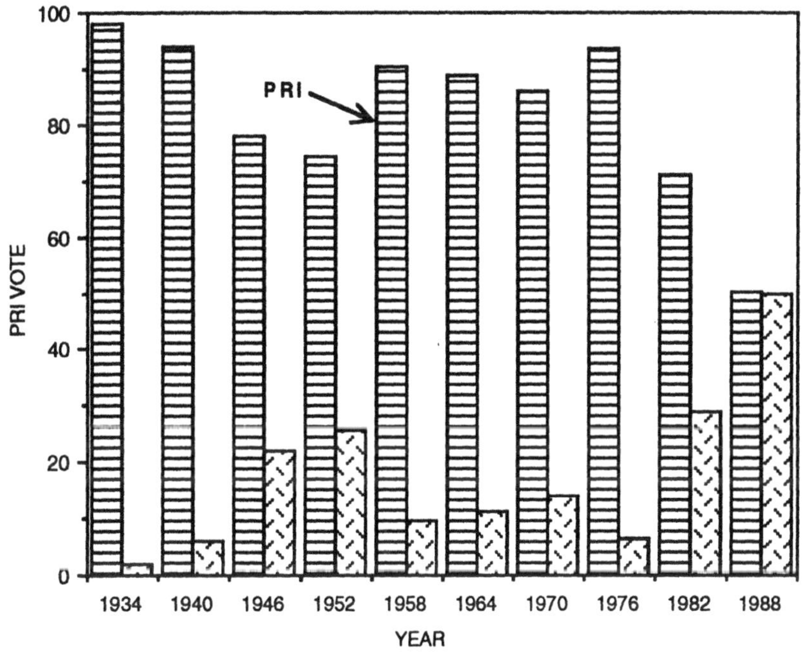

DEFINITION: Percent of official vote for the PRI candidate vs. vote for all other candidates.

SOURCE: Ponce and Alonso (1987) and Proceso Electoral Federal (July 7, 1988).

Figure 11.2
Non-PRI Vote: Mexican Presidential Elections, 1934-1988

Non-PRI Presidential Vote: National and Baja California

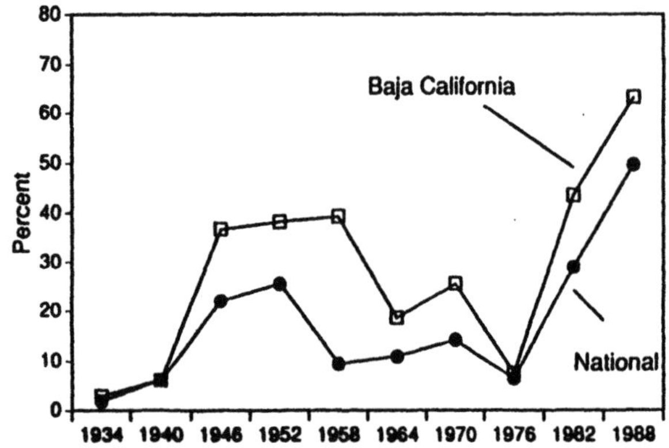

Non-PRI Presidential Vote: National and Federal District

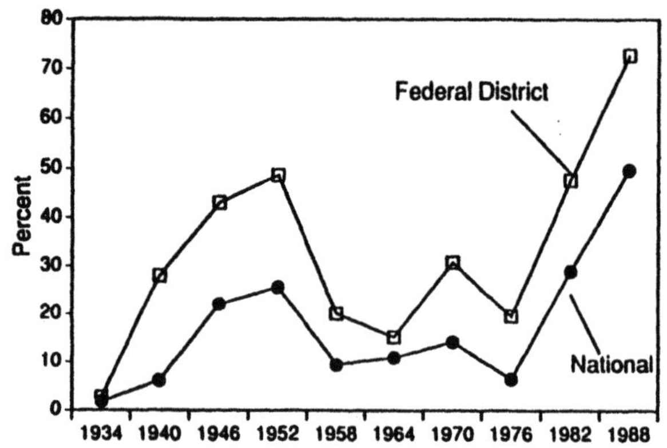

Non-PRI Presidential Vote: National and Mexico

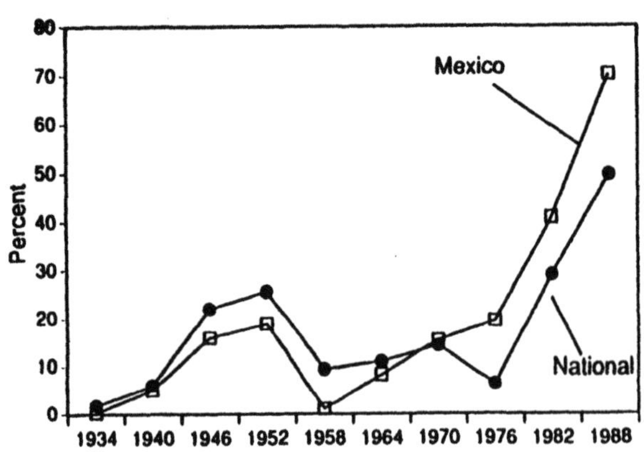

Figure 11.2 Continued
Non-PRI Vote: Mexican Presidential Elections, 1934-1988

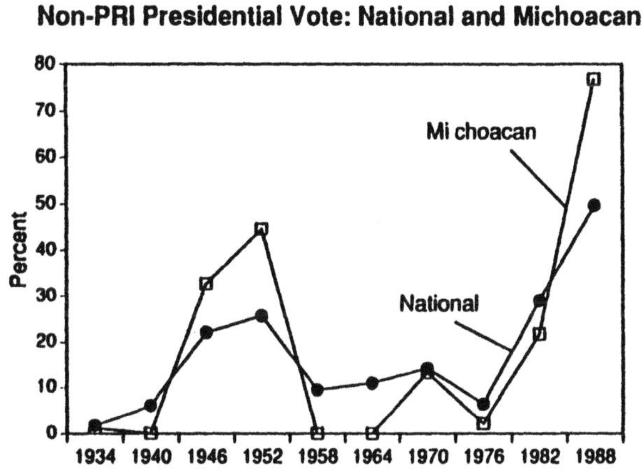

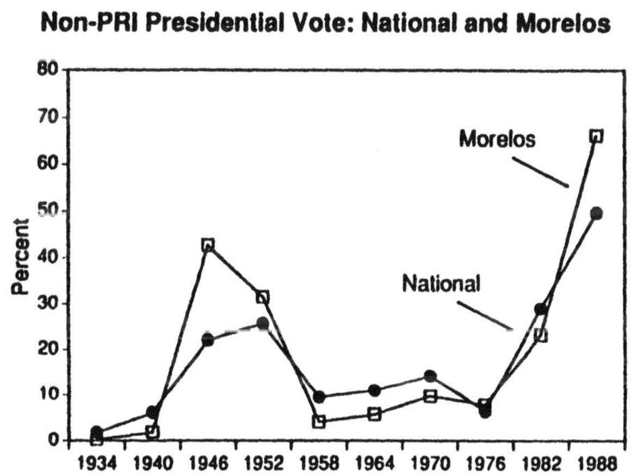

Table 11.2 Non-PRI Presidential Vote: 1934 –1988

Year	Baja California Percent	Federal District Percent	Mexico Percent	Michoacan Percent	Morelos Percent	National Average Percent
1934	2.8200	2.6800	0.2200	1.1700	0.2400	1.8100
1940	6.0800	28.0100	5.1400	0.1000	1.8700	6.1000
1946	36.7400	42.9900	15.9500	32.6700	42.6900	22.0900
1952	38.2600	48.6100	18.9400	44.6300	31.5400	25.6700
1958	39.3300	20.1300	1.0800	0.0000	4.1700	9.4400
1964	18.6100	15.2700	8.2800	0.0000	5.7900	10.9500
1970	25.6500	30.7700	15.3400	13.2300	9.7100	14.2000
1976	7.5800	19.6200	19.4300	2.2300	7.7900	6.4000
1982	43.5700	47.5900	40.8700	21.7900	23.2300	29.0000
1988	63.3400	72.7500	70.2100	76.7900	66.2600	49.6400

DEFINITION: Percent of vote for all Non-PRI parties.

SOURCE: Ponce and Alonso (1987) and Proceso Electoral Federal, July 7, 1988.

Presidential Election, 1988[1]

Prior to the Mexican presidential election of 1988, there was widespread discontent with the political process in Mexico. With the PAN on the right and the FDN on the left, virtually everyone knowledgeable about Mexico expected more formidable opposition to the PRI in 1988 than in any previous election. Election results showed great electoral opposition; at least for the moment there appeared to some to be a radical shift taking place in Mexican politics.

Of particular interest in any election is voter participation or turnout. As shown in Table 11.3, the official voter participation rate was just over 50 percent with substantial variation among states (Butler and Bustamante 1991; Proceso Electoral Federal 1988). The range was from a high of 64.39 percent in Puebla to a low of 37.9 percent in Coahuila. There was no discernible regional pattern except states surrounding the Federal District generally had higher rates of voter participation than the rest of the country and the border region had lower rates (see Map 11.1). In a statistical analysis of voter turnout and voting for the PAN, PRI, or FDN, no consistent pattern was found since voter turnout correlations with the PRI was R = .09, with the FDN - .08, and - .01 with the PAN (Butler et al. 1991). As with elections in the U.S., if a comparison is made between those totally eligible to register and to vote, the president was elected by less than a majority of the population.

As in past elections in Mexico, there was variation in voting for the PRI by state. Official voting figures gave the PRI slightly over 50 percent of the vote. According to the official election results reported in Table 11.3, the PRI candidate carried 27 of the 32 states. In three of these states, Salinas had only a relative majority—Colima, Guanajuato, and Jalisco. Table 11.3 and Map 11.2 illustrate that the major support for the PRI came from the southern states of Campeche, Chiapas, Puebla, Tabasco, and Yucatan, as well as from Nuevo Leon, San Luis Potosi, and Sonora. Statistical analyses of the 1988 election showed that the larger the urban population, the lower the PRI vote. Also, the higher the level of education in a state the lower was the vote for the PRI (Butler et al. 1991).

The PAN did not win one state vote in the 1988 election and its vote share of 17 percent was very similar to its percentage in previous elections. Clearly, it appears that despite general dissatisfaction with the political process in Mexico, the PAN was unable to capitalize upon this dissatisfaction. PAN's major support came from the states of Aguascalientes, Chihuahua, the Federal District, Guanajuato, Jalisco, and Sinaloa, with indications of strength in Nuevo Leon and Yucatan (see Map 11.3). Thus, the PAN must be considered a regional party with its primary strength being in the border region and selected urban areas. The PAN vote, however, was associated with education, literacy, and medium and higher level incomes that may bode well for future elections.

Despite being a new coalitional party, the FDN was able to mobilize almost twice the vote of the PAN, receiving 32 percent of the total vote cast, according to official election results. As shown in Table 11.3 and Map 11.4, the FDN carried

---

1 For a more extensive analysis of the 1988 presidential election, see Butler and Busatamente (1991). Also see Butler et al. (1991) for a critique of the official election results.

the adjoining states of Mexico, Morelos, and Michoacan, the candidate's home state. In the Federal District, the FDN vote was nearly a majority (49.2 percent). The FDN also carried Baja California by a slight majority and was especially strong in Colima and Guerrero. As shown on Map 11.4, the FDN's major support is in and around the Federal District, with the addition of Baja California.

Overall, the greatest distinction among state vote for particular political parties was between the PRI and FDN (r = - .78), with the relationship between the PRI and PAN being - .29, and the correlation of the FDN and PAN vote being - .38.

Both the PAN and FDN candidate parties believed that they had actually received a much larger share of the vote and charged fraud (Barberan et al. 1988; PAN 1988). Table 11.4 presents the official vote for the PRI as reported by the *Processo Electoral Federal* on July 7, 1988, immediately after the election, and PAN surveys reportedly conducted during the same time period (PAN 1988). The FDN analyzed official election results by *casillas* (e.g., precincts) and concluded that extensive fraud had been committed (Barberan et al. 1988). As Table 11.4 and Map 11.5 demonstrate, there were some states with a high correspondence between official results and PAN surveys while other states had great discrepancies.

The main caveat to remember in comparing these election results here is that the PAN surveys did not cover all of the voting districts in some states, thus the differences could be a result of fraud or of actual vote differences in voting districts of those states. For example, in Baja California the PAN surveys covered all voting districts and the comparability of results was great; however, if the PAN surveys were accurate, rather than the FDN winning the state the PRI would have!

Table 11.3 Presidential Vote, 1988

No.	State	Total Vote	Perc. Vote for PRI	Perc. Vote for FDN	Perc. Vote for PAN	Perc. Vote for Other	Perc. of Voting Pop.
1	AGUASCALIENTES	168,899	50.21	18.67	28.42	2.70	50.43
2	BAJA CALIFORNIA	413,953	36.66	37.19	24.39	1.77	50.64
3	BAJA CALIFORNIA SUR	85,643	54.02	25.87	19.00	1.10	56.96
4	CAMPECHE	116,107	70.88	16.30	12.37	0.46	50.49
5	COAHUILA	328,239	54.27	29.95	15.34	0.43	37.89
6	COLIMA	97,316	47.83	35.74	14.80	1.63	44.63
7	CHIAPAS	658,195	89.91	6.45	3.39	0.24	55.36
8	CHIHUAHUA	521,995	54.58	6.77	38.19	0.46	40.31
9	DISTRITO FEDERAL	2,904,169	27.25	49.22	22.01	1.52	57.00
10	DURANGO	356,446	63.63	18.82	16.99	0.56	52.24
11	GUANAJUATO	726,312	44.03	22.01	29.93	4.03	46.18
12	GUERRERO	510,797	60.53	35.80	2.44	1.23	42.54
13	HIDALGO	421,893	64.72	28.26	5.84	1.19	51.94
14	JALISCO	1,194,247	42.57	23.87	30.76	2.80	47.49
15	MEXICO	2,331,479	29.79	51.58	16.33	2.30	55.64
16	MICHOACAN	614,899	23.21	64.16	10.28	2.35	40.18
17	MORELOS	278,208	33.74	57.65	7.44	1.17	47.67
18	NAYARIT	205,214	56.56	36.80	5.72	0.91	50.63
19	NUEVO LEON	704,156	72.08	3.83	23.70	0.39	46.65
20	OAXACA	628,155	63.81	30.25	4.63	1.30	46.03
21	PUEBLA	1,091,658	71.55	17.69	9.87	0.89	64.39
22	QUERETARO	238,058	63.34	15.81	19.43	1.42	58.15
23	QUINTANA ROO	94,322	65.70	24.14	9.69	0.47	50.12
24	SAN LUIS POTOSI	380,418	68.25	8.81	21.15	1.79	43.81
25	SINALOA	623,904	50.81	16.75	32.07	0.37	56.01
26	SONORA	410,386	68.59	9.98	20.85	0.59	45.64
27	TABASCO	268,071	74.30	19.94	5.25	0.51	42.24
28	TAMAULIPAS	470,309	59.33	30.15	9.91	0.61	41.98
29	TLAXCALA	184,000	60.21	31.00	5.88	2.92	55.44
30	VERACRUZ	1,516,257	62.59	31.05	5.21	1.16	49.78
31	YUCATAN	307,657	67.08	1.61	31.19	0.12	51.10
32	ZACATECAS	293,650	66.17	22.31	10.77	0.76	48.72
National Total			1818.20	828.43	513.24	40.15	1578.28
Mean		598,282	56.82	25.89	16.04	1.25	49.32
Median			60.37	24.01	15.07	1.13	49.95
S.D.		615,775	15.11	15.15	9.94	0.93	6.10
C.V.		102.92	26.59	58.51	61.98	74.22	12.36
Minimum		85,643	23.21	1.61	2.44	0.12	37.89
Maximum		2,904,169	89.91	64.16	38.19	4.03	64.39

DEFINITION: Percent of official vote.

SOURCE: Proceso Electoral Federal, July 7, 1988.

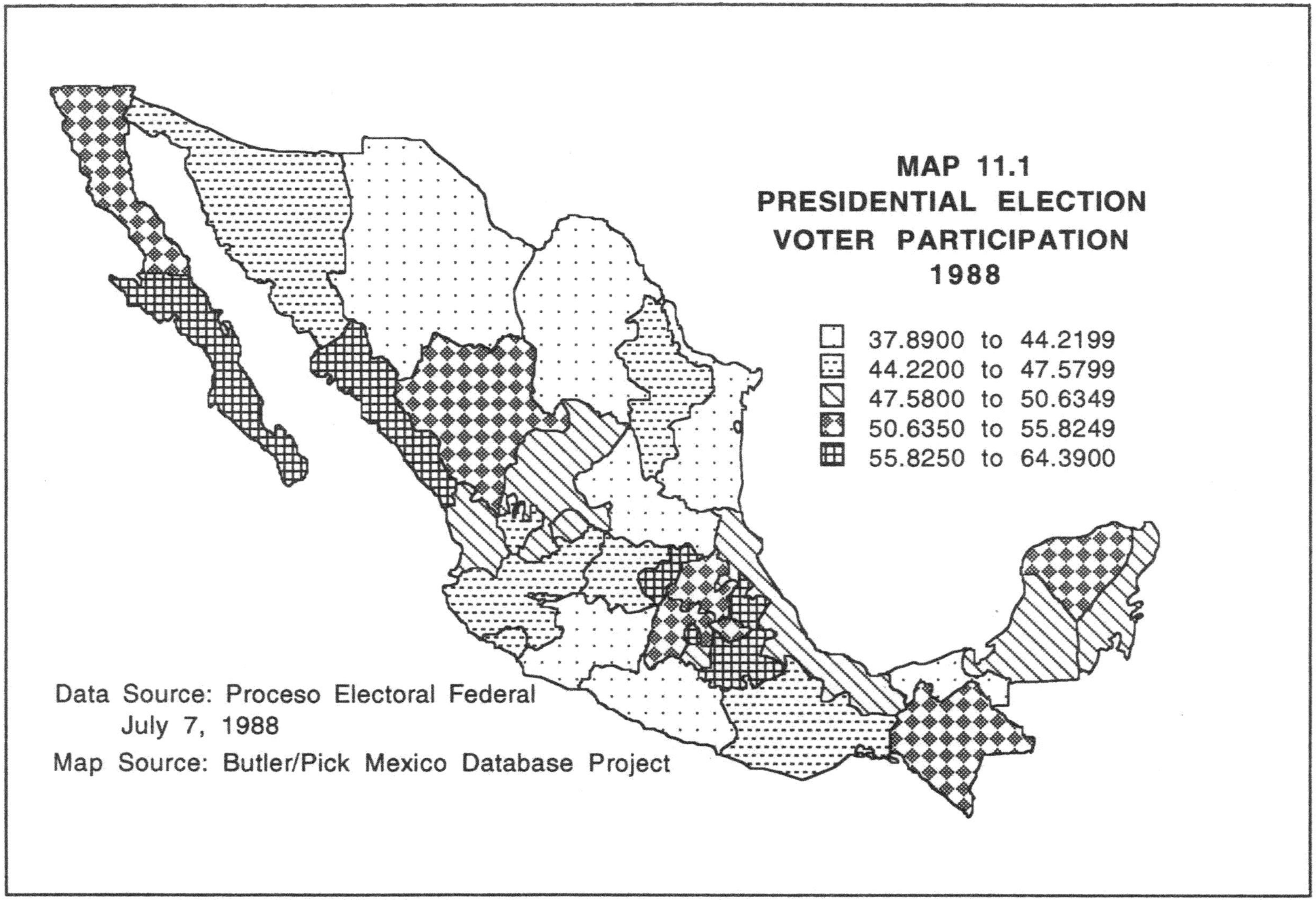

MAP 11.1
PRESIDENTIAL ELECTION
VOTER PARTICIPATION
1988

MAP 11.2
PRESIDENTIAL VOTE – PRI
1988

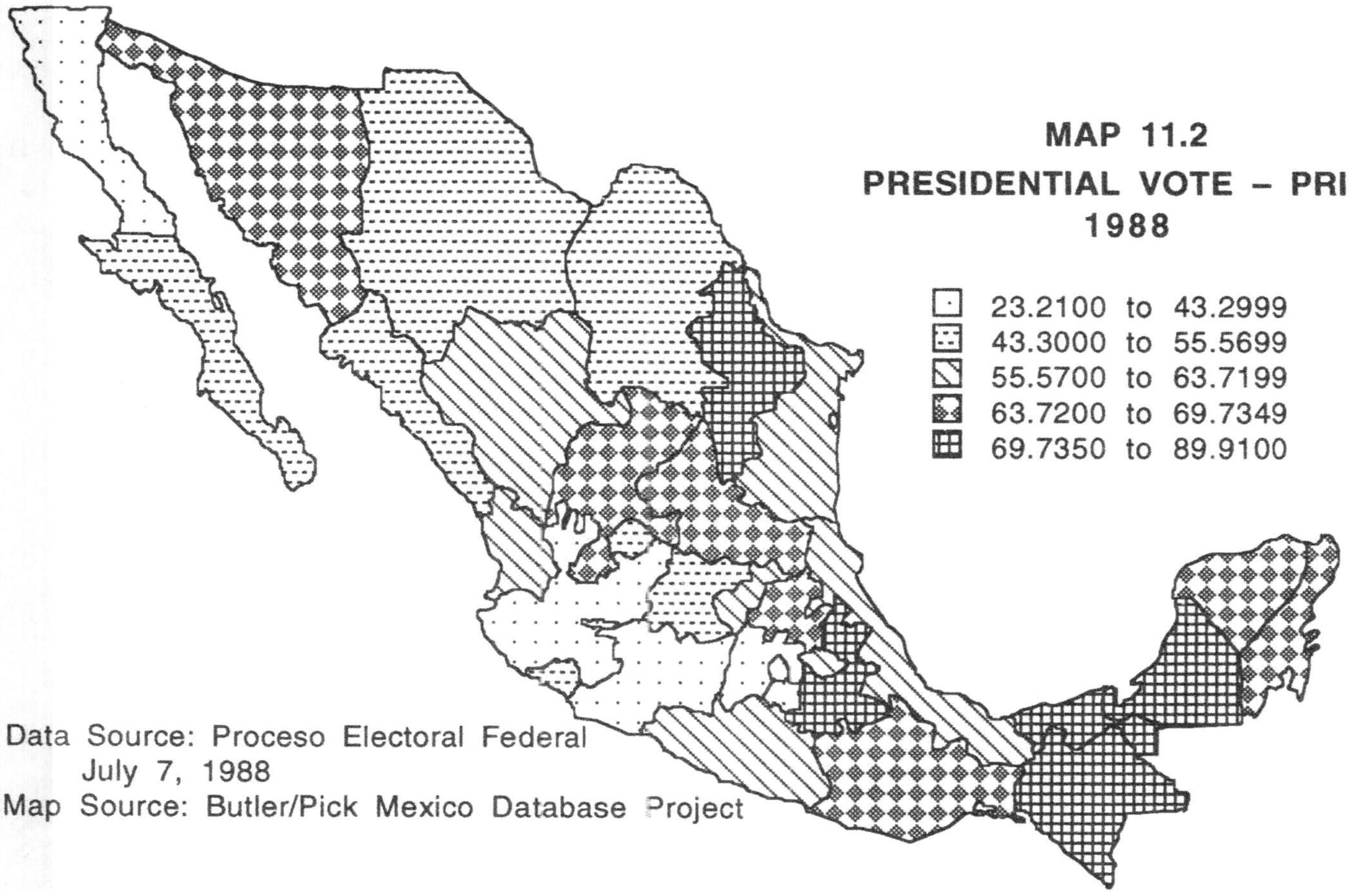

Data Source: Proceso Electoral Federal
July 7, 1988
Map Source: Butler/Pick Mexico Database Project

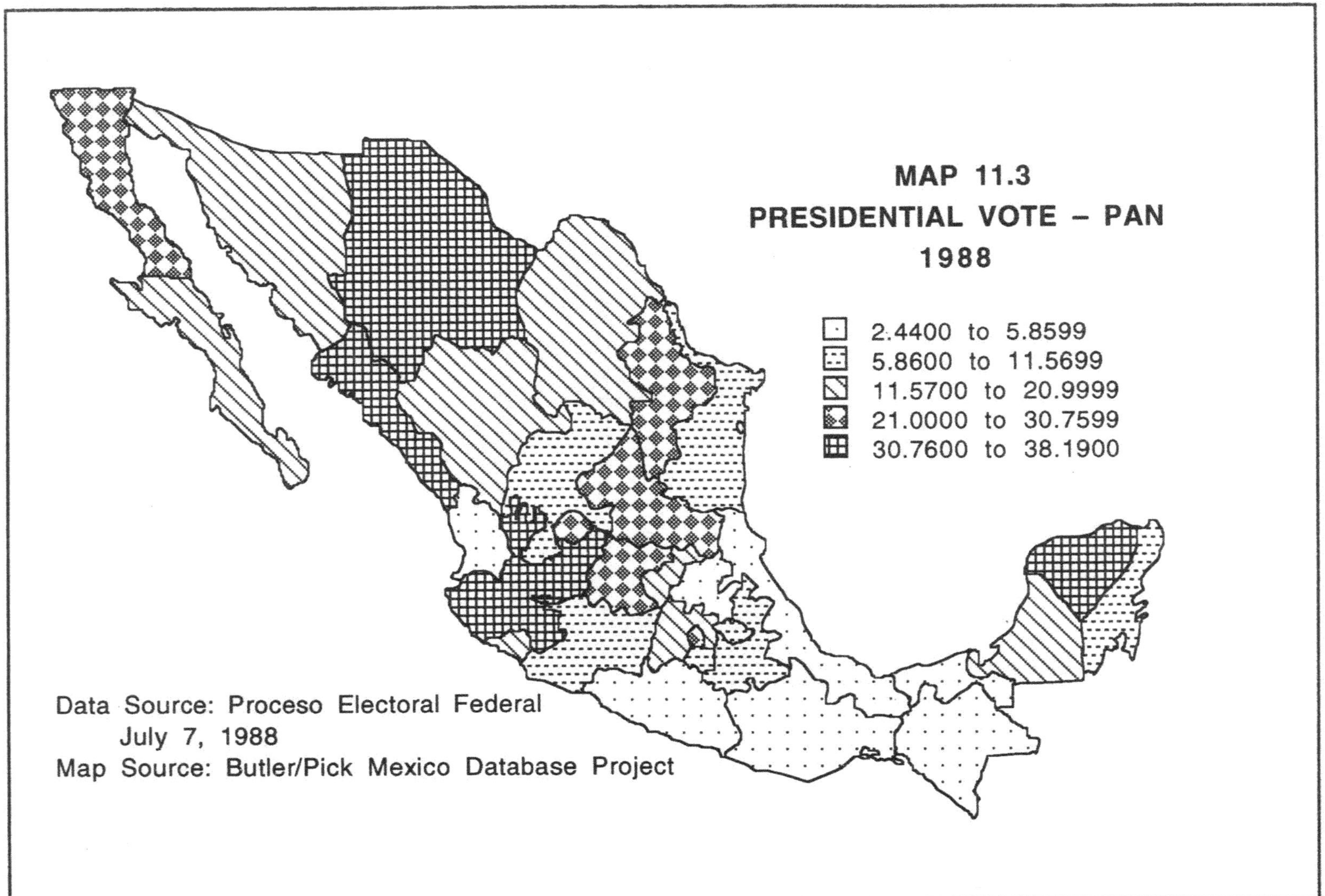
MAP 11.3
PRESIDENTIAL VOTE – PAN
1988
2.4400 to 5.8599
5.8600 to 11.5699
11.5700 to 20.9999
21.0000 to 30.7599
30.7600 to 38.1900
Data Source: Proceso Electoral Federal
July 7, 1988
Map Source: Butler/Pick Mexico Database Project

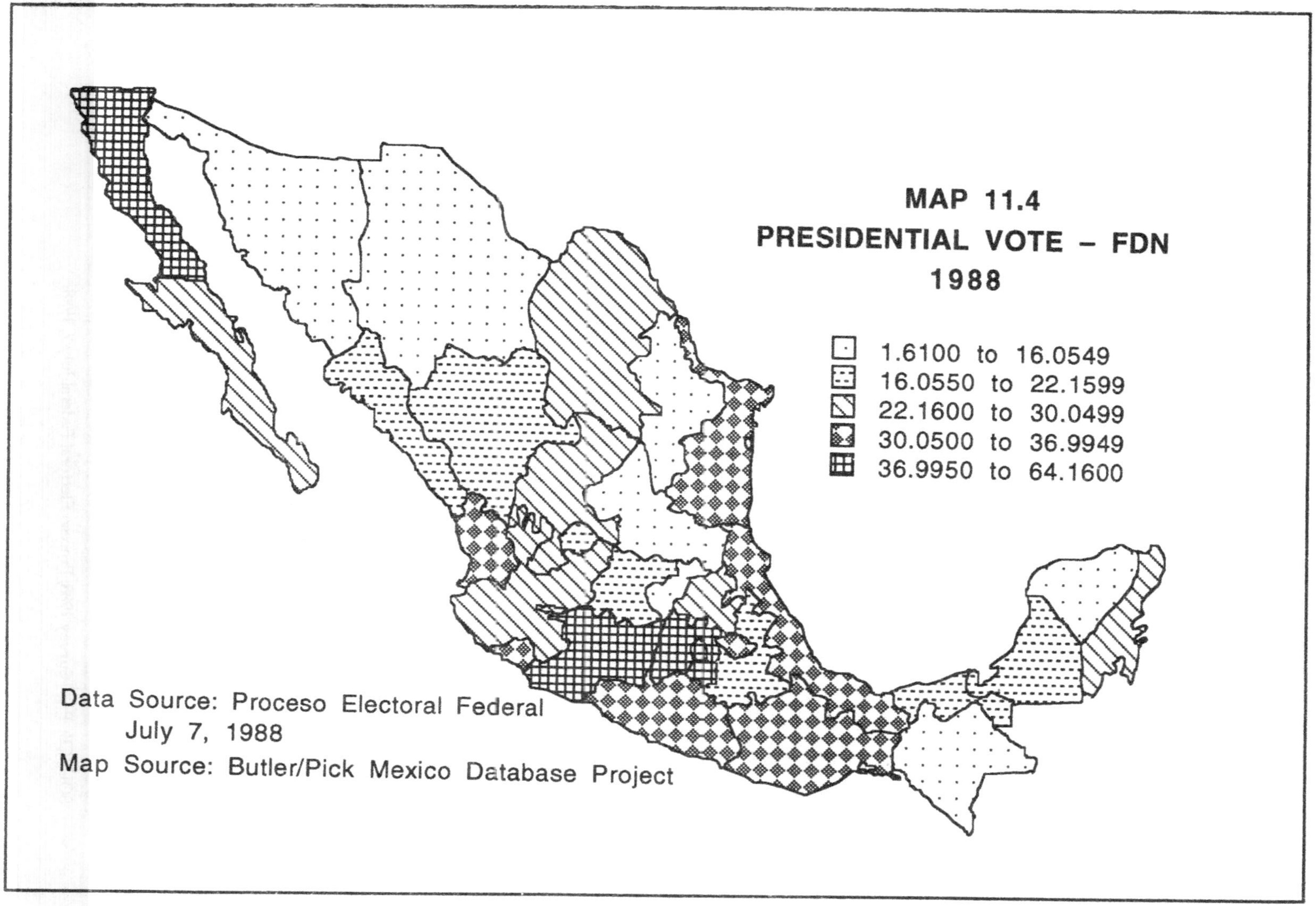
MAP 11.4
PRESIDENTIAL VOTE – FDN
1988
1.6100 to 16.0549
16.0550 to 22.1599
22.1600 to 30.0499
30.0500 to 36.9949
36.9950 to 64.1600
Data Source: Proceso Electoral Federal
July 7, 1988
Map Source: Butler/Pick Mexico Database Project

Table 11.4 Official Election Results and PAN Survey, 1988

No.	State	PAN Survey Percent Salinas	Official Election Results Perc. Salinas	Perc. Difference in Electoral Results
1	AGUASCALIENTES	45.8000	50.3000	4.5000
2	BAJA CALIFORNIA	34.2000	36.4000	2.2000
3	BAJA CALIFORNIA SUR	49.5000	53.9000	4.4000
4	CAMPECHE	44.3000	71.2000	26.9000
5	COAHUILA	46.9000	54.2000	7.3000
6	COLIMA	48.7000	47.8000	-0.9000
7	CHIAPAS	51.6000	89.8000	38.2000
8	CHIHUAHUA	44.2000	54.3000	10.1000
9	DISTRITO FERERAL	27.2000	27.1000	-0.1000
10	DURANGO	46.0000	63.5000	17.5000
11	GUANAJUATO	27.7000	43.8000	16.1000
12	GUERRERO	29.2000	60.4000	31.2000
13	HIDALGO	39.7000	64.8000	22.5000
14	JALISCO	42.3000	42.5000	0.2000
15	MEXICO	21.0000	35.4000	-4.3000
16	MICHOACAN	21.6000	23.6000	2.0000
17	MORELOS	29.2000	35.4000	6.2000
18	NAYARIT	42.2000	56.6000	14.4000
19	NUEVO LEON	51.7000	71.7000	20.0000
20	OAXACA	32.5000	64.6000	32.1000
21	PUELBA	15.5000	72.2000	56.7000
22	QUERETARO	60.2000	63.4000	3.2000
23	QUINTANA ROO	45.6000	65.7000	20.1000
24	SAN LUIS POTOSI	46.1000	68.2000	22.1000
25	SINALOA	47.4000	60.0000	12.6000
26	SONORA	42.4000	68.5000	26.1000
27	TABASCO	48.9000	74.2000	25.3000
28	TAMAULIPAS	41.6000	59.2000	17.6000
29	TLAXCALA	36.4000	60.1000	23.7000
30	VERACRUZ	33.4000	61.9000	28.5000
31	YUCATAN	53.9000	66.1000	12.2000
32	ZACATECAS			
Mean		39.6120	55.0720	14.6080
Median		44.2000	56.6000	12.6000
S.D.		11.3040	15.7601	14.5327
C.V.		28.54	28.62	99.48
Minimum		15.5000	23.6000	-4.3000
Maximum		60.2000	89.8000	56.7000

SOURCE: PAN Survey 1988; Proceso Electoral Federal July 7, 1988.

MAP 11.5
OFFICIAL ELECTION RESULTS AND PAN SURVEY, 1988

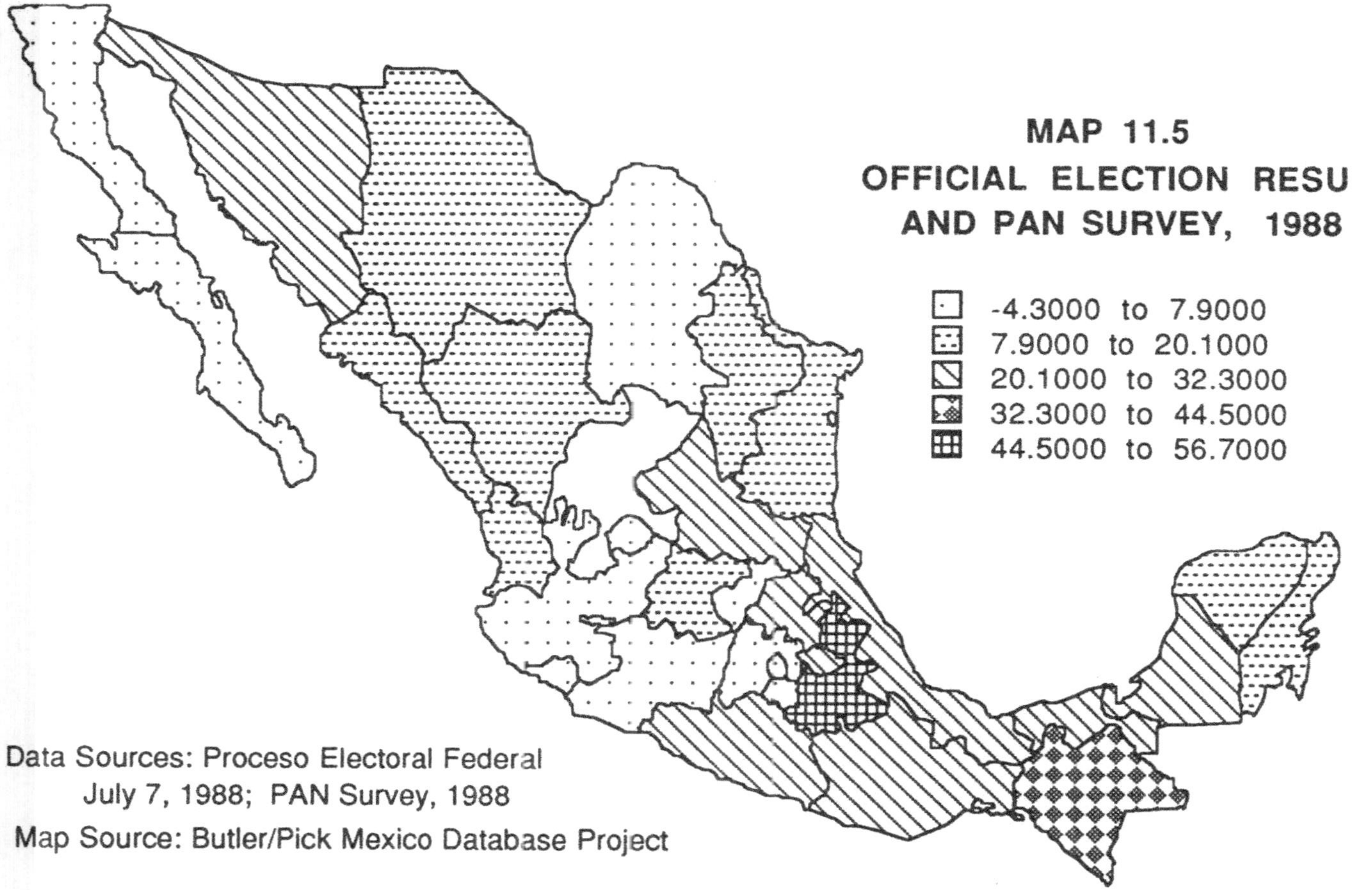

Data Sources: Proceso Electoral Federal
July 7, 1988; PAN Survey, 1988
Map Source: Butler/Pick Mexico Database Project

Congressional Elections, 1991

The most recent national elections in Mexico were the congressional elections of 1991. Table 11.5 presents the results of that election. Nationwide voter participation was 65.14 percent, substantially higher than for the 1988 presidential election. As with most elections, there was substantial variation in voter participation. Map 11.6 illustrates that the highest participation rates were in the Federal District, the state of Mexico, Baja California—long time opposition states, and Chiapas. Also, as shown on Map 11.6, states surrounding the Federal District had high participation rates. Most of these states also had high participation rates in the 1988 presidential election (see Map 11.1).

Knowing the state election results for the PRI, PAN, and FDN/PRD presidential vote in 1988 predicted very accurately the congressional vote in 1991. Thus, states and dimensions, such as agricultural labor force, urbanization, income, and educational levels that predicted the presidential vote in 1988 also were systematically associated with similar party vote in the 1991 congressional election vote, although the PRI increased its margin.

As shown on Map 11.7, congressional vote for the PRI in the 1991 elections was concentrated in the southern part of the country, much like in the 1988 presidential election (see Map 11.2). Only Tamaulipas in the northern region had a relatively high vote for PRI candidates. The 1991 congressional vote for the PAN (see Map 11.8) also was consistent with the 1988 presidential election vote (see Map 11.3) implying that the party remains a regional one with the north being its stronghold. Yucatan, as in some previous elections, also voted relatively heavily for PAN candidates. Map 11.9 shows the vote for 'other' political parties in the 1991 congressional elections. The vote is concentrated in areas where in the 1988 presidential election the FDN had shown strength. However, on the basis of this election it would have to be concluded that the FDN (as it emerged to become the PRD) has lost much of the influence it gained in the 1988 presidential election.

Table 11.5 Congressional Elections, Mexico, 1991

No.	State	Eligible Voting Pop.	Perc. of Total Pop. *	Total Vote	Perc. of Voting Pop.	Perc. PRI	Perc. PAN	Perc. PRD	Perc. Other	Perc. Non PRI, Non PAN
1	AGUASCALIENTES	313,355	43.54	215,711	68.84	63.80	18.83	0.62	16.74	17.36
2	BAJA CALIFORNIA	768,567	46.28	596,359	77.59	43.79	42.81	1.40	12.00	13.40
3	BAJA CALIF. SUR	144,112	45.35	92,865	64.44	64.56	23.82	1.44	10.19	11.63
4	CAMPECHE	221,126	41.32	155,121	70.15	74.01	3.20	3.98	18.81	22.79
5	COAHUILA	872,529	44.24	479,276	54.93	61.28	20.53	6.99	11.19	18.18
6	COLIMA	186,358	43.49	123,264	66.14	63.71	13.59	8.22	14.47	22.69
7	CHIAPAS	1,358,163	42.30	891,281	65.62	72.57	5.85	5.65	15.93	21.58
8	CHIHUAHUA	1,117,988	45.78	735,644	65.80	56.33	31.20	2.11	10.37	12.47
9	DISTRITO FEDERAL	4,511,172	54.78	3,431,829	76.07	44.25	19.03	11.51	25.22	36.73
10	DURANGO	554,710	41.11	335,794	60.54	60.11	16.00	5.62	18.27	23.88
11	GUANAJUATO	1,650,677	41.45	1,226,456	74.30	50.77	31.80	4.49	12.95	17.43
12	GUERRERO	1,011,206	38.59	509,305	50.37	60.42	2.82	23.65	13.11	36.76
13	HIDALGO	815,419	43.18	496,474	60.89	69.04	7.12	8.06	15.78	23.85
14	JALISCO	2,306,792	43.50	1,594,326	69.11	60.24	22.68	2.58	14.51	17.08
15	MEXICO	4,505,685	45.90	3,080,852	68.38	48.99	16.28	10.06	24.67	34.73
16	MICHOACAN	1,459,585	41.14	987,908	67.68	51.31	8.29	29.69	10.72	40.41
17	MORELOS	532,982	44.60	306,991	57.60	63.52	7.22	11.88	17.38	29.26
18	NAYARIT	350,160	42.46	200,202	57.17	67.39	3.90	12.34	16.38	28.71
19	NUEVO LEON	1,468,664	47.40	597,729	40.70	66.94	25.36	1.21	6.49	7.70
20	OAXACA	1,229,861	40.73	653,812	53.16	71.35	5.35	9.24	14.06	23.30
21	PUEBLA	1,853,031	44.91	1,207,300	65.15	66.63	14.29	4.40	14.68	19.08
22	QUERETARO	424,692	40.40	315,442	74.28	67.55	20.27	2.36	9.83	12.18
23	QUINTANA ROO	208,214	42.21	116,612	56.01	73.42	11.28	5.58	9.71	15.30
24	SAN LUIS POTOSI	834,981	41.68	540,368	64.72	60.87	28.91	1.29	8.94	10.22
25	SINALOA	986,004	44.74	646,693	65.59	63.81	24.71	4.70	6.77	11.47
26	SONORA	794,423	43.58	500,055	62.95	66.64	23.47	3.21	6.68	9.89
27	TABASCO	660,883	44.01	359,170	54.35	68.00	2.21	17.67	12.13	29.79
28	TAMAULIPAS	1,002,932	44.58	660,496	65.86	61.16	14.19	3.60	21.05	24.65
29	TLAXCALA	349,486	45.91	222,849	63.76	71.38	8.15	5.99	14.48	20.47
30	VERACRUZ	3,037,232	48.77	1,864,388	61.38	72.50	4.81	5.78	16.92	22.70
31	YUCATAN	615,685	45.17	380,107	61.74	59.52	34.68	0.23	5.57	5.80
32	ZACATECAS	548,686	42.99	377,020	68.71	73.47	8.76	6.87	10.90	17.77
	National Total	36,695,360	45.16	23,901,699	65.14	58.63	17.09	7.88	16.39	24.28
	Mean	1,146,730	43.94	746928.09	63.56	63.10	16.29	6.95	13.65	20.60
	Median	825,200	43.56	504680.00	64.94	63.81	15.15	5.60	13.59	19.78
	S.D.	1090970.18	2.91	780812.92	7.72	8.10	10.42	6.46	4.77	8.72
	C.V.	95.14	6.62	104.54	12.14	12.84	63.94	93.02	34.94	42.35
	Minimum	144,112	38.59	92865.00	40.70	43.79	2.21	0.23	5.57	5.80
	Maximum	4,511,172	54.78	3431829.00	77.59	74.01	42.81	29.69	25.22	40.41

NOTE: * Percent of Total Population Eligible to Vote.

SOURCE: Instituto Federal Electoral, 1991.

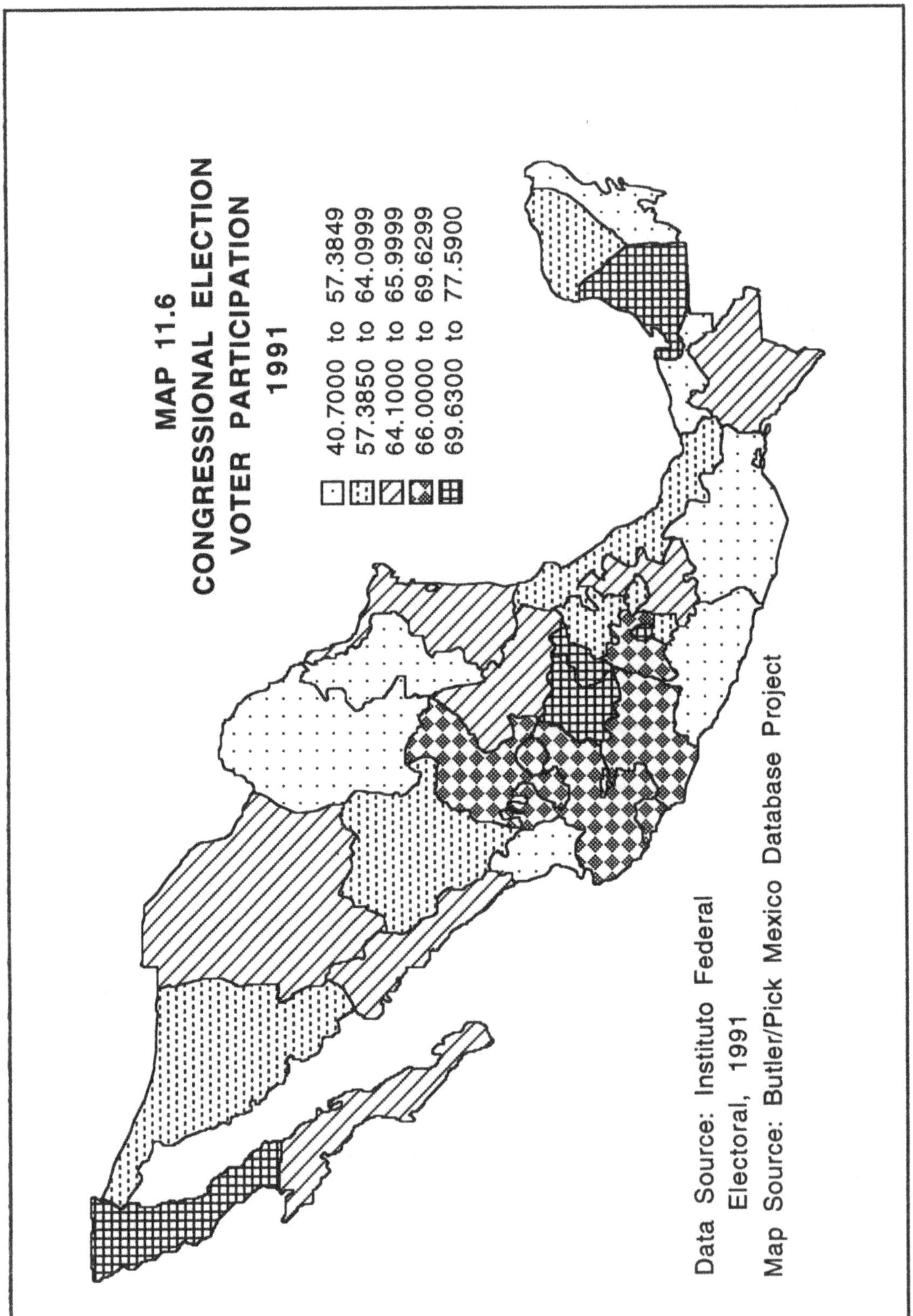
MAP 11.6
CONGRESSIONAL ELECTION
VOTER PARTICIPATION
1991
40.7000 to 57.3849
57.3850 to 64.0999
64.1000 to 65.9999
66.0000 to 69.6299
69.6300 to 77.5900
Data Source: Instituto Federal
Electoral, 1991
Map Source: Butler/Pick Mexico Database Project

MAP 11.7
CONGRESSIONAL VOTE – PRI
1991

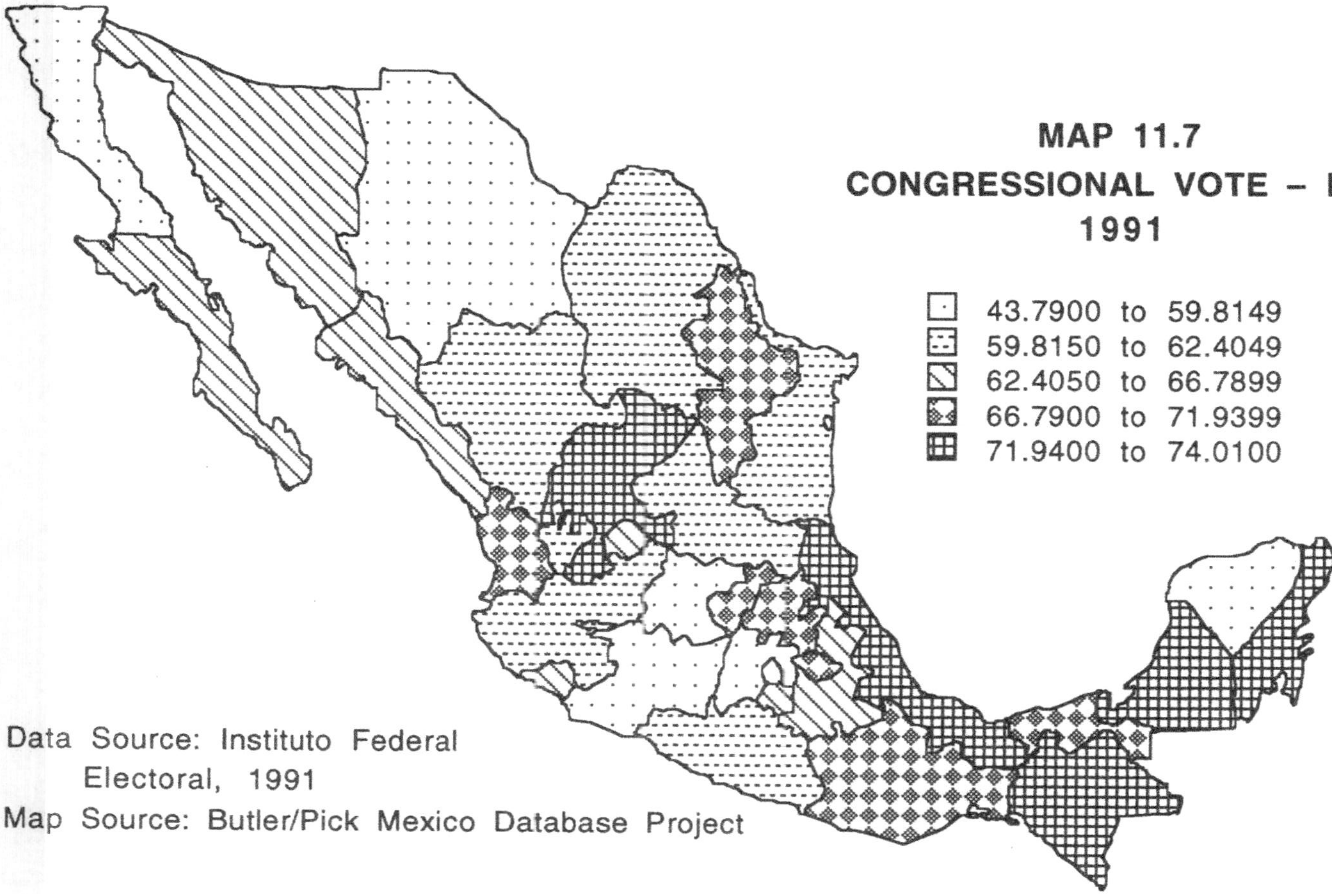

Data Source: Instituto Federal Electoral, 1991
Map Source: Butler/Pick Mexico Database Project

MAP 11.8
CONGRESSIONAL VOTE, PAN
1991

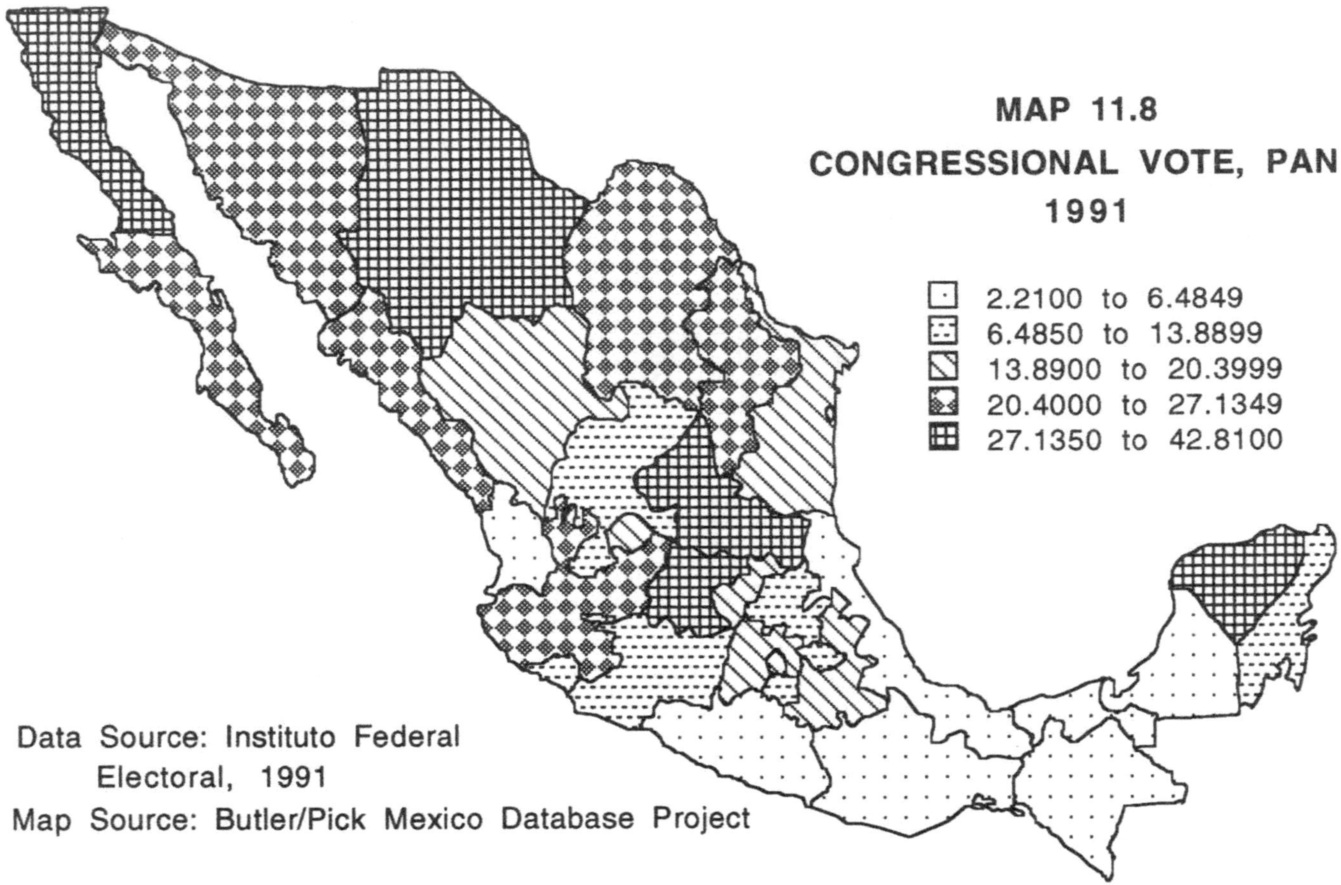

Data Source: Instituto Federal Electoral, 1991
Map Source: Butler/Pick Mexico Database Project

MAP 11.9
CONGRESSIONAL VOTE
OTHER PARTIES
1991

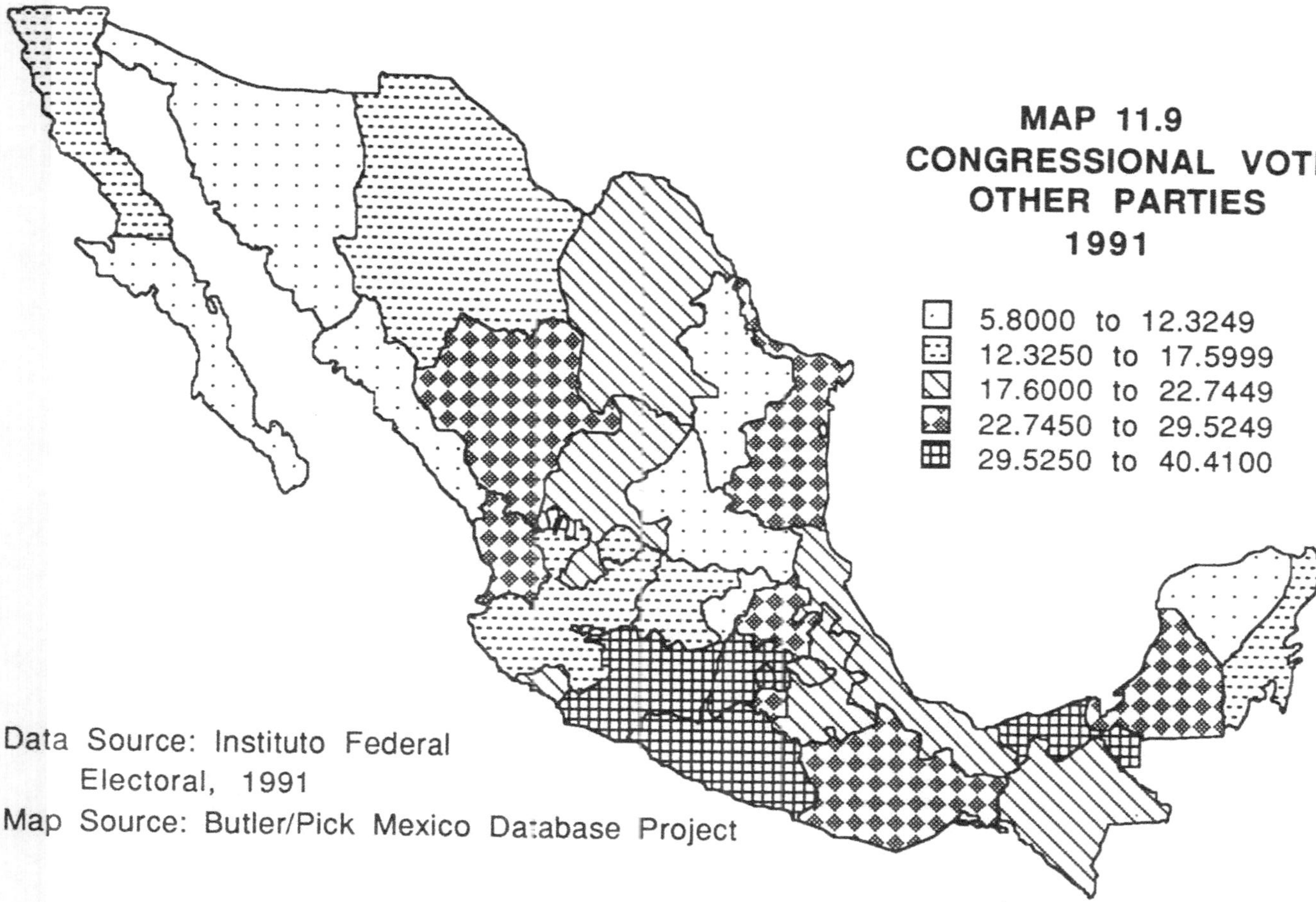

Data Source: Instituto Federal Electoral, 1991
Map Source: Butler/Pick Mexico Database Project

Projected Presidential Election, 1994

There is substantial continuity in Mexico even though there also have been great changes taking place (Butler et al. In press). Already noted is the consistency in electoral results from 1940 through the 1991 congressional elections. Thus, utilizing these past results, projections for the 1994 presidential election were carried out. Several caveats need to be noted in respect to these projections. First, they are made at the *macro* and *ecological* perspective. Second, they are mainly based upon official election results. Third, a basic assumption of the projections is that 'tradition' is particularly important in Mexico and thus it would take extremely unusual events to influence acutely the 1994 election. This assumption means explicitly that opposition states will remain opposition states, but, what is more important, PRI states will remain so. Finally, this means essentially that *who* the 1994 candidates will be is being ignored. Elsewhere we have made predictions about the 1994 and year 2000 elections utilizing other possibilities in what we labeled a 'legitimacy crisis scenario' (Guillen et al. 1990; Butler and Pick forthcoming). However, these factors only slightly decrease the likelihood of predicting the winning party to be the PRI. The statistical methodology of exponential smoothing utilized in the predictions presented here focus on prior electoral results (see Guillen et al. 1990).

The 1994 scenario assumes that 1988 was an unusual year because of a charismatic opposition candidate and because of the economic crises of debt and rampant inflation. Voters in the 1994 election, according to these predictions, will return to the PRI as the traditional majority political party. Using double smoothing procedures (see Map 11.10), the predicted vote for the PRI in the 1994 presidential election is 59.8 percent, which, of course, is much larger than the 1988 vote. The only other 1994 projection we know of anticipates a PRI vote of 63 percent, plus or minus three percent, by Ponce and Alonso (1987: 5-13). Their projection, of course, was made prior to the 1988 election. Triple smoothing procedures (see Map 11.11) results in a slightly lower predicted vote for the PRI but still winning the election handily.

As shown in Table 11.6, only in the Baja California, Federal District, the state of Mexico, and Michoacan is the opposition expected to be more than a majority. Note that these states historically have been opposition states. Maps 11.10 and 11.11 illustrate the predicted 1994 vote for the PRI candidate. The results of the projection indicate that the PRI will not only win the election in 1994 but that its candidate, regardless of who it is, will win by a larger majority in 1994 than did President Salinas in 1988.

As with previous elections, including the 1988 presidential and 1991 congressional elections, there is a consistency of voter characteristics associated with the PRI, PAN, and other party votes.

Table 11.6 National and State Presidential Election Forecast of PRI Vote, 1994

No.	State	1994 Election Results Forecast of PRI Vote Based on Double Exponential Smoothing	1994 Election Results Forecast of PRI Vote Based on Triple Exponential Smoothing
1	AGUASCALIENTES	0.6200	0.5180
2	BAJA CALIFORNIA	0.4650	0.3680
3	BAJA CALIFORNIA SUR	0.6230	0.5260
4	CAMPECHE	0.8020	0.7380
5	COAHUILA	0.6300	0.5100
6	COLIMA	0.6620	0.5480
7	CHIAPAS	0.9190	0.8970
8	CHIHUAHUA	0.5940	0.5470
9	DISTRITO FEDERAL	0.3770	0.2670
10	DURANGO	0.7060	0.6530
11	GUANAJUATO	0.5540	0.4520
12	GUERRERO	0.7140	0.6130
13	HIDALGO	0.7340	0.6400
14	JALISCO	0.5120	0.3930
15	MEXICO	0.4240	0.2480
16	MICHOACAN	0.4720	0.3040
17	MORELOS	0.5220	0.3690
18	NAYARIT	0.6710	0.5560
19	NUEVO LEON	0.7440	0.7000
20	OAXACA	0.7350	0.6450
21	PUEBLA	0.7660	0.7180
22	QUERETARO	0.7590	0.6690
23	QUINTANA ROO	0.7180	0.6500
24	SAN LUIS POTOSI	0.7530	0.6880
25	SINALOA	0.6430	0.5170
26	SONORA	0.7370	0.6620
27	TABASCO	0.8250	0.7600
28	TAMAULIPAS	0.6880	0.6000
29	TLAXCALA	0.7080	0.6060
30	VERACRUZ	0.7170	0.6200
31	YUCATAN	0.7260	0.6900
32	ZACATECAS	0.7610	0.7080
National Total		0.5980	
Mean		0.6650	0.5744
Median		0.7070	0.6095
S.D.		0.1227	0.1514
C.V.		18.45	
Minimum		0.3770	0.2480
Maximum		0.9190	0.8970

DEFINITION: Presidential Election Results 1994 projected by exponential smoothing based on presidental election data, 1934–1988.

SOURCE: Proceso Electoral Federal July 7, 1988.

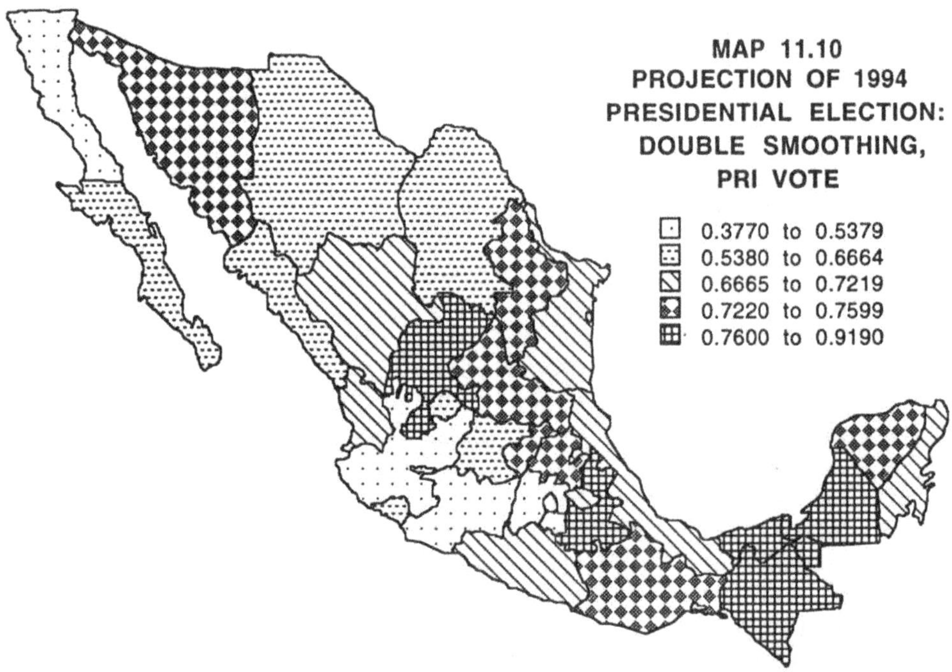

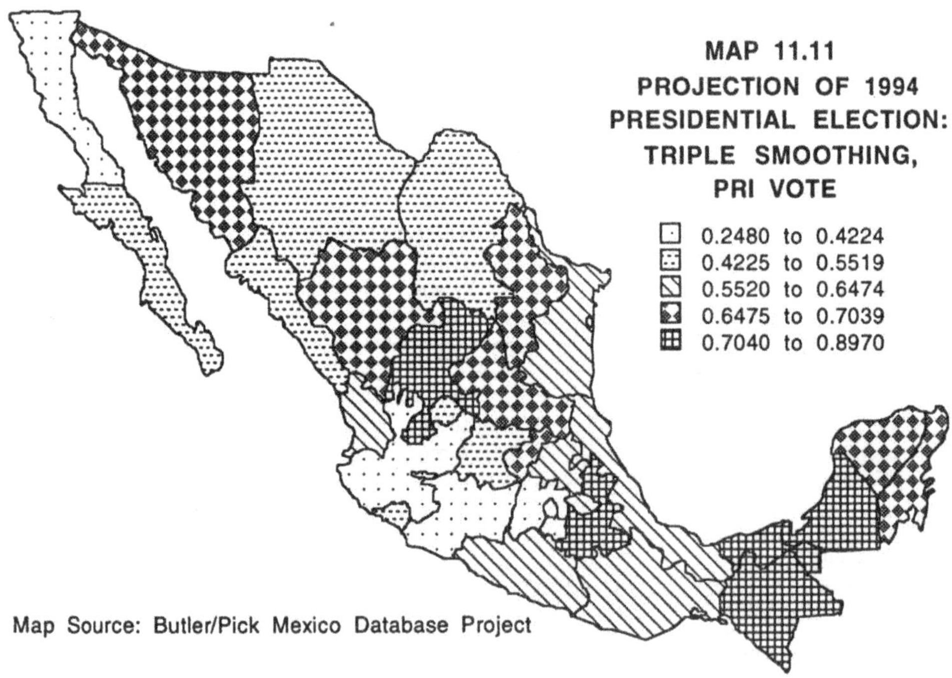

Map Source: Butler/Pick Mexico Database Project

Appendix

Unspecified Total Population from
the Mexican Census of Population, 1990

Unspecified Total Population from the Mexican Census of Population, 1990

No.	State	Total	Population Not Specifying Age: Males	Population Not Specifying Age: Females
1	AGUASCALIENTES	2,245	1,084	1,161
2	BAJA CALIFORNIA	32,223	16,131	16,092
3	BAJA CALIFORNIA SUR	3,504	1,783	1,721
4	CAMPECHE	7,603	3,813	3,790
5	COAHUILA	11,461	5,655	5,806
6	COLIMA	4,365	2,163	2,202
7	CHIAPAS	10,865	5,328	5,537
8	CHIHUAHUA	32,158	15,953	16,205
9	DISTRITO FEDERAL	28,914	13,421	15,493
10	DURANGO	2,797	1,369	1,428
11	GUANAJUATO	43,512	20,927	22,585
12	GUERRERO	31,081	15,145	15,936
13	HIDALGO	13,809	6,643	7,166
14	JALISCO	46,312	22,256	24,056
15	MEXICO	22,261	10,925	11,336
16	MICHOACAN	42,379	20,447	21,932
17	MORELOS	3,901	1,873	2,028
18	NAYARIT	9,725	4,852	4,873
19	NUEVO LEON	16,593	8,202	8,391
20	OAXACA	6,340	3,022	3,318
21	PUEBLA	10,712	5,103	5,609
22	QUERETARO	6,857	3,330	3,527
23	QUINTANA ROO	9,312	4,796	4,516
24	SAN LUIS POTOSI	8,873	4,320	4,553
25	SINALOA	12,292	6,073	6,219
26	SONORA	14,079	7,054	7,025
27	TABASCO	5,407	2,676	2,731
28	TAMAULIPAS	18,016	8,866	9,150
29	TLAXCALA	847	400	447
30	VERACRUZ	26,647	12,969	13,678
31	YUCATAN	4,080	1,983	2,097
32	ZACATECAS	3,095	1,496	1,599
National Total		492,265	240,058	252,207
Mean		15,383	7,502	7,881
Median		10,789	5,216	5,573
S.D.		13,157	6,358	6,804
C.V.		85.53	84.75	86.33
Minimum		847	400	447
Maximum		46,312	22,256	24,056

NOTE: These populations are not included in any age specific variables.

SOURCE: 1990 Mexican Census of Population, Resumen General, Table 2.

References

Afifi, A. A. and S. P. Azen. Statistical Analysis: A Computer Oriented Approach. New York, Academic Press, 1972.

Aguirre, Alejandro and Sergio Camposortega. "Evaluacion de la Information Basica Sobre Mortalidad Infantil en Mexico," in "Lecturas en Materia de Seguridad Social, Planeacion Familiar, y Cambio Demografico," Mexico, D.F.: IMSS, 1982.

Ahituv, N. and Neumann, S. *Principles of Information Systems for Management*. 3rd Edition. Dubuque, Iowa, William C. Brown, 1992.

Alba, Francisco. *La Poblacion de Mexico: Evolucion y Dilemas*. Mexico, D.F.: El Colegio de Mexico, 1984.

Alba, Francisco. "Logros y Limitaciones en la Absorcion de la Fuerza de Trabajo en Mexico." *Demografia y Economia* 18(4):557–580, 1984.

Arreloa, Daniel D. and James R. Curtis. *The Mexican Border Cities*. Tucson, University of Arizona Press, 1993.

Barberan, Jose, Cuauhtemoc Cardenas, Adrianna Lopez Monjardin, and Jorge Zavala. *Radiografia del Fraude*. Mexico: Collecion: Los Grandes Problemas Nacionales, 1988.

Barry, Tom (ed.). *Mexico: A Country Guide*. Albuquerque, New Mexico, The Inter-Hemispheric Education Resource Center, 1992.

Bassols Batalla, Angel. "La Division Economica Regional de Mexico." *Investigacion Economica* 24:387–413, 1961.

Beegle, J. Alan, Harold F. Goldsmith, and Charles P. Loomis. "Demographic Characteristics of the United States-Mexican Border." *Rural Sociology* 25:107–161, 1960.

Berry, Brian J.L. *Comparative Urbanization*. New York, St. Martins Press, 1981.

Blalock, Hubert M. *Social Statistics*, 2nd edition, New York, McGraw-Hill, 1979.

Bogue, Donald J. *The Population of the United States*. New York, The Free Press, 1985.

Bronfman, Mario and Jose Gomez de Leon (eds.). *La Mortalidad en Mexico: Niveles, Tendencias y Determinantes*. Mexico, D.F., El Colegio de Mexico, 1988.

Brown, L.A. and Jones III, J.P. "Spatial Variation in Migration Processes and Development: A Costa Rican Example of Conventional Modeling Augmented by the Expansion Method." *Demography*, 22(3):327–352, 1985.

Bruch, Hans A., Silera B. Hartman, and Jose Sanchez-Crespo. "The Health and Vital Statistics Systems in Mexico." Chapter 2 in DHHS Pub. No., (p. 115) 81–1353, Hyattsville, Maryland, National Center for Health Statistics, 1980.

Butler, Edgar W. and James B. Pick. *Geothermal Energy Development*. New York: Plenum Publishing Co., 1982.

Butler, Edgar W., James B. Pick, and Hiroshi Fukurai. "A Systematic Approach to a Demographic and Geographic Database System on Mexico." Paper presented to Simposium Binacional Sobre Poblacion y Desarollo, Ciudad Juarez, Chihuahua, Mexico, September, 1987.

Butler, Edgar W., James B. Pick, Hiroshi Fukurai, and Suhas Pavgi. "Migration to Baja California 1900–1980." The Center for Inter-American and Border Studies, The University of Texas at El Paso," *Research Paper Series*, 54 pp., 1987.

Butler, Edgar W., Hiroshi Fukurai, and James B. Pick. "Tourism and the Economies: A Case Study of Mexican States and Municipios." *Proceedings of the American Statistical Association*, Business and Economics Statistics Section, 728–733, 1987. Expanded version in *1989 Proceedings of the Business Association of Latin American Studies*, Kuklan, Hooshang (ed.), Business Association of Latin American Studies, 165–171, 1989.

Butler, Edgar W. and James B. Pick. *Codebook: States of Mexico Database.* Version 1.0. Butler/Pick Mexico Database Project, Department of Sociology, University of California, Riverside, June, 1990.

Butler, Edgar W., and James B. Pick. "Twentieth Century Migration to Baja California." *Journal of Borderlands Studies* 6(1):1–35, 1991.

Butler, Edgar W. and Jorge Bustamante. *Sucesion Presidencial: The 1988 Mexican Presidential Election.* Boulder, Colo.: Westview Press, 1991.

Butler, Edgar W. and Pick, James B. "Twentieth Century Migration to Baja California." *Journal of Borderlands Studies* 6(1):1–35, 1991.

Butler, Edgar W., James B. Pick, and Glenda Jones. "An Examination of the Official Results of the 1988 Mexican Presidential Election," in Edgar W. Butler and Jorge Bustamante (eds.), *Sucesion Presidencial: Bi-National Reflections*, Westview Press, pp. 13–44, 1991.

Butler, Edgar W., James B. Pick, and Glenda Tellis. "Political Change in the Mexican Borderlands," in Edgar W. Butler and Jorge Bustamante (eds.), *Sucesion Presidencial: Bi-National Reflections*, Westview Press, pp. 45–69, 1991.

Butler, Edgar W., James B. Pick, and Hiroshi Fukurai. "Twentieth Century Mexico: Continuity Within Change," in Leonard Hochberg, Carville Earle, and David Miller (eds.), *Geographic Information Systems: A Handbook for the Social Sciences*, Oxford, Basil Blackwell, in press.

Calderon Macias, M., Leal Rosales, M., and Soto Maldonado, D. *Geomunicipal 90*. Fundacion Arturo Rosenblueth, Mexico City D.F., Mexico, 1991.

Camposortega, Sergio. "Evaluacion y Correccion de la Poblacion Mexicana Censada en 1970." *Revista de Estadistica y Geografia* 3(10). Mexico, D.F., Secretaria de Programacion y Presupuesto, 1982.

Carbaugh, L.W. and Marx, R.W. "The TIGER System: A Census Bureau Innovation Serving Data Analysts." *Government Information Quarterly* 7(3):285–306, 1990.

Centro de Estudios Economicos y Demograficos. *Dinamica de la Poblacion de Mexico.* 2nd edition. Mexico City, D.F., El Colegio de Mexico, 1981.

Clarke, A.L. "GIS Specification, Evaluation, and Implementation," in Maguire, D.J., Goodchild, M.F., and Rhind, D.W., (eds.), *Geographical Information Systems*, Longman Scientific and Technical, Essex, England, 477–488, 1991.

Corona Vazquez, Rodolfo. "Confiabilidad de Los Resultados Preliminares de XI Censo General de Poblacion y Vivienda de 1990." *Estudios Demograficos y Urbanos* 6(1):33–68, 1991.

Densham, P.J. "Spatial Decision Support Systems," in Maguire, D.J., Goodchild, M.F., and Rhind, D.W., (eds.), *Geographical Information Systems*, Longman Scientific and Technical, Essex, England, 403–412, 1991.

Department of the Environment. *Handling Geographic Information*, Her Majesty's Stationery Office, London England, 1987.

ENFES. *Encuesta Nacional Sobre Fecundidad y Salud, 1987.* Columbia, Maryland, Institute for Resource Development/Macro Systems Inc., 1989.

Expansion. "Las Empresas Individuales Mas Importantes de Mexico," Mexico: Expansion, 1987.

Figueroa Campos, Beatriz (ed.). *La Fecundidad en Mexico: Cambios y Perspecitvas.* Mexico, D.F., El Colegio de Mexico, 1989.

Fukurai, Hiroshi, James B. Pick, Edgar W. Butler, and Swapan Nag. "An Analysis of the Interstate Migration in Mexico." *Mexican Studies* 3(2):365–395, 1987.

Fukurai, Hiroshi, James B. Pick, Edgar W. Butler. "Interstate Migration in Mexico, 1980: A Spatial Analysis." *Sociology and Social Research* 71(4): 312–322, 1987.

Fukurai, Hiroshi, James B. Pick, Edgar W. Butler, and Glenda Tellis. "An Examination of Regional Migration Patterns in Mexico: New and Old Mexican Regions." *Genus* 44(3–4):225–243, 1989.

Garcia y Garma, Irma Olaga. "Diferenciales de Fecundidad en Mexico, 1970." *Demografia y Economia* 13(1):49–91, 1979.

Garcia, Brigida. *Desarrollo Economico y Absorcion de Furza de Trabajo en Mexico, 1950–1980.* Mexico City, D.F., El Colegio de Mexico, 1988.

Garcia, Brigida. Article in *Demos*, Winter 1993.

Garza, Gustavo. *El Proceso de Industrializacion en La Ciudad de Mexico: 1821–1970.* Mexico, D.F., El Colegio de Mexico, 1985.

Garza, Gustavo (ed.). *Atlas de la Ciudad de Mexico.* Mexico City, D.F., Departamiento del Distrito Federal y El Colegio de Mexico, 1987.

Goodchild, M.F. and Rizzo, B.R. "Performance Evaluation and Work-Load Estimation for Geographic Information Systems." *International Journal of Geographical Information Systems*, 1:67–76, 1987.

Gonzalez-Arechiga and Jose Ramirez. "Definicion y Perspectiva de la Region Fronteriza." *Estudios Sociologicos* 13(23):271–304, 1990.

Guillen, Tonatiuh, Edgar W. Butler, and James B. Pick. "La Politica Electoral En La Frontera Norte de Mexico Hacia El Ano 2000." *Estudios Sociologicos* 8(23):271–304, 1990.

IMF. *International Financial Yearbook.* Washington, D.C.: International Monetary Fund, 1979 and 1991.

INEGI, *Anuario Estadistico de los Estados Unidos Mexicanos*, Instituto Nacional de Estadistica, Geografia, e Informatica, Aguascalientes, Mexico, Various Years.

INEGI. *X Censo General de Poblacion y Vivienda, 1980.* Various Volumes. Mexico, D.F., Instituto Nacional de Estadistica, Geografia, e Informatica, 1984–86.

INEGI. *Estadisticas Historicas de Mexico.* 2 Vols. Mexico City, D.F., Instituto Nacional de Estadistica, Geografia, e Informatica, 1985.

INEGI, *INEGI*, Instituto Nacional de Estadistica, Geografia, e Informatica, Aguascalientes, Mexico, 1991.

INEGI. *Censos Economicos, 1986.* Various Volumes, 1991–92.

INEGI. *XI Censo General de Poblacion y Vivienda: Estados Unidos Mexicanos, Resumen General.* Aguascalientes, Mexico, Instituto Nacional de Estadistica, Geografia, e Informatica, 1992a.

INEGI. *XI Censo General de Poblacion y Vivienda: Perfil Sociodemografico.* Aguascalientes, Mexico, Instituto Nacional de Estadistica, Geografia, e Informatica, 1992b.

INEGI, *Una Gran Cosecha Nacional,* Instituto Nacional de Estadistica, Geografia, e Informatica, Aguascalientes, Mexico, 1992c.

INEGI. *Cuaderno de Poblacion No. 3.* Aguascalientes, Instituto Nacional de Estadistica, Geografia, e Informatica, 1992d.

INEGI. *X Censo de Servicios: Resultados Definitivos.* Aguascalientes, Mexico, Instituto Nacional de Estadistica, Geografia, e Informatica, Censos Economicos, 1993a.

INEGI. Special metropolitan areas table provided on request to authors. Aguascalientes, Mexico, Instituto Nacional de Estadistica, Geografia, e Informatica, 1993b.

INEGI. *Censos Economicos, 1989.* Various Volumes, 1993c.

Instituto Federal Electoral. Mexico, D.F., 1991.

International Labour Organization. 1986. *Economically Active Population, 1950–2025,* Volume 3, Latin America. Geneva, International Labour Office, 1986.

Jarque, C.M. *Statistics, Democracy, and Development,* Instituto Nacional de Estadistica e Informatica, Aguascalientes, Mexico, 1991.

Jefferson, Mark. "The Law of the Primate City." *Geographical Review.* 29:226–232, 1939.

Kasarda, John D., J.O.B. Billy, and K. West. *Status Enhancement and Fertility.* Orlando, Florida, Academic Press, 1986.

Keyfitz, Nathan and Wilhelm Flieger. *Population: Facts and Methods of Demography.* San Francisco, W.H. Freeman, 1971.

Keyfitz, Nathan and Wilhelm Flieger. *World Population Growth and Aging.* Chicago, Illinois, University of Chicago Press, 1990.

Lorey, David E. *United States-Mexico Border Statistics Since 1900.* Los Angeles: UCLA Latin American Center Publications, 1990.

Maguire, D.J., Goodchild, M.F., and Rhind, D.W., (eds.), *Geographical Information Systems,* Longman Scientific and Technical, Essex, England in

Maguire, D.J., Goodchild, M.F., and Rhind, D.W., (eds.), *Geographical Information Systems,* Longman Scientific and Technical, Essex, England.

Maguire, D.J. and Dangermond, J. "The Functionality of GIS," in Maguire, D.J., Goodchild, M.F., and Rhind, D.W., (eds.), *Geographical Information Systems,* Longman Scientific and Technical, Essex, England, in Maguire, D.J., Goodchild, M.F., and Rhind, D.W., (eds.), *Geographical Information Systems,* Longman Scientific and Technical, Essex, England, 319–335, 1991.

Martinez, Jorge. *The Demographic Revolution in Mexico: 1970–1980.* Mexico, D.F., Mexican Institute of Social Security, 1982.

Marx, R.W. "The TIGER System: Automatic the Geographic Structure of the United States Census." *Government Publications Review,* 13, 181–201, 1986.

Mexico Database Project. *Codebook: States of Mexico: Database,* Version 1.0, Butler/Pick Mexico Database Project, Department of Sociology, University of California, Riverside, 1990.

Middlebrook, Kevin J. "Political Liberalization in an Authoritarian Regime: The Case of Mexico," in *Elections and Democratization in Latin America, 1980–1985,* Paul W. Drake and Eduardo Silva (eds.), San Diego: Center for U.S.-Mexican Studies, University of California, 1986.

Nag, Swapan. Development of a Computerized Cartographic System for Mapping Sociodemographic, Economic, and Marketing Data in Municipios of Six Mexican Border States. Masters Thesis, Graduate School of Management, University of California, Riverside, 1986.

National Center for Health Statistics. *Health, United States, 1991.* DHHS Pub. No. (PHS) 92–1232. Hyattsville, Maryland, U.S. Public Health Service, 1992.

National Center for Health Statistics. *Annual Summary of Births, Marriages, Divorces, and Deaths: United States, 1991.* Monthly Vital Statistics Report. Vol. 40, No. 13. Hyattsville, Maryland, U.S. Public Health Service, 1992.

National Center for Health Statistics. *Advance Report of Final Natality Statistics, 1990.* Monthly Vital Statistics Report. Vol. 41, No. 9, Supplement. Hyattsville, Maryland, U.S. Public Health Service, 1993.

National Center for Health Statistics. *Advance Report of Final Mortality Statistics, 1990.* Monthly Vital Statistics Report. Vol. 41, No. 7, Supplement. Hyattsville, Maryland, U.S. Public Health Service, 1993.

Negrete Salas, Maria E. and Hector Salazar Sanchez. "Zonas Metropolitanas en Mexico, 1980." *Estudios Demograficos y Urbanos* 1(1):97–290, 1986.

PAN. *Mitos y Verdades de las Elecciones Presidenciales de 1988 y Commentarios al Processo Electoral Federal de Mexico 1988.* Mexico, PAN, 1988.

PEMEX. *Statistical Yearbook 1992.* Mexico City, D.F., PEMEX, 1992.

Pick, James B., Swapan Nag, Glenda Tellis, and Edgar W. Butler. "Geographical Distribution and Variation in Selected Socioeconomic Variables for Municipios in Six Mexican Border States, 1980." *Journal of Borderlands Studies* 2(1):58–92, 1987.

Pick, James B., Glenda Tellis, and Edgar W. Butler. "Socioeconomic Characteristics of the Mexican Oil Region." *Proceedings of the American Statistical Association,* Social Statistics Section, 483–489, 1987.

Pick, James B., Swapan Nag, and Edgar W. Butler. "A Cluster Analysis Approach to Marketing Research in the Borderlands Region of Mexico," in Kuklan, Hooshang, Joan Anderson, and Denise Dimon (eds.), *1988 BALAS Proceedings,* Business Association of Latin American Studies, 19–25, 1988.

Pick, James B., Edgar W. Butler, and Suhas Pavgi. "Socioeconomic Determinants of Fertility: Selected Mexican Regions, 1976–77." *Social Biology* 35(1–2):137–157, 1988.

Pick, James B., Edgar W. Butler, and Elizabeth Lanzer. *Atlas of Mexico.* Boulder, Colorado: Westview Press, 1989a.

Pick, James B., Glenda L. Tellis, and Edgar W. Butler. "Fertility Determinants in the Oil Region of Mexico." *Social Biology* 36(1–2):45–66, 1989b.

Pick, James B., Edgar W. Butler, Swapan Nag, and Glenda Tellis. "Socioeconomic Influences on Fertility in the Mexican Borderlands Regions." *Mexican Studies* 6(1):11–42, 1989c.

Pick, James B., Glenda L. Tellis, Edgar W. Butler, and Suhas Pavgi. "Determinantes Socioeconomicas de Migracion en Mexico." *Estudios Demograficos y Urbanos* 5(1):61–101, 1990a.

Pick, James B. and Edgar W. Butler. "Socioeconomic Inequality in the U.S.-Mexico Borderlands: Modernization and Buffering." *Frontera Norte* 2(3):31–62, 1990b.

Pick, James B. and Skye Stephenson-Glade. "The NAFTA Agreement and Its Relation to Labor Force Projections." In Rivera, Juan M. and Alfred J. Hagan (eds.), *1993 Proceedings of the Business Association of Latin American Studies*, Business Association of Latin American Studies, 277–286, 1993.

Pick, James B., Edgar W. Butler, and Raul Gonzalez Ramirez. "Projection of the Mexican National Labor Force, 1980–2005." *Social Biology* 40(3), in press.

Pick, James B., Edgar W. Butler, and Sandra Tint. 1993. "Development of a Census-based Geographic Information System for Mexico." Paper presented at Conference of International Union for the Scientific Study of Population, Montreal, Canada, September, 1993.

Palladino, S.D. and Kemp, K.K., 1991, *GIS Teaching Facilities*, Technical Report 91–21, National Center for Geographic Information and Analysis, University of California at Santa Barbara.

Pirez, Pedro. "Para El Estudio de Los municipios y La Politica Regional en Mexico." *Demografia y Economia* 15(3):344–358, 1981.

Ponce, Dolores G. and Antonio Alonso C. *Politica Interna: Escenario Tendencial.* Mexico: Centro de Estudios Prospectivos AC de la Fundacion Javier Barros Sierra (Documento Preliminar), 1987.

Population Reference Bureau. "World Population Data Sheet." Washington, D.C.: Population Reference Bureau, various years.

President's Office, Mexico. *Carlos Salinas de Gotari: First State of the Nation Report*, November, 1989.

President's Office, Mexico. *Carlos Salinas de Gotari: Third State of the Nation Report*, November, 1991.

President's Office, Mexico. *Carlos Salinas de Gotari: IV State of the Nation Report*, November, 1992.

President's Office, Mexico. *Mexico: On the Record*, p. 3, July 1992.

Proceso Electoral Federal, July 7, 1988.

Rabell, Cecilia, Marta Mier, and Teran Rocha. "El Descenso de la Mortalidad en Mexico de 1940 a 1980." *Estudios Demograficos y Urbanos* 1(1): 39–92, 1986.

Rendon, Teresa and Carlos Salas. "Evolucion del Empleo en Mexico: 1895–1980." *Estudios Demograficos y Urbanos* 2(2):189–230, 1987.

Reyna, Jose Luis and Edgar W. Butler. "Political Transition in Mexico: Its Impact upon U.S.-Mexico Relations," in *Mexico and the United States: Neighbors In Crisis*, in Daniel G. Aldrich, Jr. and Lorenzo Meyer (eds.), San Bernardino, California, The Borgo Press, 1993.

Rodgriguez Sala, Maria L. "La Regionalizacion de Mexico." *Revista Mexicana de Sociologia* 22:231–248, 1960.

Salinas de Gortari, Carlos. *Third State of the Nation Report*. Mexico, D.F.: Presidencia de la Republica, Direccion General de Comunicacion Social, 1991.

Salinas de Gortari, Carlos. *Fourth State of the Nation Report.* Mexico, D.F.: Presidencia de la Republica, Direccion General de Comunicacion Social, 1992.

Sanchez Molina, Antonio. *Sintesis Geografica de Mexico.* Mexico, D.F., Editorial Trillas, 1973.

Schultz, S. and Regan, J. "The 1990 Census, GIS Technology, and Rural Data Needs." *Rural Sociologist,* 11, No. 1, 23–29, 1991.

Schteingart, Martha. "Mexico City," in Dogan, Mattei and John D. Kasarda, *The Metropolis Era,* Vol. 2, *Mega-Cities,* pp. 268–293, 1988.

Scott, Ian. *Urban and Spatial Development in Mexico.* Baltimore, The Johns Hopkins University Press, 1982.

SPP. *Encuesta Mexicana de Fecundidad.* V. I. Primer Informe Nacional. Mexico, D.F., Secretaria de Programacion y Presupuesto, 1979a.

SPP. *Encuesta Mexicana de Fecundidad.* V. II. Primer Informe Nacional. Mexico, D.F,, Secretaria de Programacion y Presupuesto, 1979b.

SPP. *Encuesta Mexicana de Fecundidad.* V. III. Tres Areas Metropolitanas. Mexico, D.F., Secretaria de Programacion y Presupuesto, 1979c.

Secretaria de Salud. *Vitales 1987.* Mexico, D.F.: Secretaria de Salud, 1991.

Secretaria de Salud, 1991. *Mortalidad 1988.* Mexico, D.F.: Secretaria de Salud, 1991.

Stoddard, Ellwyn R., Richard Nostrand, and Jonathan P. West. *Borderlands Sourcebook: A Guide to the Literature on Northern Mexico and the American Southwest.* Norman, Oklahoma, University of Oklahoma Press, 1983.

Stoddard, Ellwyn R. *Maquila: Assembly Plants in Northern Mexico.* El Paso, Texas, Texas Western Press, 1987.

Strategic Mapping Inc. *Atlas Pro.* San Jose, California, Strategic Mapping Inc.

Tamayo, Jesus and Jose Luis Fernandez. *Zonas Fronterizas.* Mexico, D.F.: Centro de Investigacion y Docencia Economicas, 1983.

U.S. Bureau of the Census. *The DIME Geocoding System,* Report No. 4, Census Use Study, U.S. Department of Commerce, Bureau of the Census, 1970.

U.S. Bureau of the Census. *State and Metropolitan Area Data Book 1991.* 4th edition. Washington, D.C., Government Printing Office, 1991.

U.S. Bureau of the Census. *1990 Census of Population and Housing: Summary Population and Housing Characteristics.* 1990 CPH-1-1. Washington, D.C., U.S. Government Printing Office, 1992a.

U.S. Bureau of the Census. *1990 Census of Population and Housing: Summary Social, Economic, and Housing Characteristics.* 1990 CPH-5-1. Washington, D.C., U.S. Government Printing Office, 1992b.

U.S. Bureau of the Census. *Households, Families, and Children: A 30-Year Perspective.* Current Population Reports, P23–181. Washington, D.C., Government Printing Office, 1992c.

U.S. Bureau of the Census. *Population Projections of the United States, by Age, Sex, Race, and Hispanic Origin: 1992 to 2050.* Current Population Reports, P25–1092. Washington, D.C., U.S. Government Printing Office, 1992d.

U.S. Bureau of the Census. *U.S. Population Estimates by Age, Sex, Race, and Hispanic Origin: 1980 to 1991.* Current Population Reports, P25–1095. Washington, D.C., U.S. Government Printing Office, 1993.

U.S. Department of Labor. *Working Women: A Chartbook.* Bureau of Labor Statistics Bulletin 2385. Washington, D.C., U.S. Government Printing Office, 1991.

U.S. Department of Labor. *Outlook, 1990–2005.* Bureau of Labor Statistics Bulletin 2402. Washington, D.C., U.S. Government Printing Office, 1992.

Van Arsdol, Maurice, Nadia Youssef, Michel Antochiw, Dennis Berg, and John Brennan, Jr. "Migration and Population Redistribution in the State of Mexico, republic of Mexico." ICP Work Agreement Reports, *Occasional Monograph Series,* 5(1), Washington, D.C., Smithsonian Institution, 133-176, 1976.

Whetten, Nathan and Robert G. Burnight. "Internal Migration in Mexico." *Rural Sociology* 21:140–156, 1956.

Wilkie, James W. *The Mexican Revolution: Federal Expenditure and Social Change Since 1910,* 2nd Edition. Berkeley, University of California Press, 1970.

Wilkie, James W. *Statistical Abstract of Latin America,* Volume 23. Los Angeles, UCLA Latin American Center Publications, 1986.

Wilkie, Richard W. *Latin American Population and Urbanization Analysis: Maps and Statistics, 1950–82.* Los Angeles, UCLA Latin American Center Publications, 1984.

Index

www.ingramcontent.com/pod-product-compliance
Ingram Content Group UK Ltd.
Pitfield, Milton Keynes, MK11 3LW, UK
UKHW051323190926
475701UK00011B/1095
* 9 7 8 0 3 6 7 3 0 9 3 1 2 *